KEYGUIDE TO INFORMATION SOURCES IN

MEDIA ETHICS

Barrie MacDonald and Michel Petheram

MANSELL

London and Washington

First published 1998 by
Mansell Publishing Limited, *A Cassell imprint*
Wellington House, 125 Strand, London WC2R 0BB, England
PO Box 605, Herndon, Virginia 20172-0605, USA

© Barrie MacDonald and Michel Petheram 1998

All rights reserved. No part of this publication may be reproduced or transmitted in any form or by any means, electronic or mechanical, including photocopying, recording or any information storage or retrieval system, without permission in writing from the publishers or their appointed agents.

The idea for this book was supplied by Michael J. Walsh, Librarian, Heythrop College (University of London).

British Library Cataloguing in Publication Data
A catalogue record for this book is available from the British Library.

ISBN 0-7201-2128-0

Library of Congress Cataloging-in-Publication Data
MacDonald, Barrie I.
    Keyguide to information sources in media ethics / Barrie MacDonald and Michel Petheram.
       p. cm.
    Includes bibliographical references and index.
    ISBN 0-7201-2128-0 (hardcover)
    1. Mass media – Moral and ethical aspects – Information resources.
I. Petheram, Michel. II. Title.
P94.M22 1998
016.175 – dc21   97-40767
                                                                                                          CIP

Typeset by York House Typographic Ltd, London
Printed and bound in Great Britain by Bookcraft (Bath) Ltd.

Contents

Introduction   vi
Acknowledgements   ix

Part I   Overview of media ethics   1

1   Media ethics   3
2   Freedom of speech   5
     2.1   Justifications of free speech   6
     2.2   Extent of free speech   10
     2.3   Access   13
     2.4   The right to know   14
     2.5   Accountability   15
3   Government and the media   18
     3.1   Internal threats   19
     3.2   External threats   21
4   Economic pressures   26
     4.1   Media ownership   28
     4.2   Advertising and marketing   29
5   Privacy   32
6   Censorship: taste, decency and pornography   38
     6.1   Freedom of expression and harm   41
     6.2   Film censorship   46

	6.3 Broadcasting	47
	6.4 Cable and the Internet	50
7	Truth and truth-telling	52
	7.1 Accuracy	56
	7.2 Understanding	58
	7.3 Fairness and bias	60
	7.4 TV news and journalism	64
	7.5 News-gathering	65
8	Confidentiality and sources	68
9	The values of journalists	73
	9.1 Conflicts of interest	76
	9.2 Professionalism, councils and codes	77
10	Quality	81
	10.1 Quality in television	83
11	Religion	87
12	Media imperialism	89
13	Advertising	92

Part II Bibliography 99

Media ethics	102
General media ethics	102
Mass media in general	114
Freedom of speech	124
Justifications of free speech	130
Extent of free speech	132
Access	135
The right to know	136
Accountability	139
Government and the media	140
Internal threats	143
External threats	147
Economic pressures	153
Media ownership	153
Advertising and marketing	156
Privacy	156
Censorship: taste, decency and pornography	166
Freedom of expression and harm	169
Film censorship	172
Broadcasting	174
Cable and the Internet	176

Truth and truth-telling	177
Accuracy	179
Understanding	182
Fairness and bias	190
TV news and journalism	196
News-gathering	199
Confidentiality and sources	201
The values of journalists	203
Conflicts of interest	208
Professionalism, councils and codes	209
Quality	212
Quality in television	213
Religion	217
Media imperialism	221
Advertising	231
Periodicals	237
Bibliographies, indexes and abstracting services	245

Part III Directory of selected organizations — 253

International	257
Europe	262
Africa	298
Asia	308
Americas	324
North America	324
Central America and the Caribbean	334
South America	339
Oceania	345

Index — **350**

Introduction

The media are spreading ever wider across the globe: they become more pervasive and gain more influence, yet the public perception in many areas of the world is of a decline in the ethical standards of the media. This apparent decline may only be a reflection of a general decline in standards of public and private life, or perhaps of a greater readiness to criticize. However, complaints about the media – of bias, inaccuracy, unfair treatment, invasion of privacy and so on – are continually increasing, with siren calls for stricter control and regulation of the press and broadcasters. There is concern not only about the media themselves, but also about the attitudes of governments throughout the world to the freedom and independence of the media. Wars, civil unrest, terrorism have all given governments excuses to curb the freedom of the media, and in many cases justify censorship in the name of national security. Therefore the need for reaffirming and upholding ethical principles in mass communications has never been greater.

The academic study of media ethics is well established in the United States, mostly within journalism and mass communications, with many university courses, a plethora of books published on the subject, and even a specialist magazine entirely devoted to it, *The Journal of Mass Media Ethics*. It is rather less well established as a separate area of study elsewhere in the world, but perhaps this volume might in a small way help stimulate or facilitate studies of media ethics.

For this book 'the media' includes mass communications and media in general, print and electronic media – the press and broadcasting, book publishing, advertising, marketing and film. There is selected coverage of the new technologies, though they are developing so rapidly that they will need a book of their own.

INTRODUCTION

For whom is this book intended? Media ethics is an area of study that traverses many academic disciplines – media, journalism, law, cultural studies, philosophy and applied ethics. In it we have tried to provide guidance and bibliographical references for students within any of those disciplines, and wherever in the world they may be studying the subject. Media practitioners may find it useful in guiding them through the ethical problems they meet in their work, with useful examples of key issues and recommendations of further reading. As well as students and practitioners, librarians, readers' advisers, information officers, journalists, and researchers for radio or television programmes or business should find this book useful in giving them an overview of media ethics and guidance as to who are the experts and specialists in the field. We hope also that the general reader with an interest in the media and its workings may find something of value in this book.

This volume, as with other titles in the Keyguide series, is arranged in three parts: an extended survey giving an overview of the subject; an extensive bibliography of annotated entries on books and other printed materials on the topic; and a directory of organizations and institutions working within the area.

In Part I we have attempted to map out the topics that fall within the heading of 'media ethics', and to give the general ideas and arguments for each. Freedom of speech, the right to know, access and accountability, democracy, censorship, privacy, truth, honesty, accuracy, fairness, objectivity, confidentiality of sources, and the values and professionalism of journalists are certainly all included. However, related issues which one might term 'ethical' are also covered – such 'taste and decency' issues in the press, film and broadcasting as violence, obscenity and pornography, or concepts of quality. Religion and cultural imperialism in relation to the media are dealt with separately. Most of these 'media ethical' issues are discussed within a context of the principles of ethics and applied philosophy, and illustrated by recent and notable cases.

The bibliography in Part II contains annotated entries for some 800 books, articles and periodicals, representing all the topics covered in Part I, and in the same subject arrangement. It is selective, as we cannot hope to list everything published, and covers English-language publications mostly from the United Kingdom, the United States, Canada and Australia; however, it deals with media issues throughout the world. Apart from a small number of items not obtainable at the time of compilation, all of the works have been personally examined by the compilers. The annotations are for the most part descriptive rather than critical, and aim to give the reader an idea of the purpose, scope and content of the book or article.

The aim of the list of institutions in Part III is to provide the user with details of those organizations which are involved in media regulation, are concerned with the provision of professional services for the media industry or personnel, or campaign on moral issues affecting the media. Many of these bodies draw up codes of ethical practice or conduct, through which they regulate the media industry, supervise self-regulation in sectors of it, or set and maintain high professional standards among practitioners within the media. The other categories include academic establishments which provide study and research programmes in the media. For any student studying ethical issues in the media – wherever they are in the world – this listing will identify some of the relevant organizations they could approach for advice, information, and examples of codes.

Acknowledgements

I would like to acknowledge the contribution of those individuals or organizations who have made this book possible.

First, I wish to record my appreciation of my collaborators in this project for their vital part in its evolution. Michel Petheram, who came to the project at a comparatively late stage, stayed the course and provided so much of the momentum to complete it. As a philosopher who has worked in the media, his great strength has been to encompass both backgrounds from which he has written with considerable knowledge and experience. His firm understanding of the ethical principles underlying issues in the media informs his writing, and adds substance to the arguments. He has written Part I and contributed to Part II. My grateful thanks also go to my previous collaborator, Nigel Harris from the University of Dundee, who provided a disciplined academic eye and a focus for the work, before he had to withdraw because of the pressure of university work. Stephen Murphy, with whom the project first began in 1986, made a crucial and valiant start on the work before having to withdraw because of ill health. He was an inspiring collaborator. His career as a notable Secretary to the British Board of Film Censors, and later as Senior Programme Officer at the Independent Broadcasting Authority, gave him tremendous experience and insight into the ethical issues of film and television. He was a wise and liberal-minded regulator. His annotations for entries in Part II were keen and perceptive, and I am grateful to Jean Murphy, his widow, for allowing us to include many of them in the completed work.

I would also like to express my gratitude to the various libraries on whose resources we have made considerable demands: the British Library, at both the Reading Room in London and the Document Supply Centre at Boston Spa; the

London Library; the Library of the World Association for Christian Communication and their Librarian, Ann Davies; the International Institute of Communications Library and their Librarian, Lydia Jackson; and the BBC Reference Library. I owe a personal debt of gratitude to the Library of the Independent Television Commission in London, and to my own loyal and supportive staff.

And finally, I would like to thank our long-suffering commissioning editors at Mansell, firstly Colin Hutchens, and latterly Veronica Higgs, for their patience and support over this long period.

Barrie MacDonald
Librarian
Independent Television Commission
London

Part I

Overview of media ethics

Note: References from the discussion of a book in this part to the full entry in Part II are indicated by a sequential number in square brackets. The source and page number of a quotation from a book used in the text are indicated by a superior number, and are in the list of notes at the end of a chapter. Full publication details of cited works are given only for those books that are not included and fully described in Part II.

1 Media ethics

When the subject of 'media ethics' is mentioned, a frequent response is 'What ethics?' or 'It can be covered in two paragraphs'. This can probably be taken as a comment on the standing of the media, particularly the newspapers in the United Kingdom in the middle and late 1990s. It also shows that the excesses of a few have tarred the many with the same brush. To take a more optimistic view, the very perception of a lack of ethics shows a need for the media to act ethically, and if this book can help, so much the better.

On the one hand, media ethics is about problems of conduct that practitioners in the media have to face as they go about their work. On the other hand, it is a crossroads where many roads meet. In thinking of the media, we first think of journalists and reporters, but of course radio and television require a wider range of professionals than newsmen and newswomen, for example, advertisers and drama producers; then there are those whom the journalists write about, who are also those who read, hear or see the media – the public. Besides the media that carry news and current affairs, there is the cinema, advertising, and the first and historically most important medium of all, books. Then, apart from what is implied by the word 'media', there is 'ethics', which in turn implies philosophers. Yet most discussion of communication has been undertaken by sociologists and historians.

Media ethics is sometimes considered to be a branch of applied ethics, but because it also raises questions of rights and politics, it can also be considered as part of social philosophy. Media ethics is usually encountered on the level of individual cases: did a certain report constitute an invasion of privacy? Was the government justified in withholding a particular piece of information? Did the language of a play unnecessarily offend? But it can soon move to more general questions: should pornography be restricted, and if so to what extent? Should journalists guarantee confidentiality for their sources? They can in fact reach the most abstract level. Part of the defence of public service television is that it guarantees quality in programmes – what really is 'quality' in television? One of the most long-winded debates about journalism is whether it can claim to be 'objective' – and here we reach a very old question: 'What is truth?'

By and large, the books that have been published on the general subject of media ethics are American textbooks for students of journalism. These nearly all work through the discussion of individual cases, but tend to be very weak when it comes to discussion of the principles involved, which is required if any consistency of approach is to be attained. These books are predominantly descriptive in character and tend to prefer stories and anecdotes to hard thinking. The fundamental topic, one which is presupposed in nearly all discussions within the subject, is freedom of speech.

2 Freedom of speech

Milton: 'Give me the liberty to know, to utter, and to argue freely according to conscience, above all liberties.'

Junius: 'The liberty of the press is the *Palladium* of all the civil, political, and religious rights of an Englishman.'

Freedom of speech is one of the key values of liberal democracies (along with freedom of worship and freedom of assembly). In the UK this freedom was acquired only after a long struggle. In the US it receives legal protection from the Constitution. The First Amendment states that 'Congress shall make no law ... abridging the freedom of speech, or of the press, or the right of the people peaceably to assemble, and to petition the Government for a redress of grievances'. It has gone on to achieve worldwide status. In 1941 President Roosevelt called it one of the 'four essential freedoms'. These were widely regarded during the Second World War as a succinct statement of the Allied war aims, and were later included in the various 'human rights' declared by the United Nations in its 1948 Declaration of Human Rights. Article 10 of the European Convention on Human Rights declares that 'Everyone has the right to freedom of expression. This right shall include freedom to hold opinions and to receive and impart information and ideas without interference by public authority and regardless of frontiers.'

What is special about the principle of free speech is that it provides a degree of immunity from government control, even when it causes some measure of harm to the public. Speech, expression, communication (whichever term is used) are deemed to have a special quality or value. In the UK and other Western democracies the merits of free speech are widely accepted; what is questioned is its scope and meaning. Still, it will be valuable to examine the justifications of free speech.

It is not, however, usually regarded as an absolute value in that it can claim to override all other values. There are grounds for limiting free speech, which are recognized in law, such as libel, slander or incitement to riot. Apart from these legal limitations, there are ethical limitations, taken in a broad sense, where the value of free speech conflicts with other values of society. These limitations lead to the issues which are the subject of media ethics and, therefore, of this book. Such limitations are often categorized as censorship. But this term 'censorship' is also often used more particularly to describe offences against taste and decency, such as pornography, violence or bad language (a particular problem in broadcasting). The other limitations include conflicts with government (for example, over reporting of war and terrorism); privacy of individuals; blasphemy (though this is not legally effective in the UK); and what might be called internal restraints in that they apply to the media as an industry, such as ownership and advertising interests.

So far, we have been talking of free speech; the quotation from Junius at the start of this chapter refers to 'liberty of the press'. Are these the same thing? Perhaps not, and for two reasons. First, the early arguments about free speech were to obtain it for individuals (see, for example, the quotation from Milton above) and for small independent publishers and presses, while the modern press largely consists of vast and complex institutions. Second, it may be that the contemporary mass media, because they are so dominant, suppress information and stifle ideas rather than promote them. The fact that there are only a few newspapers means that a smaller range of opinion and thought is expressed.

Most writers, however, treat freedom of the press as more or less the same thing as freedom of speech. In this book it may be more correct to talk of freedom of the media, but the first phrase is the most familiar, and using it when the second is more accurate should cause no confusion. What, then, are the arguments made to justify freedom of speech and of the press?

2.1 Justifications of free speech

There are three main lines of argument used to justify the principle of free speech, to say that it deserves special protection. Two of these arguments claim that this protection produces special benefits: the first is that free speech promotes the discovery of truth and error through discussion; the second is that it provides the necessary information for educated political decision-making. Then there is also an argument from principle, which asserts that silencing someone is a trespass against their dignity, and against the respect due to a free agent, a blow to their autonomy.

One of the first writers to argue for a link between freedom of speech and the discovery of truth was John Milton in his *Areopagitica* of 1644 [144], though it is important to remember that he was making an argument against licensing, that is, prior clearance for publication, against any one taking it upon themselves to decide what might or might not be published. He thought that the licensing of printing would cause 'the discouragement of all learning, and the stop of Truth'.

'Since therefore the knowledge and survey of vice is in this world so necessary to the constituting of human virtue, and the scanning of error to the confirmation of truth, how can we more safely, and with less danger, scout into the regions of sin and falsity than by reading all manner of tractates and hearing all manner of reason? And this is the benefit which may be had of books promiscuously read.'[1]

Behind this link between virtue and truth lies Milton's belief that God gave man reason and in so doing gave him freedom of choice. There can be no virtue unless it is freely chosen. So to license printing is to treat us as less than men. We must be free to seek truth, and this is to be arrived at through argument and discussion. As Milton puts it in a famous metaphor: 'And though all the winds of doctrine were let loose to play upon the earth, so Truth be in the field, we do injuriously, by licensing and prohibiting, to misdoubt her strength. Let her and Falsehood grapple; who ever knew Truth put to the worse, in a free and open encounter?'

John Stuart Mill's famous *On Liberty* of 1859 [143] includes the classic defence of the principle of freedom of thought and discussion. The main arguments occur in Chapter 2 and are perhaps the most vigorous to be found in favour of freedom of speech. 'If all mankind minus one, were of one opinion, and only one person were of the contrary opinion, mankind would be no more justified in silencing that one person, than he, if he had the power, would be justified in silencing mankind.' All subsequent discussions refer back to Mill and this work. Although he argues in a way similar to Milton that free speech generates special benefits, he does not draw any authority from God, nor does he believe that truth always triumphs over persecution. This view he describes as 'a pleasant falsehood'.

Mill believed that freedom of opinion and of the expression of opinion are necessary for the mental well-being of mankind – and it is on this well-being that all other well-being depends. His first point is that any opinion that is silenced may well be true. To deny this possibility is to assume our own infallibility. Second, even if the silenced opinion is false, it may contain a portion of the truth. And as the prevailing opinion, the belief held by society, is rarely the whole truth, only 'the collision of adverse opinions' can lead to the discovery of the remainder of truth. Third, even if the prevailing opinion is the whole truth, unless this belief is contested, belief in it will lack understanding or 'feeling of its rational grounds'. Also, the meaning of the opinion itself will be weakened, will become a mere dogma 'deprived of its vital effect on the character and conduct'. Mill's overall idea, then, is that truth is to be attained and retained through unrestricted public discussion: 'the peculiar evil of silencing the expression of an opinion is, that it is robbing the human race ... If the opinion is right, they are deprived of the opportunity of exchanging error for truth: if wrong, they lose, what is almost as great a benefit, the clearer perception and livelier impression of truth, produced by its collision with error.'

In criticism of this line of argument (which has been here much simplified), the first thing that might be said is that it assumes that it is always right to publish an opinion that is possibly true, yet it is in fact quite plausible to hold that the publication of some opinion should be banned, because disseminating it is harmful to the welfare of society, for example, what is at present called 'hate-speech' in the US, and which includes racist speech. Another point here is that Mill and Milton are concerned with expressions of belief or opinions. It can be extended to works of serious literature, but probably not to everything that is published. It is not clear how the argument applies to fields like commercial advertising or pornography (which were not topics they had to deal with). Another point is that Mill may have been over-optimistic in his assessment of the rationality of human beings, and in supposing that the truth can emerge from uninhibited discussion.

The notion here has been described as a 'free market' of ideas, though Mill himself does not use the phrase, and there is doubt as to whether such a market can operate freely. If everyone talks at once, truth will not prevail; and if powerful agencies gain an undue monopoly of the market, falsehood can prevail. If Truth cannot manage on her own, she will need help, that is, intervention.

The second major argument is that freedom of speech serves a necessary part of educated, political decision-making. The media, it is claimed, promote debate; democracy depends on debate, on the clash of opinions freely expressed, and such debate requires a forum.

This public debate rationale is perhaps the one most commonly put forward. It was made originally by American judges, then popularized by Alexander Meiklejohn in his 1948 book, *Free speech and its relation to self-government* [142]. It is a justification widely held among contemporary journalists. For example, British journalist Raymond Snoddy, in his 1992 work *The good, the bad and the unacceptable* [311], links it to the need in the UK for a Freedom of Information Act, similar to the one in the US. Anthony Lester QC is quoted: 'A modern democracy cannot function properly without a well-informed electorate. We could enjoy substantially more freedom of information in this country without endangering effective government. Greater freedom of information means more accountability and the ability to make wiser choices.' Snoddy himself adds: 'a full flow of information is essential in a democracy if citizens are to make informed judgements, and will also make government more efficient through all policy options having been discussed fully before a choice is made.'[2]

One writer has described this line of argument as 'the historically astonishing principle that *public disagreement is a creative force*'.[3]

However, the fact that this view is an 'instrumentalist' or 'consequentialist' one raises difficulties, for it may be argued that sometimes the values of a democracy, including its long-term commitment to free speech, can best be preserved by the temporary suppression of some speech. Second, it may be that the exercise of free speech in particular situations is contrary to public welfare. What if an improvement of collective decision-making through exposure to a diversity of views could be achieved only by imposing some sort of regulative regime on the press? Publicity can poison the air as well as cleanse it. Publicity, far from ensuring rationality, is a display case for human vanity, for playing to the gallery. More generally, if the maintenance of democracy is considered to be the foundation of free speech, how is one to argue against the control of that speech by the democracy?

We noted Milton's claim that freedom of speech is an expression of our God-given liberty of choice – that we as individuals must freely choose virtue and truth. Mill too had a strong belief in individual autonomy: 'It is the privilege and proper condition of a human being, arrived at the maturity of his faculties, to use and interpret experience in his own way.' These suggestions lead us to the *principled* argument for free speech, that to silence someone is an offence against their dignity and against the respect owing to a free agent. Restrictions on a person's freedom of speech are restrictions on that person's freedom. The point of the arguments already discussed is that they claim that freedom of speech leads to good consequences for society. Here the suggestion is that freedom of speech is important for individual well-being. Speech may be an integral component of self-fulfilment, it may be that it is a primary good. Put a little more strongly, it may be suggested that freedom of speech is an essential part of human dignity or autonomy. This is a comparatively recent line of argument. Two weaknesses may be mentioned here. First, it is not easy to specify exactly what the relationship is between freedom of speech and the somewhat vague notion of autonomy. Second, granted that it is true that freedom of speech is important for the individual, so are a number of other things. What then is the reason for giving freedom of speech *special* treatment?

Arguments along these lines are often based on the notion of a *right* to free speech. A remark often quoted in this context is Voltaire's 'I disapprove of what you say, but I will defend to the death your right to say it', but this is in fact apocryphal.[4] It is the case that theories of rights have a long history in political philosophy. The notion was developed in the seventeenth century in the work of philosophers like Hobbes and Locke, and became very influential in the eighteenth century. It was first explicitly applied to press freedom by Matthew Tindal in *Reasons against restraining the press*, 1704. It became commonly held that it was the proper task of the state and of positive law to safeguard such rights, lists of which can be found in the American Bill of Rights and in the French Declaration of the Rights of Man.

There are many philosophical problems and issues revolving around rights. For example, Jeremy Bentham, the early utilitarian philosopher, denied there was any such thing: 'natural rights is simple nonsense: natural and imprescriptible rights, rhetorical nonsense – nonsense upon stilts.' Are they any more than custom or convention? The main problem can perhaps be put like this: rights are appealed to as something each of us has in virtue of being a human being, irrespective of the actual form of our society. Yet there has to be some agreement among humans that they should be treated as having rights, and this presupposes a society of some kind. Mill wrote: 'To have a right is to have something society ought to protect me in the possession of.' Note the use of the word 'ought' – the language of rights is inescapably normative. Where in turn does this 'ought' come from – nature or social agreement?

Before leaving this topic, it is worth mentioning two other arguments that are sometimes made, though rarely pursued in detail. There is a negative argument in that the harms caused by speech are less significant than those caused by other actions; and, lastly, there is a pragmatic argument that speech is an area which governments are especially tempted to curtail.

2.2 Extent of free speech

Given that free speech is thought to have special claims in society and that it deserves protection, the next question is – how extensive is this freedom? Does the claim of free speech or expression mean that we may say anything at all, to anyone at all, anywhere at all?

As mentioned earlier, there are a number of legal restrictions on free speech. In the UK, for example, there are the Official Secrets Act, the Prevention of Terrorism Act, laws of libel and contempt, restrictions on the naming of victims in rape cases and of minors accused in criminal cases. Beyond this, many of the issues covered in the rest of this book are questions about whether the freedom of the press should be restricted: reporting of war and terrorism, invasions of privacy.

As far as the press is concerned, most debate has taken place in the US, largely because the Constitution (through the First Amendment) secures a large amount of freedom for the press. Histories of newspapers in that country are full of horror stories of the excesses of the 'yellow press', the sensationalism, the intrusions, all in pursuit of higher sales (the name of newspaper owner William Randolph Hearst is often cited as one of the worst offenders). The unrestricted freedom of the press comes to seem the unrestricted power of the press, the arbitrary power of an unelected minority to inflict harms free from any rule or regulation. An institution that is strong enough to act as an effective counterweight to government is also strong enough to inflict serious damage on innocent bystanders. Is liberty to be treated as a ruleless state of individual licence? This dilemma bedevils all regulation of the media.

Many critics have therefore argued that press freedom is too great or is being misused. Some have suggested that the press should show some social responsibility. This line can be taken further: other critics have argued that state intervention is justified on a theory of market failure. The state is needed to compensate for the market's deficiencies. Public debate, left to itself, or rather to the newspapers, is not, as it should be, 'uninhibited, robust and wide-open' but instead will be distorted by the forces that dominate society.

The view that the media should be left alone and that there should be no regulation is often referred to as a 'libertarian' or 'classic liberal' view. Some proponents trace it back to early writers like Locke, but it is a matter of dispute how far they would have tolerated a so-called free market. The idea is that all voices should be free to be heard in the press and, as various viewpoints contend, the public would be able to discern the truth amid the hubbub. There would be an open market place of ideas. This theory seems to assume that access to the means of publishing or disseminating information is freely available to all, or most. This last point can turn into a dispute about the ability to start a newspaper. In principle, any one can start their own newspaper; in practice, in the modern age, it is a prohibitively expensive undertaking.

The notion of a 'socially responsible press' has been argued over since the 1940s, when the Hutchins Commission was established. Robert Hutchins, Chancellor of the University of Chicago, was commissioned in 1942 to study the prospects of press freedom. It is worth noting as background that as the new media of radio and television came into existence, they had been made subject to government regulation. Regulations for radio and television had imposed requirements of social responsibility. But the press, having been an unregulated industry since its beginning in the US, was free of any government control. According to some critics, the press enjoyed a privileged position in America, through the protection of the First Amendment. But this freedom, granted by society, carried obligations to society: what were these?

The Commission published its report in 1947 under the title *A free and responsible press* [161]. The Commission identified five functions against which the performance of the press might be measured:

1. The press should give a truthful, comprehensive and intelligent account of the day's events in a context which gives them meaning.
2. The press should provide a forum for the exchange of comment and criticism.
3. The press should project a representative picture of the constituent groups in the society.
4. The press should present and clarify the goals and values of society.
5. The press should provide full access to the day's intelligence.

The report was vilified, misrepresented and then ignored by the press it had hoped to reform. Some claimed that it was a misty appeal to broad coverage and public involvement. One critic said that the Commission's theory 'reaffirms the existing social order while at the same time providing the cloak of moral rectitude for those who claim to follow the doctrine'.[5]

Similar concerns were expressed at the time in the UK by the first Royal Commission on the Press (1947–49), which, though appointed to consider the effects of monopoly of ownership of the press on freedom of expression, did seek to encourage a sense of public service and responsibility amongst the journalistic profession [255, 256, 257].

Despite the criticisms of both efforts, the general notion that the press should serve some useful social function has persisted. This is not surprising if we think back to the justifications made for free speech. If it is claimed that the media aid either the pursuit of truth or the citizens in a democracy, then they should be seen to be doing so. Nor does it seem unreasonable, put in these bland terms – 'some useful social function'. But how is 'useful social function' or 'socially responsible' to be defined? One writer summed up the five proposals of the Hutchins Commission as 'education', by which he meant a liberal education.[6] But, of course, how people are educated is controversial in itself.

The danger is that the concept is hijacked by those with a very narrow view of 'good for society'. For example, it has been argued that government should be engaged in raising the moral quality of the community and therefore must judge and limit public discussion according to the moral quality of the writer or speaker. This could mean, though, that anything that is very critical of existing institutions is considered to be 'lowering' the moral quality of the community. Similarly, it has been argued that American communists have no claim to free expression because they are 'disloyal'.

Social responsibility theory contends that since the channels of communication are now so limited, those who own the channels and those who work within them must accept a responsibility to society along with the freedom that they still enjoy from any government interference. And that responsibility is to provide a truthful, balanced and comprehensive account of the news. But who is to decide what is socially responsible? If it is the government, then freedom is lost. What kinds of sanctions will restrict irresponsible newspapers? The authors of *Media ethics* [11] sum up the problem of 'social responsibility' well: 'the term captures the two sides of a classic democratic dilemma: A press free of all constraints could easily run amok in its own drive for power and profit; a press too constrained by the power of the state would fail to achieve its lofty mission – informing citizens.'[7] As proponents of such a theory the authors go on to claim that free of state control and responsible to the public for essential democratic services, the press could flourish. It would prefer telling the truth to making profits. But they acknowledge the facts of the matter: 'A socially responsible press is a medium in tension, conscious of its obligations to enlighten readers and viewers and all too aware of its deadlines and competitors.'

A recent development in moral theory is the notion of communitarianism. This has been applied in the field of the media by Clifford Christians and colleagues in *Good news: social ethics and the press* [10]. The authors identify previous theories as libertarianism, social responsibility (which only modifies libertarianism), and collectivism (which would be the press for the good of the state, as in communist countries). 'Against these there is the integration of person and community into a communitarian whole.' They believe that human life will be better if communitarian, collective and public values guide and construct our lives. But it is not clear where the practical difference lies between responsibility to society and responsibility to the community, certainly as it affects the media. When they write that the goal of media ethics should be 'transformative social change' or 'civic transformation', one may applaud the worthiness of the aim, and at the same time ask how this differs in its effect on the press from theories of 'social responsibility' and how it avoids that theory's difficulties. Also, to make a more general point that applies elsewhere: writers, thinkers and critics who seek improvements in society naturally wish for similar improvements in the media. But it is hard to see how the media, which reflect society in so many ways, can lead the way. However, it is not possible to do much more than signal the existence of this theory here.

We should also mention at this point the influential argument of the German philosopher Jürgen Habermas on 'the public sphere' [151]. He begins with a historical argument that in the seventeenth and eighteenth centuries a range of practices and institutions, principally the newspaper press, evolved, and thereby facilitated open debate of public affairs. This public arena emerged throughout Western Europe. Going on from this notion it can be argued that modern communications media can contribute to the exercise of full citizenship in two important ways. First, they can provide people with access to the information, advice and analysis that enable them to know their rights and to pursue them effectively. Second, they can provide the broadest possible range of information, interpretation and debate on areas that involve political choices, and enable them to register dissent and propose alternatives.

2.3 Access

A claim that is sometimes made is that commitment to freedom of speech requires the provision of facilities for speech, and so the public has a right of access to newspaper columns and to appear on radio and television. Without such access, the public has no real freedom of the press, only those who own the means of communication do. It is clear that those with access to radio, television, newspapers, and magazine and book publishers have more ability to speak than those without that access. So, it is argued, as there is no true market place of ideas, something should be done (for example, by government action) to rectify the balance. A typical statement of this is: 'What supporters of the status quo mean when they saw "we" have a free press is that we don't have state-run or party-controlled newspapers . . . if democracy is to mean anything it must mean that the power to communicate is available equally to *all* groups and classes, not just the media moguls and the mighty corporations . . . a litmus test for any claims for media freedom must be whether press and broadcasting accurately or fairly represent the fullest possible range of opinion and experiences from the *whole* of society.'[8] The argument is based on ideas of freedom as a kind of power, and of democracy as entailing an equality of opportunity to communicate for everyone. It could also be seen as a conflict between freedom of speech (the individual's) and the freedom of the press. Who, though, is to regulate the press in this way?

However, in defence of the press, it can be argued that such an interpretation of press freedom takes it away, in that the important thing is editorial freedom. If individuals could force their opinions into newspapers, editors would lose their freedom of decision. A further objection is that no one is prevented by direct governmental coercion from starting a newspaper or magazine, or from publishing their own book (in Western democracies at least – many countries have licensing of newspapers by government). They are of course prevented by economic considerations from doing so, but this is a different constraint from deprivation by government or other human action. It is true that such deprivation is caused by the actions of governments and individuals, and could be cured by a redesign of society. But, it is argued, liberty and the conditions of its exercise are two different problems. Another point is that to demand a right of access is to ignore why the mass media have become so important. If unorthodox views expressed in unfashionable publications do not have the impact of other media, it is largely because the consumers of information have chosen the result. If many people choose *The Times* over the *Morning Star* this is not in itself a free speech problem. As Frederick Schauer [132] puts it: 'it is one thing to say that the state must allow a forum. It is quite another to say that the state must provide the audience.'[9]

Clearly, though, if the press (or any other media) uses the argument about the role of informing the citizens of a democracy as a justification of free speech, then the provision of a full range and diversity of opinion is important.

This debate overlaps with Chapter 4 in that those holding a dominant position in the market can use their strength to keep out or buy out new entrants. This is an accusation that has been made against Rupert Murdoch, for example. At the same time it might be argued that desk-top publishing and the Internet make it easier for ordinary people to disseminate information and ideas.

2.4 The right to know

The most radical claim in this area is what is usually called 'the right to know'. Free speech will be without value if the public cannot obtain the information it needs, from government and other bodies, to enable it to discuss important issues.[10]

Naturally, the idea is popular among journalists. In the US the news media have vigorously urged the government to recognize the people's right to know. Harold Cross has written: 'public business is the public's business. Freedom of information is their just heritage. Without that the citizens of a democracy have but changed their kings' [177]. And to quote Walter Cronkite: 'when we do fight for freedom of the press, we're not fighting for our rights to do something, we're fighting for the people's right to know. That's what freedom of the press is. It's not license to the press. It's freedom of the people to know. How do they think they're going to know? By putting news or newspapers or any other news source under government control?'[11] Among British journalists, we find the campaigning editor Harold Evans [254] declaring that 'too much secrecy perpetuates error and inefficiency. If the press will not do this work, who else can?'[12] His comment on the final victory of the *Sunday Times* against Distillers in the thalidomide affair at the European Commission of Human Rights was that the judgement relied 'not so much on the right of the press to publish as the right of an individual to information which may affect his life, liberty and happiness'.

It has been suggested that this alleged right is a journalist's invention, and a very successful one at that. On the other hand, its proponents in the US claim that the right is presupposed by or closely linked to the First Amendment.

So the notion of the public's right to know has become something of a slogan. But it is a very sweeping claim and we must ask 'the right to know what?' No one wants to know everything, nor does anyone expect to be able to have access to everything, like personal letters, diaries and confidential files. Who, then, interprets the people's right to know? The press itself. So does the notion now mean any more than the public's (unexpressed) right to know whatever a newspaper wishes to tell it. There is another weakness: freedom of speech is claimed in circumstances where there is no willing speaker wanting to impart the information. It is odd to say that the principle of freedom of speech compels a government or other body to disclose information against its will.

Taking the notion less sweepingly, it may be possible to define areas of information that the public has a right to know about. This would include, most importantly, what its government is doing (because it affects the public). Similarly, the activities of non-governmental organizations – and sometimes of private companies – affect the public. So it may be said that where the public has an *interest*, the press has a mandate to inform it. To adopt Sissela Bok's summing-up: 'the public's right to know, even where protected by statute, cannot be a right to knowledge or truth, but at best to access to information; and not to all information, but only to some. The public has a legitimate interest, however, in all information about matters that might affect its welfare, quite apart from whether a right to this information can be established.'[13]

The claim, then, is not for a right to know, but for freedom of information. Some countries, notably the US, have Freedom of Information Acts, others do not. The UK will acquire one in 1998. This topic is discussed further in Chapter 3.

2.5 Accountability

Our discussions so far have amply shown the power of the media. In the US one of their roles, which is protected by the First Amendment, is to act as a check or balance against government. In the UK the press has been described as 'the fourth estate'. More generally, 'the press has become the greatest power within Western countries, more powerful than the legislation, the executive and the judiciary. One would like to ask: By what law has it been elected and to whom is it responsible?' This quotation comes from Alexander Solzhenitsyn in 1978,[14] after some years' experience of living in the West. It is a familiar question: is the press, which is always holding others to account, itself accountable? This might be construed as a more technical question: are there mechanisms for public feedback and criticism?

One way of regulating the press is through the law (for example, laws on libel). This kind of regulation, though, is seen as an infringement on freedom of the press. Strong believers in press freedom propose instead a model of accountability through the market place. They would claim that insofar as the media are held accountable, their freedom is necessarily diminished. But through the market place the public rewards or punishes the media by buying or not buying (the newspaper, magazine or book), viewing or not viewing (the television programme), listening or not listening (the radio programme). 'Media that people accept and support will survive and thrive, media that people dislike or reject will suffer and die.'[15]

However, the market model assumes a knowledgeable and concerned audience, that when people know the good, they will see it, and that when they know the bad (for example, a newspaper), they will avoid it. But this is a large assumption if the audience is largely passive. The market model is also undermined by concentrations of media ownership, which restricts the choices available in the market (this point will be discussed further in Chapter 4).

An alternative way of dealing with accountability is through self-regulation, with the use of councils and codes. But as codes and councils are often put together by professionals for professionals, accountability tends to be an in-house matter. The problem here is whether internal self-regulation can be effective in providing accountability, or whether it is a screen behind which the media carry on much as before. (George Bernard Shaw said that all professions are conspiracies against the public.) In particular, the issue is whether these councils and codes have any force; to have none seems tantamount to an avoidance of accountability. (There is more on councils and codes in Chapter 9.)

There is another issue here, which depends on accountability to the public. Should there be a 'right to reply' available when the media make a mistake or wrong individual citizens? Do newspapers and broadcasters allow enough space or time for people to respond? In the UK the Press Complaints Commission requires newspapers to print the results of their adjudications of complaints, but they are not given prominence. Some newspapers have ombudsmen; and one can of course write a letter to the editor, but it remains an editorial decision whether to print the letter, which anyway will have much less prominence than the original article. Campaigners continue to call for a statutory right of reply to factual inaccuracies, and the continuing resistance of newspapers to this suggests a less than complete commitment to truth and accuracy.

Broadcasting in the UK, which is more heavily regulated than the press, provides a more satisfactory right of reply through complaints handling procedures by the British Broadcasting Corporation and the commercial radio and television channels, which can result in on-screen and printed apologies.

Notes

1. Milton, *Areopagitica*, Everyman edition, p. 158.
2. Snoddy, R. *The good, the bad and the unacceptable*, p. 172.
3. Stephen Holmes in Lichtenberg, J. (ed.) *Democracy and the mass media*, p. 28.
4. See Lee, S. *The cost of free speech*, p. 3.
5. Altschull, J. H. *Agents of power*, p. 304.
6. Ferry, W. H. 'Masscomm as guru' in Merrill, J. C. and Barney, R. D. (eds.) *Ethics and the press*, pp. 47–59.
7. Christians, C. G. *Media ethics*, p. 327.
8. Oakley, G. in Curran, J. and others *Bending reality*, pp. 215–16.
9. Schauer, F. *Free speech*, p. 127.
10. According to Fink, C. *Media ethics*, p. 11, the notion was first propounded by Kent Cooper in 1942.
11. Quoted in Merrill, J. C. and Barney, R. D. (eds.) *Ethics and the press*, p. 178.
12. Evans, H. *Good times, bad times*, p. 59.
13. Bok, S. *Secrets*, p. 258.
14. *National Review*, 30, 7 July 1978, p. 838.
15. Merrill, J. C. in Dennis, E. E., Gillmor, D. M. and Glasser, T. L. (eds.) *Media freedom and accountability*, p. 12.

3 Government and the media

The media, when restricted or constrained, are most likely to be so by government. On the one hand, there is the free press (most often found in Western societies), whose primary function is perhaps to provide the people with a free flow of information. On the other hand, governments have always realized that information is power and the control of information is essential to public support for its policies and mandates. So that even if government is not attempting to control the media, it is trying to present itself favourably in the media, and this might well include suppression of information harmful to itself. Governments do practise 'selective presentation' and 'economy with the truth' – not to speak of lying.

In the UK this includes the debate over whether there should be a Freedom of Information Act as is the case in Australia, New Zealand, Canada, the US (since 1966), Norway, Sweden, Denmark, France and the Netherlands. For example, Maurice Frankel[1] stated that a Freedom of Information Act would put into law the presumption that the public has the right to official information unless the government can show that disclosure would be harmful for one of a number of specified reasons: breach of privacy, or the disclosure of genuine military or trade secrets, for example, if it involved foreign relations and law enforcement. Government claims on these scores could be challenged in the courts or through an ombudsman. Many active journalists have argued for it too: Raymond Snoddy wrote that 'the single most effective way to extend press freedom would be to pass a Freedom of Information Act'.[2] The Conservative government in the UK opposed this on the grounds that it would not be constitutional for an independent body to overrule a minister. Prime Minister Thatcher was quoted as saying that 'Ministers' accountability to parliament would be reduced and Parliament itself diminished' and this view has been echoed by her successors. But Snoddy gives an example of the kind of anomaly that arises: the safety of a pesticide is under review in the UK but the details are confidential; however, anyone going to the reading room of the Environmental Protection Agency in Washington, DC can look them up.

In the UK over the last few years several cases have been fought in the courts between government and the media as to whether information should be made available to the public. An important case was that of the civil servant Clive Ponting. He passed official documents, regarding the sinking of the Argentine cruiser *General Belgrano* in the Falklands conflict, to a Member of Parliament for disclosure in a parliamentary debate. Ponting was prosecuted under the old Official Secrets Act in 1985. He defended himself on the grounds that his passing of confidential material was 'in the interests of the state'. The judge decided that, by legal definition, the 'interests of the state' meant the interests of the government of the day. But the jury rejected the direction of the judge and acquitted Ponting.

Then there was the long-running 'Spycatcher' case, where the government tried to suppress the publication of the memoirs of an agent, Peter Wright, who had worked for MI5, the British security service. However, after the Ponting trial, the government no longer trusted a jury to convict and resorted to the civil law, claiming breaches of the law of confidence. In this case the government argued that total secrecy was necessary for the efficient functioning of the security services. Any information from Wright's book would damage this. The defence argued that much of the information had already been made available. The British government pursued the case lengthily but eventually had to concede defeat: in 1988 the House of Lords rejected the government's argument that the duty of confidence was absolute and recognized that a public interest defence exists.

By the end of the 1980s the old Official Secrets Act of 1911 had become unworkable, as the Ponting case had shown. The notorious part of it was Section II, which made it an offence for any civil servant to make public any information obtained in the course of his official duties. New legislation was introduced in 1989. The UK government claimed it would lead to greater openness, but this has been disputed. Two of the criticisms made of the new Official Secrets Act of 1989 are that public interest cannot be invoked as a defence, and that a lifelong duty of confidentiality is imposed on all Crown servants and any disclosure is an offence, for whatever motive.[3]

3.1 Internal threats

In England and Wales during the Tudor period, in what was in effect the early days of the media, any criticism of state or church was severely proscribed. Seditious libel, as it was called, was a serious crime. In the present age, most democratic governments tolerate criticism of their actions. The most problematic area for a free speech principle is when this principle protects anything that suggests or advocates illegal activity. (Though this illegal activity might vary from the smoking of cannabis to assassinating the Prime Minister.)

Obviously, speech advocating illegal political action is the most crucial. It can be argued that it appears most inconsistent with the argument from democracy. If the processes of democratic government generate the free speech principle, then speech that would circumvent those processes, and that would impose a form of government other than rule by the people, cannot fall within coverage of the principle. Perhaps paradoxically, the argument from democracy can justify protecting speech advocating violation of law when, and only when, democracy does not exist.

There is a similar line based on the argument from truth. This argument presupposes a system of rational discourse. Advocacy of illegal action, especially advocacy of violence, is fundamentally inconsistent with the assumptions upon which the argument from truth is founded. Anyone who seeks to impose their views by force, or seeks to have others do so for them, can reasonably be said to have forfeited their claim to protection under a system premised on the supremacy of reason.

On the other hand, there is the point that one might want to allow the advocacy of illegal conduct under a theory of 'catharsis', that permitting such advocacy may be less likely to lead to illegal conduct.

As has already been noted, the argument from truth, the argument from democracy and those based on distrust of government are all consequentialist arguments, deriving their force from some conception of the long-range general welfare and from a conception of public interest. In the face of this it is perhaps hard to argue that disobedience of the law is in the public interest. On the other hand, arguments from autonomy and individuality are non-consequentialist and emphasize the priority of the individual over state power.

Government most strongly attempts to constrain freedom of speech when it is felt that there is a threat to 'national security'. A recent example of suppression is the government of Serbia stopping television coverage of pro-democracy demonstrations in the winter of 1996–97, as if to deny they were taking place. Still, how is the extent of this threat to be determined? That is, how great is the threat, how likely is it to occur?

In the UK, the most contentious issue between government and media was the coverage by television and radio of Northern Ireland, in particular, the terrorist activity that resulted from the Troubles. On the one hand, there was the desire of television journalists to explain what was going on, to give some understanding of the events (which of course included many deaths), to the British public. One of their methods is to interview people involved in the terrorist organizations, on both sides of the sectarian divide. On the other hand, the British government saw this terrorism as a threat to democratic government and something that had to be fought. (The terrorists themselves would say that to describe them thus is to beg the question; they are not 'terrorists' but 'freedom fighters'.) In a memorable phrase, the British Prime Minister described the media as providing the terrorists with 'the oxygen of publicity'. The strongest expression of this attitude was the introduction of the so-called Broadcasting Ban in October 1988 (not lifted until September 1994). This was a ban on direct appearance by representatives of several named organizations in Northern Ireland on radio and television. Journalists challenged the ban on the grounds that it contravened the duty laid upon broadcasters by law to observe 'due impartiality'. Supporters of the ban argued along the lines that they did not see why terrorists and their apologists should enjoy the freedoms of a civilized society; opponents that such a ban should be imposed only when the damage to society was substantial and certain, and could be demonstrated. It should also be noted that the ban did not apply to newspapers and magazines; government believed that there was a directness about the broadcasting media that made them more dangerous.

We should also mention here the nadir of the deteriorating relations between government and media over Northern Ireland. This was the showing of the controversial Thames Television documentary *Death on the Rock* about the shooting of IRA terrorists in Gibraltar, which suggested that the government had lied. It became the subject of an independent inquiry under Lord Windlesham and Richard Rampton QC [226].

3.2 External threats

By external threats is meant threats from outside the state or country. This can involve national security, as occurred with the 'Spycatcher' case discussed above, but typically it involves issues relating to war and war reporting. The conflict can be summed up by two quotations taken from *The media and the Falklands campaign* by Valerie Adams [227]. From the point of view of government, Lawrence Freedman wrote in the foreword: 'For the military commander, information is a weapon of war.' So he has an interest in accurate information being withheld and, sometimes, inaccurate information being disseminated. On the other hand, *The Times* wrote on 25 May 1982: 'the first, indeed the paramount interest in a democracy must be to inform the public as soon as possible about what is happening on its behalf.'

The issues mentioned so far in this chapter revolve around a clash between government interest and the public interest; governments usually argue that the two are the same thing. In times of war these two interests are linked together as the 'national interest' – and the national interest (that is, winning the war in which that nation is engaged) overrules many of the normal freedoms possessed by the media.

One way of solving the problem, from the military's point of view, is to withhold information entirely, as with the invasion of Grenada by the US in 1983. For the first time in living memory, reporters were not informed in advance of the operation or permitted to accompany the assault troops. For two days the press was kept away, and then for another two days was only permitted guided tours of the island. The media complained vociferously. One eminent American journalist said: 'if the press isn't there the people aren't there.'

This distrust from the US military stems from its unfounded belief that the media contributed to the Americans losing the Vietnam War. The policy in this instance was to hope for a quick and painless victory. At first, according to Fink,[4] the public was happy with the victory and not worried by being kept in the dark. Later public opinion changed, but not drastically.

Even when the military is releasing information, its aim will be to reveal as little as possible. This attitude was severely criticized by the media during the Falklands conflict of 1982. For one thing, the media professionals felt they could be trusted. One defence correspondent, Christopher Wain, wrote in a letter to *The Times*: 'For a Defence Correspondent, the rules of engagement are clear. You do not reveal British military secrets. You do not put British lives at risk. You do not put interviewees whom you know to be in possession of secret information into the position where it may be inadvertently blurted out ...' But this leaves the controversial issue of who is to decide whether publication is in the national interest. According to Valerie Adams, this question lay at the heart of the argument between the military and the media during the Falklands conflict.[5] She adds that the consensus among journalists seemed to be that, if asked to do so, they would temporarily delay the publication of material that was operationally sensitive, but that delay could not be indefinite, nor would they maintain a delay if they thought the material was going to be published elsewhere.

In the cases described so far, it was the journalists' struggle simply to get enough information with which to report. What of the crisis of conscience that would arise where a journalist is asked to conceal something of major importance? Should journalists in wartime give way to their obligations as citizens of the country they live in? Or should they continue to uphold the basic tenet of journalism, to report events in an objective and detached manner?

It may be that this clash is usually resolved in favour of journalists' obligations as citizens, but one can go on to question the narrowness of an interpretation of citizenship that ties it closely to official views and explanations of events.

What would override journalists' national loyalties? Do they fail to record war crimes by their country's armed forces? Do they report lies as truth if they know them to be lies? Or, to give a more ambiguous situation, on occasions when they are sceptical of what they have been told by official spokespersons, do they record that scepticism?

For many it is more important to win the war the country is involved in than to tell the truth about it. As Ronald Dworkin commented: 'Truth may be the first casualty of war, but some people's desire to be told the truth is a close second.'[6] But then the point at issue will shift to discussing whether this or that truth, when told, will harm or weaken the nation's attempt to win the war.

An example that illustrates this occurred during the Korean War. Tom Hopkinson, the editor of the magazine *Picture Post*, received an article from Korea which gave an account of the UK's ally South Korea treating its prisoners of war with brutality. The owner of the *Picture Post* told Hopkinson not to print the article, on the grounds that it would 'give aid and comfort to the enemy'. Hopkinson refused and was sacked. On this occasion, then, the truth was more important. But it may well be that Hopkinson did not agree that publication of the article would give aid and comfort to the enemy. Second, the British position in the war was quite different – it was not fighting for national survival.

From the military's and, probably, the government's point of view, the war correspondent should help the war effort, not only by protecting security and the lives of those involved, but also by keeping up morale at home and at the front. During the Falklands conflict the government accused the BBC of treachery for airing the views of politicians opposed to the war. As Dworkin suggested above, there has even been some doubt that the public prefers truthful reporting to loyal reporting in times of war. However, if this is the case, there must come a point where the public no longer believes the press. It is usually acknowledged that the press has a critical, questioning function in a society – should it continue to exercise this function in times of war? Or should it be said that a society is different at such times? Suppose a war is being run with great inefficiency, to the extent that it reduces the chances of winning the war. Should not a journalist report this? This was the situation with the Crimean War and perhaps the first great war correspondent, W. H. Russell, who was encouraged to report the suffering and misery he saw about him by his editor on *The Times*: 'Continue as you have done, to tell the truth and as much of it as you can, and leave such comment as may be dangerous to us, who are out of danger.'[7] Valerie Adams concludes her study with the observation that 'the limits which may be applied to the public right to information must be based on criteria which can be generally accepted by the public'.

Other issues are raised by the comparatively recent importance of television. This is now the main source of news for most people, and pictures are more vivid than print. It is one thing to state in words that, say, twenty people were killed; it is another to show film of twenty bodies, with perhaps a few faces pictured as well. So there is a temptation to 'sanitize' the coverage, to play down the fact that war means death. For Western political societies depend upon at least a certain amount of public support in prosecuting a war. There would be a fear of losing this support if large numbers of casualties occurred, either to one's own troops or to the enemy's civilians. As already mentioned, the US military believed, and perhaps still does, that it only lost the war in Vietnam because television reporting of it sapped the will of the American public to continue fighting. Whether this is true or not, and it probably is not, the US military's belief in it has affected its attitude to the media ever since: this can be seen in the media blackout during the US invasion of Grenada and careful news management during the Gulf War. One of the events of the Gulf War was the killing of 400 civilians by a missile in a bunker in Baghdad. The graphic reports of this on television, 'allowed' by the Iraqi government, were criticized by the Ministry of Defence and by certain newspapers in the UK as being unnecessary and giving comfort to the enemy.

John Tusa, former Managing Director of the BBC World Service, reported going to the Public Radio Conference in the US in May 1991, after the Gulf War.[8] There he found a strong current of criticism of the quality of coverage of the war. There was a belief that the Pentagon had lied to the press along with feelings that the war had been covered in a 'hurray' manner, with objectivity thrown out of the window. Tusa himself felt that many aspects of the war had been missed and under-reported; he concluded that what would have really tested the journalists would have been failure in the war. Would they then have been able to report directly and honestly? Dworkin, in the same article from which we quoted above, expressed a concern that some politicians believed that government may properly manipulate public opinion in order to prevent the public from criticizing the war or its conduct. He saw censorship being defended on the insidious ground 'that a pleased and supportive public is a great military advantage'.

Apart from war itself, there is the Cold War, or to put it more broadly, the furtherance of a country's foreign policy. For the US, there are the activities of the Central Intelligence Agency; for the UK, from 1948 to 1976 there was the Information Research Department. Such organizations practise disinformation, planting false stories in the press to discredit opponents of the nation's government. It is bad enough if the press is manipulated to carry falsehoods; much worse if it does so willingly.

An important case was that of the British government versus the BBC over Suez in 1956. First, it was crucial that war had not been declared. Second, the government's actions and intentions were being heavily criticized in the country. The BBC felt it should follow its duty to be fair and impartial and so should give space on television to opponents of the government. This caused great annoyance to the government. In fact, in later years there were allegations that the government had made plans to take over the BBC if it did not obey its wishes.

On the other hand, it appears that there does not always have to be an opposition between the military and the media. At the present time, the military often plays a peacekeeping, humanitarian role, and here the media can aid this aim, as in the former Yugoslavia. A commander of United Nations forces in Sarajevo said that 'the media was the only major weapons system that I had. In a number of cases the media had more impact on keeping the peace and reducing atrocities than the peacekeeping personnel.'[9]

Another topic worth mentioning here is the role of the media in diplomatic and trade relations between countries. For example, in 1980 a British television company broadcast a drama-documentary about the execution of an Arab princess for adultery, *Death of a Princess*. The British government sought to stop it rather than harm relations with Saudi Arabia. More recently the Malaysian government was angered by a press report in the *Sunday Times*, claiming a possible link between the UK government grant for the construction of the Pergau hydroelectric dam in 1991 and British arms sales, and as a result excluded British companies from tendering for new contracts. The British government had to tell Malaysia that it could not censor newspapers in the UK.

Notes

1. Frankel, M. in Buchan, N. and Sumner, T. (eds.) *Glasnost in Britain?*, p. 92.
2. Snoddy, R. *The good, the bad and the unacceptable*, p. 170.
3. Snoddy, R. *The good, the bad and the unacceptable*, p. 180f.
4. Fink, C. *Media ethics*, p. 219.
5. Adams, V. *The media and the Falklands campaign*, p. 160.
6. Dworkin, R. in *Index on Censorship*, Vol. 20, Nos. 4–5, April–May 1991, Issues 129–30, p. 2.
7. Quoted in Knightley, P. *The first casualty*, p. 12.
8. Tusa, J. *A world in your ear*, p. 36.
9. Quoted in Stewart, I. and Carruthers, S. L. *War, culture and the media*, p. 18.

4 Economic pressures

So far we have been talking about the media in abstract and perhaps grandiose terms. We have spoken of principles and rights, of conflicts with government, of democracy and truth. But there is a more down-to-earth view: 'a newspaper is a private enterprise owing nothing whatever to the public, which grants it no franchise. It is emphatically the property of its owner who is selling a manufactured product at his own risk.' This emphatic statement comes from the *Wall Street Journal*. It at least reminds us that much of the media is a business, an enterprise aimed at making money. Most radio and television around the world is financed out of advertising and, from the commercial point of view, the programmes exist in order to obtain an audience for the advertising that takes place in and around these programmes. Public service broadcasting in general, and the BBC in particular, because they are paid for by alternative means, by government grant or through a licence fee, have been insulated from the commercial imperative, but then public service broadcasting throughout the world, including the BBC, has become increasingly subject to commercial pressures. As we have seen earlier, there is a strong tradition that the press should be free from government control. But what about freedom from commercial pressures?

There is a partly historical answer to this question. It was the commercial success of newspapers (for example, *The Times* in the early nineteenth century) that gave them the independence and power to criticize government. It is also possible to see a close link between financial health and good journalism, to be able to pay for enough correspondents at home and abroad and for wider cultural coverage, to have the resources to pursue investigations over a period of time, and so on.

Still, the question is whether commercial pressures inhibit the freedom of the media. It is a central argument of defenders of the free market that freedom in the market is a necessary condition for democracy to flourish. They say that market arrangements encourage a diversity of opinion and best serve the democratic need for informed citizens. They also argue that the market is the best institutional arrangement for ensuring that the press can act as a check on government.

One worry may be about the influence of owners upon their newspapers. Their business goals may affect their editorial activities. So how much influence would be acceptable? Are they to have no involvement at all? Is it acceptable for them to make suggestions about content, but no more? Might they have a major role to play in making the larger decisions, such as design changes and marketing campaigns? A survey run in the US found that most owners and editors were in favour of this latter option, involvement in strategic decisions. The extent of acceptable influence by proprietors is crucial. There is nothing to stop owners subordinating objective and comprehensive news coverage to their commercial and political concerns (as Lord Beaverbrook did) or ruthlessly pursing their various media interests.

A more philosophical argument on the subject of economic pressures is the claim that the market undermines the relationship between journalism and democracy, for the values of journalism conflict with the requirements of the market place. To survive in the market place, it is alleged, the press has to satisfy the preferences of its customers, and this can mean that it 'rarely confronts its consumers with information, beliefs and knowledge which do not conform to their pre-existing preference'.[1] In other words, the press gives its readers only what it wants.

Then it is added that the more competitive the market, the greater the pressure in this direction, to sensationalism, to lowest common factor journalism. Fierce competition may also erode professional ethics.

There is also the more general claim that sees the press of the modern world as contaminated by the capitalist system. It is claimed that capitalists use their economic power with a commercial market system to ensure that the flow of public information is consonant with their interests. This might be termed a 'propaganda' model: 'the powerful are able to fix the premises of discourse, to decide what the general populace is allowed to hear, see and think about, and to "manage" public opinion by regular propaganda campaigns.'[2]

It may be that both these arguments, which see the media as 'simplifying' a picture of the world in order to conform to the interests of their audience or owners, are themselves oversimplifying, by exaggerating the homogeneity of the media within a society. For the 'media' includes, besides television and mass-market newspapers, periodicals and magazines of all shapes, sizes and persuasions. But this leads us to two specific phenomena which reflect the economic pressures of the modern world: first, the trend towards concentration of ownership in the media; second, the influence of advertising and marketing on the media.

4.1 Media ownership

Since the beginning of the twentieth century there has been a relentless march towards large media groups and concentration of ownership in the US and UK. Figures for the US show that in 1930 84 per cent of the nation's daily newspapers were independent; in 1987 this figure had fallen to less than 30 per cent. The successive Royal Commissions on the Press (1947–49, 1961–62, 1974–77) in the UK were established because of concerns over monopolistic tendencies in the newspaper industry [255, 256, 257].

One fear is an extension of one mentioned above, that the views of the fewer owners left in the field will be imposed. This will have two results: that fewer viewpoints will be expressed, and that there will increasing similarity between the viewpoints that are expressed. But it is not to be assumed that media concentration in itself does not result in a better product (for example, there may be a more economic use of resources). Also, while there is plenty of evidence to show that the ownership of the media is concentrated in the hands of a few capitalists, there is limited evidence demonstrating that this actually affects the *content* of the media.

A second fear is that many media institutions are owned by outside corporations that have no commitment to the qualities of journalism, and which find that they can get more profit for less quality (for example, by reducing the number of journalists). Yet this accusation need not be confined to outside corporations which own media organizations or companies.

A third concern over the concentration of media ownership is with companies expanding into different areas. The Time–Warner grouping is a huge one and links a primarily entertainment company (Warner) with a news one (Time). So there may be a temptation for the news arm to deal favourably, in news and reviews, with the entertainment company's films, for example. A company's newspapers may not investigate the activities of other companies in the group. It has happened that a newspaper has been used to pursue commercial vendettas.

A frequent source for these fears in the UK has been Rupert Murdoch. It has been argued that his formula for media success was to narrow the editorial focus of his tabloids, concentrate on sex and crime (although this has always been part of other papers), reduce news coverage, increase cheque-book journalism. And, as proprietor, he can remove and appoint editors in order to get his view of things put across. What makes this all the more worrying is that Murdoch owns a large number of media outlets: will his newspapers give favourable reviews to books from the publishing company he owns? There is certainly some evidence that they take every opportunity to praise and promote his television company, British Sky Broadcasting, and criticize its rivals, the BBC and other commercial television channels.

In the UK there have been attempts to limit concentrations of media ownership. The Broadcasting Act 1996 tackles the problem of comparing the different markets of newspapers and broadcasting with a definition of 'national voice', thereby setting limits for cross-media ownership and ensuring that no media proprietor owns a monopoly of media within an industry sector nationally or across the media within a region.

There are two other questions to be faced. First, how important is media pluralism for a fully free press? Perhaps the question is not to be judged in terms of the number of viewpoints. What of factors such as the truth or falsity of the information, differences in validity and sophistication of the views expressed, or the superficiality or thoroughness of the messages presented?

Second, has there really been a decline in media outlets? This leads to another question: how is media pluralism to be measured? Media pluralism can be judged by the number of publications and broadcast outlets in the market place, the nature of the ownership of these outlets, and also the characteristics of the content (programming and news) they deliver. The assumption is that the more outlets from different ownerships available, the healthier it is.

But to revert to the question of a decline in outlets. On the one hand, there has been increasing centralization of ownership; on the other hand, an increase of outlets from proliferation of cable and satellite television channels, the vast number of magazines available. There is diversity of opinion in book publishing too. So it can be argued that the pluralism of the system is growing. However, the real problem may be shrinkage of media providing news, a restriction of pluralism or diversity in journalism.

Domination of the press by large media companies has another detrimental effect, that of making it difficult for new entrants into the industry or for smaller, independent newspapers to survive. Large companies can buy or squeeze out smaller titles, and so restrict diversity. In the UK, *Today*, the first British national daily newspaper to be printed using colour, was begun in 1986 by an independent news proprietor, Eddie Shah. It was, however, later bought out by Rupert Murdoch's News Corporation and eventually closed down.

4.2 Advertising and marketing

It is worth repeating a point made earlier, that it was advertising which gave the press financial independence in the nineteenth century and thus freedom from political interests. But then in the early twentieth century publishers, rather than raise the price of their commodity to reflect increases in production, chose to keep the cost low and use the contented readership to attract more advertisers.

So newspapers, magazines and most television could not exist without advertising. The amount of it determines the amount of space or time available, and affects the content and structure of the paper or programme. The provision of content can be seen by the consideration that it would be highly unlikely that a newspaper would contain travel pages, if travel agencies and airlines did not advertise. Television programmes are constructed to reach a dramatic climax at a commercial break. For the 1994 World Cup in football, which took place in the

US, there was some pressure from the American television networks to divide each game into quarters rather than halves, in order to provide more opportunity for screening advertisements. Conversely, cutbacks in advertising affect the media: reduction of revenue means less money to be spent on content. There is the often cited case of the *Daily Herald*, a British newspaper that had a high readership but had to close because most of its readers were working class and so advertisers were not interested in them.

In fact there are a number of ways in which newspapers can be affected by advertising. First, newspapers may be led to increase the ratio of advertising in their products to editorial content.

Second, they may allow market criteria (that is, how many advertisers will be attracted) to determine new ventures. An example of this is as follows: the *Los Angeles Times* produces zonal papers for the different areas of this huge city, but for many years it would not produce one for the central poor districts, on the grounds that 'the audience does not have the purchasing power and is not responsive to the kind of advertising we carry'. Here it might be asked: do newspapers have an ethical obligation to provide coverage to all significant segments of their geographical areas whether they make money from them or not? Do readers have any worth to newspaper publishers other than their utility to individuals or groups?

Third, newspapers may accept editorial-style adverts. Some newspapers and magazines (mostly in the US, but also in British local newspapers) carry 'advertorials'. These are supplements paid for by advertisers but made to look like the editorial pages. So they resemble independent feature articles but are in fact advertising.

Fourth, newspapers may suppress stories when advertisers withdraw their support in protest, or suppress them in case they might. The music editor of an American newspaper was sent to cover a jazz festival sponsored by a cigarette company. 'Strange bedfellows, cigarettes and jazz', he wrote, 'Duke Ellington died of lung cancer.' He was fired because of the fear of losing five pages of regular advertising from tobacco companies.

Fifth, newspapers may provide lowest common factor content aimed to deliver the largest audience.

Sixth, newspapers may provide news space for companies that is proportionate to the advertising the company buys. The separation of advertiser's interests and feature or editorial material can be quite tenuous in the specialist magazine press (that is, consumer, style, hobby and leisure magazines).

As for television, the problem of advertising on television is well expressed in the dilemma: does commercial television exist to bring programmes to viewers, or deliver viewers to advertisers? In the UK, spot advertising and clear identification of commercial breaks (as required by *The ITC code of advertising standards and practice*) has ensured the separation of adverts and programmes. However, television companies have to make programmes around which advertisers wish to purchase airtime. Recently, sponsorship (long accepted in the US) has introduced further opportunities for indirect influence on programme planning by advertisers and sponsors. This is despite safeguards to ensure sponsors have no editorial control or direct influence over programmes they sponsor.

Marketing also can affect the content of the media. In the fight for profits, it is considered to be an essential tool. Editors and news directors are expected to package their news and information to attract a target audience. In newspapers this has the result that an increasing percentage of space is devoted to 'soft' news or features, such as articles on travel, recreation and lifestyles.

The use of marketing techniques for the press has the justification that editors and reporters are not representative of their readers and listeners; market research information gives media organizations a continuous source of feedback from readers and listeners. So a marketing approach to news is the most effective and efficient way to select and present news that is of interest to and pertinent for the audience.

This does lead to editors no longer determining what their audiences need or should have. Rather, they provide the news that the audiences say they want. The question is: which should decide what is news, the editor (or some journalistic decision-maker) or someone apart from journalism? This in fact leads us to the old debate of whether the press should give readers what they want or what they need.

But it is an inescapable economic fact that newspapers cannot give readers what they need unless they also give them what they want. A newspaper has to remain profitable.

Of course, if one assumes with the *Wall Street Journal* that the sole purpose of the media is to make money, then the ethical issues are considerably simplified. But then there can no longer be any claim to the freedom provided by the free speech principle.

Notes

1. O'Neill, J. in Belsey, A. and Chadwick, R. (eds.) *Ethical issues in journalism and the media*, p. 23.
2. Herman, E. S. and Chomsky, N. *Manufacturing consent: the political economy of the mass media*, p. xi.

5 Privacy

We asked earlier about the extent of the right of free speech. Governments, large organizations and companies with economic power seek, rightly or wrongly, to restrict this freedom. But the press also affects individual citizens. One of the functions of the press is to find out the truth in matters of public concern, and this can very often disrupt the privacy of an individual, when for instance it is revealed that a minister has had a holiday paid for by a company in return for that company being given certain contracts. On the one hand, it is a private matter how the holiday is organized; on the other, it reflects on the independence of the Minister's judgement. The aim of the media is, of course, to make things public, to interrupt privacy.

What exactly is privacy? A distinction needs to be drawn between privacy and secrecy; letters are private, but not necessarily secret. The private is the area over which individuals feel they have control, where they can invite or exclude without having to give justifications. Claims to privacy are claims to control access to what one takes to be one's personal domain. Secrecy is that which is intentionally hidden. Privacy is something we like to protect.

Isaiah Berlin has suggested that the distinction between the public and the private is in fact quite a modern idea. He writes: 'there is a province of life – private life – with which it is thought undesirable, save in exceptional circumstances, for public authority to interfere ... In the modern world ... we proceed on the assumption that there is a frontier between public and private life; and that, however small the private sphere may be, within it I can do as I please – provided this does not interfere with the similar rights of others, or undermine the order which makes this kind of arrangement possible.'[1] This is a classical liberal view, which can be traced through Locke, Thomas Paine and J. S. Mill, and is enshrined in Article 12 of the Universal Declaration of Human Rights (1948): 'No one shall be subjected to arbitrary interference with his privacy, family, home or correspondence, nor to attacks upon his honour and reputation. Everyone has the right to the protection of the law against such interference or attacks.'

It should first be noted that some areas of privacy are protected by law. Most papers avoid printing the names of rape victims. The reasoning is that rape, unlike other crimes, places a stigma on the victim, who should be spared the additional pain of being publicly identified. Women are reluctant to report rapes anyway, and by keeping their names out of the paper, newspapers can encourage the increasing number of victims who do report. There is a counterargument, which is that secrecy reinforces the social stigma, and greater openness would lead to more realistic responses to the crime and its victims. And is it fair that the accused is named, although presumed innocent until proved guilty?

Privacy can be disrupted in different ways: by publication of embarrassing private facts, such as that staple of British Sunday newspapers, the report of a vicar having an affair with one of his parishioners; by intrusion, that is, unwarranted violation of one's private space, which can come about through a journalist entering a home uninvited, or by taking photographs with telephoto lenses; by publishing information that places someone in a false light through reporting falsehoods and distortions (for example, by the mismatching of a photograph of a person in a newspaper and the caption).

The issues raised by the publication of embarrassing private facts were highlighted by the case of US Senator Gary Hart, who was campaigning to be chosen by the Democratic Party as its candidate for president in 1987. From early on in the campaign, there were reports of the rumours that Hart was a womanizer. Hart then challenged the press to follow him and look for evidence. The *Miami Herald* had already done so; a reporter had been watching his town house in Washington DC, and seen a young woman visiting him. Hart denied that she had stayed the night, but said that she had left by a back door – which is, of course, beside the point. Reports of other meetings between the two came in. At a press conference three days later Hart was asked if he had ever committed adultery. He replied that he did not have to answer the question. But the reporter who had asked that question later phoned Hart's press secretary to inform him that his paper had documented evidence of a long-standing affair between Hart and a prominent Washington social figure. The next day Hart withdrew his candidacy.

The issue here was whether Hart's involvement with the young woman was relevant to his campaign to seek the presidential nomination. In reporting it, were the press trivializing the issues, or were they showing that Hart would be less able as the President? The newspapers that defended running the story argued that Hart had showed 'poor judgement' in the affair, an insensitivity to appearances, recklessness and a lack of discipline, indifference to trust. Put more generally, the question is: is it relevant to a politician's abilities and capacities as a politician that he is in private a womanizer? (And it was later revealed that revered US President

John F. Kennedy was precisely that.)

One way of dealing with this problem of what constitutes a justifiable disruption of privacy is to say that the personal affairs of a public person are only newsworthy if relevant to another obviously newsworthy story. Take the hypothetical case of a British MP with a mistress: if he was married, a Conservative and part of a campaign for family values, then we would have a clear case of hypocrisy. It seems right that the press should bring examples of this to our attention. But if he is single, mainly interested in economics, and of any party, then where is the need to know this?

So, we have another question: do public figures have a diminished right to privacy? Does the fact that they have chosen to enter the public arena suggest a willingness to undergo rigorous scrutiny and to suffer the consequences of embarrassing revelations? Enoch Powell commented that politicians who complain about the press are like sailors who complain about the sea. One might also quote US President Harry S. Truman: 'If you can't stand the heat, get out of the kitchen.' On the other hand, in the US especially, media scrutiny is so thorough, delving far back into the past, questioning all that a person has done, that some politicians have decided it is not worth subjecting themselves and their families to the process, and have thus chosen not to run for high office. Another consideration, however, is that the demand for privacy by public figures can be used as a cloak to hide secret activities that are either illegal or blameworthy, where the media have a justifiable interest in reporting these. The British press baron Robert Maxwell was notorious for issuing writs at any attempt to investigate his activities.

It should not be forgotten, however, that besides politicians and people in positions of power, there are two other groups of people who get caught up in the media. There are, for want of a better description, public personalities, those created and sustained by publicity. Finally, there are those who become caught up in the media, thrust involuntarily into the public eye.

The second group includes the many public figures – celebrities, 'stars' – who are created and maintained by the media, or have exploited the media to promote themselves. It frequently happens that they are in turn exploited by the media. Can they complain? One might want to say to them that those who live by the sword shall die by the sword. This is a broad category, passing from Sarah, Duchess of York to minor actors from television soap operas.

To return to the question: to what extent is the information that is made public relevant to the individual's public performance? What justifies the intrusion into – not to say, removal of – that person's privacy? The common way of raising the issue is by referring to 'the public interest'. But how is this to be examined? For the media make ambiguous use of the notion. It can be taken to mean, what it is in the interests of the public to know, or, what the public is interested in (that is, what it is curious about). Since some sections of the media's public like any amount of gossip and scandal, the notion of public interest becomes whatever is newsworthy – and anything a newspaper wishes to print is, by definition, newsworthy.

We might also try to understand the public interest in terms taken from

Chapter 2. In discussion of the right to know in that chapter, it was suggested that the public may have a right to be informed about matters that might affect its welfare. Or we could refer back to the discussion of social responsibility and suggest explanations of public interest in terms like 'redeeming social value', 'reasonable benefit to society', 'social utility', 'legitimate public concern'. Many newspaper articles which claim to describe the private lives of ordinary individuals can hardly be covered by any of these, let alone the retailing of gossip and scandal about actors, actresses and pop stars, nor the press pursuit of Diana, Princess of Wales and so on.

Let us now turn to the third group, those who unwittingly enter public awareness. These are the people who are most in need of protection and least able to secure it. Another case from the US is discussed by Sissela Bok in her book *Secrets* [505]. In 1937 the *New Yorker* magazine published an article about William Sidis. Sidis had been a child prodigy, through the influence of the rigorous training of his father, a psychologist. He went to Harvard University at the age of 11. His father reported on all his successes to the press, and received front-page coverage for them. But having got a degree, Sidis dropped out, cut off relations with his family, and took up one menial job after another. He would leave each job as soon as it was discovered that he was the once famous child prodigy William Sidis.

But this *New Yorker* article cornered him. It described him at the age of 39 living in a bedsit in a poor area of Boston. He who had wanted to live in obscurity and to recover his privacy, was once more exposed to full public view. He sued for invasion of privacy but lost the case. The court held that it did not constitute punishable invasion of privacy. First, much of what was revealed about Sidis's childhood was already public knowledge. People have no legal claim to erase their childhood fame, nor to remain unconnected with it in later life. Second, courts have held that, once a public figure, one has fewer lawful claims to privacy than another person. This ruling may be legally justified but appears harsh. Privacy was something Sidis had never had – his father had destroyed it in the first place, and he had never been able to recover it.

Here again we can ask: was it in the public interest to publish this story? A possible justification is that it highlights the dangers of forced education to make prodigies and of thrusting talented children into the public eye. As it happens though, the article was not sympathetically written – and for a warning against fame, it had the effect of making Sidis famous again. The public certainly had an interest in him. And it is not wrong to be curious about another person's life, no matter whether that person is famous or not. However, what was the nature of this interest?

Another issue raised here is that the judgment confirms a standard attitude of the press, that once people have got into the public eye, then they have lost their privacy. Even if Sidis had won his case and received damages, he would still not have recovered his privacy.

The conflict between press freedom and privacy is very much a live issue in the UK, where there is considerable reluctance to legislate in favour of privacy, although the right to it is recognized by several US states and some European countries. Concern about press intrusion came to a head in 1989 when the Committee on Privacy and Related Matters, chaired by Lord Justice Calcutt, was set up by the government to report on how to deal with the problem. The case that most profoundly influenced the Committee was press intrusion against a well-known television actor who was in hospital following an operation for the removal of a brain tumour. Reporters from a Sunday newspaper walked into his hospital room, took photographs and recorded his ramblings for publication as a 'world exclusive'. His family could do nothing to stop publication, nor had any grounds for redress after. All three judges in the Court of Appeal called the newspaper's behaviour 'a monstrous invasion of privacy' but could do nothing to stop publication.

The Committee reported in June 1990 [283], coming down on the side of press self-regulation, but within a strengthened framework. Of course, the press was glad to accept this, fearing any kind of legislation. But it was slow to reform itself; the Committee re-formed and proposed, first, a press tribunal with statutory powers and, second, that the government should give consideration to the introduction of a law against the infringement of privacy. But in July 1995 the government announced that there would be no legislation on privacy. It decided to strengthen yet further the institutions already in place. For one thing it seems to have proved very difficult to define privacy legally in a way that would not make genuine reporting more difficult.

There was another period of debate following the death of Diana, Princess of Wales, and the allegations that she had been hounded to death by the paparazzi. British newspapers seemed to acknowledge that they had intruded too much into her private life, while still claiming that she had used press publicity for her own purposes. The new Labour government expressed no wish to introduce legislation on privacy. The press accepted firmer guidelines from the Press Complaints Commission. Some newspapers admitted that they would have to be more careful. Yet this still suggests that they retain their room for manoeuvre. They will be more careful, see what the public will accept – in other words, what they can get away with.

Protection of privacy works better in other countries. In France, for example, there was a successful court case against the magazine *Paris-Match* (in January 1997) for publishing photographs of President Mitterrand, taken secretly as he lay on his death bed. The court fined the proprietors of the magazine and also ordered a symbolic payment of damages to members of the Mitterrand family for violation of their privacy.

There are two other issues that should be mentioned here. The first is the moral rights of the subjects of photographs. Photos of celebrities or public figures in their public role may be fair game, but is it right to use images of ordinary people, particularly when caught up in extraordinary situations? These can be war, terrorism or other violence; people can be shown dead, dying or in distress, in poverty or suffering famine. Such images are very powerful, and are the staple diet of photojournalism, but they are an intrusion into privacy. Should there be strict guidelines in the use of such images, with provision for authorization and legal consent by the subjects of the photographs?

The other issue is intrusion into grief in the aftermath of disasters or violent incidents. Examples of this are doorstepping the famous (including those who achieve that status for only fifteen minutes) or the innocent victims of crime, thrusting microphones in front of victims, who may be in a state of shock, or asking grieving relatives how they feel. Such incidents have occurred after the Lockerbie airplane explosion and bomb outrages in Northern Ireland, and in the coverage of famine in Somalia, or civil war in Rwanda and Zaïre. There was an interesting case in Australia, where two Seven Network journalists were sacked for showing a distressed woman being told of the death of her child by ambulancemen. In the UK, broadcasters are warned that the individual's right to privacy at times of bereavement or extreme distress must be respected. The *ITC programme code* of the Independent Television Commission recently added to the section on privacy a clause on 'interviews without prior appointment' (that is, doorstepping interviews) because of this concern over abuse of privacy.

Note

1 Article on 'Liberty', *Oxford companion to philosophy*, pp. 485–7.

6 Censorship: taste, decency and pornography

In this chapter, we shall deal with matters of taste and decency, which are probably of most concern in the media that provide entertainment: issues of sex and violence on the screen (in cinema or television), of bad language in television and radio, of blasphemy. But the problems also affect the print media providing information: the realism of news photographs in the press, the under-reporting of the detail provided in grisly murder cases. The problem of pornography, in particular, is as current as it ever has been, but it can now be found in most media. There is the question of so-called 'adult' channels being available on cable television: if people wish to subscribe is that not their business? Should the government interfere? Then there is the availability of pornography on the Internet.

The situation is complicated in that the different media have different ways of handling the issues. The most obvious of these is the fact that the cinema operates a system of pre-censorship, through its system of giving certificates, which are in effect judgements of what audiences a film is suitable for. On the other hand, books may only be prosecuted for breaches of what is thought to be acceptable after publication; what is more, prosecutions of written material are very rare and nearly always unsuccessful. Pre-censorship in the theatre ended in 1968.

As for television, 'adult channels' are a reality in the UK (The Adult Channel, Playboy TV, etc.). Subscription, encrypted channels can show adult movies or videos that would be legally available in video shops and cinemas, but hard-core pornography channels have been banned. The process this works by is that the ITC recommends to the Secretary of State that the channel in question be the subject of a proscription order (as happened with Red Hot Dutch in 1993 and TV Erotica in 1995).

Like books and publishing, broadcasting in the UK (since the Broadcasting Act 1990) is now subject to post-transmission action. After the programme has been broadcast, it can be the subject of complaints from the public or from people who were subjects of or participants in the programme; the ITC can intervene (using a range of sanctions if the programme does not comply with the broadcaster's licence conditions or the *ITC programme code*), so can the Broadcasting Standards Commission. And, of course, there may be legal action (for example, if the programme is defamatory).

These are all areas where there is a dividing line between the acceptable and the offensive, but different people draw the line in different places. In each area it is possible to draw up a series of examples that provide a continuum from that which is accepted by all members of a society for all members of that society (that is, including children) to what most people consider to be extremely offensive. This leaves open the question whether there are some things that everyone would consider so offensive as to be unacceptable; an example might be 'snuff' films, but then they do have an audience otherwise they would not be made. However, there are libertarians who are opposed to all forms of moral censorship. Another consideration to be taken into account is the question of how the offending material is being presented – how public or private it is. For example, a photograph on the front page of a tabloid newspaper is far more public than a book, as is a programme shown on a terrestrial 'free-to-air' public channel as opposed to one encrypted on cable television. With the former, notions of what is socially acceptable come into play far more than with the solitary, private activity of reading a book. This contrast, incidentally, is a factor in arguments about censorship in the cinema. On the one hand, there is the film maker wanting to be taken as an artist, tending to model themselves on the author, who speaks to an audience of individuals, in the darkness (that is, privacy) of the auditorium. On the other hand, there is what might be called the public display, the cinema as a presence in a high street, with posters and large flashing signs. It seems, to those who are offended by certain things, to flaunt its wares. In 1988 the film *The Last Temptation of Christ* upset many Christians, in both the US and the UK, and led to them calling for the film to be banned, on the grounds of blasphemy and denigration of Christ. This call, of course, was not based on a viewing of the film, but on a reading of its plot from newspapers. The book, a novel by Nikos Kazantzakis, had been available in English since 1960.

At the beginning of the discussion on privacy in Chapter 5, we referred to Isaiah Berlin's comments on the distinction between the public and the private. This forms a good starting point for the discussion here. The general question is: what sorts of conduct may the law properly seek to suppress? The answer that is most widely accepted in British society, as in many others, is that no conduct should be suppressed by law unless it can be shown to cause harm to someone. (This principle can be found in John Stuart Mill's *On liberty*.) The Williams Committee report on obscenity and film censorship published in 1979 [342] commented that almost all the evidence it received stated something like the harm condition or took it for granted. However, people differed about what harms are caused by obscene material, and about what might count as harmful.

Before discussing this 'harm principle' in more detail, we should first consider an older attitude, which still has its adherents. This can broadly be understood as a paternalistic attitude. A society involves a shared history, culture and values. It rests upon a moral consensus. Whatever threatens that moral consensus threatens society. And the description or portrayal of immoral activity by definition threatens that moral consensus. But it is the business of law to protect society; it can therefore be used to protect the moral consensus. Even if there is no demonstrable harm caused by the viewing or reading of pornographic material, this material should be controlled, simply because it offends society's standards. (One of the classic sources for this view is Lord Devlin, *The enforcement of morals* [324].)

In the 1960s and 1970s in the UK a campaigner from this standpoint was Mary Whitehouse with her Clean Up Television Campaign, which was later rechristened more grandiosely as the National Viewers' and Listeners' Association. In the US one of the most vocal critics of television has been the self-styled Moral Majority, a group set up in 1979 and largely comprised of evangelical Christians. It is dedicated to stemming what it believes is a tide of liberalism engulfing America. (This group is now called the Liberty Federation.)

In this type of view, there are kinds of acts which are not necessarily harmful in themselves, but which are morally disapproved of by a majority of citizens. According to this argument, if these acts are not discouraged, then certain moral and social harms will follow. But these moral and social harms do not follow simply from the kind of act they are – there is the additional consideration that the act is morally disapproved of by that society's citizens. In another society these acts might not be disapproved of, and if they were not, no harms would follow. This looks like sacrificing people's rights to do things that are otherwise harmless to other people's prejudice. To sum up, according to this paternalistic line of thought, something is wrong if it offends a majority of people in society. Opponents argue that this taking of offence has to be in some way justified, by the fact that it causes harm, and not simply because it is not the sort of thing that society is used to.

Another point is that this view exaggerates the identity and extent of the moral consensus required by a society, and so overstates the harms that supposedly follow if moral opinion is not made into law. Moral opinion does change without the disintegration of society. A society can move to a new consensus, or it can support a degree of variety and pluralism.

Even if such things as obscene publications are significant expression of things wrong with our society, it is still another question of whether it is justifiable or effective to legislate against them. To be the identifiable cause of harms is one thing, to be the expression of underlying ills in society is another.

6.1 Freedom of expression and harm

As mentioned above, John Stuart Mill was an important advocate of the harm condition. In *On liberty* [143] he stated that 'the only purpose for which power can be rightfully exercised over any member of a civilized community, against his will, is to prevent harm to others'. Now, freedom of expression is a very special and fundamental form of freedom. Mill believed that human beings have no infallible source of knowledge about human nature or how human affairs may develop, and so do not know in advance what arrangement or forms of life may make people happy or enable them to be, as he wanted them to be, creative, tolerant and strong individuals. Since we do not have knowledge in advance, we do not know what new ideas or forms of expression may contribute to the development of man and society. For Mill, the value of freedom of expression is connected with the open future of human development. Because of this it seems wrong to suppress certain publications, not just restrict them, on the grounds that they offend contemporary standards. This seems to allow, more than is justified, present views to determine the future.

This may seem high-minded when applied to pornography. But two points should be stressed: first, as we have seen throughout this book, there is a general presumption in favour of free expression, and second, that censorship is in its nature a blunt and treacherous instrument. But, though the presumption in favour of freedom of expression is strong, it is a presumption, and we may want to overrule it in consideration of the harm which the speech or publication in question may cause. The first question that arises is: harm to whom? Is supposed harm to consumers, just in itself, to count? Mill and others who advance the harm condition would say not. This is because they accept the principle that, if one is dealing with adult persons, it is best to assume that each person is the best judge of whether they are being harmed.

Is there an *independent* test of whether the given activity produces harm? The physical and mental condition of taking drugs would be bad even if caused by something other than taking drugs. But what are the bad effects of reading pornography or watching blue movies? If the only sign of this apparently deplorable state of mind is just wanting to read or watch pornography, this would not be much of an argument.

But a lot of the argument about harm with regard to pornography is that the harm is not done to the consumers, but to those affected by consumers (for example, that exposure to pornography leads to sexual crime). Or again, pornography persistently depicts women as subservient, leading to mistreatment of women. 'Pornography exists because men despise women, and men despise women because pornography exists', wrote Andrea Dworkin. Feminists writing on pornography often invoke their disgust that it should continue as well as their moral indignation. But this returns to the issue mentioned above with regard to moral disapproval. To reject the harm principle in one area would be both taking a step backwards and setting a dangerous precedent. Some feminists have made a particularly virulent attack on pornography from this point of view, though it is worth noting that in recent years there has been an increasing availability of erotic material written specifically for women by women. This suggests that there is no necessary link between pornography and downgrading of women.

It has also been claimed that pornography leads to a distortion of human experience, by hindering the development of the human personality or corrupting the imagination. Sometimes there is reference to 'cultural pollution', and this would be a serious matter. But there is real difficulty in identifying what the harmful *effect* is supposed to be.

To evaluate the harm caused by pornography, there are two important principles to be borne in mind. One is the requirement, for legal purposes, that the causation of the harm should lie 'beyond reasonable doubt'. The second is the question of whether pornography constitutes a class of publications to which, as such, there belongs a tendency to cause harm. (And not whether a given book has harmed anyone, for the Bible might cause harm.)

The report of the Williams Committee provides a long review of the evidence for a connection between pornography and the alleged harms. On whether there is a link with sex crimes and violence, they conclude with a verdict of not proven. As for other effects on human behaviour in general, there was a lack of concrete evidence. Again, there was very little evidence for concerns that readers of pornography might be led into deviant sexual practices, or that pornography could damage human relationships and lead to marital breakdown.

On the question of the degradation of women, the position is a little more complicated. For in this case pornography was seen as but one form of sexism, a blatant one perhaps, but a sexism encountered in advertising, entertainment and other areas. In this case, then, pornography should not be singled out for special treatment under the law, since the desire is to alter fundamentally society's attitudes towards the role of women, rather than to legislate against one symptom of those attitudes.

The broadest harms mentioned were those concerning social harms – the weakening of our civilization and the demoralization of society. But how do you distinguish symptom from cause in this instance? Also, what happens here is that the attack on pornography is really aimed at a broader target, an alleged sickness throughout the culture, and so is not very closely connected with pornography and still less with the laws on obscenity. To regard it as having a crucial or even a significant effect on essential social values, is to get the problem of pornography out of proportion with the many other problems that face society today.

Wherever the line is drawn, if it is drawn, on pornography, there is a separate question of whether material that is *offensive* should be restricted in some way, though not suppressed. Pornography not only exists for private consumption, it may also be publicly displayed. People may be forced to see things which they do not wish to see, which they may think should not be seen. The Williams Committee, although sceptical about the harms alleged to be caused by pornography and violence, was sensitive to this consideration, and content to fall in with traditionally accepted rules protecting the interest in public decency. But as the question of offensiveness touches other matters in this chapter, we shall return to it later.

Many of the issues and arguments discussed with regard to pornography also apply to violence in the media. There is the same basic problem – that is, given the presumption in favour of free speech, it is very difficult to establish that harm is caused by violent material. Usually, this would be by seeing it: violence is a problem raised in the context of films, television and videos, though there are also anxieties about comics. Very many research studies have been carried out in recent years, and though some have claimed to have found evidence one way or another, nothing conclusive has been brought forward to prove or disprove a causal link between violence on screen and violent behaviour. And yet, the deep, as yet unfounded suspicion remains, with the result that after any particularly violent crime, questions are asked, or assumptions are made, about the perpetrator's viewing habits. Commentators make an equation: violent crime comes from watching violent films or videos, which comes from a sick and amoral society. One might want to say that violent people tend to watch violent television or videos, but viewing violence would not change the behaviour of a normally non-violent person. But this does not take us very far in identifying the causes of violence.

Although the effects of watching such material have not been established, it is plausible to argue that there must be some effect. Hardly anyone claims that there is no effect. Clearly the makers of a film actively seek a tangible response from the audience. Are these responses then left behind when the viewer leaves the cinema? On the other hand, it has been pointed out that Britain's film censorship is the most restrictive in the Western world, and yet this has not led to a reduction in violent crime. There is, however, a consensus that children should be protected from such material, hence the concern over 'video nasties' which children are able to gain access to. (In the UK videos are classified by the British Board of Film Classification using the same rules and guidelines as for film.)

(There is a separate discussion that gets involved here, which is not within our scope. This is the historical argument as to whether our society is becoming more violent. But what is the reach of the comparison? If the comparison is with fifty years ago, the answer is perhaps yes; if with a hundred years ago, then perhaps not.)

But the issues here are very complex: there are differences between film and television in the way they are received; the 'messages' being received by audiences are more subtle than simply 'be violent'; how causes are to be distinguished from symptoms; and so on.

However, there is one difference between sex and violence which may make a difference to how they should be treated. This is that violence is in itself harmful, and so it may be right to exercise greater caution. This was in fact the feeling of the Williams Committee when considering violence in films.

Films, plays and books which are accused of being obscene are sometimes defended on artistic grounds, that their artistic merit outweighs the bad effects they may have. Throughout the twentieth century, there has been a succession of trials of books (to give just three examples: *The well of loneliness* by Radclyffe Hall, *Ulysses* by James Joyce, *Tropic of Cancer* by Henry Miller). Since the Second World War these have ended in the failure of the prosecution. The most famous was the trial of *Lady Chatterley's lover* by D. H. Lawrence in 1960. More recently, there has been the case of an exhibition of homoerotic photographs by Robert Mapplethorpe. They produced an outrage when exhibited in the US, but little controversy when the exhibition came to the UK in 1996.

The problem here is that it is very difficult to describe the merits of a work in terms of what are causal concepts, good and bad effects.

We have referred frequently to the work of the Williams Committee, and so it may be useful to refer briefly to its recommendations, which were not acted upon by the government. The Committee thought that the printed word should not be restricted, and that the principal object of the law should be to prevent certain kinds of material causing offence or being made available to young people. It would have done away with the old terms like 'obscene', 'indecent' and 'deprave and corrupt', and replaced them with the notion of material *offensive to reasonable people*. Only a small class of material should be forbidden to those who want it, because an objective assessment of likely harm does not support a wider prohibition. The printed word should be neither restricted nor prohibited.

So far, in discussing pornography and violence, the point at issue has been whether access to them should be denied to those who want that access. This leaves much else that may be considered 'offensive', material that people can come across without wanting to or expecting to. And, of course, material with sexual or violent content is used on television. A difficulty here is that some people are easily offended. In their discussions of censorship, the Williams Committee, as noted, came up with the notion of 'offensive to reasonable people'. In other words, there should be a broad social consensus. If it came to a legal prosecution and trial by jury, that consensus would be provided by twelve men and women. That said, it is a cliché of the time, and true, that the UK is a pluralistic society, with a mixture of races, religions, regions, ideas and beliefs.

Now, how do these considerations affect the media? If readers find the contents of a book or magazine offensive, then they have only to close it. However, more 'public' media, even individual newspapers, have to deal with the problem. They have to take a view as to what the consensus of their own readers will be. This will, of course, differ from one newspaper to another, from one medium to another.

As far as news reporting is concerned, the offensive material will be in conflict with the journalist's pursuit of the true and newsworthy. This can range from passing over the full details of a horrific murder (an example given earlier) to the watering down, not to say improving, of the language of a sportsman with a limited and coarse vocabulary. Here it will be for editors to decide on the susceptibilities of their readership.

With 'entertainment' programming, particularly broadcast drama, the issue will often be one of 'realism' for those authors who aim to make their work as 'lifelike' as possible. Thus a drama executive, Nick Elliott, argues that today's society is one of rape, murder and violent attacks: 'surely, you as a society, expect us to have some of our drama reflecting the world ... There is nothing wrong with drama tackling dark and violent themes.'[1] Others argue that viewers have become desensitized to violence on the screen. At the same discussion from which the quotation just given comes, another drama producer dismissed the argument that programmes containing violence reflected the world: 'We have violence on television because we like it. People find it entertaining.'

How should material including sex or violence be handled? Guidelines for the broadcasters can be proposed. With regard to violence, these may include considerations such as: no violence for violence's sake; the realistic portrayal of character; a reasonable manner of portrayal; avoidance of portrayal of specific techniques; it should not be shown as a justified means to an end. However, where this last consideration would leave Westerns is an interesting question.

Then there are the specific problems of visual material. Some photographs are so graphic that they will shock the viewer in a way that a written report of the same events would not. Journalists who offend can be subject to charges ranging from poor taste to voyeurism. Such material can include grieving families after an accident, the accident itself, shootings, casualties in war. After the massacre of children by a gunman in Scotland, Independent Television News was criticized by the Broadcasting Standards Council for transmitting pictures of a distraught mother who had just learned her child was one of the victims. ITN defended its choice: 'they were harrowing, heart-wrenching pictures. But we are not in the business of sanitising news. You can't create a make-believe world in which people don't cry ...'[2] Pictures of casualties in war raise other questions: it is thought to be bad for the morale of the citizens back home, whose support for the war may be reduced; on the other hand, can it be wrong to remind people that wars cause casualties? This brings us back to the special vividness of pictures.

In all of these, newsworthiness competes against the audience's sensibilities. But should the viewers' sensibilities always be protected? In this respect, there may be a difference between photographs and television, film or video. One of the characteristics of television is that it is such a domestic medium – the television set is usually part of the living-room furniture, and often the one source of family entertainment.

6.2 Film censorship

As noted earlier, the cinema in the UK and in the US is subject to a system of pre-censorship. It is a common view that films should be freed of this burden and, like other media, be subject to the laws of the land.

Almost everywhere the cinema is more closely regulated than any comparable media of communication. The reasons for this are partly historical, in that the cinema was the first provider of mass entertainment. Also, it has been suggested that there are political reason, in that the cinema's early public was almost entirely working-class, which the elites felt to be most open to corruption.

The cinema is the only area subject to a sophisticated system of pre-censorship. This means that the censoring body can exercise tight control on the material presented to the public. The British Board of Film Censors, which was established in 1912 and which, since 1985, has been operating under the more neutral title of the British Board of Film Classification, considered itself the guardian of public morality until the 1960s. It considered film primarily as family entertainment, allowed no departures from accepted codes of conduct and behaviour, and remained shy of the representation of anything controversial.

But this system has operated with a good degree of public acceptance. Almost everywhere in the world there is a system for the prior vetting of films. In the US this is only to categorize films with regard to their suitability for children; the system is purely voluntary and aims solely at classifying films in order to provide advance information to help parents judge whether their children should be allowed to see particular films. Belgium, the Netherlands and Denmark concentrate on protecting children, and take the view that there should be no prior controls on what adults are able to see.

The arguments against this system of pre-censorship will be familiar. There should be no barriers to the free communication of facts and ideas, and the worlds of the arts and entertainment may be considered to be inseparable from these; adults should have the freedom to choose what they wish to see and not have others judge what is right or wrong for them to see; there should be the same artistic freedom as in the other arts.

Those who oppose film censorship would like the cinema to have the same treatment as the theatre: there should be no prior restraint, and films which are challenged should be able to fight for their rights before a jury in open court. Interestingly, this attitude is not shared by the major film distributors. For them, there are two advantages. The first is a commercial one, in that a lot of money is put into a film; once completed, it cannot easily be changed (unlike a play in the theatre). The sense of certainty that a certificated film could be shown throughout the country without any legal interference is a real commercial benefit. Second, prior censorship is also required because seeing a film is different from reading, and the cinema, catering as it does for a mass audience unlike the theatre, penetrates far deeper into society than the theatre. Geoffrey Wood, who worked at the BBFC, wrote in *Index on Censorship* that film censorship is only one of a number of interventions made in the course of the product's progress from studio to screen, interventions which include corporate decisions to do with production and distribution. He commented: 'the BBFC provides a comparatively cheap testing of the waters and an umbrella against litigious storms.'[3]

This can be seen in the case of the film *Last Tango in Paris* in 1972 in the UK. A press outcry preceded the advent of the film. The BBFC passed it with a cut of ten seconds, but some fifty local authorities banned it (without seeing it). However, the film was widely defended by film critics, audiences made the longer journeys to cinemas in areas that had not banned it, and the film was a commercial success. It is not surprising that the film industry prefers to have a system that avoids running the gauntlet of all British local authorities.

On the other hand, the interests of the industry are not the only ones to be considered, and this system of pre-censorship works against individual film makers, who feel that they are thus made to suffer constraints additional to those operated in other media.

The director, Nigel Wingrove, of a short video called *Visions of Ecstasy*, was refused a certificate for the film on the grounds of blasphemy, and took his case to the European Court of Human Rights, which decided in November 1996 that the British authorities were fully entitled to consider that the refusal to grant a certificate was 'justified as being necessary in a democratic society for the protection of the rights of others'. The point here is that the BBFC had concluded that the video would infringe the law of blasphemy and that a jury would convict it of doing so. The film maker, however, could reasonably argue that a jury should be given the opportunity to make its own decision, after a full trial, as would occur with a book, for example. It was not for the Board to set themselves up as the judge of what a jury would decide.

Perhaps the most famous 'banned' film in the UK has been *A Clockwork Orange*, which was given a certificate for public showing by the BBFC but later withdrawn by the director, Stanley Kubrick, and the distributors, Warner Brothers. This followed the blaming on the film of a real-life case of violent rape. The curious factor is that it was the director who withdrew the film and who has continued to restrict its showing in the UK.

6.3 Broadcasting

Anxieties about broadcasting, and the wide influence it might have on behaviour and standards, led to the foundation in the UK of the Broadcasting Standards Council in 1988. In its Code of Practice, published in 1989, decency was described as 'the reflection of individuals' enduring regard for one another' and as 'acknowledging our common humanity'. The Council's Annual Review of 1991 (which had the title 'Taste and decency in broadcasting') added that 'good taste is one of the ways in which, at a particular time, decency may be observed'.

The issues covered by the Code of Practice with regard to taste and decency are the limits of language, offences against religious sensibilities, stereotypes, people with disabilities, questions of race, privacy, occasions of grief and bereavement, portrayal of smoking, alcohol and drugs. According to the 1991 Annual Review over half the complaints to the BSC in that year were to do with taste and decency, and of these the highest proportion (about a third) were about bad language, with a further 17 per cent about language that offended religious sensibilities.

The use of 'bad' language has long been a problem for broadcasters. If we go back to the notion of a continuum, in this case of words ranked according to their strength, individuals would each draw the line differently between what is acceptable and what is not. Also, the consensus would draw the line differently from, say, ten years ago. So there are shifts of taste in this matter, as elsewhere.

Now, in so far as one can know what the consensus is, should broadcasters adhere to it? The first point to make is that even given a consensus across society, the audience at any given point is not necessarily homogeneous with that society. Different people watch different kinds of programmes at different times. The clearest demonstration of this is the 'watershed' in British television, where it is generally accepted that 9 p.m. is the point of division between programmes that are acceptable to the whole of the family, children included, and those that can be aimed at an adult audience. Another way of dealing with this is a form of signposting, indicating beforehand, or through other clues, what kind of programme can be expected.

A second point is that some broadcasters and writers claim the ability to challenge accepted social mores. As Carla Lane puts it in *A matter of manners?* [368], should writers inhibit their work to appease? What of the 'right' to be truthful and authentic? This applies not only to drama and comedy. In the same book Roger Graef writes: 'our task as broadcasters engaged in factual programming is to bring to viewers as full and accurate accounts of the world as we can manage within the resources available and the law of the land.' So, of a programme about young offenders, whose language is riddled with swearing, he adds: 'It is not my job to protect viewers from reality, but rather to present reality in a form that brings it alive in a meaningful way.' Sanitizing language is, in his view, to sanitize reality.

There remain some subjects that are considered to be taboo. In 1995 there was a fuss when the BBC decided to show a documentary on euthanasia, which showed a man dying after requesting a lethal injection from a doctor. Anti-euthanasia groups wanted the programme banned, but this seems a clear example of wanting to stifle discussion of an important issue. In fact, it seems one of the clearest illustrations in this book of Mill's argument for the freedom of expression of opinion.

In 1996 another taboo subject was treated on British television. The popular Channel 4 soap opera *Brookside* depicted an incestuous relationship between a brother and sister. The couple were seen in bed together, after having sex. Neither the ITC nor the Broadcasting Standards Council considered that the programme was wrong to have treated the subject of incest. It was the 'how' that was important. The BSC considered that 'the great care and sensitivity' that was required had not been shown and that there was an absence of insight and a tendency to glamorize. The ITC felt that the showing of the episode at 8 p.m. was 'just acceptable', but certainly not the earlier time of 5 p.m. (for the repeat, omnibus edition) when large numbers of children might have been watching.

Blasphemy is another issue. There is a law on blasphemy which is now thought to be virtually unenforceable and applies only to Christianity. However, it is not perhaps a dead issue, because people's feelings about their religion are particularly strong. On its first showing on British television, the film *The Last Temptation of Christ* (see also p. 39) produced a record number of complaints to the ITC (though most were before the film was shown). The complaints were not upheld as the film had a BBFC certificate for cinema release. The ITC recognized that the film might be offensive to some people, but concluded that it was a serious and thoughtful film from a modern literary classic, and did not contravene the *ITC programme code*.

Still, on this and other matters, how far ahead (if ahead they are) of the audience may broadcasters be? And this question will answered differently, depending on whether one is looking at programme output as a whole, or at individual programmes. Here one might turn to Hugh Greene, perhaps the most forward-thinking of BBC Director-Generals: 'I believe that we [broadcasters] have a duty to take account of the changes of society, to be ahead of public opinion rather than always to wait upon it.' In discussing how far ahead broadcasters may go, he adds: 'Relevance is the key. Outrage is impermissible. Shock is not always so. Provocation may be healthy and indeed socially imperative.'[4] This formulation is not as helpful as it might be, since the divisions between these are not clear-cut. It is in fact what Bertrand Russell would have called an 'emotive conjugation' (for example, 'I have reconsidered, you have changed your mind, he has gone back on his word'). But it also conveniently brings us back to the notion of a continuum of reaction and sensitivity.

Studies in the US have shown a wide difference in social profile between programme makers and their audiences.[5] To what extent, then, are the broadcasters inflicting their values on the audience? This in turn raises questions about the passivity of the audience. Do they unthinkingly adopt the values of behaviour of the characters they observe?

Here we enter on an important question in research into the effects on media, which is linked to issues of sex and violence. For recent research (see, for example, the work of Sonia Livingstone) suggests that audiences are rather more active in their interpretations than has often been assumed.

Yet there is a market for the 'shocking' and 'outrageous'. At one time the most popular radio programme in New York was that of the 'shock jock' Howard Stern, and it was also broadcast in several other American cities. His talk might be described as bold and provocative. However, this did not lie in its originality but in its blatant appeal to the prejudices of his audience, frequently commenting on women's physical appearance, for example. Defenders of the programme will suggest that those who think the material indecent are merely being prudish. Then there is Rush Limbaugh who takes a more insulting line, for whom liberals are 'commie libs', who cuts off listeners who disagree with his views on abortion with the sounds of a vacuum cleaner and a woman screaming. Again, he has a large audience. Should the popularity of these two shows be censored? One does not have to listen, after all. They certainly cross the boundaries of widely acceptable conduct. The question, here, may be the extent to which a radio or television programme can be treated like public space. One may want to go further and say that these programmes cross the boundaries of the conduct, the tolerance, for a democracy to work.

6.4 Cable and the Internet

These two forms for the dissemination of information are comparatively recent, have a growing audience and raise similar problems to those already discussed, though in different combinations. Since cable and satellite channels appear on the homely television set, they are faced with some of the expectations for television programmes that are broadcast on terrestrial channels (that is, available to all). On the one hand, there is the paternalist or authoritarian view that the viewing of pornography on cable and satellite channels must be controlled. On the other hand, there is the libertarian attitude that such channels are voluntarily subscribed to by mature adults, and as such they should be free to watch what they wish to. They pay for the service and are fully aware of the content.

As things stand in the UK, cable and satellite programme channels are subject to lighter regulations than the terrestrial channels, but are still subject to the *ITC programme code*. The wider problem is that satellite television cuts across national borders but also differing country views on taste and decency issues.

The Internet can also make pornography available, as well as, according to a tabloid newspaper, tracts on white supremacy, the formula for crack cocaine, details of women for sale in Thailand and the Philippines, and how to make Molotov cocktails. Most of what is available on the Internet is in fact available in print form, and so could be found in a good public library. But it is clear that it is not the material itself that is always the problem so much as the availability in the home, its ease of access.

The additional problem with the Internet is locating the source. Take the example of a tract on white supremacy that offends the UK's laws on race relations. In 1995, and not for the first time, Lady Birdwood was convicted of distributing a racist pamphlet. In this case there was a physical object and someone handing it out in person. But what is the law to do with the same text on a computer network? It could be very difficult to track down the source, which may well be in a foreign country. Should an online service be treated as a common carrier (like a telephone company that cannot be held responsible for what people say on it) or should it be treated as a publisher (which can be)?

In September 1996 the UK established a system of self-regulation, which had been agreed by the largest UK Internet service providers, the government and the police. Called R3/Safety Net, the proposal included setting up an industry-run complaints hotline, establishing monitoring and investigation procedures and adopting a self-regulatory code. It relies on co-operation between service providers and police. Will it be powerful enough to be effective?

Notes

1. At the Edinburgh Television Festival, 1996, quoted in *Ariel*, 27 August 1996.
2. At the Edinburgh Television Festival, 1996, quoted in *Ariel*, 27 August 1996.
3. Wood, G. in *Index on Censorship*, Vol. 24, No. 6, November–December 1995, Issue 167, p. 153.
4. Greene, H. C. *The third floor front*, pp. 101 and 103.
5. See references in Limburg, V. E. *Electronic media ethics*, p. 99.

7 Truth and truth-telling

To what extent can the whole truth be told?

Both Milton and Mill saw freedom of speech as an aid to finding truth. The freedom to discuss different ideas is a process that leads to the one that is true. The more modern argument, that it is the role of the media to inform citizens, assumes that they should be given correct, truthful information, to enable them to make informed decisions. Now, immediately we have to make a distinction, for some media provide fictions, as do the cinema and much of television, and others' main aim is to persuade, as do advertising and public relations. In this chapter, then, we shall be concerned with the provision of news, as in newspapers, magazines, factual television programmes and so on.

The press's aim and obligation to print the truth have become part of its rhetoric. What might be called the current doctrine evolved in the nineteenth century, as the press claimed to be emancipating itself from political influence (whether it has ever done so completely is another question). It can be found in a pair of important leading articles published in *The Times* in 1852.

'The press lives by disclosures; whatever passes into its keeping becomes a part of the knowledge and history of our times; it is daily and for ever appealing to the enlightened force of public opinion – anticipating, if possible, the march of events – standing upon the breach between the present and the future, and extending its survey to the horizon of the world . . . of all journals, and of all writers, those will obtain the largest measure of public support who have told the truth most constantly and most fearlessly . . . the first duty of the press is to obtain the earliest & most correct intelligence of the events of the time, and by disclosing them, to make them the common property of the nation.'

These claims were being quoted approvingly as recently as 1991 by John Tusa, when Managing Director of the BBC World Service, in his *A world in your ear*.

Nor should we omit C. P. Scott's famous declaration, in a special centenary edition of the *Manchester Guardian* (6 May 1921), that a newspaper's 'primary office is the gathering of News. At the peril of its soul it must see that the supply is not tainted. Neither in what it gives, nor in what it does not give, nor in the mode of presentation, must the unclouded face of Truth suffer wrong. Comment is free, but facts are sacred. Propaganda, so called, by this means is hateful. The voice of opponents, no less than that of friends, has a right to be heard. Comment is also justly subject to a self-imposed restraint. It is well to be frank: it is even better to be fair.' In the present day nearly all ethics codes begin with the journalist's duty to tell the truth under all conditions. This is usually thought of, in the first instance, as applying to the journalist's reports, what the audience actually reads or hears. But it can also be applied to the methods used by journalists in gathering news – can not telling the truth be justified in order to gain important information?

The first problem was raised as long ago as Plato. In *The Republic* (Book III, 414b–415d) he puts forward a suggestion that is usually known as the 'noble lie', though an alternative translation is the 'grand myth'. In order that the rest of the city may be persuaded of its community of interest, the rulers, the philosopher-kings, may have to tell them a myth, namely, that they are all brothers born from earth, and that some are made from gold, some from silver, and others from bronze or iron. The type of work that each does should depend, each must be told, on which metal he is made of. The rulers must be on guard lest this principle be violated, and especially lest the city be ruled by someone of bronze or iron.

The myth is not told in order to convince the rulers, but it may be necessary to convince the rest. The rulers will be able themselves to understand the principles the myth contains, both of the essential community of interest of the city and of the need for each person to do the work he is fitted for. Underlying this argument is a suggestion that human survival or social cohesion is more important than telling the truth. This is also of course the justification of censorship.

Now, to focus on the notion of truth. We must begin by making a distinction between truth and truth-telling or, as Sissela Bok puts it in *Lying* [380], 'between two domains: the *moral* domain of intended truthfulness and deception, and the much vaster question of truth and falsity in general. The moral question of whether you are lying or not is not *settled* by establishing the truth or falsity of what you say. In order to settle the question, we must know whether you *intend your statement to mislead*.' Truth and truthfulness, then, are not identical. She goes on: 'We must single out, therefore, from the countless ways in which we blunder misinformed through life, that which is done with the *intention to mislead*; and from the countless partial stabs at truth, those which are intended to be truthful. Only if this distinction is clear will it be possible to ask the moral question with rigour. And it is to this question alone – the intentional manipulation of information – that the court addresses itself in its request for "the truth, the whole truth and nothing but the truth".' That is to say, one is not expected to give the whole truth on a given subject – for who could do that? – but to be wholly truthful, to tell all the truth that one knows.

As far as journalism is concerned, a larger question should be mentioned, though it is far too large to be answered here: is truth-telling necessary to society? Fortunately for our purposes it is widely accepted that we do need it. Reasons that may be put forward are: lack of integrity in human communications undermines the autonomy of the individual or, in other terms, it treats them as a tool to be manipulated rather than an end; and, trust is based on truthful communication and without it lying and deception undermine the foundations of society. Certainly, the Old Testament inveighs against it, in the ninth commandment, and in all societies perjury is severely treated.

For journalists, however, there are further questions, since they are not just supposed to be telling the truth but finding it out. They need to do more than achieve truthfulness. One can ask of journalists, how much care have they taken in finding out the truth? How much care have they taken to be truthful? These questions raise the notion of laziness. Then we might also ask: is there an attempt to be fair, to be balanced, to avoid bias? This last question, with its alternatives, is a recognition that the whole truth is elusive and sometimes, perhaps always, impossible.

The press's desire to report the truth is opposed by those who sometimes have reason to fear the truth, including, of course, governments. They are also increasingly faced by the practices of press agents or, as they are now often termed, 'spin doctors'. These operate mostly in politics and negotiate access to the politicians they represent. They are thus in a position to lay down the conditions under which their employer will appear on television, for example: who the interviewer will be, what questions are 'off-limits', who else will appear on the programme.[1]

Now, clearly the reporting of the truth is often harmful to others. For many years the press was discreet in obituaries about the cause of a person's death if it resulted from AIDS. This spared the family's feelings; however, by not admitting that people died of AIDS, the practice of non-reporting confirmed people's prejudices about it. Further, if a person died young and no reason was given, then this in itself led to speculation about the cause of death.

A striking example is given by Ibsen's play *An enemy of the people*, which also illustrates the fact that the issue of reporting the truth is not confined to the media. The protagonist of the play, Dr Stockmann, finds that the waters of the baths in the town where he lives are contaminated. He insists on telling the truth, despite the harm that will be done to the town and to his own family, when everyone prefers to keep this information quiet, including the townspeople themselves.

Sometimes the reporting of the truth may cause what is felt to be unnecessary trouble, as with the reporting of terrorist threats against an airline, for example. Should passengers be told of a general threat against the airline? To do so would increase paranoia, which is just what the terrorists desire. It is easy to make threats, harder to carry them out. And what if there is no proof of any immediate danger?

What makes for truth in news reporting? Louis Day [18] suggests three criteria. The first is accuracy: the facts should be based on solid evidence. Second, a news story should promote understanding. A story should contain as much relevant information as is available and essential to provide the average reader or viewer with some understanding of the facts and the context of the facts. His third criterion leads to the most controversy, to which we shall return. This is that reporting should be fair and balanced.

But before we go on to consider each of these topics in more detail, we should discuss here the consideration that the press is not so much interested in the 'truth' as in the 'news' (that is, there is a notion of newsworthiness that is more important to the actual practice of newspapers than any high-minded assertions about truth). This is a charge often made by sociologists examining the press, but goes back at least as far as Walter Lippmann. He made a distinction between truth and 'news': because news reporting and truth seeking have different ultimate purposes, Lippmann postulated that 'news' could be expected to coincide with truth in only a few limited areas – such as sports scores or elections, where the results are definite and measurable. In political life, where the outcome is always in dispute, news reports could not be expected to exhaust, or perhaps even indicate, the truth of the matter.[2]

So it is stated by Colin Seymour-Ure [94] that academic studies have confirmed the obvious; that events make news if they are clear, unusual, unexpected or unpredictable; if they fit a medium's cycle (for example, a daily paper or an hourly news bulletin); if they involve well-known people or groups, places, countries; if they are close to home (literally or figuratively); if they are negative (accidents) or reach a certain volume (for example, in terms of numbers hurt or goals scored).[3]

Or again, Paul Rock 'illustrates with great clarity how news consists of the unusual event occurring within the rubric of the "usual" characterizations of journalists and press officers. The paradigm of the usual "taken for granted" world view of the journalist becomes stylized into a number of almost reflexive clichés evoked effortlessly in the face of a deluge of events which face him in his work.'[4]

Michael Schudson [205] argues that news is a form of culture: related to, but not the same as ideology; related to, but not the same as information. He calls the form of culture 'public knowledge': the news is produced by people who operate, often unwittingly, within a cultural system, a reservoir of cultural meanings and patterns of discourse. News as a culture makes assumptions about what makes sense, what time and place we live in, what range of considerations we should take seriously. However, this may not take us as far as he would like, since most forms of communication make assumptions about time and place, and what is to be taken seriously or not. Schudson goes on to say that 'public knowledge' comes from the fact that when the media offer the public an item of news, they confer upon it public legitimacy. They bring it into a common public forum where it can be discussed by a general audience.[5]

This much is clear: of all the events that a newspaper could report, it selects those which it considers important or interesting (that is, newsworthy), and ranks them accordingly, by their prominence in the paper and by size of headline.

7.1 Accuracy

The reporting of a story should be accurate. The facts presented in a report should be based on solid evidence. A notorious instance of a failure to do this was when the *Washington Post* ran a detailed report of an 8-year-old heroin addict. The piece won a Pulitzer Prize, which had to be returned when it was found that the story was false. The journalist who wrote it was sacked.

Accuracy as a requirement is threatened, first, by the competitive practices of journalism. Where speed is of the essence, information may be broadcast before it has been verified. Then, on the other hand, the demand for verification could be taken too far. It has been suggested that the BBC was unnecessarily reluctant to report on the existence of concentration and death camps in Germany during the Second World War, because it felt the evidence, before the invasion of Germany and liberation of the camps, was not strong enough.

But many journalists are simply lazy or casual about accuracy. Once an inaccuracy gets into the news, it can often be repeated and magnified, as journalists' research rarely goes further back or more deeply than previous newspaper stories. What is more, given a newsworthy story, there is little temptation for further research that might show the story to be false and so leave the journalist with a space to fill. In 1995 the European Commission felt impelled to publish a booklet rejecting many of the stories published about it as false, and explaining how the misunderstandings came about. As the Commission commented,[6] newspapers are reluctant to publish corrections, and if something appears in many papers that automatically gives it authenticity. The failure to check things carefully enough (the excuse usually given) has resulted in some famous hoaxes, including the Hitler diaries in the *Sunday Times*.

A specific issue raised by the requirement of accuracy is whether it is permissible to stage or restage events. This applies particularly to photographs and film or video material. On the most trivial, 'harmless' level there is the practice of television news to introduce interviews over footage of the interviewee, walking along, or on the telephone, or reading a document, all activities staged for the camera. To move to a more serious level, the famous photograph of American soldiers raising the US flag at Iwo Jima was a re-enactment of the original event. It was not a depiction of reality; does it still tell the story faithfully? Then, what is to be said of a photographer on his way to cover a motor accident, who goes into a toy-shop to buy a couple of dolls to place at the scene, in order to get a more poignant photograph?

Photographs, because of their high degree of selectivity and what might be termed their credibility in showing reality, can easily give a misleading impression.

US President Jimmy Carter was out jogging, stumbled and fell, before quickly recovering his feet. The incident lasted a second, but the photograph of the stumble and his surprised expression was shown across the country. Similarly, in the 1996 US presidential campaign, a photograph of candidate Bob Dole falling from a podium was considered to have damaged his chances. However, it might be argued that the photograph would not have become a metaphor for his campaign unless the campaign itself was already seen to be failing.

These problems have been sharpened by recent improvements in technology. It is now very easy to alter photographs; it is now possible to create photographs – that is, to create photograph-like images of events that have not happened. Is any alteration of a photograph to be treated as a deliberate inaccuracy, an intention to mislead?

Many news reports include quotations. These should be accurate, but many people are unable to speak in well-formed sentences. Is it wrong for the reporter to tidy up faulty grammar? Or, as in a case mentioned in Chapter 6, remove unnecessary expletives? It might be said that if there is a problem, indirect quotes or paraphrases can be used. But then, journalists are very reluctant to relinquish the vividness of direct quotation.

There are other manipulations possible: interviews on television can be edited so that an answer to one question can be moved so as to seem the answer to a quite different question. This might put a quite different slant on what was said. The 'letters page' of a newspaper can be manipulated to suggest support for the newspaper, even when most readers might be against it.

Though not directly involving news and reporting, this is probably the appropriate place to provide some discussion of the genre of docudramas (that is, blends of fact and fiction on television). They have become a popular entertainment format. The problem here may simply be one of presentation. It occurs only with television, and because the 'fiction' uses its documentary techniques. Television now has various blends of fact and fiction. 'Reconstructions' are enactments of confidential public events – here there is still a strong element of creation in that the script has to be written. Also, it may well be that as soon as actors are used, there will be a distortion of fact. This stricture also applies to perhaps a more neutral mixture – 'reality' television which tends to be the re-enactment of crimes or rescue attempts. These seem to be relatively innocuous in that they are short and aim largely at being informative (for 'reconstruction' television clearly has entertainment interest). Of course, novels and the cinema have represented and misrepresented historical events through fiction for a long time. The only problem would be the claim, implicit or explicit, that the events shown happened in that way.

The case of *The Monocled Mutineer* illustrates the issues well. This was a British television series broadcast in 1986, based on a book published in 1978. The series dramatized the life of a soldier in the First World War, Percy Topliss, who was alleged to have led an army mutiny. The problems began with the claim of wide discrepancies between the original book and the dramatization. Then a historian who had been used as an adviser said that the series bore no relation to the facts he had discovered and presented to the producer and the writer (the well-known television dramatist Alan Bleasdale). Others complained of exaggerations and distortions in the series. Unfortunately the issue also became a political one in that the BBC was going through a period of heavy criticism from the Conservative Party. Bleasdale, who never made a secret of his own left-wing leanings, had taken an anti-establishment line in the dramatization. One of the writers of the original book joined the fray, to defend their research and to say that the BBC adviser had never made contact with them. So there was a dispute between historians about the quality of their research; but the main problem was caused by the claim of the BBC publicity that it was a 'true story'. Bleasdale himself said that he never claimed that the work was anything other than fiction, which suggests that the problems were the result of a failure in labelling, but also that in any work which contains both factual and fictional elements, the fictional undermines the factual.

7.2 Understanding

Merely observing accuracy in an article or report might be described as a minimal virtue. The facts reported may be correct, but they might still give a poor picture of what has occurred. On the other hand, not all the facts about an event can be reported – a book would not be large enough. In this sense, the whole truth is impossible. The journalist has to provide an account that, as Louis Day puts it, promotes understanding.

A politician is speaking in public. Suppose that what they say contains claims that the reporter believes may be untrue? They can be seen to be doing their job if they simply quote the speaker accurately – and they may not have the time to check all the assertions they heard. But this grey area was exploited by Senator Joseph McCarthy in the US in the 1950s. He took advantage of the fact that journalists were content to report what he said about the prevalence of communists in American life and did not check the truth of his claims, with the result that these false assertions reached the audience directly. In American books on the subject there are many references to the way McCarthy exploited news procedures. With him, it ceased to be enough to report the facts, which in this case was what McCarthy said – that is, his lies and libels. He added to the manipulation by speaking in time for television news deadlines, so that there was no opportunity to question him before the reports had to go out.

So it is not always enough to provide an accurate record of the facts. The journalist will often have to provide background information or context. But some media are better at doing this than others. It is perhaps a limitation of TV news that it is all foreground. The immediacy of the pictures precludes sober analysis. And TV news is also very lavish of time. Very little is conveyed in 30 minutes compared to what can be read in that time. This is not to assume that the media which are more capable of sober analysis always provide it. Newspapers vary greatly in how much effort they put into promoting understanding. As Harold Evans put it, writing of the thalidomide campaign pursued by the *Sunday Times*: 'There are occasions when it is no use publishing the truth once . . . the erratic nature of the interest in the Thalidomide children was also a reflection of the way newspapers and television news programmes work. "News" is defined too episodically and too topically . . . journalism has not learned how to write about processes, rather than about events.'[7]

So far, this might be considered a failing of the journalist's craft or skills. But the criticism can be made at a deeper level. Psychology has a concept called 'availability error', which is the strong disposition to make judgements or evaluations in light of what is already available to the mind. So uncritical news reporting tends to bolster conventional wisdoms. It is too often anchored to 'what everybody knows', to simplistic analogies, to whatever is most readily available, psychologically. This criticism, an extension of the point made above about newsworthiness, has often been made of journalists. Here is a typical example: 'recurrent interpretations take the form of conventional explanations, legitimations and evaluations of social phenomena which have been incorporated into journalism's stocks of knowledge. As conventional wisdoms, they enable him to make sense of the world and enable him to produce public accounts that are acceptable to his various audiences (editors, readers, sources).'[8]

The suggestion is that journalists are too ready to accept and use conventional explanations. This is often unconscious and unstated, as can be seen in the case of stereotypes. In fact, the criticism above may be summed up as this: reality is translated into stereotypes, including stereotypical stories and explanations. There is also a general lack of understanding by Western media of the Third World, which is seen only in terms of war and famine, for example; South America means drugs and dictators, Islam means fundamentalism.

Stereotyping in the media most commonly affects racial minorities, the elderly, the handicapped and women, which altogether makes up over half the human race. It hardly needs be added that stereotyping is even more prevalent in advertising (see p. 97).

Women have long been stereotyped by the press. Betty Friedan's book *The feminine mystique*, first published in 1963 [423], showed how the American cultural ideal of 'the happy-housewife heroine' was constructed in women's magazines and advertisements. The book was a bestseller and contributed to the revival of the women's movement. Even after thirty years, the press still puts an overemphasis on clothes and physical appearance, a glorification of domesticity, a portrayal of women as empty headed or at least non-intellectual. A woman tends to be treated in the media as a mother, a wife, a housewife or a sex object.

The problem has been recognized for some time, but it is so deeply embedded in our culture that the media are having difficulty in eradicating it. Stereotypes are an economical way of viewing the world, but they are too economical. They are a tool for communicating with a mass audience and as such they appeal to prejudices. They exploit the fact that we do need some categories, some classification of the world. They ignore or dismiss the differences between individuals.

7.3 Fairness and bias

We now enter a minefield. This is the claim that an article or report should be, and here we find a repertoire of terms, 'fair' and 'balanced', 'without bias', 'impartial'. Or, rather more controversially, they should be objective. To ask for fairness and balance is to ask that evaluative language be avoided, that the material should not be slanted. The request for objectivity can be seen as something stronger and is felt by many critics to be impossible. Also, the press, and to an increasing extent radio and television, use columnists and commentators who are opinionated, who have a point of view to put over. Here, though, we are concerned with the purity of the news report.

The history of newspapers does not present much evidence of fairness and impartiality. There seem to have been two major influences in bringing it forward as a journalistic value: broadcasting and the rise of press agencies.

When radio was created in the early 1920s, in both the US and the UK the airwaves available for broadcasting were scarce. So those who were given licences were required to operate their stations in some sense as public trustees. Thus in 1929 in America there was a court case involving the Federal Radio Commission, with the judgment that 'the public interest requires ample play for the free and fair competition of opposing views'. This became the so-called Fairness Doctrine and applied to broadcast news (but *only* broadcast news). It became law in 1959. This was an obligation that broadcasters had to represent various points of view in their public affairs programming. The Doctrine was seen as a guarantee that the privately owned American broadcasting system would provide the valuable social service of balanced, unbiased information. (It did not apply to newspapers.) Another important factor was the alleged scarcity of wavebands available to those wishing to put their views forward.

The major argument against the Doctrine was that it appeared to be a violation of the First Amendment protection of free speech; some asserted that it verged on content control of broadcasters. The claim of scarcity was also attacked; in many cities there are fewer newspapers than television stations. It was also argued that the Doctrine actually discouraged broadcasters from covering controversial public issues, that it had a so-called 'chilling effect'. In 1987 the Federal Communications Commission decided they would no longer enforce the Doctrine. Of the arguments against the Fairness Doctrine, the claim of a 'chilling effect' was at least open to empirical evidence. It has been suggested (for example, by Patricia Aufderheide [453]), that the record of broadcasters' airing of controversial issues since the 1987 decision does not support the FCC's contention that the Doctrine constrained broadcasters from airing controversy and airing it fairly.

In the UK, the BBC's charter imposes obligations of impartiality, fairness and balance, as does the Broadcasting Act upon Independent Television (ITV). Here the criticisms are that it leads to the broadcasting organizations staying safely in the middle of any issue. Philip Schlesinger [487] commented: 'It can confidently be stated that impartiality, by which is meant an uncritical adherence to parliamentary forms of political behaviour, and an absence of political commitment, is the required ideological stance for the BBC newsman.'[9] He also provides a thorough discussion of how the BBC achieves an impartial, neutral style in its news programmes.

Oliver Boyd-Barrett [620] argues that the major international press agencies introduced a second factor. They promoted the idea of 'impartiality' as a valued journalistic objective. Because they supplied the same news to clients whose individual circumstances varied, they constructed a product that was at once standardized and flexible. As a further consequence, the standardized nature of the product helped bring about the substantial measure of uniformity in professional theory and practice far beyond the confines of their initial markets.[10]

A general criticism of notions of fairness and balance is that they are limited virtues, take a middle way, and thus exclude views that are extreme or, as their proponents would describe them, more *radical*. If we turn to the more philosophical notion of objectivity, the arguments become sharper.

How 'fair' and 'balanced' can journalists be? Is it possible for them 'to report an event or series of events in a way that does not reflect the reporter's attitudes about the events and people involved'?[11] It is a dogma of sociology that the media fail to be 'objective'. This implication can be seen in the titles of many books about journalism: *Bending reality*, *The manufacture of news* and *Putting reality together*. To quote from a recent textbook by Brian McNair: 'Journalism, regardless of the integrity of individual journalists and editors, is always a selective, partial account of reality which can never be known in its entirety by anyone.'[12] The point being made here is that objectivity is not just very difficult, but impossible.

Now it is certainly true that journalism is selective, but this is actually a quite trivial criticism. As has been mentioned earlier, it is impossible to write down all the true statements there are about any one topic. To even try and get close to this would mean a single story filling a newspaper. No one would want that amount of detail. No one would pick up a newspaper or turn on the radio or television if one did not know one was going to be offered a selection.

Where the criticism has any force is in the suggestion that anything one writes must be partial – not in the sense of 'incomplete', but in the sense of 'favouring one party or side in a controversy'. It is claimed that it is impossible to exhibit the actual facts not coloured by the feelings or opinions of the writer. As the American historian Charles Beard wrote in another context: 'Whatever acts of purification the historian may perform, he yet remains human, a creature of time, place, circumstance, interests, predilections, culture.'[13] So, by extension, it is argued that anything journalists write must reflect their feelings, opinions and values. Can journalism be value-free?

James Cameron in his autobiography *Point of departure* [457] addresses the problem. Of his reporting during the Vietnam War, he remarks that his belief that North Vietnam was inhabited by human beings earned him criticism for not being objective. He says of books on journalism: 'they seem to argue that the writer himself has no viability, no raison d'être, other than well outside the situation he describes. This is objective journalism and I am obliged to salute it, if only as a ritual gesture to something I never really achieved. Of course "objective journalism" is necessarily to be found in court reports or accounts of, shall we say, earthquakes. Yet it has always seemed to me that a reporter involved, however fortuitously, in a situation concerning genuine ethical values will find this famous "objectivity" not only virtually impossible, but even maybe undesirable.' Here, it would seem, Cameron is defying the belief that journalism should always be neutral. He makes another remark: 'I have always tended to argue that objectivity was of less importance than truth.'

This points to something curious – that in discussing objectivity it is easy to slip past the notion of truth. As Judith Lichtenberg [468] says, 'Our most fundamental interest in objectivity is an interest in truth'.[14] And it has not been shown that the possession of values prevents us from seeing and telling the truth.

If it is admitted that journalism cannot be completely neutral, this does not go very far. If news in the relevant sense of the word is to be written, the journalist must select in a value-judging way because 'news' in this sense is a quasi-evaluative notion, the notion not just of the events, but also of significant or memorable events. But then, all inquiries are selective in this sense, even in the natural sciences. In making their selections, scientists, like historians, follow their interest and betray their values. If journalists cannot avoid it, then nor can anyone else. If we cannot find criteria for comparing 'ultimate commitments' in the media, we cannot do it for any other intellectual activity: history, ethics, aesthetics. It may be possible to find the required objectivity in physics, but even here there are problems. Whatever the claim made about the media, one can reply, it is just the same in sociology – no more and no less.

So, to sum up: if journalism's failure to be objective is because it is selective, then the claim is false. If journalism's failure to be objective is because it cannot free itself of value judgements, then we are all in the same boat, including the critics of journalistic objectivity. But it still looks as if it is possible for a journalist to produce a story that is accurate, promotes understanding and is free of prejudice.

In practice there are many difficulties in the way of objective journalism, but unless we maintain the notion of objectivity, we cannot criticize journalists for not trying to overcome these. What we need to do is examine each piece of journalism on its merits, and one of the merits should be the extent to which it is objective. Even if you fail to tell the whole truth, this does not mean you have not told the truth. We call a man a good man, without implying that he is a saint. Or, to reverse the metaphor, if everyone is blamed, then the worst offenders get off lightly.

McNair concludes his chapter on objectivity thus: 'Is journalism biased, then? On the basis of the evidence gained by content analysis over a period of more than twenty years, we can state with some confidence that the news media of a particular society – press and broadcasting – tend to construct accounts of events which are structured and framed by the dominant values and interests of that society, and to marginalise (if not necessarily exclude) alternative accounts.'[15]

Frankly, it would be very surprising if the media of a society did not have the same criteria of importance and did not make the same value judgements as that society.

It should be recognized, however, that behind the criticism of journalism's objectivity, there is a more substantive claim. It is one thing to criticize the media for distorting the truth; it is another to claim that these distortions flow from certain ideological positions. More specifically, there is the assertion that failures of understanding, which some might want to call intellectual laziness, are ideologically motivated. This issue has already been touched on in the discussions of newsworthiness and journalists' reliance on conventional wisdom.

Thus, among sociologists in the 1960s and 1970s there was, according to Jock Young [417], a general agreement on the notion of a 'consensual paradigm'.[16] The events reported or depicted were the '*translation* of reality into a paradigm or world view. This contains a preconceived notion of social order (a consensus), a concept of normal human nature (free and voluntaristic) and a conception of deviance (either a determined sickness or an act of corruption) ... The consensual paradigm then, is a lens through which reality is seen: it focuses on certain events, it obscures and obfuscates others, it leads to certain questions being asked and others being ignored.' Similarly, Oliver Boyd-Barrett in 1980 [620] summarized recent studies of news selection: 'the issue of selection is seen to involve consideration of the structure, ownership and management of media organisations; the social backgrounds, career patterns, and attitudes of professional communications; patterns of interaction between communications and other related occupational groups; and the influence of prevailing cultural values. Increasingly the media are seen in relation to the characteristic mode of production in society, as functional sustainments of the "corporate economy".'[17]

This type of analysis is often called the hegemonic model. It argues that the media portray only one view of the world. This is the one subscribed to by society's privileged classes and is the dominant set of ideas. The media are ideological, carrying a world-view which structures the world and also explains it to the audience. Some views are rendered acceptable, normal or common-sense. Others are marginalized as extremist, irrational, utopian or impractical. This is the line taken by the Glasgow University Media Group in a well-known series of studies [459]. However, the proponents of the hegemonic model have little evidence to offer to show that the media do have an effect on the audience.

In this type of criticism, two assumptions are often made. The first is that there is no real world to be objective about, which is controversial to say the least, but is often asserted without any argument. The second is that journalism, the media, should provide a fully representative picture of society. On this point, it will be best to quote a journalist, Gerald Priestland [535]: 'unless they are to embed the relatively small number of events that are actually new and striking within a great mass of what is everyday, humdrum, and rather boring, journalists can never present a completely accurate model of the life we all lead. But to create such a model is not our purpose, and I do not think many people would buy one if we made it. Few people would have the time to read their way through it. And so we select. We are bound to select and we are expected to select.'[18]

7.4 TV news and journalism

We have been discussing what the truth-telling of journalism involves and the extent to which it can succeed. These questions are raised more sharply when television news and journalism are specifically looked at. For one thing, television news is the most common source of the public's information and has been since about 1960. It reaches a wider audience than any one newspaper. According to the annual ITC survey *Television: the public's view*, in 1995 the prime sources of world news were 71 per cent television, 16 per cent newspapers and 11 per cent radio.

The main issue is whether the form of television makes it unsuitable as a medium for providing news. This has been argued, for example, by Philip Schlesinger in *Putting 'reality' together* [487]. First, the fact that the news has to fill a time slot is a goal and a constraint; it determines what is to be left out. For a 30-minute programme can only convey about the same amount of information as the front page of a newspaper. Second, television news is nearly all foreground, with very little background; there is a bias towards immediacy as against providing a context, and this weakens the promotion of understanding. Third, in selecting items to fill that space of time, there will be a bias towards those that go more easily with visual material. Each of these is a criticism of television's ability to impart information.

Other aesthetic considerations might be introduced, such as changes of pace and variety to keep the audience interested. A blatant example of this kind of thing is quoted from an NBC news executive: 'Every news story should, without any sacrifice of responsibility, display the attributes of fiction or drama. It should have structure and conflict, problem and denouement, rising action and falling action, a middle and an end.'[19] This may be extreme, but the same point is made when we note the widespread practice of finishing a news bulletin with a light-hearted or humorous item.

The reliance on pictures leads to other effects. One of these is the 'staging' of news for the convenience of the cameras by, for example, press conferences and interviews. These are not important events that take place and so need to be reported; they are events staged so that the cameras can be present. This staging of scenes is perhaps at its most ridiculous in the currently universal practice that has the journalist reporting from the spot what could easily have been narrated from the studio (for example, a journalist giving a report from outside a government office).

This kind of consideration has led some to dismiss the notion that television portrays 'reality' in any way, but instead creates it: 'The core argument in theories of representation (within modernism) is that, despite appearances, television does not represent (re-present) a piece of reality but rather produces or constructs it. Reality does not exist in the objectivity of empiricism, but is a product of discourse. The television camera and microphone do not record reality, but encode it: the encoding produces a sense of reality that is ideological. What is re-presented, then, is not reality but ideology.'[20]

Another facet of television's influence on the world is that it can become an active participant by the mere fact of turning its cameras on events. This was clearly illustrated in the race riots in Brixton, south London, in 1981. Lord Scarman, in his report on the disorders [483], declared that the broadcasters 'do bear a responsibility for the escalation of the disorders . . . and for the imitative element in the later disorders elsewhere' (that is, riots in other cities). He believed that television should have shown much less of the riots on the news.

7.5 News-gathering

Here the concern is with deception, economy with the truth, and even straightforward lying as an aid to obtaining information. For instance, undercover reporting is a common practice, and this obviously entails deception. Is this justifiable? For some people and some philosophers, all deception is morally wrong. Augustine and Aquinas held that lying is always prohibited. Kant judged that a lie violates a duty to oneself and to others, because rational beings owe each other truthfulness in communication. Mill severely condemned almost all lying as injurious to human trust and therefore to the social fabric, but judged it right on rare occasions, as when only thus can some great and unmerited evil be averted.

Those who defend such practices argue that journalists are representatives of the public, and deception in the name of the public interest is sometimes necessary, to uncover corruption, social ills and other shady activities. This is in effect a utilitarian justification – a greater good is served.

We might want to draw a distinction between active and passive deception. It is passive when a person does not reveal their true identity; for example, a restaurant critic seems to be justified in withholding his identity. But what of a reporter who dons a white coat and pretends to be hospital staff? This is an active deception, amounting to a lie. It may be possible to say that we should never lie, but that always avoiding deception is too high a demand to be achieved. Then what of a case where journalists break the law to illustrate the malfunctioning of institutions, such as placing fake bombs to test airport security?

In the UK in 1994 a *Sunday Times* journalist posing as a businessman offered ten MPs £1000 to put down a question in the House of Commons on behalf of a non-existent company. The newspaper subsequently claimed that two agreed to do so. (The exercise was set up as a straw poll, prompted by claims from a genuine businessman who did not want to go on the record.) The justification given by the editor of the *Sunday Times* for using deception to highlight the readiness of these Tory MPs to take cash for tabling parliamentary questions was that the paper was performing a public service.[21]

Nicholas Tomalin [540] wrote: 'the gathering of newspaper information almost invariably involves guile, subterfuge, humiliation, lying, cheating and a healthy amount of straightforward criminality.'[22] No doubt there is a healthy amount of journalistic exaggeration here. But many journalists feel that subterfuge is the only way to expose those who would prefer to stay unexposed, and so is necessary for a vigorous, strong press. And the code of the Press Complaints Commission allows for subterfuge 'in the public interest'.

Of course, as we have already seen, 'the public interest' is hard to define. The greater goods used to justify a lie include: avoiding harm to others; promoting fairness and justice; protecting the truth by counteracting another lie or by furthering some more important truth; or by preserving the confidence of others in our own truthfulness. Can good ends justify bad means? If a utilitarian viewpoint is adopted, then yes. And it is the case that the justifications offered by the press are firmly utilitarian. But it still needs to be taken into account that a newspaper that uses lying and what might be called the exploitation of deception becomes involved in a web of deceit that pervades the news-gathering process. Taking short-cuts in one area can easily lead to short-cuts in another (that is, the truth of the facts reported). Second, journalists can be taking part in practices they criticize in others, notably government, and which they would protest against strongly if carried out on themselves, as newspaper organizations or individuals. Further, the function of investigative journalism can be said to identify responsibility for wrongdoing, and allocate guilt and blame. It is taking on a moral role.

In deciding whether a specific lie would be justified we have to weigh the importance of the good at which we aim by telling it against the harm involved in or arising from its being told. Here we can use the notion of a 'publicity test', testing our views against those of others. (This idea comes from Sissela Bok.) It can play two roles: to check how our reasoning stands up to analysis in discussion and to check the reliability of the information on which we base our judgements (for example, as to the necessity of the lie or the degree to which it undermines others' trust). A point to bear in mind here is that where discussion of the possible lie might give it away, and so make the 'publicity test' difficult, one might be able to deliberate in private against a background of informed and open public debate of like cases. The informed public's reaction to past cases may then give guidance.

Sissela Bok, in her important book *Lying* [380], outlines a three-level procedure for determining whether a lie is justifiable, and for this to take place after the honest alternatives have been thoroughly considered and debated. First, we scrutinize our own conscience. Second, we examine precedents and consult with friends, elders and colleagues. Third, and most important, there should be an opportunity for public debate among the public at large. Her overall point is that the person making or intending to make the lie should not be the judge of its justification.

Overall the preceding discussion should not be taken to mean that the lies of journalists are justified, for very many are not, but that it is possible to have a justification.

There is a tendency for journalists to argue that if the crime or malpractice being exposed is worse than the deception required to expose it, then it is justified. But this will nearly always be the case, especially if the practice of journalistic deception is very common and so devalued.

On the other hand, there is concern, particularly in the US, about the use of deceptive practices. The Pulitzer Prize has twice been refused to newspapers for stories based on undercover reporting. Some newspapers have a policy of not using surreptitious techniques except when alternative approaches have failed, and when the story is of extreme public interest.

Notes

1. Jones, N. *Soundbites and spin-doctors.*
2. Quoted in Merrill, J. C. and Barney, R. D. (eds.) *Ethics and the press*, p. 60.
3. Seymour-Ure, C. *British press and broadcasting since 1945*, p. 126.
4. According to Cohen, S. and Young, J. in *The manufacture of news*, p. 24.
5. Schudson, M. *The power of news*, pp. 1–33.
6. As reported in *The Guardian*, 2 October 1995.
7. Evans, H. *Good times, bad times*, p. 64.
8. Cohen, S. and Young, J. (eds.) *The manufacture of news*, Rev. ed. 1981, p. 87. Other examples can be found in the same book at pp. 12 and 163.
9. Schlesinger, P. *Putting 'reality' together*, p. 191.
10. Boyd-Barrett, O. *The international news agencies*, p. 19.
11. Olen, J. *Ethics of journalism*, p. 85.
12. McNair, B. *News and journalism in the UK*, p. 31.
13. Quoted in Dray, W. *Philosophy of history*, 2nd ed. (New York: Prentice-Hall, 1993), p. 35.
14. Curran, J. and Gurevitch, M. (eds.) *Mass media and society*, 2nd ed., p. 227.
15. McNair, B. *News and journalism in the UK*, p. 38.
16. Cohen, S. and Young, J. (eds.) *The manufacture of news*, Rev. ed. 1981, p. 393.
17. Boyd-Barrett, O. *The international news agencies*, p. 73.
18. Priestland, G. *The dilemmas of journalism*, p. 42.
19. Quoted in Epstein, E. J. *News from nowhere: television and the news* (New York: Random House, 1973).
20. Fiske, J. in Curran, J. and Gurevitch, M. (eds.) *Mass media and society*, 2nd ed. 1996, pp. 56–7.
21. *UK Press Gazette*, 30 January 1995.
22. Tomalin, N. *Nicholas Tomalin reporting*, p. 93.

8 Confidentiality and sources

The issue of confidentiality is one that is strongly associated with journalism, usually when journalists are asked to reveal the source of their information, who may wish to remain secret. But it also appears in many other areas of professional life, for the medical profession, lawyers, priests, accountants, social workers and so on.

Sissela Bok in her book *Secrets* [505] has a chapter with the title 'The limits of confidentiality'. In this she argues that the justification for confidentiality rests on four premises, of which three support the general practice of confidentiality, and the fourth supports professional secrecy in particular. The first premise is that of individual autonomy over personal information; people can have secrets. The second holds that it is not only natural but often also right to respect the secrets of intimates and associates, secrets which might have been shared with one, and that human relationships could not survive without such respect. The third premise holds that a pledge of silence, should one be made, creates an obligation beyond the respect already provided for by the two previous premises, for persons and for existing relationships. A promise raises the stakes. But then, as Bok points out, there may be times when these premises have to be overridden; an example might be if maintaining confidentiality would lead to violence being done to innocent persons, or to someone becoming an unwitting accomplice in crime. In such circumstances, she says, a promise of silence can be breached. But her fourth premise 'enters in to add strength to the particular pledges of silence given by professionals. This premise assigns weight beyond ordinary loyalty to professional confidentiality, because of its utility to persons and to society.'

This point about the social utility of the silence of the professional is important, because it is easy for professionals in any field to advance confidentiality as a shield (the medical profession is particularly prone to do this). An absolute insistence on confidentiality can be unreasonable. It can be used as a means for deflecting legitimate public attention. (And indeed it may be this kind of confidentiality that journalists often need to breach to discover something of public concern.) Bok concludes her chapter: 'The premises supporting confidentiality are strong, but they cannot support practices of secrecy – whether by individual clients, institutions, or professionals themselves – that undermine and contradict the very respect for persons and for human bonds that confidentiality was meant to protect.' A system of ethics cannot excuse any group from the rules of moral reasoning predicated simply on the role of that group within society.

So confidentiality is something that can be overridden by other, weightier considerations. But the burden of proof lies with those who wish to override it. As it affects journalism, the principle of confidentiality imposes a duty to withhold the names of sources of information from third parties under certain circumstances. Sometimes, also, there is the issue of whether a news organization should publish secret or confidential information provided to it by a source. Here there is not only the source's confidentiality, but also whether the media should release the information at all.

Some of the confidential relationships mentioned above are considered important enough to receive recognition by the law (for example, between lawyers and clients, priests and penitents, bank managers and clients). This is not the case with journalism. There was an important case in the US in 1972, which ruled by a majority in the Supreme Court to deny constitutional protection for the reporter–source relationship. According to this judgment, reporters had no privilege under the First Amendment to refuse to testify before grand juries. Nevertheless many lower federal courts and state courts have protected journalists, following the dissenting opinion of one of the judges in the case. This judge proposed a three-part test, which had to be met before government could compel grand jury testimony from a journalist. First, there should be probable cause to believe that the journalist has information 'clearly relevant to a specific probable violation of the law'. The second was that the information sought could not be obtained by alternative means less destructive of First Amendment values. The third was that there should be a 'compelling and over-riding need' for the information.

The law apart, journalists believe in the need for confidentiality for sources. Raymond Snoddy writes in *The good, the bad and the unacceptable* [311] of the 'need to maintain confidentiality of sources. It is impossible to exaggerate the importance for a journalist of being able to obtain information in confidence from a private source and then being allowed to protect the confidentiality of that source.' He refers to the still secret identity of 'Deep Throat' who helped Bob Woodward and Carl Bernstein in the Watergate investigation, and then describes two recent British cases, where journalists were prosecuted under the Contempt of Court Act 1991. The crucial ethical issue is whether anonymity should be promised in the first place, as the journalist knows that this may well come into conflict with other demands. There are times when journalists believe that they will not get the information unless confidentiality can be promised, and thus the readers would not be informed about matters of public interest. It can hardly be doubted that the reporter–source relationship is an important one.

In individual cases, this can put journalists in conflict with the police, if the former have information that the latter believe they need when investigating a crime. Journalists feel that the police should develop their own sources, and resent becoming an arm of law enforcement.

So far, we have been assuming, with journalists, that the reporter's privilege of keeping confidences is a good thing. It may sometimes, perhaps often, be necessary. However, in principle, sources should be made known. For one thing, readers are often only able to judge the value of the information provided if they are able to evaluate the source from which it comes. Confidentiality can act as a smokescreen. As an editorial from the *Washington Post* put it, 'Walter and Ann Source (née Rumor) had four daughters (Highly Placed, Authoritative, Unimpeachable, and Well-Informed). The first married a diplomat named Reliable Informant. (The Informant brothers are widely known and quoted here; among the best known are White House, State Department, and Congressional.) Walter Speculation's brother-in-law, Ian Rumor, married Alexandre Conjecture, from which there were two sons, It Was Understood and It Was Learned.'[1]

Thus confidentiality deprives the audience of the opportunity to decide for itself how much faith to put in the information. In other words, the names of the sources are an important part of the story.

In addition, news sources act from a variety of motives, not all of which are praiseworthy. They may be providing information out of self-interest or for revenge. How are the journalists to know whether this information has been altered, edited or selected out of context? What interest are they serving? There is a very real danger that journalists, and through them the public, can be deceived by this use of confidentiality. In the UK, the government uses a system of informal unattributed briefings to the press, known as the 'lobby system'. This has allowed governments and individual politicians to manipulate the news to the point of 'disinformation'.[2] 'When journalists are presented with secret information about issues of great import, they become, in a very real sense, agents for the surreptitious source.'[3]

It may not be in journalists' long-term interests to connive in such practices. The extensive use of unattributed sources promotes distrust and even cynicism towards reported stories. Journalists should not let their desire to obtain information undermine the long-term credibility of the information they present to their readers. More generally, journalists stand for openness in public discourse; they challenge secrecy. They should, therefore, avoid it in their own practices, and reliance on reporter's privilege can lead to accusations of hypocrisy.

In a case in the UK in 1984, when *The Guardian* published a confidential document that had been leaked to it by a civil servant, the newspaper was taken to court and relinquished the name of the person involved, who was then sent to prison for six months. It is hard to tell to what extent this discouraged potential 'leakers' or 'whistle-blowers'. If it is a matter of providing documents to a newspaper, this can be done anonymously.

A more famous case was the leaking of the *Pentagon papers*, a confidential report detailing American involvement in Vietnam since the Second World War. The government claimed that the papers contained 'information relating to the national defense of the United States' and that publication was prohibited by law. The *New York Times*, which was publishing a selection from the papers, replied that 'it is in the interest of the people of this country to be informed of the material contained in this series of articles'. There were two important questions. First, was it ethically permissible to publish classified material? (This was the issue in the legal battles and was settled by the Supreme Court in favour of the press.) Nearly all ethical frameworks permit civil disobedience under certain circumstances. We can repeat a point made when discussing media and government: that the government's interest is not the same as the public interest. Second, should the newspapers have used stolen documents as their source? From some ethical perspectives, theft is always wrong. The newspapers justified themselves on utilitarian grounds. The managing editor of the *New York Times* contended that publication was in the best interests of the country. Is it possible to steal a decision that was made three years ago and has caused such consequences? He was in fact suggesting that you cannot steal information on public matters.

An important case in the UK was the publication of the diaries of Richard Crossman, a government minister in the 1960s, which gave a vivid picture of confidential and often rancorous discussions in cabinet meetings. The *Sunday Times* wanted to publish them, the Cabinet Office wished to prevent publication. The newspaper's editor, Harold Evans, took a calculated risk by publishing some extracts, but without giving advance warning, so that the government could not take out an injunction to prevent publication. With each week of publication, Evans introduced increasingly confidential information from the diaries and the Attorney-General eventually took the paper to court, appealing for the material to be banned as an infringement of the law of confidence. The newspaper won.

Away from the press there is the general issue of loyalty, which does not always have an express promise. Should a doctor write of his patient's illnesses, even when the patient is dead? After Sir Winston Churchill's death, his doctor, Lord Moran, wrote of the statesman's illnesses while Prime Minister, and was criticized for breaking medical confidentiality. Does this apply after the patient's death?

Another recent case was that of a woman who had worked for the Kennedy family and then wrote a book about it. From one point of view her obligations as a confidante ended with her official employment. But she would not have held that earlier privileged position if her employers had known what she would do with the information. So, even if she made no promise of confidentiality, had she committed a betrayal of loyalty?

Finally, it may be useful to note what journalists think of the issue. In a survey carried out in the US in the mid-1980s, publishers, editors and journalists were asked about their view of confidentiality. Twenty-five per cent of the total said that a pledge of confidentiality to a source should always be kept no matter what the circumstances, even if it means a long jail term for the reporter and heavy financial cost to the newspaper (though, interestingly, this broke down into 40 per cent of the journalists, 18 per cent for publishers, and 20 per cent for editors; the latter two categories worry more about financial consequences). Sixty-two per cent thought that a pledge of confidentiality should always be taken seriously, but that it can be violated in unusual circumstances.[4]

Notes

1. Quoted in Hulteng, J. L. *The messenger's motives*, p. 79.
2. Cockerell, M. and others. *Sources close to the Prime Minister: inside the hidden world of the news manipulators.*
3. Epstein, E. J. in Merrill, J. C. and Barney, R. D. (eds.) *Ethics and the press*, pp. 60–8.
4. Meyer, P. *Ethical journalism*, pp. 208–9.

9 The values of journalists

What makes a good journalist? This is an ambiguous question. For a reporter the first sense will be something like a person's abilities at getting a story, range of contacts, good background knowledge, research skills, writing skills and perhaps the knack of being in the right place at the right time. A succinct and down-to-earth journalist's view is Nicholas Tomalin's: 'the only qualities essential for real success in journalism are ratlike cunning, a plausible manner, and a little literary ability.'[1] Of course, other skills are used in putting a newspaper together, such as the sub-editor's flair for headlines and the layout of a page. In the context of media ethics, however, the question asks whether the journalist goes about their professional activities in a moral way.

For our purposes the question can be rephrased as follows: what values should journalists pursue? What are their professional skills for? Not all the definitions one comes across are helpful. For example, 'good journalism, which means information of high quality, well written and well presented' (Everette Dennis, *Reshaping the media* [558]) merely replaces one evaluative term 'good' with others; in particular we need to know, what is meant by 'of high quality'?

Here is a journalist's encapsulation: 'the basic commitment of journalism remains, however, the same as always. It is identical for all. It is to report honestly, to comment fearlessly, and to hold fast to independence.'[2]

Newspapers themselves claim that the pursuit of truth is their primary aim. The 1975 code of ethics of the Associated Press Managing Editors Association says: 'A good newspaper is fair, accurate, honest, responsible, independent and decent. Truth is its guiding principle.' The 1973 code of the Society of Professional Journalists, Sigma Delta Chi, begins: 'The Society believes the duty of journalists is to serve the truth.'³ In such codes this claim is supported by references to 'public welfare', the role of mass communication as a carrier of 'public discussion and information', notions which we have discussed in Chapter 2. There is also a tendency in these codes of ethics to refer to the public's 'right to know'; for example, the Society of Professional Journalists' code states that: 'the public's right to know of events of public importance and interest is the overriding mission of the mass media.' Apart from problems about a blanket 'right to know' (criticized earlier), we have here an implicit declaration of passing on information and knowledge.

Other suggestions for the virtues of a journalist are mostly in the same area:

- Journalists must observe a responsibility to the public welfare; their impressive power should be employed for the general good, not for private advantage.
- Journalists should provide a news report that is sincere, true and accurate; accounts should be thorough, balanced and complete.
- Journalists should be impartial; they should function as the public representatives, not as the mouthpieces of partisan groups or as special interest.
- Journalists must be fair. They must give space or airtime to the several sides of a dispute; private rights should not be invaded; correction of errors should be prompt and wholehearted.
- Journalists should respect the canons of decency, insofar as those canons can be identified in a society with ever-changing values.⁴

There seems, then, to be widespread agreement that at the base of journalistic ethics is an allegiance to truth. To put this in more philosophical terms, we can say that certain human activities have goals which make them the kinds of activity they are. Medicine and education are examples of areas or practices which provide the arena in which virtues are exhibited. So health is an internal and constitutive end of medicine; in the same way truth-telling about significant contemporary events is an internal and constitutive end of journalism.⁵

These goals of journalism then define the qualities characteristic of a good practitioner of the profession – the particular virtues and excellence of a journalist as a journalist, which include the technical skills, clarity of style and ability to construct a story.

Of course, journalism does not always deliver the truth, as medicine does not always deliver health. We have to bear in mind that journalism is a business – or, more specifically, as Rupert Murdoch once said, 'we are in the entertainment business' following the discovery that the *Hitler diaries*, which his papers had been publishing, were fakes.⁶ This reminds us that the journalist lives in two worlds: in a craft or profession that has a commitment to telling the truth, and also as an employee in a particular market. Sometimes the pressure of the market will have to be resisted through the virtue of integrity. The history of journalism is full of principled resignations by editors and journalists.

A more damaging criticism was made by Edward Jay Epstein in an article on the American press, and what he says can be applied to British journalism. 'The problem of journalism in America proceeds from a simple but inescapable bind: journalists are rarely, if ever, in a position to establish the truth about an issue for themselves.' Even if they were to avoid the restraints imposed by space, time and financial resources, 'they would still lack the forensic means and authority to establish the truth about a matter in serious dispute'. They cannot cross-examine witnesses or their own sources, they lack the technical competence to evaluate evidence, they cannot identify their sources, let alone document their claims. 'Gathering news is a very different enterprise from establishing truth, with different standards and objectives.' This links to the suggestion made earlier, that the journalist's primary aim is the pursuit of the newsworthy. The main thrust of Epstein's argument is that journalists are too dependent on their sources to be able to claim the role of truth-seekers. Journalism can 'serve as an important institution for conveying and circulating information, and signalling changes in the direction of public policy and discourse, but it cannot serve as a credible investigator of the "hidden facts" or the elusive truths which determine them'.[7]

Another sceptical note comes from Nicholas Tomalin: 'to say a journalist's job is to record facts is like saying an architect's job is to lay bricks – true, but missing the point. A journalist's real function, at any rate, his required talent, is the *creation of interest*.'[8] This fits in well with our earlier discussion of newsworthiness.

Before leaving this discussion of journalistic truth, let us quote a journalist in the field, Gerald Priestland [535]: 'When I presented a nightly news programme we had an unofficial motto: "We hope this is the truth. We're sure it isn't the whole truth. It'll be a miracle if it's nothing but the truth".'[9]

This comment reflects an honesty of purpose, the aim of truth-telling, rather than claiming to have the whole truth. Thus in 1994 *The Spectator* revealed that a journalist on *The Guardian* had received payment from the KGB, and so it was no longer possible to believe that he had been writing honestly, with no hidden agenda. This leads us to the issue of conflicts of interest, which will be treated separately.

There is also an ideal of campaigning journalism, exemplified by W. T. Stead in the nineteenth century, and represented by Harold Evans in the UK since the Second World War. In the afterword to *Good times, bad times* [254] he writes of the effectiveness of the *Sunday Times* in areas of public policy. He then talks about two schools of journalism. On the one hand, there is the horizontal school of journalism, which waits on events and is characterized by moral torpor. On the other hand, 'the effort to get to the bottom of things, which is the aspiration of the vertical school of journalism, cannot be indiscriminate. Judgements have to be made about what is important; they are moral judgements. The vertical school is active. It sets its own agenda.'

A 1995 survey of British journalists asked a number of ethical questions, the answers to which are worth recording here:

- Eighty-six per cent say it may be justified to 'use confidential business or government documents without authorization'.

- Over half say it may be justified to 'agree to protect confidentiality and not do so'.
- Half say it may be justified to 'use personal documents such as letters without permission'.[10]

Of course, what is left out here is the conditions under which such actions may or may not be justified. But it is clear enough that journalists tend to take a robustly consequentialist line in ethics. The important question is: who decides that a course of action is justified? It should not be the journalists themselves.

9.1 Conflicts of interest

As we have just mentioned, journalists are often subject to a conflict of interest. This occurs where there is a clash between professional loyalty and outside interests. Few cases are as obvious as that of a journalist on the *Wall Street Journal* who used his position on the paper to find out which stocks and shares were going to be mentioned in an influential column. He passed on this information to friends before publication. With this advance information his friends could buy and sell the stocks and shares in advance of the rest of the market and make large profits which they shared with the journalist. Not only was he fired for violating the newspaper's rules; what he had done was against the law, and the journalist went to jail.

At a quite different level, is it wrong for a journalist to accept any gift or favour from vested interests or news sources? Although a meal provided by a news source in itself may not be a problem over time, the reporter's professional detachment may be undermined, even if no favour is promised in return. This would apply more strongly to free trips (sometimes including food and lodging) paid for by a vested interest. Expense-paid trips are valuable public relations tools; for journalists they provide useful access, but are they then able to write in a fully balanced way? Travel writers are often offered free trips to holiday destinations. They may not be able to afford go otherwise, or their newspaper to send them, but are they going to be able to write a critical piece? Many newspapers have firm policies about not accepting this kind of favour.

Another question is whether journalists should be involved in public organizations and, in particular, in politics. Some news organizations discourage participation in any community organizations, because journalists become part of the system they are assigned to cover. On the other hand, civic participation and activism may be useful in that it keeps journalists in touch with the community and provides them with news sources. Outright political activism, however, would be widely frowned upon.

Then there are conflicts of interest that involve personal relationships. Reporters are sons and daughters, wives and husbands; they also have friends. Perceptions can vary greatly here, as was brought out neatly in an American survey reported in Philip Meyer's *Ethical journalism* [42]. Respondents were asked whether the reporter's background was a help or a hindrance in particular case:

- A reporter who was raised on a farm is assigned to cover agriculture (+94 per cent).
- A black reporter is assigned to cover civil rights (+8 per cent).
- A reporter whose parents runs an oil-exploration business is assigned to cover energy (−25 per cent).
- A reporter whose close friend is elected mayor is assigned to cover city hall (−74 per cent).

The above is just a sample, but we have the striking contrast between attitudes to agriculture and oil exploration. Meyer suggested that the difference reflects contrasting attitudes of approval for the two businesses. He also drew the conclusion that apparent conflict needs to be treated as seriously as real conflict. To put this point in other terms, journalists need public credibility. Individual newspapers need it, and the profession as a whole needs it.

Beyond this, because conflicts of interest are so varied, it is difficult to say anything that is both general and useful about them. To say that every effort should be made to avoid them does not take us very far. At least perhaps, if conflicts cannot be avoided, they should be acknowledged, so that the audience or readership can take this factor into account.

9.2 Professionalism, councils and codes

There is a debate over whether journalism counts as a profession, or is something rather less, merely a craft, for instance. Much depends on how 'professionalism' is defined. The term is associated with competence, with training, with a body of knowledge, with standards of evaluation and improvement. Professions also draw esteem, respectability, and, its members hope, better pay. A 1995 survey in the UK found that 51 per cent of journalists saw their occupation as a 'profession', a figure which probably reflects the aspirations of graduates, who now constitute 49 per cent of journalists.

But beyond this, is it possible to give a more exacting definition? It can be argued, against the belief that professionalism can be applied to journalists, that there are no formal minimum entrance requirements, that no journalist is expected to abide by a code of ethics, that no journalist is certified or licensed, and that no professional standards are commonly agreed upon, as, for instance, in the medical and legal professions. A person writing for the *Sunday Sport* is just as much a journalist as one writing for the *Financial Times*. (Actually, journalists are less professional than librarians in this respect, for the latter have to have an appropriate qualification.) Nor is there any 'body of knowledge'.

In defence of professionalism, it might be said that journalism is still evolving, and so does not yet have all the accoutrements of a profession. But it does now provide 'a public service – the free flow of information and ideas'.[11] A journalist has an expertise that a layman does not, namely, in news-gathering. Also, minimum levels of education are required. People can be put out of the profession – informally, by not being given a job. Journalism does have codes of ethics, and on some newspapers failure to adhere to them can result in dismissal.

One way of asserting professionalism is to have self-regulatory councils and codes of practice. These have come into being in an attempt at self-regulation in the face of public criticism, and also in an attempt, it might be suggested, to gain or maintain public credibility, to establish journalism as a profession. The adoption of a code can be seen as an important symbol of the fact that the occupation is seeking to justify itself in terms of professional norms. Codes for journalists have been adopted in a wide range of countries, but as Nigel Harris [5] points out, they are only a part, and perhaps quite a minor part, of the regulatory framework within which journalists operate. The most important constraining factor remains the law.[12]

In favour of councils and codes, it can be said that the press can be improved if there are formal channels for public comment and criticism and if professionals have standards against which they can make individual decisions. Are the press above criticism? No. Then how is the criticism to be made? Councils observe the work of the press, comment and criticize. So they have a role to play, both for the journalist and the press themselves on defending press freedom and improving professional standards, and for the public in opening a channel for complaints about press treatment and making the press accountable.

However, self-regulation has not been completely successful. In the UK the Press Complaints Commission, set up and paid for by the press themselves, appears to some a toothless watchdog. It can only apply the pressure of publicity.

Another criticism that is made is that self-regulation through codes and councils has an idealistic belief that the quality of the press is determined by the qualities of individual journalists, and fails to account for the way in which the organization of the press constrains what journalists do and shapes their perceptions of what is 'professional' and what is not. To put this point another way, professionalism is not assured within media organizations which do not have as their goal the realization of professional norms (for example, a journalist on a newspaper which is only concerned to make money). Unlike medicine and the law, the media is an industry.

There is still strong resistance to press councils, based on the belief that they impede the freedom of the press. It is claimed that press councils inevitably set up universal standards and these then lead to conformity. A council would define what 'good practice' and proper ethical behaviour are, and there is a danger of pushing the press in the direction of a monolithic conformity. There would be a group setting itself up as an arbiter of media conduct. It is true that press councils can impede the freedom of the press. That is, surely, exactly the point, to curtail the press's freedom to harm others through the various abuses to which it is prone. It is hard to see that a press council can formulate and impose commandments that can easily be followed.

On the question of codes of conduct for journalists, there is a similar debate. There are many ways in which the media can offend without straying beyond the law: inaccuracy, lies, distortions, bias, propaganda, sensationalism, trivialization, lapses of taste, vulgarity, sexism, racism, smears, character assassination, deception, invasions of privacy. Andrew Belsey and Ruth Chadwick in *Ethical issues in journalism and the media* [5] argue that a start to dealing with these can be made by introducing a code of conduct which would prohibit these journalistic malpractices and provide that journalists be accountable for their actions. But they do not really deal with the problem of how codes of conduct can be made binding, what force they can be given. For it does seem that there must some measure of adherence to a code if it is to have any value. Also, it would be no small problem with some of the journalistic sins listed above to define them for a code of conduct.

Against codes, it is claimed that most are platitudes, drawn up merely to improve public relations. Furthermore, a code is useless because it cannot cover all the problems which a journalist will encounter. Codes are where editors rationalize and idealize their practices.

One problem with codes raised above is how detailed they should be. It might seem that detailed specifications of what is deemed to be unethical, rather than a few general principles, might be better. However, a lot of detail can encourage journalists into a 'loophole-seeking attitude of mind'. In addition, short codes consisting of a few broad principles can often be applied to new situations, while detailed codes are more cumbersome.

Most of the codes in Europe were adopted by journalists themselves. According to a survey by Tiina Laitila [563],[13] no one principle was present in every one of the thirty-one codes surveyed. The most common were:

1.	Truthfulness, honesty, accuracy of information	90%
2.	Correction of errors	90%
3.	Prohibition of discrimination on basis or race or religion	87%
4.	Respect for privacy	87%
5.	Prohibition on accepting bribes or other benefits	87%

Naturally, with all these criticisms of how the press actually functions, there have been many suggestions for press reform. A convenient summary of recent ideas can be found in the article by James Curran entitled 'The different approaches to media reform' in *Bending reality* [73].

See also the discussion of codes and councils in the section on Accountability in Chapter 2.

Notes

1. Tomalin, N. *Nicholas Tomalin reporting*, p. 77.
2. Williams, F. *Dangerous estate*, p. 291.
3. Quoted in Meyer, P. *Ethical journalism*, pp. 250 and 252.
4. Examples taken from Hulteng, J. L. *The messenger's motives*.
5. For an argument that truth-telling should be an internal goal of the media quite generally, fictional as well as factual, see Mepham, J. 'Television fictions: quality and truth-telling', *Radical Philosophy* 57 (1991), pp. 20–7.
6. Evans, H. *Good times, bad times*, p. 404.
7. Epstein, E. J. in Merrill, J. C. and Barney, R. D. (eds.) *Ethics and the press*, pp. 60–8.
8. Tomalin, N. *Nicholas Tomalin reporting*, p. 83.
9. Priestland, G. *The dilemmas of journalism*, p. 113.
10. Quoted in *The Guardian*, 16 October 1995.
11. Dennis, E. E. and Merrill, J. C. *Media debates*, p. 156.
12. Harris, N. in Belsey, A. and Chadwick, R. (eds.) *Ethical issues in journalism and the media*, p. 65.
13. Laitila, T. 'Journalistic codes of ethics in Europe', *European Journal of Communication* 10 (4), December 1995, pp. 527–44.

10 Quality

Though considerations of quality can be applied in any area of the media, there are two in particular that have caused discussion. There is a desire both for 'quality' newspapers and for 'quality' television. In both areas quality is seen as threatened by the pursuit of profit, by which is meant the pursuit of large audiences. In television for instance, it is believed that bad programmes drive out good ones. (We have already touched on this subject in Chapter 4.)

As far as newspapers are concerned, there has been a modification in recent years, in that some advertisers (who of course make it possible for newspapers and commercial television to exist) have sought a 'quality' audience, in the belief that those parts of the population who have plenty of money to spend are likely to include a large enough proportion of people with a taste for 'quality' in the newspaper they read. There is here a tacit definition of 'quality' as referring to high culture, art in a traditional sense. Debate has focused on whether a free market will automatically deliver quality as demanded by the consumer, or whether the pursuit of the highest ratings (or readership) at the lowest cost will not inevitably erode the standards of quality we have come to expect (in the UK at least).

But there are some general questions that are worth asking: is there a natural conflict between high culture, which is, almost by definition, minority culture, and the mass media? Do not the mass media have their own standards of quality? What makes good television? What makes a good newspaper? Even if everyone agreed that soap operas are not 'quality' television, they still raise questions of quality. What makes one soap opera better than another? What makes one episode better than another episode of the same soap opera?

It has also been argued that quality is a non-issue, that it is just a legitimation of the old hierarchies of judgement, a concept drained of meaning by years of abuse by those in power. This question is at least worth raising. Do we need to worry about quality in the sense of ranking what we are looking at? I enjoyed X, I enjoyed Y – not, X is better than Y, because . . . On the other hand, in any branch of the media, selections and choices are made on criteria other than price. Programme controllers in broadcasting evaluate programme proposals when choosing which to finance; the Independent Television Commission evaluates proposals for television franchises and applies a 'quality threshold'; newspaper editors select writers and individual articles. So even if it is not possible to arrive at a satisfactory definition of 'quality', it will remain a concept much invoked.

This said, the debate about quality in the media tends to be sharpest around the issue of entertainment. The question becomes whether the media have an obligation to elevate tastes or whether providing escapist fare is sufficient. Though there are television programmes that are well conceived and brilliantly written and produced, there is little doubt, according to some, that sensationalism and escapism are ubiquitous in American culture. It is also the case that entertainment values have entered news and journalism (but this complaint has been made for over a century).

The argument against escapism is that it may distance people from important social issues and direct them from useful social participation and action. The diversion from real life can lead to individual and group apathy as well as to lower cultural standards and popular tastes. Two key sources on (and polemics against) escapism in entertainment, and people living on a diet of trivia, are Neil Postman's *Amusing ourselves to death* [574] and Aldous Huxley's *Brave new world*, with its prophecy of people being controlled by pleasure.

Must all material produced for a mass audience have at least some social worth? Is it possible or even morally desirable to devise strategies that will meet the demands of a mass audience without resorting exclusively to content that does nothing more than trivialize the human condition and then provide an escape from it?

Still, at the very least, we must allow for some pure escapism. As the journalist Francis Williams pointed out in his history of the press [100]: 'the conception of the newspaper as properly concerned only with large matters of public interest is almost entirely Victorian, a solemn interlude in two and a half centuries of boisterous existence . . . the development of the newspaper as a daily magazine is a reversion to an earlier pattern.' And at the beginning of the book he speaks of 'the dual role of the press, to inform and to entertain'.[1]

10.1 Quality in television

There is a large literature attacking television as a medium. Two well-known polemics are Neil Postman's *Amusing ourselves to death* [574], mentioned in the previous section, and Jerry Mander's *Four arguments for the elimination of television* [89]. To quote from another book of Neil Postman's: the emphasis of television is on 'imagery, narrative, presentness, simultaneity, intimacy, immediate gratification, and quick emotional response'.[2] Television values imagery and immediacy. And these values spread from the entertainment programmes into the informative ones. Anthony Smith in *The politics of information* [96]: 'the electorate, the great audience of politics has become one with the great mass audience of entertainment.'[3] Given that television is subject to this kind of criticism, and that it is the most popular medium, it is not surprising that television is the scene of the most virulent debates about quality. They begin with the ethos of public service broadcasting, promulgated by Lord Reith, to justify the BBC's long monopoly on broadcasting in the UK. Talking of radio, he wrote in 1924: 'I think it will be admitted by all that to have exploited so great a scientific invention for the purpose and pursuit of "entertainment" alone would have been a prostitution of its powers and an insult to the character and intelligence of the people.' (With the word 'entertainment' he was making a distinction between the usual sense of the word – which he dubbed 'erroneous' – of diversion or amusement and the 'full sense' of the term.) From the same book we might also quote: 'It is occasionally indicated to us that we are apparently setting out to give the public what we think they need – and not what they want – but few know what they want and very few what they need ... In any case it is better to over-estimate the mentality of the public than to underestimate it.'[4]

Asa Briggs commented: 'Reith's theory of public service began with a conception of the public. Without such a conception, the conception of public service itself becomes bleak and arid. Reith may have erred somewhat on the side of high-mindedness, but he never lost his respect for his audience.'[5] The notion of public service broadcasting has always relied on notions of cultural value, and has always intended 'to provide programmes of information, education and entertainment' (according to the 1996 BBC Royal Charter). As Francis Williams implied, this ideal of service to the public interest derives from the Victorians, in particular the middle class.

But, to make Briggs' point about Reith in different terms, it may be that Reith only wanted an audience he could respect. The debate about the advent of commercial television to Britain raised the issue of quality and public service broadcasting. A. J. P. Taylor said that in the debate about commercial television in the UK that preceded ITV, the high-mindedness of its opponents was one of the things people objected to.[6] To quote Reith again, this time in a debate in the House of Lords, 'Somebody introduced dog-racing into England ... And somebody introduced Christianity and printing and the uses of electricity. And somebody introduced smallpox, bubonic plague and the Black Death. Somebody is minded now to introduce sponsored broadcasting into this country.'[7] Why should people be denied programmes they enjoyed and be given only those which did them good? This mood was also felt within the BBC; Grace Wyndham Goldie [383] said of the popularity of *Tonight*, a BBC programme of the 1950s: 'its popularity was an expression of relief from the Reithian attitudes, which were suffused by intellectual condescension. The audience was no longer content to be the grateful recipients of opinions of those who were supposed to know better.'[8]

The argument about commercial television was won and the BBC's monopoly of British broadcasting broken. However, because there was a fear that commercial television would import some of the worst excesses of American television, a public service ethos was clearly spelt out for Independent Television in the Television Act 1954, and in the subsequent codes drawn up by the Independent Television Authority. Independent television companies were required from the beginning to meet certain standards in terms of news, information and education programmes. They were not able to follow fully commercial criteria, no sponsorship was allowed, and spot advertising was quite limited and contained. In recent years the debate has been similar, but with the boot on the other foot, for it is public service broadcasting that has sought to justify itself in the face of the onslaught of commercial channels in television and radio, with the proliferation of channels on satellite and cable. For it is believed that the existence of public service broadcasting guarantees quality broadcasting. Free of the demands of the market place, that is, with income assured, programme makers can get on with making 'good' programmes. (In British discussions related to public service broadcasting and its defence, a contrast is very often drawn with American television, which was characterized as 'wall-to-wall *Dallas*'.) The ability to provide 'quality' justifies the continuing existence of public service broadcasting.

So what makes 'good television'? There is no consensus here, and there has been little consistent effort to answer the question. For one thing, television consists of a variety of genres, a fact which makes it difficult to talk of television as a single whole.

However, there does seem to be a consensus as to what makes bad television – not bad television programmes, but a bad television system. This emerges in the feared effects of the huge expansion of channels from cable, satellite and digital television. First, there has been a drive to maximize audiences, a pressure to come up with successful programmes. Second, there is the incentive to tailor programmes for acceptability in multiple markets. Third, advertisers will gain more power. All of these factors will work against variety in television and against controversy, risk-taking, and appealing to specialized audiences.

The notion of quality is going to vary with views as to what television is for. This because it is easier to define quality in terms of fulfilment of function. But there seems to be very little agreement about that. It may turn out that we cannot say what television is for, any more than we can say what books, taken en masse, are for.

Some writers, however, have tackled this question. Geoff Mulgan [586] is one:

'the most important question we need to ask of any broadcasting system is whether it is adequate for its society: does it really reflect and express its experiences, its pleasures and pains, its insights and understandings, its differences as well as its similarities? Does it function adequately as a set of channels for groups and individuals to communicate to each other?'[9]

This idea that broadcasting should reflect its society is common among sociologists, and perhaps can also be applied to the press. But as it stands, it is merely an assertion. In one sense, of course, any broadcasting system will reflect its society, but that is not what is meant here, for there is implicitly an assertion of what the media should do (for example, not neglect minorities and minority views). However, this assertion needs independent argument, for otherwise there is no need for those who think of television as a money-making industry to accept it.

Many people have come to feel that talk of quality is paternalistic, and prefer to talk of 'diversity' instead (for example, *Quality assessment of television*, edited by Sakae Ishikawa [583]). But is this much help? According to John Ellis 'diversity' is a term 'which ducks all the major questions'. It does so because it establishes no priorities, no mechanisms for planning. Diversity is a countervailing force. It says there are some people or ideas which are under-represented, and establishes their right to be represented. But on its own it cannot establish what the basic priorities of representation should be. As a criterion it applies only on the level of choosing what subjects programmes should be about, but does not help the quality of individual programmes.[10] But in reply to this we might say that the notion of diversity operates as a factor at a general level, leaving quality of programmes to individual programme makers. There also needs to be discussion of how diversity can be measured. It is not just multiplicity of choice, for several channels might provide little variation of a basic diet of programmes.

John Mepham proposes a similar, but somewhat more tendentious, definition to that of Mulgan: 'I propose a conception of quality which will be anchored in the social project of preserving the possibilities for cultural pluralism and extending the possibilities for democratisation of society.'[11] This does seem a long way from the individual television programme. To be fair, he does go on to be more specific: high quality television is television which is excellent as measured by its faithfulness to certain principles – the rule of diversity, the cultural purpose of providing usable stories, and the ethic of truth-telling.

By contrast, it is believed that the private sector operates to different dictates. The profit motive will lead to a homogeneous diet of ineffectual programmes which will impoverish national culture, stifle natural creative ability and fail to challenge prevailing orthodoxy. Here we can see an implicit political criterion emerge – if a programme challenges prevailing orthodoxy then it is a good one.

At this point, one needs to say, not enough attention is being given to what are sometimes called the production values of individual programmes, what makes a programme good of its kind, what makes a good soap opera, a good documentary and so on.[12]

There is a similarly sociological approach to quality in the American media system as a whole by Michael Gurevitch and Jay Blumler who begin: 'the American media system is presumably animated by certain democratic principles', and go on to say that democracy is an exacting creed, and that it 'requires' the media to provide a number of functions and services. They give a list of eight, only the first two of which are obviously part of present functions.[13]

Finally, another discussion in this area is the moral role of television. The argument runs that television has, in many cases, taken the place of parental guidance on moral issues. Drama, and particularly soap operas, bring before wide audiences the ethical dilemmas of everyday life. There is therefore an obligation on producers, given the 'power' of popular soap operas, to design story lines with full awareness of their responsibilities.

Notes

1. Williams, F. *Dangerous estate*, pp. 284 and 10.
2. Postman, N. *Technopoly*, p. 16.
3. Smith, A. *The politics of information*, p. 25.
4. Reith, J. C. W. *Broadcast over Britain*, pp. 17 and 34.
5. Quoted in MacCabe, C. and Stewart, O. (eds.) *The BBC and public service broadcasting*, p. 59.
6. Taylor, A. J. P. in *New Statesman*, 21 July 1961, p. 85.
7. Hansard, House of Lords, 22 May 1952.
8. Goldie, G. W. *Facing the nation*, p. 216.
9. Mulgan, G. *The question of quality*, p. 8.
10. Ellis, J. 'What's the point?' in Mulgan, G. (ed.) *The question of quality*.
11. Mepham, J. 'The ethics of quality in television' in Mulgan, G. (ed.) *The question of quality*.
12. One attempt in this direction is Timothy Leggatt's article 'Quality in television: the views of professionals' in Ishikawa, S. (ed.) *Quality assessment of television*.
13. Lichtenberg, J. (ed.) *Democracy and the mass media*, pp. 269–89.

11 Religion

This is not a subject that occurs much in discussions of the media, which may in itself be a recognition that the media are overwhelmingly secular.

The problems of religious broadcasting stem from the fact of its changing importance in society. When the BBC was established in the UK, it could reasonably be claimed that as it was a Christian country, Christian values should be promoted. This claim can no longer be justified; we now have an increasingly secular society and, in terms of the religions that are practised, an increasingly pluralistic one. The problem for religious groupings is that each believes it has the truth, yet has to operate in a system that asserts freedom of expression for different opinions.

In the US the problems are centred around the rise of televangelism or, as it is sometimes called, the electronic church. At the beginning of television, Catholics and liberal Protestants were prepared to work within the agenda of the secular broadcasting industry and, in the process, to abandon any attempt at directly proclaiming the 'gospel'. Some might see this as the church's abdication to secularism.

The rise of proselytizing, evangelistic channels (at the expense of the mainstream church) stems from 1960 when the Federal Communications Commission allowed television stations to fulfil their public service obligations to religion by buying programmes; channels no longer had to provide airtime to the mainstream churches, who were ousted by those willing to pay.

There are now several of these channels in the US, and their owners intend to make use of satellite to spread their word around the world. The extent of televangelism's influence is a difficult empirical question. For one thing, the channels themselves are very prone to inflate the size of their audiences. It may be that their influence has been exaggerated and that in actual terms relatively few people watch it. Also, it may be that television is not particularly good at influencing people, and so the channels preach only to the converted.

In the UK the legislation of the Broadcasting Act 1990 trod carefully in this area. Religious groups may apply for television and radio licences, but the new code states that 'religious programmes may not be designed for the purpose of recruiting viewers to any particular faith' nor may an organization whose aims are religious appeal for money. For evangelists, of course, not being able to try and recruit to the faith is an unacceptable restriction.

12 Media imperialism

This is the idea that the world's mass media of communication are essentially 'Western'. The West dominates the world news flow. It might even be said to have a world information monopoly, with an unrelenting one-way flow of ideas from Western countries to the Third World. Four large news agencies dominate the international flow of news. All are Western: two American, one British-based, the other French. Thus the prevailing image in the Western world of most Third World nations is controlled by the West. The further accusation is that most of this coverage is of natural disasters and coups.

As a result of this, the media promote Western values to the detriment of the Third World. Advertising, magazines and TV programmes are seen as instruments of cultural domination, transmitting to the developing countries messages which are harmful to their cultures, contrary to their values and detrimental to their development aims and efforts.

There have been attempts to counter this domination. There is the Gemini News Service, founded in 1967, which promotes English-language news from and about the Third World. Also, many developing countries have their own news agencies, to disseminate news to the outside world. But it is very difficult for them to compete with the major agencies.

In radio broadcasting there is the domination of the BBC World Service, Voice of America and Deutsche Welle. In television the economies of scale and the ability to recover most of the production costs in the domestic markets mean that Western countries, especially the US, can make programme material available at relatively low cost – cheaper than local programmes. This is even a problem in Europe, where the prevalence and cheapness of American television programmes has meant that several countries have introduced quotas to restrict them, including the UK and France.

These problems are still current in that new and established broadcasters, with CNN as an example of the first, the BBC of the second, are quickly developing a genuinely global journalism. A contemporary buzzword is 'globalization', mainly applied to trade, but the notion is extended to culture, and is facilitated by satellite broadcasting.

The 'cultural imperialism' thesis was first proposed by Herbert Schiller in *Mass communications and American empire* (New York: A. M. Kelley, 1969). The term 'media imperialism' was a later coinage, and comes from the work of Oliver Boyd-Barrett.[1] He defines this as 'the process whereby the ownership, structure, distribution or content of the media in any country are ... subject to substantial pressure from the media interests of any other country or countries without proportionate reciprocation of influence by the country so affected' (that is, any imbalance of power between countries). It has been suggested, however, that this is too broad a definition and, in particular, weakens the concept of imperialism.

It has also been pointed out that there has been little research on the cultural impact on Third World countries.[2] There has been a tendency to assume a manipulative model of the mass media, in which the effects can simply be read off from how many episodes of any one American television series are shown in any Third World country. As we have seen elsewhere in this book, recent research has given more attention to how people use the media, and argued that audiences are more active in what they take from programmes than they are given credit for on the manipulative model.

It also seems to be the case that regional markets are stronger than has been realized. The authors of *New patterns in global television* [647] argue that much of television programming is of 'an inescapably local, untranslatable nature'. Apart from television, some Third World countries, of which India is the best example, have large film industries.

On the other hand, Jeremy Tunstall, in the introduction to the 1994 edition of *The media are American* [655], admits the popularity of local programming but adds that American television 'will continue to be successful because it is the nearly universal second choice, and because it is conveniently available, familiar, and an expensive product at an affordable price'.

A separate question is: is the European and US ideal of freedom of the press transferable? Is it appropriate for other countries and continents? For example, in many African countries the press and broadcasting are controlled, on the grounds that this promotes national unity, economic development and stability.

The differences in attitude between the West and the Third World surfaced in the discussions that went into the UNESCO report edited by Sean MacBride, *Many voices, one world* [658], which were quite bitter. There was the Third World belief that it was for governments to rule what was true and erroneous and that controls of the press were justified as a means of achieving political, economic or social objectives. (This is reminiscent of the debates about social responsibility: see pp. 11–13). On the other hand, this was opposed by Western governments, stimulated by Western journalists, who were totally opposed to any wording that would include state control. The report concluded by endorsing the traditional values of the free flow of information and freedom of speech and the press, and also made a strong argument for the need to improve Third World mass media. The UNESCO declaration in 1980, following the MacBride Report, sought to reconcile the objective of media freedom with a positive role for the media in social change and nation building.

For the future, there is perhaps a possibility of correcting the imbalance through such new technologies as desktop publishing, video cameras and the Internet. These may make it possible for small countries to bypass the traditional channels of communication in order to make information available for a wider audience.

Notes

1. For example, chapter 5 of Curran, J. and others (eds.) *Mass communication and society*, 1977.
2. See Reeves, G. *Communications and the Third World*.

13 Advertising

Probably our first associations with the word 'advertising' are the advertisements seen on television or on large hoardings. We should begin by pointing out that this, if the most expensive and most prominent part of the advertising industry, is not all of it. In the UK in 1990, 27 per cent of advertising expenditure was on classified advertisements, property, situations vacant, cars for sale and so on, while 73 per cent came from commercial advertisers. Most discussion of advertising focuses on commercial advertising and its ubiquity in contemporary Western society.

A fundamental fact about advertising is that it is usually aiming to sell something, such as a product or service, and sometimes aiming to impart an opinion, as with political advertising. Where financial benefits are at stake, the temptations to misinform or lie are stronger, to say the least.

There have long been concerns about the ethics of advertising, but there are two other important issues which should be mentioned in passing, because they are often referred to in more general debates of the subject. First, there is the economic issue, whether advertising does actually help improve the performance of an economy. Is it wasteful or, by increasing sales, does it lead to economies of scale? Needless to say, its supporters all argue for the economic benefits, but there is no consensus on the issue.

The second issue concerns the effects of advertising. What exactly is its influence? This is relevant to the issue of ethics; obviously, the weaker its effects, the less we have to worry about its ethics.

Advertising has long been a target of criticism. It is accused of appealing to people's materialism, self-interest, hedonism, hopes, fears and insecurities, to the lower impulses, to the lowest common factor. In a word, it seeks to persuade and, it is added, it does this by avoiding use of rationality.

Advertising is sometimes defended as 'the right of freedom of commercial speech'. This argument has the strategy of claiming that commercial speech is just a subcategory of speech in general and so able to claim the same freedom. However, we need to recall the discussions of free speech in Chapter 2, where three main arguments were made to justify the claim for a right of free speech. One was that it led to informed citizens making free and democratic political choices. Clearly, this has nothing to do with selling products or services. Sometimes the attempt is made: 'Advertising is an essential part of any real democracy, which is always based on freedom of choice', says the Director-General of the International Advertising Association.[1] What is true is that democracies require political freedom of choice, but not economic choice, and the remark reveals a typically American link between unregulated markets and politics.

A second argument gave weight to the autonomy of the individual, but this has nothing to do with the autonomy of the commercial organizations which advertise.

The third argument was that freedom of speech aids the pursuit of truth. Mill thought of this as the truth in religious, moral and social matters, which does not apply here. Advertisers might maintain that it aids the pursuit of truth as to which are good and useful products and services available to the public.

This brings us to a common justification of advertising, that it provides an information service. It is true that much advertising does provide information – in particular, classified advertising. But it is also true that for many advertisements, providing information is not the only aim, and it seems absurd to maintain otherwise. (In fact, the most prominent advertisements – those on posters and on television – are the least informative.) A more sophisticated version here is to admit that an advertisement does not provide full information, but that its purpose in drawing attention to a brand is just the starting point, which then leads to other information sources, trial or personal experience, labelling, in-store advice, consumer tests and so on. Still, this avoids the question of how attention is drawn to the brand and the persuasiveness involved.

A picture of the rational consumer is presented in a ruling of the US Supreme Court in 1976: 'Advertising ... is dissemination of information as to who is producing and selling what products, for what reason and for what price. So long as we preserve the predominantly free-enterprise economy, the allocation of our resources in large measure will be made through numerous private economic decisions. It is a matter of public interest that these decisions ... be intelligent and well informed. To this end, the free flow of commercial information is indispensable.'[2]

Perhaps the most famous book written on advertising is *The hidden persuaders* by Vance Packard, published in 1957, which sold millions of copies [686]. For example, he wrote: 'large-scale efforts are being made, often with impressive success, to channel our unthinking habits, our purchasing decisions and our thought processes by the use of insights gleaned from psychiatry and the social sciences.' But he did not provide much evidence that such attempts actually worked. In many ways his book was a response to the grandiose claims being made in the 1950s by behavioural psychologists. There were fears that minds could be manipulated.

More recent research has suggested that audiences select and interpret the messages of advertising in their own way.[3] Consumers are more sophisticated than they have been given credit for. A very similar argument is made about television viewers in general.

Still, if advertising can persuade people to buy products and services, can it not influence behaviour? As part of its persuasion, advertising sells attitudes and social behaviour as well, which are glamourized and legitimized by being shown on television or on large hoardings. Against this, it is claimed that people know their own minds. This in fact is a tacit admission that these attitudes are being 'sold' – the question is: are they 'bought'? There is a tendency to assert that the influence of advertising goes only as far as advertisers want it to go – that is, it sells the products – and no more. As it is, the advertising industry is in the odd position of arguing that advertisements have little effect on overall sales – in effect, they argue for the ineffectiveness of their product.

However, there are more general attacks on advertising. It can be attacked from the right as promoting liberal, secular values, and from the left as turning the working classes into passive consumers, bought off by the promise of material well-being. Further, advertising creates false needs in consumers, needs that can only be fulfilled through the purchase of goods in the marketplace.[4] But what are 'false needs'? Are we to ask for anything beyond nourishment, clothing and housing? What are 'true needs'?

However, this is a different criticism from one that accuses advertising of appealing to our 'needs' for emotional security, say, or self-esteem. With these, critics would say that advertising, or rather the products advertised, do not really satisfy.

Advertisements are then accused of being purveyors of ideology, an ideology which endorses and so helps to perpetuate the economic conditions of society. There is also the danger of using criticism of advertising as a target when it is really the capitalist society that is the target. However, to this it may be replied that advertising enforces the status quo of capitalism, and so slows down change.

We mentioned that advertisers claim limited effectiveness for advertising. They would say that they do not create new needs, but change the shape of individual markets. An example of this is the tobacco market from 1918 to 1940. In this period the overall consumption of cigarettes increased steadily, but the consumption of tobacco remained constant. This suggests that if advertising was having an effect, it was to switch cigar and pipe smokers to cigarettes. In short, advertising follows, it does not lead. What has not been pointed out, though, is that for a market to continue, even at a constant level, it needs new consumers – to replace the older ones, who die (and nowhere is this more the case than with tobacco).

And this is reflected by the fact that many more women smoke now than before. But the advertising industry continues to take the line that its function is to increase market share within a particular product group.

But even its defenders would admit that advertising is a form of communication that adopts a very limited perspective on society and the way people aspire, act and interact in it. It reflects an image of life governed by merchandising objectives by marketing criteria – so it should not be surprised that people find fault with this.[5]

Given the anxieties about advertising's role as a persuader, the industry seems to admit that it will always be regulated. The question is: how? Industry organizations argue that the path of self-regulation is to be preferred, as a way of preventing (that is, pre-empting) regulations, restrictions and even bans on advertising. If advertisers were to say as a whole, as some do, 'we don't have any social responsibility – our responsibility is to our clients to help sell their products', then the state would have to impose the regulations.

The Advertising Standards Authority in the UK claims to be the most developed and effective self-regulating system in the world. (Television advertising is governed by the Independent Television Commission.) But worldwide it is one of the concerns of the advertising industry to promote self-regulation as against statutory regulation. It is claimed the advantages of self-regulation are: that it is usually faster and less expensive; it does not require proof of any injury, as would be the case with laws; it can complement statutory regulations; it generates greater moral adherence. The criticisms of self-regulation are that: it impairs competition and innovation; it is a sop to statutory regulation; it lacks bite; it does not represent consumers; it may not receive enough financing and publicity. This latter consideration is really only a technical difficulty and, in its 1995 Annual Report, the ASA claimed that much of its effectiveness lies in the wide publicity given to its decision on complaints. In other words, justice is being seen to be done.

The ASA 'operates in the public interest' and in co-operation with the whole of the advertising industry by ensuring that everyone involved with advertisements observes the codes of advertising practice. Together the codes require that advertisements and sales promotions should be:

- legal, decent, honest and truthful;
- prepared with a sense of responsibility to consumers and society;
- in line with the principles of fair competition generally accepted in business.

Primary responsibility for observing the codes falls on advertisers. They must be able to produce documentary evidence needed to support any claim, whether explicit or implicit, made in an advertisement.

The main problem for self-regulation is how it deals with the problem of 'rogue' members of the industry. Two factors come into play. First, advertising is inherently visible; any failings are easily detectable and traced. Second, in the UK at least, about 90 per cent of advertisements rely on the print and broadcast media or on postal services. Thus there is a screening mechanism between the advertiser and the public.

The most difficult area to regulate in that of taste and decency. Here the problems are very similar to those encountered in broadcasting (see Chapter 6).

The accusation is that advertisements can seem to legitimize 'unacceptable' or 'unsocial' behaviour. For example, the Italian clothing manufacturer Benetton has established a reputation for striking photographs in its advertisements: a newborn baby still covered in blood; the blood-smeared clothes of a dead Croatian soldier. The photographs in themselves are not necessarily shocking, since they depend upon their context. But their use on large hoardings, to promote a brand of clothes, gives them a quite different currency, and it was this that many people found shocking. Perhaps the point was to suggest to young people that as a brand, Benetton is also young, streetwise, unafraid of being controversial. In this case, the pressing against accepted limits of decency may be the only message. But then the advertisers need the barriers to show that they can leap over them, that they are liberated.

The area of advertising most under attack is that of tobacco advertising. All the member states of the European Union operate severe restrictions, and there is pressure for a total ban. The main argument against it is that it persuades people to engage in something that is damaging to their health, to which the industry has several replies. The first is that selling tobacco is legal and so it is unfair to ban promotion of it. Second, there are many other products (such as alcohol and motorbikes) whose use and misuse give rise to health risks and which are not banned, but here the links between use of these products and ill health are by no means so clear-cut. Third, the intention is not to start people smoking, but to get them to switch brands. Still, as noted earlier, to maintain a static market, new consumers are required.

The advertising of alcohol has also caused concern, in that drinking can affect health and lead to antisocial behaviour. There have been proposals to ban advertising it on television. On the other hand, according to the Advertising Standards Authority, few complaints are made about alcohol advertising in the UK.

This may be because the British codes on advertising practice are very careful in what they permit. Advertisements should be socially responsible, with no suggestion that drinking alcohol leads to social acceptance or is a specific challenge. Suggestions that drinking is an essential attribute of masculinity should be avoided. Advertisements should not suggest that a drink is sensible or desirable. Interestingly, all these caveats are evidence for the argument that advertising in general does sell attitudes as well as products, and that the audience might be susceptible to the messages. Or is all this merely to pacify the public?

It is believed that one group in the audience that might be more susceptible and therefore needing more protection is that of children. Thus there are concerns about the advertising of sweets, snacks and soft drinks aimed at children, and of toys. With these foods concern has been expressed about the effect on children's diets and overall health. The Advertising Association commissioned some research on the subject in 1994: 'the findings in summary were that parents do not believe that advertising is a major influence on their children's diet and do not believe that children are continually pestering them for specific advertising foods.' This quotation is a good example of the ambiguity in the advertising industry's presentation of its effects. For the companies making these foods might conclude that this research shows that they no longer need to advertise their products. But this conclusion is never reached; this less than major influence is still significant for them, in which case it should be significant for those anxious about their children's diet.

Children are also protected in the area of toy advertising in many countries of Europe (including the UK), either by statutory legislation or self-regulation. Sweden, for example, has a ban on all TV advertising to children under the age of 12. There have been arguments that restriction should be more uniformly severe throughout Europe. In reply, the advertising industry argues that advertising bans are harmful to trade, proper competition and consumer choice; and more specifically, that without advertising, it would not be possible for commercial television to finance its programmes.

A final issue is that of stereotyping, and of women, in particular. The fashion, cosmetic and magazine industries present very limited images of women, say, as mindless sex objects or mindless housewives. (We discussed the problems of stereotyping earlier: see p. 59.) Now, the purpose of an advertisement is to get across a message in a short space of time or amount of copy. So advertising tends to need some kind of shorthand, and stereotypes fill this role. A survey of the issue published by the Advertising Association (*A woman's place*, by Sue Phipps, 1991) argued that the repertoire of roles and emotions ascribed to women needs to be increased. There has been some pressure for a code of practice for women in the UK, with a broad aim that traditional images of women in the media should be challenged, and positive ones promoted. The argument against this is that not only would it be very difficult to produce guidelines, but also that it would be undesirable in that women are not a homogeneous group.

There is also racist stereotyping – the suggestion that advertisements do not adequately reflect the numbers of Asian and Afro-Caribbean in the population.

These questions again involve the notion of social responsibility. For advertisers it is not their prime concern, but can they ignore this? Can the industry ignore the issues that concern society, and simply reflect conventional attitudes?

Notes

1. Boddewyn, J. J. *Global perspectives on advertising self-regulation*, Foreword by Norman Vale, pp. xiii–xiv.
2. Quoted in Boddewyn, J. J. *Global perspectives on advertising self-regulation*, p. 1.
3. One example is Jamieson, G. H. *Communication and persuasion*.

4. The accusation that advertising plays a role in creating demands for goods can be found in Galbraith, J. K. *The affluent society*, 1958, and *The new industrial state*, 1967.
5. See, for example, Leiss, W., Kline, S. and Jhally, S. *Social communication in advertising*. This book contains an excellent summary of the ethical and sociological discussions of advertising.

Part II

Bibliography

Part II Bibliography

The main aim of this bibliography is to provide a representative selection of the literature on the key issues of media ethics, and to give the reader a good starting point for study and research into the subject.

It can only be selective given the enormous number of books and articles that have been written in this area. The emphasis is on recent and contemporary items, though many earlier and often historic items are included so that the evolution of the study of media ethics is well represented. The coverage is worldwide, though all the works are in the English language, and mostly published in the United Kingdom, the United States, Canada and Australia. As most comparable bibliographies on the media are American, it is hoped that the British emphasis of this work will complement them. Most of the items are scholarly works written by academics, though some are by media practitioners and some more journalistic or popular items are also included.

The method of compilation was through systematic recourse to various general and specialist indexing and abstracting services, databases, journals, bibliographies and lists of further reading in books on media ethics. Among the generalist indexing services used were *British Humanities Index* and *Reader's Guide to Periodical Literature*. Specialist indexing and abstracting services included *Communication Abstracts, International Index to Television Periodicals, Nordicom: Bibliography of Nordic Mass Communication Literature*, and the UNESCO *List of Documents and Publications in the Field of Mass Communications*. Database host services consulted were *FT Profile* and *Dialog*, particularly the *PsycINFO: Psychological Abstracts* and *Sociological Abstracts* databases. Long runs of several specialist periodicals were systematically analysed for articles on media ethics issues, in particular the only one devoted entirely to the subject, *Journal of Mass Media Ethics*, but also other key media journals: *British Journalism Review*; *Communication Research*; *Communications and the Law*; *European Journal of Communication*; *InterMedia*; *International Journal of Advertising*; *Journal of Broadcasting & Electronic Media*; *Journal of Communication*; *Media & Values*; *Media, Culture and Society*; *Media Development*; *Media International Australia*; *Media Studies Journal*; *Public Opinion Quarterly*; and *Television Quarterly*. Many subject bibliographies were used, but special mention should be made of two model works which were of particular value both in their content and by their example: *Mass media bibliography*, by Eleanor Blum and Frances Wilhoit, and *Television and ethics: a bibliography*, by Thomas W. Cooper. All these sources have full entries in the last two sections 'Periodicals' and 'Bibliographies, indexes, and abstracting services', of this bibliography.

There are some 800 entries, virtually all of them annotated through personal examination by the compilers. The initials in brackets at the end of each entry indicate whether the annotation was written by Barrie MacDonald (BM), Michel Petheram (MP) or Stephen Murphy (SM). The annotations are mostly descriptive rather than critical; they aim to give the reader the bibliographical details, and an idea of the purpose, scope and content of the book or article.

To facilitate easy reference between the overview of media ethics and the bibliography, this part is arranged by exactly the same subject arrangement. Only the last two sections in this bibliography are additional.

Media ethics

General media ethics

1 Adams, Julian. *Freedom and ethics in the press.* New York: Richards Rosen Press, 1983. 126pp.
Primarily concerned with press freedom in the US, this book is intended for both professionals and students, and discusses such issues as freedom of expression, fairness, right to know, confidential news sources, privacy and obscenity, with reference to the First Amendment and Supreme and Federal Court decisions. Reprints codes of the American Society of Newspaper Editors and the Society of Professional Journalists. (BM)

2 Allen, Lois and **Voss, Dan**. *Ethics in technical communication: shades of gray.* New York: Wiley, 1997. xxi, 410pp.
Text for professional technical communicators in which the authors explore the theoretical and philosophical foundations of ethical and moral issues of the information age, looking at codes of practice, honesty, legality, privacy, conflict of interest, and professional advancement, and, through the use of case studies and scenarios, give practical advice for analysing and resolving moral dilemmas in the areas of copyright, intellectual property, software licensing, non-disclosure agreements, privacy and confidentiality. (BM)

3 Altschull, J. Herbert. *Agents of power: the media and public policy.* 2nd ed. White Plains, New York: Longman, 1995. xxvi, 461pp.

Prominent American media academic and former journalist argues that the power of the media is not just the sum total of their structural, environmental, political and economic aspects, but something less tangible to do with information and the mesmerizing uses made of it. This thoughtful analysis covers the press and democracy, news media and social control, in particular the power and freedom of the press (including the rise of Ted Turner and CNN), the political arena, free flow of information, and the ethics of journalism (with reference to the issues of social responsibility and accountability raised by the Hutchins Commission report, *A free and responsible press*, in 1947). (BM)

4 Becker, Lawrence C. and **Becker, Charlotte B.** (eds.) *Encyclopedia of ethics.* New York: Garland, 1992. 2 vols.

Section on 'mass media' (pp. 775–8) covers such issues in the print and electronic media as consciousness shaping and agenda setting, cultural production, function of the media to evaluate and not just reinforce, confidentiality and protection of information sources, the requirement of advertising to be 'truthful', the damage to race and gender by the use of stereotypes, violence and pornography. (BM)

5 Belsey, Andrew and **Chadwick, Ruth** (eds.) *Ethical issues in journalism and the media.* London: Routledge, 1992. xiii, 179pp. (Professional ethics)

Central to the practice of journalism are several basic ethical concepts – of freedom of speech, democracy, truth, objectivity, honesty and privacy – concepts which have come under intense scrutiny in the UK in recent years, in relation to both broadcast and print journalism. This collection of essays by academics is part of a series on professional ethics, edited from the Centre for Applied Ethics at the University of Wales College of Cardiff. It addresses such issues as quality (Andrew Belsey and Ruth Chadwick), freedom of speech and the law (David Burnet), codes of conduct for journalists (Nigel G. E. Harris), honesty in investigative journalism (Jennifer Jackson), terrorism and reporting restrictions (Paul Gilbert), and ethical issues in war reporting (Kevin Williams). Bibliography. (BM)

6 Bertrand, Claude-Jean. 'Media ethics in perspective'. *Journal of Mass Media Ethics*, Vol. 2, No. 1, 1986–87, pp. 7–16.

7 Blum, Eleanor and **Christians, Clifford**. 'Ethical problems in book publishing'. *Library Quarterly*, Vol. 51, No. 2, April 1981, pp. 155–69.

Summary of inquiry into the ethics of 140 book publishing personnel in the US, which found a fundamental devotion to quality content and provision of accurate and informative material. Other findings included: a rejection of all forms of censorship and commitment to the free flow of ideas; hostility to government intervention; concern to handle morally the tensions between author and editors; and promoting publications truthfully. Attitudes reflect a classical liberal framework. (BM)

8 Chadwick, Ruth (ed.) *Encyclopaedia of applied ethics*. San Diego, California: Academic Press, 1997. 3 vols.

Reference work covering all aspects of applied ethics, with several articles relating to the media: censorship, confidentiality of sources, freedom of speech, investigative journalism, media ethics overview, media depiction of ethnic minorities, objectivity in reporting, pornography, tabloid journalism, truth-telling as constitutive of journalism, violence in films and television. (MP)

9 Christians, Clifford G. 'Fifty years of scholarship in media ethics'. *Journal of Communication*, Vol. 27, No. 4, Autumn 1977, pp. 19–29.

Useful survey of American study of and writings on media ethics. (BM)

10 Christians, Clifford G., Ferre, John P. and **Fackler, Mark**. *Good news: social ethics and the press*. New York: Oxford University Press, 1993. xvi, 265pp.

An erudite and highly theoretical account by three American academics of the evolution of social ethics and the press, from its roots in the eighteenth-century age of enlightenment, through to the media theories of the twentieth century. It proposes an alternative philosophical foundation for media ethics, based on recent communitarian thought. Comprehensive bibliography. (BM)

11 Christians, Clifford G., Fackler, Mark and **Rotzoll, Kim**. *Media ethics: cases and moral reasoning*. 4th ed. White Plains, New York: Longman, 1995. xiv, 350pp.

Student textbook which aims to improve ethical awareness and analytical skills by integrating media theory and practice through case studies, taken from actual experience, and commentaries. Beginning with a clear explanation of the stages in moral reasoning and selected ethical guidelines, it illustrates such key issues as truth-telling, protection of sources, invasion of privacy, persuasion and advertising, violence and censorship with many well-known cases from both sides of the Atlantic, such as the reporting of the trial of two 11-year-old boys for the murder of 2-year-old James Bulger in England, and the FBI raid on an obscure religious cult community at Waco in Texas, both in 1993. (BM)

12 Christians, Clifford G. and **Traber, Michael** (eds.) *Communication ethics and universal values*. Thousand Oaks, California: Sage, 1997. xvi, 384pp.

Communications ethics is at a crossroads of opposing directions of cultural homogenization and cultural resistance. This work aims to get away from the narrow study of professional and journalistic ethics, and identify a broader-based ethical theory of communications and universal moral imperatives. Issues touched on are ethical foundations, comparative ethics from the perspectives of particular cultures (Arab-Islamic, India, Latin America, Africa), and the need in this *fin-de-siècle* to vigorously analyse the crisis in values and to develop common values for a twenty-first century of powerful transnational media and information systems. (BM)

13 Cooper, Alison. *Media power?* London: Franklin Watts, 1997. 32pp. (Viewpoints)
One of a series on contemporary social issues designed for younger students. It collects notable recent examples, with quotations and extracts, from the UK, the US and Australia of key issues of media ethics – the impact of advertising, violence on television, trial by media, state censorship, media ownership, invasion of privacy and the need to know. (BM)

14 Cooper, Thomas W. 'Communication and ethics: informal and formal curricula'. *Journal of Mass Media Ethics*, Vol. 2, No. 1, 1987, pp. 71–9.
Children can learn more through the media than from formal school education. (BM)

15 Cooper, Thomas W. (ed.) *Communications ethics and global change.* White Plains, New York: Longman, 1989. xxx, 385pp. (Communications series)
Media professionals throughout the world broadly share common ethical values, though ethics in the West is a system of rights and obligations that differs considerably from other cultures. This work questions the values that the global media are communicating, the responsibility of communicators, and whether traditional journalistic ethics can still apply with the new technologies, or whether entirely new ethical systems are required. Three general essays on media ethics in a universal context are followed by thirteen, separately authored, essays on various countries worldwide, with comparison of national codes of ethics. Selected international and national codes are reprinted as appendices. Bibliography. (BM)

16 Creech, Kenneth C. *Electronic media law and regulation.* 2nd ed. Boston: Focal Press, 1996. xxv, 502pp.
Overview of the major American legal and regulatory issues facing broadcasting, cable and the emerging new media through discussion of legislation, cases, regulations and legal documents. Issues discussed include legal and regulatory structure, First Amendment free speech, defamation and libel, invasion of privacy, and conflict of rights between free press and fair trial. (BM)

17 Cunningham, Stanley B. 'A place in the sun: making room for media ethics'. *Journal of Mass Media Ethics*, Vol. 8, No. 3, 1993, pp. 147–55.
Author argues for giving greater prominence to the study of communication ethics in academic disciplines and structures. (BM)

18 Day, Louis A. *Ethics in media communications: cases and controversies.* 2nd ed. Belmont, California: Wadsworth Publishing, 1997. xiv, 450pp.
A media ethics text and case book for students and practitioners, one of the best. It offers a comprehensive systematic approach to moral reasoning and making ethical judgements by combining ethical theory with real practical examples from media professionals. Part One provides the theoretical foundations and principles

of ethics and moral reasoning. Part Two provides over 70 hypothetical cases to illustrate some of the major issues and ethical dilemmas likely to face media practitioners: truth; privacy; confidentiality and the public interest; conflict of interest; coverage of antisocial behaviour; morally offensive material and freedom of speech; social justice; use of stereotypes; and special ethical concerns regarding a juvenile audience. Codes of practice of the Society of Professional Journalists, American Society of Newspaper Editors, Radio–Television News Directors Association, and Public Relations Society of America are reprinted. Bibliography. (BM)

19 Dennis, Everette E. and **Merrill, John C**. *Media debates: issues in mass communications.* 2nd ed. White Plains, New York: Longman, 1996. xiii, 236pp.

American university media studies textbook, first published in 1984 as *Basic issues in mass communication*, which presents the arguments in some key media debates in a standard format of neutral description of the issue, followed by a challenge and a response, topics for further discussion and research, and bibliography. Topics include freedom of the press, media–government relationship, people's right to know, access to the media, bias, quality of media content, journalistic ethics, propaganda, race and ethnicity, advertising, public relations, and globalism of the media. (BM)

20 Fink, Conrad. *Media ethics: in the newsroom and beyond.* New York: McGraw-Hill, 1988. xxv, 323pp. (McGraw-Hill series in mass communication)

Conrad Fink was formerly a reporter, editor and foreign correspondent, becoming Vice-President of Associated Press, before going on to teach advanced reporting and newspaper and broadcast station management at the University of Georgia. His reader, 'field-tested for twenty-five years, then classroom-tested', is designed to assist teachers and students in discussion of ethical issues, and also to contribute to the current ethical debates in the print and broadcast industries. Part One aims to help students and trainee reporters in a critical self-examination of ethical conduct in the pursuit of news. Part Two focuses on the corporate ethics of either a print or broadcasting organization, and its responsibility to society. Part Three speculates on society's attitude to the media as it evolves and grows more powerful. Illustrated with practical examples, it has lists of references and various codes of practice reprinted. (BM)

21 Funiok, Rudiger. 'Basic questions concerning audience ethics'. *Media Development*, Vol. 42, No. 4, 1995, pp. 37–40.

Audience choice, though private, has a public meaning, and is an exercise of moral judgement. (BM)

22 Gill, Karamjit S. (ed.) *Information society: new media, ethics and postmodernism.* London: Springer, 1996. xxxii, 390pp. (Human-centred systems)

Based partly on the proceedings of the 'New Visions of the Post-industrial Society' international conference held at the University of Brighton in 1994, and originating in the debate on 'The Changing Society, the New Technologies' initiated by the European Commission the previous year. Together these papers form an exploration and ethical reflection on the potential, limitations and implications of the growing convergence between information, communication and media technologies. (BM)

23 Gordon, A. David, Kittross, John M. and **Reuss, Carol.** *Controversies in media ethics.* White Plains, New York: Longman, 1996. xvi, 317pp.

American textbook for media students and practitioners focusing on a dozen major media controversies, giving brief commentary and two contrasting points of view for the following topics: freedom of expression; individual autonomy and ethical decisions; codes of ethics; truth, fairness and objectivity; the ethics of 'correctness' in gender, race and ethnicity; privacy; violence and sexual pornography; media ethics and the market place; and the ethics of advertising. The final chapter briefly identifies other ethical controversies facing the media, including manipulation of photographs and conduct of interviews. An overview of general ethical principles by John C. Merrill places media ethics in context. (BM)

24 Greenberg, Karen Joy (ed.) *Conversations on communication ethics.* Norwood, New Jersey: Ablex Publishing, 1991. xii, 188pp. (Communication and information science)

Contributions by American academics on aspects of ethics in communication, including a history of communication ethics, a review of scholarship into the topic, tolerance and understanding, principles of fidelity and veracity, ideological gatekeeping, democratization of communication, and a case study of the rhetoric and situational ethics of the symbol of the 'refugee' in the Israeli–Palestinian Arab conflict. (BM)

25 Hamelink, Cees J. 'Ethics for media users'. *European Journal of Communication*, Vol. 10, No. 4, December 1995, pp. 497–512.

Professor of International Communications at the University of Amsterdam argues that media consumers have responsibility, as well as media producers, in ensuring high standards of media ethics, and should contribute to the public debate on the crucial moral issues connected with the mass media by demanding accountability from the media and by taking an active interest through civil and pressure groups. (BM)

26 Haselden, Kyle. *Morality and the mass media.* Nashville, Tennessee: Boardman, 1968.

27 Henry III, William A. 'Why journalists can't wear white'. *Media Studies Journal*, Vol. 6, No. 4, Fall 1992, pp. 17–29.

Time senior writer thinks that 'Properly speaking, the American press has no ethics', noting that public resentment of the media has not improved over the years. He reviews areas of concern – accuracy, patriotism, political and social bias, reporting techniques, privacy and fairness. (BM)

28 Hulteng, John L. *The messenger's motives: ethical problems of the news media.* 2nd ed. Englewood Cliffs, New Jersey: Prentice-Hall, 1985. xii, 239pp.
A routine volume of case studies, largely anecdotal, fleshed out by some references to the history of ethics. One chapter on the implications of cable. Annotated bibliography. (SM)

29 Ignatieff, Michael. 'Is nothing sacred?: the ethics of television'. *Daedalus. The Journal of the American Academy of Arts and Sciences*, Vol. 114, No. 4, Fall 1985, pp. 57–78.
Because of the impact on the world and Western charity of the coverage of the Ethiopian famine, broadcasters can no longer claim the media's function is only informative, and they cannot escape the moral consequences (and responsibilities) of their power. (BM)

30 Iyengar, Shanto. *Is anyone responsible?: how television frames political issues.* Chicago: University of Chicago Press, 1991. viii, 195pp.
There are many conflicting views on television's impact on public opinion on questions of political responsibility and accountability. Some feel it has impoverished national, political discourse but at the same time has moulded Americans' political consciousness. (BM)

31 Johannesen, Richard L. *Ethics in human communication.* Prospect Heights, Illinois: Waveland Press, 1983. 243pp.
Basically a college textbook which aims to provide information about a number of ethical approaches rather than to argue a case. A meaty work, not easy to read, it contains a useful discussion of the value of voluntary codes, and four American case studies. Its value to the general reader is perhaps reduced by the form of the work, and its frequent lists of questions suggests it was written primarily for use in seminars. Bibliography. (SM)

32 Kieran, Matthew. *Media ethics: a philosophical approach.* Westport, Connecticut: Praeger, 1997. ix, 168pp.
Examination of what constitutes ethical media practice, and why, by a lecturer in philosophy at the University of Leeds. Employing a primarily dialectical method of argument, he examines philosophical ethics and the media, the news media, impartiality, deceit, lies and privacy, sex and sexuality, violence in the media, and media censorship. Extensive bibliography. (BM)

33 Lambeth, Edmund B. 'Marsh, mesa, and mountain: evolution of contemporary study of ethics of journalism and mass communication in North America'. *Journal of Mass Media Ethics*, Vol. 3, No. 2, Fall 1988, pp. 20–5.
Summary of developments in the study of journalism and media ethics – books, journals, courses, workshops and conferences in North America. (BM)

34 Limburg, Val E. *Electronic media ethics.* Boston: Focal Press, 1994. x, 188pp.

Dr Limburg, Head of Broadcast Program at the Edward R. Murrow School of Communications of Washington State University, has written a clear and accessible text for media students and practitioners on basic ethical principles and their application (partly through case studies) to the business, programming and advertising of broadcasting. Entirely within an American context, he looks at the ways broadcasters *encode* social and moral values, and how audiences *decode* them. Of interest is the discussion of how codes formulated by the industry determine what is considered ethical in professional conduct, and the standards and practice established in the media, in particular the National Association of Broadcasters' *Code of good practice* of 1929, its eventual demise and later replacement with a new *Statement of principles of radio and television broadcasting* in 1990. (BM)

35 Lowenstein, Ralph L. and **Merrill, John C.** *Macromedia: mission, message and morality.* New York: Longman, 1990. x, 309pp.

'Designed as a catalyst to thought', this student text covers selected basic issues in mass communications, stressing morality and ethics. Sections on 'Freedom and responsibility', covering ethical perspectives with a suggestion of an ethical formula ('truthful, unbiased, full, and fair'), and 'Media and society', covering propaganda, fairness, right to know, integrity of reporting and 'reporter or moralist?'. (BM)

36 Meiden, Anne van der. 'The basic issues of media ethics'. *WACC Journal*, Vol. 26, No. 4, 1979, pp. 3–6.

Theoretical and practical discussion of media ethics covering, among other topics, freedom of speech and right to communicate. (BM)

37 Meiden, Anne van der (ed.) *Ethics in mass communication.* Utrecht: State University of Utrecht, 1980. 237pp.

A collection of essays in English, ranging in subject from the political pamphlets of John Milton to a discussion of the work of the Korean Press Ethics Commission by a contributor from the University of Seoul. The book is in typescript, the contributors are of very mixed quality, with some suffering because they were writing in their second or third language, and it has no index. Nevertheless, some of the essays represent a valuable attempt to face ethical problems squarely and the difference in national attitudes are themselves fascinating, from a Finnish work which comes close to embracing the Soviet arguments, to a US contribution which indicates that American newspaper editors may be more interested in consensus than in moral issues. (SM)

38 Merrill, John C. *The imperative of freedom: a philosophy of journalistic autonomy.* New York: Hastings House, 1974.

39 Merrill, John C. and **Barney, Ralph D.** (eds.) *Ethics and the press: readings in mass media morality.* New York: Hastings House, 1975. xiii, 338pp. (Humanistic studies in the communication arts)

A collection of 35 articles and papers intended, according to the editors, to fill a gap in studies of ethical problems in journalism. There was, they remark, a good deal of discussion of journalistic morality in the 1920s and 1930s, but little more in the next four decades. The essays are of varying quality, the press figures prominently and the book is firmly centred on the US. Part One is on general ethical foundations; Part Two expounds particular ethical dilemmas. Bibliography. (SM)

40 Merrill, John C. and **Odell, S. Jack**. *Philosophy and journalism*. New York: Longman, 1983. xiii, 190pp.

Philosophical context for consideration of journalistic problems, questions and issues. Odell, a philosophy professor, covers fundamentals of deductive and inductive reasoning, conceptual analysis, and ethics. Merrill, a journalism professor, discusses the implication of those philosophical problems for journalism. (BM)

41 Meyer, Philip. *Editors, publishers and newspapers ethics*. Washington, DC: American Society of Newspaper Editors, 1983.

42 Meyer, Philip. *Ethical journalism: a guide for students, practitioners and consumers.* New York: Longman, 1987; reprint Lanham, Maryland: University Press of America, 1991. x, 262pp.

This clearly written American reader begins with the history and principles of the First Amendment, which underlie the ethics of the press in the US, followed by an examination of various codes of journalism, sections on advertiser influence, objectivity, conflict of interest and privacy, newspaper ethical judgements in practice, and the 'ethical audit'. Appendices include an American Society of Newspaper Editors survey on newspaper ethics, and reprints of four codes. (BM)

43 Moore, Roy L. *Mass communication law and ethics*. Hillsdale, New Jersey: Lawrence Erlbaum Associates, 1994. viii, 610pp.; *1996 update*. 1996. 81pp. (Communication textbook series)

Within an American context this textbook examines the ethical dimensions of key legal issues in the media, detailing landmark cases and demonstrating where the law ends and ethics begins. Issues covered include the US legal and judicial system, libel, right of privacy, press and public access to judicial processes and records, intellectual property rights, obscenity and pornography. Appendices reprint codes of the Society of Professional Journalists, National Press Photographers Association, American Society of Newspaper Editors, American Association of Advertising Agencies, Radio-Television News Directors Association, and the National Association of Broadcasters. (BM)

44 Olen, Jeffrey and **Barry, Vincent**. *Applying ethics: a text with readings*. 4th ed. Belmont, California: Wadsworth Publishing, 1992. ix, 470pp.

Reader on applied ethics: Part One on moral reasoning; Part Two on various issues, including pornography, obscenity and censorship, with discussion of the moral issues, arguments, readings and case presentations. (BM)

45 Overbeck, Wayne and **Pullen, Rick D.** *Major principles of media law.* Rev. ed. New York: Holt, Rinehart & Winston, 1991. xx, 359pp.

Basically a US college textbook, it includes chapter summaries, for example, as well as a whole chapter on the freedom of the student press. The authors recognize that they are writing at a time of significant change in the media, and that some of the material will date quickly (indeed some has already done so). So they revert to 'principles', which include basic ethical considerations. It is written with commendable clarity. (SM)

46 Patterson, Philip and **Wilkins, Lee.** *Media ethics: issues and cases.* 2nd ed. Wisconsin, Madison: Wm C. Brown Communications, 1994. xx, 280pp.

Student textbook providing a collection of real-life and hypothetical cases with discussion points supplied by over 40 authors from academic and media backgrounds, illustrating basic philosophical and ethical issues – truth, fairness, loyalty, privacy, the position of the media in a democratic society, and photojournalism. (BM)

47 Rivers, William L. and **Mathews, Cleve.** *Ethics for the media.* Englewood Cliffs, New Jersey: Prentice Hall, 1988. xi, 307pp.

Ethical questions across the media – press, broadcasting, advertising, photography and public relations – 'their similarities more important than the differences'. Chapters cover democracy and ethics, journalistic virtues, news-gathering, investigative reporting, packaging the news, advertising and persuasion, sexism, codes and press councils. Useful features include profiles in each chapter of key figures (John Stuart Mill, David Halberstam, Sissela Bok, Wilbur Schramm, Susan Sontag, etc.), practical exercises and reprints of various American codes of practice. (BM)

48 Rivers, William L., Schramm, Wilbur and **Christians, Clifford G.** *Responsibility in mass communication.* 3rd ed. New York: Harper & Row, 1980. 378pp.

A classic work on media ethics, though some of the sharp edges of the argument have been blunted by time. Originally commissioned by the Federal Council of the Churches of Christ in America. A statement of the social responsibility theory of the media, strongest on the press. It makes the customary US assumptions about economic resources of the media, and predates the argument about intellectual imperialism. But it raises many of the dilemmas of the 'free' media, and keeps its feet firmly on the ground. It is well written, and free from sociological jargon. Bibliography. (SM/BM)

49 Robertson, Geoffrey and **Nicol, Andrew G.** *Media law.* 2nd rev. ed. London: Penguin Books, 1992. lxv, 667pp.

Authoritative textbook on the legal rights of journalists, broadcasters, editors, film and TV producers and all who publish news or views through communications media, written for lawyers, journalists and students. Enormous in scope, given the extent of media regulation in the UK, it covers in detail (and with case law) freedom to communicate, defamation, obscenity, blasphemy, racism, confidence and privacy, contempt of court, reporting the courts, Parliament and government, film and video censorship, and broadcasting law. (BM)

50 Roth, John K. (ed.) *International encyclopedia of ethics.* London: Fitzroy Dearborn Publishers, 1995. xvi, 988pp.

Comprehensive encyclopedia examining the various areas of (mainly) applied ethics. Contains 819 alphabetically arranged articles, mostly by American academics, varying in length from 250 to 3000 words. Standard format articles offer descriptors of type of ethics, date, definition, significance, and bibliography. No main entry for 'media ethics', but contains many media ethics-related topics, including entrapment, American Society of Newspaper Editors, journalistic ethics, libel, sources of information, etc. (BM)

51 Rubin, Bernard (ed.) *Questioning media ethics.* New York: Praeger, 1978. x, 310pp.

Despite some distinguished contributors from the press, television and film worlds, including Nora Beloff and Roger Manvell, this is a routine collection of 'for instances' of ethical problems facing media practitioners. (SM)

52 Russell, Nick. *Morals and the media: ethics in Canadian journalism.* Vancouver: UBC Press (University of British Columbia), 1994. xii, 250pp.

Because this is the first book on Canadian journalism ethics, the author, a journalism teacher and former journalist, aims to make it a broad introduction covering all the fundamental moral questions and ethical dilemmas of journalism across the major print and electronic media. He emphasizes the coverage is exclusively anglophone, not encompassing the French or ethnic media of Canada, as their value systems are significantly different, and also stresses the Canadian perspective on ethics as being distinct from the American in many respects (greater concern for rights to privacy, more likely to consider the right to fair trial outweighs the public's right to know, and less tolerance for sensational news coverage or the right to publish pornography). (BM)

53 Sobel, Lester A. *Media controversies.* New York: Facts on File, 1981. 179pp.

A chronology of media controversies during the 1970s in the US. The relationship between the media and the Nixon administration forms a substantial section, with other topics including broadcasters under pressure, the regulation of radio and television, ownership and control of the media, libel laws and media curbs, and protection of sources. The conflict between the right to a free press, in the First Amendment, and the right to fair trial, in the Sixth Amendment, is illustrated with examples of notable cases. (BM)

54 Tester, Keith. *Media, culture and morality.* London: Routledge, 1994. 138pp.
Cultural and media studies text by a University of Portsmouth lecturer, which examines moral and cultural values in a media-dominated world. Citing media coverage of global problems, the author identifies a paradox: on the one hand television has the potential to communicate moral values and responsibilities because it is for many individuals and audiences the channel through which they become aware of what is said to be right and wrong, but on the other hand it can minimize if not trivialize the moral impact through constant, though brief and superficial exposure to the issues. He concludes that the media will not, because they cannot, act as channels for the communication of values. (BM)

55 Thayer, Lee (ed.) *Ethics, morality and the media: reflections on American culture.* New York: Hastings House, 1980. 302pp.
A collection of papers, lectures and articles written by both media practitioners and academics. Some were written specially, and some are reprints from elsewhere, almost all are lightweight and the book is highly parochial. There is, however, an introductory essay by Professor Thayer in which he questions many assumptions about the media, and poses a number of interesting questions. Bibliography. (SM)

56 Traber, Michael (ed.) *The myth of the information revolution: social and ethical implications of communication technology.* London and Beverly Hills, California: Sage Publications, 1986. viii, 146pp. (Sage communications in society)
This is a committed book, whose copyright is vested in the World Association for Christian Communication. Many of the contributors are from Third World countries. The more factual essays constitute a valuable introduction to the 'information revolution': the final chapter, 'Communication and religion in the technological era', summarizes from a mainly Christian viewpoint some of the challenges to established religion. (SM)

57 White, Robert A. 'From codes of ethics to public cultural truth: a systematic view of communication ethics'. *European Journal of Communication*, Vol. 10, No. 4, December 1995, pp. 441–59.
The author, Director of the Centre for Interdisciplinary Study of Social Communications at the Gregorian University in Rome, rejects the accepted definition of media ethics as solely in terms of the professional ethics of media practitioners, but thinks it must be seen as an integral part of the responsibility of all members of society – legislators and policy makers, owners and administrators of the media, media academics, the general public, as well as editors and journalists – and that media policy or reform based on public interest depends on a concordance of the moral claims and concerns of all of them. (BM)

58 Whitehorn, Katharine. *Ethics and the media.* Guildford: University of Surrey, 1988. 17pp. (Leggett Lectures, 12)

Respected British journalist and columnist surveys the various ethical dilemmas faced by media journalists and the attempts to preserve professional standards through codes of practice. In surveying the role of the media, she concludes, by quoting from American Judge Gurfein (on the publication of the *Pentagon papers*), that 'a cantankerous press, an obstinate press, a ubiquitous press must be suffered by those in authority to preserve the even greater values of freedom of expression and the right of the people to know'. (BM)

Mass media in general

Essential, basic works on mass communications, the press and broadcasting which contain, *inter alia*, discussion of ethical issues.

59 Agee, Warren K., Ault, Phillip H. and **Emery, Edwin**. *Introduction to mass communications*. 9th ed. New York: Harper & Row, 1988. xvi, 589pp.

Comprehensive student text, first published in 1960, with substantial section on social and ethical responsibilities of the media. Beginning with a discussion of the moral law within which communications operate, it covers such issues as media portrayal of violence, terrorism, obscenity and pornography, with examples, citations of research studies, ethical codes and their enforcement – all from an American context. Bibliography. (BM)

60 Agee, Warren K., Ault, Phillip H. and **Emery, Edwin**. *Maincurrents in mass communications*. New York: Harper & Row, 1986. xiv, 457pp.

American reader offering cross-media approach to controversies in mass communications by writers prominent in media, grouped by themes – media in society, ethical and legal challenges, technology revolution, communicators, media trends and techniques, and the information society, all from a US viewpoint. (BM)

61 Barnouw, Erik. *A history of broadcasting in the United States*. New York: Oxford University Press, 1966–70; *A tower in Babel: Volume 1 – to 1933*. 1966. 344pp.; *The golden web: Volume 2 – 1933 to 1953*. 1968. 391pp.; *The image empire: Volume 3 – from 1953*. 1970. 396pp.

Comprehensive standard history of broadcasting in the US covering legislative, technical, administrative, business and programming aspects of radio and television. *The tube of plenty: the evolution of American television* (New York: Oxford University Press, 1975. 518pp.) is a condensed and updated version, concentrating on the emergence of television as a dominant factor in American society. (BM)

62 Berger, Arthur Asa (ed.) *Television in society*. New Brunswick, New Jersey: Transaction Books, 1986. 282pp.

Collection of articles from *Society* magazine dealing with television in sociological terms, and how it both reflects and affects society, with some articles on 'ethical' issues – on violence in programme content, mass media values, satellite television and cultural intrusion, freedom of speech, reporting Vietnam and nuclear war. (BM)

63 Bittner, John R. *Mass communication.* 6th ed. Boston: Allyn & Bacon, 1996. xxx, 514pp.

American students' class textbook with chapter on ethics and social issues, summarizing, with examples, the more common ethical issues confronting media practitioners. (BM)

64 Briggs, Asa. *The history of broadcasting in the United Kingdom.* London: Oxford University Press, 1961–95.
Volume 1: *The birth of broadcasting.* (1896–1927). 1961. xiii, 425pp.
Volume 2: *The golden age of wireless.* (1927–1939). 1965. xvi, 688pp.
Volume 3: *The war of the words.* (1939–1945). 1970. xviii, 766pp.
Volume 4: *Sound and vision.* (1945–1955). 1979. xiv, 1082pp.
Volume 5: *Competition.* (1955–1974). 1995. xxvi, 1133pp.

Lord Briggs is a distinguished historian and educationalist who for a number of years wrote 'house histories'. This massive work is rather more. It traces the stages by which the BBC acquired from its first Director-General a sense of social purpose, and also its years of triumph as the principal mouthpiece of democracy during the Second World War. The leisured pace at which successive volumes were published indicates the considerable amount of archive material used, but also means that the perspective changes somewhat from the first to the last volume. The work is, however, in the tradition of house histories, being well-disposed towards the institution which commissioned it. Not only is the book a massive quarry for historians, it has also given Lord Briggs a substantial and scholarly background from which to write other works on British broadcasting. (SM)

65 Campaign for Press and Broadcasting Freedom. *Twenty-first-century media: shaping the democratic vision: media manifesto.* London: Campaign for Press and Broadcasting Freedom, 1996. 12pp.

Produced by a pressure group for media reform, this work is aimed as a contribution to the wide-ranging debate on policy issues for the 1997 British General Election. It covers the case for regulation, ownership, the right to report, secrecy, trade union rights and equal opportunities, among other topics. (BM)

66 Cantor, Muriel G. and **Cantor, Joel M.** *Prime-time television: content and control.* 2nd ed. Newbury Park, California: Sage, 1992. viii, 135pp. (Sage commtext series)

Analysis of American television programme content and how the networks and producers adapted it to the demographic, economic and political shifts in the viewing audience. Ethical, legal, regulatory, selection and editorial issues are covered. (BM)

67 Chilton, Paul and **Crispin, Aubrey** (eds.) *Nineteen eighty-four in 1984: autonomy, control and communication.* London: Comedia, 1983. 120pp.

George Orwell's *Nineteen eighty-four*, first published in 1949, has become a symbol of a future wired-up totalitarian world of surveillance and alienation. This collection of essays takes the novel as its starting point and examines, from a left-wing viewpoint, how far his prophecies, and surprising omissions (like computers), are relevant to the information revolution of the real 1980s. Some of the essays are stimulating. (SM/BM)

68 Collins, Richard (ed.) *Media, culture and society: a critical reader.* London: Sage Publications, 1986. 346pp.

The journal *Media, culture and society* began publication in 1979, providing a bridge between the American empirical school of communications studies and the more theoretical, frequently Marxist, approach of Europe. This anthology of some of the more important papers published between 1979 and 1985 is arranged under three headings: 'Approach to cultural theory'; 'Intellectuals and cultural production'; and 'British broadcasting and the public sphere'. (SM)

69 Collins, Richard and **Murroni, Cristina**. *New media, new policies: media and communications strategies for the future.* Cambridge: Polity Press, 1996. ix, 243pp.

Study undertaken at the Institute for Public Policy Research (IPPR), a British centre–left think-tank, of media and communication policy, covering organization of the infrastructure, the balance between markets and regulation, the link between ownership and control of the media, universal service obligation, and priority given to freedom of expression in questions of regulation of media content. (BM)

70 Comstock, George. *Television in America.* Beverly Hills, California: Sage, 1980. 155pp.

Analysis from viewpoints of psychology, politics, sociology and communications of television in the US, and its influence and impact on society. (BM)

71 Cranfield, G. A. *The press and society: from Caxton to Northcliffe.* London: Longman, 1978. vii, 242pp. (Themes in British social history)

History of the press in Britain from the Tudor era to the launch and rise to dominance of the *Daily Mail* by Alfred Harmsworth in the late nineteenth century. Three themes – of intelligence, instruction and entertainment – emerge, as do the ambivalent attitudes of authority to the press – regarding it both as a tool of power and as a subversive force. The press's position as a powerful factor for social change dates back to Caxton. (BM)

72 Curran, James (ed.) *The British press: a manifesto.* London: Macmillan, 1978. viii, 339pp. (Communication and culture)

This book is a product of the Acton Society Press Group, formed in 1974 to ensure that the UK Royal Commission on the Press (the McGregor Commission) received some evidence from independent bodies. Much of the content of the book has been overtaken by events: nevertheless it has some importance as an analysis by distinguished, mainly left-wing, contributors of the ills of the British press in the 1970s. (SM)

73 Curran, James, Ecclestone, Jake, Oakley, Giles and **Richardson, Alan**. *Bending reality: the state of the media*. London: Pluto Press, 1986. ix, 243pp.
The title is splendidly ironic: a number of the nineteen papers and articles in this left-wing propaganda pamphlet by the Campaign for Press and Broadcasting Freedom do indeed seem to bend reality a long way. The book is redeemed by one or two essays of quality: in particular James Curran on the different approaches to media reform, in which he torpedoes several of the other more strident contributions. A parochial work. (SM)

74 Curran, James and **Gurevitch, Michael** (eds.) *Mass media and society*. 2nd ed. London: Edward Arnold, 1996. 378pp.
Successor to a British Open University textbook, *Mass communication and society* (1977), which now takes in the new revisionism that has developed in mass communications research in the past couple of decades. Seventeen essays by distinguished international media scholars, including Peter Golding, Graham Murdock, Jay Blumler, Ien Ang, Sonia Livingstone and the editors themselves, are grouped into three broad topics – mass media and society, media production, and mediation of meaning. Of particular interest are 'Media in the public interest' by Denis McQuail (pp. 66–80), 'The sociology of news production' by Michael Schudson (pp. 141–59), and 'In defence of objectivity revisited' by Judith Lichtenberg (pp. 225–42). (BM)

75 Curran, James and **Seaton, Jean**. *Power without responsibility: the press and broadcasting in Britain*. 5th ed. London: Routledge, 1997. ix, 420pp.
Survey of the British press and broadcasting, tracing their historical development to the present-day concepts and structures. It argues that the media and politics have inspired, reflected and shaped each other more than has been generally realized or accepted. The move towards moral censorship in the 1980s gave rise to changes in media regulation – the Broadcasting Standards Council and the Broadcasting Act 1990 bringing broadcasters under the Obscene Publications Act, among others. This demand for increased moral and ethical regulation in broadcasting could be accommodated by existing structures of control, whereas those for stricter regulation of the press (caused by reactions to tabloid journalism excesses) could not. In making proposals for reform, the authors identify the contradictions in current public and political attitudes to the media – the traditional left–right battle lines crossing those of libertarianism versus paternalism. Extensive bibliography. (BM)

76 Dennis, Everette E. *Of media and people*. Newbury Park, California: Sage Publications, 1992. vii, 187pp.

Collection of articles and speeches, edited and revised in many cases, by Executive Director of the Freedom Forum (formerly the Gannett Center) Media Studies Center at Columbia University, on the theme of the relationship of the mass media with their audience. Divided into seven parts: media performance (including the effects of news gathering processes on journalistic values, the dangers in blurring the line between politicians and journalists, and the question of faked coverage, 're-creations' or 'simulations' on television); international communications; educating communicators; consequences of convergence; reporter's imperatives; media at war. (BM)

77 Eldridge, John, Kitzinger, Jenny and **Williams, Kevin**. *The mass media and power in modern Britain.* Oxford: Oxford University Press, 1997. x, 199pp. (Oxford modern Britain)
Overview for students of sociology, politics and media of the role, influence and power of the media in contemporary British society, including media ownership, public service broadcasting, 'moral panics' and media scares, photojournalism and propaganda. (BM)

78 Friendly, Fred W. *Due to circumstances beyond our control...* New York: Random House, 1967. xxvi, 326pp.
Critique by former CBS news division president of US television networks, and the Federal Communications Commission's failure to police them, to plan and understand the true meaning of television. (BM)

79 Gitlin, Todd. *Inside prime time.* New York: Pantheon Books, 1983. ix, 372pp.
Professor of Sociology at University of California at Berkeley looks in detail at the American television production industry. He is critical of a commercial television which aims only to encourage its audience to think of themselves as consumers and which does not take its responsibility to inform the public, of the decision-making processes that produce unchallenging, stereotyped programming for the lowest common denominator audience, and of the regulators who have been persuaded that the market place should be its own regulator. 'The predicament of American television is the predicament of American culture and politics as a whole.' (BM)

80 Heren, Louis. *The power of the press?* London: Orbis, 1985. 205pp.
A popular history of the press in Britain and the US, with a chapter on the white Commonwealth, by a journalist and former Deputy Editor of *The Times*. The stress is on personalities (press barons and editors) and papers at the height of their success or the major controversies. He argues strongly that radio and television have not reduced the need for printed newspapers. But, as the question mark in the title indicates, he is not convinced of the power and influence of the press. As Lord Windlesham argued in *Communication and political power*, it is news, not newspapers or television programmes, which governs the course of events. Bibliography. (SM)

81 Hiebert, Ray Eldon (ed.) *Impact of mass media: current issues.* 3rd ed. White Plains, New York: Longman, 1995. xv, 472pp.

Comprehensive student reader covering a range of issues in print and broadcast media, film, advertising and public relations. Section on ethical values includes articles on public exposure of private grief, press responsibility in reporting, privacy and the First Amendment, revealing the identity of the accused in court cases, journalists' personal involvement in issues, digital retouching of photographs, and the use of hidden cameras in obtaining news stories. (BM)

82 Hood, Stuart. *On television.* 3rd ed. London: Pluto Press, 1987. 133pp.

A short popular work, now largely out-of-date, aimed at students and teachers of the media, and those 'who are active in trade unions and in the political parties and groups to the left'. Its continuing interest lies in the fact that Stuart Hood has been a senior figure in the BBC and ITV, a prominent trade unionist and a Professor at the Royal College of Art. Brief bibliography. (BM/SM)

83 Humphreys, Peter J. *Mass media and media policy in Western Europe.* Manchester: Manchester University Press, 1996. ix, 349pp.

The rapid and revolutionary changes that the press and television are undergoing in Western Europe are raising profound questions for public policy. The author looks in particular at media freedom and pluralism, and the threat to them from both political pressures and the concentration of media ownership and markets. (BM)

84 Inglis, Kenneth Stanley. *This is the ABC: the Australian Broadcasting Commission 1932–1983.* Carlton, Victoria: Melbourne University Press, 1983. x, 521pp.

A house history by a Professor of History in the Research School of Social Sciences at the Australian National University. It focuses primarily on broadcast programmes rather than institutions, and, in the manner of house histories, is a work of record rather than critical assessment. Nevertheless it has wider interest and relevance to media ethics. Though Australia is a prosperous society, it has had to struggle to emerge from cultural as well as institutional imperialism. Second, the ABC has battled to free itself from governmental control and censorship. Third, the ABC has always had to live with commercial rivals. (SM)

85 McLuhan, Marshall. *The Gutenberg galaxy: the making of typographic man.* Toronto: University of Toronto Press, 1962; London: Routledge & Kegan Paul, 1962. 294pp. *Understanding media: the extension of man.* New York: McGraw-Hill, 1964; Routledge & Kegan Paul, 1964. 359pp.

The initial astonishment and controversy which surrounded the publication of these two best-known works of Marshall McLuhan have now subsided, and it is possible to make a more considered assessment of his work. Much media research is long on information, but short on ideas and judgements. In McLuhan's work ideas sparkle like firecrackers, often infuriating, always thought-provoking. He raises profound questions. It becomes increasingly clear that the supremacy of print is being challenged in many fields of study, though it will never be superseded as the most ardent McLuhanites once argued. If it is true that the medium is the message the relevance and validity of much research are limited: they are distorted by the medium in which they are reported. The developing investigation of effective and cognitive perception, too, owes something to McLuhan's work. McLuhan's books are required reading for any serious student of the media. (SM)

86 McNair, Brian. *News and journalism in the UK: a textbook.* London: Routledge & Kegan Paul, 1994. xi, 212pp. (Communication and society)

A student reader which comprehensively surveys the economic, political and regulatory developments of British press and broadcast journalism during a period of radical change from the 1980s. It covers the consequences of an increasingly competitive press, with more titles competing for a generally declining readership, as well as the effects of new political ideologies, technological advances and competition from emergent satellite channels on public service broadcasting. On the debate on press freedom versus individual right to privacy, the author surveys recent political and royal invasion of privacy cases, and the findings of the Calcutt Committee on Privacy, and concludes that continuation of the regulatory status quo for the British press is no longer tenable. (BM)

87 McQuail, Denis. *Communication.* 2nd ed. London: Longman, 1984. xiii, 266pp. (Aspects of modern sociology. Social processes)

The author, Professor of Mass Communication at the University of Amsterdam, analyses the nature of mass communications as part of the study of human communications within a sociological framework. He examines the complex relationships in the process of mass communication, and in particular the three basic elements of communicator, channel of communication and audience; and the crucial role of the media organizations who control access to the vital intermediary channels of communication and have a direct influence in the content of the media. The consequence of this dominance of the media institutions, frequently large centralized monoliths accountable to the public, if not government control, is a tendency of the mass media to favour dominant social values and the existing power structures of society. (BM)

88 McQuail, Denis. *Mass communication theory: an introduction.* 3rd ed. London: Sage Publications, 1994. xvi, 416pp.

This introductory book has quickly established itself as scholarly, thoughtful and a good deal more comprehensive than many longer works. Initially conceived as a successor to the same author's *Towards a sociology of mass communication*, which itself was an attempt to use sociological theory to supply coherence to the mass of research findings, but necessarily wider in scope. Starting with a historical approach to mass communication, it surveys a number of approaches to media theory, and differing ideas of function and purpose, with discussion on social responsibility and media codes of conduct. It examines relationships between media institutions and culture, then media content and effects before a final chapter on the limits of media theory. The list of references amounts, in itself, to a selected bibliography. (BM/SM)

89 Mander, Jerry. *Four arguments for the elimination of television*. New York: William Morrow, 1978; Brighton, Sussex: Harvester Press, 1980. 371pp.
A well-known, hilarious polemic against television by an ex-advertising director turned saint. Written in a populist style, the book is based on fairly elementary arguments about the changing face of culture. It is part of the author's argument that his thoughts cannot be condensed (at least for television), so no summary is attempted here. The book never rises above the anecdotal, but is occasionally stimulating, though there are no positive arguments. Bibliography. (SM)

90 Merrill, John C. and **Lowenstein, Ralph L**. *Media, messages and men*. 2nd ed. New York: Longman, 1979. vii, 264pp.
Introductory text on many of the contemporary issues and controversies in journalism and mass communication; Part Three, 'Media concepts and ethics', covers media freedom, propaganda, objectivity and journalistic ethics. (BM)

91 Postman, Neil. *Technopoly: the surrender of culture to technology*. New York: Knopf, 1992. xii, 225pp.
The author defines 'technopoly' as totalitarian technocracy, society in which culture submits to the dominance of technology. This book aims to describe when, how and why technology came to this dominant position. In particular he points out the dangers of the information explosion, and argues that cultures suffer from information glut, information without meaning, and information without control mechanisms. Technopoly flourishes when the link between information and human purpose has been severed. (BM)

92 Robinson, Glen O. *Communications for tomorrow: policy perspectives for the 1980s*. New York: Praeger, 1978. xiv, 528pp.
The American Aspen Institute for Humanistic Studies set up a task force to re-examine and explore basic philosophical and policy issues in communications. Though the study was internationally based, the focus is largely American. Chapters by lawyers, economists, political scientists and technologists look at the electronic media, and, *inter alia*, propose new policies and regulatory institutions. (SM)

93 Sendall, Bernard. *Independent Television in Britain*. London: Macmillan, 1982–83; Volume 1: *Origin and foundation, 1946–62*. 1982. xviii, 418pp.; Volume 2: *Expansion and change, 1958–68*. 1983. xvii, 429pp.
This house history of commercial television in the UK differs from Asa Briggs' monumental study of the BBC [64] in that the author was himself an important

participant in many of the events he recounts – he was a senior member of staff of the Independent Television Authority (later Independent Broadcasting Authority) in which he became the Deputy Director-General. This double stance is more noticeable, and more awkward, in the first volume. The nature of the subject means that most of the ethical issues about a television service financed by advertising are raised, as are many of the issues involved in the relationship between government and broadcasters. Series continued by Jeremy Potter: *Independent Television in Britain*, Volume 3: *Politics and control, 1968–80* (London: Macmillan, 1989. ix, 352pp.); *Independent Television in Britain*, Volume 4: *Companies and programmes, 1968–80* (London: Macmillan, 1990. xi, 428pp.) (SM/BM)

94 Seymour-Ure, Colin. *The British press and broadcasting since 1945*. Oxford: Basil Blackwell, 1991; 2nd ed. 1996. xiii, 289pp. (Making contemporary Britain)

In a series of student readers sponsored by the Institute of Contemporary British History, this work by Professor Seymour-Ure (University of Kent at Canterbury) surveys post-war development of the press and broadcasting in the UK, concentrating on media accountability and the relations between government and media, particularly on policy, regulation and freedom of information. (BM)

95 Smith, A. C. H. *Paper voices: the popular press and social change, 1935–1965*. London: Chatto & Windus, 1975. 262pp.

This book is an expanded version of a research report, *The popular press and social change*, published by the Birmingham University Centre for Contemporary Cultural Studies. It is based on an intensive content analysis of two high-circulation British newspapers, the *Daily Express* and the *Daily Mirror*, and particularly the campaigns they conducted during the post-war general elections. An attempt is made to relate this to academic sociological analyses, and it also involves literary/linguistic analysis. The book has largely been overtaken by events (for example, neither of the newspapers was able to continue its market dominance), but it is an interesting example of the work of what was for some years the most forward-looking academic institution in the UK. Bibliography. (SM)

96 Smith, Anthony. *The politics of information: problems of policy in modern media*. London: Macmillan, 1978. xii, 252pp. (Communications and culture)

This is a slight collection of essays, most of which had previously been published elsewhere. Some of them, however, retain their value. The book is of interest as containing the early work of one of the few media practitioners who successfully transferred to the academic world. Includes a paper on 'news values and the ethic of journalism'. (SM/BM)

97 Tunstall, Jeremy. *The media in Britain*. London: Constable, 1983. 304pp. (Communication and society)

Though this sets out to be little more than an introductory textbook, it is comprehensive, well written and, at times, provocative. It is particularly strong on relationships between the various media. Ethical issues covered include relationship of the media with government and politics, media bias, and the work of Royal Commissions and Committees. Excellent bibliography. (SM)

98 Vivian, John. *The media of mass communication.* Boston: Allyn & Bacon, 1991. xix, 411pp.

Popularly written media students' textbook, mostly from an American context, including chapters on mass media law and regulation (covering First Amendment, censorship, privacy, libel, obscenity and pornography issues), and ethics and the mass media. (BM)

99 Whale, John. *The politics of the media.* 2nd ed. London: Fontana, 1980. 176pp. (Political issues of our times)

Summary of developments in the press and broadcasting since 1945, covering the institutions and pressure groups concerned (media owners, trade unions, the state and the law), and strongly arguing for regulated diversity in the media in future. (BM)

100 Williams, Francis. *Dangerous estate: the anatomy of newspapers.* London: Longmans Green, 1957; facsimile ed.: Cambridge: Patrick Stephens, 1984. xi, 304pp.

A minor classic by one of the greatest of British newspapermen (though he was not a great editor), reprinted here with a preface by journalist and politician Michael Foot. The core of the book is a history of the British press of sufficient merit to have influenced many later studies. There are problems of perspective – for example, much space is devoted to the circulation war of the 1930s, and to the *Daily Herald*, of which Francis Williams became editor. Of equal interest, however, are the chapters of comment and analysis. *Plus ça change* ... until, perhaps, the new technology. (SM)

101 Williams, Raymond. *Communications.* 3rd ed. Harmondsworth, Middlesex: Penguin, 1976. 192pp.

Influential introduction to role and influence of communications within modern society, looking at the history, institutions, means and controversies of communications. (BM)

102 Williams, Raymond. *Television: technology and cultural form.* 2nd ed. London: Routledge, 1990. 164pp.

In his influential exploration of some of the relationships between television as a technology and as a cultural form, Professor Williams concluded that television could be a tool for education and wider democracy, but it could also limit individual and collective responses to different situations to a choice between programmed possibilities. (BM)

103 Windlesham, Lord. *Broadcasting in a free society.* Oxford: Basil Blackwell, 1980. 172pp. (Mainstream series)

A sparkling, well-written primer; the author has extensive experience in television, and has been a government minister. Brief though it is, the book finds space for some history, some account of relations between the media (including the press) and government, and some discussion of the rise of 'professionalism' as a criteria of media excellence. (SM)

Freedom of speech

104 *African Charter on Human and Peoples' Rights.* Banjul, Gambia: African Commission on Human and Peoples' Rights, 1986.
Adopted by most African countries (35 by 1989), the charter does not protect freedom of opinion nor the right to seek and impart information and ideas. Article 9: '1. Every individual shall have the right to receive information. 2. Every individual shall have the right to free association provided he abides by the law.' (BM)

105 Allaun, Frank. *Spreading the news: a guide to media reform.* London: Spokesman (for the Campaign for Press and Broadcasting Freedom), 1988. 112pp.
Left-wing treatise by former British Labour Member of Parliament, which proposes that the impact of new technologies on the newspaper and television industries, together with declining professional standards of journalism, make reforms in the media necessary, in particular a statutory right of reply, anti-monopoly measures and freedom of information legislation. (BM)

106 *American Convention on Human Rights.* Washington, DC: Organization of American States (OAS), 1969.
Follows the 'American Declaration of the Rights and Duties of Man' of 1948, and now ratified by many countries of Central and South America. Article 13 provides a strong statement on protection of freedom of expression, including injunction against prior censorship and recognizing a right of reply. (BM)

107 Article 19. *Freedom of expression handbook: international and comparative law, standards and procedures.* London: Article 19, 1993.
International organization which publishes reports on, and campaigns against, censorship throughout the world.

108 Article 19. *Information, freedom and censorship: world report 1991.* London: Library Association, 1991. xv, 471pp.
Comprehensive survey of censorship in 77 countries around the world. Each country report contains a factual account of the media laws with some demographic and media statistics, followed by a survey of the press, broadcasting, film, publishing and journalism, and details of abuse of freedom of expression and censorship cases with action taken by Article 19. A reference section on themes

and issues lists international treaties which protect freedom of expression. Overview of censorship issues across the world. Bibliography. (BM)

109 Barbrook, Richard. *Media freedom: the contradictions of communications in the age of modernity*. London: Pluto Press, 1995. xii, 218pp.
Academic study of the contradiction between participation and democracy within the media through an analysis of the history of the media in France, from the right of freedom of publication proclaimed in the 1789 revolution to the bicentenary celebrations and new communications law of 1989. (BM)

110 Barendt, Eric. *Freedom of speech*. Oxford: Clarendon Press, 1985. xxiv, 314pp.
Discussion of the legal questions connected with fundamental free speech principles, with a detailed account of the law in various jurisdictions. British standpoint, but American case law dominates some chapters, and there is also recourse to German law and European Commission and the Courts of Human Rights (of increasing importance as a defence of fundamental freedoms in the UK) when relevant. Though the UK does not yet have constitutional protection (for example, a Bill of Rights) for freedom of expression, politicians and the law have always regarded it as a basic value. This mixture of law and philosophy covers freedom of the press, access to information, film and theatre censorship, politics and official secrets, libel, invasion of privacy, public order and obscenity. (BM)

111 Berns, Walter. *Freedom, virtue and the First Amendment*. Baton Rouge: Louisiana State University Press, 1957. xiii, 264pp.
Critical of the liberal conception of law and politics in the US underlying the decisions of the Supreme Court in the 1950s in First Amendment cases, this book surveys issues of government censorship, obscenity and freedom of the press. Despite the assumption that free speech and press is a *right*, the Court generally acknowledges that freedom of speech is not *absolute*. (BM)

112 Blanchard, Margaret A. 'The business of a free press'. *Gannett Center Journal*, Vol. 4, No. 4, Fall 1990, pp. 17–29.
Eastern European countries can learn from the American model that a free press is the best way to ensure all the freedoms they have so painfully won. (BM)

113 Boutros-Ghali, Boutros. 'Opinion: the new authority'. *Media Studies Journal*, Vol. 9, No. 3, Summer 1995, pp. 21–4.
United Nations Secretary-General (1992–96) argues the media today are as important as the branches of government (executive, legislature and judiciary), and have an impact on them, as well as democracy itself, and it is essential they are free and independent. (BM)

114 Campbell, Tom and **Sadurski, Wojciech** (eds.) *Freedom of communication*. Aldershot, Hampshire: Dartmouth Publishing, 1994. xii, 304pp. (Applied legal philosophy series)

Academic essays on the fundamental philosophical issues concerning freedom of communication, published within a series which adopts a theoretical approach to the study of areas of the law, focusing on issues of practical, moral and political concern. Emanating from a Freedom and Communication in Australia workshop, held at the Australian National University in 1993, these essays address the traditional rationale for free speech, political advertising, freedom of information, pornography, racism, and media self-regulation. (BM)

115 Collins, Richard. 'Public service broadcasting and freedom'. *Media Information Australia*, No. 66, November 1992, pp. 3–15.
Though the concept 'public service broadcasting' may have different meanings around the world depending on memory and past experience of services that have gone under that name (for example, in Eastern Europe there has been no experience of independent public service broadcasting as understood in the West), there must evolve a commonly accepted public service ethos to ensure freedom. (BM)

116 Demszky, Gabor. 'Breaking censorship: making peace'. *Media Studies Journal*, Vol. 9, No. 3, Summer 1995, pp. 79–85.
Mayor of Budapest looks at the growing appreciation of free expression in the post-Cold War Eastern Europe and that it is the best guarantee of the demise of censorship. (BM).

117 Europe. Committee of Ministers. *Declaration of freedom of expression and information*. 1982.
'... in the field of the mass media the following objective has to be achieved: the protection of the right of everyone, regardless of frontiers, to express himself, to seek and receive information and ideas, whatever their source, as well as to impart them under conditions set out in Article 10 of the European Convention on Human Rights.' (BM)

118 *European Convention on Human Rights*. Strasbourg: Council of Europe, 1950.
Central treaty instrument within the European Council's framework. Article 10: '1. Everyone has the right to freedom of expression. This right shall include freedom to hold opinions and to receive and impart information and ideas without interference by public authority and regardless of frontiers. This article shall not prevent states from requiring the licensing of broadcasting television or cinema enterprises.' (BM)

119 Goldberg, David. *Free media: report on the CSCE Human Dimension Seminar on Free Media*. Wivenhoe Park, Essex: Human Rights Centre, University of Essex, 1993. (Papers in the theory and practice of human rights, No. 8)

120 Graham-Yooll, Andrew. 'New dawn for press freedom?: a personal and prejudiced opinion'. *Media Studies Journal*, Vol. 7, No. 4, Fall 1993, pp. 21–7.

Former editor of *Index on Censorship* argues that freedoms now available in Eastern Europe after the end of the Cold War, replacing decades of state censorship, have not been tested in many cases, but the press and international human rights community must be alert to defending those freedoms and to a resurgence of censorship. (BM)

121 Haiman, Franklyn S. *Freedom of speech.* Skokie, Illinois: National Textbook Company, 1978. xiv, 221pp. (To protect these rights)
Student reader, sponsored by the Civil Liberties Union, tracing the evolution of the concept of freedom of speech, explores controversies that surround the issue in contemporary America, and provides key excerpts from landmark US Supreme Court decisions and from other historic documents (John Stuart Mill, Thomas Emerson, etc.). (BM)

122 Haiman, Franklyn S. *Speech and law in a free society.* Chicago: University of Chicago Press, 1981. x, 499pp.
The First Amendment to the US Constitution, the bedrock legal instrument which governs communication and freedom of speech in America, is seemingly simple and absolute, but in the 200 years since it was adopted its meaning has universally been regarded as neither simple nor absolute. The author discusses this, arguing that it is not so much whether there should be any legal restraints but where the line should be drawn. Covers other topics such as defamation, privacy, spreading hatred and prejudice, fair trial, lies, government involvement, and secrecy. He seeks a coherent set of principles to resolve the conflict between freedom of expression and the competing interests with which it clashes, and to counteract the tendency of the mass media to a homogenization of ideas. (BM)

123 Helsinki Watch and **The Fund for Free Expression**. *Restricted subjects: freedom of expression in the United Kingdom.* New York: Human Rights Watch, 1991. v, 66pp.
Helsinki Watch was formed in 1978 to monitor and promote observance of domestic and international compliance with the human rights provision of the 1975 Helsinki Accords (European Agreement on Security and Co-operation). The Fund for Free Expression was created in 1975 to monitor and combat censorship around the world. It believes that the UK, despite a strong tradition of protection of freedom of speech, has become increasingly hostile to the freedom of the media to report defence, military policy and intelligence matters. This report examines official secrecy, libel, public order and broadcasting issues, with proposals for reform and recommendations, including the repeal of the Official Secrets Acts. One-sided and full of inaccuracies. (BM)

124 Journalism Quarterly. 'The First Amendment: the third century'. *Journalism Quarterly* (Special Issue), Vol. 69, No. 1, Spring 1992.
The US Constitution and the Bill of Rights are a stone dam against powerful currents trying to limit free expression, and suppress dissent and trim opinions not

regarded as politically correct. Articles in this special issue of *Journalism Quarterly* trace the history of the First Amendment and argue for being ready to protect it in the twenty-first century. (BM)

125 Lanier, Gene D. 'Censorship: the enemy is us'. *Media Studies Journal*, Vol. 6, No. 3, Summer 1992, pp. 81–9.
Censorship of both printed and non-print material continues at an ever-increasing pace in the US according to recent surveys – despite the guarantee of the First Amendment. (BM)

126 Milne, John. 'Different views of press freedom'. *Media Information Australia*, No. 57, August 1990, pp. 43–9.
Comparison of cultural differences between Australia and Indonesia, particularly with regard to press freedom, and their effect on media relations between the two countries. (BM)

127 Plotkin, Adam S. 'The First Amendment and democracy: the challenge of new technology'. *Journal of Mass Media Ethics*, Vol. 11, No. 4, 1996, pp. 236–45.
The author addresses the challenges to government and public in adapting appropriate philosophies to regulation of the new electronic media. Media convergence has rendered inadequate some approaches to regulation but has produced services capable of greater access and availability of information. (BM)

128 Reporters Sans Frontières. *1996 report: freedom of the press throughout the world.* Luton: University of Luton Press, 1996. v, 381pp.
Reporters Sans Frontières, an independent international organization with a secretariat in Paris and national branches in several countries, monitors and publicizes violation of press freedom throughout the world. It has consultative status with the Council of Europe and UNESCO, and encourages the debate on press freedom through seminars and conferences for journalists on professional ethics and on relationships with the law. The annual report is a country-by-country compilation of attacks on press freedom. (BM)

129 Righter, Rosemary. 'UNESCO: declarations, promises and practice'. *Inter-Media*, Vol. 7, No. 1, January 1979, pp. 6–7.
The 'Declaration on the media', finally endorsed in November 1978 by UNESCO's 146 member states, inevitably represents a compromise, and papers over the basic differences between those who think of the media as a vehicle of free speech and diverse sources of information and opinion, and those who view them as tools of state policy. Nonetheless it asserts the freedom of journalists to report and to full access to information. (BM)

130 Robertson, Geoffrey. *Freedom, the individual and the law.* 7th ed. London: Penguin Books, 1993. xxiv, 582pp.

Authoritative guide to citizen's rights, first published in 1963 (then written by Professor Harry Street) and now in its seventh edition, authored by Geoffrey Robertson, a Queen's Counsel who has acted in many landmark cases involving civil liberties in British and Commonwealth courts as well as at the European Court of Human Rights. The scope of the book is confined to law in force in England and Wales, and covers such areas as personal liberty, public protest, privacy, official secrecy, censorship, pornography, blasphemy, the regulation of film, video and broadcasting, and freedom of expression. Issues are illustrated by analysis of notable cases, such as Clive Ponting and the *Belgrano* papers, Martin Scorsese's film *The Last Temptation of Christ*, the publication of Salman Rushdie's *The satanic verses*, and the video *Visions of Ecstasy* on St Teresa of Avila's mystic trances. He concludes that such improvements as have been achieved in the UK have come about largely as a result of the country's obligations under the European Convention on Human Rights, and makes a case for a Bill of Rights. (BM)

131 Scharff, J. Laurent. 'Needed: a first-class First Amendment for television journalism'. *Television Quarterly*, Vol. 25, No. 1, 1990, pp. 83–8.
The First Amendment rights enjoyed by the print media in the US are not all available to broadcasters owing to content regulation by the Federal Communications Commission. Today the greater diversity of expression communicated in many more forms and through many more media outlets than ever before makes a review of the First Amendment necessary. (BM)

132 Schauer, Frederick. *Free speech: a philosophical enquiry*. Cambridge: Cambridge University Press, 1982. xiv, 237pp.
A comprehensive philosophical study of the subject, the book aims to give a thorough account and a secure justification for free speech. The author asks what is it for a society to recognize the right to free speech and assesses the different arguments that have been made for it. He goes on to present his own analysis and defence of an intelligent political principle of free speech. (MP)

133 Schwarz, Ted. *Free speech and false profits: ethics in the media*. Cleveland, Ohio: Pilgrim Press, 1996. 272pp.
The author, a Professor of Journalism and Mass Communications at Northern Arizona University, has written an entertaining and thoughtful, if rather anecdotal book on a wide range of ethical issues that confront the media, including press freedom, invasion of privacy, interviewing techniques, cheque book journalism and pornography. He questions how to regulate the content of television, the press, films, music lyrics and the Internet and World Wide Web, and whose standards and ethics should prevail. He concludes: 'You cannot legislate morality, but you can be a more discerning user of the media, eliminating what is ethically wrong by the choices you make.' Consumers *can* force more ethical standards in the media in part by what they choose to read or view. (BM)

134 Trauth, Denise M. and **Huffman, John L.** 'Heightened judicial scrutiny: a test for the First Amendment rights of children'. *Communications and the Law*, Vol. 2, No. 2, Spring 1980, pp. 39–58.
Discussion of extending the First Amendment rights of adults to children as activist group efforts, such as Action for Children's Television, try to limit types of communication available to children. (BM)

135 United Nations. *Universal Declaration of Human Rights*. New York: United Nations, 1948.
Despite being non-binding on member nations, this declaration has served as a powerful statement of aspiration for the protection of human rights, and its provisions have been incorporated into many constitutions throughout the world. Article 18: 'Everyone has the right to freedom of thought, conscience and religion.' Article 19: 'Everyone has the right to freedom of opinion and expression ... to seek, receive and impart information and ideas through any media and regardless of frontiers.' (BM)

Justifications of free speech

136 Bindman, Geoffrey. 'The case for a Freedom of Expression Act'. *British Journalism Review*, Vol. 5, No. 1, 1994, pp. 30–4.
The British legal establishment has always been deeply suspicious of broad statements of principle; however, the influence of international human rights laws is beginning to change attitudes, and a freedom of expression law is now more likely. (BM)

137 Bunker, Matthew D. 'Lifting the veil: ethics bodies, the citizen critic and the First Amendment'. *Journalism Quarterly*, Vol. 70, No. 1, 1993, pp. 98–107.
Silencing the criticism of judges, lawyers and public officials is not consistent with constitutional guarantees of free speech. (BM)

138 Dworkin, Ronald. *Taking rights seriously*. London: Duckworth, 1977. xv, 293pp.
Philosophical defence of liberalism and a liberal theory of law, though critical of the related theories of legal positivism and utilitarianism, which includes discussion on concepts of liberty and the individual's right to liberty. (BM)

139 Forgan, Liz. 'Trampling over Britain'. *Index on Censorship*, No. 19, June–July 1990, pp. 31–3.
Right to free expression must be enshrined in law to ensure right decisions about press and broadcasting freedom in Britain. (BM)

140 Jenkinson, Clay. 'From Milton to media: information flows in a free society'. *Media & Values*, No. 58, Spring 1992, pp. 3–6.
Historical look at the liberty of the press from early days, with its origins in John Milton's defence of 'free and open encounter' in *Areopagitica* (1644), to the

electronic bulletin boards and desktop publishing of the late twentieth century. (BM)

141 Lichtenberg, Judith (ed.) *Democracy and the mass media.* Cambridge: Cambridge University Press, 1990. xi, 410pp.
The Institute for Philosophy and Public Policy of the University of Maryland established a Working Group on News, Mass Media and Democracy, which discussed moral, philosophical and legal foundations of mass media regulation. All but one of the papers of this collection were written specifically for this group. They provide a wide-ranging discussion of issues raised by regulation of the press. Though with some American bias, this collection contains fundamental discussions by eminent scholars in the field. (MP)

142 Meiklejohn, Alexander. *Free speech and its relation to self-government.* Harper Brothers, 1948; reissued by Kennikat Press, 1972. xiv, 107pp. (Also contained in *Political freedom: the constitutional powers of the people.* New York: Oxford University Press, 1965)
The author argues for an absolute reading of the First Amendment, which he felt had been curtailed by legal judgments of the US Supreme Court and, further, by the Cold War atmosphere of the late 1940s in America. He argues that freedom of speech is closely related to notions of self-government enshrined in the US constitution. Open debate and public deliberation are an intrinsic and indispensable feature of any society premised on the principle of self-government. The First Amendment does not balance intellectual freedom against public safety, 'its great declaration is that intellectual freedom is the bulwark of the public safety'. (MP)

143 Mill, John Stuart. *On liberty.* Various editions. *On liberty and other essays.* Oxford: Oxford University Press, 1991. (Also *On liberty in focus.* London: Routledge, 1991)
A classic work of political theory, this long essay puts forward the 'one very simple principle' that 'the sole end for which mankind are warranted, individually or collectively, in interfering with the liberty of action of any of their number, is self-protection'. Chapter 2 is devoted to the 'liberty of thought and discussion' and here Mill argues strongly that no opinion should be silenced, as they all, the true and the false, have a contribution to make to the pursuit of truth. (MP)

144 Milton, John. *Areopagitica: a speech by Mr John Milton for the liberty of unlicensed printing, 1644.* Various editions.
The earliest comprehensive defence of freedom of speech. Milton argues that the absence of government restrictions on publishing (particularly the absence of licensing) will enable society to locate truth and reject error. His aim was to remove prior restraints on freedom of printing, but not subsequent punishment. (MP)

145 Schudson, Michael. 'Creating public knowledge'. *Media Studies Journal,* Vol. 9, No. 3, Summer 1995, pp. 27–32.
News is a vital democratic function and the power of the press lies in its responsibility to distribute news and information to an informed citizenry. (BM)

Extent of free speech

146 Anawalt, Howard C. 'Is the MacBride Commission's approach compatible with the United States Constitution?' *Journal of Communication,* Vol. 31, No. 4, Autumn 1981, pp. 122–8.
The commitment of the International Commission for the Study of Communication Problems (MacBride Commission) to independence of journalism and the abolition of censorship is largely compatible with the US First Amendment. (BM)

147 Boccardi, L. D. 'Press responsibility: the journalist's view'. *Mass Comm Review,* Vol. 14, No. 3, 1987, pp. 11–13.

148 Bogart, Leo. 'Media and democracy'. *Media Studies Journal,* Vol. 9, No. 3, Summer 1995, pp. 1–10.
The media can be used to undermine democracy as well as enhance it, but it can only serve democracy if those who manage it have a commitment and responsibility to create and maintain it. (BM)

149 Francis, Richard. *What price free speech?* London: BBC, 1982. 16pp.
Paper given by the Director, News and Current Affairs, BBC, to the Law Society Conference in 1982, on the external restrictions on the press – editorial, societal and legal – which to some extent define the limits of free speech. (BM)

150 Gerald, J. Edward. *The social responsibility of the press.* Minneapolis: University of Minnesota Press, 1963. 214pp.
Author considers the mass media as a social institution, rather like political and economic institutions, in serving society by the gathering and disseminating of news. Surveys the nature of the media, newspaper business, publishing, proprietors, press content and freedoms in the US. Speculates on a new form of organization for the discussion and application of ethical standards of journalism to strengthen the media. (BM)

151 Habermas, Jürgen. *The structural foundation of the public sphere: an inquiry into a category of bourgeois society.* Translated by T. Burger from the German. London: Polity Press, 1989.
Perhaps his most accessible work. He focuses on the notion of a bourgeois public sphere as it emerged in Europe, appearing for the first time in seventeenth-century England, although its character and role were transformed by the growth

of capitalism, the rise of the mass media, and the development of the modern state. His concern is with the rise of an informed public in the UK, France and Germany and its decline with the emergence of modern social-welfare states. (MP)

152 Hill of Luton, Lord. *Freedom of the communicators.* London: BBC, 1968. 14pp.
Speech given by the (then) Chairman of the BBC to the Guild of British Newspaper Editors. It stresses the responsibilities, particularly to the public, which come with the freedom to communicate. (BM)

153 Hocking, William Ernest. *Freedom of the press: a framework of principle. A report from the Commission on the Freedom of the Press.* Chicago: University of Chicago Press, 1947. xi, 243pp.
Special study and personal statement by a member of the Hutchins Commission, which argues that freedom of speech and the press is close to the central meaning of liberty, and can be seen as a protector and promoter of the other liberties, and is thus inseparable from the general meaning of freedom in a modern state. But there can be no complete or absolute freedom, there are inevitably some limitations as well as responsibilities. A free press cannot only be on the basis of the rights of free expression of the producers of opinion, though it should be free to all who have something worth saying, but the interests of the reader must also be considered, to be served by independent, substantial and honest information to enable them to take an informed part in the democratic processes. (BM)

154 Lee, Simon. *The cost of free speech.* London: Faber, 1990. x, 149pp.
The author challenges the widely held view, apocryphally ascribed to Voltaire, of defending the right to free speech even though one may not agree with what is said. He affirms that there is a *cost* to free speech through detailed examination of two cases – Salman Rushdie's right to publish *The satanic verses*, and Sinn Fein and the IRA's right to free speech in Northern Ireland issues. The fatwa issued by Ayatollah Khomeini against the publication of *The satanic verses* did result in the assassination of the Belgian Muslim leader Imam Abdullah Al-Ahdal for speaking out against the death threat, and many died in riots over the book in Bombay and Kashmir. Such issues as blasphemy, propaganda, pornography and secrecy are considered, and the author concludes that, despite the often high cost, society must overcome threats to free speech. (BM)

155 Lloyd, Scott. 'A criticism of social responsibility theory: an ethical perspective'. *Journal of Mass Media Ethics*, Vol. 6, No. 4, 1991, pp. 194–209.
The author challenges the moral foundations of the 1947 Hutchins Commission concept of the 'socially responsible press' and proposes an alternative solution. (BM)

156 Merrill, John C. *The dialectic in journalism: toward a responsible use of press freedom.* Baton Rouge: Louisiana State University Press, 1989. vii, 259pp.

'Dialectics', the principle of contradiction (*thesis*, challenged by the opposite, *antithesis*, finally reconciled in *synthesis*), applied to two concepts in journalism – freedom and responsibility – their contradiction, but need for reconciliation. Concludes that though press freedom is vitally important, a viable ethics must control or limit it. (BM)

157 Murphy, Paul L. *The meaning of freedom of speech: First Amendment freedoms from Wilson to F.D.R.* Westport, Connecticut: Greenwood Publishing, 1972. 401pp.
The subtitle gives a better clue to the contents of the book. A scholarly work of history, particularly legal history, concerned with how the First Amendment was interpreted during the 1920s and 1930s. (SM)

158 Ng'Weno, Hilary. 'All freedom is at stake'. *InterMedia*, Vol. 5, No. 1, 1977, pp. 20–3.
The editor of *The Weekly Review* in Nairobi analyses the complex arguments on the role of the press and the media in the international flow of information, but concludes that it is 'the freedom of millions of inhabitants of the Third World that is at stake, not only the freedom of journalists'. (BM)

159 Rees-Mogg, William. 'Bring the press to heel'. *The Times*, 3 November 1994, p. 18.
Former Editor of *The Times* looks at the case of Peter Preston (Editor of *The Guardian*) and the 'cash for questions' affair, and argues the press cannot be above the law. (BM)

160 Tusa, John. 'The problems of freedom and responsibility in broadcasting'. *Terrorism and Political Violence*, No. 2, Winter 1990, pp. 544–53.
Responsibility of broadcasters to help citizens towards freedom of political choice. (BM)

161 United States of America. The Commission on Freedom of the Press. *A free and responsible press.* Chicago: University of Chicago Press, 1947. xii, 139pp.
First suggested by Henry R. Luce of *Time* magazine, this American 'inquiry into the present state and future prospects of the freedom of the press', under its Chairman Robert M. Hutchins, expanded its remit to include all 'the major agencies of mass communication' – radio, newspapers, motion pictures, magazines and books. Its report concluded that 'freedom of speech and press is close to the central meaning of all liberty' and that it was in danger for three reasons: though the importance of the press had increased the proportion of people who could express their opinions and ideas through it had decreased; media owners had not provided a service adequate to the needs of society; and they had engaged in practices contrary to the public interest, which if continued society would need to control and regulate. The report's recommendations cover courses of action from government (including the courts), the press itself and the public, including

constitutional guarantees of freedom of the press, monitoring of increased concentration of press ownership, legislation to protect injured parties as an alternative to the law, the press itself to be accountable, and supportive of innovation and the independence of its journalists. (BM)

162 Warnock, Mary. *The social responsibility of the broadcasting media.* Liverpool: Liverpool University Press, 1985. 17pp. (Eleanor Rathbone Memorial Lecture, 1985)
Distinguished British philosopher argues that the broadcasting media have a social responsibility because of their power to educate and inform. (BM)

Access

163 Ansah, Paul A. V. 'The right to communicate: implications for development'. *Media Development*, Vol. 39, No. 1, 1992, pp. 53–6.
Independence in African countries has not always brought greater freedom or respect for human rights. Many of them require licences to start up newspapers, have state monopoly of broadcasting, impose direct censorship and harass journalists. Author argues that the remedy is for activist groups, trade unions and church communities to mobilize and educate people on their rights. (BM)

164 Black, Charles. 'A human right to broadcast "television speech"?' *Communications Law*, Vol. 1, No. 1, 1996, pp. 8–16.
In the past the right to impart information and ideas by broadcasting has been subject to tighter regulation than has the right to free speech or freedom of expression in print, but the author argues within a UK, US and European context that now that cable technology and 'Internet broadcasting' permit an unlimited number of broadcasters it is possible to construct a supra-legislative right to broadcast. (BM)

165 Fisher, Desmond. 'The achievement of a new right to communicate'. *InterMedia*, Vol. 11, No. 3, May 1983, pp. 36–40.
A new right to communicate would complement the existing rights in communications – freedoms of opinion, of speech, of the press, and from censorship. (BM)

166 Grossman, Lawrence K. 'Television and the future of the First Amendment'. *Television Quarterly*, Vol. 25, No. 4, 1992, pp. 63–71.
Former President of NBC News believes that the challenges facing the First Amendment as it enters its third century, from the explosion of new channels and services and from concentration of media ownership, will be met by keeping government out of content, the press in many different hands, and ensuring citizens have access to information. (BM)

167 Harmon, Mark D. 'Hate groups and cable public access'. *Journal of Mass Media Ethics*, Vol. 6, No. 3, 1991, pp. 146–55.

Broad public debate is a legal and philosophical mandate in the US, so more harm than good would be done in preventing activist groups expressing unpopular or antisocial views on the public access cable channels. (BM)

168 Harms, L. S. and **Richstad, Jim**. 'The "right to communicate": a practical concept'. *InterMedia*, Vol. 5, No. 4, August 1977, pp. 14–16.
The authors chart the evolution of the concept 'the right to communicate', and the present need to put it into practical terms at various levels of society and countries. (BM)

169 Reid, Traciel V. 'An affirmative First Amendment access right'. *Communications and the Law.* Vol. 10, No. 3, June 1988, pp. 39–58.
Recent interpretations of the First Amendment by local courts in the US, favouring the requirement of government officials to comply with citizens' requests for official information and right of access, may lead to more open government. (BM)

170 Whitaker, Brian. *News limited: why you can't read all about it.* London: Minority Press Group, 1981. 176pp.
An account, by one of the journalists involved, of the unsuccessful attempts to establish an 'alternative' newspaper in a provincial city (in this case, Liverpool). (SM)

The right to know

171 Anderson, Rob, Dardenne, Robert and **Killenberg, George M**. 'The American newspaper as the public conversational commons'. *Journal of Mass Media Ethics*, Vol. 11, No. 3, 1996, pp. 159–65.
Academics often dismiss journalism as a force in the public sphere, partly because of journalists' own self-defined role as mere transmitters of the news. Here the authors advocate a philosophy for public journalism in which newspapers become a forum for public debate accessible to all citizens. (BM)

172 Barnett, Anthony. 'Change and effect'. *Index on Censorship*, Vol. 22, Nos. 5–6, May–June 1993, pp. 5–6.
New Right to Know Bill, currently before the British Parliament, has raised the public debate. (BM)

173 Benn, Tony. *The right to know: the case for freedom of information to safeguard our basic liberties.* Nottingham: Institute for Workers' Control, 1978. 15pp. (IWC pamphlet, 62)
Lecture to the British Association for the Advancement of Science by British Member of Parliament and long-time campaigner for a Freedom of Information Act, on open government and greater access for all interests, opinions and faiths to the media. (BM)

174 Birkinshaw, Patrick. *Freedom of information: the law, the practice and the ideal.* London: Weidenfeld & Nicolson, 1988. xxii, 291pp.
Analysis of freedom of information in a British framework, written by Professor of Law at the University of Hull, primarily for students of constitutional, administrative and public law. Though centring on the relationship between government and society and on the topic of provision of information, it inevitably strays into other related topics – freedom of speech, the right to remain silent, freedom of assembly and so on. Overseas experience in the US, Canada, Australia and New Zealand, and briefly with Sweden and France, is detailed. Concludes with proposals for a Freedom of Information Act. (BM)

175 Clurman, Richard M. *Beyond malice: the media's years of reckoning.* New Brunswick, New Jersey: Transaction Publishers, 1988. 306pp.
Former *Time* journalist surveys the often stormy media history of the 1980s in the US, focusing on two major libel cases – General Westmoreland against CBS, and Israel's General Ariel Sharon and *Time*. Both highlighted the troublesome relationship between the media, government and the public, and raised questions about the balance of privacy with the people's right to know. He concludes the relationship would be improved if the news media covered and criticized their own performance and practices with the same determination they report everyone else's, and provision of adequate right of reply. (BM)

176 Cooper, Kent. *The right to know: an exposition of the evils of news suppression and propaganda.* New York: Farrar, Straus & Cudahy, 1956. xiii, 335pp.
Formerly of the Associated Press news service, the author, who coined the slogan 'the right to know', feels there cannot be political freedom without it, and that there is an increasing totalitarian tendency of news suppression and use as political censorship in wartime or propaganda in peacetime. Truthful mutual news exchange would treat citizens honestly by not withholding news from them. (BM)

177 Cross, Harold L. *The people's right to know: legal access to public records and proceedings.* Morningside Heights, New York: Columbia University Press, 1953. xxiv, 405pp.
Report to the American Society of Newspaper Editors, whose Committee on Freedom of Information was concerned that newspapers were allowing the people's right to information to go by default. The author argues that 'public business is the public's business', and newspapers have a responsibility to ensure that right. (BM)

178 Grade, Michael. 'The state of the nation'. *Index on Censorship*, Vol. 23, Nos. 1–2, May–June 1994, pp. 207–13.
Speech, given at the Campaign for Freedom of Information Awards, on the freedom of information being the journalist's right to publish and the public's right to know. (BM)

179 Grant, Myrna Reid. 'Investigative journalism in Britain is under government threat'. *Media Development*, Vol. 39, No. 2, 1992, pp. 26–8.
Because British media have been restrained by various Acts of Parliament, the author argues that citizens are being deprived of basic human rights, particularly over such recent events as the government reaction to the *Death on the Rock* television documentary about the killing of three IRA suspects in Gibraltar. However, British journalists can now have recourse to appeal under various international and European instruments of freedom of expression and information. (BM)

180 Hamelink, Cees J. 'The right to knowledge: a balancing act'. *Media Development*, Vol. 40, No. 2, 1993, pp. 3–7.
Difficulty in finding a proper balance between protection of intellectual property rights ownership and a citizen's right to knowledge. (BM)

181 Meyers, Christopher. 'Justifying journalistic harms: right to know vs. interest in knowing'. *Journal of Mass Media Ethics*, Vol. 8, No. 3, 1993, pp. 133–46.
In obtaining a news story, journalists must weigh up the possible harm caused to others with the greater moral purpose of satisfying the public's right to know, and not confuse having a need to know with just having a curiosity in knowing. (BM)

182 *The right to know: Freedom of information*, by Floyd Abrams, *Media law reform – beyond Shangri-la*, by Michael Kirby, *The right to know*, by Lord Scarman. London: Granada Publishing, 1985. 79pp. (Granada Guildhall Lectures, 1985)
Three lectures on aspects of freedom of information. Lord Scarman argues that in the UK confusion and lack of principle have rendered the law obscure, and at times seemingly arbitrary, so that legislation is now needed to provide a sound basis of principle to safeguard the conflicting interests of confidentiality, privacy and the accessibility of information, and that these rights are as powerfully protected by the judicial system as are liberty of person and freedom of speech. (BM)

183 Wicker, Tom. *The right to know: an unending battle*. Tucson: University of Arizona, 1984. 13pp.
Speech by the Associate Editor of the *New York Times*, accepting the University of Arizona's annual John Peter Zenger Award for Freedom of Press and the People's Right to Know in 1984, in which he champions the role of a free press in its dedication to the goal of an informed public. (BM)

184 Zerbinos, Eugenia. 'The right to know: whose right and whose duty'. *Communications and the Law*, Vol. 4, No. 1, Winter 1982, pp. 233–49.
Addresses the question whether the right to know is a fundamental right derived directly from the US Constitution or stems from a broader societal goal, to determine the press role in fulfilling the right to know. (BM)

Accountability

185 Aucoin, James. 'Implications of audience ethics for the mass communicator'. *Journal of Mass Media Ethics*, Vol. 11, No. 2, 1996, pp. 69–81.
'Audience ethics' means that audiences have responsibilities as well as the media producers, but it also assumes collective accountability is possible and a theory of mass communication that assumes an active audience, and a role for audience members. (BM)

186 Dee, Juliet Lushbough. 'Media accountability for real-life violence: a case of negligence or free speech?' *Journal of Communication*, Vol. 37, No. 2, Spring 1987, pp. 106–38.
Blaming the media has been one of many attempts to find direct and therefore remediable solutions to the problems of violence in society, but this review of fifteen US court decisions on cases in which a child or young adult was the victim of violence said to be induced by the media suggests that courts are reluctant to hold media organizations accountable for inciting the violent acts of individuals. (BM)

187 Dennis, Everette E., Gillmor, Donald M. and **Glasser, Theodore L.** (eds.) *Media freedom and accountability*. New York: Greenwood Press, 1989. x, 210pp. (Contributions to the study of mass media and communications, 14)
The means of people talking back to the media have improved in some ways, but the death of the American National News Council in 1984 would suggest that journalists and broadcasters do not want an organized system of feedback. However, there is still a need for forms of accountability that do not damage the freedom of the press. This collection of articles by distinguished writers on media ethics, including Clifford G. Christians and John C. Merrill, addresses the problems of media freedom and accountability, covering regulation, self-regulation and codes of ethics in an American context. (BM)

188 Glasser, Theodore L. and **Craft, Stephanie**. 'Public journalism and the prospects for press accountability'. *Journal of Mass Media Ethics*, Vol. 11, No. 3, 1996, pp. 152–8.
Many journalists, while embracing the principles of public journalism, fail to recognize that the press is bound by the same standards of accountability and openness to public scrutiny as other public institutions. One improvement the authors suggest is for the press to account for itself on the editorial page – to identify, explain and defend the newspapers' policies and priorities. (BM)

189 Hannaford, Peter. *Talking back to the media*. New York: Facts on File, 1986. v, 184pp.
An anecdotal work which has some value in illustrating the mounting tide of criticism of the lack of responsibility of the American media. (SM)

190 Hazell, Robert. 'Freedom of information: the implications of the ombudsman'. *Public Administration*, Vol. 73, No. 2, Summer 1995, pp. 263–70.
Freedom of information, once thought by the British government to be incompatible with the Westminster system of ministerial accountability to Parliament, may now have a code of practice to be policed by the ombudsman. (BM)

191 Johnson, Nicholas. *How to talk back to your television set*. Boston: Little, Brown, 1967. ix, 278pp.
Former member of the Federal Communications Commission is critical of American television, and the Commission as a regulator, and urges reform through the encouragement of the ordinary citizen (both as an individual and through activist groups) to express their views and complaints, and try to influence or challenge hearings and regulatory decisions. (BM)

192 Porter, Vincent and **Gabriel, Martin**. 'A right too far: ten obstacles to the exercise of a right to reply to transfrontier television broadcasts'. *Communications Law*, Vol. 1, No. 1, 1996, pp. 2–7.
The requirement (in the Council of Europe Convention on Transfrontier Television and the European Union 'Television Without Frontiers' Directive) for European Union member states to make provision for a right of reply, or an equivalent remedy, to domestically licensed television broadcasts, is less likely to provide the ordinary citizen with the chance to set the record straight concerning television reportage, than to help the wealthy transnational corporations with sophisticated legal departments. (BM)

193 Singer, Jane B. 'Virtual anonymity: online accountability and the virtuous virtual journalist'. *Journal of Mass Media Ethics*, Vol. 11, No. 2, 1996, pp. 95–106.
Explores the ethical implications and concerns of electronic publishing and communication, which now offer alternatives to traditional methods of dissemination, and the role and accountability of the journalist in this computer-mediated world. (BM)

Government and the media

194 Buchan, Norman and **Sumner, Tricia**. *Glasnost in Britain?: against censorship and in defence of the word*. London: Macmillan, 1989. xiv, 190pp.
Anthology of essays by writers covering a wide spectrum of political and social ideas, though predominantly left-wing, who hold the opinion that censorship of the written and spoken word in the UK, direct and indirect, has increased in recent years. Issues covered include: Peter Fiddick on government confrontation with broadcasters in the 1980s; Steven Barnett on the dangers to public service broadcasting from the proliferation of channels and uncontrolled commercial interests; Maurice Frankel on the right to know and freedom of information; and

barrister Heather Rogers on issues raised by government attempts to suppress Peter Wright's *Spycatcher*. (BM)

195 Cockerell, Michael, Hennessy, Peter and **Walker, David**. *Sources close to the Prime Minister: inside the hidden world of the news manipulators*. London: Macmillan, 1984. 255pp.
Three journalists argue that British governments have consistently sought to manipulate the news, sometimes to the point of 'disinformation'. This has usually been done, the authors argue, through the system of informal, unattributable briefings institutionalized in the UK as 'the lobby system'. (SM)

196 Gottschalk, Jack A. '"Consistent with security ...": a history of American military press censorship'. *Communications and the Law*, Vol. 5, No. 3, Summer 1983, pp. 35–52.
The media and the public must remain determined both to inform and to be informed, but must also accept that national security interests may still require use of censorship by military and civil authorities. (BM)

197 Kaplar, Richard T. and **Maines, Patrick D**. *The government factor: undermining journalistic ethics in the information age*. Washington, DC: Cato Institute, 1995. xi, 101pp.
The authors, from the Media Institute in Washington, argue that in the US the government has hindered the development of journalistic ethics through intervention of laws and communications policy, which have had the effect of substituting government ethics for private ethics, and by arresting the development of new media that would be more hospitable to ethical conduct. (BM)

198 Leigh, David. *The frontiers of secrecy: closed government in Britain*. London: Junction Books, 1980. x, 291pp.
Self-described as a polemic against secrecy in the UK, this book makes a strong case for free access to many internal official documents. The author surveys information control by Parliament, government and civil service, such issues as Official Secrets Acts, libel, privacy and national security, and makes a case for a Freedom of Information Act. (BM)

199 Long, Gerald. 'Governments and the journalist'. *InterMedia*, Vol. 4, No. 5, October 1976, pp. 8–10.
Managing Director of Reuters discusses the responsibility of individual journalists in a free and democratic society. (BM)

200 Merrett, Christopher. *A culture of censorship: secrecy and intellectual repression in South Africa*. Cape Town: David Phillip, 1995; Macon, Georgia: Mercer University Press, 1995. xv, 296pp.

This book considers state-initiated political censorship, secrecy and intellectual oppression in South Africa from colonial times to 1994. Almost inevitably South Africans are taking this legacy, an inherited lack of openness and accountability, into the post-apartheid future, despite the era of glasnost initiated by President de Klerk's speech in 1990, and the first fully democratic elections of 1994. (BM)

201 Neil, Andrew and **Whitaker, Anthony**. 'Spycatcher's lessons for press and law'. *The Times*, 27 November 1991, p. 15.

Lessons to be learnt from the Strasbourg ruling against the UK government ban on *Spycatcher*, Peter Wright's revelations about British espionage activities. (BM)

202 Ponting, Clive. *The right to know: the inside story of the Belgrano affair*. London: Sphere, 1985. 214pp.

Clive Ponting was the British civil servant tried at the Old Bailey in 1985, under the Official Secrets Act, for 'disclosing official information without authority' by passing confidential government documents, about the sinking of the Argentinian cruiser *General Belgrano* in May 1982 during the Falklands conflict, to an opposition Member of Parliament for use in a parliamentary debate. The first part of his book covers the general topic of official secrecy, the Official Secrets Act and the blocking of any reform of it, based on his researches into the subject in preparing his defence for the trial. The second part gives a detailed account of the background to, and circumstances of, the sinking of the *Belgrano*, his decision to make public 'secret' documents, and a diary of the trial. (BM)

203 Ponting, Clive. *Secrecy in Britain*. Oxford: Basil Blackwell, 1990. viii, 87pp. (Historical Association studies)

In this book Clive Ponting studies the growth of secrecy in government, the media and everyday life in the UK. He examines the passing of the Official Secrets Acts and some of the famous prosecutions under them, including those of Compton Mackenzie, the Richard Crossman diaries, Peter Wright for *Spycatcher* and his own case. Chronology. Bibliography. (BM)

204 Raboy, Marc, and **Dagenais, Bernard**. *Media, crisis and democracy: mass communication and the disruption of social order*. London: Sage, 1992. viii, 199pp. (Media, culture and society series)

Papers by media academics and practitioners, including George Gerbner, Douglas Kellner and John Keane, from an international conference on 'Media and Crisis' held at Laval University, Quebec, in 1990. They examine the relationship between the media and the state in periods of crisis, instancing the Gulf War, terrorism and Eastern Europe. Mustapha Masmoudi, a member of the UNESCO MacBride Commission and one of the architects of the New World Information and Communication Order, discusses media ethics in a period of crisis, and proposes a code of conduct for journalists in their role of informing the public without reservation or preconception. (BM)

205 Schudson, Michael. *The power of news*. Cambridge, Massachusetts: Harvard University Press, 1995. 269pp.
Watergate was not the beginning of an adversarial relationship between government and the press in the US – that was probably Vietnam – but it was crucial in the increase in investigative reporting. The author, Professor of Communications and Sociology at the University of California, San Diego, explodes certain myths about media power, and analyses the production and reception of the news, in particular the evolution and authenticity of the news interview. (BM)

206 Tusa, John. 'Fourth estate or fifth column?: media, the government and the state'. *Combroad*, Issue 94, January–March 1992, pp. 1–5.
Address to the Nigerian Institute of International Affairs by the Managing Director of the BBC World Service, on the relationship between the press and the state, which concludes that a free and independent press able to criticize government and governments able to react rationally to such criticism are evidence of a civilized state. He rejects the notion of two different codes of journalistic ethics – a higher set of editorial standards for the developed world, and looser discipline for developing nations. (BM)

207 Wright, Peter. *Spycatcher: the candid autobiography of a senior intelligence officer*. New York: Viking, 1987. 392pp.
These reminiscences of a British secret service agent are more remarkable for the controversy they caused than for the actual content. He had access to many secrets in his time, knew many of the key British spies of the Cold War era (Guy Burgess, Donald Maclean, Kim Philby and Anthony Blunt), and does shed light on British relations with the USSR and the KGB, Suez and many other security issues. However, it is the action of the UK government in trying to ban publication, the subsequent ruling from Strasbourg against the ban, and the issues raised of confidentiality and free speech that make the book a defining event in government–media relations. (BM)

Internal threats

208 Alali, A. Odasuo and **Eke, Kenoye Kelvin**. *Media coverage of terrorism: methods of diffusion*. Newbury Park, California: Sage Publications, 1991. 148pp. (Sage focus editions)
A proliferation of terrorist incidents in the 1970s and 1980s has resulted in concern over the role of the media in the diffusion of news and information on terrorism, particularly the question of whether or not media coverage has a contagious effect. As Mrs Thatcher once said: does terrorism thrive on the 'oxygen of publicity'? This, and other issues such as journalists' role in the coverage of terrorist events, the portrayal of the victims of terrorism, and examination of the TWA hostage crisis in 1985 and the IRA on British television, are covered by these essays by American media academics. (BM)

209 Article 19. *No comment: censorship, secrecy and the Irish troubles*. London: Article 19 International Centre Against Censorship, 1989. vi, 110pp.

Report on the restrictions on media coverage of Northern Ireland. On 19 October 1988 the British government invoked a power of control over the media few were aware existed, by issuing a notice to the BBC and the Independent Broadcasting Authority banning the broadcast of any spoken words by members of paramilitary organizations; a ban was predated in the Republic of Ireland by an even more restrictive ban on interviews, or reports of interviews. This report questions the validity and effectiveness of government attempts to impose censorship, and argues that it only impedes debate and delays a possible resolution of the conflict. (BM)

210 Bassiouni, M. Cherif. 'Media coverage of terrorism: the law and the public'. *Journal of Communication*, Vol. 32, No. 2, Spring 1982, pp. 128–43.

Professor of Law at De Paul University wonders whether the public's right to know interferes with their protection, and examines US First Amendment issues. Proposals for media self-regulation include: the delaying of reporting details that could inflame an incident; balanced reporting; co-operating with the police; non-involvement in the negotiation process; and education of public and terrorists in the undesirability of resorting to violence. (BM)

211 Bolton, Roger. *Death on the Rock, and other stories*. London: W. H. Allen, 1990. x, 318pp.

Roger Bolton edited BBC current affairs programmes, *Tonight*, *Panorama* and *Nationwide*, before joining Thames Television in 1986 to edit *This Week*. His *Death on the Rock* documentary in the *This Week* series about the shooting of three alleged IRA terrorists on Gibraltar, shown on ITV on 28 April 1988, was one of the most controversial programmes of the 1980s. It brought the broadcasters, the Independent Broadcasting Authority and Thames Television, into unprecedented conflict with government ministers, and raised crucial questions about the relationship between government and an independent television industry. An invaluable insider's view of the role of investigative television journalism in a free society. (BM)

212 Butler, David. *The trouble with reporting Northern Ireland: the British state, the broadcast media and nonfictional representation of the conflict*. Aldershot: Avebury, 1995. vii, 170pp.

Historical survey of broadcasting in Northern Ireland, and examination of the various influences shaping the non-fictional representation of the conflict in Ulster and the seemingly irreconcilable aspirations of Irish nationalism and Ulster unionism. (BM)

213 Campaign for Free Speech on Ireland. *The British media and Ireland – truth: the first casualty*. London: Campaign for Free Speech on Ireland, 1978. 56pp.

Campaigning pamphlet containing a dossier of articles, extracts from newspapers, books and broadcasts on the media coverage of the Northern Ireland situation, calling for it to be put it in context, with events clearly explained and solutions for the future, and, above all, calling for an end to censorship of reporting the troubles. (BM)

214 Cathcart, Rex. *The most contrary region: the BBC in Northern Ireland 1924–84.* Belfast: Blackstaff Press, 1984. ix, 306pp.

This account of the BBC in Northern Ireland is a kind of lengthy case study. A broadcasting organization which has long prided itself on its essential liberalism and its sturdy independence has had to live in the midst of violence. Both those who argue for complete freedom of information, and those who fear that the media can exacerbate tense situations, will find material of interest. Professor Cathcart is an academic, a broadcaster, and for some time a senior broadcasting executive. The book assumes, perhaps, rather too much knowledge of Ulster politics in the reader, but it does illustrate vividly some of the ethical dilemmas of the media and relations between media and government. (SM)

215 Clutterbuck, Richard. *The future of political violence: destabilization, disorder and terrorism.* London: Macmillan, 1986. xv, 206pp. (RUSI defence studies)

An account of two conferences held under the auspices of the Royal United Services Institute and Control Risks Ltd. Part of the book consists of regional surveys and assessments of terrorism, but some of the papers consider more general issues of civil rights in a liberal society at risk, and the role and responsibility of the media. Bibliography. (SM)

216 Clutterbuck, Richard. *The media and political violence.* 2nd ed. London: Macmillan, 1983. xlv, 191pp.

Richard Clutterbuck is one of the few modern representatives of the soldier-scholar, a regular army officer who has been on the staff of Exeter University. The result is a refreshing directness coupled with a concern for evidence, though this is not an academic work (at least in the conventional sense). It is based largely on British case studies: it considers, albeit briefly, the importance of television documentaries and drama. The central question is how in a liberal democracy the media can ensure that they do not become the allies of terrorism and political violence. Not everyone will agree with his proposed solutions, but the book offers a number of new thoughts. (SM)

217 Curtis, Liz and Jempson, Mike. *Interference on the airwaves: Ireland, the media and the Broadcasting Ban.* London: Campaign for Press and Broadcasting Freedom, 1993. 92pp.

Part One of this campaigning tract looks at the events leading to the introduction of the British government's 'Broadcasting Ban' in 1988, reactions to it, and its subsequent effect on media reportage from Ireland; it firmly supports journalists' freedom to report and the public's right to know. Part Two is a catalogue of radio and television programmes on Northern Ireland that had been delayed, censored or banned since 1959. (BM)

218 Grant, Myrna Reid. 'Gibraltar killings: British media ethics'. *Journal of Mass Media Ethics.* Vol. 7, No. 1, 1992, pp. 31–40.
In the author's view, the controversial 1988 British television documentary *Death on the Rock*, about the killing of three IRA members by the Special Air Service (SAS) in Gibraltar, provided a clear example of government attempts at media control using the various legislative instruments of restraint, as well as direct coercion, and raised serious issues of the basic rights of freedom of expression and information, and the need to embody them in a formal Bill of Rights for the UK. (BM)

219 Kelly, Tom. *Politics, terrorism and the media in Northern Ireland: the reporter's role in a polarised society.* London: British Petroleum, 1986. 22pp.
Discussion paper for the 1986 BP Press Fellowship at Wolfson College, Cambridge, arguing for the media taking on the role of telling people what is happening in Northern Ireland, of providing an objective account because the accounts provided by the parties involved will be (in varying degrees) selective and self-interested. (BM)

220 Miller, Abraham H. (ed.) *Terrorism, the media and the law.* Dobbs Ferry, New York: Transnational Publishers, 1982. xi, 221pp.
Project undertaken under contract from the National Institute of Justice, the US Department of Justice, and based on revised versions of some papers presented at an earlier conference at De Paul University. Contributors include journalists, lawyers, psychologists, police, and range widely over legal and ethical issues for the media in dealing with terrorism. One of the appendices reprints some current guidelines of newspapers and government agencies. Extensive bibliography. (SM)

221 Murdock, Graham. 'Patrolling the Border: British broadcasting and the Irish question in the 1980s'. *Journal of Communication*, Vol. 41, No. 4, Autumn 1991, pp. 104–15.
Director of Communications and Media Studies at Loughborough University surveys the difficult relationship between the UK government and broadcasters in reporting Northern Ireland, concludes that repealing the Broadcasting Ban on direct broadcasts by members of paramilitary organizations and the introduction of a Freedom of Information Act would aid British democracy and its ability to resolve the Irish question. (BM)

222 Paletz, David L. and **Schmid, Alex P**. *Terrorism and the media.* Newbury Park, California: Sage, 1992. viii, 250pp.
Collection of papers, originating from the 'Towards a European response to terrorism' conference held in Leiden in 1989, on the relationship between

insurgent terrorism (social-revolutionary, separatist and single issue terrorism aimed at the state) and the media. (BM)

223 Schlesinger, Philip, Murdock, Graham and **Elliott, Philip**. *Televising 'terrorism': political violence in popular culture.* London: Comedia, 1983. vii, 183pp.
Three academics consider the contradictory accusations that television can promote the cause of terrorist violence, and that the established media deny access to alternative voices. They arrive at the conclusion that public service television in the UK, despite occasional lapses from its own high standards, deserves neither criticism. (SM)

224 Shanor, Donald R. 'The "hundred flowers" of Tiananmen Square'. *Gannett Center Journal*, Vol. 3, No. 4, Fall 1989, pp. 128–36.
The violent suppression of dissent in Tiananmen Square in 1989 shows that despite embracing free market philosophy China will still not allow free speech, and the Communist Party maintains a strict control on what information must be kept secret and what may be published. (BM)

225 Wardlaw, Grant. 'Terrorism and the media: a symbiotic relationship'. *Media Information Australia*, No. 22, November 1981, pp. 49–55.
Research criminologist with the Institute of Criminology in Canberra examines the conflict of interest in reporting terrorism between the public's right to know, and the need to deny the terrorist access to the media for their own purposes, and concludes the media must adopt a more ethical stance. (BM)

226 Windlesham, Lord and **Rampton, Richard**. *The Windlesham/Rampton report on Death on the Rock.* London: Faber, 1989. viii, 145pp.
The showing of the documentary *Death on the Rock*, in the *This Week* series, on 28 April 1988, against the government's wishes, led to widespread controversy and the establishing of an independent inquiry. Lord Windlesham, a former government minister and broadcasting administrator, and Richard Rampton, a leading barrister with experience in defamation and media law, were commissioned (by the producing company Thames Television) to investigate the circumstances of the making of the programme about the shooting of three IRA terrorists in Gibraltar. The inquiry found it a thorough and vividly presented programme even though it divided public opinion, but then 'diverse values freely expressed are unmistakable marks of a free society'. (BM)

External threats

227 Adams, Valerie. *The media and the Falklands campaign.* London: Macmillan, 1986. x, 224pp.
The facilities for reporting the Falklands conflict were deplorable. This was due in part to simple inefficiency, in part to the historic antipathy between the armed

forces and the media, and in part to the assumed consequences of the freedom with which the media reported the Vietnam War. After the close of hostilities and the *Report of a Study Group on Censorship* (the Beach Report) the Ministry of Defence commissioned academic studies. This is a well-researched study by Valerie Adams, of the Department of War Studies at King's College London, though not everyone would accept her central focus on the media's use of armchair strategists to speculate on the probable course of the conflict. Chronology. Bibliography. (SM)

228 Arno, Andrew and **Dissanayake, Wimal** (eds.) *The news media in national and international conflict.* Boulder, Colorado: Westview Press, 1984. xii, 250pp.

The core of this book is a series of case studies ranging through India, Pakistan, China, Hong Kong and Sri Lanka, but dominated by the American obsession with Iran. But its main interest may lie in a group of more general speculative papers on news as conflict: on 'salvation through communication', which dares to advance the thesis that less communication may sometimes be better; and one which proposes an international code of ethics for the media. There are some original ideas in this volume but, sadly, much of it is written in the most opaque jargon. Bibliographies. (SM)

229 Article 19. *Forging war: the media in Serbia, Croatia and Bosnia-Hercegovina.* London: Article 19 International Centre Against Censorship, 1994. xiv, 272pp.

Detailed study of the role of the media in the war in three of the republics of the former Yugoslavia, looking at the way in which their governments were controlling and using the media as an instrument of war. It focuses on two aspects: the relationship between the media and government both before and during the war; and the 'messages' carried by the media. For both the warring sides and the peacekeepers, the media were a strategic concern; one incidental benefit of the presence of television cameras was the recording of agreements where no other record might be possible. This conflict provides a casebook example of 'truth being the first casualty of war' with abuse of the media by all sides through disinformation, distortion and propaganda. Article 19, an international human rights organization, takes its name and purpose from Article 19 of the Universal Declaration of Human Rights supporting freedom of opinion and expression. (BM)

230 Bolling, Landrum R. (ed.) *Reporters under fire: US media coverage of conflicts in the Lebanon and Central America.* Boulder, Colorado: Westview Press, 1985. xvi, 155pp.

Edited account of seminars organized by the Institute for the Study of Diplomacy at Georgetown University, at which participants were active journalists and retired diplomats. The debate is largely at the anecdotal level, and the perspective is specifically American. Nevertheless, in the course of much breast-beating, some ethical problems do emerge. (SM)

231 Cohen, Yoel. *Media diplomacy: the Foreign Office in the mass communications age.* London: Frank Cass, 1986. x, 197pp.
American researchers were the first to point out that, in the continuing crises in the Middle East, governments had frequently made use of the media to signal diplomatic moves. In this quiet, scholarly and likeable book an Israeli academic shows that the media have played an important role in diplomacy for over a century. Whilst there is little that is startlingly new, the perspective is very different from more conventional studies of the media. It raises, often indirectly, major ethical questions about media responsibility. As the subtitle implies the book is almost entirely concentrated on British diplomacy. Bibliography. (SM)

232 Glasgow University Media Group. *War and peace news.* Milton Keynes: Open University Press, 1985. 355pp.
This book came about almost by accident: a proposed study of media coverage of defence and disarmament issues was overtaken by the Falklands conflict. The resulting book is, therefore, in two sections. It follows the familiar pattern of the Group's work, and pays particular attention to reaction within the BBC to outside influences and criticism. As with their other books it tends to illustrate the old dictum that people go to the media for the reinforcement of their own prejudices: the Group obviously wishes that more people shared their views. (SM)

233 Great Britain. Parliament. House of Commons. *First report from the Defence Committee: the handling of the press and public information during the Falklands conflict.* (Session 1982–83: HC 17-I, 17-II) London: HMSO, 1982.
Among the conclusions of this British Parliamentary Select Committee post-mortem on the media coverage of the Falklands conflict were that in future UK governments should not rely on the sense of fairness and objectivity of the world's media, but should appreciate the importance of propaganda. (BM)

234 Great Britain. Parliament. House of Commons. *Report from the Defence Committee ... The D-Notice system.* (Session 1979–80: HC 773, HC 640-I-v) London: HMSO, 1980.
British Parliamentary Select Committee report on the 'D-notice' system of voluntary self-censorship by the press and broadcasters in reporting defence matters. (BM)

235 Hallin, Daniel C. *The 'uncensored war': the media and Vietnam.* New York: Oxford University Press, 1986. viii, 285pp.
The unfortunate thing about this book is its title, which may give the impression that it is simply yet another study of how Vietnam was reported. In fact, though it is a detailed and scholarly study of that coverage, it uses Vietnam as an extended case study in the growing rift between government and the media in the US, a

development which can be paralleled elsewhere in Western society. One basic argument of the book is the contradiction inherent in two claims by the media: on the one hand to 'objectivity' but on the other a strengthening of the concept of 'the fourth estate'. The work also considers the consequences of the growth of 'professionalism' in journalism, and the use governments seek to make of the media. An important work. Bibliography. (SM)

236 Hampson, Françoise J. *Incitement and the media: responsibility of and for the media in the conflicts in the former Yugoslavia.* Wivenhoe Park, Essex: Human Right Centre, University of Essex, 1993. (Papers in the theory and practice of humans rights, No. 3)

237 Harris, Robert. *Gotcha!: the media, the government and the Falklands crisis.* London: Faber & Faber, 1983. 158pp.

A journalist's account of the way the Falklands conflict was reported in the UK, and the internecine quarrels within government, the armed forces and the media, and between the three parties. Though strident and overstated, the book does face seriously the problems of freedom of information in wartime – in particular the fear that the media's demands to know more can aid the enemy or cause casualties. (SM)

238 Knightley, Phillip. *The first casualty: the war correspondent as hero, propagandist and myth maker from the Crimea to Vietnam.* London: André Deutsch, 1975. 465pp.

According to Senator Hiram Johnson in 1917, 'the first casualty when war comes is truth'. This history of war reporting begins with William Howard Russell, according to his epitaph in St Paul's Cathedral 'the first and greatest war correspondent', whose despatches from the Crimea are considered to be the beginnings of war reportage. Through many theatres of war worldwide since then – the American Civil War, the Boer War, two world wars, Spain, Algeria, Korea and Vietnam – the author chronicles the work of many correspondents, including Rudyard Kipling, Sir Winston Churchill, John Reed, Ernest Hemingway and Donald McCullin. He covers press and, latterly, film and broadcasting, looking at front-line reporting, censorship and wartime propaganda. (BM)

239 Masterman, Len. *Television and the bombing of Libya: an independent analysis.* Elston, Newark: MK Media Press, 1987. 24pp.

A slight paper by an influential British media academic analysing a BBC news bulletin to which the Chairman of the British governing Conservative Party objected, on the grounds of bias. His action in writing to the Chairman of the BBC was widely seen as an indirect attempt to assert government influence over the content of BBC programmes. In retrospect, it seems more likely to have been a temporary aberration. (SM)

240 Dennis, Everette E. and others. *The media at war: the press and the Persian Gulf conflict. A report of the Gannett Foundation.* New York: Gannett Media Center, 1991. xii, 116pp.
Analysis and evaluation of the news media coverage of the Gulf War, examining press censorship, journalists covering the conflict, news media technology, media and editorial, and public opinion. Among the findings were that the military placed considerable restriction on the media, particularly on access to the war zone (in contrast to Vietnam), and the military used the media not only to promulgate its own policies but also to spread misinformation to the Iraqis. (BM)

241 Mercer, Derrik, Mungham, Geoff and **Williams, Kevin.** *The fog of war: the media on the battlefield.* London: Heinemann, 1987.

242 Morrison, David and **Tumber, Howard.** *Journalists at war: the dynamics of news reporting during the Falklands conflict.* London: Sage, 1988. xiv, 370pp.
Examination of journalism in wartime through interviews with reporters who sailed with the Task Force to cover the Falklands conflict in the South Atlantic. It shows how the professional codes and established standards of accuracy to which reporters work were tested to the limits, as was the commonly accepted balance between the public's right to know and a government's legitimate right to withhold information on the grounds that its release might endanger its nationals' lives or jeopardize the security of the military campaign. As well as issues of censorship and the media's relationship with the government and military, it surveys public opinion on the coverage of the conflict and attitude to the independence of the media. (BM)

243 Newhagen, John E. 'The relationship between censorship and the emotional and critical tone of television news coverage of the Persian Gulf War'. *Journalism Quarterly*, Vol. 71, No. 1, Spring 1994, pp. 32–42.
Content analysis of over 400 news stories during the Gulf War looking at censorship and the use of disclaimers found that both Iraq and the US exercised tight control on news and that disclaimers curiously did not work. (BM)

244 O'Heffernan, Patrick. 'Television and the security of nations: learning from the Gulf War'. *Television Quarterly*, Vol. 25, No. 2, 1991, pp. 5–10.
Television and news organizations were manipulated by the US military, Department of State and the White House during the Gulf War. In this examination of the media–military relationship the author concludes that it will only improve in future if a new international co-ordinating and consultative body is established to monitor the media–security relationships, formulate guidelines and keep all sides informed, most importantly the emerging global audience. (BM)

245 Pilger, John. 'Myth-makers of the Gulf War'. *The Guardian*, 7 January 1991, p. 21.

British broadcaster and journalist challenges assumptions about the Gulf War, and discusses journalists' responsibility for truthful reporting. (BM)

246 Putnam, John. 'Britannia rules the airwaves'. *Television Quarterly*, Vol. 19, No. 3, 1982, pp. 21–5.
American journalist in London examines the difficult relationship between the media and the British government during the Falklands conflict. (BM)

247 Royle, Trevor. *War report: the war correspondent's view of battle from the Crimea to the Falklands.* [Edinburgh]: Mainstream Publishing, 1987. 240pp.
Less a history of war reporting, than a study of six leading correspondents, ranging from William Howard Russell for *The Times* in the Crimea, through Edgar Wallace for the *Daily Mail* on the Boer War, up to Chester Wilmot for ABC in the Second World War and James Cameron in Korea, chronicling the various problems they all faced covering wars far away from the home base, dealing with the vagaries of editorial control and the uncertainties of military or political censorship. (BM)

248 Simic, Predrag. 'Instant publicity and foreign policy'. *Media Studies Journal*, Vol. 7, No. 4, Fall 1993, pp. 149–59.
The outbreak of war in the former Yugoslavia in 1991 was the first serious crisis in Europe after the end of the Cold War, and confronted by the complexities of the Balkan War the international press, without any clear guidance from their governments on how to view the situation or any truly viable solutions, reported it in a biased way and were manipulated by the warring parties in the Bosnia conflict. (BM)

249 Stewart, Ian and **Carruthers, Susan L.** *War, culture and the media: representations of the military in twentieth-century Britain.* Trowbridge, Wiltshire: Flicks Books, 1996. vi, 202pp. (Studies in war and film, 3)
Essays by academic staff of the Royal Miltary Academy at Sandhurst, and others, which address presentation of war and the military by film makers, broadcasters and the press. It covers the practical and political aspects of bringing reports of armed conflict to the screens, the control and management of information (with particular reference to the Falklands conflict and the Gulf War), fairness in representation of British military and the enemy, and the ethics of reporting terrorism. (BM)

250 Traber, Michael and **Davies, Ann.** 'Ethics of war reporting'. *Media Development* (Special Issue), October 1991, pp. 7–10.
War reporting accentuates the ethical dimensions of public communications. The responsibility of journalists is to ensure not only that the public is informed but also that they *understand*. One lesson from the Gulf War is that ethics of journalism cannot now be done on an ad hoc basis, and left until the next war, otherwise government and the military will make the rules again. (BM)

Economic pressures

Media ownership

251 Bagdikian, Ben H. *The media monopoly.* 5th ed. Boston: Beacon, 1997. xlix, 289pp.
Warning about the dangers of increasing concentration of control over the American media, and the insidious power which comes from unchallenged dominance over public information. The author sees a possible solution in the rising standards of ethics and competence of trained professionals in news and public affairs, and their challenging the narrow and self-interested direction of their work by the media owners. (BM)

252 Cohen, Roger. 'The ethics of cross-ownership: the example of Silvio Berlusconi in Italy'. *Gannett Center Journal*, Vol. 4, No. 2, Spring 1990, pp. 111–19.
The case of Italian media magnate Silvio Berlusconi, who has become a kind of paradigm of this age of growing media concentration, has lessons for the US. It illustrates that the quality of news and information can be undermined by the growth of conglomerates, and the constraint that can be placed on journalistic activity, particularly investigative reporting, by controlling too large a proportion of the advertising. (BM)

253 Curran, James. 'Press freedom as a property right: the crisis of press legitimacy'. *Media, Culture and Society*, Vol. 1, No. 1, January 1979, pp. 59–82.
Economic transformation of the British press during the post-war period has called into question the liberal theory of a free press by rendering unconvincing the traditional view of the free market on which it is based. The author discusses the issues through examination of the findings of the Royal Commissions on the Press, and various other inquiries. (BM)

254 Evans, Harold. *Good times, bad times.* 3rd ed. London: Phoenix (Orion Books), 1994. xxviii, 498pp.
After a distinguished career as journalist and editor of the *Sunday Times*, where he pioneered the highly regarded Insight investigative reports, Harold Evans was appointed editor of *The Times* by its new proprietor, Rupert Murdoch, but resigned after only a year. This fascinating and detailed account of the relationship between proprietor and editor shows how Murdoch acquired *the* newspaper of record, one of unimpeachable integrity and independence, and gradually subordinated its editorial independence to his own commercial interests. In addition the media tycoon acquired other newspaper, publishing and satellite television interests, clearly in breach of the spirit of government regulations on cross-media ownership, and against declared views that media concentration and monopoly are bad for democracy. (BM)

255 Great Britain. Royal Commission on the Press, 1947–1949. *Report.* (Chairman: Sir William David Ross) (Cmd 7700) London: HMSO, 1949. 363pp.

The first Royal Commission on the Press was set up following increasing concern from the public and the National Union of Journalists about the growth of monopolistic tendencies in the ownership of newspapers in the UK. The Commission inquired into the control, management and ownership of the press and news agencies, with the object of ensuring free expression of opinion and accuracy in the presentation of the news. It did not find the degree of concentration of ownership then current so great as to prejudice freedom of opinion, or contrary to the public interest. However, it did recommend establishing a General Council of the Press to safeguard the freedom of the press and encourage a sense of public service and responsibility among journalists. (BM)

256 Great Britain. Royal Commission on the Press, 1961–1962. *Report.* (Chairman: Lord Shawcross) (Cmnd 1811) London: HMSO, 1962. 239pp.

The second Royal Commission began by noting that since the first had reported in 1949 seventeen daily and Sunday newspapers had ceased publication, and the ownership of those remaining was concentrated in fewer hands. It aimed to inquire into the economic and financial factors affecting the press, rather than performance or ethical issues. (BM)

257 Great Britain. Royal Commission on the Press, 1974–1977. *Interim report: the national newspaper industry.* (Chairman: Professor O. R. McGregor) (Cmnd 6433) London: HMSO, 1976. x, 116pp.; *Final report.* (Cmnd 6810) 298pp.; *Appendices.* (Cmnd 6810-1) London: HMSO, 1977. ii, 166pp.

This third Royal Commission inquired into factors affecting the maintenance of the independence, diversity and editorial standards of newspapers, with particular investigation into the economics of newspaper publishing and distribution, concentration of ownership, and the functioning of the Press Council. The interim report, *The national newspaper industry*, concluded that the financial position of the industry was poor, particularly for the quality papers, with no immediately better prospects, and, that as a healthy, independent and diverse press was indispensable to a democratic society, some special consideration should be given to the newspaper industry. The final report recommended various measures to prevent undue concentration of ownership in the press and media generally, to protect press freedom, and strengthen the effectiveness of the Press Council in handling cases of invasion of individual privacy by newspapers or their reporters. Other publications from the third Royal Commission were Research Papers, Working Papers (including *Review of sociological writing on the press*, by Denis McQuail, 1976), and a minority report (*The press*, by Geoffrey Goodman and David Basnett, London: Labour Party, 1977. 18pp.). (BM)

258 Hollingsworth, Mark. *The press and political dissent: a question of censorship.* London: Pluto Press, 1986. viii, 367pp.

A passionate pamphlet about the current state of the press in the UK centred on the familiar arguments on press ownership. It does not face up to the difficult questions, for example, why is a press so corrupt and powerful so ineffective? Bibliography. (SM)

259 Horvat, Janos. 'How free are East European media without state control'. *Media Development*, Vol. 39, No. 4, 1992, pp. 36–8.
After four decades of censorship the public in Eastern Europe do not know quite what to expect from a free press, but they are moving to responsible and independent journalism, though market deficiencies and foreign media ownership may cause concern. (BM)

260 Howard, Michael W. 'Self-management, ownership and the media'. *Journal of Mass Media Ethics*, Vol. 8, No. 4, 1993, pp. 197–206.
Qualified case for worker control of the media, newspapers in particular, which argues that free expression can be enhanced without compromising press freedom either through government control or through corporate and market dominance. (BM)

261 McDonald, Donald. 'The media's conflict of interests'. *InterMedia*, Vol. 5, No. 3, June 1977, pp. 14–19.
Threats to a free press from the big-business nature of the media and the increasing ownership concentration can only be remedied by a de-concentration of ownership, facilitating new entry to the media, expanding public access, and developing ethical and legal grounds for asserting journalists rights to protected professional status. (BM)

262 *Media ownership and control in the age of convergence.* London: International Institute of Communications, 1996. viii, 303pp.
As broadcasting, telecommunications, information technology and print media converge, there are increasing fears about how the media will be controlled and by whom, and with related issues of national identity, freedom of speech and democratic values. These essays by distinguished writers compare and contrast developments worldwide. (BM)

263 Tunstall, Jeremy. *Newspaper power: the new national press in Britain.* Oxford: Clarendon Press, 1996. xi, 441pp.
Professor of Sociology at City University (London) surveys the British national press following the 'death of Fleet Street' in 1986, triggered by Rupert Murdoch. Through over 200 interviews with some of the most senior and powerful newspaper people he examines the power of the press, and questions 'whether it is compatible with, or healthy for a democracy to have so much power residing in so few unregulated hands'. (BM)

264 Murdock, Graham. 'The new Mogul empires: media concentration and control in the age of convergence'. *Media Development*, Vol. 41, No. 4, 1994, pp. 3–6.

It is likely that the age of convergence will witness an explosion of plurality but a reduction of diversity, which would erode existing institutions of democracy. New strong independent sources are essential to combat the concentration of cultural power in the hands of major communications operators. (BM)

Advertising and marketing

265 Barnouw, Erik. *The sponsor: notes on a modern potentate*. New York: Oxford University Press, 1978. 220pp.

Sponsorship of television and radio programmes, long a reality in the US, has recently been introduced in the UK and Europe. The author looks at the impact of the advertiser and sponsor on American network programme planning. Despite protestations to the contrary by the networks, the sponsors' choices of programmes with which they wish their company or product to be associated inevitably influence programming decisions. (BM)

266 Hesterman, Vicki. 'Consumer magazines and ethical guidelines'. *Journal of Mass Media Ethics*, Vol. 2, No. 2, Spring–Summer, 1987, pp. 93–101.

Results of a pilot study of 100 American consumer magazines indicate considerable lack of standard practices, and the need for ethical guidelines on such issues as separation of editorial from advertorial and business interests, conflict of interest, advertiser influence, advertiser supplied stories and so on. (BM)

267 Meeske, Milan D. 'Editorial advertising and the First Amendment'. *Journal of Broadcasting*, Vol. 17, No. 4, Fall 1973, pp. 417–26.

Editorial advertisements, or 'advertorials', commercial announcements paid for by citizens' action groups expressing opinions on controversial public issues, raise legal and ethical issues. (BM)

Privacy

268 Braman, Sandra. 'Global surveillance, media policies and civil liberties'. *Media Development*, Vol. 40, No. 2, 1993, pp. 36–40.

Development of global communications and surveillance systems raise policy issues, and potential concerns for abuse of civil liberties. (BM)

269 Branscomb, Anne Wells. *Who own information?: from privacy to public access*. New York: Basic Books, 1994. xii, 241pp.

A communications and computer lawyer examines, from an American though not parochial perspective, the problems presented by the emergence of information as a commodity, now calling out for protection and definition of ownership rights, and by the technologies of dissemination and transmission of information so far outstripping the law. In a most readable way she poses such thought-provoking questions as who owns your name, medical history and image, and more generally who owns government and religious information (for example the Dead Sea Scrolls). In a fascinating chapter on who owns your image, in which it seems (at least according to US law) that if you are a public figure you have waived your privacy rights with respect to intrusion, she looks at the rights of the subject and the photographer, and the integrity of the images in an age of computer 'enhancements', and concludes that in future the subjects of electronic images are going to seek more control over the use of their likeness. (BM)

270 Bremner, Charles. 'Privé, égalité, fraternité'. *The Times*, 20 November 1993, Magazine, pp. 12–13, 15.
A look at the effects on the press in France of the French privacy laws, some of the toughest in Europe, which protect private life from public scrutiny. (BM)

271 Brook, Tom. 'Shooting pain'. *The Listener*, Vol. 122, No. 3131, 14 September 1989, p. 19.
Report on the ethics of the media coverage of the crash of the Pan Am Flight 103 at Lockerbie in Scotland in 1988. (BM)

272 Bryant, Garry. 'Ten-fifty P.I.: emotion and the photographer's role'. *Journal of Mass Media Ethics*, Vol. 2, No. 2, Spring–Summer, 1987, pp. 32–9.
Salt Lake City newspaper staff photographer believes that photographs can still be the most powerful form of communication but offers a personal testimonial, with his 'soul-searching checklist' regarding intrusion into an individual's right to privacy, including consideration of the effect his photographs will have on the subject, being unobtrusive, and acting with compassion. (BM)

273 Childers, Doug. 'Media practices in AIDS coverage and a model for ethical reporting on AIDS victims'. *Journal of Mass Media Ethics*, Vol. 3, No. 2, Fall 1988, pp. 60–5.
Study of coverage of AIDS-related stories in the *Washington Post*, the *New York Times*, *Newsweek* and *Time*, and the ethical problems in balancing the interests of the public and the AIDS victims, and the moral limitations that restrict coverage. (BM)

274 Cochran, Wendell. 'Computers, privacy and journalists: a suggested code of information practices'. *Journal of Mass Media Ethics*, Vol. 11, No. 4, 1996, pp. 210–22.
To reassure public fears about the privacy of information held on electronic databases journalists need to be more sensitive to privacy concerns, and to create a Code of Information Practices that would provide guidance in making decisions about the use of private information in computer format. (BM)

275 Coleman, A. D. 'Private lives, public places: street photography ethics'. *Journal of Mass Media Ethics*, Vol. 2, No. 2, Spring–Summer 1987, pp. 60–6.
Ethical dilemmas in photographing private persons in public places. Subjects have a right to control use of own image and not just be 'camera fodder'. (BM)

276 Dauncey, Hugh. 'French "reality television": more than a matter of taste'. *European Journal of Communication*, Vol. 11, No. 1, 1996, pp. 86–106.
Recent development in France of 'télé-réalité' programmes, initially greeted by a storm of controversy about their legality, are now a popular and established form but still raise fears of invasion of privacy and voyeurism, and concerns over their morality and attempts to undermine traditional values and aspirations. (BM)

277 Edelman, Bernard. *Ownership of the image.* Translated by Elizabeth Kingdom from the French, *Le Droit saisi par la photographie.* London: Routledge & Kegan Paul, 1979. xii, 217pp.
French philosopher discusses from a Marxist viewpoint the law relating to photography and the cinema, in particular the role of the subject in law. There is a conflict between the photographer as the creator of the image, and owner of it as a property, and the subject of the image, who is 'real' and also has established rights in the work. (BM)

278 Fisher, Mark. 'Press clipping'. *The Listener*, 9 August 1990, pp. 10–11.
British Labour Member of Parliament argues for statutory protection of individual privacy to be balanced with equal protection for the freedom of the press. (BM)

279 Glasser, Theodore L. 'Resolving the press–privacy conflict: approaches to the newsworthiness defense'. *Communications and the Law*, Vol. 4, No. 2, Spring 1982. pp. 23–42.
The defence of newsworthiness, however tenuous, in the conflict between freedom of the press and intrusion of privacy can be overpowering. (BM)

280 Glasser, Theodore L. and **Jassem, Harvey**. 'Indecent broadcasts and the listener's right of privacy'. *Journal of Broadcasting*, Vol. 24, No. 3, Summer 1980, pp. 285–99.
Case law in the United States established listeners' right to hear, and not the broadcasters' right to be heard, but a Supreme Court ruling in 1978 introduced a new concept of the listeners' right *not* to hear in the case of indecent broadcasts, which may constitute a form of intrusion and thus violate the listeners' right of privacy. (BM)

281 Great Britain. Department of National Heritage. *Review of press self-regulation.* (Cm 2135) London: HMSO, 1993. xiv, 88pp.
Two years after the publication in 1990 of the *Report of the Committee on Privacy and Related Matters*, its Chairman, David Calcutt QC, reviews its impact on the regulation of the press in the UK, in particular the operation of the Press Complaints

PRIVACY   159

Commission since its establishment in 1991. He concludes that the PCC has not become an effective regulator, and does not command the confidence of the public, because of the way it was set up as self-regulator by the press themselves, and the lack of a code of practice. In its place he recommends a statutory complaints tribunal with firm powers, and other measures, such as the introduction of a new tort of infringement of privacy and legislation covering interception of telecommunications, to ensure that privacy is protected from unjustifiable intrusion and by a body commanding respect of the press and public. (BM)

282 Great Britain. Home Office, Lord Chancellor's Office and **Scottish Office**. *Report of the Committee on Privacy*. Chairman: The Rt. Hon. Kenneth Younger. (Cmnd 5012) London: HMSO, 1972. xi, 350pp.

British government Committee of Inquiry, set up in 1970 'to consider whether legislation is needed to give further protection to the individual citizen ... against intrusions into privacy by private persons, and organizations, or by companies'. Triggered off by the Right of Privacy Bill and conclusions reached then that a general right of privacy should be created. Investigations included written memoranda from 130 organizations, oral evidence from witnesses, and commissioning a public attitudes survey. Covered all areas, including press and broadcasting (unethical methods of obtaining material, unwanted publicity concerning private persons or private affairs, and so on). The report concludes that the question of privacy embodies values essential to a free society, and that the law has its part to play in the protection of privacy, but it saw no need to extend it any further. (BM)

283 Great Britain. Home Office. *Report of the Committee on Privacy and Related Matters*. Chairman: David Calcutt, QC. (Cm 1102) London: HMSO, 1990. xii, 124pp.

The UK government set up the Committee on Privacy and Related Matters following allegations of declining press standards and concern about growing intrusion into individual privacy. The Committee's remit was to improve recourse by the individual citizen against the press, and was concerned with two distinct categories of violation of privacy – physical intrusion by press reporters or photographers, and publication of intrusive material. Its recommendations included defining certain acts of physical intrusion as criminal offences (with some defences), new legal restrictions on press reporting, and the establishment of a Press Complaints Commission (replacing the Press Council). (BM)

284 Great Britain. Lord Chancellor's Department and **Scottish Office**. *Infringement of privacy*. London: Central Office of Information for the Lord Chancellor's Department, 1993. 90pp.

UK government Consultation Paper on the introduction of a civil remedy for the infringement of privacy, issued in response to the recommendation of Sir David Calcutt's Review of Press Self-Regulation. Proposes citizens shall have legal right over infringement of privacy causing substantial distress, and defines privacy to include matters appertaining to health, personal communications, and family and personal relationships, and a right to be free from harassment and molestation. (BM)

285 Gross, Larry, Katz, John Stuart and **Ruby, Jay**. *Image ethics: the moral rights of subjects in photographs, film and television.* New York: Oxford University Press, 1988. xvii, 382pp.
Since the invention of photography in the mid-nineteenth century a stream of visual images have poured into our consciousness, accelerating rapidly in the twentieth century with film, television and video. This interesting book addresses the ethical and moral issues raised by the production of images. Do we have the right to photograph anything we have a right to look at? What are the moral or legal rights of those individuals or groups whose images are used by photographers, film makers and television/video producers. Topics covered include: the question of informed consent by the subjects of photographs or film; privacy issues such as intrusion, causing embarrassment, showing subjects in a false light, and appropriation; who owns a star's image (for example, Elvis Presley or Bela Lugosi); and the treatment of those outside the mainstream or on the margins of society. Balancing ethical considerations with the exigencies of film making is difficult. The solution to such ethical problems is usually reached through accommodation and compromise, without which no work would get done. Working ethics change constantly, not by application of unchanging standards to new situations but by their continual re-interpretation and working practice in the light of new technical or organizational situations. Extensive bibliography. (BM)

286 Gunaratne, Shelton A. 'Invading privacy of mourners and victims'. *Media Development*, Vol. 39, No. 4, 1992, pp. 11–13.
Death, sickness and suffering are a staple diet of news media content, but news values and 'public interest' are often placed before ethics in their coverage. (BM)

287 Henry, Georgina. 'Trespassers beware!' *The Guardian*, 10 June 1992, p. 19.
In the light of calls for privacy law in the UK, author looks at privacy issues in the US, France and Germany. (BM)

288 Hewitt, Patricia. *Privacy: the information gatherers.* London: National Council for Civil Liberties, 1977. 98pp.
Campaigning pamphlet on citizens' right to control the personal information collected and stored on them. National and local government, education, medical, employment and police records are covered. On privacy and the media it recognizes the conflicting claims of privacy and journalistic freedom, and why any attempts to legislate in this area have been strongly resisted as privacy laws could restrict the legitimate investigation of matters of public concern. (BM)

289 Hyde, H. Montgomery (ed.) *Privacy and the law.* London: Thornton Butterworth, 1947.

290 Jenkins, Simon. 'Public lives, private pain'. *The Times*, 10 June 1992, p. 16.
Editors' decisions on the recent publication in the UK of royal secrets were not helped by the Calcutt Committee's code of practice on privacy. (BM)

291 Jones, Mervyn (ed.) *Privacy.* Newton Abbot, Devon: David & Charles, 1974. 230pp. (David & Charles sources for contemporary issues series)
Useful compilation of extracts from key texts on privacy, prompted by the publication of the *Report of the Committee on Privacy*, under the Chairmanship of Sir Kenneth Younger in 1972. Topics covered include threats to privacy from the new technologies and techniques of intrusion, the power of the state and the mass media. Views from Members of Parliament and Younger Committee members on the privacy debate, and the right to privacy are also anthologized. (BM)

292 Kilborn, Richard. '"How real can you get?": recent developments in "reality television"'. *European Journal of Communication*, Vol. 9, No. 4, December 1994, pp. 421–39.
'Reality programming', mostly dramatized reconstructions of real-life events, often crime, or candid camera-type of programmes, has given a new twist to questions of journalism ethics, particularly methods of obtaining material, invasion of privacy, exploitation and voyeurism, and represents a further erosion of codes of fair dealing and consent. (BM)

293 Lander, Estelle. 'AIDS coverage: ethical and legal issues facing the media today'. *Journal of Mass Media Ethics*, Vol. 3, No. 2, Fall 1988, pp. 66–72.
Coverage of AIDS by the media raises issues of privacy, terminology and disclosure, but also the educational role they could assume. (BM)

294 Lennon, Peter. 'It started with a kiss'. *The Guardian*, 16 December 1992, Supplement, pp. 4–5.
The subjects of Robert Doisneau's photograph 'Baiser de l'Hôtel de Ville' sued the photographer under a French law which gives individuals a right to their own image. (BM)

295 Lester, Paul Martin. *Photojournalism: an ethical approach.* Hillsdale, New Jersey: Lawrence Erlbaum, 1991. xii, 202pp. (Communication textbook series)
American student textbook aiming to give insights into the various ethical perspectives of photojournalists, editors, subjects of photos, and readers in the use of photographs in the press. It covers ethical problems arising from images of dead or grieving victims of violence, invasion of (and rights to) privacy by the subjects of photos, picture manipulation by traditional or computer methods, staged or posed news stories, and such other concerns as images of nudity, children in dangerous situations and context-excluded shots. The inevitable conflict between photojournalists' principles of telling the truth, objectivity and newsworthiness,

and humanistic ethical values makes adherence to a code of ethics necessary. The author examines the US National Press Photographers Association (NPPA) code of ethics. Review of selected literature, and bibliography. (BM)

296 Lind, Rebecca Ann and **Rarick, David**. 'Public attitudes toward ethical issues in TV programming: multiple viewer orientations'. *Journal of Mass Media Ethics*, Vol. 7, No. 3, 1992, pp. 133–50.

Survey of viewers in St Paul in Minneapolis on how they evaluate ethical issues and problematic content in TV news and entertainment, such as the use of hidden cameras, showing grieving, use of classified information, violence and invasion of privacy. (BM)

297 Long, Gerald. 'No innocence, no privacy: that is the world as it is'. *InterMedia*, Vol. 22, No. 1, February 1994, pp. 39–43.

Discussion on the definition of privacy and whether it constitutes a universal right. (BM)

298 McKie, David. 'Self-regulation and the Calcutt report'. *Index on Censorship*, No. 19, August 1990, pp. 2–3.

The government-appointed Calcutt Committee on privacy and newspapers brings in press self-regulation in the UK, but with threats of statutory action if these reforms fail. (BM)

299 McLean, Deckle. 'Press and privacy rights could be compatible'. *Communications and the Law*, Vol. 8, No. 2, April 1986, pp. 13–25.

Courts and the media might be more eager to protect privacy from invasion if the US Supreme Court had used Alexander Meiklejohn's distinction between the two kinds of freedom of speech – the first (on points of democratic principle) is absolute and protected by the First Amendment, the second (all other forms of speech) need not be absolute. (BM)

300 McLean, Deckle. 'Privacy invasion tort: straddling the fence'. *Communications and the Law*, Vol. 7, No. 3, June 1985, pp. 15–30.

American privacy law is ineffective – it discourages the media from taking responsibility for privacy, while failing to provide a solid opportunity for recompense. (BM)

301 Mallam, Paul and **O'Dea, Jacqueline**. 'Privacy and communications: the example of Australia'. *InterMedia*, Vol. 22, No. 5, October–November 1994, pp. 32–40.

General discussion of issues relating to the protection of privacy, and outline of legislation and regulation of privacy in telecommunications in Australia. (BM)

302 Maxwell, Kimera, and **Reinsch, Roger**. 'The Freedom of Information Act privacy exemption: who does it really protect?' *Communications and the Law*, Vol. 7, No. 2, April 1985, pp. 45–59.

The right of privacy has generally been accepted as an implied US constitutional right, but a recent Supreme Court case recognized *personal* privacy but not that of government agencies. (BM)

303 Merryman, John Henry and **Elsen, Albert E**. *Law, ethics and the visual arts*. New York: Matthew Bender, 1979. xv, 650pp.
Anthology of American cases, statutes, treaties and articles on a range of legal and ethical issues regarding art and artists, including interpretation of the First Amendment to protect artistic freedom, censorship of art, and artists' moral and legal rights in their work. (BM)

304 Pilgrim, Tim A. 'Docudramas and false-light invasion of privacy'. *Communications and the Law*, Vol. 10, No. 3, June 1988, pp. 3–37.
In the US false-light invasion of privacy occurs when publication or broadcast of some matters concerning a person places them before the public in such a way that is highly offensive to a reasonable person or the material was broadcast or published with the knowledge of its falsity or with disregard as to its falsity. Docudramas, the fictionalizing of factual material, can fulfil both criteria. (BM)

305 Powell, Di. 'Media intrusion into grief'. *Media Information Australia*, No. 57, August 1990, pp. 24–9.
The debate in Australia on media intrusion into private grief was highlighted by the sacking of two Seven Network journalists in Perth after showing a distressed woman being told by an ambulance officer of the death of her child. (BM)

306 Samarajiva, Rohan. 'The democratic test is: can individuals negotiate their own boundary conditions in telecoms?' *InterMedia*, Vol. 22, No. 1, February 1994, pp. 34–8.
Paper by American academic, presented at the International Institute of Communications annual conference in 1993, which addresses privacy issues in the provision of telecommunications services. (BM)

307 Samoriski, Jan H, and **Huffman, John L**. 'Electronic mail, privacy and the Electronic Communications Privacy Act of 1986: technology in search of law'. *Journal of Broadcasting & Electronic Media*, Vol. 40, No. 1, Winter 1996, pp. 60–76.
Examination of electronic privacy, particularly in relation to e-mail and related communications in the computer environment, and the need for the legal system to adapt to this evolving and potentially great medium of communication and to resolve the competing interests, particularly of government versus citizen. (BM)

308 Shearer, Ann. *Survivors and the media*. London: John Libbey, 1991. v, 73pp. (Broadcasting Standards Council, research monograph series, 2)
Report based on two research surveys. One is of those who had survived acts of violence, and the other is of audiences for their attitudes to media coverage of the

aftermath of man-made disasters, rape, assault or sudden and violent death. (BM)

309 Sherer, Michael D. 'Photojournalism and the infliction of emotional distress'. *Communications and the Law*, Vol. 8, No. 2, April 1986, pp. 27–37.
Those captured in the powerful images of news photography may experience emotional distress by being displayed before the public, and may wish to seek redress before the courts in a classic confrontation between the right of photojournalists to communicate and individuals' rights to privacy. (BM)

310 Simmons, Charles E. 'Privacy in the age of the microcomputer'. *InterMedia*, Vol. 15, No. 2, March 1987, pp. 31–7.
The author argues that instant global communications and computer databanks require new standards and procedures for the collection and publication of personal data, and a redefinition of privacy in future. (BM)

311 Snoddy, Raymond. *The good, the bad and the unacceptable: the hard news about the British press.* London: Faber, 1992. xiv, 210pp.
The author, media correspondent of the *Financial Times* from 1983 to 1997, examines the tension between the need to protect individuals from invasion of privacy or insensitive reporting by a sensationalist press intent on journalistic scoops, and the equally important need to maintain the freedom of the press and the right of free expression. Drawing on examples of good and bad practice from past and contemporary British newspapers, the findings of various post-war inquiries into the press, including the 1989 Calcutt Committee on Privacy and Related Matters, and comparison with the US, he presents a valuable contribution to the debate on press standards. (BM)

312 Sontag, Susan. *On photography*. New York: Farrar, Straus & Giroux, 1977; London: Allen Lane, 1978. 207pp.
Collection of thoughtful and stimulating essays, first published (in slightly different form) in the *New York Review of Books*, on the 'insatiability of the photographing eye', and the aesthetic and moral problems posed by the omnipresence of photographic images. The author's concern is over the ever more peremptory rights of the photographer 'to interfere with, and invade or ignore whatever is going on', and to appropriate the thing photographed. On the power of the photographic image she argues that 'the naked South Vietnamese child just sprayed by American napalm, running down a highway towards the camera ... screaming in pain – probably did more to increase public revulsion against the war than a hundred hours of televised barbarities'. (BM)

313 Stovall, James Glen and **Cotter, Patrick R**. 'The public plays reporter: attitudes toward reporting on public officials'. *Journal of Mass Media Ethics*, Vol. 7, No. 2, 1992, pp. 97–106.

Tennis player Arthur Ashe's forced admission that he had AIDS (in 1992) again raises the questions of media exposure of private facts about public figures; this article, based on a survey, compares attitudes of journalists with the public as to how far the media should go. (BM)

314 Taylor, S. J. *Shock! horror!: the tabloids in action.* London: Bantam Press, 1991. 476pp.
'Tabloid journalism is the direct application of capitalism to events and ideas, with profit, and not ethics, as the prevailing motivation.' With a total absence of hypocrisy about paying high prices for stories, the tabloid press handle information as a commodity with little regard for moral or ethical implications. This anecdotal but entertaining book surveys tabloids in the UK and the US through interviews with reporters, paparazzi, gossip columnists and editors. It concludes that society needs an irreverent popular press, but that if it goes too far society will seek to control it and all press freedom. (BM)

315 Wacks, Raymond. *Privacy and press freedom.* London: Blackstone Press, 1995. xvi, 181pp.
Professor of Law at Hong Kong University argues that the freedom of the press can be reconciled with the individual's right to privacy. He examines common law in England relating to intrusion by the media and publication of intimate facts, the recommendations of the Younger Committee on Privacy (1970), and the Calcutt Committee on Privacy and Related Matters (1990), various attempts at Privacy Bills, and the work of the Press Complaints Commission, with comparisons with US case law and the international dimension. He concludes that recent developments, such as expanding the remedy for breach of confidence, action over infliction of emotional stress, and international recognition, will help provide judicial recognition of individual rights to privacy. (BM)

316 Winch, Samuel P. 'Moral justifications for privacy and intimacy'. *Journal of Mass Media Ethics*, Vol. 11, No. 4, 1996, pp. 197–209.
Historical and philosophical examination of privacy (and intimacy) as basic moral and social rights in democratic societies, which argues for the protection of the personal intimacy of public figures. (BM)

317 Winsbury, Rex. 'A clash of freedoms: defending "private space" against the communications intruder'. *InterMedia*, Vol. 21, No. 4–5, August–September 1993, pp. 18–20.
Author argues that under the pressure of advancing technology in communications, there is an increasing need for a universal legal right to privacy for the individual, and for a comprehensive definition of the right to privacy that will encompass different branches of communications activity and national legislations. (BM)

318 Winsbury, Rex. 'Royal tapes, tax returns, personality profiles, junk calls and encryption: making the rights connection'. *InterMedia*, Vol. 21, No. 4–5, August–September 1993, pp. 21–5.
Survey of the main areas in which privacy is now a key issue – the press, information held by government, databases in general, and intelligent telecom networks – with reprints of some attempts at definition of privacy. (BM)

319 Winsbury, Rex. 'The right to be let alone: the most comprehensive of rights'. *InterMedia*, Vol. 21, No. 4–5, August–September 1993, pp. 26–8.
Brief overview of the law on privacy in various countries in Europe, Australasia and North America. (BM)

320 Wischmann, Lesley. 'Dying on the front page: Kent State and the Pulitzer Prize'. *Journal of Mass Media Ethics*, Vol. 2, No. 2, Spring–Summer 1987, pp. 67–74.
Citing the example of John Filo's 1971 Pulitzer Prize-winning photograph of a young man's body after the killing of four students by National Guardsmen at Kent State University, the author examines the problems of privacy for innocent victims of news events, and photojournalists' responsibility for the publication of their pictures. (BM)

321 Wober, J. Mallory. 'Psychologists and the intrusion of broadcast "prygrammes" on personal privacy'. *Bulletin of the British Psychological Society*, Vol. 31, January 1978, pp. 1–2.
The author addresses the concerns raised by the privacy of individuals whose problems have been publicized in the mass media, and calls for further inquiry into the issue. (BM)

322 Young, John B. (ed.) *Privacy*. Chichester: John Wiley, 1978. viii, 350pp.
Seminal collection of essays by British academics offering a multi-disciplinary approach to the issue of privacy, beginning with a look at the concept of privacy as an individual right and value by a philosopher, a psychologist and a sociologist, followed by articles on the effect of external sources, including 'The mass media and privacy' by Denis McQuail, and concluding with the topic of business and privacy, and the role of electronics in crime detection and spying. (BM)

Censorship: taste, decency and pornography

323 Brown, Jennifer E. 'News photographs and the pornography of grief'. *Journal of Mass Media Ethics*, Vol. 2, No. 2, Spring–Summer 1987, pp. 75–81.
Photographers should never forget their humanity in getting good photographs. This article outlines the ethical dilemmas photographers face when capturing grief and tragedy, and the lack of guidelines on the issue. (BM)

324 Devlin, Patrick. *The enforcement of morals.* New York: Oxford University Press, 1965. xiv, 139pp.
In this series of lectures on aspects of the relationship between the law and morals, Lord Devlin argues that society cannot live without morals, and its morals are those standards of conduct of which the reasonable man approves; he makes a case for toleration of the maximum individual freedom that is consistent with the integrity of society. A common morality is the price paid for social cohesion. (BM)

325 Gauntlet, David. *Moving experiences: understanding television's influences and effects.* London: John Libbey, 1995. viii, 148pp. (Acamedia research monograph, 13)
Comprehensive and objective overview of the body of research into the possible effects of television on its viewers, examining all major studies in the field. The author addresses (and sometimes refutes) the prevailing academic arguments and findings on such vexed issues as television violence, campaigns and advertising, and pro-social effects of television. He concludes that the search for direct effects of television is over (and not proven), and that television must now be considered within a wider social context and as only one of many influences in people's lives. (BM)

326 Hannabuss, Stuart. 'Explicit representations: approaches to censorship'. *ASLIB Proceedings*, Vol. 46, No. 10, October 1994, pp. 249–55.
Information is not just facts and figures, neutral and objective, but often value-laden and liable to controversy and moral censorship. Its wide availability in the global village does not relieve us of the responsibility for deciding what it represents, who has generated it, and its likely effects. The author looks at examples of censorship in literature and the media, with reference to codes of conduct. (BM)

327 Jenkins, Simon. 'A pot can judge a kettle'. *The Times*, 10 November 1993, p. 18.
Pressure from other newspapers can be more effective as a regulation of taste than statutory control by privacy laws. (BM)

328 Lloyd, Peter. *Not for publication.* London: Bow Group, 1968. 80pp.
This report from a British right-wing research group works from the assumption that 'the truth and public well-being are also best served by the free play of ideas, knowledge and comment, and the fullest opportunity for each adult to make up his own mind what books he will read or what film he will see'. Its influential and prophetic recommendations included: theatre censorship to be abolished leaving the law of libel and obscenity the only restrictions; film censorship for adults to be abolished; the obscene publications law to be amended; Official Secrets Acts to be repealed; for broadcasting, government reserve powers over content of programmes to be surrendered. (BM)

329 Medved, Michael. *Hollywood vs. America: popular culture and the war on traditional values.* New York: HarperCollins, 1992. xiii, 386pp.

Controversial polemic blaming the Hollywood film, television and popular music industries for, what the author sees as, the moral collapse of the US. He claims that Hollywood is out of touch with the traditional values of the ordinary citizen, and he is concerned with the moral and ethical problems presented by too much violence, nudity and bad language in popular entertainment. (BM)

330 Roberts, Churchill L. 'Attitudes and media use of the Moral Majority'. *Journal of Broadcasting,* Vol. 27, No. 4, Fall 1983, pp. 403–10.

The Moral Majority, an American activist group comprised largely of evangelical and fundamentalist Christians, founded in 1979 by radio and television minister Jerry Falwell, considers itself as dedicated to stemming what it believes to be a tide of liberalism, and has been involved in many morality-related political controversies. This survey of a local group of the Moral Majority in 1981 found that their views on issues such as abortion, pornography and gay rights were significantly different and to some extent out-of-step with those of the country at large. (BM)

331 Tracey, Michael and **Morrison, David**. *Whitehouse.* London: Macmillan, 1979. 216pp. (Communications and culture)

One of the few serious attempts by academics to record and analyse the way the cultural right-wing functions in its attack against the 'liberalism' of the media – television, drama, cinema and magazines. The phenomenon associated with Mrs Mary Whitehouse is not simply of importance in the UK. It has spread over much of the 'white Commonwealth'; has political and religious implications; and has some parallels (though they are by no means exact) in the US. (SM)

332 Whitehouse, Mary. *Cleaning up TV: from protest to participation.* London: Blandford Press, 1967. 240pp.

Since she launched the Clean Up TV Campaign in 1964, Mary Whitehouse has become a household name in the UK. The conviction of this former school mistress that declining standards of taste and decency on television were having harmful effects on her pupils led her to found the campaign, and later in 1965 the National Viewers' and Listeners' Association which became an influential and vocal activist group. She chronicles her movement, the inadequacies, as she sees them, of the system of regulation of television, and her solutions to the problems, including a proposal for making broadcasters more publicly accountable through a Viewers' and Listeners' Council. (BM)

333 Whitehouse, Mary. *Mightier than the sword.* Eastbourne: Kingsway Publications, 1985. 160pp.

The leading campaigner on standards of taste and decency on British television outlines her own Christian beliefs and urges action among those who share them. (BM)

334 Whitehouse, Mary. 'Popular taste and the exercise of moral judgement'. *Television: the journal of the Royal Television Society,* Vol. 19, No. 4, July–August 1982, pp. 3–6.
After tirelessly campaigning against 'permissiveness in broadcasting' for nearly twenty years, Mrs Whitehouse surveys violence, swearing, blasphemy, and taste and decency issues on British television, and concludes that we should accept that television is 'the most powerful medium ever to affect the thinking and behaviour of people' (Sir Hugh Greene) and act on it. (BM)

Freedom of expression and harm

335 Beaver, Frank. 'The awkward embrace: the legal battle over obscenity'. *Gannett Center Journal,* Vol. 2, No. 1, Winter 1988, pp. 81–90
Study of obscenity laws and prosecutions, and regulation of pornography in the US. (BM)

336 Carol, Avedon. *Nudes, prudes and attitudes: pornography and censorship.* Cheltenham: New Clarion Press, 1994. x, 213pp.
Feminist case against official censorship of sexual portrayal and pornography on the grounds that it would give enormous powers to the state, and would promote the very repression that is implicated in causing sexual violence – a law that is made to suppress racist and sexist hate expression (in speech or print) can be easily turned against anti-racist or feminist opinion, and in silencing all dissent or alternative views. (BM)

337 Chandos, John (ed.) *'To deprave and corrupt...': original studies in the nature and definition of 'obscenity'.* London: Souvenir Press, 1962. xii, 207pp.
Collection of essays on 'obscenity', and the conflicting demands of the principles of freedom and control of written communication, including Lord Birkett (former Lord Justice of Appeal) on the law of obscene publications, Maurice Girodias (of the Olympia Press and publisher of Vladimir Nabokov and Jean Genet) against moral censorship, and the author Walter Allen on the writer and the frontiers of tolerance. (BM)

338 Collins, Richard and **Purnell, James** (eds.). *Reservoirs of dogma.* London: Institute for Public Policy Research, 1996. 55pp.
Selection of papers from an IPPR seminar on 'Expression and Censorship' in 1995, which addresses the question as to whether there are harmful effects from the representation of violence, sexual behaviour and sexual differences, and, more importantly, whether there should be censorship. Most contributors are strongly libertarian, including Erica Jong ('I am against censorship. I prefer the chaos of uncontrollable communication. The urge towards obscenity is nothing more or less than the urge towards freedom'), Bernard Williams, who argues for some restriction of access to pornography, and Michael Grade (Chief Executive, Channel 4), promoting the public's right to free and fair communication. (BM)

339 Cumberbatch, Guy and **Howitt, Dennis**. *A measure of uncertainty: the effects of the mass media.* London: John Libbey, 1989. vii, 88pp. (Broadcasting Standards Council, research monograph series, 1)
An overview of research evidence on mass media effects – women and sex roles, racism, ageism, disablement, sex and violence, followed by two in-depth studies of violence and the mass media, and the debate on pornography. (BM)

340 Dhavan, Rajeev and **Davies, Christie** (eds.) *Censorship and obscenity.* London: Martin Robertson, 1978. x, 187pp. (Law in society series)
Collection of papers by experts on aspects of obscenity and the law. John Trevelyan (former Secretary of the British Board of Film Censors), in his fair-minded preface, states we must try to achieve a balance between human freedom and the risk of harm, not an easy balance to determine but it is the core of the problem. Contributions include David Morrison and Michael Tracey on the case of Mary Whitehouse and the National Viewers' and Listeners' Association, Professor D. N. McCormick on privacy and obscenity, Trevelyan on film censorship and the law, and Dr Patricia Gillan (Guy's Hospital) on the therapeutic uses of pornography. (BM)

341 Easton, Susan M. *The problem of pornography: regulation and the right to free speech.* London: Routledge, 1994. xviii, 197pp.
The author, a barrister and lecturer in law, questions whether a commitment to free speech can be reconciled with the control of pornography, but (taking John Stuart Mill's test of harm principle as a starting point) concludes that it can, and proposes a legal action of 'incitement to sexual hatred' as the best means of regulating pornography. (BM)

342 Great Britain. Home Office. *Report of the Committee on Obscenity and Film Censorship.* Chairman: Bernard Williams. (Cmnd 7772) London: HMSO, 1979. vii, 270pp.
British government Committee of Inquiry appointed in 1977 'to review the laws concerning obscenity, indecency and violence in publications, displays, and entertainments in England and Wales, except in the field of broadcasting, and to review the arrangements for film censorship'. Among the Committee's conclusions were that any proposals should translate into effective legislation; that the terms 'obscene', 'indecent' and 'deprave and corrupt' should be abandoned as having outlived their usefulness. It recommended that new laws should rest partly on the basis of *harms* caused by the existence of the material (taking up John Stuart Mill's concept of 'harms'), and that the principal object of the law must be to prevent certain kinds of material causing offence to reasonable people or being available to young people. A short version was published: **Williams, Bernard**. *Obscenity and film censorship: an abridgment of the Williams Report.* Cambridge: Cambridge University Press, 1981. x, 166pp. (BM)

343 Kamp, John. 'Obscenity and the Supreme Court: a communication approach to a persistent judicial problem'. *Communications and the Law*, Vol. 2, No. 3, Summer 1980, pp. 1–42.

Continuing debate over the role of government in the censorship of sexually explicit material focusing on US Supreme Court judgments in obscenity cases. (BM)

344 Kendrick, Walter. *The secret museum: pornography in modern culture*. New York: Viking, 1987; Berkeley: University of California Press, 1996. xiv, 318pp.

Author looks at the definitions and origins of pornography, relating it to issues of censorship and freedom of expression. He covers the obscenity trials of Gustave Flaubert's *Madame Bovary*, *The well of loneliness* by Radclyffe Hall, and D. H. Lawrence's *Lady Chatterley's lover*, and more recent issues such as Robert Mapplethorpe's homoerotic photographs, Madonna's book of erotica, *Sex*, cable TV and Internet pornography. (BM)

345 Marcuse, Ludwig. *Obscene: the history of indignation*. Translated by Karen Gershon from the German. London: MacGibbon & Kee, 1965. 327pp.

Professor Marcuse's philosophical work analyses definitions and differing attitudes to 'obscenity' through key trials of (alleged) obscene publications, most notably of Gustave Flaubert's *Madame Bovary* in France in 1857, D. H. Lawrence's *Lady Chatterley's lover* in London in 1960, and Henry Miller's *Tropic of Cancer* in Los Angeles in 1962. (BM)

346 Noble, Grant. 'Children, television and morality'. *Media Information Australia*, No. 30, November 1983, pp. 56–65.

Examines the effects of television viewing on the moral development of children. (BM)

347 *Pornography: the Longford report*. London: Coronet Books, 1972. 520pp.

Report of the Committee Investigating Pornography, under Chairman Lord Longford, and with a group of 50 distinguished members including authors Kingsley Amis and Malcolm Muggeridge, Archbishop of York Donald Coggan, and former Attorney-General Lord Shawcross, and witnesses that included BBC and ITA Directors-General, and film censors John Trevelyan and Stephen Murphy. It looked into questions of pornography in publishing, broadcasting, advertising and films, and among its recommendations were a new statutory definition of 'obscene' and reform of the Obscene Publications Act. (BM)

348 Postman, Neil. *The disappearance of childhood*. New York: Delacorte Press, 1982; London: W. H. Allen, 1983. xiii, 177pp.

The media in general, television in particular, are largely responsible for the erosion of the dividing line between childhood and adulthood. Since, however, Professor Postman also argues in a historical survey that contemporary ideas of childhood derive from the invention of the printing press, it is not easy to see the significance of the argument. It is a beautifully written book, with a wide range of reference, and an elegant entertainment. The influence of Marshall McLuhan is not difficult to perceive, though the American stance of the book, historical review apart, is parochial. (SM)

349 Thompson, Margaret E., **Chaffee, Steven H**. and **Oshagen, Hayg H.** 'Regulating pornography: a public dilemma'. *Journal of Communication*, Vol. 40, No. 3, Summer 1990, pp. 73–83.

Despite strong opinions by both men and women that pornography has negative and harmful social effects, especially on interpersonal relationships between men and women, this study finds that a large proportion believe that pornographic materials should be protected by freedom of speech and the press. (BM)

350 United States Attorney General's Commission on Pornography. *Final report.* Washington, DC: US Government Printing Office, 1986.

351 Winn, Marie. *The plug-in drug: television, children and the family.* New York: Viking Press, 1977; Harmondsworth, Middlesex: Viking Press and Penguin Books, rev. ed., 1985. xiv, 288pp.

A journalistic work by a writer of children's books. It avoids the customary discussions of violence, sexuality and so on, and instead examines some of the less popular theories – for example, cognitive and affective communications – in an almost McLuhanite way: the content of programmes is not so important as the experience of watching. Sadly the argument is related specifically to US society, and the evidence used is highly selective. Some of the studies cited have yielded different results when replicated in Europe. (SM)

Film censorship

352 Black, Gregory D. *Hollywood censored: morality codes, Catholics and the movies.* New York: Cambridge University Press, 1994. xi, 362pp.

353 Hunnings, Neville March. *Film censors and the law.* London: Allen & Unwin, 1967. 474pp.

Lawyer and film historian looks at censorship of films in the UK, the US and several other countries worldwide, and discusses the nature of film censorship. (BM)

354 Index on Censorship. *The subversive eye*, edited by Sally Sampson. *Index on Censorship*, Vol. 24, No. 6, November–December 1996, 192pp.

Special issue of *Index on Censorship* devoted to film censorship as a contribution to the cinema's centenary, edited by a former examiner for the British Board of Film Classification. More than 40 essays cover the violence debate, sexual portrayal, political censorship and propaganda. Contributions include: 'No end in sight' by Philip French on the history of film censorship in the UK and abroad; 'Clockwork crimes' by Julian Petley on the interesting case of Stanley Kubrick's *A Clockwork Orange* – passed by the British film censors but withdrawn from distribution by the director himself after a sustained campaign of press vilification; and 'The case for quotas' by Bertrand Tavernier on American market forces acting as a kind of censorship of foreign films. (BM)

355 Mathews, Tom Dewe. *Censored*. London: Chatto & Windus, 1994. 298pp.
In this entertainingly written and well-researched history of film censorship in the UK, the author argues that the country has one of the most rigorous systems in the world. He began by believing 'that a centralised system of delegated censorship was not too high a price to pay in order to protect those too young to discriminate for themselves', but came to doubt its value and 'that films should find their audience in the market-place without intervention'. (BM)

356 Millar, Gavin. 'Witness to rape'. *The Listener*, Vol. 122, No. 3131, 14 September 1989, pp.8–9.
Moral issues raised by the depiction of rape on film and television, particularly the potential for offence and exploiting the victim, the attacker and the audience. (BM)

357 Phelps, Guy. 'Censorship and the press'. *Sight and Sound*, Vol. 42, No. 3, Summer 1973, pp. 138–40.
The case of Bernardo Bertolucci's *Last Tango in Paris*, which brought attention to the role of local authorities in film censorship and their assumption of moral guardianship of their electors, also highlighted exploitative and sensationalist reporting by the press. (BM)

358 Robertson, James C. *The British Board of Film Censors: film censorship in Britain, 1896–1950*. London: Croom Helm, 1985. 213pp.
History of film censorship in the UK since its inception, tracing events leading up to the founding of the BBFC in 1912 and chronicling its work during the rise of the cinema to become the most important medium of communication by 1950, with comparisons with film censorship in the US. (BM)

359 Trevelyan, John. *What the censor saw*. London: Michael Joseph, 1973. 276pp.
The Secretary of the British Board of Film Censors for many years, and an enlightened 'censor' noted for his liberal policy on films, writes of guiding the BBFC through a period of changing attitudes to censorship, and gives insight into the evolution of this working institution and social phenomenon. (BM)

360 Vaughn, Stephen. 'Hollywood regulation: a look back'. *Gannett Center Journal*, Vol. 2, No. 1, Winter 1988, pp. 91–8.
Films have always been a controversial mass entertainment, and a wide range of civic and religious groups have attempted to censor them over the past 80 years. This article chronicles the regulation of Hollywood films, the rise (and eventual

demise) of the notorious Hays Code of self-regulation of the film industry, and the belated according of protection against prior restraint under the First Amendment in 1952. (BM)

Broadcasting

361 British Broadcasting Corporation. *Violence and the media.* London: BBC, 1987. 59pp.
The BBC, always concerned about violence in its programmes, first published a code on violence in the 1950s. These papers are a contribution to the continuing process of editorial discussion and examination of principles, and cover research, legal, moral and programming issues. (BM)

362 British Broadcasting Corporation. *Violence on television: the report of the Wyatt Committee.* London: BBC, 1987. 23pp.
Violence may not be the only area of complaint about television, but along with bad taste, sexual morality and language, it puts television in the dock, for its own alleged transgressions as well as for reflecting a society which is itself a cause for concern. The BBC asked its (then) Head of Documentary Features, Television, Will Wyatt, to chair an internal committee to review the BBC's guidelines on the portrayal of violence, and survey such issues as scheduling, the 'watershed', and the wider context of what is acceptable to society at large. (BM)

363 Cooper, Cynthia A. *Violence on television: congressional inquiry, public criticism, and industry response. A policy analysis.* Lanham, Maryland: University Press of America, 1996. ix, 201pp.
Major focus of this study are the 28 American congressional hearings to investigate television violence since 1954, which provided a forum for government inquiry and public criticism, and have played a significant role in the development of the debate over 40 years. (BM)

364 Donnellan, Craig (ed.) *Television and censorship.* Cambridge: Independence, 1996. 40pp. (Issues for the nineties, Vol. 27)
One of a series of student texts offering a reference source on contemporary social issues, this volume looks at violence, bad language and sex on television and the issue of censorship, through a variety of different original key sources – government reports, regulatory bodies' codes, lobbying and campaign literature, and research studies. (BM)

365 Duval, Robin. 'Not before 9 o'clock'. *InterMedia*, Vol. 20, No. 3, May–June 1992, pp. 28–31.
Deputy Director of Programmes at the Independent Television Commission discusses the regulation of programme content on British television, particularly sexual representation, and the concern for standards of taste and decency. (BM)

366 Feldman, Charles and **Tickton, Stanley**. 'Obscene/indecent programming: regulation of ambiguity'. *Journal of Broadcasting*, Vol. 20, No. 2, Spring 1976, pp. 273–82.
In the US the Federal Communications Commission has recently considered cases of obscene and indecent programming, but its efforts to clarify its standards on obscenity have only clouded this issue, which perhaps should be left to the courts. There is no simple solution as to how a free society can protect itself from what it finds morally objectionable without infringing upon citizens' rights. (BM)

367 Gunter, Barrie. *Dimensions of television violence*. Aldershot: Gower, 1985. ix, 282pp.
Violence in society, and the influence of the media in promoting social violence, has long been one of the most persistent strains of media research. Academic interest appears to be declining, but politicians, journalists and one small sector of public opinion continue to pursue the 'effects' study, even though a quarter of a century's work has produced relatively little positive results. This book explores, rather than 'effects', the audience's perceptions of violence, which has never been satisfactorily defined. Though it is essentially a pilot study, it contains a useful critique of some of the established gurus. (SM)

368 Hargrave, Andrea Millwood. *A matter of manners?: the limits of broadcast language*. London: John Libbey, 1991. v, 105pp. (Broadcasting Standards Council research monograph series, 3)
Broadcasters receive a huge volume of complaints about bad language and swearing in broadcasts. These are research findings on the offence caused by bad language, with seven essays by distinguished contributors on aspects of the problem, including Phil Redmond on 'Class, decency and hypocrisy', Colin Morris on 'Blasphemy' and Professor Rom Harré on 'Obscenity and blasphemy from the linguistic point of view'. (BM)

369 Hargrave, Andrea Millwood. *Sex and sexuality in broadcasting*. London: John Libbey, 1992. v, 146pp. (Broadcasting Standards Council, public opinion and broadcasting standards, 3)
Research report examining the portrayal in broadcasting of sexual conduct, particularly explicit sex, and how much offence and genuine outrage are really caused. (BM)

370 Hargrave, Andrea Millwood. *Taste and decency in broadcasting*. London: John Libbey, 1991. 53pp. (Broadcasting Standards Council, annual review 1991, public opinion and broadcasting standards, 2)
Survey of public attitudes to areas of taste and decency in radio and television in the UK, including bad language, depiction of stereotypes, issues raised by invasion of privacy, and the role of programme scheduling to avoid causing offence. (BM)

371 Hawes, William. 'Television censorship: myth or menace?' *Television Quarterly*, Vol. 4, No. 3, Summer 1965, pp. 63–73.
Changes in programme 'censorship' on American television since the Second World War, and the influence of the National Association of Broadcasters' voluntary code, pressure groups, advertisers, sponsors and the networks. (BM)

372 Pierson, W. Theodore. 'The active eyebrow: a changing style for censorship'. *Television Quarterly*, Vol. 1, No. 1, 1962, pp. 14–21.
Author argues against the intrusion of government into television programming. (BM)

373 Samoriski, Jan H., Huffman, John L. and **Trauth, Denise M.** 'Indecency, the Federal Communications Commission and post-Sykes era: a framework for regulation'. *Journal of Broadcasting & Electronic Media*, Vol. 39, No. 1, Winter 1995, pp. 51–72.
Evolution of broadcast indecency in the US, its interpretation by the courts, and its enforcement by the FCC, with a proposal for a new framework for regulating indecency aiming at a new formulation of the concept of indecency, but also consistency. (BM)

374 Comstock, George A. and **Rubinstein, Eli A.** (eds.) *Television and social behaviour: a technical report to the Surgeon General's Scientific Advisory Committee on Television and Social Behaviour.* Vols. 1–5. Washington, DC: US Government Printing Office, 1972.
Five volumes of technical reports resulting from research 'from a broad scientific inquiry about television and its impact on the viewer' in the US. *Television and growing up: the impact of televised violence* (1972) summarized the report. (BM)

Cable and the Internet

375 Bridger, Francis. *Videos, permissiveness and the law.* Bramcote, Nottinghamshire: Grove Books, 1984. 26pp. (Grove booklet on ethics, No. 54)
Examination of the moral and legal issues raised by the video revolution, particularly the genre of films popularly known as 'video nasties', from a theological perspective. (BM)

376 Dupagne, Michel. 'Regulation of sexually explicit videotex services in France'. *Journalism Quarterly*, Vol. 71, No. 1, Spring 1994, pp. 121–34.
Author describes how the French judicial system copes with the rising phenomenon of sexually explicit message services and places the legal responsibility for them; French courts have made little reference to a defence of freedom of speech and the press. (BM)

377 Kleiman, Howard M. 'Indecent programming on cable television: legal and social dimensions'. *Journal of Broadcasting & Electronic Media*, Vol. 30, No. 3, Summer 1986, pp. 275–94.

The American cable television industry does not want to adhere to the self-regulation codes of the National Association of Broadcasters, particularly in relation to adult or sexual material, nor to adopt a degree of responsibility to the right of viewers not to be confronted with such material. (BM)

Truth and truth-telling

378 **Barney, Ralph D**. 'Community journalism: good intentions, questionable practice'. *Journal of Mass Media Ethics*, Vol. 11, No. 3, 1996, pp. 140–51.
The author argues that communitarianism, currently at the centre of the media ethics debate, denies individuals rights to develop their own moral reasoning which is essential for an individualistic society, and that communitarian journalism devalues truth in favour of community loyalty and conformity. (BM)

379 **Blumler, Jay G**. and **Gurevitch, Michael**. *The crisis of public communication.* London: Routledge, 1995. vi, 237pp.
Collection of old and new essays on the role of the media in political communication over the past 25 years, addressing the crisis in public confidence in both the media and politics, with British and American examples. (BM)

380 **Bok, Sissela**. *Lying: moral choice in public and private life.* New York: Pantheon, 1978; Hassocks, Sussex: Harvester Press, 1978. xxii, 328pp.
Examination of the many types of situations in which deception becomes an issue – white lies, excuses, justification, lies in a crisis, lying to liars and to enemies, lying for the public good, and lying to the sick and dying. Whether to lie, equivocate, be silent or tell the truth in these situations is often a hard choice and results in a moral quandary. The author concludes that truth and integrity are precious resources, easily squandered and hard to regain; they can only survive on a foundation of respect for veracity. (BM)

381 **Cooper, Thomas W**. *Time before deception: truth in communication culture and ethics.* Santa Fe, New Mexico: Clear Light, 1995.

382 **Dayan, Daniel** and **Katz, Elihu**. *Media events: the live broadcasting of history.* Cambridge, Massachusetts: Harvard University Press, 1992. xi, 306pp.
An original and thought-provoking study of a recent media phenomenon, the live televising of major historic events, which combines the disciplines of sociology, anthropology and political science. Drawing on such examples as the Olympic Games, the funeral of John F. Kennedy, moon landings, papal visits, and the wedding of the Prince of Wales and Lady Diana Spencer, the authors examine how the live broadcasting of these media events has redefined the power of organizers, intermediaries, broadcasters and audiences (for whom it has become a unique form of ceremonial experience), and the very essence of a public event. (BM)

383 Goldie, Grace Wyndham. *Facing the nation: television and politics, 1936–76.* London: Bodley Head, 1977. 368pp.

The author was a major influence in British television for over 20 years, latterly as BBC Head of Television Talks and Current Affairs, during which time her achievements included *Tonight, Panorama* and *That Was The Week That Was*. She writes of the delicate relations between broadcasters on the one hand and politicians and governments on the other, particularly the symbiotic relationship which developed between television and politics over a 40-year period, and some of the flashpoints – the Suez Crisis, General Election broadcasts, and the attitudes to television of various Prime Ministers, including Harold Macmillan, Harold Wilson and Edward Heath. (BM)

384 Jensen, Carl and **Project Censored**. *Censored: the news that didn't make the news – and why: the 1995 Project Censored yearbook.* New York: Four Walls Eight Windows, 1995. 332pp.

Project Censored is a national media research project on news media censorship founded in 1976 by Carl Jensen at Sonoma State University. The yearbook, previously a self-published resource book, seeks to highlight annually the news and information not published or broadcast by the mainstream media in the US. It contains a survey of censorship in America, the top 25 censored news stories, the over-covered 'junk food news' stories, and a directory of alternative organizations, news services, publications, civil groups and so on. (BM)

385 Jones, Nicholas. *Soundbites and spin doctors: how politicians manipulate the media – and vice versa.* Rev. ed. London: Indigo, 1996. vii, 272pp.

BBC political correspondent looks at the pursuit of publicity by politicians in the UK, and their attempts to manipulate the media, and examines the work of the all-powerful press agents, or 'spin doctors', who control and negotiate media access to politicians. (BM)

386 Leslie, Larry Z. 'Lying in prime time: ethical egoism in situation comedies'. *Journal of Mass Media Ethics*, Vol. 7, No. 1, 1992, pp. 5–18.

'Lying is rampant in America and Americans are good at rationalizing their lies', so the author thinks it is not surprising that a content analysis has found a high incidence of lying in such network situation comedies as *Roseanne* and *Family Matters*. (BM)

387 Pares i Maicas, Manuel. 'The ethics of political communication'. *European Journal of Communication*, Vol. 10, No. 4, December 1995, pp. 475–95.

Professor of Communication Sciences at the Universitat Autónoma de Barcelona analyses from an ethical perspective the political communication process, and concludes that the increasing use of untruths and deception through propaganda, disinformation, political advertising and public relations makes an ethical approach more urgent. (BM)

388 Phelan, John M. *Disenchantment: meaning and morality in the media.* New York: Hastings House, 1980. 191pp. (Humanistic studies in the communications arts)
A stimulating book, slightly marred by the air of self-satisfaction with which it is written. It is basically an attack on the concept that functionalism – the facts and figures effects study – increases our understanding of the media. The author pleads instead for a 'humanist' approach which might employ a multiplicity of methods, but would always be concerned with value judgements. He challenges many received truths – for example, by pointing out that Ralph Nader-type consumerism is a form of concealed censorship; but because so many of the references are topical and trivial the book falls nearer to the category of high-class journalism than to the search for absolute truth. (SM)

389 Read, Donald. *The power of the news: the history of Reuters, 1849–1989.* Oxford: Oxford University Press, 1992. xv, 431pp.
Julius Reuter established his news agency in London in 1851, which was to eventually extend throughout the world, first as the news agency of the British Empire and then as the supplier of economic information to the world trading community. Beginning modestly with a carrier pigeon service from Aachen to Brussels, Reuters was quick to realize the potential of new technologies, from the laying of submarine cable under the English Channel from Dover to Calais in 1851, through to the satellite communications and data networks of the late twentieth century. Despite tensions with the British government in the 1930s and at the beginning of the Second World War, Reuters has maintained its pre-eminence and reputation for independence and commitment to the truth. (BM)

390 Scott, George. *Reporter anonymous: the story of the Press Association.* London: Hutchinson, 1968. 307pp.
A house history of the only British national news agency. George Scott is himself a journalist, and most of the emphasis is on 'news' itself. There is coverage, however, of relations with government, censorship and technical developments. (SM)

Accuracy

391 Daviss, Bennett. 'Touching up reality: new technologies shake old beliefs in news photography'. *Media & Values,* No. 50, Spring 1990, pp. 10–11.
New technologies have changed images into electronic information, and have destroyed the photograph as a reliable record of reality. (BM)

392 Denton, R. E. (ed.) *Ethical dimension of political communication.* New York: Praeger, 1991.
Essays on ethical concerns of political communication, such as whether image projection is more important than political discussion, and television's impact on democracy. (BM)

393 Forsyth, John. 'I've got you taped ...'. *British Journalism Review*, Vol. 2, No. 2, Winter 1990, pp. 30–4.
BBC Radio producer discusses the ethical aspects of editing and cleaning up (or distorting) taped interviews in favour of the subject. (BM)

394 Gitlin, Todd. *The whole world is watching: mass media in the making and unmaking of the New Left*. Berkeley: University of California Press, 1980. xiii, 328pp.
This book by a respected sociologist is of particular interest because he was himself president of one of the New Left movements in the 1960s. He analyses the way in which the media distort the nature of protest movements, and detach the leaders from their base by making them celebrities. In this closely argued work, he is saying that the modern media have inevitably altered the nature and course of social protest. (SM)

395 Harris, Christopher R. 'Digitization and manipulation of news photographs'. *Journal of Mass Media Ethics*, Vol. 6, No. 3, 1991, pp. 164–74.
Despite the ethical concerns about digital retouching and its effect on the perception of the truthfulness of photographs, it should not be completely outlawed as they are useful to photojournalism, but protocols (rather than rigid codes) should be devised for practical consideration in the use and identification of manipulated images. (BM)

396 Lessing, Doris. 'Never the whole truth'. *British Journalism Review*, Vol. 1, No. 2, Winter 1990, pp. 18–22.
Distinguished writer bemoans the lack of commitment to the truth in newspaper interviews or profiles. (BM)

397 Linn, Travis. 'Staging in TV news'. *Journal of Mass Media Ethics*, Vol. 6, No. 1, 1991, pp. 47–54.
'Staging for the camera' can be any action that alters what would have happened or taken place without the presence of the camera, whether intentional or unintentional (effect of the very presence of the camera); its use by TV news editors is ethically dangerous. (BM)

398 Martin, Edwin. 'Against photographic deception'. *Journal of Mass Media Ethics*, Vol. 2, No. 2, Spring–Summer, 1987, pp. 49–59.
There are many forms of deception possible in the use of photographs – through captions, context, photographer's impact on the subject of the picture, and so on. (BM)

399 Martin, Edwin. 'On photographic manipulation'. *Journal of Mass Media Ethics*, Vol. 6, No. 3, 1991, pp. 156–63.

Clearly articulated policies and guidelines on standards for manipulation of photographs are needed to prevent deception and a public loss of faith in their veracity. (BM)

400 O'Brien, Sue. 'Eye on Soweto: a study of factors in news photo use'. *Journal of Mass Media Ethics*, Vol. 8, No. 2, 1993, pp. 69–87.
The experience of Gregory Marinovich, who took the 1991 Pulitzer Prize-winning photograph of the murder of an accused Zulu spy by African National Congress sympathizers in Soweto, and who tried to – but could not – stop the murder, shows the moral dilemmas that face photographers. Such images must be used carefully, in context. (BM)

401 Parker, Douglas. 'Ethical implications of electronic still cameras and computer digital imaging in the print media'. *Journal of Mass Media Ethics*, Vol. 3, No. 2, Fall 1988, pp. 47–59.
'Manipulation of photographs is not new, it just has never been as easy to do before.' This examination of the ethical problems presented by the new digital technologies, conducted partly through interviews with eleven leading American photographers and editors, calls for agreement on setting ethical standards. (BM)

402 Real, Michael. 'The great quiz show scandal: why America remains fascinated'. *Television Quarterly*, Vol. 27, No. 3, 1995, pp. 2–27.
Media academic looks at the ethical questions of the notorious quiz show rigging scandal of the 1950s (where the production team of *The $64,000 Question* devised a system of cheating to increase dramatic appeal and ratings), which became a defining moment in the American public's attitudes to and trust in television. (BM)

403 Reaves, Shiela. 'Digital alteration of photographs in consumer magazines'. *Journal of Mass Media Ethics*, Vol. 6, No. 3, 1991, pp. 175–81.
Digital manipulation raises different concerns for magazine editors than for newspaper reporters and editors. In interviews with thirteen American consumer magazines (including *Time* and *National Geographic*) it is clear that they would refuse to manipulate *news* photographs but opinions varied on the use of manipulation for features and cover photographs, depending partly on the editorial policy of the magazine. (BM)

404 Reaves, Shiela. 'Digital retouching: is there a place for it in newspaper photography?' *Journal of Mass Media Ethics*, Vol. 2, No. 2, Spring–Summer, 1987, pp. 40–8.
Digital retouching can alter and synthesize photographs to the point that the alteration is undetectable, but it raises many ethical questions about the 'integrity' of photographs. Is there agreement that it is not acceptable in news photographs,

but all right in feature sections? Deadlines, layout problems and ease of altering pictures all make for potentially unethical decisions. (BM)

405 Warburton, Nigel. 'Varieties of photographic representation: documentary, pictorial and quasi-documentary'. *History of Photography*, Vol. 15, No. 3, Autumn 1991, pp. 203–10.

Author discusses what he sees as the inadequacies of philosophical analysis of photography, and proposes a general framework which can be applied in discussion of specific images. Analysis of the controversy over Robert Capa's famous photograph *Spanish Republican soldier at the very instant of his death*, regarding the power of the image, 'staging' of photographs and the questions of deception and responsibility. (BM)

406 Winston, Brian. *Claiming the real: the Griersonian documentary and its legitimations.* London: British Film Institute, 1995. 301pp.

The status of the photographic image has reached a turning point, digital image manipulation is now widely used in the press, along with a parallel technology for the moving image. The implication of this undetectable digital retouching for the integrity and veracity of the photograph is profound and far-reaching. This, and other ethical issues concerning documentary film making from John Grierson and Robert Flaherty to recent *cinéma-vérité* and direct cinema movements, are covered by the author, who is Director of the University of Wales Centre for Journalism Studies. He particularly addresses the ethics of 'actuality' and the legal position and restraints on film makers with regard to consent from the subjects of documentaries, and the exposure (or exploitation) of suffering in the victim documentary. (BM)

407 Young, Hugo. 'Can television tell the truth?' *British Journalism Review*, Vol. 2, No. 1, Autumn 1990, pp. 11–16.

British author and political journalist questions whether television is capable of telling the truth. Using examples of notable and controversial documentaries (including Thames Television's *Death on the Rock*) and drama-documentaries (the BBC's *Tumbledown* and *The Monocled Mutineer*), he argues that the need to keep the audience tuned in, and the rules that it might follow to satisfy that audience, are more important than the truth. While based on fact, these programmes were factually inaccurate, and claims of truth and accuracy in these facsimiles of reality were widely challenged. Despite its undeniable impact and technical brilliance television is often a deeply flawed medium for truth-telling. (BM)

Understanding

408 Adams, William C. *Television coverage of the Middle East.* Norwood, New Jersey: Ablex Publishing, 1981. x, 167pp. (Communication and information science)

This claims to be the first thorough content analysis of the American network's news coverage of the Middle East, stimulated by the Iranian taking of US hostages crisis in 1979. It is enlivened only by one interesting paper by David Altheide on the Iranian affair. (SM)

409 Aubrey, Crispin (ed.) *Nukespeak: the media and the bomb.* London: Comedia, 1982. vii, 135pp. (Comedia/Minority Press Group series, 9)
A propagandist pamphlet critical of the media's treatment of the nuclear disarmament in the UK. Oddly, and unconvincingly, the central target is the BBC. (SM)

410 Baehr, Helen and **Dyer, Gillian** (eds.) *Boxed in: women and television.* London: Pandora Press (Routledge & Kegan Paul), 1987. xi, 233pp.
Collection of original essays by British and American women academics and media practitioners showing the range of feminist approaches to the media – women working in the medium of television, as viewers, and as represented on screen. (BM)

411 Baehr, Helen and **Gray, Ann** (eds.) *Turning it on: a reader in women and media.* London: Arnold, 1996. xiii, 226pp.
One achievement of feminist media studies of the past two decades has been that it is now impossible to make sense of the mass media without some reference to gender issues. This selection of key texts on women and the media covers the areas of representation, genre, audiences and industry working practices. (BM)

412 Benthall, Jonathan. *Disasters, relief and the media.* London: I. B. Tauris, 1993. xiv, 267pp.
Director of the Royal Anthropological Institute, London, takes as his central theme the relationship between the relief agencies and the media. He identifies the moral predicament they face: the agencies benefit from the public's exposure to images of disaster and relief efforts through media coverage, but are often unhappy with the negative representation of misery. The adoption by the General Assembly of European Non-Governmental Organizations in 1989 of its *Code of conduct on images and messages relating to the Third World* represents an effort by the agencies to impose their own guidelines on television journalists in the honest and truthful depiction of disasters which respects the human dignity of people. (BM)

413 Birt, John and **Jay, Peter**. 'Can television news break the understanding-barrier?' *The Times*, 28 February 1975, p. 14; 'Television journalism: the child of an unhappy marriage between newspapers and film'. *The Times*, 30 September 1975, p. 12; 'The radical changes needed to remedy TV's bias against understanding'. *The Times*, 1 October 1975, p. 14. London: Times Newspapers, 1975.
Influential three-part analysis of television news, known as 'Bias against understanding', written by John Birt (Director-General of the BBC since 1993) and Peter Jay (an economic journalist). The main thesis is that news and current affairs programmes aggravate the difficulties of society in solving its problems and

reconciling its differences, by failing to devote enough time to important news stories or putting them in a full enough context, and therefore not informing their audience about the circumstances which shape the world in which they live. (BM)

414 Black, Jay and **Steele, Bob**. 'Beyond Waco: reflections and guidelines'. *Journal of Mass Media Ethics*, Vol. 8, No. 4, 1993, pp. 239–45.

Final section from the report of the Task Force appointed by the Society of Professional Journalists to examine journalists' conduct in covering the stand-off between federal agents and David Koresh and his Branch Davidian followers at Waco in Texas in 1993. It highlights press attitudes to reporting on religious cults and sects as well as problems in covering ongoing crises and hostage situations, and suggests guidelines. (BM)

415 Cohen, Phil and **Gardner, Carl** (eds.) *It ain't half racist, mum: fighting racism in the media.* London: Comedia, 1982. vi, 120pp. (Comedia/Minority Press Group series, 10)

Sponsored by the Campaign Against Racism in the Media, this collection of pieces by media workers on aspects of racial prejudice in the British press and broadcasting, both in employment and in reporting of ethnic minority issues. An examination of press coverage of the 1981 race riots in Brixton, South London which claims to reveal a 'conspiracy' in the reporting of race relations issues between sections of the media and the police, who both skilfully exploit their own record of events to suit their own purposes, but leading to a perpetuation of the view that black equals crime. Lord Scarman's report on the riots blamed the media, particularly television, for escalation of the disorders in Brixton. (BM)

416 Cohen, Stanley. *Folk devils and moral panics: the creation of the mods and rockers.* London: MacGibbon & Kee, 1972; Oxford: Martin Jackson, 1980.

An interesting early case study of the British 'mods and rockers' phenomenon of the 1960s. A relatively unimportant press story, at a time when 'news' was in short supply, escalated to the point at which legislation was passed in Parliament. This, Professor Cohen argues, is because of the media's need for 'devils' and because the population at large needs to express moral indignation. Though the book is British based it has implication for many societies. (SM)

417 Cohen, Stanley and **Young, Jock** (eds.) *The manufacture of news: social problems, deviance and the mass media.* Rev. ed. London: Constable; Beverly Hills, California: Sage Publications, 1981. 506pp. (Communication and society)

A valuable reader. The second edition contains 30 papers; seven have been dropped from the first edition and twelve added. The basic theme is how the media respond to deviant behaviour and social problems, grouped into four sections: the selection (and creation) of news; how it is presented, and what images of society are revealed; what the consequences are for the public and for the development of social policy. A final section makes some suggestions for do-ityourself research. There are brief but useful critical introductions by the editors to each section. (SM)

418 Creedon, Pamela J. (ed.) *Women in mass communication.* 2nd ed. Newbury Park, California: Sage Publications, 1993. x, 398pp.
Women working in the communications industries, and images of women in the media, examined by American media academics from a feminist theoretical viewpoint. The editor concludes that the situation had not improved in the four years since her first edition because feminist theory has had little effect on communications research, media education has remained essentially unchanged, and that the increased numbers of women in the field has had no significant effect on practice. (BM)

419 Council of Europe. *Human rights and gender: the responsibility of the media. Proceedings: Seminar: Strasbourg 29 June – 1 July 1994.* Strasbourg: Council of Europe Press, 1995. 97pp.
This seminar address the exercise of two fundamental rights: the freedom of expression, exercised through the media, and the right to equality between the sexes. Includes contributions from Andrea Millwood Hargrave (of the Broadcasting Standards Council) on 'The media: pornography, violence and gender equality', and Bettina Peters (of the International Federation of Journalists) on 'The value of and limits to the self-regulatory approach to gender equality in the media'. (BM)

420 Cumberbatch, Guy and **Negrine, Ralph.** *Images of disability on television.* London: Routledge, 1992. xii, 180pp.
Report on the portrayal of people with disability on British television, partly from content analysis and partly from interviews with disabled people, their families and carers, which concludes that representation is inadequate and does not promote greater understanding of disability by the public. (BM)

421 Dahlgren, Peter and **Sparks, Colin** (eds.) *Journalism and popular culture.* London: Sage Publications, 1992. x, 210pp. (Media culture and society)
Cultural studies papers by international scholars presented at a Stockholm University Colloquium in 1990. Looking at broadcast and print journalism in a context of popular culture, the contributors consider a variety of topics, including personalities in the popular media, news, photojournalism and the tabloid press, attitudes to and representation of sexual minorities, and two special (American) case studies of the Oliver North affair and the San Francisco earthquake. Rather academic but addresses interesting issues. (BM)

422 Davis, Richard H. and **Davis, James A.** *TV's image of the elderly.* Lexington, Massachusetts: Lexington Books, 1985. xvi, 265pp.
Television has such influence over people's view of society, while its largest audience are older viewers, and yet it virtually ignores them as an audience and

presents negative stereotyped images of the elderly. A gerontologist and an educator explore the issues of ageing and the media, and propose strategies for combating ageism in American television. (BM)

423 Friedan, Betty. *The feminine mystique.* New York: W. W. Norton, 1963; London: Victor Gollancz, 1963; Harmondsworth, Middlesex: Penguin, 1965. 367pp.
Pioneering text of the Women's Movement, by a founder of the American National Organization for Women in 1966, which analyses the position of women in Western society and their long battle for emancipation and greater fulfilment. Media-related issues covered include images of women in magazines and television, and the use of the 'sexual sell' in advertising. (BM)

424 Gallagher, Margaret. 'Communication and human dignity: a women's rights perspective'. *Media Development*, Vol. 42, No. 3, 1995, pp. 6–9
Author discusses women's rights in the context of the mass media, advertising, pornography and violence, and concludes that freedom of expression is incomplete unless women's rights to freedom of expression form an integral part of it. (BM)

425 Gallagher, Margaret. 'Women and men in the media'. *Communication Research Trends*, Vol. 12, No. 1, 1992, pp. 1–36.
Special issue devoted to patterns of male and female representation in media content, facing the underlying and serious issues in this debate of fairness and justice. List of current worldwide research on gender and mass media. Annotated bibliography. (BM)

426 Godfrey, Donald R. 'Ethics in practice: analysis of Edward R. Murrow's WWII radio reporting'. *Journal of Mass Media Ethics*, Vol. 8, No. 2, 1993, pp. 103–81.
Ed Murrow's Second World War reports were legendary, and this article examines his decision processes and ethical choices in reporting on an American bombing mission over Germany. His reports enhanced audiences' involvement and understanding; through superb command of language he 'spoke to the heart of audiences'. (BM)

427 Goode, Erich and **Ben-Yehuda, Nachman.** *Moral panics: the social construction of deviance.* Cambridge, Massachusetts: Blackwell, 1994. xi, 265pp.
'Moral panics' result from the fears and concerns of individuals and societies, often irrational, which focus on groups or movements branded as deviant or a threat, and find expression as moral outrage. The concept, first articulated by Jock Young and Stanley Cohen in the 1970s, may be fairly recent, but the manifestations have been around for quite a long time. The authors, sociology academics from the State University of New York and the Hebrew University of Jerusalem respectively, examine the phenomenon and the role of the media, particularly the press, in the creation of moral panics. (BM)

428 Harrison, Paul and **Palmer, Robin**. *News out of Africa: Biafra to Band Aid.* London: Hilary Shipman, 1986. x, 147pp.
A journalistic account, based on experiences of Frederick Forsyth, Jonathan Dimbleby, Mohamed Amin and Michael Buerk in reporting Africa. Interest lies in the description of the random, almost incidental way in which news stories surface; the authors express concern at the implications for the reporter of the new technologies. (SM)

429 Herman, Edward S. and **Chomsky, Noam**. *Manufacturing consent: the political economy of the mass media.* New York: Pantheon Books, 1988. xvi, 413pp.
The authors apply a 'propaganda' model to the performance of the media in the US, because 'managing' public opinion and fixing the premise of discourse have become a significant part of the overall service. This bias in the news results not from 'conspiracy', but from the realities of source and media organizational requirements of and adaptation of media personnel to the constraints of ownership and market forces. The proposition is tested against media coverage of El Salvador, Guatemala, Nicaragua and Vietnam. Commercialization of the publicly owned airwaves should be resisted as a democratic political society requires far wider control of and access to the media. (BM)

430 Levin, Ellen. 'The victim: twice wounded'. *Media Studies Journal,* Vol. 6, No. 1, Winter 1992, pp. 45–51.
The founder of the Justice For All victims' rights political action committee pleads for respectful, dignified and compassionate treatment by the media of victims of crime. (BM)

431 Lester, Paul Martin (ed.) *Images that injure: pictorial stereotypes in the media.* Westport, Connecticut: Praeger, 1996. xii, 282pp.
Essays by America academics and media professionals that examine images in the media that harm and perpetuate misleading myths through use of ethnic, gender, age, physical disability and sexual orientation stereotypes. General overview, including 'Ethical and moral responsibilities of the media' by Deni Elliott, is followed by 30 essays on different individual stereotypical situations. Bibliography. (BM)

432 MacDonald, J. Fred. *Television and the red menace: the video road to Vietnam.* New York: Praeger, 1985. xii, 278pp.
There is a scarcity of books which take 'popular' television programming (including fiction) seriously. This work argues that American television became 'politicized' at the time of the Cold War and was influential in creating the climate of opinion – chauvinistic, anti-communist – which allowed the US to drift into the Vietnam War. Though the book conscientiously records the American television diet over these years, from news and current affairs through action-adventure to situation comedy, it makes little attempt to provide evidence that this programming was necessarily influential. Bibliography. (SM)

433 McFarlane, Janice J. 'The cultural censorship of women'. *Media Development*, Vol. 38, No. 2, 1991, pp. 18–19.

Author argues that the inevitable censorship of women inherent in language and culture is often reinforced by a high degree of self-censorship generated by institutional inequality. Journalists and broadcasters who have privileged access to the printed and broadcast word have a responsibility to correct this wherever possible. (BM)

434 McLeod, Douglas M. 'Communicating deviance: the effects of television news coverage of social protest'. *Journal of Broadcasting & Electronic Media*, Vol. 39, No. 1, Winter 1995, pp. 4–19.

Research study testing the concerns that media news coverage may unfairly bias audiences against social protesters by portraying them as deviant, and that such negative portrayal may act against protest as a legitimate form of democratic participation. (BM)

435 Meyers, Marian. *News coverage of violence against women: engendering blame.* Thousand Oaks, California: Sage Publications, 1997. xii, 148pp.

The author, from the Department of Communication at Georgia State University and former reporter and news editor, argues that journalists need to be educated about violence against women and to become more sensitive to both the victim and the effects of coverage on the victim, if they are not to perpetuate traditional and damaging stereotypes of victim and perpetrator. (BM)

436 Minear, Larry, Scott, Colin and **Weiss, Thomas G.** *The news media, civil war and humanitarian action.* Boulder, Colorado: Lynne Rienner, 1996. xi, 123pp.

A study of the three sides of the triangle – media, governments and humanitarian organizations – in the media coverage of war and famine, and the immense power it has to change policy and shape the public and humanitarian response. (BM)

437 Pickering, Michael. 'Race, gender and broadcast comedy: the case of the BBC's "Kentucky Minstrels"'. *European Journal of Communication*, Vol. 9, No. 3, September 1994, pp. 311–33.

Blackface minstrelsy has been a popular and traditional form of entertainment in the UK dating back to the 1830s, one more recently picked up by the BBC for radio in the *Kentucky Minstrels* and a long-running television series with *The Black and White Minstrel Show*; however, it is cultural transmission of prejudice which raises questions of racism and sexism in popular humour. (BM)

438 Rocheron, Yvette and **Linne, Olga.** 'AIDS, moral panic and opinion polls'. *European Journal of Communication*, Vol. 4, No. 4, December 1989, pp. 411–34.

British media coverage of AIDS, as a threat to society, is a classic moral panic. (BM)

439 Ross, Karen. *Black and white media: black images in popular film and television.* Oxford: Polity Press, 1996. xxv, 206pp.

The author, from the Centre for Mass Communications Research at the University of Leicester, provides a textbook on media representation of black people, and the relationship between black communities and popular media in the UK and the US, and covers ethnicity, racism and 'blaxploitation'. (BM)

440 Said, Edward W. *Covering Islam: how the media and the experts determine how we see the rest of the world.* New York: Pantheon Books, 1981; London: Routledge & Kegan Paul, 1981; rev. ed. London: Vintage, 1997. lxx, 202pp.

This is an odd book. It begins with a scholarly inquiry into the difficulties one society finds in understanding another with a quite different social ethos, and suggests that 'Islam' as the West understands it is a fiction created not only by the media, but also by academics and government 'experts'. It then falls to a much less exalted examination of particular cases (for example, the British television documentary *Death of a Princess*). Said, born in Jerusalem and educated in Egypt and at Harvard, has taught at Harvard, Princeton, Johns Hopkins and Columbia Universities in the USA. (SM/BM)

441 Scott, Colin. 'The humanitarian response to war: who are the drivers – policymakers, and agencies or the media?'. *InterMedia*, Vol. 25, No. 1, February 1997, pp. 8–10.

Looking at the media coverage of humanitarian crises in Iraq, Liberia, Somalia, the former Yugoslavia, Rwanda and Haiti, the author proposes ways in which the media, agencies and policy makers can take the opportunity with regard to educating public opinion, not only about the reality of famine and war, but also about the causes and the real effectiveness of international responses. (BM)

442 Thoveron, Gabriel and others. *How women are represented in television programmes in the EEC.* Part One: *Images of women in news advertising, and series and serials.* 59pp.; Part Two: *Positive action and strategies.* 39pp.; Part Three: *EEC television and the image of women.* 28pp. Luxembourg: Office for Official Publications of the European Communities, 1987.

Study of the representation of women's place and role in the various types of television programmes across the countries of the European Community (in 1984). (BM)

443 Traber, Michael. 'Death and the media: an introduction'. *Media Development*, Vol. 39, No. 4, 1992, pp. 3–5.

Western societies are in varying degrees death-denying and this is particularly evident in the lack of representation in the mass media of natural death and dying, despite an obsession with violent death in war and terrorism reportage. (BM)

444 Tuchman, Gaye, Daniels, Arlene Kaplan and **Benet, James.** *Hearth and home: images of women in the mass media.* New York: Oxford University Press, 1978. xi, 333pp.

Pioneering examination of sex-role stereotyping in American media, partially using survey findings, contributors such as George Gerbner, Muriel Cantor and Larry Gross look at television, women's magazines, newspapers and television's effects on children in the development of sex-role attitudes and behaviour. (BM)

445 Wahl, Otto F. *Media madness: public images of mental illness.* New Brunswick, New Jersey: Rutgers University Press, 1995. xiv, 220pp.
American psychology academic argues that media portrayals of mental illness are at best insensitive, inaccurate and unfavourable, and at worst, harmful stereotype images that have such profoundly negative consequences as to demand action for change. (BM)

446 Watney, Simon. *Policing desire: pornography, AIDS and the media.* 3rd ed. London: Cassell, 1997. xvi, 172pp.
Analysis of media coverage of the AIDS epidemic (and representation of homosexuality), which places it within the theory of moral panics, periods when society defines certain conditions, persons or groups of persons as a threat to its values and interests, and the potential long-term consequences for fair reporting and public understanding. (BM)

447 Williams, Kevin. 'AIDS stories covered up'. *Media Development*, Vol. 39, No. 4, 1992, pp. 9–11.
AIDS is a story of ignorance, prejudice, exclusion and callousness, and reporting of the fatal disease and deaths from it has exposed fears and taboos. Media response to AIDS has largely been characterized by denial, fear, blame and fatalism. (BM)

448 Ziesenis, Elizabeth. 'Suicide coverage in newspapers: an ethical consideration'. *Journal of Mass Media Ethics*, Vol. 6, No. 4, 1991, pp. 234–44.
Ethical problems in media coverage of suicide, and possible implications of imitative suicide and effects of suicide stories on people in crisis. Suggested guidelines for treatment, which would not detract from press freedom but might save lives, would provide for avoidance of romanticizing, stating general method of death but no details, discussing options to suicide, and handling carefully cases of adolescent suicide. (BM)

Fairness and bias

449 Alter, Jonathan, 'The cloak of fairness'. *Gannett Center Journal*, Vol. 2, No. 1, Winter 1988, pp. 73–80.
Fairness is by far the most problematic journalistic concept, such simple definitions as 'giving both sides' are wholly inadequate, and if pursued it would deny journalism its edge and make an interesting and provocative piece bland and equivocal. (BM)

450 Altheide, David L. and **Snow, Robert P.** *Media logic.* Beverly Hills, California and London: Sage Publications, 1979. 256pp. (Sage library of social research, Vol. 89)

An intensely parochial and frequently superficial work. The theme is post-McLuhan: our perception of society is governed by the way the media report and reflect on it. The media, however, by their format and 'logic' condition, or even alter fundamentally, the events they purport to cover. Typically, the book is strongest in dealing with news and politics, much weaker with entertainment, religion and sport. Its value lies in providing some context to the (then) current television programmes; perhaps a similar, or better, book is called for in each society. (SM)

451 Altschull, J. Herbert. 'Fairness, truth and the makers of images'. *Media Studies Journal*, Vol. 6, No. 4, Fall 1992, pp. 1–15.

Public dissatisfaction with the media, which has long been a fixture of American politics, reached a new peak with the 1992 presidential election season and raised questions of fairness in reporting, not only of major issues, of which many watchdogs exist to adjudicate, but also of less prominent or immediate stories. (BM)

452 Altschull, J. Herbert. 'A crisis of conscience: is community journalism the answer?' *Journal of Mass Media Ethics*, Vol. 11, No. 3, 1996, pp. 166–72.

The author argues that the press should put public and community interest ahead of maximization of profit or rigid adherence to journalistic objectivity and detachment, and advocates participatory community journalism in which journalists become activists on behalf of the process of self-government. (BM)

453 Aufderheide, Patricia. 'After the Fairness Doctrine: controversial broadcast programming and the public interest'. *Journal of Communication*, Vol. 40, No. 3, Summer 1990, pp. 47–72.

Author examines the effects on the broadcasting of public interest and controversial issues on American television, since the Federal Communications Commission announced in August 1987 that it would no longer enforce the Fairness Doctrine requiring broadcasters to give fair airtime to a broad range of views. (BM)

454 Boyer, John H. 'How editors view objectivity'. *Journalism Quarterly*, Vol. 58, No. 1, Spring 1981, pp. 24–8.

Objectivity as an ethical standard is one of the most pervasive of all journalism. This factor analysis of editors found general agreement about objectivity, though some saw it as an unobtainable goal, but clear differences of emphasis on some aspects. (BM)

455 Brennan, Timothy J. 'The Fairness Doctrine as public policy'. *Journal of Broadcasting & Electronic Media*, Vol. 33, No. 4, Fall 1989, pp. 419–40.

The American Fairness Doctrine, whereby broadcasters were obliged to represent a spectrum of opinion in public affairs programming, had come under criticism from both regulators and academics. In 1987 the Federal Communications Commission decided that the Doctrine was a counter-productive and unconstitutional interference with the freedom of broadcasters. (BM)

456 Byrd, Joann. 'Fair's fair – unless it isn't'. *Media Studies Journal,* Vol. 6, No. 4, Fall 1992, pp. 103.

Author, ombudsman for the *Washington Post,* claims 'journalism has a different definition of fairness than the people it serves', but news judgements can be fair so long as journalists have only the interests of keeping the public informed and have no personal (or corporate or political) axes to grind. (BM)

457 Cameron, James. *Point of departure.* London: Barker, 1967; Stocksfield, Northumberland: Oriel Press, 1978. 318pp.

Not so much an autobiography from this celebrated reporter, as reflections on a life in journalism and of covering news stories from Korea, Lambaréné, Tibet, South Africa, and his involvement with the Campaign for Nuclear Disarmament (CND). (BM)

458 Donahue, Hugh Carter. *The battle to control broadcast news: who owns the First Amendment?* Cambridge, Massachusetts: MIT Press, 1989. xiv, 238pp.

The author, from Ohio State University School of Journalism, and former television news writer, charts the evolution of the concepts of fairness and equal time in American broadcasting, and their subsequent erosion by the explosion of channels and First Amendment rights for speakers. The Fairness Doctrine (1949) had become accepted because the scarcity of frequencies made it against the public interest to let any radio or TV channel be devoted to single or partisan views. It placed two obligations on broadcasters: to broadcast balanced coverage of controversial news and public issues with reasonable opportunities for presentation of contrasting viewpoints and all sides of opinion; and the right of reply on controversial or public issues. The ebbtide came in the 1980s with deregulation, new technology and broadcasters' claims that they stifled good news reporting and inhibited editorials. (BM)

459 Eldridge, John (ed.) *Glasgow Media Group reader:* Volume 1: *News content, language and visuals.* xi, 399pp.; **Philo, Greg** (ed.) *Glasgow Media Group reader:* Volume 2: *Industry, economy, war and politics.* xiii, 241pp. London: Routledge, 1995.

The Glasgow University Media Group has been influential over the past twenty years in the study of the mass media and society, and controversial in its views of the role the media has played in shaping audience understanding of current events. These volumes assemble a representative selection of readings from four of the Group's earlier published works: *Bad news* (1976), *More bad news* (1980), *Really bad news* (1982) and *War and peace news* (1985). The first volume covers news content, language and visual images in news reporting, with case studies including reportage of nuclear protest, and the 'Church and the bomb', with the second volume concentrating on reporting of industrial and economic affairs, Northern Ireland, the Falklands conflict and the Gulf War, and the media strategies (and attempts to manage the media) of political parties in the UK. (BM)

460 Galician, Mary-Lou and **Pasternack, Steve**. 'Balancing good news and bad news: an ethical obligation?' *Journal of Mass Media Ethics*, Vol. 2, No. 2, Spring–Summer, 1987, pp. 82–92.
The author, using findings from her own American national survey of television news directors' policies, practices and perceptions of good/bad news, asks whether they have an ethical responsibility in the selection and presentation of news, given the potentially negative effects on individuals and society of excessive amounts of bad news. (BM)

461 Haarsager, Sandra. 'Choosing silence: a case of reverse agenda setting in depression era news coverage'. *Journal of Mass Media Ethics*, Vol. 6, No. 1, 1991, pp. 35–46.
Moral implications of selected coverage, strategic silence and reverse-agenda setting. (BM)

462 Halloran, James, Elliott, Philip and **Murdock, Graham**. *Demonstrations and communications: a case study*. Harmondsworth, Middlesex: Penguin Books, 1970. 334pp.
This was the first European study of the way in which a single event – the anti-Vietnam War demonstration on 27 October 1968 – was presented by a cross-section of the media, in fact the BBC, ITV and two national newspapers. An overwhelmingly peaceful event was anticipated by journalists largely in terms of an expectation of violence; and the presentation did, indeed, seek out some isolated scenes of violence. Yet no one told 'lies'. This is a pioneering study of the assumptions journalists make. It is open to criticism, but remains an invaluable work. (SM)

463 Harrison, Martin. *TV news: whose bias?* Hermitage, Berkshire: Policy Journals, 1985. 408pp.
The author has published the text of the relevant passages from the news bulletins from ITN (though not unfortunately the BBC as well) on which the Glasgow University Media Group purportedly based its *Bad news* studies. The evidence made available is accompanied by a commentary highly critical of the Group's scholarship and integrity. Some account is given of the damage done to the relationship between academics and broadcasters by the Group's activities. In the ten years following publication, *Bad news*, despite some critical voices, established itself as an authoritative critique of television news in universities and academic institutions in many countries. While only the naive ever assumed that objectivity

and impartiality were the prerogative and the hallmark of the academic, this book, part reputation, part indictment, is a cautionary tale for media students. (SM)

464 Hetherington. Alastair. *News, newspapers and television.* London: Macmillan, 1985. ix, 329pp.

This is basically a journalist's counterblast to much of the academic criticism of journalism. The author was at one time editor of *The Guardian*, then a senior executive of the BBC before becoming Research Professor of Media Studies at the University of Stirling. Apart from a brief review of some of the relevant literature the core of the book is a series of case studies of newspapers, ITN and the newsroom of the BBC. In particular it focuses on coverage of the coal dispute (the miners' strike) of 1984, and on the ethical problems of journalists reporting war (the Falklands) and terrorism (Northern Ireland). The author was unable to gain the co-operation of the more strident popular newspapers, but his general conclusion is that journalism is considerably more 'responsible' than most academic studies would allow. (SM)

465 Hinshaw, Ed. 'Life with the Fairness Doctrine'. *Television Quarterly*, Vol. 21, No. 3, 1985, pp. 37–42.

Author examines the arguments for and against the Fairness Doctrine, and concludes that while a spirit and sense of fairness are sound policy for any journalistic organization which aims to secure public confidence, regulated fairness is by its nature harmful. (BM)

466 Jones, Nicholas. *Strikes and the media: communication and conflict.* Oxford: Basil Blackwell, 1986. 220pp.

The title is misleading. This is primarily a case study of the British miners' strike of 1984–85, mentioning also two earlier strikes in the automobile and railway industries. It is essentially journalistic rather than scholarly, though well written. Its value lies in its analysis of the way in which managements employed communications techniques, some old, some new, to outflank union leaderships. (SM)

467 Killory, Diane S. and **Bozzelli, Richard J**. '"Fairness", the First Amendment and the public interest'. *Gannett Center Journal*, Vol. 2, No. 1, Winter 1988, pp. 62–72.

In abandoning its enforcement of the so-called Fairness Doctrine in August 1987, the Federal Communications Commission repudiated the role of the government as a referee and enforcer of the presentation of contrasting viewpoints, and returned to broadcasters the right to make their own editorial judgements. (BM)

468 Lichtenberg, Judith. 'In defence of objectivity revisited'. In **Curran, James** and **Gurevitch, Michael** (eds.) *Mass media and society.* 2nd ed. London: Edward Arnold, 1996, pp. 225–42.

Objectivity is regarded as a cornerstone of the professional ethics of journalists in democratic societies, inextricably linked to truth, fairness, balance and neutrality, yet it has recently come under fire. The author examines the issue, largely from a theoretical stance, and concludes in defence of the objective, professional model of journalism. (BM)

469 Lower, Elmer. 'Fairness, balance and equal time'. *Television Quarterly*, Vol. 9, No. 4, 1970, pp. 46–53.
President of ABC News discusses the principles of fairness and equal time, and the entitlement of all citizens to fair and balanced treatment in news programming. (BM)

470 McNair, Brian. *Images of the enemy: reporting the new Cold War*. London: Routledge, 1988. viii, 216pp. (Communication and society)
Examination of British television news coverage of the Soviet Union and East–West relations through interviews with BBC and ITN journalists and correspondents, based in London and Moscow, by a University of Ulster media studies lecturer. Using examples of the disarmament talks, the Korean airline disaster and Chernobyl, it challenges the concept of impartial or neutral news, and highlights the xenophobic perspective of past Western reportage of the 'Soviet threat'. It concedes that part of the problem has been Soviet secrecy, but now that Glasnost has improved information flow and East–West rhetoric has softened, reportage may improve. (BM)

471 MacNeil, Robert. 'The media and the public trust'. *Television Quarterly*, Vol. 22, No. 1, 1986, pp. 63–70.
Author believes the answer to American public disillusion with the media is for them to take more journalistic responsibility, in particular ensuring greater fairness in reporting. (BM)

472 Meech, Peter. 'Death in a Scottish tabloid'. *Media Development*, Vol. 39, No. 4, 1992, pp. 14–16.
The *Daily Record* is a popular and best-selling Scottish tabloid newspaper, read by one in two Scots, though not well-known outside Scotland. This article analyses its treatment of death (an average of thirteen deaths per issue), and the most striking example of the paper's values in ignoring AIDS as a subject for serious reporting or analysis despite the huge incidence of AIDS in Edinburgh. (BM)

473 Mellencamp, Patricia (ed.) *Logics of television: essays in cultural criticism*. Bloomington: Indiana University Press; London: BFI Publishing, 1990. viii, 307pp. (Theories of contemporary criticism, 11)
Cultural studies essays, including 'Techno-ethics and tele-ethics' by Andrew Ross, on video piracy in the wider context of the ethics of the television industry. (BM)

474 Meyers, Marian. 'News of battering'. *Journal of Communication*, Vol. 44, No. 2, Spring 1994, pp. 47–63.

An examination of how the media have reported wife abuse since Erin Pizzey exposed it as a serious social problem in 1974 concludes that myths and stereotypes combine to blame the victim for the crime, and that the news codes of 'balance' and 'objectivity' ironically collude in this by requiring both sides of the story be covered. (BM)

475 Schoenbrun, David. 'Is "perfect fairness" possible? *Television Quarterly*, Vol. 13, No. 1, 1976, pp. 77–9.

Former CBS News Paris correspondent examines the question of fairness, and argues for eliminating equal time provisions, revising views on objectivity, and a greater stress to the principle of fairness. (BM)

476 Williams, Betty Anne. 'Sins of omission'. *Media Studies Journal*, Vol. 6, No. 4, Fall 1992, pp. 49–56.

News media in the US need to be more reflective of the country, more honest, more fair and more consistent with the way people live their lives. (BM)

TV news and journalism

477 Altheide, David L. *Creating reality: how TV news distorts events*. Beverly Hills, California and London: Sage Publications, 1976. 221pp. (Sage library of social research, Vol. 33)

A study of the dynamics of television news by an American academic, based on research that spanned the 1972 presidential campaign, Watergate and the resignation of President Nixon. Professor Altheide observed the news process in action in the newsroom of a US network affiliate television station, rather as Philip Schlesinger did for his pioneering study of the BBC television news in *Putting 'reality' together* [487]. He developed his theory of 'the news perspective' for that combination of factors – economic, organizational and personal – which determine the shape, bias and slant of the news. (BM)

478 Altheide, David L. *Media power*. Beverly Hills, California: Sage Publications, 1985. 288pp. (Sage library of social research, Vol. 158)

Professor Altheide's previous works addressed the television news process (*Creating reality*) and media impact on society (*Media logic*), while in this he analyses the diffusion of media formats and perspectives into other areas of life. Rather academic sociological study, but with interesting analysis of television coverage (and distortion) of the 1979 Iran hostage crisis. Bibliography. (BM)

479 Croteau, David and **Hoynes, William**. 'Democracy, diversity and television news'. *Television Quarterly*, Vol. 25, No. 1, 1990, pp. 95–101.

Authors look at the various types of diversity in television news – demographic, political, national and topical – essential if it is to serve the public interest, but conclude that they have fallen victim to the narrow boundaries established by the major news media. (BM)

480 Epstein, Edward Jay. 'The values of newsmen'. *Television Quarterly*, Vol. 10, No. 2, 1973, pp. 9–21.
From an American perspective this article challenges the accusation that newsmen's personal views and values influence television news, by examining the diverse backgrounds of the 'collaborators' in the news-gathering process – reporters, technicians, producers and news editors. (BM)

481 Gans, Herbert J. *Deciding what's news: a study of CBS evening news, NBC nightly news, Newsweek and Time*. New York: Pantheon Books, 1979; London: Constable, 1980. xvii, 395pp.
In the years since it was first published this book has rightly established itself as a standard work. Cool, as far as possible objective (the author questions his own objectivity), and riding easily on a foundation of considerable scholarship, it is a model of its type. As the title implies, it is based exclusively on American journalism, and not all of it can immediately be applied to the media in other societies. (SM)

482 Golding, Peter and **Elliott, Philip**. *Making the news*. London: Longman, 1979. xi, 241pp.
An important book, which analyses news broadcasting in Sweden, Ireland and Nigeria. Though obvious differences emerge, the authors are more impressed by the similarities thrown up by the news operation in these three dissimilar organizations and countries. Historical studies of the development of news broadcasting, and of sociological studies of news give the book depth. A final chapter rejecting the concept of 'objectivity' argues a plurality of more subjective treatments of the news. Extensive bibliography. (SM)

483 Great Britain. Home Office. *The Brixton disorders 10–12 April 1981: Report of an Inquiry by the Rt. Hon. The Lord Scarman, O.B.E.* (Cmnd 8427) London: HMSO, 1981. viii, 168pp.
British government investigation into the causes of street riots (of a largely racial nature) in Brixton in south London. During that weekend (10–12 April 1981) 'the British public watched with horror and incredulity an instant audio-visual presentation on their television sets of scenes of violence and disorder in their capital city'. Lord Scarman found that it was this very coverage by the media which had an effect on the escalation and continuation of the disorders, and on the imitative or copycat element in the later disorders elsewhere. He urged editors and producers to accept a responsibility in assessing the likely impact on events of their own reporting of them, and that in cases like this rioters will respond violently before cameras in what they see as the encouraging presence of TV. (BM)

484 Hoyt, James L. 'Courtroom coverage: the effects of being televised'. *Journal of Broadcasting*, Vol. 21, No. 4, Fall 1977, pp. 487–95.
'Free press and fair trial' – debate on the effect cameras have on jurists and witnesses in televising court proceedings. Study seems to prove some beneficial effects with witnesses giving more articulate and correct answers. (BM)

485 MacLeish, Rod. 'The ethics of television news'. *Television Quarterly*, Vol. 25, No. 1, 1990, pp. 89–94.
Former CBS correspondent takes a historical view of television journalism, and concludes that only the technology has changed but not the timeless ethical standards. (BM)

486 Pavlik, John V. 'Television news: a crisis of opportunity'. *Television Quarterly*, Vol. 28, No. 1, 1996, pp. 21–8.
American academic looks at the ethical and social issues that are beginning to arise from revolutionary changes in television technology, and the possible profound implications of virtual news experiences. (BM)

487 Schlesinger, Philip. *Putting 'reality' together: BBC news.* London: Constable, 1978. 303pp. (Communication and society); rev. ed. London: Methuen, 1987; new ed. London: Penguin Books, 1992.
For the research for this seminal sociological study of news production Professor Schlesinger was allowed privileged access to BBC newsrooms, observing the way in which news bulletins are assembled and how this affects the final version of reality. He poses many questions on the processes involved in producing news, journalistic concepts of the audience, the BBC and its corporate ideology, the 'impartiality' of BBC news, and the special topic of reporting Northern Ireland. He concluded that the production cycle of broadcast news – planning, deployment of reporters, film crews and other resources, copy deadlines, running time and so on – determines the shape and stance of the news and often results in routine and predictable coverage of events. He questions the official BBC claim of value-free, impartial and objective news; as Sir Hugh Greene once pointed out, there are limits to the BBC neutrality concerning basic moral values as it could hardly be 'impartial about racialism or extreme forms of political belief'. A thorough, scholarly account, with a critique of some sociological theories on the 'construction' of news. (BM)

488 Tuchman, Gaye. *Making news: a study in the construction of reality.* New York: Free Press, 1978. xi, 244pp.
The author argues that the act of making news is the act of constructing reality itself, and sets the context in which people discuss public issues. (BM)

489 Tumber, Howard. *Television and the riots: a report for the Broadcasting Research Unit of the British Film Institute.* London: BFI, 1982. viii, 54pp.
A series of urban riots hit the UK in 1981 – in Brixton in London, in Toxteth in Liverpool, in Manchester, Leicester, Coventry and other places. There was

immediate criticism of the role of the media. This slender volume is no more than a quick response by an academic researcher; it questions a number of the myths which arose. (SM)

490 Wulfemeyer, K. Tim and **Frazier, Lowell**. 'The ethics of the video news releases: a qualitative analysis'. *Journal of Mass Media Ethics*, Vol. 7, No. 3, 1992, pp. 151–68.

Authors identify sixteen potential ethical problems with the use (and abuse) of video news releases (VNRs) from public relations practitioners and electronic journalists, including inaccurate or misleading information, offensive material, manipulation of the media, failure to identify source, paying broadcasters to use them, need to validate information and so on. Both the Society of Professional Journalists Code of Ethics and the Radio–Television News Directors Association Code of Broadcast News Ethics provide guidance. (BM)

News-gathering

491 Bell, Martin. 'TV news: how far should we go?' *British Journalism Review*, Vol. 8, No. 1, 1997, pp. 7–16.

Renowned BBC foreign and war correspondent writes of his career 'from the killing fields of Vietnam to the *barrios* of Nicaragua'. He raises questions regarding reporters' indifference to the consequences of the power of the news medium, the possibility (or impossibility) of true objectivity, and what justification there could be for disengaged journalism which would require practitioners to close their hearts to pity. (BM)

492 Borden, Sandra L. 'Empathic listening: the interviewer's betrayal'. *Journal of Mass Media Ethics*, Vol. 8, No. 4, 1993, pp. 219–26.

Sympathetic interviewing by journalists can deceive the subjects into expecting to be portrayed favourably in news stories, therefore fairer practice would be to always obtain informed consent beforehand as an automatic news-gathering routine. (BM)

493 Bovee, Warren G. 'The end can justify the means – but rarely'. *Journal of Mass Media Ethics*, Vol. 6, No. 3, 1991, pp. 135–45.

Journalists must use reason in consideration of the means used in obtaining news stories; failure to do so may cause not only moral laxity but also its opposite, a false 'scrupulosity'. (BM)

494 Browne, Christopher. *The prying game*. London: Robson Books, 1996. viii, 159pp.

Newspaper journalist examines the role of the British news media, and their powerful influence on the public. Are they a social commentator, moral guardian, wise counsellor? Or just a relentless predator systematically undermining most institutions – the state, the establishment, the judiciary, the church, the royal family and so on. He concludes that they have become the vice rather than the voice of the people. (BM)

495 Dennis, Everette E. 'News, ethics and split-personality journalism'. *Television Quarterly*, Vol. 27, No. 1, 1994, pp. 29–35.
Discussion of the effect that the faster and more efficient news-gathering, processing and dissemination, brought about by the convergence of new technologies, is having on journalistic quality and values. (BM)

496 Elliott, Deni and **Culver, Charles.** 'Defining and analyzing journalistic deception'. *Journal of Mass Media Ethics*, Vol. 7, No. 2, 1992, pp. 69–84.
Definition of the conditions for deception in investigative reporting, interviewing and disclosure (or non-disclosure) of information. (BM)

497 Ettema, James S. and **Glasser, Theodore L.** 'Narrative form and moral force: the realization of innocence and guilt through investigative journalism'. *Journal of Communication*, Vol. 38, No. 3, Summer 1988, pp. 8–26.
Television news investigative journalism tells moral tales by defending traditional virtue through skilfully defining the plight of the innocent victim and assigning allocation of guilt, but often sidesteps thorough analysis of basic moral issues involved. (BM)

498 Goldstein, Tom. 'The news at any cost: how far should a journalist go to get a story'. *Media & Values*, No. 50, Spring 1990, pp. 16–17.
Of all unethical practices used by journalists the author (a former *Wall Street Journal* and *New York Times* reporter) considers deception the worst. (BM)

499 Gumpert, Gary and **Drucker, Susan J.** 'Respect for life even at public executions'. *Media Development*, Vol. 39, No. 4, 1992, pp. 17–18.
Ethical conflict in televising executions – if one opposes the death penalty and believes in the sanctity and responsibility of a free press, one reaches a disturbing conclusion that they should be televised, though regular viewing would desensitize viewers. (BM)

500 Hodges, Louis W. 'Undercover, masquerading, surreptitious taping'. *Journal of Mass Media Ethics*, Vol. 3, No. 2, Fall 1988, pp. 26–36.
Author looks at the morality of undercover investigation methods, and whether there is a justification for deception and secret taping in gathering information. He suggests posing three questions for justifying them: 'is the information of overriding importance in revealing wrong doing?'; 'can the information not be obtained by straightforward interview or research?'; and 'is there a risk of an innocent party being harmed?' (BM)

501 Lake, James Burges. 'Of crime and consequence: should newspapers report rape complainants' names?' *Journal of Mass Media Ethics*, Vol. 6, No. 2, 1991, pp. 106–18.
The cases for both concealment and disclosure examined, and suggestions for determining whether or not to publish the names of rape victims. (BM)

502 McLean, Deckle. 'Recognizing the reporter's right to trespass'. *Communications and the Law*, Vol. 9, No. 5, October 1987, pp. 31–42.
American courts may soon have to recognize a First Amendment right to gather news that includes not only a right of access to criminal trials, but also the right to follow demonstrations on to public and quasi-public property without fear of trespass prosecutions. (BM)

503 Mollenhoff, Clark R. *Investigative reporting: from courthouse to White House*. New York: Macmillan, 1981. xxii, 381pp.
Author defines 'investigative reporting' as reporting through one's own work, product and initiative on matters of importance which some persons or organizations want to keep secret. The classic example was Watergate, when *Washington Post* reporters Bob Woodward and Carl Bernstein revealed the secrets of the Watergate break-in and eventual cover-up which, from the President down, the most powerful people in Washington were determined to keep secret. Mollenhoff opines that the survival of American democracy is to a large degree contingent upon whether people understand the problems of their society, and only if the press can establish and maintain a corps of effective, professional non-partisan investigative reporters and editors can these problems be aired. They must have high standards to test their work, and be consistently honest, responsible, fair and non-partisan. The book explores free speech, use of records, use of vice and pay-offs, exposure of corruption, fraud, secrecy, security risks and ethical practice. (BM)

504 Pippert, Wesley G. *An ethics of news: a reporter's search for truth*. Washington, DC: Georgetown University Press, 1989.

Confidentiality and sources

505 Bok, Sissela. *Secrets: on the ethics of concealment*. New York: Pantheon, 1982; Oxford: Oxford University Press, 1984. xviii, 332pp.
Author explores the ethics of secrecy as it pervades public and private life, such issues as when a promise of secrecy may be breached, whether there are times when it must be broken, and whether secrecy is corrupting when it permits unchallenged exercise of power. A chapter on investigative journalism argues that the press is the best counterbalance against secrecy, but questions justifications given by the press for its more questionable activities, and whether there is a blanket 'right to know'. Also discusses invasion of privacy, reporters in disguise and deception in obtaining stories. (BM)

506 **Bunker, Matthew D.** and **Splichal, Sigman L.** 'Legally enforceable reporter–source agreements: chilling news gathering at the source?' *Journalism Quarterly*, Vol. 70, No. 4, Winter 1993, pp. 939–46.
The promise of confidentiality between reporter and source has long been considered a vital ethical obligation of the press. A recent court judgment on reporter–source agreements may have marked out dangerous new ground of liability for media organizations. (BM)

507 **Day, Louis A.** 'Shield laws and the separation of powers'. *Communications and the Law*, Vol. 2, No. 4, Fall 1980, pp. 1–15.
A reporter's right to protect confidential sources, a cornerstone of investigative reporting, and the 'newsman's privilege' (under the First Amendment), can impede the course of justice by withholding evidence. (BM)

508 **Kase, K. M.** 'When a promise is not a promise: the legal consequences for journalists who break promises of confidentiality to sources'. *Comm/ent: a Journal of Communications and Entertainment Law*, Vol. 12, No. 4, Summer 1990, pp. 565–91.

509 **Navasky, Victor S.** *Naming names*. New York: Viking Press, 1980; London: John Calder, 1982. xxvi, 482pp. (Platform books)
Playing the informer is not the American way, so said actor Larry Parks before the House Committee on Un-American Activities in 1951 for being a member of the Communist Party. He had the options to invoke the First Amendment (with its guarantee of free speech and association) but risk going to prison for contempt of Congress, cite the Fifth Amendment but be blacklisted, or co-operate with the Committee, name names and hope to work again. The ground rules were set in this shameful episode in American history for informing on others. This book examines the effect of this 1950s witch-hunt initiated by Senator Joseph McCarthy, the moral issues it raised, and the long-term consequences for the media and the entertainment industry. (BM)

510 **Newsom, David D.** 'Scoops and secrets: diplomacy and the press'. *Gannett Center Journal*, Vol. 3, No. 4, Fall 1989, pp. 175–87.
'Diplomats attempt to keep secrets and journalists try to reveal them.' American policy makers, from the President down, seek not so much secrecy as control over information. (BM)

511 **Van Gerpen, Maurice**. *Privileged communication and the press: the citizen's right to know versus the law's right to confidential news*. Westport, Connecticut: Greenwood Press, 1979. xi, 239pp.
Legal protection of personal privacy is crucial in constitutional democracies and through protection of communication between parties who have preferred to keep their conversations private and confidential. However, the argument for a press privilege has proved controversial. This book examines from an American

viewpoint the moral and legislative arguments for journalistic protection of sources. (BM)

The values of journalists

512 Barney, Ralph D. 'Responsibilities of the journalist: an ethical construct'. *Mass Comm Review*, Vol. 14, No. 3, 1987, pp. 14–22.

513 Brislin, Tom and **Williams, Nancy**. 'Beyond diversity: expanding the canon in journalism ethics'. *Journal of Mass Media Ethics*, Vol. 11, No. 1, 1996, pp. 16–27.
Ethics courses preparing journalists for the twenty-first century need to take more account of diversity, so that young journalists can bring a greater knowledge of the ethics of non-Western, non-white cultures and values to the news-gathering process. (BM)

514 Brown, William J., Singhal, Arvind and **Rogers, Everette M**. 'Pro-development soap operas: a novel approach to development'. *Media Development*, Vol. 36, No. 4, 1989, pp. 43–7.
Television soap operas, designed to educate as well as entertain, and which can be a useful tool for moral education in developing countries, began with the *telenovelas* in Mexico and Latin America and have now spread to other Third World countries. (BM)

515 Crawford, Nelson Antrim. *The ethics of journalism*. New York: Alfred A. Knopf, 1924. viii, 264pp.
Pioneering, early American text on contemporary journalistic practice and the press's ethical standards, with reference to news, editorial, advertising and various codes of ethics. Author has a strong commitment to the professional status of journalism and setting professional standards. 'It is of the utmost importance that its standards of practice shall be such as to further the best interests of society.' (BM)

516 Elliott, D. 'Creating the conditions for ethical journalism'. *Mass Comm Review*, Vol. 14, No. 3, 1987, pp. 6–10.

517 Elliott, Deni (ed.) *Responsible journalism*. Beverly Hills, California: Sage, 1986. 187pp.
Collection of essays by American academics, including John C. Merrill, Theodore L. Glasser, Everette E. Dennis and Clifford G. Christians, on aspects of the theoretical background to press journalism, and the practice of responsible journalism. (BM)

518 Flint, Leon Nelson. *The conscience of the newspaper: a case book in the principles and problems of journalism*. New York: D. Appleton, 1925. x, 470pp.

Early American case book on newspaper editing and journalism. The first part, 'Newspaper practice and the editor's conscience', covers truth, suppression of news, independence, impartiality and fairness, handling antisocial acts, and business-ethical problems (offensive, dishonest or untruthful advertising), each with actual cases. Second and third parts cover the nature of journalism, and professional training and codes of ethics for journalists. (BM)

519 Gibbons, William Futhey. *Newspaper ethics: a discussion of good practice for journalists.* Ann Arbor, Michigan: Edwards Bros, 1926.

520 Goodwin, Gene and **Smith, Ron F.** *Groping for ethics in journalism.* 3rd ed. Ames: Iowa State University Press, 1994. x, 371pp.

Lively account of the declining state of ethics in American journalism, written from the two authors' personal experience as journalism academics and former reporters, as well as from observation and interviews with 170 journalists. The third edition aims to be more prescriptive and judgemental than the previous editions in its coverage of the rights and wrongs of journalistic behaviour, and look at codes and professional status, reporters and their sources, deception, fakery, privacy, errors and accountability. (BM)

521 Greenwood, Catherine. 'Publish or perish: the ethics of publishing in peer-reviewed journals'. *Media Information Australia*, No. 68, May 1993, pp. 29–35.

Editors of peer-reviewed journals are aware of unethical behaviour among contributors anxious to amass a publication record, ranging from multiple submission of a paper to honorary authorship. (BM)

522 Gunter, Barrie. 'Television as a facilitator of good behaviour amongst children'. *The Journal of Moral Education*, Vol. 13, No. 2, October 1984, pp. 152–9.

Author looks at the impact of television's pro-social content on audiences' values and behaviour, particularly those of children whose early understanding of good and bad behaviour comes partly from television programmes, some of which deliberately emphasize good behavioural traits. (BM)

523 Henning, Albert F. *Ethics and practice in journalism.* New York: Long & Smith, 1932.

524 Henningham, J. P. 'Comparisons between Australian and US broadcast journalists' professional values'. *Journal of Broadcasting*, Vol. 28, No. 3, Summer 1984, pp. 323–32.

Australian journalists admire the freedoms enjoyed by their American counterparts, but this survey finds a remarkable similarity in their professional approach and values. (BM)

525 Hulteng, John L. *Playing it straight: a practical discussion of the ethical principles of the American Society of Newspaper Editors.* Chester, Connecticut: Globe Pequot Press, 1981.

526 Killenberg, G. Michael. 'What is a quote?: practical, rhetorical and ethical concerns for journalists'. *Journal of Mass Media Ethics*, Vol. 8, No. 1, 1993, pp. 37–54.
Ethical issues of quoting practices by journalists. (BM)

527 Kirkhorn, Michael J. 'The virtuous journalist'. *British Journalism Review*, Vol. 1, No. 4, Summer 1990, pp. 6–24.
Former American journalist suggests that clearer views of journalistic integrity and responsibility would result in a journalism which explains (and even entertains) more, but is less frivolous and wasteful than at present. (BM)

528 Kocher, Renate. 'Bloodhounds or missionaries: role definition of German and British journalists'. *European Journal of Communication*, Vol. 1, No. 1, March 1986, pp. 43–64.
A comparative study of British and German journalists found significant differences in their perception of their role, evaluation of objectivity and views on acceptable methods of obtaining information. German journalists place emphasis on their role of taking up grievances as spokesmen for the underdog, whereas their British counterparts value being neutral in reporting of events. (BM)

529 Lambeth, Edmund B. *Committed journalism: an ethic for the profession.* Bloomington: Indiana University Press, 1986. xi, 208pp.
In his textbook for journalism students and practitioners, Professor Lambeth, from the University of Kentucky School of Journalism, identifies a framework of principles of ethical journalism from articulated ideals, codes and accepted best practice as a useful approach for thinking through ethical problems, considering differences of judgement and evaluating the performance of the news media. Topics examined are social responsibility of the press (Hutchins Commission on the Freedom of the Press, 1947), ethical theory and applying principles to actual situations requiring moral reasoning, organizational pressures on journalists, government–media conflicts and investigative journalism. (BM)

530 McMane, Aralynn Abare. 'Ethical standards of French and US newspaper journalists'. *Journal of Mass Media Ethics*, Vol. 8, No. 4, 1993, pp. 207–18.
Simultaneous surveys of newspaper journalists in France and the US on ethical standards in reporting find some differences but many shared values and a cross-cultural consensus, particularly in support of keeping the promise of source confidentiality. (BM)

531 Marks, Jeffrey A. 'TV news photographer as equipment: a response'. *Journal of Mass Ethics*, Vol. 2, No. 2, Spring–Summer 1987, pp. 18–20.
The News Director of Maine Broadcasting System argues that TV news photographers are often treated as pieces of equipment, not as journalists whose insights and judgements should be taken into consideration, causing their perceptions of

reality (through a lens) to be different from normal ethical decision making. (BM)

532 Merrill, John C. 'Freedom and the growth of the ethical dimension in journalism'. *Mass Comm Review*, Vol. 16, No. 1–2, 1989, pp. 3–13.

533 Nunez Encabo, Manuel. 'The ethics of journalism and democracy'. *European Journal of Communication*, Vol. 10, No. 4, December 1995, pp. 513–26.
Taking as its starting point the Council of Europe Resolution on the ethics of journalism and the duty of proprietors, publishers and journalists to consider the information they disseminate as a fundamental citizens' right, the author, Professor of Moral and Political Philosophy at the Complutense University of Madrid, believes it is the responsibility of media managers to approve codes of journalistic ethics for guaranteeing both freedom of speech and the accuracy and honesty of information and opinion. (BM)

534 Olen, Jeffrey. *Ethics of journalism.* Englewood Cliffs, New Jersey: Prentice Hall, 1988. xiv, 127pp. (Occupational ethics series)
The author of this volume, one of a series on the ethical dimensions of 'professions' and occupations, examines from a philosopher's viewpoint the ethical problems of journalists, and how they may resolve them by applying moral reasoning. He looks at the conflict a journalist may have between the wider moral principles of society and the narrower aims of journalism to serve the interests of the reader, viewer or listener. Through the ethical code of Sigma Delta Chi, the (American) Society of Professional Journalists, he focuses on particular issues – public interest, responsibility to question, accuracy, objectivity, fairness and fair play. Other topics covered include right to privacy, protection of sources, investigative reporting, partisanship and advocacy, and agenda setting. (BM)

535 Priestland, Gerald. *The dilemmas of journalism.* Guildford, Surrey: Lutterworth Press, 1979. 120pp.
Based on two lectures, 'The moral dilemmas of journalism' and 'Journalism and terrorism', a respected BBC broadcaster writes from a religious (Quaker) viewpoint of the practice of press and broadcasting journalism, and argues for a more moral outlook. 'A Christian journalist's Christianity should help him withstand the dehumanising, cynical effects of his experiences and give him his sense of vocation.' (BM)

536 Schmuhl, Robert. *The responsibility of journalism.* Notre Dame, Indiana: University of Notre Dame Press, 1984. ix, 138pp.
Papers presented at a conference on the responsibility of journalism held at the University of Notre Dame in 1982 exploring the moral dimension of journalism, and mechanisms to use for fostering journalistic responsibility, such as codes, internal and external criticism, news councils and education. (BM)

537 Steele, Robert M. 'Video ethics: the dilemma of value balancing'. *Journal of Mass Media Ethics*, Vol. 2, No. 2, Spring–Summer, 1987, pp. 7–17.
Results of a participation/observation study, conducted in two American television stations, of television news photographers and their dilemmas in balancing their own personal and professional ethical beliefs, and the practical requirements imposed by competition, careerism, peer pressure, technology and organizational expectations. (BM)

538 Sutherland, John C. 'The treatment and resolution of moral violations on soap operas'. *Journal of Communication*, Vol. 32, No. 2, Spring 1982, pp. 67–74.
The depiction of moral truths and dilemmas on television is perhaps most evident in soap operas, but it is unclear whether they condone immorality or present satisfactorily moral resolutions in which violators of society's rules are punished. (BM)

539 Swain, Bruce M. *Reporters' ethics*. Ames: Iowa State University Press, 1978. 153pp.
This book reprints nine American codes, or statements of principle, and examines how such codes are interpreted by 67 working journalists in 16 metropolitan daily newspapers in ten US cities. The result is largely anecdotal, with its feet firmly on the ground but never delving deeply into the assumptions of the reporters' trade. Bibliography. (SM)

540 Tomalin, Nicholas. *Nicholas Tomalin reporting*. London: André Deutsch, 1975. 317pp.
Collection of articles from highly respected *Sunday Times* journalist who was killed covering a war in 1974. Contains four sharp articles on journalism itself, with pieces on war reporting and what it takes to be a journalist. (MP)

541 Tomlinson, Don E. 'Coalesce or collide?: ethics, technology and TV journalism 1991'. *Journal of Mass Media Ethics*, Vol. 2, No. 2, Spring–Summer 1987, pp. 21–31.
New digital technologies will soon be able to easily manipulate video and audio in utterly fundamental ways, with potential for unethical practices. (BM)

542 Weaver, David H. and **Wilhoit, Cleveland**. 'Journalists: who are they, really?' *Media Studies Journal*, Vol. 6, No. 4, Fall 1992, pp. 63–79.
Journalists in the US in some ways fit the description of a cultural elite (by Jonathan Alter) as being 'less connected to conventional standards of morality than most of the public'. This survey proves in some ways they are out of step with public opinion – they are more likely to be white, less religious, more liberal and more willing to sanction questionable reporting methods (use of hidden microphones, getting employment to obtain information). (BM)

543 Whale, John. *Journalism and government.* London: Macmillan, 1972. 120pp.
John Whale, a 'serious' journalist with experience of radio, television and the quality press, wrote this book by way of a personal apologia justifying his decision to return to the printed word after the electronic media. He argues in favour of the precision of 'the word', and is suspicious of emotion in politics. He instances ethical dilemmas which have come his way, and argues that journalists often have an influence on individual politicians. Brief bibliography. (SM)

Conflicts of interest

544 Bailey, Charles W. *Conflict of interest: a matter of journalistic ethics. A report to the National News Council.* Minneapolis: Journalism Center, University of Minnesota, 1984.

545 Francis, Richard. 'The journalist cannot survive as an informer, except when ...' *The Listener*, Vol. 105, No. 2699, 12 February 1981, pp. 206–7.
Discussion of the delicate, ethical value judgements a journalist has to make when obtaining information, and the conflict with their duties as a responsible citizen. (BM)

546 Goldstein, Tom. *The news at any cost: how journalists compromise their ethics to shape the news.* New York: Simon & Schuster, 1985.

547 O'Brien, Conor Cruise. 'A journalist doesn't stop being a citizen'. *The Listener*, Vol. 105, No. 2696, 22 January 1981, p. 108.
Irish writer and former diplomat proposes that there is nothing in the function of being a journalist which absolves them from the requirements of decency, and that often their behaviour is considered unacceptable to the public. (BM)

548 Tumber, Howard. 'Bystander journalism, or the journalism of attachment'. *InterMedia*, Vol. 25, No. 1, February 1997, pp. 4–7.
In covering war journalists cannot always remain detached and 'objective', but must make a choice between professional commitment and participatory loyalties. (BM)

549 Vergobbi, David J. 'Journalist as source: the moral dilemma of news rescue'. *Journal of Mass Media Ethics*, Vol. 7, No. 4, 1992, pp. 233–45.
Ethical and legal concerns with staff members of news agencies taking a story suppressed by their own agency to another. Raises questions of loyalty, ownership of information (news agency proprietor or the public), the right to information, right to legitimate dissent or for disclosure. Some of these must be personal choices. (BM)

Professionalism, councils and codes

550 Bertrand, Claude-Jean. 'Ethics in international communications'. *InterMedia*, Vol. 13, No. 2, March 1985, pp. 9–13.
Western commercial media have developed more interest in ethical rules, and the author identifies three motives for this: political – to avoid restrictive legislation; economic – to be more credible and acceptable to the consumers; and in response to pressure from their own staff, conscious of the need to improve journalistic standards and exert self-discipline. (BM)

551 Bertrand, Claude-Jean. 'Media accountability: the case for press councils'. *InterMedia*, Vol. 18, No. 6, November–December 1990, pp. 10–14.
Despite a worldwide failure of press councils, the author believes the concept is right; he analyses the reasons why they have not succeeded and restates their two basic functions of defending media freedom and improving professional standards, stressing the importance of accountability. (BM)

552 Black, Jay and **Barney, Ralph D**. 'The case against mass media codes of ethics'. *Journal of Mass Media Ethics*, Vol. 1, No. 1, 1985–86, pp. 27–36.

553 Blom-Cooper, Louis. 'The last days of the Press Council'. *British Journalism Review*, Vol. 2, No. 3, Spring 1991, pp. 34–9.
The last Chairman of the Press Council writes of its demise after 37 years of attempting to maintain standards of journalism in the UK, and the proposals for new self-regulatory system for the newspaper industry. (BM)

554 Boeyink, David E. 'Casuistry: a case-based method for journalists'. *Journal of Mass Media Ethics*, Vol. 7, No. 2, 1992, pp. 107–20.
Casuistry – a case-centred methodology – applied to the development of a code of ethics on use of anonymous sources at daily newspapers. (BM)

555 Brogan, Patrick. *Spiked: the short life and death of the National News Council.* Dallas, Texas: Priority Press, 1985.

556 Christians, Clifford G. 'Enforcing media codes'. *Journal of Mass Media Ethics*, Vol. 1, No. 1, 1985–86, pp. 14–21.

557 Courtright, Jeffrey L. 'An ethics code postmortem: the National Religious Broadcasters' EFICOM'. *Journal of Mass Media Ethics*, Vol. 11, No. 4, 1996, pp. 223–35.
The author questions the value of ethics codes, which are often, he claims, designed to improve public opinion and fend off government legislation regulation, and in practice they often limit public discussion of the issue at hand. To remedy this he suggests regular maintenance and revision, with the public and within the profession. (BM)

558 Dennis, Everette E. *Reshaping the media: mass communication in an information age.* Newbury Park, California: Sage, 1989. 205pp.
Anthology of speeches, lectures and articles by foremost American media academic, and Executive Director at the Gannett Center for Media Studies at Columbia University, touching on news media, journalism and journalism education, particularly journalistic ethics and values. (BM)

559 Elliott-Boyle, Deni. 'A conceptual analysis of ethics codes'. *Journal of Mass Media Ethics*, Vol. 1, No. 1, 1985–86, pp. 22–6.

560 Harris, Nigel G. E. *Professional codes of conduct in the United Kingdom: a directory.* 2nd ed. London: Mansell, 1996. 438pp.
Directory listing over 500 UK organizations with codes of practice, many of which are within the 'media', giving either full text or summaries, with introduction on the development and purpose of codes and a subject index. (BM)

561 Jones, J. Clement. *Mass media codes of ethics and councils: a comparative international study on professional standards.* Paris: UNESCO, 1980. 80pp.
A study of national codes of ethics in the media. The country-by-country survey of different codes is obviously dated, but the general discussion of the development of ethical codes and comparative analysis of various provisions and common approaches to the content, formulation and administration of codes of practice are of lasting value. (BM)

562 Kruckeberg, D. 'The need for an international code of ethics'. *Public Relations Review*, Vol. 15, No. 2, Summer 1989, pp. 6–18.

563 Laitila, Tiina. 'Journalistic codes of ethics in Europe'. *European Journal of Communication*, Vol. 10, No. 4, December 1995, pp. 527–44.
Survey of 31 codes of journalism from 29 European countries, and whether they cover similar rules and ideals, prompted by the suggestion of establishing a media ombudsman and common set of ethical principles for Europe, by the 1993 Council of Europe Resolution on ethics of journalism. Three ideals found to be common to all national codes could form the basis of a European code: accountability to the public, accountability to sources and protection of journalists' integrity and independence. (BM)

564 Levy, H. Phillip. *The Press Council: history, procedure and cases.* London: Macmillan, 1967. xiv, 505pp.
In the UK the main form of recourse outside the judicial system for an individual whose privacy had been or was about to be intruded upon by the press was the Press Council. It was established in 1953 as the General Council of the Press following a recommendation from the first Royal Commission on the Press. Its objectives were to preserve the freedom of the press, maintain high professional and commercial standards, and consider and adjudicate on complaints about

press conduct. This account of its history, constitution and procedures also gives details of its cases classified to illustrate the principles they establish on confidential material, embargoes, fair comment, misreporting, privacy, sensationalism, taste, reporting court proceedings and crime, and cheque-book journalism. Criticism to the Calcutt Committee on Privacy and Related Matters of the Council as ineffective as an adjudicating body and working to an 'unwritten code of ethical conduct' resulted in its replacement by the Press Complaints Commission in 1991. (BM)

565 Loevinger, Lee. 'The journalistic responsibility of broadcasting'. *Television Quarterly*, Vol. 8, No. 1, 1969, pp. 70–81.
American attorney calls for a non-government institution to oversee the quality of broadcast journalism, hear grievances and adjudicate on fairness and accuracy in reporting. (BM)

566 Logan, Robert A. 'Jefferson's and Madison's legacy: the death of the National News Council'. *Journal of Mass Media Ethics*, Vol. 1, No. 1, 1985–86, pp. 68–75.

567 Nordenstreng, Kaarle. *The mass media declaration of UNESCO*. Norwood, New Jersey: Ablex Publishing, 1984. 475pp. (Communication and information science)
This imposing work is really four books in one. The first reviews historically the emergence of the 1978 UNESCO Mass Media Declaration, with a commentary on the text. The second examines the concept of an International Law of Mass Communications. Then there is discussion of professional codes of ethics. Almost half the volume is devoted to 27 appendices containing various drafts of the Declaration from commentators in the US, USSR and India. The author argues that much of the Western criticism of the Declaration is based on a simplistic and mistaken view of its content. (SM)

568 Peters, J. D. and **Cmiel, K**. 'Media ethics and the public sphere'. *Communication*, Vol. 12, No. 3, 1991, pp. 197–215.
Authors recommend placing more emphasis on citizenship than professionalism in discussion of media ethics. (BM)

569 Summers, John B. 'The judicial death of the NAB codes'. *Gannett Center Journal*, Vol. 2, No. 1, Winter 1988, pp. 99–106.
The National Association of Broadcasters codes in the US began with radio in 1929, and extended to television in 1952. They covered programming and advertising topics such as violence, drugs, gambling, obscenity and children. Broadcasters subscribed to them; they were not mandatory but were a democratic form of industry self-regulation which had much to recommend it over direct government regulation. They served the public interest but were disbanded in 1983 through action of the Department of Justice. (BM)

570 Weibull, Lennart and **Borjesson, Britt**. *Perspectives on changes in Swedish press ethics in the early 1990s.* Göteborg: Göteborgs Universitet, 1993. 19pp.
Based on results of research programme on Swedish media ethics, this report looks at the code of ethics, conduct of the Swedish press and the Press Council. (BM)

Quality

571 Belsey, Andrew and **Chadwick, Ruth**. 'Ethics as a vehicle for media quality'. *European Journal of Communication*, Vol. 10, No. 4, December 1995, pp. 461–73.
One of the roles of the media is to enhance the level of participation in democratic processes by providing information, opinion, comment and debate on a wide range of social and political issues. Crucial to this is the freedom of the media, but also the quality of the information and opinion they make available. The authors examine the legal (both positive and restrictive) and ethical routes to media quality. The advantages and disadvantages of the latter route in attempting to encapsulate ethical principles and standards in a code of practice are examined through the example of the British Press Complaints Commission code. (BM)

572 Dyson, Kenneth and **Homolka, Walter** (eds.) *Culture first!: promoting standards in the new media age.* London: Cassell, 1996. xv, 175pp.
Essays by academics which examine the challenge from the new digital age to traditional concepts of standards and quality in the media. Neil Postman, in 'Defending ourselves against the seduction of eloquence', warns against unconditional acceptance of new technologies, though it is only dangerous if we abdicate our responsibility for its control. 'The ethics of media use: media consumption as a moral challenge', by Hermann Lubbe, argues that the ethics of the usage of the media have now become more important than the ethics of the media themselves and their regulatory framework. (BM)

573 Keane, John. *The media and democracy.* London: Polity Press, 1991. xiii, 202pp.
The author, Director of the Centre for the Study of Democracy at the University of Westminster, analyses the relationship between the media and democracy. He questions contemporary arguments for the justification of public service media (as constituting a 'natural monopoly' or as standard bearers of 'balanced' or 'quality' programming) to that of the free-market case for total freedom of the media promising 'freedom and choice, rather than regulation and scarcity' (Rupert Murdoch). Finding those arguments wanting, Professor Keane proposes a revised public service model of non-state and non-market media in which it would be for public use and benefit, and not for the private gain or profit of political rulers or business. Rapid expansion of channels of communication may further this ideal of genuinely democratic media. (BM)

574 Postman, Neil. *Amusing ourselves to death: public discourse in the age of show business.* New York: Viking, 1986; London: Heinemann, 1986.
Influential polemic on the inherent dangers of television replacing the printed word at the centre of our culture, and in doing so making people into an audience, distracting them from the serious reality of life with a diet of trivia and entertainment – fulfilling Aldous Huxley's prophecy in *Brave new world* of people controlled by pleasure, worshipping the very technologies which undo their capacities to think.(BM)

Quality in television

575 Blumler, Jay G. (ed.) *Television and the public interest: vulnerable values in West European broadcasting.* London: Sage, 1992. viii, 242pp.
The established order of broadcasting in Western Europe, essentially unchanged for over half a century, was challenged in the 1980s by technological, economic, social, structural and legislative change. Such issues as breaking the monopoly of public service broadcasting, the shift from spectrum scarcity to multi-channel explosion, accelerated competition for audiences and revenue, and transnational invasion all presented governments with problems of regulating new services to ensure conformity to the public interest and preservation of those values and standards thought to be relevant in the last decade of the twentieth century. Edited by Jay Blumler, Emeritus Professor at Leeds University, where he directed the Centre for Television Research, these essays by media academics examine how eight countries are meeting these challenges, and in particular, the inherent moral concerns and issues. (BM)

576 Briggs, Asa. *Governing the BBC.* London: BBC, 1979. 291pp.
The BBC has a Board of Governors appointed by the Queen-in-Council on the advice of the government; the Governors have been traditionally charged with acting as 'trustees of the national interest in broadcasting' (Crawford Report, 1926). However, the conception of 'public interest' has changed considerably since the 1920s, and the role of the Governors increasingly been questioned. Distinguished historian Asa Briggs looks at the powers and performance of the Governors, and a series of case histories of difficult and sometimes controversial issues they have had to handle, including some highlighting the difficult relationship between broadcasters and government – coverage of the Suez crisis in 1956, the showing of *Yesterday's Men*, a television documentary on the impact of losing the General Election in 1970 on the Labour Party, and the transmission of *The Question of Ulster* in 1972 against the publicly expressed wishes of the Home Secretary. (BM)

577 Brown, Les. 'Is the public interested in the public interest?' *Television Quarterly*, Vol. 16, No. 3, 1979, pp. 21–6.

Viewers anxious about television's effect on the moral fabric of society can become an effective force in the broadcasting system though joining citizen action groups. (BM)

578 Burns, Tom. *The BBC: public institution and private world.* London: Macmillan, 1977. xviii, 313pp. (Edinburgh studies in sociology)
While now obviously dated, this remains the classic analysis by an academic (though it is by no means conventionally academic) of the nature of a major broadcasting institution. Professor Burns made a preliminary study in 1963, and a further exploration in 1973. The book, therefore, includes a picture of a decade of development which now needs a further study. The essential paradox incorporated in the title remains, however – and indeed the work is full of paradoxes. How can a major public establishment, and an industry, still remain a creative force in the arts? (SM)

579 Curran, Charles. *A seamless robe: broadcasting – philosophy and practice.* London: Collins, 1979. 358pp.
Former BBC Director-General (1969–77) emphasizes the importance of broadcasting as a public service in his survey of the BBC. The main tenets of his faith were to give direction and encouragement to programme makers, defend them against politicians and the 'morality' activist groups when necessary, while upholding standards of truthfulness and taste. He felt that the proper philosophy of the BBC was in considering how much to reflect dissenting views which fall outside of the consensus, as well as mainstream ideas, in order to provide a balance of opinion for an informed public. (BM)

580 Greene, Sir Hugh. *The third floor front: a view of broadcasting in the sixties.* London: Bodley Head, 1969. 143pp.
Collection of speeches, lecture and broadcasts by the Director-General of the BBC from 1960 to 1969, a time of fundamental changes in broadcasting, many of which he was responsible for as an innovator who believed in pushing forward the boundaries. Mary Whitehouse might have blamed him for 'the moral collapse which characterised the Sixties', but he believed he had a duty to take account of changes in society and to keep ahead of public opinion, and certainly to resist disguised censorship. (BM)

581 Groombridge, Brian and **Hay, Jocelyn** (eds.) *The price of choice: public service broadcasting in a competitive European market place.* London: John Libbey, 1995. vi, 154pp.
The citizen's rights in broadcasting was a theme in these proceedings of the second Voice of the Listener and Viewer international conference on the future of public service broadcasting, held at the Royal Society of Arts in London in 1994, with keynote speakers including Albert Scharf (President of the European Broadcasting Union) and Henriques Francisco da Silva (European Commission). (BM)

582 Harriott, John F. X. 'Television, St George or the dragon?' *The Journal of Moral Education*, Vol. 13, No. 2, October 1984, pp. 147–51.
British television regulator argues that ethical considerations pervade the whole broadcasting process, at the heart of which is the integrity of the programme maker, but an alert, intelligently critical audience also plays a part as a stimulus to good broadcasting. (BM)

583 Ishikawa, Sakae (ed.) *Quality assessment of television.* Luton: John Libbey Media at the University of Luton Press, 1996. ix, 309pp.
An urgent need in the regulation of television has been to establish a method of assessing quality. This collection, the result of joint research undertaken in five countries (the UK, Japan, Sweden, Canada and the US) and sponsored by the NHK Broadcasting Culture Research Institute, examines the concept of diversity as a measure of broadcasting quality, and analyses the criteria that professionals themselves use in making judgements about individual programmes in an attempt to establish a common framework of objective measurement. Marc Raboy, in his chapter 'Towards a new ethical environment for public service broadcasting', argues that though the concept of public service remains central to broadcasting, and the strongest argument against abandoning it to the market place, it needs to be reaffirmed through meaningful public participation in decision making. (BM)

584 Jenkins, Roy. *Government, broadcasting and the press.* London: Hart-Davis, MacGibbon, 1975. 32pp. (Granada Guildhall Lectures, 1975)
Lecture on the freedom of the press by the (then) British Home Secretary, who concludes that the quality of the press – and of broadcasting – must depend upon responsible independence in the exercise of editorial judgement. (BM)

585 MacCabe, Colin and **Stewart, Olivia** (eds.) *The BBC and public service broadcasting.* Manchester: Manchester University Press, 1986. viii, 116pp.
The consensus view of radio and television in the UK of public service broadcasting has been challenged by rapid technological change and a new political climate. Prompted particularly by the appointment of the Peacock Committee on Financing the BBC in 1985, the John Logie Baird Centre for Research in Television and Film organized a seminar to examine present concerns and future prospects for British broadcasting. These papers, by such eminent practitioners as Anthony Smith, Janet Morgan, David Elstein and Jeremy Isaacs, argue, in many cases from committed, though diverse viewpoints, for holding fast to the ideals of public service broadcasting while still advocating reform of institutions of broadcasting. (BM)

586 Mulgan, Geoff (ed.) *The question of quality.* London: British Film Institute, 1990. 72pp. (The broadcasting debate, 6)

In his introduction, Anthony Smith argues that each stage in the history of broadcasting in the UK has been characterized by a debate about a word – 'monopoly' in the 1920s, followed by 'diversity', 'regionalism', 'commercial', 'professionalism', 'access', 'public service broadcasting' and now, in the 1990s, 'quality'. In this continuing and deeply ethical debate, each stage has been accompanied by fresh institutional changes, new channels, new regulatory regimes. This collection of essays explores the concept of 'quality', and its maintenance in a future broadcasting landscape of a multiplicity of channels and the highly competitive pursuit of audiences, and tries to show that the question of quality has an essential ethical dimension. One essay by John Mepham, 'The ethics of quality in television', questions what television is for, in particular what its social and cultural purposes are within a context of a culturally plural society. He proposes an 'ethics of truth telling' as an overriding principle and ethical value to be served by television and, in particular, to be exemplified in fictional programming. (BM)

587 Raboy, Marc. 'Towards a new ethical environment for public service broadcasting'. *Studies of Broadcasting: an International Annual of Broadcasting Science*, No. 29, 1993, pp. 7–35. Tokyo: NHK Broadcasting Culture Research Institute, 1993.
The author discusses, through an analysis of the current state of broadcasting in Canada, the idea that broadcasting is a sphere in which public participation is a legitimate and an essential part of democracy. (BM)

588 Reith, J. C. W. *Broadcast over Britain*. London: Hodder & Stoughton, 1924. 231pp.
The British Broadcasting *Company* was formed in 1922, at the invitation of the Post Office, by a group of wireless manufacturers to provide central broadcasting of programmes, but from the beginning saw itself as a public service. John Reith, the first Managing Director, always saw its responsibility to preserve a high moral standard as of paramount importance. In one of the earliest books on the BBC (and on the philosophy of broadcasting), he outlines its ideals and policy. He believed the function of broadcasting was to bring relaxation and interest, but even more information to enable listeners to take greater interest in events previously 'outside of their ken', and 'to carry into the greatest possible number of homes everything that is best in every department of human knowledge, endeavour and achievement'. (BM).

589 Wenham, Brian. 'Broadcasting and the moral imperative: patrolling the perimeters'. *The Journal of Moral Education*, Vol. 13, No. 2, October 1984, pp. 160–7.
The (then) BBC Television Director of Programmes gives an outline of programme decision-making processes in the BBC, and accounts of some overt ethical judgements made during his time at the Corporation. (BM)

Religion

590 Abelman, Robert and **Hoover, Stewart** (eds.) *Religious television: controversies and conclusions.* Norwood, New Jersey: Ablex Publishing, 1990. x, 366pp.

591 Alley, R. S. *Television: ethics for hire?* Nashville, Tennessee: Abingdon, 1977. 192pp.
Through interviews with over 40 American directors, writers, producers and actors, the author provides insight into the aims and ethics of the television industry in most areas of programming (drama, comedy and so on) and on such issues as violence and pornography. In particular he looks at television as usurping the roles of home and school in imparting moral instruction and direction to children, but concedes that with its potential for conveying ideas and values through entertainment television could be a bridge between the traditional nuclear family and changing cultures and society. (BM)

592 Arthur, Chris (ed.) *Religion and the media: an introductory reader.* Cardiff: University of Wales Press, 1993. xii, 302pp.
Collection of essays on a range and diversity of topics on religion and the mass media and aspects of media examined from multi-denominational religious viewpoints, including Islamic perspectives on news, soap operas as modern morality plays, and reconciling the values of advertising with Christian tradition values. (BM)

593 Bruce, Steve. *Pray TV: televangelism in America.* London: Routledge, 1990. xii, 272pp.
Televangelism in the US looked at within the tradition of American protestantism. Evangelists look on the medium of television as a new means to express their beliefs and values, and to achieve increasing acceptance and respectability. (BM)

594 Cardwell, Jerry D. *Mass media Christianity: televangelism and the great commission.* New York: University Press of America, 1984. xvi, 215pp.
A pamphlet by the Professor of Sociology at Western Kentucky University, which represents a systematic study of the televangelists and makes some attempt to relate them to the sociology of religion. (SM)

595 Carr, Wesley. *Ministry and the media.* London: SPCK, 1990. 156pp.
Study of the media's importance to the church, particularly for religious education. (BM)

596 Christians, Clifford G. and **Fortner, Robert S.** 'The media gospel'. *Journal of Communication*, Vol. 31, No. 2, Spring 1981, pp. 190–9.
Essay review of several books on and the general issues surrounding the electronic church and televangelism. (BM)

597 Christians, Clifford G. and **Gjelsten, Gudmond**. *Media ethics and the church.* Kristiansand, Norway: International Mass Media Institute, 1981.

598 Devereux, Eoin. 'Good causes, God's poor and telethon television'. *Media, Culture and Society,* Vol. 18, No. 1, January 1996, pp. 47–68.
A look, partly within an Irish context, at the moral issues resulting from the emergence of charity television, in particular telethons, and whether or not entertainment-based fund-raising helps social action on poverty and inequality. (BM)

599 Elvy, Peter. *Buying time: the foundations of the electronic church.* Great Wakering, Essex: McCrimmons, 1986. 159pp.
Canon Elvy is a journalist as well as a vicar. This is a bright, breezy pamphlet describing the wave of electronic evangelism which swept the US in the late 1970s and early 1980s. Yet, while admiring the achievements, he is concerned at the consequences for mainline religion, worried by the overt political stance of the evangelists, and apprehensive about the future in the age of satellites. The electronic church appears to be going the way of the multinationals, towards cultural imperialism. (SM)

600 Elvy, Peter (ed.) *Opportunities and limitations in religious broadcasting.* Edinburgh: Centre for Theology and Public Issues, New College, University of Edinburgh for the Jerusalem Trust, 1991. 176pp.
Collection of papers on the opportunities presented by the new technologies in offering a greater range and pluralism in religious channels and services, but also the limitations of such proliferation. In addition it questions the suitability of television as an evangelical medium. Contributors include Eric Shegog (Director of Communications, General Synod of the Church of England), Jim McDonnell (Director, Catholic Communications Centre, London), and Robert Towler (Commissioning Editor, Religion, Channel 4). (BM)

601 Felton, Daniel J. 'The unavoidable dialogue: five interfaces between theology and communication'. *Media Development* (Special Congress Issue), October 1989, pp. 17–23.
Article identifies and discusses the relationship between theology and communications, and issues of ethics and moral questions raised by communications. (BM)

602 Gentry, Richard H. 'Broadcast religion: when does it raise Fairness Doctrine issues?' *Journal of Broadcasting,* Vol. 28, No. 3, Summer 1984, pp. 259–70.
The Fairness Doctrine in the US, a set of Federal Communications Commission policies evolving since the 1940s, which requires broadcasters to devote reasonable time to the coverage of important and public interest issues and to allow an opportunity for contrasting opinions, has been applied to religious programming, and such 'religious' or moral issues as abortion and gay rights. Two accompanying

articles in this issue of *Journal of Broadcasting* discuss the importance of the Doctrine to coverage of moral and spiritual issues and to the right of free speech: 'The necessity of the Fairness Doctrine given the religious right televangelists', by Anthony Podesta (pp. 271–2); and 'Let's be fair about Fairness', by Jerry Falwell (pp. 273–4). (BM)

603 Hoover, Stewart M. *Mass media religion: the social sources of the electronic church.* Newbury Park, California: Sage, 1988. 251pp. (Communication and human values)

A consideration of the implications of religious television primarily on a social and cultural level. The electronic church has crossed denominational boundaries in the US, and moved from the margins to centre stage, and now represents a challenge to the established, traditional church. (BM)

604 Horsfield, Peter G. *Religious television: the American experience.* New York: Longman, 1984. xv, 197pp. (Communication and human values)

Review of the history, research and policy of religious television in the US, both mainstream religious programming and the electronic church of evangelicals and fundamentalists. Author argues that because of its own economic and functional interests commercial television has exercised a powerful censoring effect on the expression of religious faith in the country, resulting in an exaggerated influence over the development of American religious culture and institutions. (BM)

605 Milner, Don and **Wesson, John**. *God or mammon?: a Christian ethic for the market place.* Bramcote, Nottinghamshire: Grove Books, 1976. 24pp. (Grove booklet on ethics, 10)

A Christian viewpoint on advertising and marketing, by the (then) Chaplain and Lecturer in Marketing at the Polytechnic of Central London. It takes as its starting point Christ's saying 'You cannot serve God and mammon' (Matthew 6:2). This tract examines such ethical issues as misleading promotional material, and the emphasis on the social attributes and symbolic values of products over their intrinsic properties in trying to influence the consumer. He emphasizes the necessity of adherence to codes of practice to ensure that advertising is 'legal, decent, honest and truthful'. (BM)

606 Morris, Colin. *God-in-a-box: Christian strategy in the television age.* London: Hodder & Stoughton, 1984. 238pp. (Hodder Christian paperbacks)

Colin Morris was a missionary in Africa before he became the BBC's Head of Religious Broadcasting. As a result he came full-time to broadcasting with few preconceptions. The result may not be a conventionally academic work, but it is a perceptive and sometimes profound one. It begins with a brisk canter round the field of media theory and new technologies before a more speculative section on Christian communication. It is not centred on the BBC and the UK: he explores, for example, the television evangelism of the US. A stimulating book. (SM)

607 Muggeridge, Malcolm. *Christ and the media*. London: Hodder & Stoughton, 1977. 127pp.

Malcolm Muggeridge worked in the press and broadcasting for many years, before retiring from them to become their most bitter critic. This collection of three lectures and some responses to them has as its theme 'television as a Frankenstein monster', exerting its influence 'without reference to any moral or intellectual, still less spiritual guidelines whatsoever'. The whole case is so overstated as to become at times absurd. (SM)

608 Quicke, Andrew and **Quicke, Juliet**. *Hidden agendas: the politics of religious broadcasting in Britain, 1987–1991*. Virginia Beach, Virginia: Dominion Kings Grant Publications, 1992. 276pp.

The controversy of whether religious programmes can proselytize, and if not whether it is a restriction on freedom of speech, is at the heart of this critique of the formulation of policy of religious broadcasting in the UK by government and the regulator (the Independent Television Commission), and the provision in the *ITC programme code* that religious programmes on non-specialist channels may not be designed to recruit viewers to any particular faith or denomination. (BM)

609 Soukup, Paul A. *Media, culture and Catholicism*. Kansas City, Missouri: Sheed & Ward, 1996.

610 Soukup, Paul A. 'Spirituality, popular culture and television'. *Media Development*, Vol. 40, No. 3, 1993, pp. 6–8.

Television can provide information about religion and religious experience, but powerful and culturally deeply-rooted counterforces at work in programming as well as shortcomings in regards to spirituality indicate that it has its limits. (BM)

611 Stout, Daniel A. and **Buddenbaum, Judith M**. *Religion and mass media: audiences and adaptations*. Thousand Oaks, California: Sage Publications, 1996. 294pp.

Interdisciplinary approach to religion and media. Topics covered include the relationship between religiosity and media-related behaviour, the presentation of religion in the news and entertainment media, and the attitudes to the media, and particularly censorship, of religious institutions in the US – Roman Catholics, mainstream Protestant, Evangelicals, Fundamentalists, Mormons and others. The case of *The Last Temptation of Christ* is dealt with in one chapter; the denunciation of this 1988 Martin Scorsese film on the grounds of blasphemy, distortion of scriptural facts and blatant disrespect for Christian sensibilities brought grass-roots boycotts and threats of economic reprisal against the sponsors. (BM)

612 Warnock, Mary. 'Broadcasting ethics: some neglected issues'. *The Journal of Moral Education*, Vol. 13, No. 2, October 1984, pp. 168–72.

Eminent British philosopher, academic, writer and Member of the Independent Broadcasting Authority from 1973 to 1981 looks at the moral and ethical effects of television, and particularly its role as a moral educator. (BM)

613 Wolfe, Kenneth M. *The churches and the British Broadcasting Corporation, 1922–1956: the politics of broadcast religion.* London: SCM Press, 1984. xxiv, 627pp.

A considerable work of scholarship written by a Research Fellow at the University of Kent Centre for the Study of Religion and Society. It is a saddening book: the broadcasters sought to encourage broadcast religion, but the churches, partly because they were sceptical about the influence of broadcasting, partly because of the sectarian schism, failed to take the opportunities they were offered. A number of controversies which are often thought of as recent, and specifically related to television, did in fact emerge quite early in the history of radio. A substantial book. (SM)

Media imperialism

614 Adams, William C. *Television coverage of international affairs.* Norwood, New Jersey: Ablex Publishing, 1982. xi, 253pp. (Communication and information science)

An extended content analysis, based on the Vanderbilt Television Archive, of the treatment of international news by three major American networks. It begins with two general chapters, turns to Third World coverage (with the UNESCO debate in mind), and looks at coverage of the developed world before turning to South East Asia. The final chapter, based on audience comprehension, or rather incomprehension, of one news item, comes near to destroying the major theses of the rest of the work. It reflects many of the findings of the 1950s radio research based on the BBC's *Topic for Tonight.* (SM)

615 Ansah, Paul A. V. 'The ethical dimension of development communication'. *Journal of Development Communication,* Vol. 2, No. 2, December 1990, pp. 57–75.

The pursuit and defence of social justice and recognition of individual dignity and rights are the ethical dimension of new communication approaches and strategies. (BM)

616 Ansah, Paul A. V. 'The path between cultural isolation and cultural dependency'. *Media Development,* Vol. 36, No. 2, 1989, pp. 12–18.

Ghanaian media academic argues that foreign cultural material coming into African and Third World countries has had a largely negative effect on the development of their own national cultural identities. (BM)

617 Barrett, Richard J. and **Muller, Ronald E.** *Global reach: the power of the multinational corporations.* New York: Simon & Schuster, 1974. 508pp.

This massive study is essentially journalistic – indeed, parts of it originally appeared in the *New Yorker.* It is highly critical of the multinationals, and some of the proposals for control and disclosure read quaintly today. Oddly, since electronics provide the basis on which the multinationals operate, relatively little attention is paid to communications, more to political and ethical questions. (SM)

618 Bertrand, Claude-Jean. 'Strange media, getting less so'. *Media Studies Journal,* Vol. 9, No. 4, Fall 1995, pp. 99–108.

Though American media have many unique qualities the hypercommercialism of it and lack of regulation are in marked contrast to the public service ideals of much European media. US media should develop a greater awareness of the importance of the rest of mankind as originators of news, and generators of entertainment and culture. (BM)

619 Bourne, Richard. *News on a knife-edge: Gemini journalism and a global agenda.* London: John Libbey, 1995. viii, 216pp.

This is an account of a brave (and mostly successful) attempt to redress the North–South, or Third World–West media imbalance, and challenge the dominance of the large, international news agencies. The Gemini News Service was founded in 1967 as a small agency aiming to supply the Western media with news stories from developing countries, written from their viewpoint by local journalists, with the aim of promoting greater understanding of the Third World in the English-language Western press. (BM)

620 Boyd-Barrett, Oliver. *The international news agencies.* London: Constable, 1980. 284pp.

A storehouse of information about the history, organization and operations of news agencies, inevitably concentrating on the 'Big Four' – AP, UPI, Reuters and AFP. The information is so densely packed that 'reading' is difficult; inevitably too, some of the statistical information is dated; and the new technology has made swift advance. Nevertheless, this meticulously detailed study makes it difficult to accept some of the more emotive and generalized attempts to cast the agencies as the backstage villains of the world of communications. Indeed, among the author's own (by no means uncritical) conclusions is that 'some of the Third World criticisms of the "Big Four" agency operations need to be carefully reconsidered'. An important book. Bibliography. (SM)

621 Boyd-Barrett, Oliver and **Thussu, Daya Kishan.** *Contra-flow in global news: international and regional news exchange mechanisms.* London: John Libbey, 1992. 154pp. (Acamedia research monograph, 8)

The severe imbalance in the dissemination of news and information between the developed and the developing nations of the world, as highlighted notably in the 1980 MacBride Commission Report for UNESCO, *Many voices, one world,* is examined again through this summary of the results of a UNESCO survey on recently established news exchange mechanisms. It concludes that although prospects are not encouraging for any radical change in the world information order, there are opportunities raised by the receding ideological confrontation between East and West, and an increasingly multipolar world, for a greater plurality of information sources and better understanding of regional, subregional and national aspirations. (BM)

622 Breen, Myles. 'Identity crisis down under: Australia assesses its future'. *Media Development*, Vol. 36, No. 2, 1989, pp. 9–12.
Following its bicentenary, Australia is reflecting on its cultural identity. Long under the cultural imperialism of the British Empire, it is now a polyglot immigrant nation taking its national identity from a diversity of peoples from all over the world, and coming to terms with internationalization and the geographical realities of close proximity with Asia. (BM)

623 Dunn, Hopeton S. 'Caribbean islands: the world's most culturally beleaguered region'. *Media Development*, Vol. 36, No. 2, 1989, pp. 25–7.
The post-colonial English-speaking Caribbean countries have problems of cultural identity, with European heritage dominating most walks of life, language and culture, but now the development of more appropriate forms of technology and the cultural and creative renovation offered by such innovations as community-based video and desktop publishing may strengthen the indigenous and popular cultures. (BM)

624 French, David and **Richards, Michael** (eds.) *Contemporary television: Eastern perspectives*. New Delhi: Sage, 1996. 371pp. (Communication and human values)
Collection of papers about the importance of television in South and South East Asia as an increasingly dominant form of leisure pursuit, as a source of information and news, and as an important influence upon the cultural life in those societies. Individual topics covered include the conflict between the concern to preserve distinctive national and regional cultural identities, and the irresistible pressure of global media. (BM)

625 Gerbner, George and **Siefert, Marsha** (eds.) *World communication: a handbook*. New York and London: Longman, 1984. xv, 527pp.
'Compendium' might be a better word than 'handbook' for this vast compilation of articles and papers from all over the world, including a number from the *Journal of Communication*. They are grouped into five sections: 'Global perspectives on information'; 'Transnational communications: flow of news and images'; 'Telecommunications: satellites and computers'; 'Mass communications: development within national contexts'; and 'Intergovernmental systems: towards international policies'. There are four appendices, including a useful glossary. Bibliography. (SM)

626 Golding, Peter. 'The communications paradox: inequality at the national and international levels'. *Media Development*, Vol. 41, No. 4, 1994, pp. 7–9.
Globalizing tendencies of communications media should not be allowed to disguise the very real inequalities which persist at both international and intra-

national levels if the liberalizing potential of the communications media is to be realized. (BM)

627 Halloran, James D. 'What we urgently require is a globalisation of moral responsibility'. *InterMedia*, Vol. 21, No. 2, March–April 1993, pp. 4–7.

Professor Halloran reports on an International Institute of Communications Conference in Montreal in 1992, and the debate on the responsibility of the global media to inform all and to address the problems of inequality and democracy. (BM)

628 Hamelink, Cees J. *Cultural autonomy in global communications.* New York: Longman, 1983. xiv, 143pp. (Communication and human values)

The growth of information has led to a worldwide domination by the giant American companies. Not only economic independence but cultural autonomy is at risk: the author argues that the only way out for Third World countries (and perhaps some Western states) is 'cultural dissociation'. It is more successful in its analysis of the problem than in the almost despairing unrealistic solutions it proposes. The author, Senior Lecturer at the Institute for Social Studies at The Hague, writes: 'I am conscious that ... the plea for cultural dissociation may meet the reproach of *naïveté*.' In fact its *naïveté* lies more in the academic presumptions on which the idea of dissociation is based. However, it is a useful book, which spans a wide spectrum from Coca-Cola to informatics. (SM)

629 Hanns Seidel Foundation. *Freedom of information: a human right.* Munich: Hanns Seidel Stiftung, Institute for International Meeting and Co-operation, 1978. 122pp.

Papers given at a Symposium at the United Nations in Geneva in 1978 on freedom of information in the Third World, covering international agencies and global information imbalance, transnational broadcasting, and the presentation and reception of news of Third World issues. (BM)

630 Herzog, William. 'Issues of development communication ethics'. *Journal of Mass Media Ethics*, Vol. 6, No. 4, 1991, pp. 210–21.

Ethical consideration of the policies, programmes and models used to project successful development, and the opportunities offered by the newly emerging communications technologies. (BM)

631 Hoover, Stewart. 'All power to the conglomerate: if information is a commodity what price is international understanding?' *Media & Values*, No. 61, Winter 1993, pp. 2–5.

Discussion of the global role of the media and 'commoditization' of the media. (BM)

632 Jakubowicz, Karol. 'Equality for the downtrodden, freedom for the free: changing perspectives on social communication in Central and Eastern Europe'. *Media, Culture and Society*, Vol. 16, No. 2, April 1994, pp. 271–92.

Examination of the role of the media in some Eastern European countries under the communist system, and since the downfall of communism in 1989, questioning whether freedom to communicate has followed in the newly free states. (BM)

633 Katz, Elihu and **Wedell, George**. *Broadcasting in the Third World: promise and performance*. Cambridge, Massachusetts: Harvard University Press, 1977; London: Macmillan, 1978. xvi, 305pp.

This book is the result of a co-operative study between Manchester University and the Hebrew University of Jerusalem. Broadcasting systems in 91 countries were studied at various levels of intensity. It is inevitable that some of the political and institutional structures have changed since it was published, and communications satellites have opened up new possibilities. This does not detract, however, from the thoughtful generalizations and analyses which distinguish this book from the more purely descriptive works. Though the authors, and their teams, make good use of the academic research, and give an account of it, the perspectives here are wider and more level-headed. A valuable work. (SM)

634 Kunczik, Michael. *Communication and social change: a summary of theories, policies and experiences for media practitioners in the Third World*. Bonn: Friedrich-Ebert-Stiftung, 1984. 295pp.

The extended title exactly describes this admirable work, which ranges from the development of media theory to a final chapter on the outlook for the international flow of data. Scholarly, heavily condensed and extensively referenced, it provides a synoptic view of the whole field, and should become a standard work. Bibliography. (SM)

635 Lee, Chin-Chuan. *Media imperialism reconsidered: the homogenizing of television culture*. Beverly Hills, California: Sage Publications, 1980. 277pp. (People and communication, 10)

A refreshingly 'middle-of-the-road' book, critical of the analyses of neo-Marxists and non-Marxists alike. Case studies of Canada and Taiwan reinforce the author's argument that broad generalizations about the Third World and Western capitalism are no substitute for detailed examination of individual broadcasting systems. Though marred by some factual errors, it is nevertheless thoughtful and stimulating, with a firm foundation in empirical research. Bibliography. (SM)

636 Lee, Philip (ed.) *Communication for all: New World Information and Communication order*. Maryknoll, New York: Orbis Books, 1986. xiii, 160pp.

A revised version of a book originally published in 1985 in India. There are seven essays, some by Third World authors, and an annotated bibliography by Colleen Roach. It is a committed work, the copyright of which is held by the World Association for Christian Communication. One essay, by Washington Uranga, is excellent. For the rest, a disappointing book, though there are a few interesting points. Bibliography. (SM)

637 McAnany, Emile G. and **Wilkinson, Kenton T**. 'From cultural imperialists to takeover victims?' *Communication Research*, Vol. 19, No. 6, December 1992, pp. 724–48.
The term 'cultural imperialism', so popular in the 1970s, has largely been abandoned in today's academic discussion, though some of the issues underpinning the earlier debate (for example, the argument about perceived American cultural domination) have not entirely disappeared, and the question of how television might influence cultural values and social behaviour is as important as ever. (BM)

638 McPhail, Thomas L. *Electronic colonialism: the future of international broadcasting and communication.* 2nd ed. Beverly Hills, California: Sage Publications, 1987. 312pp. (Sage library of social research)
A sensible, orderly account of the debates on the New World Information Order up to the MacBride Report. A valuable introduction to the subject. (SM)

639 Mansell, Gerard. *Let the truth be told: 50 years of BBC External Broadcasting.* London: Weidenfeld & Nicolson, 1982. x, 300pp.
A house history, largely concentrated on the war years. Much of the book is special pleading; it is nevertheless of interest, because some of the current problems of sovereignty over air space were being considered half a century ago. The changing shape and objectives of external broadcasting in the 1960s and 1970s are discussed. As a broadcaster, Gerard Mansell does not share the doubts and inhibitions of UNESCO delegates about cultural imperialism. Bibliography. (SM)

640 Mowlana, Hamid. *Global communication in transition: the end of diversity?* Thousand Oaks, California: Sage Publications, 1996. xiv, 233pp. (Communication and human values)
A discursive text on the history, theories, processes and issues of international communication, covering community and national and global development, Islamic perspectives and concepts of ethics, nationalism versus universalism, and the erosion of nation-state sovereignty. (BM)

641 Mowlana, Hamid. *Global information and world communication: new frontiers in international relations.* 2nd ed. London: Sage, 1997. xiii, 270pp.
Overview of international and intercultural relations, examining the 'information revolution' of mass communications, telecommunications and new media in various contexts – political, economic, cultural, technological and legal. The author's suggested ethical framework includes four basic principles: to prevent war and promote peace; to respect culture, traditions and values; to promote human rights and dignity; and to preserve home, family and community. He concludes the ultimate ethical power the communications institutions have is to serve the public. (BM)

642 Murphy, Brian M. *The international politics of new information technology*. London and Sydney: Croom Helm, 1986. 306pp.
The present imbalance of the world information technology market, which is due to the overwhelming dominance of the US (largely through one corporation – IBM), has meant that technological neo-colonialism exists not only in the Third World, but also increasingly in Europe and other developed countries. Many such countries, conscious of the necessity to control the supply and application of their own information technology systems if they are to retain true independence, are concerned about the impact of transborder data flows upon their national sovereignty, and social, economic and cultural identity. The author, Executive Secretary to the British Parliamentary Information Technology Committee, charts the history of computerized information, the IT industries and policies of developed and Third World countries, efforts by international agencies to face the problems and lay down standards, and the necessity of technology transfer to improve the world distribution of information technology. Bibliography. (SM)

643 Organ, Christine. 'Video's great advantage: decentralised control of technology'. *Media Development*, Vol. 36, No. 4, 1989, pp. 2–5.
Video is a medium with perhaps more promise than other communication technologies for developing countries, enabling them to take control of creation and distribution of programming away from centralized authority and placing it in the hands of the peoples themselves, perhaps helping survival of indigenous cultures. (BM)

644 Pigeat, Henri. 'The new international news disorder'. *InterMedia*, Vol. 17, No. 3–4, August–September 1989, pp. 10–16.
Former President of Agence France-Presse reflects on the important role of news agencies in the dissemination of news. The enormous growth in the media, and thousands of dispatches sent out daily, do not automatically contribute to the development of truthful news, and there are still 'black holes' in news leading to a misinformed world. (BM)

645 Reeves, Geoffrey. *Communications and the 'Third World'*. London: Routledge, 1993. xiv, 277pp. (Studies in culture and communication)
Transnationalization and informationalization raise fundamental questions for all societies whether advanced or developing. Third World countries, as importers of advanced information and communications technologies, as well as a vast range of cultural commodities, seem virtually powerless to resist and establish a real means of control over their own cultural production processes. This work addresses cultural domination and subordination, control of communications, cultural production and distribution, regulation of transborder data flows, development of indigenous cultural and technological production capacity, and the creation of a New World Information Order. (BM)

646 Schiller, Herbert I. 'Freedom from the "free flow"'. *Journal of Communication*, Vol. 24, No. 1, Winter 1974, pp. 110–17.
Governments and international organizations are considering ways of ensuring that societies keep their own cultures from being homogenized by the international free flow of information and the domination of Western media. (BM)

647 Sinclair, John, Jacka, Elizabeth and **Cunningham, Stuart**. *New patterns in global television: peripheral visions*. Oxford: Oxford University Press, 1996. xii, 238pp.
Three Australian academics challenge the idea that the powerful metropolitan nations at the centre of the world media system are breaking down the integrity and autonomy of the cultures of peripheral countries, by showing that some such countries have now developed strong television industries, in this series of overviews of the major regions of television programme production and distribution, including Australia, Latin America, India, Middle East, China and Canada. (BM)

648 Singh, Kusum and **Gross, Bertram**. '"MacBride": the report and the response'. *Journal of Communication*, Vol. 31, No. 4, Autumn 1981, pp. 104–17.
Examination of the background to and the key tenets of the MacBride Report on a New World Information Order, published as *Many voices, one world* [see 658], and subsequent response to it. The Voice of Freedom Conference at Talloires in 1981 upheld the concept of press freedom as a basic right, but rejected the call for an international code of journalistic ethics because the plurality of views made it impossible. (BM)

649 Smith, Anthony. *The geopolitics of information: how Western culture dominates the world*. London: Faber, 1980. 192pp.
The development of communications systems is so swift that much of the statistical information in this book is now out of date. Nevertheless, it retains much of its value as a realistic assessment of the divide between North and South, the developed world and the Third World, and grimly argues that the inequalities will increase in the future. It ranges from news agencies to informatics, is not tendentious, and keeps its feet firmly on the ground, though much of it is quite new territory. Particular attention is paid to communications in India. (SM)

650 Smith, Anthony. 'Media globalism in the age of consumer sovereignty'. *Gannett Center Journal*, Vol. 4, No. 4, Fall 1990, pp. 1–16.
Globalization of the world's information and entertainment business, now beyond the power of nations to control, may eventually undermine democratic institutions and subvert and erode national cultures. (BM)

651 Smith, Anthony. 'The natives are restless'. *Media Studies Journal*, Vol. 9, No. 4, Fall 1995, pp. 1–6.

Author looks at the fears over the ownership of media and the values which we are trying to protect – cultural products can be absorbed, enjoyed, neglected – but deeper forms of sovereignty are at stake. National policies need to be developed to deal with the problems and that suit their own cultural and political needs. (BM)

652 Tomaselli, Keyan. 'Transferring video skills to the community: the problem of power'. *Media Development*, Vol. 36, No. 4, 1989, pp. 11–15.
South African academic looks at the new opportunities for true community media provided by video, and its impact on democracy and participation. (BM)

653 Tomlinson, John. *Cultural imperialism*. London: Pinter, 1991. 187pp.
Critique of the theoretical basis and principles of the 'cultural imperialism' debate. (BM)

654 Tunstall, Jeremy. 'Are the media still American?' *Media Studies Journal*, Vol. 9, No. 4, Fall 1995, pp. 7–16.
American domination of world media and entertainment, while still strong in some areas, is like the general position of the US on the world stage: it is in gradual decline against the world as a whole. (BM)

655 Tunstall, Jeremy. *The media are American: Anglo-American media in the world*. 2nd ed. London: Constable, 1994. 352pp. (Communication and society)
Despite the title, this is basically a mini-encyclopedia on the world's media. However, there is a shrewd organizing intelligence behind the mass of facts, and the thesis is well documented. Professor Tunstall's central theme is that, given the economics of media production and distribution, it was destined to be a winner-take-all industry, and successive waves of American media – popular press, movies, popular music, television programmes – have ensured that the US dominates world media, and to the disadvantage of national cultural industries and identity. As always, Jeremy Tunstall's judgements are individual and independent. Bibliography. (SM/BM)

656 Tunstall, Jeremy and **Walker, David**. *Media made in California: Hollywood, politics and the news*. New York and London: Oxford University Press, 1981. vi, 204pp.
Academic studies of the media often seem remote from the 'real' media world of newspapers, films and records. This book, written jointly by an academic and a journalist from *The Economist*, goes to the other extreme. For the most part it is descriptive rather than analytical, a little clouded by stardust. But from the macro-world of *The media are American* this smaller study focuses on Californian culture and its influence on the US generally as well as the wider world. The Californian media, the authors argue, have created some false images of America. Bibliography. (SM)

657 Tusa, John. *A world in your ear: reflections on change.* London: Broadside Books, 1992. 176pp.

Renowned journalist and broadcaster, latterly Managing Director of the BBC World Service, justifies (as if it needs it) international broadcasting in its role in contributing to the free flow of information, satisfying the universal need to know and for the truth. (BM)

658 UNESCO. *Many voices, one world: communication and society today and tomorrow.* London: Kogan Page, 1980. xx, 312pp.

The final report of UNESCO's International Commission for the study of 'the totality of communication problems in modern societies' (also known as the MacBride Report), though in fact it falls a long way short of this. Members were drawn from 16 countries, with six additional 'collaborating consultants'. The aim of the Commission was (unrealistically) to reach a consensus view, but the Soviet delegate entered a brief minority report. This is a primary source, though it suffers from the faults of any work produced by committee, and is written in the jargon of international bureaucracy. Though the Commission set out to 'investigate the collection and dissemination of news', its discussions were soon enlarged to cover a wider historical, political and sociological perspective. Its value is increased by an orderly layout and excellent sub-headings which make it easy to use. The report set out, in the words of its President Sean MacBride, 'to meet the challenge of reaching the broadest possible consensus in our views', a consensus that proved illusory. From 1980 the UNESCO General Conference began to debate the implementation of the New World Information and Communication Order policies, based on the MacBride Commission conclusions, though with little agreement. However, some consensus had emerged by the end of the decade, and found its place in UNESCO's strategy for the 1990s which seeks to encourage 'the free flow of information at international as well as national levels'. (SM/BM)

659 Varis, Tapio. 'The influence of international television: a case study'. *The Journal of Moral Education*, Vol. 13, No. 2, October 1984, pp. 173–82.

Dr Varis takes as his main theme what happens to international communication in conditions of international tension when the media are transnationally highly concentrated and controlled by only a few. (BM)

660 Wilson II, Clint C. and **Gutierrez, Felix**. *Race, multiculturalism and the media: from mass to class communication.* Thousand Oaks, California: Sage, 1995. xvi, 274pp.

Authors argue that rapid and sweeping changes in the demographic composition of the US will force the media to change approach from trying to appeal to a homogenized 'mass' audience, to a strategy of targeting individual audience segments along racial or ethnic lines (for example, black, Latino or American-Asian). (BM)

Advertising

661 Arthur, Chris. 'Agony in advertising: appraising recent media images of suffering and death'. *Media Development*, Vol. 39, No. 4, 1992, pp. 19–23.
A recent advertising campaign by Italian clothes manufacturer Benetton using a series of controversial news photographs of suffering, including a dying AIDS patient, brought official criticism and public protest, and was banned in the UK and several other European countries. It raised religious and moral questions, though the author argues that shocking pictures may be a healthy antidote to bland consumer dream-world images. (BM)

662 Barnes, Michael (ed.) *The three faces of advertising*. London: Advertising Association, 1975. vii, 277pp.
The 'three faces' are ethics, economics and effects. Though inevitably the debate on advertising has moved on, this collection of 16 articles, extracts and lectures has continuing value because it brings together some classic pieces, both 'for' and 'against'. For example, Nicholas (later Lord) Kaldor's paper, written in 1943 but not published until 1951, 'The economic aspects of advertising' was a seminal piece which dominated the Left's view of advertising for decades. Other essays are by Richard Williams, Richard Crossman, Harry Henry and Harold Lind. (BM/SM)

663 Bennett, Roger. 'Effects of horrific fear appeals on public attitudes towards AIDS'. *International Journal of Advertising*, Vol. 15, No. 3, 1996, pp. 183–202.
Advertising intended to induce fear is illegal in several Western countries, and banned under voluntary self-regulatory codes of practice in others, yet fear appeals are commonly used in government health and safety campaigns. This article assesses research findings on the impact on the audience of such campaigns, particularly warnings of AIDS. (BM)

664 Bishop, F. P. *The ethics of advertising*. London: Robert Hale, 1949. 256pp.
Included here because for many years, with its companion *The economics of advertising*, it was regarded as a classic defence of advertising, but it is of less value today. (SM)

665 Blakeney, Michael and **McKeough, Jill**. 'The right to advertise: the cigarette debate'. *Media Information Australia*, No. 31, February 1984, pp. 42–6.
The validity of the free speech and free enterprise arguments in relation to cigarette advertising examined with reference to the belief that 'if a product is legal to sell, it should be legal to advertise'. (BM)

666 Boddewyn, Jean J. *Global perspectives on advertising self-regulation: principles and practices in thirty-eight countries*. Westport, Connecticut: Quorum Books, 1992. xv, 235pp.

In this book, supported by the International Advertising Association (IAA), the author, Professor of Marketing and International Business at City University New York, staunchly defends the freedom of commercial speech and consumer choice, and sees the encouragement and development of advertising self-regulation as the best means of preventing the undesirable imposition of regulations and restrictions. After making the case for self-regulation, the author surveys the situation in over 30 countries throughout the world, and includes various codes of practice as appendices. (BM)

667 **Bush, Alan J.** and **Bush, Victoria Davies**. 'The narrative paradigm as perspective for improving ethical evaluations of advertisements'. *Journal of Advertising*, Vol. 23, No. 3, 1994, pp. 31–41.

Proposal for a narrative approach to identifying unethical aspects or elements of advertisements. (BM)

668 **Chonko, Lawrence B.**, **Hunt, Shelby D.** and **Howell, Roy D.** 'Ethics and the American Advertising Federation principles'. *International Journal of Advertising*, Vol. 6, No. 3, 1997, pp. 265–74.

The American Advertising Federation provides ethical guidelines to the industry. This article looks at their adherence and effectiveness. (BM)

669 **Courtney, Alice E.** and **Whipple, Thomas W**. *Sex stereotyping in advertising.* Lexington, Massachusetts: Lexington Books, 1983. xv, 239pp.

Two North American marketing lecturers examine the overwhelming research evidence and literature that advertisements present traditional, limited and often demeaning stereotypes of men and women in order to convey images quickly and clearly, and that these pervasive stereotypes have considerable impact on the attitudes and behaviour of society. Strategies for change, including major areas of research, and proposals for regulation as well as self-regulation are put forward. (BM)

670 **Cowton, Christopher J**. 'The ethics of advertising: do investors care?' *International Journal of Advertising*, Vol. 11, No. 2, 1992, pp. 157–64.

Ethical and green investment has grown considerably in the UK recently, and advertising of such ethical products and services might become more important, and may itself become an issue, particularly if claimed to be deceptive. (BM)

671 **Crowley, John H**. 'The advertising industry's defense of its First Amendment rights'. *Journal of Mass Media Ethics*, Vol. 8, No. 1, 1993, pp. 5–16.

An ethical defence by advertisers of 'banned' tobacco and alcohol advertising is based on freedom of speech and the public's right to know. (BM)

672 **Garrett, Thomas M**. *An introduction to some ethical problems of modern American advertising.* Rome: Gregorian University Press, 1961. vii, 209pp.

This exploratory thesis recognizes a previous general lack of any systematic efforts to evaluate advertising in the light of ethical principles, and highlights for further study such areas as the ethics of persuasion and consumption, and the power of advertising. (BM)

673 Gould, Stephen J. 'Sexuality and ethics in advertising: a research agenda and policy guideline perspective'. *Journal of Advertising*, Vol. 23, No. 3, 1994, pp. 73–9.
Sexual appeals in advertising are all pervasive, but do raise ethical and moral concerns; this article suggests areas of further research into the topic, and the formulation of guidelines for sexual advertising. (BM)

674 Haefner, Margaret J. 'Ethical problems of advertising to children'. *Journal of Mass Media Ethics*, Vol. 6, No. 2, 1991, pp. 83–91.
Author argues for introducing ethical values into corporate decision-making policies regarding children and advertising. (BM)

675 Hyman, Michael R. and **Tansey, Richard**. 'The ethics of psychoactive advertisements'. *Journal of Business Ethics*, Vol. 9, No. 2, February 1990, pp. 105–14.
Discussion of the ethics of advertisements designed to arouse emotions, their possible harmful effects and the need for careful pre-testing. (BM)

676 Hyman, Michael R., Tansey, Richard and **Clark, James W.** 'Research on advertising ethics: past, present and future'. *Journal of Advertising*, Vol. 23, No. 3, 1994, pp. 5–15.
American review of the literature, with survey findings on attitudes to research in this field and relative importance of different topics to the study of advertising ethics, which concludes that the research should become both more scientific (for example, better samples or better research design) and more applied (that is, useful to the advertising practitioners). (BM)

677 Jhally, Sut. *The codes of advertising: fetishism and the political economy of meaning in the consumer society.* New York: Routledge, 1990. ix, 225pp.
Examination of advertising as a cultural phenomenon whose social significance far outweighs its economic influence, not just a persuader or informer of consumerism, but a mediator between culture and the economy, and people and products. (BM)

678 Jamieson, G. H. *Communication and persuasion.* London: Croom Helm, 1985. 170pp. (Croom Helm communication series)
Human communication in all its forms includes a substantial persuasive element. This discussion on persuasion looks at the ethical issues raised concerning the contents of messages and their form of presentation, as well as the 'media manipulation' of the press, film and television. The deployment of persuasion for commercial gains, so central to the advertising and marketing industries, and its effects on the 'audience' are discussed. (BM)

679 La Tour, Michael and **Henthorne, Tony L**. 'Ethical judgements of sexual appeals in print advertising'. *Journal of Advertising*, Vol. 23, No. 3, 1994, pp. 81–90.

The findings of this American study of consumers' perception of sexual appeals indicates that both men and women have potential ethical concerns about the use of strong and overt sexual images in advertisements. (BM)

680 Lehtonen, Jaakko. 'Freedom and responsibility: global village and the power of communication'. In Lehtonen, Jaakko and Leena (eds.) *Critical perspectives on communication research and pedagogy*. St Ingbert, Finland: Röhring Universitätsverlag, 1995, pp. 31–45.

The author examines the morals of advertising and marketing, and the new communications and information environment. (BM)

681 Leiss, William, Kline, Stephen and **Jhally, Sut**. *Social communication in advertising: persons, products and images of well-being*. 2nd ed. Scarborough, Ontario: Nelson Canada, 1990. x, 426pp.

This book goes a long way to justifying its claim that it 'is the first genuinely comprehensive study of advertising'. It is multi-disciplinary, ranging from history and economics to social anthropology. Because it is Canadian it draws on both US and European cultural traditions. It surveys the literature in a number of fields, and contains more original thinking than many more traditional studies. It is unfortunate that the attempt to marry the techniques of semiology with content analysis is marred by the poor quality reproduction of the advertisements on which it is based; the weakest part of the book is the rather perfunctory proposals for new social policies towards advertising, some of which have already been tried, and others of which are obviously impractical. Nevertheless a major work. Bibliography. (SM)

682 Lester, Anthony and **Pannick, David**. 'Advertising and freedom of expression'. *InterMedia*, Vol. 13, No. 2, March 1985, pp. 25–9.

Two lawyers consider the limitations and restrictions on the right to advertise imposed by states and public authorities, with reference to the European Commission Green Paper *Television without frontiers*, and the guarantee to the right to freedom of expression under Article 10 of the European Convention on Human Rights. (BM)

683 Mander, Michael. 'Freedom to advertise: the principles of choice'. *Advertising*, No. 67, Spring 1981, pp. 32–5.

The right of the individual to advertise legitimate goods and services, and the contribution of advertising to free and fair competition, and freedom of the media. (BM)

684 Myers, Kathy. *Understains: the sense and seduction of advertising*. London: Comedia, 1986. 157pp.

This is a political pamphlet, important because it represents one stage in the Left's abandonment of many of its traditional, moralistic and economic/rational hostilities towards advertising. Highly relevant illustrations. (SM)

685 Nevett, Terence. 'The ethics of advertising: F. P. Bishop reconsidered'. *International Journal of Advertising*, Vol. 4, No. 4, 1985, pp. 297–304.
F. P. Bishop's spirited and influential defence of advertising, and advocacy of self-regulation, *The ethics of advertising* (1949), now looks inappropriate for our times. (BM)

686 Packard, Vance. *The hidden persuaders.* New York: David McKay, 1957; London: Longmans Green, 1957. 275pp.; London: Penguin Books, new ed., 1991. 256 pp.
This book was influential internationally in increasing the distrust in which some forms of advertising are held. Packard was not anti-advertising, but was concerned by the use of mass psychoanalysis to guide campaigns of persuasion. (BM/SM)

687 Rieken, Glen and **Yavas, Ugur.** 'Advertising and the professions'. *International Journal of Advertising*, Vol. 3, No. 4, 1984, pp. 311–19.
Regulatory restrictions on advertising by professional groups have changed dramatically in recent years, though traditional attitudes still make some medical practitioners wary of advertising; this article looks at the ethics of advertising by doctors and dentists. (BM)

688 Rijkens, Rein and **Miracle, Gordon E.** *European regulation of advertising: supranational regulation of advertising in the European Economic Community.* Amsterdam: North-Holland, 1986. xxxiv, 375pp.
This lavishly produced volume is the work of a former President of the European Association of Advertising Agencies and the Professor of Advertising at Michigan State University. They argue that the European Economic Community, in seeking a formula for the control of advertising at an international level, was originally influenced by consumerist pressure groups into seeking too strict controls, to the detriment of freedom of choice and running counter to the present tide of deregulation. An overly partisan work that nevertheless contains valuable material and is a useful counterbalance to more extreme consumerist arguments. Bibliography. (SM)

689 Rotzoll, Kim B. and **Christians, Clifford G.** 'Advertising agency practitioners' perceptions of ethical decisions'. *Journalism Quarterly*, Vol. 57, No. 3, Autumn 1980, pp. 425–31.
Survey (through questionnaire) of 123 employees of advertising agencies, which identifies difficult moral dilemmas with accurate representation of products, meaningful disclosure and exaggerated claims, and the difficulty in resolving these problems. (BM)

690 Scharlott, Bradford W. 'The First Amendment protection of advertising in the mass media'. *Communications and the Law*, Vol. 2, No. 3, Summer 1980, pp. 43–58.
First Amendment protection of advertising may still be acceptable for the print media (as free speech) but not for broadcast advertising. (BM)

691 Schultze, Quentin J. 'Professionalism in advertising: the origin of ethical codes'. *Journal of Broadcasting*, Vol. 31, No. 2, Spring 1981, pp. 64–71.
Author argues that ethical codes and self-regulatory mechanisms in advertising originally derived from the industry's desire to appear to be acting in the public interest and to create the impression of professionalism. (BM)

692 Tansey, Richard and **Hyman, Michael R.** 'Ethical codes and the advocacy advertisements of World War II'. *International Journal of Advertising*, Vol. 12, No. 4, 1993, pp. 351–66.
The Advertising Federation of America in 1942 drew up an ethical code for wartime advertising; this article looks at those guidelines to promote intelligent patriotism, glorify the fighting forces and arouse the enthusiasm of the worker, and draws lessons for advocacy advertising today. (BM)

693 Tomlinson, Don E. 'Where morality and law diverge: ethical alternatives in the *Soldier of Fortune* cases'. *Journal of Mass Media Ethics*, Vol. 6, No. 2, 1991, pp. 69–82.
Though serious crimes have resulted from the 'guns-for-hire' personal classified advertisements in *Soldier of Fortune*, an American magazine for professional adventurers, the courts can find no liability for dissemination of advertisements that cause harm. They can be defended on the grounds that, though they are morally irresponsible, they are protected by the freedoms embodied in the First Amendment. (BM)

694 Treise, Debbie and others. 'Ethics in advertising: ideological correlates of consumer perceptions'. *Journal of Advertising*, Vol. 23, No. 3, 1994, pp. 59–69.
Survey of consumers' perceptions of ethical controversies in advertising, in particular advertising to children, minority groups, and the use of sex and appeals to fear. (BM)

695 Voorhoof, Dirk. 'Restrictions on television advertising and Article 10 of the European Convention on Human Rights'. *International Journal of Advertising*, Vol. 12, No. 3, 1993, pp. 189–210.
Professor Voorhoof discusses the guarantee of rights to freedom of expression enshrined in Article 10 of the European Convention on Human Rights and the protection it affords to freedom of communications by means of radio and television, and the freedom of commercial speech or advertising, in the light of a European Court of Human Rights ruling that 'information of a commercial nature falls within the Convention'. (BM)

696 **Williams, David**. *Advertising and the Christian conscience*. London: Advertising Association, 1975. 20pp.
'Advertising: the Churches' view' conference (Salisbury, 14–15 October 1975) addresses advertising, and the conflict for Christians between materialism and spirituality. (BM)

Periodicals

697 *Advertising Age*. New York: Crain Communications, 1930–. Weekly.
International trade newspaper of advertising and marketing, featuring news, articles (occasionally on media ethics), product and new technology reviews, and special reports. Indexed in *Business Periodicals Index* and *Telecommunications Abstracts*. (BM)

698 *American Journalism*. Tulsa, Oklahoma: American Journalism Historians Association, Communications Department, University of Tulsa, 1982–. Quarterly.
American academic journal on the history of journalism and mass media – both print and broadcast – in the US. Indexed in *Communication Abstracts*. (BM)

699 *Article 19*. London: Article 19, 1987–. Three issues a year.
Newsletter of the international campaign for the freedom of expression. (BM)

700 *Australian Journalism Review*. Brisbane, Australia: Journalism Education Association, c/o School of Media and Journalism, Queensland University of Technology, 1979–. Biannual.

701 *British Journalism Review*. Luton: John Libbey Media at the University of Luton for BJR Publishing, 1989–. Quarterly.
British review whose primary aim 'is to help journalists themselves reflect on the changing character and problems of their job'. Distinguished journalists, broadcasters and academics write on freedom of the press, censorship, the newspaper industry, war reporting, privacy and other aspects of the practice of journalism. (BM)

702 *Broadcast*. London: EMAP Media, 1973–. Weekly.
Formerly *Television Mail* (1959–73), and incorporating *Television Weekly* (1983–85). The principal trade magazine for the British broadcasting industry, covering television, radio, cable and satellite television, video and facilities houses. It contains news, analysis, articles, statistics, letters, diary of events and so on. Indexed in *International Index to Television Periodicals*. (BM)

703 *Broadcasting & Cable*. Washington, DC: Broadcasting Cable/Cahners Publishing, 1931–. Weekly.
Weekly trade magazine for the American broadcasting and cablecasting industries, containing news and articles on legislation and regulation issues, the Federal

Communications Commission, television stations' programming and business news, new technologies and conferences. Indexed in *Telecommunications Abstracts*. (BM)

704 *The Bulletin.* Reston, Virginia: American Society of Newspaper Editors, 1970–. Nine issues a year.
Short essays and articles on press controversies, including ethics of investigative reporting. (BM)

705 *Business and Professional Ethics Journal.* Gainsville, Florida: Center for Applied Philosophy, University of Florida, 1981–. Quarterly.

706 *Canadian Journal of Communication.* Waterloo, Ontario: Wilfrid Laurier University Press, 1974–. Quarterly.
Scholarly articles on Canadian communications policy and research. Indexed in *Communication Abstracts*. (BM)

707 *Cardozo Arts & Entertainment Law Journal.* New York: Benjamin N. Cardozo School of Law, Yeshiva University, 1981–. Semi-annual.
Features scholarly discussion on a broad range of current issues in the law, ethics, policy and the regulation of communications and the media. (BM)

708 *Columbia Journalism Review.* New York: Graduate School of Journalism, Columbia University, 1962–. Bimonthly.
Renowned review of journalistic issues which aims to 'help stimulate continuing improvement in the profession and to speak out for what is right, fair and decent'. (BM)

709 *Combroad.* London: Commonwealth Broadcasting Association, CBA Secretariat, BBC, 1966–. Quarterly.
Journal for member organizations and individuals of the Commonwealth Broadcasting Association, containing articles, written mainly by senior broadcasters in the Commonwealth, on broadcasting policies, structures and administration in their countries. Indexed in *International Index to Television Periodicals*. (BM)

710 *Communication.* London: Gordon & Breach Science Publishers, 1975–. Quarterly.
Academic journal with articles from a broad range of disciplines contributing to the study of communication. Indexed in *Communication Abstracts*. (BM)

711 *Communication Quarterly.* Geneseo, New York: Eastern Communication Association, Department of Communications, State University of New York, 1953–. Quarterly.
American scholarly journal covering the role of communication in all disciplines. Indexed in *Communication Abstracts*. (BM)

712 *Communication Research.* Thousand Oaks, California: Sage, 1974–. Bimonthly.
American academic journal of research-based articles from communication scholars and researchers on a broad range of communication issues, including content analysis and effects of television, public opinion and so on. Indexed in *Communication Abstracts*. (BM)

713 *Communication Research Trends.* St Louis, Missouri: Center for the Study of Communication and Culture, Saint Louis University, 1980–. Quarterly.
Religious-based review of research and publications on communication research. (BM)

714 *Communications and the Law.* Littleton, Connecticut: Fred B. Rothman, 1979–. Quarterly.
Review devoted to the study and discussion of legislative, legal and judicial aspects of communications and the media. Indexed in *Current Law Index*. (BM)

715 *Communications Law (Tolley's Communications Law).* Croydon, Surrey: Tolley, 1980–. Bimonthly.
Formerly *Journal of Media Law and Practice* (London: Frank Cass, 1980–95). A journal designed for academics, practitioners and those working in communications, providing information, articles, case notes and law reports, and book reviews on the law and regulation of communications, information technology and entertainment industries. (BM)

716 *Critical Studies in Mass Communications.* Annandale, Virginia: Speech Communication Association, 1984–. Quarterly.
American academic journal on the study and understanding of mass communications, ranging over many issues such as freedom of speech, pornography, television content analysis and political broadcasting. (BM)

717 *Daedalus.* Cambridge, Massachusetts: American Academy of Arts and Sciences, 1846–. Quarterly.
American scholarly journal on the arts, literature and sciences, with articles from distinguished academics and writers on a diverse range of issues. Many issues of *Daedalus* are published in expanded form as books, including *The moving image* (1985) on the social and cultural implications of film and television. Indexed in *Historical Abstracts* and *Psychological Abstracts*. (BM)

718 *Diffusion.* Geneva, Switzerland: European Broadcasting Union, 1992–. Quarterly.
Formerly the *EBU Review* (1950–90). Magazine containing articles written by broadcasting executives on radio and television in Europe, particularly regulation and legislation of broadcasting, programming, audience research, statistics and broader issues such as public service broadcasting and social, political and economic context of broadcasting services. (BM)

719 *European Journal of Communication.* London: Sage, 1986–. Quarterly.
Academic journal reflecting communication theory and research in Europe, particularly mass media, comparative analysis and research on Europe and the rest of the world. It contains scholarly articles (many on ethical issues concerning broadcast or print media or film), periodic overviews of national communications literature, and book reviews. Indexed in *International Index to Television Periodicals.* (BM)

720 *Federal Communications Law Journal.* Los Angeles: School of Law, University of California, Los Angeles, 1977–. Three issues a year.
Formerly *Federal Communications Bar Journal* (1937–76). Scholarly review of First Amendment issues, pornography and so on. (BM)

721 *Free Press.* London: Campaign for Press and Broadcasting Freedom, 1979–. Bimonthly.
Journal of a British pressure group for freedom, choice and diversity in the press and broadcasting, and against concentration of ownership in the media, and government censorship. (BM)

722 *Hastings Communication and Entertainment Law Journal.* San Francisco: Hastings College of the Law, University of California, 1977–. Quarterly.
Formerly *Comm/ent: a Journal of Communications and Entertainment Law.* A journal aimed at the legal profession covers telecommunications, broadcasting, cable, print media advertising and the arts, and such topics as First Amendment issues, privacy and copyright. Indexed in *Communication Abstracts.* (BM)

723 *Historical Journal of Film, Radio and Television.* Oxfordshire: Carfax Publishing, 1981–. Three issues a year.
'Interdisciplinary journal concerned with the evidence produced by the mass media for historians and social scientists, and with the impact of mass communications on the political and social history of the 20th century.' Indexed in *International Index to Television Periodicals.* (BM)

724 *Index on Censorship.* London: Writers & Scholars International, 1972–. Bimonthly.
Containing reports of denials of free speech and censorship throughout the world, it publishes commentaries on their effects and prints examples of banned literature. (BM)

725 *The Information Society.* Washington, DC: Taylor & Francis, 1985–. Quarterly.
Journal providing a forum for discussion of broad issues of the political, social, economic and cultural implications of mass communication, telecommunications and the new information society, covering such topics as regulation and control of communications, and transborder information flows. (BM)

726 *InterMedia.* London: International Institute of Communications, 1974–. Bimonthly.
Journal for broadcasters and academics on international communications and broadcasting, particularly such issues as satellite broadcasting, copyright, telecommunications law, international news flow, the New World Information Order, and new technologies. Features include authoritative articles by practitioners, surveys, news briefings, book reviews and conference reports. Indexed in *International Index to Television Periodicals.* (BM)

727 *International Journal of Advertising.* Oxford: Blackwell, 1983–. Quarterly.
Formerly *Advertising Quarterly* (1964–78), *Advertising* (1979–81) and *Journal of Advertising* (1982). Journal on advertising and marketing from the academic, practitioner and public policy perspectives, containing lengthy, often research-based articles, statistics and book reviews. (BM)

728 *Journal of Advertising Research.* New York: Advertising Research Foundation, 1960–. Bimonthly.
Research-based rather than theoretical articles on advertising and marketing research issues – effects, methodologies, techniques and findings. (BM)

729 *Journal of Broadcasting & Electronic Media.* Washington, DC: Broadcast Education Association, 1957–. Quarterly.
Formerly *Journal of Broadcasting* (1957–84). This American academic journal contains substantive research articles on the role of the electronic media in a global society. Radio, television and telecommunications in an international context. Indexed in *International Index to Television Periodicals.* (BM)

730 *Journal of Business Ethics.* Dordrecht, Netherlands: Kluwer Academic, 1982–. Monthly.
Indexed in *Communication Abstracts.* (BM)

731 *Journal of Communication.* Cary, North Carolina: Oxford University Press, 1951–. Quarterly.
An official publication of the International Communication Association, this scholarly journal on communication theory, research, policy and practice contains research-based articles and book reviews. Indexed in *Communication Abstracts, International Index to Television Periodicals,* and *Psychological Abstracts.* (BM)

732 *Journal of Information Ethics.* St Cloud, Minnesota: St Cloud University, 1992–. Semi-annual.
American journal covering ethics in all areas of the production and dissemination of information, articles on library and information science, cyberspace and computers, from philosophical and practitioner viewpoints.

733 *Journal of Mass Media Ethics.* Provo, Utah: Department of Communications, Brigham Young University, 1985–89. Semi-annual; Mahwah, New Jersey: Lawrence Erlbaum, 1989–. Quarterly.
'Devoted to issues in mass media ethics' with the aim of providing a dialogue between academics and practitioners on aspects of media morality. Each issue features articles, philosophical discussion and literature reviews on ethics in print and broadcast journalism, often each issue grouping articles on one theme, and covering such issues as ethical, legal and moral responsibilities of media professionals, and the ethics of photojournalism. (BM)

734 *The Journal of Moral Education.* Abingdon, Oxfordshire: Carfax Publishing, 1971–. Three issues a year.
Interdisciplinary journal on moral education and development, published for the Social Morality Council. Indexed in *Psychological Abstracts.* (BM)

735 *Journal of Popular Culture.* Bowling Green, Ohio: Popular Press, Bowling Green State University, 1967–. Quarterly.
Indexed in *Communication Abstracts.* (BM)

736 *Journalism History.* Northridge, California: Department of Journalism, California State University, 1974–. Quarterly.
Academic journal of research-based articles on the history of American media. (BM)

737 *Journalism Quarterly and Mass Communication.* Columbia, South Carolina: Association for Education in Journalism and Mass Communication, 1924–. Quarterly.
Long-established scholarly journal devoted to study and research into journalism and mass communication. (BM)

738 *The Listener.* London: BBC, 1929–91. Weekly.
BBC weekly magazine, now sadly ceased publication, for the serious listener and viewer, containing features on broadcast, media and arts-related issues, transcripts of programmes and broadcast talks, book and programme reviews. Indexed in *International Index to Television Periodicals.*

739 *Mass Comm Review.* Columbia, South Carolina: Association for Education in Journalism and Mass Communication, 1973–. Three issues a year.
Research articles on all aspects of mass communication, print and broadcast journalism, advertising and telecommunications, including journalism ethics. Indexed in *Communication Abstracts.* (BM)

740 *Media & Values.* Los Angeles: Center for Media and Values, 1977–. Quarterly.

Magazine, sponsored by a confederation of religious denominations, on values presented by the mass media, and their impact on family, youth and children. (BM)

741 *Media, Culture and Society.* London: Sage, 1979–. Quarterly.
British academic journal intended as a forum for research and discussion on the media within their social, political, cultural and historical contexts. Substantial articles by distinguished media academics from the UK and overseas cover such topics as media and politics, women and the media, media images of society and public service broadcasting. Indexed in *International Index to Television Periodicals.* (BM)

742 *Media Development.* London: World Association for Christian Communication, 1970–. Quarterly.
Formerly *WACC Journal.* Magazine with a religious and humanitarian viewpoint on international development and mass communication issues. Contributors are academics, journalists, and churchmen and women. Articles cover many ethical and moral aspects of the media, particularly in Third World countries. (BM)

743 *Media International Australia.* North Ryde, New South Wales: Australian Film Television and Radio School, 1975–. Quarterly.
Formerly entitled *Australian Media Notes*, and then *Media Information Australia.* Academic journal of substantial articles on a range of media topics, including ethical issues. Indexed in the *International Index to Television Periodicals.* (BM)

744 *Media Law Reporter.* Washington, DC: Bureau of National Affairs, 1977–. Weekly, with annual cumulations.
Guide to the decisions of Federal or State Courts in areas of the media. (BM)

745 *Media Studies Journal.* New York: Freedom Forum Media Studies Center, Columbia University, 1992–. Quarterly.
Formerly *Gannett Center Journal* (1987–91). Scholarly journal of articles by academics and media practitioners on aspects of mass media and society, from a largely American viewpoint, including such issues as the First Amendment, fairness, obscenity laws and pornography, and the ethics of journalism. (BM)

746 *News Media and the Law.* Washington, DC: Reporters Committee for the Freedom of the Press, 1973–. Quarterly.
Covers press freedom and censorship. (BM)

747 *News Photographer.* Durham, North Carolina: National Press Photographers Association, 1946–. Monthly.
Formerly *National Press Photographer.* Journal on issues specific to photojournalists, including news photographers' codes of ethics. (BM)

748 *Nieman Reports.* Cambridge, Massachusetts: Nieman Foundation, Harvard University, 1947–. Quarterly.
Forum for discussion of media-related issues by journalists and academics, Nieman Fellows of Harvard University. (BM)

749 *Philosophy and Rhetoric.* University Park: Pennsylvania State University Press, 1968–. Quarterly.
Scholarly articles on the relationship between philosophy and rhetoric, and rhetoric in relation to new electronic technologies. (BM)

750 *Political Communication and Persuasion.* Bristol, Pennsylvania: Taylor & Francis, 1980–. Quarterly.
International journal which looks at the roles of national and supranational governments and non-governmental organizations as communicators. Indexed in *Communication Abstracts.* (BM)

751 *Public Opinion Quarterly.* Chicago, Illinois: University of Chicago Press, 1937–. Quarterly.
Scholarly journal published for the American Association for Public Opinion Research, and covering public opinion and communication research, and related issues. Indexed in *Communication Abstracts, Psychological Abstracts* and *Sociological Abstracts.* (BM)

752 *Public Relations Quarterly.* Rhinebeck, New York: Public Relations Quarterly, 1955–. Quarterly.
Journal devoted to the theory and practice of public relations, marketing public affairs and general communications issues. Indexed in *Communication Abstracts.* (BM)

753 *Quill.* Greencastle, Indiana: Society of Professional Journalists, 1912–. Ten issues a year.
Journal on news reporting and free press, in particular ethical issues. (BM)

754 *Screen.* Oxford: Oxford University Press for the John Logie Baird Centre (University of Glasgow), 1959–. Quarterly.
Now incorporating *Screen Education*, this scholarly journal with articles from academics, critics, writers and film makers covers media education, film and television criticism, and theory of film. Indexed in *International Index to Television Periodicals.* (BM)

755 *Sight and Sound.* London: British Film Institute, 1932–. Monthly.
Incorporating *Monthly Film Bulletin*, this long-established popular film and television magazine contains illustrated articles, interviews and book, film and video reviews. Indexed in the *International Index to Film Periodicals.* (BM)

756 *Studies in Broadcasting.* Tokyo: Broadcasting Culture Research Institute, Nippon Hoso Kyokai, 1963–. Annual.
International annual review of 'broadcasting science', with substantial articles by media academics and practitioners on all aspects of broadcasting, including public service broadcasting issues. (BM)

757 *Telecommunications Policy.* Oxford: Butterworth, 1977–. Bimonthly.
Journal on the economic, policy and regulatory aspects of the technological and changes in telecommunications. Indexed in *Telecommunications Abstracts.* (BM)

758 *Television: the Journal of the Royal Television Society.* London: Royal Television Society, 1928–. Bimonthly.
The world's earliest journal for television professionals, with articles on the creative, administrative and historical aspects of television. Indexed in *International Index to Television Periodicals.* (BM)

759 *Television Quarterly.* New York: National Academy of Television Arts and Sciences, 1962–. Quarterly.
Magazine on the television industry, mostly in the US, covering programming issues and such topics as censorship, television news, and violence on television. (BM)

760 *UNDA News.* Brussels, Belgium: UNDA – International Catholic Association for Radio and Television. Bimonthly.
Newsletter on broadcasting, advertising and general media issues from a Catholic religious perspective. (BM)

761 *World Press Review.* New York: Stanley Foundation, 1961–. Monthly.
Formerly *Atlas* (1961–72) and *Atlas World Press Review* (1972–80). Collects together material from worldwide sources on the press. (BM)

Bibliographies, indexes and abstracting services

762 Alali, A. Odasuo. *Mass media sex and adolescent values: an annotated bibliography.* Jefferson, North Carolina: McFarland, 1991. v, 138pp.
Bibliography of research findings, articles and studies of mass media products and their impact on adolescent values, sexual attitudes and behaviour, arranged into sections on sex-role portrayals, sexual curricula and media use, adolescent attitudes and values, and pregnancy and health issues. Entries with citation and full annotations. Index. (BM)

763 Alali, A. Odasuo and **Byrd, Gary**. *Terrorism and the news media: a selected, annotated bibliography.* Jefferson, North Carolina: McFarland, 1994. 213pp.

764 Atkin, Charles K, Murray, John P. and **Nayman, Oguz B**. *Television and social behaviour: an annotated bibliography of research focusing on television's impact on children.* Rockville, Maryland: National Institute of Mental Health, 1971. ix, 150pp.

By-product of the research programme initiated by the US Surgeon General's Scientific Advisory Committee on Television and Social Behaviour, this bibliography has fully annotated entries for books and articles arranged in three sections for television content and programming, audience viewing patterns and effects of television, and impact of television on children and youth. Author index. (BM)

765 Block, Eleanor S. and **Bracken, James K**. *Communication and the mass media: a guide to the reference literature.* Englewood, Colorado: Libraries Unlimited, 1991. xii, 198pp. (Reference sources in the humanities series)

Bibliographic guide to basic English-language sources in communication, mostly published in the US since 1970. Over 480 annotated entries arranged by form – bibliographies, dictionaries, encyclopedias, indexes, biographical sources and so on, including sections on research centres, archives and societies. Author, title and subject indexes. (BM)

766 Blum, Eleanor and **Wilhoit, Frances Goins**. *Mass media bibliography: an annotated guide to books and journals for research and reference.* Urbana and Chicago: University of Illinois Press, 1990. viii, 344pp.

The successor to *Basic books in the mass media* (1972; 2nd ed. 1980), now with 1947 fully annotated entries for books within subject categories for 'General communication', 'Broadcasting media', Print media', 'Film', 'Advertising and public relations', and with form categories of 'Bibliographies', Directories', 'Journals' and 'Indexes to mass communications literature'. Individual author, title and subject indexes. Many index references under 'Ethics'. (BM)

767 Carothers, Diane Foxhill. *Radio broadcasting from 1920 to 1990: an annotated bibliography.* New York: Garland, 1991. xi, 564pp. (Garland reference library of the humanities)

Comprehensive bibliography on radio in the US and throughout the world. The 1700 entries, each containing a full bibliographic citation with a short descriptive annotation, are arranged by topic – history, economic aspects, production, programming, international broadcasting, public broadcasting, regulation and legal aspects, amateur radio, women and minorities, careers and reference sources. Author and title indexes. (BM)

768 Cassata, Mary and **Skill, Thomas**. *Television: a guide to the literature.* Phoenix, Arizona: Oryx Press, 1985. xi, 148pp.

Guide to the literature of television providing evaluative bibliographic essays arranged by broad topic (for example, 'Historical development of television', 'Television news' and 'Television and politics'). Author, title and subject indexes. (BM)

BIBLIOGRAPHIES, INDEXES AND ABSTRACTING SERVICES

769 Cates, Jo A. *Journalism: a guide to the reference literature.* 2nd ed. Englewood, Colorado: Libraries Unlimited, 1997. xv, 317pp. (Reference sources in the humanities series)

770 Christians, Clifford G. 'Fifty years of scholarship in media ethics'. *Journal of Communication*, Vol. 27, No. 4, Autumn 1977, pp. 19–29.
Review of the literature on media ethics with bibliography. (BM)

771 *Communication Abstracts.* Newbury Park, California: Sage, 1978–. Bimonthly.
Abstracting service of books and periodical articles (mostly American) covering a range of communications issues (broadcasting, print journalism, advertising and public relations) with full bibliographic citations, substantial abstracts and identification of subject headings used in the index (facilitating useful cross-referencing). Author and subject indexes. (BM)

772 *Communication Booknotes* (formerly *Mass Media Booknotes*). Columbus, Ohio: Center for Advanced Study in Telecommunications, Ohio State University, 1969–. Bimonthly.
Recent titles in telecommunications, information and the media. (BM)

773 Cooper, Thomas W. *Television and ethics: a bibliography.* Boston: G. K. Hall, 1988. xlvi, 203pp.
A bibliography designed 'to assist readers and researchers interested in the relationships between television and ethics'. Dr Cooper, Professor in Mass Communications at Emerson College, provides a useful introduction providing definitions, outline of the work's scope, criteria for selection and findings with summary, and methodology used by the research editor. This valuable bibliography of some 1170 books and periodical articles, mostly North American (473 with descriptive annotations), covers ethical contexts, and such areas of television and ethics as programming, advertising, children, news, politics, effects, regulation and codes. (BM)

774 *Ethics and candour in public relations and organizational communication: a literature review.* San Francisco: International Association of Business Communicators Foundation, 1984. 89pp.

775 Fisher, Kim N. *On the screen: a film, television, and video research guide.* Littleton, Colorado: Libraries Unlimited, 1986. xii, 209pp. (Reference sources in the humanities series)
Bibliographic guide of 731 entries for reference works published in the US, the UK, Canada and Australia. Arranged in broad form categories (for example, 'Bibliographic guides' and 'Dictionaries and encyclopedias') and generally subdivided by film, television and video. Sections on research centres and archives, societies and associations. Author, title and subject indexes. (BM)

776 **Gillmor, Donald M.**, **Glasser, Theodore L.** and **Smith, Victoria**. *Mass media law: a selected bibliography*. Minneapolis: Silha Center for the Study of Media Ethics and Law, University of Minnesota, 1987.

777 **Greenfield, Thomas Allen**. *Radio: a reference guide*. New York: Greenwood Press, 1989. 172pp. (American popular culture)

778 **Higgens, Gavin** (ed.) *British broadcasting, 1922–1982: a selected and annotated bibliography*. London: BBC Data Publications, 1983. 279pp.
Produced for the BBC celebration of 60 years of broadcasting in 1982, this bibliography contains annotated entries for over 1200 books, government publications and research reports on British broadcasting. (BM)

779 **Hill, George H.** and **Davis, Lenwood**. *Religious broadcasting, 1920–1983: a selectively annotated bibliography*. New York: Garland, 1984. 243pp. (Garland reference library of social sciences)

780 **Hill, Susan M.** *Broadcasting bibliography: a guide to the literature of radio and television*. Washington, DC: National Association of Broadcasters, 1989. 74pp.
Selective bibliography of books arranged into sections for fundamentals, business, law, technology, broadcasting and society, comparative broadcasting and so on. Index. (BM)

781 **Hoffman, Frank W**. *Intellectual freedom and censorship: an annotated bibliography*. Metuchen, New Jersey: Scarecrow Press, 1989. 244pp.

782 *International Index to Television Periodicals*. London: International Federation of Film Archives. 1979–.
Companion to the *International Index to Film Periodicals*, started in 1972, this specialist indexing service co-ordinates the collaborative indexing of librarians and archivists in over 20 countries of more than 50 worldwide film, television and media journals. Covers film, advertising, television programmes and production, cable and satellite television, sociological aspects of the media, and specifically 'Ethics and TV', 'Fairness', 'Privacy and TV' and so on. Now an updated CD-ROM, with printed cumulated volumes. (BM)

783 **Langham, Josephine** and **Chrichley, Janine** (comps.) *Radio research: an annotated bibliography, 1975–1988*. 2nd ed. Aldershot, Hampshire: Avebury (Gower Publishing), 1989. ix, 357pp.
A project commissioned by the Radio Academy and funded by the Independent Broadcasting Authority in the UK, this bibliography includes sources of information about radio audiences, and the way listeners use and perceive radio. It covers BBC, IBA and other British research, and foreign research from around the world. Entry includes citation and annotation. Author and subject indexes. (BM)

784 Lent, John A. *The new world and international information order: a resource guide and bibliography.* Singapore: Asian Mass Communication Research and Information Center, 1982. 103pp.

785 Lent, John A. (ed.) *Women and mass communications: an international annotated bibliography.* New York: Greenwood Press, 1991.

786 Linton, David and **Boston, Ray** (eds.) *The newspaper press in Britain: an annotated bibliography.* London: Mansell, 1987. xvii, 361pp.
Comprehensive bibliography of over 2900 entries, mostly annotated, in one alphabetical arrangement by author. The emphasis is on printed news journalism, but not magazine and periodical publishing. Appendices include a chronology of the British newspaper industry, 1476–1986, and a location list of important papers and other archives. (BM)

787 Loughney, Katharine. *Film, television and video periodicals: a comprehensive annotated list.* New York: Garland, 1991. xv, 431pp.
Bibliography of current periodicals on film, television and video – worldwide coverage, predominantly English-language, though some foreign language titles are included. Main alphabetical sequence by journal title (with full annotated entries), followed by indexes for country of publication, by genre (film, television and video), fan magazines, scholarly journals, technical and professional journals, and annuals. (BM)

788 McCavitt, William E. (comp.) *Radio and television: a selected, annotated bibliography.* Metuchen, New Jersey: Scarecrow Press, 1978; *Supplement One: 1977–1981.* 1982; *Supplement Two: 1982–1986,* by Peter K. Pringle and Helen H. Clinton. 1989.
American bibliography and supplements covering books published in the US and the UK from 1926 to 1986 on all aspects of broadcasting, radio, television, cable, new technologies and home video, including reference works, audience research, law and regulation, history, programmes and production. Author and title indexes. (BM)

789 McKerns, Joseph P. *News media and public policy: an annotated bibliography.* New York: Garland, 1985. xxi, 171pp. (Garland reference library of social science)
Bibliography intended for scholars of public policy and administration, as well as mass communications, on the relationship between news media and government. Thematic arrangement – mass communications theory, government and the press, newsmaking and journalistic ethics and values, relationships with the executive, legislative, bureaucracy and judiciary, and news management and agenda-setting. Full citations and short annotations. Author and subject indexes. (BM)

790 *Nordicom: bibliography of Nordic mass communication literature.* Århus, Denmark: Nordic Center for Mass Communication Research, 1975–. Annual.

Bibliography of books, articles from composite works and periodicals, dissertations, research reports, conference and seminar papers on media, journalism and communication published in Scandinavian countries, many of which are in the English language. Work has two sections: document list of fully annotated entries; indexes – keyword (including terms as 'Ethics' and Values') and author. Online through NCOM database. (BM)

791 Passarelli, Anne B. *Public relations in business, government and society: a bibliographic guide.* Englewood, Colorado: Libraries Unlimited, 1989. 129pp. (Reference sources in social sciences series)

792 Schwarzlose, Richard A. *Newspapers: a reference guide.* New York: Greenwood Press, 1987. 417pp. (American popular culture)

793 Shearer, Benjamin F. and **Huxford, Marilyn** (comps.) *Communications and society: a bibliography on communications technologies and their social impact.* Westport, Connecticut: Greenwood Press, 1983. ix, 243pp.
Bibliography of over 2700 entries on the diversity of communication technologies and their impact on society arranged into sections for mass communication theory, history, shaping of mass media content (including gatekeeping, censorship, regulation and bias), social effects, media creation and reflection of public opinion (including sex and race stereotyping), politics, advertising and future prospects. Author and subject indexes. (BM)

794 Slide, Anthony (ed.) *International film, radio and television journals.* Westport, Connecticut: Greenwood Press, 1985. xiv, 429pp. (Historical guides to the world's periodicals and newspapers)
Bibliographic guide to some 300 journals, mostly American but some British. The entries, arranged in alphabetical title sections, contain a general essay with historical background and evaluation of the periodical. Appendices include fan club journals, fan magazines and in-house journals. Bibliography. Index. (BM)

795 Signorielli, Nancy and **Gerbner, George** (comps.) *Violence and terror in the mass media: an annotated bibliography.* New York: Greenwood Press, 1988. xxi, 234pp. (Bibliographies and indexes in sociology)
Originating from a UNESCO Commission, this bibliography of research and scholarly works relating to violence and terror covers four major areas: violence and media content, mass media effects, pornography, and terrorism and the media. Over 780 books, articles, government reports and conference papers. Author and subject indexes. (BM)

796 Sloan, David W. *American journalism history: an annotated bibliography.* New York: Greenwood Press, 1989. 344pp. (Bibliographies and indexes in mass media and communications)

797 Snorgrass, J. William and **Woody, Gloria T.** (comps.) *Blacks and media: a selected, annotated bibliography, 1962–1982.* Tallahassee: University Presses of Florida, 1985. xiv, 150pp.
Selected bibliography of over 700 books and periodical articles concerning blacks in the US and their relationship to the mass media, arranged by media – print, broadcast, advertising and public relations, film and theatre. Author and title indexes. (BM)

798 Snow, Marcellus S. and **Jussawalla, Meheroo**. *Telecommunication economics and international regulatory policy: an annotated bibliography.* New York: Greenwood Press, 1986. 216pp. (Bibliographies and indexes in economics and economic history, 4)

799 Soukup, Paul A. (comp.) *Christian communication: a bibliographical survey.* New York: Greenwood Press, 1989. xiv, 401pp.
Bibliography of over 1300 entries arranged in sections for history/issues, resources, communication theory (including media ethics), history, rhetoric, interpersonal communication, mass communication, international communication and other media. Author, title and subject indexes. (BM)

800 UNESCO. *List of documents and publications in the field of mass communications.* Paris: UNESCO, 1976–. Annual.
Comprehensive international bibliography of documents and publications held by the UNESCO Communication Documentation Centre. Main entries contain full bibliographic details with keyword abstracts, followed by subject and author indexes. (BM)

801 Wedell, George, **Luyken, George-Michael** and **Leonard, Rosemary** (eds.) *Mass communication in Western Europe: an annotated bibliography.* Manchester: European Institute for the Media, 1985. 327pp. (Media monograph, 6)
Bibliography comprising over 700 annotated entries for books, legislation and reports published between 1980 and 1985, on mass communications in twenty European countries, including the UK. Areas covered include the press, radio, television, film, telecommunications and informatics. (BM)

Part III

Directory of selected organizations

Part III   Directory of selected organizations

This part lists institutions concerned in some way or other with ethics in the media, either media organizations that have within their remit the responsibility for making ethical judgements, operating services requiring ethical principles, setting and adjudicating on standards of practice, producing codes of conduct or practice, and campaigning on ethical issues in the media, or teaching media ethics or training for media practitioners. Not all the government or public bodies positively promote media rights, but by a variety of direct or indirect means limit or even suppress the rights to freedom of expression and information within their country. Libraries have not been given a separate category as most of the professional associations, universities and research centres and institutes can be assumed to have a library for their members or students.

Many of the organizations listed here have been mentioned in Parts I and II, sometimes with reference to their activities, sometimes as corporate authors or publishers, or sometimes as the institutions in which the authors are teaching or working.

The arrangement is first by international organizations, then by continent and country within the continent. Within each geographical entity the entries are arranged by the following categories of organizations:

A. **Government and public bodies**. Government departments responsible for the media, public bodies responsible for regulating sections of the media, providing national or 'public service' broadcasting services, or setting and adjudicating on standards of practice
B. **Industry organizations**. Trade or employers' associations representing sec-

tions of the media, trade unions or employees' associations representing media practitioners, industry self-regulating bodies, many of whom produce codes of practice.
C. **Professional organizations.** Societies, associations and institutes for professions within the media, responsible for establishing and maintaining high standards of professional conduct, often through codes of conduct.
D. **Pressure groups.** Campaigning and activist organizations for monitoring and promoting press and broadcasting freedom, standards and values.
E. **University institutes, research centres and departments.** University departments and research institutes devoted to the study and teaching of media ethics, or areas which include ethical issues of the media (cultural studies, communications, journalism, public policy or applied philosophy).
F. **Independent research institutes and centres.** Learned societies, institutes and centres for study and research, or for training in the various professions within the media (for example, journalism and television reporting).

We have tried to ensure that the information for each organization includes address, telephone and fax number, with function and publication of codes of practice and standards where possible or useful. Unfortunately it has not always been possible to give as much detail as we would like, but we felt that it would be useful to include the names of relevant organizations no matter how brief the information.

Many of the organizations listed are known to the compilers, or have connection with the authors and editors whose works are cited in Part II. However, the following reference sources have also been used to compile this directory:

American Council on Education. *American universities and colleges.* 14th ed. New York: De Gruyter, 1992.

Centres and bureaux: a directory of UK concentrations of effort, information and expertise. 2nd ed. Beckenham, Kent: CBD Research, 1993.

Commonwealth Universities Yearbook. London: Association of Commonwealth Universities. Annual.

Encyclopedia of associations. 32nd ed. Detroit: Gale, 1997.

The Europa World Year Book. London: Europa Publications. Annual.

Harris, Nigel G. E. *Professional codes of conduct in the United Kingdom.* 2nd ed. London: Mansell, 1996.

International research centers directory. 9th ed. Detroit: Gale, 1997.

Jones, J. Clement. *Mass media codes of ethics and councils.* Paris: UNESCO, 1980.

Raboy, Marc (ed.) *Public broadcasting for the twenty-first century.* Luton: John Libbey at the University of Luton Press, 1996. (Acamedia monograph, 17)

Research centers directory. 18th ed. Detroit: Gale, 1994.

Robillard, Serge. *Television in Europe: regulatory bodies status, functions and powers in fifteen European countries.* London: John Libbey, 1995. (Media monograph, 9)

TBI: Television Business International Yearbook. London: FT Media & Telecoms. Annual.

World guide to scientific associations and learned societies. 6th ed. Munich: K. G. Saur, 1994.

The World of Learning. London: Europa Publications. Annual.

World Radio TV Handbook. Amsterdam: Billboard. Annual.

Yearbook of International Organizations. Munich: K. G. Saur, 1994. Annual.

International

International Telecommunications Union (ITU)
Address: Place des Nations, 1211 Geneva 20, Switzerland.
Tel: (+41) (22) 730 5111; Fax: (+41) (22) 733 7256.
Aims: Intergovernmental organization, which became a specialized agency of the United Nations in 1947, and which aids development of telecommunications facilities and promotes at international policy level the adoption of a broader approach to issues of telecomunications in the global information economy and society.

United Nations
Address: United Nations Plaza, New York, NY 10017, USA.
Tel: (+1) (212) 963 1234; Fax: (+1) (212) 963 4879.
Note: Human Rights Committee.
Code: *Universal Declaration of Human Rights* (1948).

United Nations Educational, Scientific and Cultural Organization (UNESCO)
Address: 7 place de Fontenoy, F-75352 Paris, France.
Tel: (+33) (1) 45 68 10 00; Fax: (+33) (1) 45 67 16 90.
Aims: Established 1946 'for the purpose of advancing, through educational, scientific and cultural relations of the peoples of the world, the objectives of international peace and the common welfare of mankind'.

World Intellectual Property Organization (WIPO)
Address: 34 chemin des Colombettes, Case Postale 18, 1211 Geneva 20, Switzerland.
Tel: (+41)(22) 730 9111; Fax: (+41)(22) 733 5428.
Aims: To promote protection of intellectual property rights throughout the world.

B.

Arab States Broadcasting Union
Address: 22A Taha Hussein Street, Zamalek, Cairo, Egypt.
Tel: (+20) (2) 805825.
Aims: Union of Arab radio and television organizations in Africa and Asia, founded in 1969 to provide professional training, research and meetings.

Association for the Promotion of the International Circulation of the Press (DISTRIPRESS)
Address: Beethovenstrasse 20, 8002 Zurich, Switzerland.
Tel: (+41) (1) 202 4121; Fax: (+41) (1) 202 1025.

Aims: Founded in 1955 to assist in the promotion of the freedom of the press throughout the world, supporting UNESCO in promoting the free flow of ideas.

Broadcasting Organization of Non-Aligned Countries (BONAC)
Address: c/o Cyprus Broadcasting Corporation, POB 4824, Nicosia, Cyprus.
Tel: (+357) (2) 422231; Fax: (+357) (2) 314050.
Aims: Founded in 1977 to ensure an equitable, objective and comprehensive flow of information through broadcasting in non-aligned countries of the world.

Federation of Arab Journalists (FAJ)
Address: PO Box 6017, 14 Ramadhan Street, Al-Mansour, Baghdad, Iraq.
Tel: (+964) (1) 5513994.
Aims: Founded in 1964 for national unions of journalists in Arab countries.

International Advertising Association (IAA)
Address: 342 Madison Avenue, Suite 2008, New York, NY 10127-0073, USA.
Tel: (+1) (212) 557 1133; Fax: (+1) (212) 988 0455.

International Chamber of Commerce (ICC)
Address: 38 Cours Albert 1er, F-75008 Paris, France.
Tel: (+33) (1) 49 53 28 75; Fax: (+33) (1) 49 53 29 42.
Aims: World business organization which acts to promote greater freedom of world trade and high standards of ethics in advertising and marketing.
Codes: *International code of advertising practice* (used by many national advertising self-regulatory bodies); *International codes of marketing practice*.

International Committee of Entertainment and Media Unions
Address: International Press Centre, Boulevard Charlemagne 1, Boîte 5, B-1041 Brussels, Belgium.

Tel: (+32) (2) 238 08 08; Fax: (+32) (2) 230 00 76.

International Federation of Journalists (IFJ)
Address: 266 rue Royale, 1201 Brussels, Belgium.
Tel: (+32) (2) 238 22 65; Fax: (+32) (2) 219 29 76.
Aims: Formed 1952 as an international trade union body to safeguard the freedom of the press and journalists.
Code: *Declaration of Principles on the Conduct of Journalism.*

International Federation of Newspaper Publishers (FIEJ)
Address: 25 rue d'Astorg, F-75008 Paris, France.
Tel: (+33) (1) 47 42 85 00; Fax: (+33) (1) 47 42 49 48.
Aims: Established 1948, to defend the freedom of the press, and safeguard the ethical and economic interests of newspapers.

World Federation of Advertisers
Address: 18–24 rue des Colonies, Boîte 6, B-1000 Brussels, Belgium.
Tel: (+32) (2) 502 5740; Fax: (+32) (2) 508 4240.
Aims: To defend freedom of commercial expression, advocate self-regulation of advertising, and assist national advertising associations.

C.

Association of European Journalists
Address: Kastanienweg 26, D-53177 Bonn, Germany.
Tel: (+49) (228) 321712; Fax: (+49) (228) 321712.
Aims: Founded in 1963, to promote deeper knowledge of European problems and appreciation by the public of the work of the European institutions, and to

facilitate journalists' access to sources of information.

Catholic Media Council
Address: Anton Kurze Allee 2, Postfach 1912, D-52021 Aachen, Germany.
Tel: (+49) (241) 73081; Fax: (+49) (241) 73462.

Commonwealth Broadcasting Association
Address: CBA Secretariat, Room 312, BBC Yalding House, 152–156 Great Portland Street, London W1N 6AJ, UK.
Tel: (+44) ((0)171) 765 5144/5151; Fax: (+44) ((0)171) 765 5152.
Aims: Formed in 1945 as an association of national public service broadcasting organizations in 53 Commonwealth countries.

Commonwealth Journalists Association (CJA)
Address: 18 Nottingham Street, London W1M 3RD, UK.
Tel: (+44) ((0)171) 486 3844; Fax: (+44) ((0)171) 486 3822.

Commonwealth Press Union (CPU)
Address: 17 Fleet Street, London EC4Y 1AA, UK.
Tel: (+44) ((0)171) 583 7733; Fax: (+44) ((0)171) 583 6868.
Aims: Formed 1909 (as the Empire Press Union) for news agencies, publishers, newspaper proprietors and journalists, in order to promote concept and ideals of the Commonwealth.

International Catholic Association for Radio and Television (UNDA)
Address: General Secretariat, rue de l'Orme 12, 1030 Brussels, Belgium.
Tel: (+32) (2) 734 4708; Fax: (+32) (2) 734 7018.
Aims: Membership association of 139 national and 26 Catholic organizations which co-ordinates worldwide network involved in broadcasting.

International Catholic Union of the Press (Union Catholique Internationale de la Presse – UCIP)
Address: 37–39 rue de Vermont, Case Postale 197, 1211 Geneva 20, Switzerland.
Tel: (+41) (22) 734 0017; Fax: (+41) (22) 734 0053.
Aims: Founded 1927 to link Catholic journalists and inspire a high standard of professional conscience.

International Christian Media Commission (ICMC)
Address: PO Box 70632, Seattle, WA 98107, USA.
Tel: (+1) (206) 781 0461; Fax: (+1) (206) 781 0571.
Aims: Association of Christian media professionals from 121 countries.

International Communication Association (ICA)
Address: 12750 Merit Drive, Suite 710, LB-89 Dallas, Texas, USA.
Tel: (+1) (214) 233 3889; Fax: (+1) (214) 233 2813.

International Federation of Catholic Journalists
Address: 163 Boulevard Malsherbes, F-75859 Paris Cedex 17, France.

International Federation of Free Journalists
Address: 4 Overton Road, London N14 4SY, UK.
Tel: (+44) ((0)171) 360 2991.

International Federation of Societies of Authors and Composers
Address: 11 rue Keppler, F-75116 Paris, France.
Aims: Protection of the rights of authors.

International Humanist and Ethical Union (IHEU)
Address: Nieuwegracht 69A, LG Utrecht, 3512 Netherlands.
Tel: (+31) (30) 231 21 55; Fax: (+31) (30) 236 41 69.

International Organization of Journalists
Address: Calle Mayor 81, Madrid 28013, Spain.
Tel: (+34) (1) 242 24243; Fax: (+34) (1) 242 23853.
Aims: Founded in 1946, for national journalists' organizations and individuals, to defend the freedom of the press and journalists.

International PEN (World Association of Writers)
Address: 9–10 Charterhouse Buildings, Goswell Road, London EC1M 7AT, UK.
Tel: (+44) ((0)171) 253 4308; Fax: (+44) ((0)171) 253 5711.
Aims: Formed in 1921 to promote worldwide co-operation between writers; national branches in many countries.

International Press Institute (IPI)
Address: Spiegelgasse 2/29, A–1010 Vienna, Austria.
Tel: (+43) (1) 512 90 11; Fax: (+43) (1) 512 90 14.
Aims: Association of editors, publishers and news broadcasters who support the principles of a free and responsible press.

International Publishers' Association
Address: Avenue de Miramont 3, 1206 Geneva, Switzerland.
Tel: (+41) (22) 346 3018; Fax: (+41) (22) 347 5717.

National Religious Broadcasters
Address: 7839 Ashton Avenue, Manassas, VA 22110, USA.
Tel: (+1) (703) 330 7000; (+1) (703) 330 7100.
Aims: Association of over 800 international and national religious broadcasting organizations throughout the world.

Pan-Arab Media Association
Address: Media Centre, 4th Floor, Accaoui Street, Achrafieh, Beirut, Lebanon.
Tel: (+961) (1) 448 152.

Union Internationale des Journalistes et de la Presse de Langue Française
Address: 3 Cité Bergère, F-75009 Paris, France.
Tel: (+33) (1) 47 70 02 80; Fax: (+33) (1) 48 24 26 32.

World Association of Women Journalists and Writers
Address: 3945 St Martin Boulevard W, Laval, Quebec H7T 1B7, Canada.

World Communication Association
Address: Westfield State College, Westfield, MA 01086, USA.
Tel: (+1) (413) 568 3311; Fax: (+1) (413) 568 3613.

World Wide Ethical Society
Address: 264 Chien Kang Road, Taipei, Taiwan.
Tel: (+886) (2) 7670401.
Publication: *Morality Quarterly*.

D.

Amnesty International
Address: 1 Easton Street, London WC1X 8DJ, UK.
Tel: (+44) ((0)171) 413 5500; Fax: (+44) ((0)171) 956 1157.

Article 19 – The International Centre Against Censorship
Address: 90 Borough High Street, London SE1 1LL, UK.
Tel: (+44) ((0)171) 403 4822; Fax: (+44) ((0)171) 403 1943.
Aims: Independent human rights organization, established in 1986, to promote freedom of expression, and monitor and combat censorship worldwide. Organization name comes from the nineteenth article of the *Universal Declaration of Human Rights*. Extensive publishing programme includes regular reviews of information, freedom and censorship throughout the world, and in-

depth reports on the status of freedom of expression and information in individual countries.

European Christian Radio Conference (CERC)
Address: place Saint-Irénée 7, 69321 Lyon Cedex 05, France
Tel: (+33) (4) 72 38 20 22; Fax: (+33) (4) 72 38 20 57.
Aims: To promote common interests of Christian radio stations throughout the world, respect for human rights, pluralism and democracy.

Human Rights Watch (Helsinki Watch)
Address: 485 Fifth Avenue, New York, NY 10017, USA.
Tel: (+1) (212) 972 8400; Fax: (+1) (212) 972 0905.
Aims: To monitor and report on human rights practices (censorship and so on).

International Freedom of Expression Exchange (IFEX)
Address: 490 Adelaide St West, Suite 205, Toronto, Ontario M5V 1TJ, Canada.
Tel: (+1) (416) 867 1154; Fax: (+1) (416) 867 1034.

International League for Human Rights
Address: 432 Park Avenue South, Room 1103, New York, NY 10016, USA.
Tel: (+1) (212) 684 1221; Fax: (+1) (212) 684 1896.
Aims: To promote application of the *Universal Declaration of Human Rights*.

Reporters sans Frontières – International
Address: 13 rue de Mail, F-75002 Paris, France.
Aims: Founded 1985, and with consultative status with UNESCO.

World Press Freedom Committee
Address: 11600 Sunrise Valley Drive, Reston, VA 22091, USA.
Tel: (+1) (703) 648 1000; Fax: (+1) (703) 620 4557.

Aims: Journalists' activist organization to support freedom of the press.

Writers and Scholars Educational Trust
Address: Lancaster House, 33 Islington High Street, London N1 9LH, UK.
Tel: (+44) ((0)171) 278 2313; Fax: (+44) ((0)171) 278 1878.
Aims: To help victims of censorship and to inform the world about current issues of censorship and freedom of expression, through investigation of individual cases, study, research and discussion. Publication: *Index on Censorship*.

F.

Arab States Regional Broadcasting Centre
Address: PO Box 5333, Damascus, Syria.
Tel: (+963) (11) 661206.

Institut International du Droits de l'Homme
(International Institute of Human Rights)
Address: 1 quai Lezay-Marnesia, F-67000 Strasbourg, France.
Tel: (+33) (3) 88 35 05 50.

International Association for Mass Communication Research (IAMCR)
Address: IAMCR Administrative Office, Baden Powellweg 109-111, 1069 LD Amsterdam, Netherlands.
Tel: (+31) (20) 6101581; Fax: (+31) (20) 6104821.
Aims: Founded in 1957 to improve communication practice, policy and research, and training for journalism.

International Foundation for Ethical Research (IFER)
Address: 53 W Jackson Boulevard, Suite 1552, Chicago, IL 60604-3702, USA.
Tel: (+1) (1312) 427 6025; Fax: (+1) (1312) 427 6524.

International Institute of Communications
Address: Tavistock House South, Tavistock Square, London WC1H 9LF, UK.

Tel: (+44) ((0)171) 388 0671; Fax: (+44) ((0)171) 380 0623.
Aims: Formed 1969, originally the International Broadcast Institute, to link broadcasting and telecommunications organizations and their staff through conferences, publications and research.

International Institute of Journalism
Address: Mülenstrasse 1–2, D-12587 Berlin, Germany.
Tel: (+49) (30) 644 01 13; Fax: (+49) (30) 645 28 87.

International Journalism Institute
Address: Ruzova 7, 110 00 Prague, Czech Republic.
Tel: (+420) (2) 264 123; Fax: (+420) (2) 267 108.

International Mass Media Institute
Address: Kristiansand, Norway.

Islamic States Broadcasting Services Organization
Address: PO Box 6351, Jeddah 21442, Saudi Arabia.
Tel: (+966) (2) 66721121; Fax: (+966) (2) 6722600.
Aims: Propagation of Islamic teaching and heritage, through production and exchange of radio and television programmes, research and training for Islamic states worldwide.

World Association for Christian Communication (WACC)
Address: 357 Kennington Lane, London SE11 5QY, UK.
Tel: (+44) ((0)171) 582 9139; Fax: (+44) ((0)171) 735 0340.
Aims: Founded in 1975 to promote more effective use of all forms of media by churches and church-related organizations, with particular reference to ethical and social issues, through study courses, publications and research.

World Association for Public Opinion Research
Address: School of Journalism and Mass Communication, University of North Carolina, Howell Hall, Chapel Hill, NC 27599-3365, USA.
Tel: (+1) (919) 962 6396; Fax: (+1) (919) 962 4079.

Europe

A.

Council of Europe
Address: 67075 Strasbourg Cedex, France.
Tel: (+33) (3) 88 41 20 00; Fax: (+33) (3) 88 41 27 81.
Aims: Founded in 1949 to uphold principles of parliamentary democracy and respect for human rights; Steering Committee on the Mass Media.
Codes: *European Convention on Human Rights* (1950), *Declaration on the protection of journalists in situations of conflict and tension* (1996).

European Union
Address: Council of the European Union, 170 rue de la Loi, 1048 Brussels, Belgium.
Tel: (+32) (2) 234 6111; Fax: (+32) (2) 234 7397.
Code: *Declaration of Rights and Obligations of Journalists.*

B.

Association of Commercial Television (ACT)
Address: 7 Square Ambiorix, 1000 Brussels, Belgium.
Tel: (+32) (2) 736 0052; Fax: (+32) (2) 735 4172.

European Advertising Standards Alliance
Address: Brussels, Belgium.

European Association of Advertising Agencies (EAAA)
Address: 28 avenue du Barbeau, B-1160 Brussels, Belgium.
Tel: (+32) (2) 672 4336; Fax: (+32) (2) 672 0014.

European Broadcasting Union (EBU)
Address: Ancienne Route 17A, 1218 Grand-Saconnex, Geneva, Switzerland.
Tel: (+41) (22) 717 2111; Fax: (+41) (22) 717 2481.
Aims: Professional association of broadcasting organizations formed in 1950 to assist the development of broadcasting services in Europe, particularly in programme, legal and technical areas.

European Committee of Entertainment and Media Unions
Address: International Press Centre, Boulevard Charlemagne 1, Boîte 5, B-1040 Brussels, Belgium.
Tel: (+32) (2) 238 0808; Fax: (+32) (2) 230 0076.

European Newspaper Publishers Association
Address: Gossetlaan 30, B-1702 Groot-Bigaarden, Belgium.
Tel: (+32) (2) 466 8875; Fax: (+32) (2) 466 1500.

European Publishers Council (EPC)
Address: c/o Daily Telegraph, 1 Canada Square, Canary Wharf, London E14 5DT, UK.
Tel: (+44) ((0)171) 538 6246; Fax: (+44) ((0)171) 538 7860.
Aims: To promote freedom of commercial expression as guaranteed by the European Convention on Human Rights, and to ensure European Single Act is not misused by regulators.

Nordic Union of Journalists
Address: Finland Journalistførbund, Sandrikgatan 2, B-22, SF-00180 Helsinki, Finland.

C.

Association of European Journalists
Address: Kastanienweg 26, 5300 Bonn, Germany.
Tel and Fax: (+49) (228) 321712.

F.

Central European Mass Communication Research Documentation Centre
Address: ul. Wisina 2, 31-007 Cracow, Poland.
Tel: (+48) (12) 22 06 44; Fax: (+48) (12) 22 63 06.

European Association of Education and Research in Public Relations
Address: St Pietersnieuwstraat 160, B-9000 Ghent, Belgium.
Tel: (+32) (9) 223 0808; Fax: (+32) (9) 233 0949.

European Audiovisual Observatory
Address: allée de la Robertsau 76, 67000 Strasbourg, France.
Tel: (+33) (3) 67 14 44 00; Fax: (+33) (3) 67 14 44 19.
Note: Pan-European institution, under the Council of Europe, providing legal, economic and market information on the television, film and video sectors.

European Institute for the Media (Europäisches Medieninstitut)
Address: Kaistrasse 13, D-40221 Düsseldorf, Germany.
Tel: (+49) (211) 901040; Fax: (+49) (211) 9010456.
Aims: Research institute covering multimedia concentration, privacy, copyright, regulation and related issues.

European Journalism Centre
Address: Boschstraat 60, NL-6211 AX Maastricht, Netherlands.
Tel: (+31) (43) 3254030; Fax: (+31) (43) 3212626.

Institut de l'Audiovisuel et de Télécommunications en Europe (IDATE)
Address: BP 4167, 34092 Montpellier Cedex 5, France.
Tel: (+33) (5) 67 14 44 44; Fax: (+33) (5) 67 14 44 40.
Note: Study and research for socio-economic analysis of communication and information industries in Europe.

Nordic Documentation Center for Mass Communication Research (NORDICOM)
Address: Göteborg University, Sprängkullsgatan 21, S-411 23 Göteborg, Sweden.
Tel: (+46) (31) 773 12 19; Fax: (+46) (31) 773 46 55.

Nordic Journalism Centre
Address: Vennelystparken, DK-8000 Århus, Denmark.
Tel: (+45) 86 13 62 33; Fax: (+45) 86 18 58 22.

Robert Schuman Institute of Journalism – European Media Studies
Address: rue de l'Association 32–34, B-1000 Brussels, Belgium.
Tel: (+32) (2) 217 2355; Fax: (+32) (2) 219 5764.

Albania (+355)

A.

Ministeria e Kulturës
(Ministry of Culture)
Address: Bulevardi Zhan d'Ark, Tirana.
Tel: (42) 29715; Fax: (42) 27878.

Radiotelevisioni Shqiptar (RTVSH)
(Albanian Radio-Television)
Address: Rruga Ismail Qemali 11, Tirana.
Tel: (42) 27512; Fax: (42) 27745.

B.

Bashkimi i Gazetarëve te Shqipërisë
(The Union of Journalists of Albania)
Address: Bulevardi Deshmoret e Kombit, Tirana.
Tel: (42) 27977.

Lidhja e Gazetarëve te Shqipërisë
(The League of Journalists of Albania)
Address: Tirana.

C.

Lidhja e Shkrimtarëve e Artistëve të Shqipërisë
(Union of Writers and Artists of Albania)
Address: Rruga Konferenca e Pezës 4, Tirana.
Tel: (42) 29689.

Austria (+43)

A.

Bundeskanzleramt
(Federal Chancellory – Media Division)
Address: Sektion 5, Ballhausplatz 2, A-1014 Vienna.
Tel: (1) 531150; Fax: (1) 531152699.

Kommission zur Wahrung des Rundfunkgesetzes (RFK)
(Commission for Observance of the Broadcasting Law)
Address: Bundeskanzleramt Verfassungsdienst, Abteilung V/4, Ballhausplatz 2,
A-1014 Vienna.
Tel: (1) 531150; Fax: (1) 5350338.

Österreichischer Rundfunk (ORF)
Address: Würzburggasse 30, A-1136 Vienna.
Tel: (1) 878780; Fax: (1) 87878-2250.
Note: State-owned broadcasting company which controls all radio and television in Austria.

B.

Fachverband Werbung und Marktkommunikation
Address: Wiedner Hauptstrasse 63, A-1045 Vienna.
Tel: (1) 501050; Fax: (1) 50206285.

EUROPE 265

Hauptverband des Österreichischen Buchhandels
(Association of Austrian Publishers)
Address: Grünangergasse 4, A-1010 Vienna.
Tel: (1) 5121535; Fax: (1) 5128482.

Österreichischer Journalistengewerkschaft
(Austrian Union of Journalists)
Address: Bankgasse 8, A-1010 Vienna.
Tel: (1) 631402.

Österreichischer Werberat
(Austrian Advertising Standards Council)
Address: Wiedner Hauptstrasse 63, A-1045 Vienna.
Tel: (222) 501053519; Fax: (222) 50206285.
Code: *Code of advertising practice.*

Österreichischer Zeitschriftenverband
(Association of Periodical Publishers)
Address: Hörlgasse 18/5, A-1090 Vienna.
Tel and Fax: (1) 3197001.

Verband Österreichischer Zeitungsherausgeber und Zeitungsverleger
(Austrian Newspaper Publishers' Association)
Address: Renngasse 12, A-1010 Vienna.
Tel: (1) 53379790; Fax: (1) 533797922.

E.

Universität Salzburg – Department of Journalism and Communications/Austrian Documentation Centre for Media and Communication Research
Address: Kapitelgasse 6, A-5020 Salzburg.
Tel: (662) 8044-0; Fax: (622) 8044214.

Universität Wien – Department of Journalism and Communications
Address: Dr Karl Lueger-Ring 1, A-1010 Vienna.
Tel: (222) 40103-0; Fax: (222) 4088725.

F.

Gesellschaft für Film und Medien (SYNEMA)
Address: Neubaugasse 36, A-1070 Vienna.
Tel and Fax: (222) 933797.

Mediacult – Internationales Forschungsinstitut für Medien, Kommunikation und kulturelle Entwicklung
Address: Schönburgstrasse 27, A-1040 Vienna.

Österreichische Gesellschaft für Filmwissenschaft, Kommunikations- und Medien Forschung
(Austrian Society for Film Science, Research on Communications and Media)
Address: Rauhensteingasse 5, A-1010 Vienna.
Tel: (222) 5129936.

Österreichische Gesellschaft für Kommunikationsfragen
(Austrian Society for Communications)
Address: Bankgasse 8, A-1010 Vienna.
Tel: (222) 3197977.

Österreichische Werbewissenschaftliche Gesellschaft (WWG)
(Austrian Society for Advertising Research)
Address: Augasse 2–6, A-1090 Vienna.
Tel: (222) 340525.

Belarus (+375)

A.

Ministerstva Suvjazi i Informatyki
(Ministry of Telecommunication and Information)
Address: pr. F. Skaryny 10, 220050 Minsk.
Tel: (17) 2272157; Fax: (17) 2267848.
Note: Responsible for audiovisual sector, in particular programme content – pornography and violence; State Committee on Television and Radio.

Nacyjanalnaja Dzjarzaunaja Telerady Jokampanija Belarusi
(National State Television and Radio Company of Belarus)
Address: vul. A. Makayenka 9, 220807 Minsk.
Tel: (17) 2647505; Fax: (17) 2648182.

B.

Belarusian Journalists' Association
Address: Minsk
Tel and Fax: (17) 2270558.

Belarusian Union of Journalists
Address: vul. Rumyantsava 3, 220005 Minsk.
Tel and Fax: (17) 2365195.

Belgium (+32)

1. Flemish-speaking community

A.

Kabinet van de Vlaamse Minister van Economic, KMO, Landbouw en Media
Address: Kreupelenstraat 2, 1000 Brussels.
Tel: (2) 227 2311; Fax: (2) 227 2303.

Mediaraat
(Media Council)
Address: Parochiaanstraat 15–23, 1000 Brussels.

Belgische Radio en Televisie (BRTN)
Address: Omroepcentrum, 52 August Reyerslaan, 1043 Brussels.
Tel: (2) 741 3111; Fax: (2) 734 9351.
Note: State broadcasting organization for Flemish-language broadcasts.

2. French-speaking community

A.

Ministère de la Culture et des Affaires Sociales – Direction de L'Audiovisuel
Address: 44 Boulevard Leopold II, 1080 Brussels.
Tel: (2) 413 3501; Fax: (2) 413 3050.

Conseil de l'Audiovisuel (CSA)
Address: 44 Boulevard Leopold II, 1080 Brussels.
Tel: (2) 413 3502; Fax:(2) 413 3050.

Commission d'Ethique de la Publicité
(Advertising Standards Council)
Address: 44 Boulevard Leopold II, 1080 Brussels.
Code: *Code of standards.*

Radio-Télévision Belge de la Communauté Française (RTBF)
Address: Cité de la Radio-Télévision, B-1040 Brussels.
Tel: (2) 737 2111; Fax: (2) 737 2556.
Note: State broadcasting organization for French-language broadcasts.

3. Flemish and French Communities

B.

Association Belge des Éditeurs de Journaux/Belgische Vereniging van de Dagbladuitgevers
(Belgian Association of Newspaper Publishers)
Address: 22 Boulevard Paepsem, BP 7, 1070 Brussels.
Tel: (2) 522 9660; Fax: (2) 522 6004.

Association Générale des Journalistes Professionnels de Belgique/Algemene Vereniging van de Beroepsjournalisten in Belgie
(General Association of Professional Journalists in Belgium)
Address: 9B Quai à la Houille, 1000 Brussels.
Tel: (2) 229 1460; Fax: (2) 223 0272.

Conseil de la Publicité
(Advertising Council)
Address: 18–24 rue des Colonies, 1000 Brussels.

Tel: (2) 502 7070; (2) 502 7733.
Note: Self-regulatory body which appoints a Jury d'Ethique Publicitaire/Jury voor Eerlijke Praktijken (JEP) to examine complaints on advertising in the light of the *Réglementation de la publicité.*

Fédération de la Presse Périodique de Belgique/Federatie van de periodieke pers van België (FPPB)
Address: 54 rue Charles Martel, 1040 Brussels
Tel: (2) 230 0999; Fax: (2) 231 1459.

C.

Association des Écrivains Belges de Langue Française
(Association of Belgian Writers in the French Language)
Address: Maison Camille Lemonnier – Maison Écrivains, 150 chaussée de Wavre, 1050 Brussels.
Tel and Fax: (2) 512 2968.

Société des Auteurs, Compositeurs et Éditeurs
Address: 75-077 rue d'Arlon, 1040 Brussels.
Tel: (2) 230 2660; Fax: (2) 231 1800.

E.

Universiteit Gent – Faculty of Law (Communication Science and Media)
Address: St Pietersnieuwstraat 25, 9000 Ghent.
Tel: (9) 264 3067; Fax: (9) 264 3597.

F.

Centre for the Study of New Media, Information and Telecommunications
Address: Vrije Universiteit Brussels, Pleinlaan 2, 1050 Brussels.
Tel: (2) 629 2111.

Bosnia and Herzegovina (+387)

A.

Ministry of Transport and Communications
Address: 71000 Sarajevo.

Radio Televizija Bosne i Hercegovine (RTVBiH)
Address: VI Proleterske Brigade 4, 71000 Sarajevo.
Tel: (71) 455107; Fax: (71) 455166.

Bulgaria (+359)

A.

Parliamentary Committee for Radio and Television
Address: 2 Kn. Dondukov Bul., Sofia 1000.

Bulgarian Committee for Television and Radio
Address: ul. San Stefano 29, 1504 Sofia.
Tel: (2) 446329.

Bâlgarsko Nationalno Radio
Address: 4 Dragan Tzankov Bul., 1040 Sofia.
Tel: (2) 661954; Fax: (2) 662215.

Bâlgarska Nationalno Televizija
Address: ul. San Stefano 29, 1504 Sofia.
Tel: (2) 446329; Fax: (2) 662388.

B.

Union of Bulgarian Journalists
Address: Graf Ignatiev St 4, 1000 Sofia.
Tel: (2) 872773; Fax: (2) 883047.

Union of Journalists in Bulgaria
Address: Exzarh Yossif St 37, 1000 Sofia.
Tel: (2) 831227; Fax: (2) 835484.

C.

Union of Bulgarian Writers
Address: Angel Kanchev 5, 1040 Sofia.
Tel: (2) 898346; Fax: (2)874757.

E.

Sofiiski Universitet 'Sveti Kliment Ohridsky' – Faculty of Journalism and Mass Media
Address: Tsar Osroboditel 15, 1504 Sofia.
Tel: (2) 8581; Fax: (2) 463589.

Croatia (+385)

A.

Ministartsvo Pomorstva Prometa i Veza
(Ministry of Maritime Affairs, Transport and Communications)
Address: Prisavlje 14, 1000 Zagreb.
Tel: (1) 6112017; Fax: (1) 6110691.

Hrvatska Radio-Televizija (HRT)
(Croatian Radio and Television)
Address: Dezmanova 10, 1000 Zagreb.
Tel: (1) 6163691; Fax: (1) 6163692.

B.

Croatian Publishers' and Authors' Business Union
Address: Klaiceva 7, 1000 Zagreb.
Fax: (1) 171624.

Cyprus (+357)

A.

Ministry of Communications and Public Works
Address: Demi. Severis Avenue, CY-1424 Nicosia.
Tel: (2) 303441; Fax: (2) 465462.

Advisory Broadcasting Commission
Address: Ministry of Communications and Public Works, Demi. Severis Avenue, CY-1424 Nicosia.

Cyprus Broadcasting Corporation
Address: Broadcasting House, PO Box 4824, CyBC Street, CY-1397 Nicosia.
Tel: (2) 422231; Fax: (2) 314050.
Code: *Code on advertising standards for radio and television.*

B.

Union of Cyprus Journalists
Address: POB 3495, 2 Kratinos Street, Strovolos, Nicosia.
Tel: (2) 454680; Fax: (2) 4644598.

E.

European University of Lefke – Department of Journalism and Broadcasting
Address: Gemikonagi, Lefke, Mersin 10, (Northern Cyprus) Turkey.
Tel: (Turkey 392) 7277362.

Czech Republic (+420)

A.

Ministry of Culture
Address: Milady Horákové 139, Prague 6.
Tel: (2) 24 31 80 51; Fax: (2) 24 32 33 04.

Rada Ceské Televize
(Council of Czech Television)
Address: Krátká 10, 10000 Prague 10.
Tel: (2) 781 3830; Fax: (2) 781 0885.

Cesky Rozhlas
(Czech Radio)
Address: Vinohradska 12, 120 99 Prague 2.
Tel: (2) 24 09 41 11; Fax: (2) 24 22 22 23.

Ceská Televize
(Czech Television)
Address: Kavcí Hory, 140 70 Prague 4.
Tel: (2) 61 21 16 02; Fax: (2) 42 15 62.

B.

Rada Pro Reklamu
(Advertising Council)
Address: Skretove 6/44, 120 59 Prague
Tel: (2) 2421 5373; Fax: (2) 2422 5692

Syndikát Novináru Ceske Republiky
(Syndicate of Journalists of the Czech Republic)
Address: Parízská 9, 116 30 Prague 1.
Tel: (2) 232 51 09; Fax: (2) 232 63 37.

C.

Obec Spisovatelu
(Society of Writers)
Address: POB 669, 111 21 Prague 1.
Tel: (2) 235 89 68; Fax: (2) 26 90 72

Denmark (+45)

A.

Kultur Ministeriet
(Ministry of Culture)
Address: POB 2140, Nybrogade 2, DK-1015 Copenhagen.
Tel: 33 92 33 70; Fax: 33 91 33 88.
Note: Broadcasting legislation, licensing and regulation of commercial channels.

Radio and Television Advertising Commission/Advertisements Board
Address: POB 2140, Nybrogade 2, DK-1015 Copenhagen.

DR Radio (Danmarks Radio)
Address: Radiohuset, Rosenørns Allé 22, DK-1999 Frederiksberg C.
Tel: 35 20 30 40; Fax: 35 20 43 71.
Note: Independent statutory corporation for national and regional stations.

DR TV
Address: TV-Byen, DK-2860 Søborg.
Tel: 35 20 30 40; Fax: 35 20 26 44.

B.

Dansk Fagpresse
(Danish Periodical Press Association)
Address: Sommerstedgade 7, DK-1718 Copenhagen V.
Tel: 31 22 12 10; Fax: 31 15 01 86.

Dansk Journalistforbund
(Danish Journalists' Union)
Address: Gammel Strand 46, DK-1202 Copenhagen K.
Tel: 33 14 23 88; Fax: 33 14 23 01.

Danske Dagblades Forening
(Danish Newspaper Publishers' Association)
Address: Pressens Hus, Skindergade 7, DK-1159 Copenhagen K.
Tel: 33 12 21 15; Fax: 33 14 23 25.

Den Danske Forlaeggeforening
(Danish Publishers' Association)
Address: Købmagergade 11, DK-1150 Copenhagen K.
Tel: 33 15 66 88; Fax: 33 18 65 88.

Reklameradet
(Danish Advertising Council)
Address: Læderstræde 32–34, DK-1201 Copenhagen K.
Tel: 33 14 43 46; Fax: 33 14 05 03.
Note: Established jointly by agencies and advertisers – voluntary guidelines.

C.

Dansk Forfatteforening
(Danish Writers' Association)
Address: Tordenskolds Gård, Strandgade 6, DK-1401 Copenhagen.
Tel: 32 95 51 00; Fax: 31 54 01 15.

E.

Ålborg Universitet – Department of Communications
Address: PO Box 159, Frederik Bajers Vej 5, DK-9100 Ålborg.
Tel: 98 15 85 22; Fax: 98 15 22 01.

Århus Universitet – Nordic Documentation Center for Mass Communication Research
Address: Universitetsparken, DK-8000 Århus.
Tel: 89 46 20 69; Fax: 89 46 20 50.

F.

Det Danske Filminstitut (DFI)
(Danish Film Institute)
Address: Vogmagergade 10, DK-1120 Copenhagen.
Tel: 33 74 34 30; Fax: 33 74 34 55.

Dansk Journalisthøjskole
(Danish School of Journalism)
Address: Olof Palmes Allé 11, DK-8200 Århus.
Tel: 86 16 11 22; Fax: 86 16 89 10.

Dansk Pressehistorisk Selskab
Address: c/o Berlingske Tidende,
Pilstraede 34, DK-1147 Copenhagen.
Tel: 33 15 75 75; Fax: 33 13 10 12.

Sammenslutningen af Medieforskere i Danmark
(Association of Media Researchers in Denmark)
Address: c/o Institut for Uddannelese og Socialisering, Ålborg Universitetscenter, DK-9100 Ålborg.

Estonia (+372)

A.

Ministry of Culture
Address: Suur-Karja 23, EE-0001 Tallinn.
Tel: (6) 282 201; Fax: (6) 313 486.

Council for Radio and Television Broadcasting
Address: c/o Ministry of Culture, Suur-Karja 23, EE-0001 Tallinn.
Note: Supervises public service channels – Eesti Raadio and Eesti Televisioon.

Eesti Raadio
(Estonian Broadcasting Co)
Address: Gonsiori 21, EE-0100 Tallinn.
Tel: (2) 243 4115; Fax: (2) 243 4457.

Eesti Televisioon (ETV)
(Estonian Television)
Address: 12 Faehlmanni St, EE-0100 Tallinn.
Tel: (2) 434 113; Fax: (2) 434 155.

B.

Estonian Newspaper Association
Address: Parnü mnt 67A, EE-0010 Tallinn.
Tel: (2) 683 018; Fax: (6) 311 210.

Estonian Journalists' Union
Address: Narva mnt 30, EE-0010 Tallinn.
Tel: (2) 449 889; Fax: (2) 433 583.

Estonian Publishers' Association
Address: POB 3366, Laki 17, EE-0006 Tallinn.
Tel: (6) 505 592; Fax: (6) 505 590.

Finland (+358)

A.

Liikenneministrioe
(Ministry of Transport and Communications)
Address: POB 235, Eteläesplanadi 16, FIN-00131 Helsinki.
Tel: (9) 160246; Fax: (9) 1602596.

Yleisradio Oy (YLE)
(Finnish Broadcasting Company)
Address: Radio and TV Centre, Radiokatu 5, POB 99, FIN-00024 Helsinki.
Tel: (0) 14801; Fax: (0) 14803390.
Note: State-owned broadcasting organization.

B.

Aikakauslehtien Liitto
(Periodical Publishers' Association)
Address: Lönnrotinkatu 11, FIN-00120 Helsinki.
Tel: (9) 22877280; Fax: (9) 603478.

Mainostajien Liitto
(Finnish Association of Advertising Agencies)
Address: Vuorikatu 22 A 3, FIN-00100 Helsinki,
Tel: (9) 6253000; Fax: (9) 6253005.

Sanomalehtien Liitto – Tidninggarnas Förbund
(Finnish Newspaper Publishers' Association)
Address: Lönnrotinkatu 11, FIN-00120 Helsinki.
Tel: (9) 22877300; Fax: (9) 607989.

Suomen Journalistiliitto
(Union of Journalists)
Address: Hietalandenkatu 2B, FIN-00180
Helsinki.
Tel: (9) 647326; Fax: (9) 644120.

C.

Suomen Kirailijaliitto
(Association of Finnish Writers)
Address: Runeberginkatu 32C, FIN-00100
Helsinki.

E.

University of Tampere – Nordic Documentation Center
Address: Box 607, FIN-33101 Tampere 10, Finland.
Tel: (31) 2157045; Fax: (31) 2157150.

France (+33)

A.

Ministry of Culture
Address: 3 rue de Valois, F-75042 Paris.
Tel: (1) 40 15 80 00; Fax: (1) 40 15 81 62.

Conseil Supérieur de l'Audiovisuel (CSA)
Address: Tour Mirabeau, 39–43 quai André Citroën, F-75015 Paris.
Tel: (1) 40 58 37 09; Fax: (1) 45 79 41 22.
Note: Independent authority for the supervision and regulation of all French radio and television channels, in particular licensing and programme standards.
Code: *La signalétique pour la protection de l'enfance et de l'adolescence à la télévision*;
Terrorisme et information: un échange de vues CSA/diffuseurs (1995).

TF1
Address: 1 quai du Pont-du-Jour, F-92656 Boulogne Cedex.
Tel: (2) 41 41 12 34; Fax: (2) 41 41 28 40.
Note: Privatized first national television channel.

France Télévision
Address: 42 avenue d'Iéna, F-75116 Paris.
Tel: (1) 44 31 60 00; Fax: (1) 47 23 56 48.
Note: Supervisory authority for two national TV networks – France 2 and France 3.

Société Nationale de Radiodiffusion (Radio France)
116 avenue du Président Kennedy, F-757786 Paris Cedex 16.
Tel: (1) 42 30 22 22; Fax: (1) 42 30 14 88.
Note: State-controlled radio, planning and production of radio programmes.

Centre National de la Cinématographie (CNC)
Address: rue de Lübeck 12, F-75016 Paris.
Tel: (1) 44 34 34 40; Fax: (1) 47 55 04 91.
Note: Government body responsible for film regulation.

B.

Bureau du Vérification de la Publicité (BVP)
(Advertising Control Bureau)
Address: 5 rue Jean Mermoz, F-75008 Paris.
Note: Self-regulation for advertising in all media.
Code: *ICC international code of advertising practice*; Laws and Regulations.

Comité de Liaison de la Presse
Address: 6 bis rue Gabriel Laumain, F-75010 Paris.
Tel: (1) 42 46 67 82.

Union des Annonceurs (Commission Consultative d'Autodiscipline)
(Union of Advertisers)
Address: 53 avenue Victor Hugo, F-75016 Paris.
Tel: (1) 45 00 79 10; Fax: (1) 45 00 55 79.
Note: Consultative Commission on Advertising Self-regulation.
Code: *Ethical code*.

Fédération Nationale de la Presse Française
Address: 7 rue de Madrid, F-75376 Paris.
Tel: (1) 44 90 43 90; Fax: (1) 44 90 43 91.

Journalistes
(affiliated to Confédération Générale du Travail (CGT))
Address: Case 570, 263 rue de Paris, F-93514 Montreuil Cedex.
Tel: (1) 48 18 81 78: Fax: (1) 48 51 58 08.

Syndicat National de l'Édition
Address: 115 Boulevard Saint-Germain, F-75006 Paris.
Tel: (1) 44 41 40 50; Fax: (1) 44 41 40 77.

Syndicat National des Journalistes
Address: 33 rue de Louvre, F-75002 Paris.
Tel: (1) 42 36 84 23.

C.

Association des Écrivains Combattants
Address: 8 rue Roquepine, F-75008 Paris.
Tel: (1) 42 65 04 30.

Société des Auteurs et Compositeurs Dramatiques
Address: 11 bis rue Ballu, F-75009 Paris.
Tel: (1) 40 23 44 44; Fax: (1) 45 26 74 28.
Note: Protection of authors' rights.

E.

Université d'Aix-Marseille II – School of Journalism and Communication
Address: 21 rue Virgile Marron, F-13392 Marseille Cedex 05.
Tel: (4) 91 24 32 00; Fax: (4) 91 48 73 59.

Université Michel de Montaigne (Bordeaux III) – Institute of Information and Communication Sciences
Address: Esplanade Michel-Montaigne, Domaine Universitaire, F-33405 Talence Cedex.
Tel: (5) 56 84 50 50; Fax: (5) 56 84 50 90.

Université Lumière Lyon 2 – Institute of Communication, Information and Performing Arts
Address: 86 rue Pasteur, F-69365 Lyon Cedex 07.
Tel: (4) 78 69 70 00.

Université de Paris IV (Paris-Sorbonne) – Institute of Information and Communication
Address: 1 rue Victor Cousin, F-75230 Paris Cedex 05.
Tel: (1) 40 46 22 11; Fax: (1) 40 46 25 88.

Université de Rennes I – Institut de Formation Supérieure en Informatique et Communication
Address: avenue du Général Leclerc, F-35042 Rennes Cedex.
Tel: (2) 99 84 71 00.

Université de Strasbourg III – Université Robert Schuman – Centre for Journalistic Studies
Address: 1 place d'Athènes, BP 66, F-67045 Strasbourg.
Tel: (3) 88 41 42 00.

F.

Ecole Supérieure de Journalisme
Address: 4 place Saint-Germain des Prés, F-75006 Paris.
Tel: (1) 42 22 68 06.

Institut Français de Presse et des Sciences de l'Information
Address: 92 rue d'Assas, F-75006 Paris.
Tel: (1) 44 41 57 93; Fax: (1) 44 41 57 04.

Institut National de l'Audiovisuel (INA)
Address: 4 avenue de l'Europe, F-94360 Bry-sur-Marne, Cedex.
Tel: (1) 49 83 20 00; Fax: (1) 49 83 31 95.
Aims: Government body for research, documentation, publication and training on broadcasting, and production of television cultural and documentary programmes.

Germany (+49)

A.

Bundesministerium für Post und Telekommunikation (PTT)
(Federal Ministry for Posts and Telecommunications)
Address: Heinrich von Stephan Strasse 1, 53175 Bonn.
Tel: (228) 14-0; Fax: (228) 148872.
Code: Article 5 of Basic Law guarantees freedom of communication and no censorship; Inter-State Treaty on Broadcasting.

Direktorenkonferenz der Landesmedienanstalten (DLM)
(Conference of Directors of the Regional Media Authorities)
Address: Mörikestrasse 21, 70178 Stuttgart.
Note: Co-ordinating body for the fifteen regional media authorities for the Länder.

Arbeitsgemeinschaft der Öffentlich-Rechtlichen Rundfunkanstalten der Bundesrepublik Deutschland (ARD)
(Association of Public Law Broadcasting Organizations)
Address: Bertramstrasse 8, 60320 Frankfurt-am-Main.
Tel: (69) 590601; Fax: (69) 1552075.
Note: Co-ordinating body for regional public-right radio and television organizations in the Länder or regions of Germany.

Zweites Deutsches Fernsehen (ZDF)
Address: Postfach 4040, 55100 Mainz.
Tel: (6131) 702050; Fax: (6131) 702157.
Note: Second national television channel.

B.

Bundesverband Deutscher Zeitungsverleger (BDZV)
(Federal Association of German Newspaper Publishers)
Address: Riemenschneiderstrasse 10, 53175 Bonn.
Tel: (228) 810040; Fax: (228) 8100415.

Deutsche Presserat (DPR)
(German Press Council)
Address: Thomas Mann Strasse, 53111 Bonn.
Tel: (228) 98572-69; Fax: (228) 98572-0.
Code: *Press code, guidelines for journalists, and complaints procedure of the German Press Council.*

Deutschen Journalisten-Verband (DJV)
(German Journalists' Association)
Address: Bennauerstrasse 60, 53115 Bonn.
Tel: (228) 222971; Fax: (228) 214917.

Deutscher Werberat
(German Advertising Council)
Address: Zentralausschuss der Werbewirtschaft (ZAW) (Advertising Federation), Villichgasse 17, Postfach 20 14 14, 5300 Bonn.
Note: Self-regulatory body.

Freiwillige Selbstkontrolle Fernsehen (FSF)
Note: Voluntary review body, founded in 1993 by German broadcasters themselves to introduce self-regulation for television.

Freiwillige Selbstkontrolle der Filmwirtschaft (FSK)
Address: Kreuzberger Ring 56, 65205 Wiesbaden.
Tel: (611) 778910; Fax: (611) 7789139.
Note: Voluntary self-regulation for the film industry.

Industriegewerkschaft Medien (IG Medien)
(Trade Union for the Media)
Address: Friedrichstrasse 20, 70174 Stuttgart.
Tel: (711) 20180; Fax: (711) 2018282.

Markenverband
(Association of Advertisers)
Address: Schöne Aussicht 59, 65193 Wiesbaden.
Tel: (611) 58670; Fax: (611) 586721.

DIRECTORY OF SELECTED ORGANIZATIONS

Verband Deutscher Zeitschriftenverleger (VDZ)
(Association of German Periodical Publishers)
Address: Winterstrasse 50, 53177 Bonn.
Tel: (228) 38203-21; Fax: (228) 38203-40.

E.

Universität Bremen – German Press Research Institut
Address: Postfach 330440, 28334 Bremen.
Tel: (421) 2181; Fax: (421) 218-4259.

Heinrich Heine Universität, Dusseldorf – Institut für Internationale Kommunikation
Address: Hillebrandtstrasse 4, Düsseldorf.

Universität Hamburg – Institut für Medienforschung
Address: Heimhuderstrasse 21, 20148 Hamburg.
Tel: (40) 502170; Fax: (40) 5021777.

Universität Hillesheim – Institute for Media and Theatre
Address: Marienburger Platz 22, 31141 Hillesheim.
Tel: (5121) 8830; Fax: (5121) 867558.

Universität zu Köln – Das Institut für Rundfunkrecht
Address: Cologne.

Johannes Gutenberg Universität Mainz – Department of Journalism/Faculty of Philosophy
Address: 550099 Mainz.
Tel: (6131) 39-0; Fax: (6131) 392919.

Universität Mannheim – Institut für Kommunikations- und Medienforschung
Address: Schloss, 681 31 Mannheim.
Tel: (621) 2920; Fax: (621) 2982-2587.

Universität Saarland – Arbeitstelle Medienrecht
(Media Legislation Centre)
Address: Postfach 1150, 66041 Saarbrücken.

F.

Akademie für Publizistik in Hamburg
Address: Magdalenestrasse 64A, 20148 Hamburg.
Tel: (40) 447142.

Catholic Media Council
Address: Anton-Kurz Allee 2, 52074 Aachen.
Tel: (241) 73081; Fax: (241) 73462.

Deutsche Gesellschaft für Kommunikationsforschung
Address: Willroider Strasse 6, 81545 Munich.
Tel: (89) 646948.

Deutsche Gesellschaft für Publizistik- und Kommunikationswissenschaft
Address: Lehrstuhl für Journalistik, Katholisches Universität Eichstätt, Ostenstrasse 26, 85071 Eichstätt.
Tel: (8421) 20564; Fax: (8421) 20553.

Deutsche Studiengesellschaft für Publizistik
Address: Königstrasse 1a, 70173 Stuttgart.
Tel: (711) 293165.

Gemeinschaftswerk der Evangelischen Publizistik
Address: Emil von Behring Strasse 3, 60394 Frankfurt-am-Main
Tel: (69) 580980.

Hochschule für Fernsehen und Film
(Academy for Television and Film)
Address: Frankenthaler Strasse 23, 81539 Munich.
Tel: (89) 680004-0; Fax: (89) 680004-89.

INCA–FIEJ Research Association
Address: Washingtonplatz 1, 64287 Darmstadt.
Tel: (6151) 70050; Fax: (6151) 784542.

Institut für Urheber- und Medienrecht
Address: Wiedermayerstrasse 32, 80538 Munich.
Tel: (89) 2913474; Fax: (89) 221528.

Institut für Zeitungsforschung
Address: Wissstrasse 4, 44122, Dortmund.
Tel: (231) 5023221.

Münchner Kreis (Übernational Vereinigung für Kommunikationsforschung)
Address: Tal 16, 80331 Munich.
Tel: (89) 223238; Fax: (89) 225407.

Greece (+30)

A.

Ministry of Press and Mass Media
Address: Odos Zalokosta 10, 106 71 Athens.
Tel: (1) 3630911; Fax: (1) 3609682.
Note: Regulation of matters relating to the electronic (radio and television) market.

National Council for Radio and Television
Address: Odos Zalokosta 3, 106 71 Athens.
Tel: (1) 3646032; Fax: (1) 3622979.
Note: Regulatory body for public and commercial broadcasting sector.
Codes: *Code of ethics*; *Professional code of practices relating to advertising*.

Elliniki Radiophonia-Tileorassi (ERT)
(Greek Radio and Television Corporation)
Address: Leoforos Messoghion 432, 153 42 Athens.
Tel: (1) 6390583; Fax: (1) 6390652.

B.

Enosis Diagmisticon Eterion Ellados (EDEE)
(Greek Advertising Agencies Association)
Address: 12 Ravine Street, 115 21 Athens.
Tel: (1) 7226990; Fax: (1) 7225885.
Code: *Code of advertising practice*.

Enosis Syntakton Imerission Ephimeridon Athinon
(Union of Athens Daily Newspaper Journalists)
Address: Odos Akademias 20, 106 71 Athens.
Tel: (1) 3632601; Fax: (1) 3632608.

Enosis Syntakton Periodikou Tipou
(Union of the Periodical Press Journalists)
Address: Odos Valaoritou 9, 106 71 Athens.
Tel: (1) 3636039; Fax: (1) 3644967.

Hellenic Federation of Publishers and Booksellers
Address: Odos Themistokleus 73, 106 33 Athens.
Tel: (1) 3300924; Fax: (1) 3301617.

E.

Athinisin Ethnikon kai Kapodistriakon Panepistimiou
(National and Capodistrian University of Athens)
Address: Odos Panepistimiou 30, 106 79 Athens.
Tel: (1) 3614001; Fax: (1) 3602145.

University of Thessalonika – School of Journalism and Mass Media Communications
Address: Aristeleio Panepistimiou Thessalonikis, University Campus, 540 66 Thessalonika.
Tel: (31) 996703.

Hungary (+36)

A.

Ministry of Transport and Telecommunications
Address: Dob ut. 75-81, H-1077 Budapest.
Tel: (1) 122 0220; Fax: (1) 122 8695.

Országos Rádió-Televízió Testület (ORTT)
(National Radio and Television Body)

Magyar Rádió
Address: Bródy Sándor u. 5-7, H-1800 Budapest.
Tel: (1) 138 8388; Fax: (1) 138 7004.

Magyar Televízió (MTV)
Address: Szabadság Sq, Ter 17, H-1810 Budapest.
Tel: (1) 153 3200; Fax: (1) 153 4568.

B.

Hungarian Newspaper Publishers' Association
Address: Bécsi ut. 122-124, H-1034 Budapest.
Tel: (1) 168 8674; Fax: (1) 188 6707.

Magyar Könyvkiadók és Könyvkerjesztök Egyesülése
(Hungarian Publishers' and Booksellers' Association)
Address: Budapest.
Tel: (1) 118 4758; Fax: (1) 118 4581.

Magyar Reklamszövetsége
(The Committee for Ethics in Advertising of the Hungarian Advertising Association)
Address: Dob ut. 45, H-1074 Budapest.
Code: *Ethical code of Hungarian advertising.*

Magyar Ujságirók Országos Szövetsége (MUOSZ)
(National Association of Hungarian Journalists)
Address: Andrássy ut 101, H-1062 Budapest.
Tel: (1) 322 1699; Fax: (1) 322 1881.
Code: Supervised by an Ethical Committee.

C.

Magyar Irók Szövetsége
(Association of Hungarian Writers)
Address: Bajza ut. 18, 1062 Budapest.
Tel: (1) 322 8840.

Iceland (+354)

A.

Ministry of Communications
Address: Hafnarhúsinu vid Tryggvagötu, 150 Reykjavik.
Tel: 5609750; Fax: 5621702.

Ministry of Education, Culture and Science
Address: Sölvhólsgata 4, 150 Reykjavik.
Tel: 5609500; Fax: 5623068.

Ríkisútvarpid (RUV)
(Icelandic National Broadcasting Service)
Address: Broadcasting Centre, Efstaleiti 1, 150 Reykjavik.
Tel: 5153000; Fax: 5153010.

Ríkisútvarpid – Sjónvarp
(Icelandic National Broadcasting Service – Television)
Address: Laugavegur 176, 105 Reykjavik.
Tel: 5153000; Fax: 5153010.

B.

Advertisers Association of Iceland
Address: Kringlunni 7, 103 Reykjavik.

Bladamannafelag Islands
(Union of Icelandic Journalists)
Address: Sidumula 23, Reykjavik.
Tel: 5539155; Fax: 5539177.

Félag Íslenskra Bókaútgefenda
(Icelandic Publishers' Association)
Address: Sudurlandsbraut 4A, 108 Reykjavik.
Tel: 5538020; Fax: 5888668.

Samtök Bæjar- og Héradsfréttablada
(Association of Local Newspapers)
Address: Bæjarhraun 16, 220 Hafnafjördur.
Tel: 5651945; Fax: 5650745.

E.

University of Iceland – Ethical Research Institute
Address: Sudurgata, IS-107 Reykjavik.
Tel: 5254000; Fax: 5521331.

University of Iceland – Nordic Documentation Center
Address: Odda, Sturlugötu, IS-101 Reykjavik.
Tel: 5254519; Fax: 5526806.

Ireland (+353)

A.

Department of Arts, Culture and the Gaeltacht
Address: Dún Aimhirgin, 43–49 Mespil Road, Dublin 4.
Tel: (1) 667 0788; Fax: (1) 667 0827.

Department of Transport, Energy and Communication
Address: Telecommunications and Radio Regulatory Division, 7 Ely Place, Dublin 2.
Tel: (1) 670 7444; Fax: (1) 662 2150.

Broadcasting Complaints Commission
Address: c/o Department of Arts, Culture and the Gaeltacht, Dún Aimhirgin, 43–49 Mespil Road, Dublin 4.

Independent Radio and Television Commission (IRTC)
Address: Marine House, Clanwilliam Place, Dublin 2.
Tel: (1) 676 0966; Fax: (1) 676 0948.
Note: Licensing and regulation of commercial television.

Radio Telefís Éireann (RTE)
Address: Donnybrook, Dublin 4.
Tel: (1) 208 3111; Fax: (1) 208 3080.
Note: National broadcasting corporation operating two national television channels and three radio networks.
Code: *Code of standards for broadcast advertising*.

Film Censors Office
Address: 16 Harcourt Terrace, Dublin 2.
Tel: (1) 676 1982; Fax: (1) 676 1898.

B.

Advertising Standards Authority for Ireland (ASAI)
Address: IPC House, 35–39 Shelbourne Road, Dublin 4.
Note: Self-regulatory body for all advertising.
Code: *Code of advertising standards for Ireland*.

Association of Advertisers in Ireland
Address: Rock House, Main Street, Blackrock, Co. Dublin.
Tel: (1) 278 0499; Fax: (1) 278 0488.
Note: Advisory body to ensure highest ethical standards of practice.

Institute of Journalists (Irish Region)
Address: EETPU Section, 5 Whitefriars, Aungier Street, Dublin 2.
Tel: (1) 478 4141; Fax: (1) 475 0131.

Irish Book Publishers' Association
Address: The Irish Writers Centre, 19 Parnell Square, Dublin 1.
Tel: (1) 872 9090; Fax: (1) 872 2035.

National Newspapers of Ireland
Address: Clyde Lodge, 15 Clyde Road, Dublin 4.
Tel: (1) 668 9099; Fax: (1) 668 9872.

National Union of Journalists (Irish Council)
Address: Liberty Hall, 9th Floor, Dublin 1.
Tel: (1) 874 8694; Fax: (1) 874 9250.
Code: *Code of ethics* observed by Irish journalists.

C.

Institute of Advertising Practitioners in Ireland (IAPI)
Address: 35 Upper Fitzwilliam Street, Dublin 2.
Tel: (01) 676 4876; Fax: (01) 661 4589.

E.

Dublin City University – Centre for Communications Technology and Culture Research
Address: Dublin 9.
Tel: (1) 704 5000; Fax: (1) 836 0830.

Italy (+39)

A.

Ministero delle Poste e Telecomunicazioni
(Ministry of Post and Telecommunications)
Address: Viale Europa, 00144 Rome.
Tel: (6) 59581; Fax: (6) 680031.

La Commissione Parliamentare per l'Indirizzo Generale e la Vigilanza dei Servizi Radiotelevisione
(Parliamentary Supervisory Committee for Broadcasting services)

Ufficio del Garante per l'Editoria e la Radiodiffusione
(Office of the Guarantor for Broadcasting and the Press)
Address: Via Santa Maria 12, 00187 Rome.
Aims: Regulatory body for broadcasting, publishing and freedom of the press.

Consiglio Consultivo degli Utendi
(Users' Consultative Committee)
Aims: Advises the Guarantor on programme matters and ethical concerns.

RAI – Radiotelevisione Italiana
Address: Viale Mazzini 14, 00195 Rome.
Tel: (6) 38781; Fax: (6) 3226070.

B.

Associazione Italiana Editori
Address: Via delle Erbe 2, 20121 Milan.
Tel: (2) 86463091; Fax: (2) 89010863.

Federazione Italiani Editori Giornali (FIEG)
(Federation of Newspaper Proprietors)
Address: Via Piemonte 64, 00187 Rome.
Tel: (6) 4881683; Fax: (6) 4871109.

Federazione Nazionale della Stampa Italiana
(National Federation of the Italian Press)
Address: Corso Vittorio Emanuele 349, 00186 Roma.
Tel: (6) 6833879; Fax: (6) 6871444.
Code: *Code of ethics.*

Federazione Radio Television (FRT)
Address: Viale Regina Margherita 286, 00195 Rome.
Tel: (6) 4402104; Fax: (6) 4402096.

Istituto dell'Autodisciplina Publicitaria (IAP)
(Institute of Advertising Self-Regulation)
Address: Via Larga 15, 20122 Milan.
Tel: (2) 58303975.
Code: *Codice di autodisciplina publicitaria.*

Sindicato Nazionale Autonomo Giornalisti
Address: Van San Sisto 3, 20123 Milan.
Tel: (2) 8056704.

Unione Stampa Periodica Italiana (USPI)
Address: Via Nazionale 163, 00184 Rome.
Tel: (6) 6783117; Fax: (6) 6795798.

Utenti Pubblicità Associati (UPA)
Address: Via Larga 23, 20122 Milan.
Tel: (2) 58303741; Fax: (1) 58304443.

C.

Società Italiana degli Autori ed Editori
Address: Viale della Letteratura 30, 00144 Rome.

E.

Pontificia Universitas Gregoriana – Interdisciplinary Centre on Social Communication
Address: Piazza della Pilotta 4, 00187 Rome.
Tel: (6) 67011; Fax: (6) 67015413.

Pontificia Università Salesiana – Faculty of Social Communication Sciences
Address: Piazza Ateneo Salesiano 1, 00139 Rome.
Tel: (6) 872901; Fax: (6) 87290318.

Pontificia Universitas Urbaniana – Department of Social Communication
Address: Via Urbano VIII 16, 00165 Rome.
Tel: (6) 69882351; Fax: (6) 69881871.

Università degli Studi di Macerata – Centre for Studies on the Means of Mass Communication and Information Law
Address: Piaggi Università 2, 62100 Macerata.
Tel: (733) 2581; Fax: (733) 232639.

F.

Centro di Documentazioni Giornalistica
Address: Piazza di Pietra 26, 00186 Rome.
Tel: (6) 6791496; Fax: (6) 6797492.

Centro Internazionale di Documentazione e Communicazione
(International Documentation and Communication Centre)
Address: Via S. Maria dell'Anima 30, 00186 Rome.
Tel: (6) 686332; Fax: (6) 6832766.

Centro Sperimentale di Giornalismo
Address: Viale Caldara 13, 20122 Milan.
Tel: (2) 584223.

Istituto Italiano de Pubblicismo (IIP)
Address: c/o Facoltà di Scienze Statistiche, Universita degli Studi, Piazzale della Scienze 2, 00185 Rome.

Latvia (+371)

A.

Ministry of Communications
Address: 41–43 Elizabetes St, LV-226010 Riga.
Tel: (2) 322 550; Fax: (2) 728 001.
Note: Regulatory government division for broadcasting and telecommunications.

Nacionala Radio in Televizijas Padome
(National Radio and TV Council)
Address: Smilsu Iela 1–3, LV-1939 Riga.
Tel: (2) 206 509; Fax: (2) 206 562.
Note: Regulatory body for radio and television, which defends social interests and maintains free access to information.

Latvijas Radio
Address: Doma Laukuma 8, LV-1505 Riga.
Tel: (2) 206 722; Fax: (2) 206 709.

Latvijas Televizija
Address: Zakusalas Krastmala 3, LV-1509 Riga.
Tel: (2) 200 314; Fax: (2) 200 025.

B.

Latvijas Televiziju Asociacija
(Association of Television Broadcasters of Latvia)
Address: 4A Vizvalza St, 14–61 Stabu St, LV-1001 Riga.

Latvijas Zurnalistu Savieniba
(Latvian Journalists' Association)
Address: Marstalu 2, LV-1050 Riga.
Tel: (2) 211 433; Fax: (2) 820 233.

Liechtenstein (+41 75)

A.

Medienkommission
Address: Regierung des Fürstentums Liechtenstein, 9490 Vaduz.
Tel: 2366111.
Aims: Advisory and supervisory body for media.
Code: *Law of national radio and television* (1996).

Lithuania (+370)

A.

Rysiu ir Informatikos Ministerja
(Ministry of Communications and Informatics)
Address: Vilnius 33, LT-2001 Vilnius.
Tel: (2) 620 443; Fax: (2) 225 070.

Lietuvos Radijas ir Televizija (LRT)
(Lithuanian Radio and Television)
Address: Konarskio 49, LT-2674 Vilnius.
Tel: (2) 235 487; Fax: (2) 263 282.
Note: Public body for national radio and television services.

B.

Lietuvos Radijo ir Televizijos Asociacija
Address: PO Box 2210, Architecty 79, LT-2049 Vilnius.
Tel: (2) 269 121; Fax: (2) 269 293.

Luxembourg (+352)

A.

Ministère des Communications
Address: Avenue Monterey, 2945 Luxembourg.
Tel: 4786818; Fax: 408940.

Service des Médias et de l'Audiovisuel
Address: Maison de Cassal, 5 rue Large, 1917 Luxembourg.
Tel: 4782160; Fax: 475662.
Aims: Government agency to advise on media policy, and assist the Conseil National des Programmes.

B.

Compagnie Luxembourgeoise de Télédiffusion (CLT)
Address: Boulevard Pierre Frieden 45, 1543 Luxembourg.
Tel: 421 421; Fax: 421 4214.

Association Luxembourgeoise des Éditeurs de Journaux
Address: 2 rue Christophe Plantin, 2988 Luxembourg.

Macedonia (+389)

A.

Makedonska Radiotelevizija (MKRTV)
Address: Goce Delcev bb, 91000 Skopje.
Tel: (91) 112 200; Fax: (91) 113 246.

C.

Drustvo na Pisatelite na Makedonija
(Society of Writers of Macedonia)
Address: Maksim Gorki 18, 91000 Skopje.
Tel: (91) 236 205.

Malta (+356)

A.

Ministry of Transport, Communications and Technology
Address: Lascaris, Valletta CMR 02.
Tel: 243 880; Fax: 243 758.

Malta Broadcasting Authority
Address: Mile End Road, Hamrun.
Tel: 247 908; Fax: 240 855.
Note: Statutory regulatory body responsible for radio and television.

Public Broadcasting Service
Address: 75 St Luke's Road, PO Box 82, Msida, MSD 09.
Tel: 225 051; Fax: 244 601.

Moldova (+373)

A.

Ministerul Comunicatiilor si Informaticii
(Ministry of Communications and Informatics)
Address: Bul. Stefan cel Mare 134, MD-2012 Chisinau.
Tel: (2) 221001; Fax: (2) 241553.

Consilul Coordonator al Audiovizualului
(Radio and Television Co-ordinating Council)
Address: Bul. Stefan cel Mare 73, MD-2001 Chisinau.
Tel: (2) 721855.

Compania de Stat Teleradio-Moldova
(State Radio and Television Company of Moldova)
Address: Str. Miorita 1, MD-2028 Chisinau.
Tel: (2) 721077; Fax: (2) 723352.

B.

Union of Journalists of Moldova
Address: Chisinau.
Tel: (2) 233419.

F.

Centre for the Study of Marketing Problems
Address: Bul. Stefan cel Mare 1, MD-2001 Chisinau.
Tel and Fax: (2) 262391.

Netherlands (+31)

A.

Ministry of Education, Culture and Science
Address: Europaweg 4, PO 25000, 2700 Zoettermeer.
Tel: (79) 531922; Fax: (79) 531953.
Note: Government department responsible for broadcasting legislation.

Commissariaat voor de Media
(Media Commission)
Address: Emmastraat 51-53, PO Box 1426, 1200 BK Hilversum.
Tel: (35) 672 1721; Fax: (35) 672 1722.
Note: Regulatory public body for television channels.
Code: *Beleidslijn televisie en jeugd (Guidelines on television and youth)* (1996).

Mediaraad
(National Media Council)
Address: Ministry of Education, Culture and Science, Europaweg 4, PO 25000, 2700 Zoettermeer.
Aims: To advise on policy for radio, television and the press.

Nederlandse Omroep Stichting (NOS)
(Netherlands Broadcasting Foundation)
Address: Sumatralaan 45, 1217 Hilversum.
Tel: (35) 6779222; Fax: (35) 6772849.
Note: State-owned body, co-ordinating national public broadcasting services.

B.

Nederlandse Organisatie van Tijdschrift-Uitgevers
(Netherlands Association of Periodical Publishers)
Address: PO Box 100, 1243 ZJ s'Graveland.
Tel: (35) 6559100; Fax: (35) 6563254.

Nederlandse Vereniging van Journalisten
(Netherlands Union of Journalists)
Address: Johannes Vermeerstraat 22, PO Box 75997, 1070 AZ Amsterdam.
Tel: (20) 676771; Fax: (20) 6624901.

Stichting Reclame Code
(Advertising Code Foundation)
Address: Paasheuvelweg 15, 1105 BE Amsterdam.
Code: *Dutch advertising code.*

Vereniging van de Nederlandse Dagbladpers (NDP)
(Association of Dutch Daily Newspaper Publishers)
Address: Johannes Vermeerstraat 14, 1071 DR Amsterdam.
Tel: (20) 6763366; Fax: (20) 6766777.

E.

University of Amsterdam – Institute of Information Law
Address: Rokin 84, 1012 KX Amsterdam.

University of Amsterdam – International Communications
Address: Spiri 21, 1012 WX Amsterdam.
Tel: (20) 5259111.

University of Utrecht – Research School for Human Rights
Address: Heidelberglaan 8, PO Box 80125, 3508 TC Utrecht.
Tel: (30) 2539111; Fax: (30) 2533388.

Universitet voor Humanistiek – Faculty of Philosophy and Ethics Research Institute
Address: Postbus 797, 3500 AT Utrecht.
Tel: (30) 2390100; Fax: (30) 234738.

F.

Stichting Nederlands Filminstitut
Address: Steynlaan 8, PO Box 515, Hilversum.

Norway (+47)

A.

Ministry of Cultural Affairs
Address: Akergt. 59, PO Box 8030 DEP, N-0030 Oslo.
Tel: 22 249090; Fax: 22 349550.
Note: Government department for the audiovisual industry, broadcasting legislation and advertising standards; Complaints Tribunal adjudicates on offence by programmes or infringement of privacy.

Statens Medieforvaltning
(Mass Media Authority)
Address: PO Box 444, N-1601 Frederikstad.
Tel: 69 319030; Fax: 69 319280.
Function: Public body to authorize and regulate national and local public service radio and television.

Norsk Rikskringkasting (NRK)
(Norwegian Broadcasting Corporation)
Address: Björnstjerne Björnsons Plass 1, N-0340 Oslo 3.
Tel: 22 457882; Fax: 22 457333.

B.

Norsk Journalistlag
(Norwegian Union of Journalists)
Address: Storgatan 14, N-0184 Oslo.
Tel: 22 170117; Fax: 22 171782.

Norsk Presseforbund
(Norwegian Press Association)
Address: Prinsengt. 1, PO Box 46, Sentrum, N-0101 Oslo.
Tel: 22 415680; Fax: 22 411980.
Code: *Code of ethics.*

Norske Avisers Landsforening (NAL)
(Norwegian Newspaper Publishers' Association)
Address: Stortorvet 2, N-0155 Oslo.
Tel: 22 861200; Fax: 22 861201.

Reklamebyråforeningen
(Norwegian Association of Advertising Agencies)
Address: Munkedamsveien 96, PO Box 7658, Skillébekk, N-0205 Oslo 2.
Tel: 22 446722; Fax: 22 449305.
Aims: Self-regulation of advertising through an Ethics Committee.
Code: *Code of ethics.*

C.

Norske Forfatterforening
(Norwegian Authors' Society)
Address: Rådhusgata 7, Oslo 1.

E.

University of Bergen – Institute of Communication
Address: Fosswinckelsgatan 6, N-5007 Bergen, Norway.
Tel: 55 589140; Fax: 55 589149.

University of Oslo – Department of Media and Communication Research
Address: PO Box 1072, Blindern, N-0316 Oslo.
Tel: 22 855050; Fax: 22 854442.

Poland (+48)

A.

Ministerstwo Lacznosci
(Ministry of Communications)
Address: Pl. Malachowskiego 2, 00-940 Warsaw.
Tel: (22) 261411; Fax: (22) 264840.

Krajowa Rada Radiofonii i Telewizja (KRRT)
(National Broadcasting Council)
Address: Skwer Ks. Kardynata, Wyszynskiego 9, 01-015 Warsaw.
Tel: (22) 8381647; Fax: (22) 8388197.
Aims: Regulatory body to protect freedom of speech and public interest in broadcasting and the independence of broadcasters.

Komitet do Spraw Radia i Telewizji
(Radio and Television Committee)
Address: Polskie Radio i Telewizja, ul.
Woronicza 17, 00-950 Warsaw.
Tel: (22) 446260; Fax: (22) 430141.

Polskie Radio i Telewizja (PRT)
Address: ul. Woronicza 17, 00-950 Warsaw.
Tel: (22) 478501; Fax: (22) 437408.
Code: *Ethical rules of journalism in Polish public television.*

B.

Stowarzyszenie Dziennikarzy Polskich (SDP)
(Polish Journalists' Association)
Address: ul. Foksal 3/5, 00-366 Warsaw.
Tel (and Fax): (22) 278720.
Code: *Code of conduct.*

C.

Stowarzyszenie Autorów
(Society of Authors)
Address: Hipoteczna 2, 00-92 Warsaw.
Tel: (22) 276061; Fax: (22) 6351347.

Zwiazek Literatow Polskich
(Union of Polish Writers)
Address: Krachowskie Przedmiescie 87-89,
00-079 Warsaw.
Tel: (22) 265785.

E.

Katholicki Uniwersytet Lubelski – Department of Ethics
Address: Al Raclawickie 14, 20-950 Lublin.
Tel: (81) 30426; Fax: (81) 30433.

Uniwersytet Jagiellonski – Press Research Centre
Address: Golebia 24, 31-007 Cracow.

Uniwersytet Marie Curie-Sklodowskiej – Department of Ethics
Address: 20-031 Lublin.
Tel: (81) 375107; Fax: (81) 375102.

Uniwersytet Slaski (University of Silesia) – Faculty of Radio and Television
Address: Bankowa 12, 40-007 Katowice.
Tel: (32) 599601; Fax: (32) 599605.

Uniwersytet Warszawski – Faculty of Journalism and Political Science
Address: Krachowskie Przedmiescie 26-28,
00-325 Warsaw.
Tel: (22) 200381; (22) 267520.

Portugal (+351)

A.

Ministerio das Obras Publicas, Transportes e Comunicações
(Ministry of Public Works, Transport and Communications)
Address: Rua São Mamede Alcodes, P-1100 Lisbon.
Tel: (1) 847 0445; Fax: (1) 866 1895.

Alta Autoridade para Comunicação Social
(High Authority for Mass Communication)
Address: Avenida Don Carlos Primeiro 130, P-1200 Lisbon.
Tel: (1) 395 1352; Fax: (1) 395 1449.
Aims: To ensure freedom, pluralism and independence of the media.

Conselho de Publicidade
(Advertising Council)
Address: Rua do Século 51, P-1200 Lisbon.
Tel: (1) 346 2751; Fax: (1) 346 5727.
Code: *Advertising code.*

Instituto Português das Arte Cinematografica e Audiovisual (IPACA)
Address: Rua San Pedro de Alcântara 45-1,
P-1250 Lisbon.
Tel: (1) 346 6644; Fax: (1) 347 2777.
Aims: To assist with regulation and promotion of the television and film industry.

Radio Televisão Portuguesa (RTP)
Address: Avenida 5 de Outubro 197, Apdo 2934, P-1000 Lisbon.
Tel: (1) 793 1774; Fax: (1) 793 1758.

B.

Associação Nacional da Imprensa Diaria
(National Association of the Daily Press)
Address: Rua de Artilharia Um 69, 2, P-1200 Lisbon.
Tel: (1) 657 584; Fax: (1) 387 3541.

Associação da Imprensa Não-Diaria
(Association of the Non-Daily Press)
Address: Rua Gomes Freire 183 Esq, P-1150 Lisbon.
Tel: (1) 355 8118; Fax: (1) 314 2191.

Associação Portuguesa de Editores e Livreiros
Address: Avenida dos Estados Unidos da America 97 Esq, P-1700 Lisbon.
Tel: (1) 848 9136; Fax: (1) 848 9377.

Instituto Civil da Autodisciplina da Publicidade (ICAP)
(Civil Institute for Advertising Self-Regulation)
Address: Avenida da Republica, 62F, 6th Floor, P-1000 Lisbon.
Code: *Code of conduct.*

Instituto das Comunicacões de Portugal (ICP)
Address: Avenida José Malhoa 21, P-1070 Lisbon.
Tel: (1) 726 9223; Fax: (1) 721 1001.

Sindicato dos Jornalistas
Address: Rua dos Duques de Bragança 7-2, P-1200 Lisbon 2.
Tel: (1) 364 354.

C.

Associação Portuguesa de Escritores
Address: Rua de S. Domingos à Lapa 17, P-1200 Lisbon.

Sociedade Portuguesa de Autores
Address: Avenue Duque de Loulé 31, P-1098 Lisbon.
Tel: (1) 357 8320; Fax: (1) 353 0257.

F.

Escola Superior de Communicação Social
Address: Rua Carolina Michaelis de Vasconcelos, P-1300 Lisbon.
Tel: (1) 716 4876.

Romania (+40)

A.

Ministry of Communications
Address: Boulevard Libertatii 14, RO-70060 Bucharest.
Tel: (1) 400 1062; Fax: (1) 400 1742.

Consiliul National al Audiovizualului (CNA)
(National Audiovisual Council)
Address: Boulevard Libertatii 14, RO-70060 Bucharest.
Tel: (1) 312 6004; Fax: (1) 312 4634.
Aims: Regulatory body for radio and television to establish standards for programming, advertising, sponsorship and right of reply.

Societatea Româna de Televiune
(Romanian Television)
Address: Calea Dorobantilor 191, RO-79757 Bucharest.
Tel: (1) 212 0710; Fax: (1) 312 0381.

Societatea Româna de Radiodifuziune
Address: str General Berthelot 60–62, RO-70747 Bucharest.
Tel: (1) 222 5647; Fax: (1) 312 1057.

B.

Societatea Ziaristilor din România – Federatia Sindicatelor din Intreaga Presa
(Society of Romanian Journalists – Federation of All Press Unions)
Address: Piata Presei Libere 1, Bucharest.
Tel (and Fax): (1) 612 8266.

Uniunea Scriitorilor din România
(Romanian Writers' Union)
Address: Calea Victorei 115, RO-71102 Bucharest.
Tel: (1) 650 7245; Fax: (1) 312 9634.

E.

Universitatea Bucuresti – Faculty of Journalism and Communication Sciences
Address: B-dul M. Kogalniceanu 64, RO-70609 Bucharest.
Tel: (1) 312 0419.

Russia (+7)

A.

Ministerstvo Svyazi
(Ministry of Communications)
Address: ul. Tverskaya 7, 103375 Moscow.
Tel: (095) 292 7070; Fax: (095) 201 2128.

Federal Radio and Television Broadcasting Commission
Address: ul. Pyatnitskaya 25, 113326 Moscow.
Tel: (095) 217 9838; Fax: (095) 215 9356.

Vserossiiskaya Gosudasrtvennaya Teleradiokompaniya
(All-Russia State Television and Radio Broadcasting Company)
Address: ul. Yamskogo Polya 5-ya 19–21, 125124 Moscow.
Tel: (095) 251 4050; Fax: (095) 250 0105.

B.

Russian Association of Advertising Agencies
Address: ul. Novaya Basmannaya 14-3-37, 107078 Moscow.
Tel: (095) 262 2184; Fax: (095) 262 7037.

Union of Journalists
Address: Zubovskii bul. 4, 119021 Moscow.
Tel: (095) 201 7770; Fax: (095) 201 4891.

C.

Union of Russian Writers
Address: ul. Vorovskogo 52, Moscow.
Tel: (095) 291 6350.

E.

Moscow State University – Centre for Mass Media Law
Address: Moscow.
Tel: (095) 203 3270; Fax: (095) 203 6831.

Moscow M. V. Lomonosov State University – Faculty of Journalism
Address: Leninskiegory, 117234 Moscow.
Tel: (095) 939 5340.

St Petersburg State University – Faculty of Journalism
Address: Universitetskaya hab. 719, 199034 St Petersburg.
Tel: (812) 218 9788; Fax: (812) 218 346.

Urals A. M. Gorkii State University – Faculty of Journalism
Address: pr. Lenina 51, 620083 Ekaterinburg.
Tel: (3432) 557420; Fax: (3432) 555964.

F.

State Institute of Cinematography
Address: ul. Vilgelma Pika 3, 129226 Moscow.
Tel: (095) 181 3868.

Serbia (+381)

A.

Jugoslovenska Radio-Televizija (JRT)
Address: Generala Zdanova 28, 11000 Belgrade.
Tel: (11) 330194; Fax: (11) 434023.

B.

Savez Novinara Jugoslavije
(Federation of Yugoslav Journalists)
Address: Trg Republiki 5/111, 11000 Belgrade.
Tel: (11) 624993.

E.

University of Belgrade – Institute for Theatre, Film, Radio and Television
Address: Kosancicev venac 29, 11000 Belgrade.
Tel: (11) 625166; Fax: (11) 629785.

Slovakia (+421)

A.

Slovak Radio and Television Broadcasting Council
Address: Mlinská Dolina 28, SK-845 45 Bratislava.
Tel: (7) 72 59 48; Fax: (7) 72 23 41.

Slovensky Rozhlas
Address: Mytna 1, SK-812 90 Bratislava.
Tel: (7) 39 897; Fax: (7) 39 89 23.

Slovenska Televizia
Address: Mlinská Dolina 28, SK-845 45 Bratislava.
Tel: (7) 72 84 00; Fax: (7) 72 94 40.

B.

Slovensky Syndikat Novinarov
(Slovak Syndicate of Journalists)
Address: Zupne nam 9, SK-815 68 Bratislava.
Tel: (7) 531 3493; Fax: (7) 533 4534.

Zdrzenie Slovenskych Novinarov
(Association of Slovak Journalists)
Address: Safarikovo nam 4, SK-811 02 Bratislava.
Tel (and Fax): (7) 36 31 84.

C.

Asociacia Organizacii Spisovatel'ov Slovenska
(Association of Writers' Organizations in Slovakia)
Address: Laurinska 2, 815 08 Bratislava.
Tel: (7) 533-5368; Fax: (7) 533-4117.

Slovenia (+386)

A.

Ministry of Transport and Communications
Address: Presernova 23, SL-1000 Ljubljana.
Tel: (61) 125 6256; Fax: (61) 218 707.
Note: Regulation of radio and television delegated to Broadcasting Council of the Republic of Slovenia.

Radiotelevizija Slovenija
Address: Kolodvorska Ulica 2-4, SL-1550 Ljubljana.
Tel: (61) 131 1333; Fax: (61) 131 9171.

Spain (+34)

A.

Ministerio de Obras Publicas, Transportes y Medios Ambientes
Address: Plaza de Cibeles, 28071 Madrid.
Note: Government department responsible for broadcasting and regulation of television channels.

Dirección General de Medios de Comunicación Social
Address: Ayala 5, 28001 Madrid.
Tel: (1) 448 7000; Fax: (1) 402 0057.

Dirección General de Correos y Telecomunicaciones
Address: Plaza de Cibeles, 28071 Madrid.
Tel: (1) 521 6500; Fax: (1) 396 2777.

Ente Publico Radiotelevisión Española
Address: Casa de la Radio, Prado del Rey, 28223 Madrid.

RTVE – Radiotelevisión Española
Address: Centro RTVE, Prado del Rey, 28223 Madrid.
Tel: (1) 346 8000; Fax: (1) 346 9835.

Radio Nacional de España (RNE)
Address: Casa de la Radio, Prado del Rey, 28223 Madrid.
Tel: (1) 346 2144; Fax: (1) 346 1249.

B.

Asociación de Editores de Diarios Españoles
Address: Espronceda 32, 6A, 28003 Madrid.
Tel: (1) 442 1992; Fax: (1) 442 8621.

Asociación de la Prensa de Madrid
(Madrid Press Association)
Address: Juan Bravo 6, 28006 Madrid.
Tel: (1) 585 0010; Fax: (1) 585 0070.

Autocontrol de la Publicidad
(Advertising Self-Regulation Body)
Address: Avenida de Burgos 14, Torre III 2B, 28036 Madrid.
Tel: (1) 302 5702; Fax: (1) 766 8574.
Code: *ICC international code of advertising practice.*

Asociación Española de Anunciantes (AEA)
(Association of Spanish Advertisers)
Address: Paseo de la Castellana 121, 28046 Madrid.
Tel: (1) 556 0351; Fax: (1) 597 0483.

Federación de Asociaciones de la Prensa de España
(National Press Federation)
Address: Plaza del Callao 4, 7, 28003 Madrid.
Tel: (1) 522 1950; Fax: (1) 521 1573.

Federación de Gremios de Editores de España
(Federation of Publishers' Associations of Spain)
Address: Juan Ramón Jiménez 45, 9, Izda, 28036 Madrid.
Tel: (1) 350 9105; Fax: (1) 343 4351.

Union de Periodistas
Address: Silva 22, 28004 Madrid.
Tel: (1) 522 4810; Fax: (1) 522 5179.

C.

Sociedad General de Autores de España (SGAE)
Address: Fernando VI 4, Apdo 484, 28004 Madrid.

E.

Universitat Autónoma de Barcelona – Faculty of Communication Sciences
Address: Campus Universitari, 08193 Bellaterra, Barcelona.
Tel: (3) 581 1100; Fax: (3) 581 2000.

Universidad Complutense de Madrid – Moral and Political Philosophy
Address: Ciudad Universitaria, 28040 Madrid.
Tel: (1) 549 0250; Fax: (1) 394 3437.

Universidad de Navarra – Faculty of Public Communication (Mass Media Law, Theory and Journalism)
Address: Ciudad Universitaria, 31080 Pamplona.
Tel: (48) 25 27 00; Fax: (48) 17 36 50.

Universitat Pompeu Fabia – Institut Universitari de l'Audiovisual
Address: Plaça de la Mercè 10–12, 08002 Barcelona.
Tel: (3) 542 2000; Fax: (3) 542 2002.

Sweden (+46)

A.

Ministry of Culture
Address: Jakobsgatan 26, 103 33 Stockholm.
Tel: (8) 4051000; Fax: (8) 216813.
Note: Government department for broadcasting legislation and regulation.
Legislation: Freedom of the Press Act; Radio and Television Act 1996.
Code: *Regler och rillkor för privatradio (Rules and conditions for private radio).*

Granskningsnämden för Radio och TV
(Swedish Broadcasting Commission)
Address: PO Box 244, Nämndhuset Stores Grand 20, 13622 Haninge
Tel: (6) 6067970; Fax: (6) 7410588.
Note: Government agency controlling radio and television programmes, advertising, sponsorship and right of reply.

DIRECTORY OF SELECTED ORGANIZATIONS

Radio- och TV-Verket
(Radio and Television Authority)
Address: PO Box 123, Nämndhuset Stores Grand 20, 13622 Haninge.
Tel: (6) 6069086: Fax: (6) 7410870.
Note: Founded 1994 to license commercial radio, cable and satellite.

Sveriges Radio (SR)
Address: Radiohuset, Oxenstiernsgatan 20, 105 10 Stockholm.
Tel: (8) 7840000; Fax: (8) 6628336.

Sveriges Television
Address: Oxenstierngatan 26-34, 105 10 Stockholm.
Tel: (8) 7840000; Fax: (8) 784150.

Statens Biografbyrå
(Swedish National Board of Film Censors)
Address: Box 7728, 103 95 Stockholm.
Tel: (8) 243425; Fax: (8) 210178.

B.

Annonsörföreningen
(Advertisers' Association)
Address: PO Box 1327, 113 86 Stockholm.
Tel: (8) 235100; Fax: (8) 235510.

Svenska Bokförläggareföreningen
(Swedish Publishers' Association)
Address: Drottninggatan 97, 113 60 Stockholm.
Tel: (8) 7361940; Fax: (8) 7361944.

Svenska Journalistförbundet
(Swedish Union of Journalists)
Address: Journalisternas Hus, Vasagatan 50, 111 20 Stockholm.
Tel: (8) 6137500; Fax: (8) 212680.

Svenska Tidningsutgivareföreningen
(Swedish Newspaper Publishers' Association)
Address: Kungsholmstorg 5, PO Box 22500, 104 22 Stockholm.
Tel: (8) 6924600; Fax: (8) 6924638.

Code: *Rules*.

Svenska Veckopressens Tidningsutgivareförening (VECTU)
(Swedish Magazine Publishers' Association)
Address: Kungsgt. 33, 111 56 Stockholm.
Tel: (8) 201510; Fax: (8) 213520.

Sveriges Reklamförbund
(Advertising Agencies' Association of Sweden)
Address: Norrlandsgatan 24, 111 43 Stockholm.
Tel: (8) 6790800; Fax: (8) 6790801.

C.

Sveriges Författarförbund
(Swedish Writers' Union)
Address: Drottninggatan 88B, 111 36 Stockholm.
Tel: (8) 7912280; Fax: (8) 7912285.

E.

Göteborgs Universitet – Department of Journalism and Mass Communication
Address: Vasaparken, 41124 Göteborg.
Tel: (31) 7731000; Fax: (31) 7731064.

Högskolan i Kalmar – Department of Communication and Media Studies
(University of Kalmar)
Address: Box 905, 391 29 Kalmar.
Tel: (480) 446000.

Stockholms Universitet – Department of Media and Communication
Address: 106 91 Stockholm.
Tel: (8) 162000; Fax: (8) 159522.

Umeå Universitet – Department of Mass Communication
Address: 901 87 Umeå.
Tel: (90) 165000; Fax: (90) 165488.

Switzerland (+41)

A.

Department of Transport, Communications and Energy
Address: Radio/TV Department, Bahnhofplatz 10B, 3030 Berne.
Tel: (31) 614 111; Fax: (31) 229 576.

Office Fédéral de la Communication (OFCOM)/Bundesamt für Kommunikation (BAKOM)
Address: 44 rue de l'Avenir/ 44 Zukunftstrasse, Postfach 1003, 2503 Biel-Bienne.
Tel: (32) 285 511/31; Fax: (32) 285 533.

Authorité Indépendente d'Examen des Plaintes en Matière de Radio-Télévision
(Independent Authority for Examining Complaints about Radio and Television)
Address: Case Postale 8547, Haslerstrasse 8, 3000 Biel-Bienne.
Tel: (31) 615 538; Fax: (31) 615 558.

Société Suisse de Radiodiffusion et Télévision (SSR)/Schweizerische Radio- und Fernsehgesellschaft/Società Svizzera di Radiotelevisione
(Swiss Broadcasting Corporation)
Address: Giacomettistrasse 3, 3000 Berne 15.
Tel: (31) 350 92 31; Fax: (31) 350 92 56.

B.

Association Suisse des Éditeurs de Journaux et Périodiques/Schweizer Verband der Zeitungs- und Zeitschriftenverleger
(Swiss Newspaper and Periodical Publishers' Association)
Address: Baumackerstrasse 42, Postfach 1465, 8050 Zurich.
Tel: (1) 318 64 64; Fax: (1) 318 64 62.

Association Suisse des Éditeurs de Langue Française
Address: 2 avenue Agassiz, 1011 Lausanne.
Tel: (21) 319 71 11; Fax: (21) 319 79 10.

Commission Suisse pour la Loyauté en Publicité/Schweizerische Kommission für die Lauterkeit in der Werbung
(Swiss Commission for Fair Practices in Advertising)
Address: Kappelergasse 14, Postfach 4675, 8022 Zurich.
Code: *ICC international code of advertising practice.*

Schweizer Verband der Journalistinnen and Journalisten/Fédération Suisse des Journalistes/Federazione Svizzera Giornalisti
(Swiss Union of Journalists)
Address: Postfach 316, Grand-Places 14A, 1701 Fribourg.
Tel: (37) 811 200; Fax: (37) 231 202.

Schweizerischer Büchhändler- und Verleger-Verband
Address: Baumackerstrasse 42, 8050 Zurich.
Tel: (1) 318 64 00; Fax: (1) 318 64 62.

Union Suisse d'Agences-Conseil en Publicité/Bund Schweizer Werbeagenturen
Address: Winkelriedstrasse 35, 8033 Zurich.
Tel: (1) 361 37 60; Fax: (1) 361 38 10.

C.

Schweizerische Gesellschaft fur Kommunikations- und Medienwissenschaft (SGKM)
Address: c/o SRG Forschungsdienst, Giacomettistrasse 1, Postif, 3000 Berne 15.
Tel: (31) 439 430; Fax: (31) 439 436.

E.

Université de Fribourg – Institut für Journalistik und Kommunikationswissenschaft
(Institute for Journalism and Social Communications)
Address: 1700 Fribourg.
Tel: (26) 297 111; Fax: (26) 299 700.

Universität St Gallen – Institute for Business Ethics
Address: Dufourstrasse 50, 9000 St Gallen.
Tel: (71) 224 21 11; Fax: (71) 224 28 16.

Universität Zürich – Department of Journalism
Address: Rämistrasse 71, 8006 Zurich.
Tel: (1) 257 11 11; Fax: (1) 257 23 04.

Turkey (+90)

A.

Ministry of Transport and Communications
Address: Ulastirma Bakanligi, Sok 5, Emek, Ankara.
Tel: (312) 212 4416; Fax: (312) 212 4930.

Supreme Council for Radio and Television
Address: Atatürk Bulvari 169/2, Bakaniklar, Ankara.
Tel: (312) 417 0370; Fax: (312) 417 0551.

Türkiye Radyo-Televizyon Kurumu (TRT)
(Turkish Radio and Television Corporation)
Address: TRT Sitesi, Merkez Kutuphane, Oran, 06450 Ankara.
Tel: (312) 490 4983; Fax: (312) 490 4985.
Note: Controls Turkish radio and television services.

B.

Reklamcilar Dernegi (RD)
(Turkish Advertising Agencies' Association)
Address: Yildiz Posta Caddesi, No. 26, A-Block, D 18, Gayrettepe, 80280 Istanbul.
Tel: (212) 166 9088; Fax: (212) 173 1293.

Türkiye Gazeteciler Sendikasi
(Turkish Journalists' Union)
Address: Basin Sarayi Kal-2, Cagaloglu, Istanbul.
Tel: (212) 527 8534.

Türkiye Yagincilar Birligi Demegi
(Turkish Publishers' Association)
Address: Kazim Ismail, Gürkan Caddesi 12, Ortaklar Han Kat 1/11, Cagaloglu, Istanbul.
Tel: (212) 512 5602; Fax: (212) 511 7794.

E.

Anadolu Üniversitesi – Faculty of Communication Sciences
(University of Anatolia)
Address: Yunus Emre Kampüsü, 26470 Eskisehir.
Tel: (222) 335 0580; Fax: (222) 335 3616.

Ankara Üniversitesi – Centre for Journalism and Communications
Address: Tandogan, 06100 Ankara.
Tel: (312) 223 4361; Fax: (312) 223 6070.

Istanbul Üniversitesi – Faculty of Communications
Address: Beyazik, Istanbul.
Tel: (212) 528 0701; Fax: (212) 520 5473.

Ukraine (+380)

A.

Ministerstvo Zvyazku ta Informatiki
(Ministry of Communications and Informatics)
Address: vul. Khreshchatyk 22, 252001 Kiev.
Tel: (44) 2262140; Fax: (44) 2286141.
Note: The Supreme Council Committee for Legislative Safeguards of Freedom of Speech and Mass Media legislates on media issues.

Derzhteleradio (Derzhavna Teleradiomovna Kompania Ukrainy)
(Ukrainian State Television and Radio Committee)
Address: vul. Khreshchatyk 26, 252001 Kiev.

Natsionalna Rada z Pytan Telebachennya i Radiomovlennya
(National Council for Radio and Television Broadcasting)
Address: Kiev.

E.

Taras Shevchenko University of Kiev – Institute of Journalism
Address: Volodymyrska vul. 64, 252601 Kiev.
Tel: (44) 2252082; Fax: (44) 2246166.

United Kingdom (+44)

A.

Department of Culture, Media and Sport
Address: 2–4 Cockspur Street, London SW1Y 5DH.
Tel: ((0)171) 211 6000; Fax: ((0)171) 211 6270.
Note: Government department responsible for arts, film, broadcasting and media.

British Board of Film Classification (BBCF)
Address: 3 Soho Square, London W1V 6HD.
Tel: ((0)171) 439 7961; Fax: ((0)171) 287 0141.
Note: Classification of films for public showing in the UK, and of videos for sale and distribution to the public.

British Broadcasting Corporation
Address: Broadcasting House, London W1A 1AA.
Tel: ((0)171) 580 4468; Fax: ((0)171) 637 1630.
Note: Public service broadcaster.
Codes: *Producers' guidelines; Guidelines for factual programmes; Guidelines for the portrayal of violence on BBC Television.*

Broadcasting Standards Commission
Address: 5 The Sanctuary, London SW1P 3JS.
Tel: ((0)171) 233 0544; Fax: ((0)171) 233 0397.
Note: Statutory body for both standards and fairness in broadcasting; conducts research and investigates public complaints. Formed in 1997 from merger of the Broadcasting Standards Council and Broadcasting Complaints Commission.
Code: *A code of practice; Draft code on fairness and privacy.*

Independent Television Commission
Address: 33 Foley Street, London W1P 7LB.
Tel: ((0)171) 255 3000; Fax: ((0)171) 306 7800.
Note: Licenses and regulates commercial terrestrial, cable and satellite television.
Codes: *ITC programme code; ITC code of advertising standards and practice; ITC code of programme sponsorship.* Library.

Office of Telecommunications (Oftel)
Address: 50 Ludgate Hill, London EC4M 7JJ.
Tel: ((0)171) 634 8700; Fax: ((0)171) 634 8943.
Note: Regulatory body for monitoring and enforcing telecommunication licences and competition legislation in relation to these services. Library.

Radio Authority
Address: Holbrook House, 14 Great Queen Street, London WC2B 5DG.
Tel: ((0)171) 430 2724; Fax: ((0)171) 405 7062.
Note: Licenses and regulates commercial radio.
Codes: *The Radio Authority programme code; The Radio Authority code of advertising standards and practice and programme sponsorship.*

B.

Advertising Association
Address: Abford House, 15 Wilton House, London SW1V 1NJ.
Tel: ((0)171) 828 2771; Fax ((0)171) 931 0376.

DIRECTORY OF SELECTED ORGANIZATIONS

Note: Represents advertisers, agencies, the media and support services, and develops codes of conduct. Library.
Code: *Code of practice: covering the use of personal data for advertising and direct marketing purposes.*

Advertising Standards Authority
Address: Brook House, 2–16 Torrington Place, London WC1E 7HN.
Tel: ((0)171) 580 5555; Fax: ((0)171) 631 3051.
Note: Supervises *The British codes of advertising and sales promotion* (drawn up by the Committee of Advertising Practice), and ensures all advertisements and promotions are legal, decent, honest and truthful.

Broadcasting, Entertainment, Cinematograph and Theatre Union (BECTU)
Address: 111 Wardour Street, London W1V 4AY.
Tel: ((0)171) 437 8506; Fax: ((0)171) 437 8268.
Note: Trade union for broadcasting industry employees.

Commercial Radio Companies Association
Address: 77 Shaftesbury Avenue, London W1V 7AD.
Tel: ((0)171) 306 2603.

Committee of Advertising Practice
Address: 2 Torrington Place, London WC1E 7HW.
Tel: ((0)171) 580 5555: Fax: ((0)171) 631 3051.
Note: Self-regulatory body that devises and enforces the codes.
Codes: *The British codes of advertising and sales promotion.*

ITV Network Centre (and ITV Association)
Address: 200 Gray's Inn Road, London WC1X 8HF.
Tel: ((0)171) 843 8000; Fax: ((0)171) 843 8158.

Note: Centralized scheduling and commissioning body for the ITV network, and trade association for the Channel 3 commercial television companies.
Code: *Factual drama on ITV: statement of best practice.*

Incorporated Society of British Advertisers (ISBA)
Address: 44 Hertford Street, London W1Y 8AE.
Tel: ((0)171) 499 7502; Fax: ((0)171) 629 5355.

Institute of Practitioners in Advertising (IPA)
Address: 44 Belgrave Square, London SW1X 8QS.
Tel: ((0)171) 235 7020; Fax: ((0)171) 245 9904.
Note: Trade and professional body for advertising agencies and staff. Library.
Codes: *Bye-laws.*

London Film Commission
Address: 12 Raddington Road, Ladbroke Grove, London W10 5TG.
Tel: ((0)181) 968 0968; Fax: ((0)181) 968 0177.
Code: *Film-makers' code of practice.*

National Union of Journalists (NUJ)
Address: Acorn House, 314–320 Gray's Inn Road, London WC1X 8DP.
Tel: ((0)171) 278 7916; Fax: ((0)171) 837 8143.
Note: Trade union for journalists in broadcasting and the press.
Codes: *Code of conduct* (Appendix A in *Rules of the National Union of Journalists*).

Newspaper Publishers Association
Address: 34 Southwark Bridge Road, London SE1 9EU.
Tel: ((0)171) 928 6928; Fax: ((0)171) 928 2067.
Note: Trade association for national daily and Sunday newspapers.

Newspaper Society
Address: Bloomsbury House, 74–77 Great Russell Street, London WC1B 3DA.
Tel: ((0)171) 636 7014; Fax: ((0)171) 631 5119.
Note: Trade body for the regional and local press.

Periodical Publishers Association
Address: Imperial House, 15–19 Kingsway, London WC2B 6UN.
Tel: ((0)171) 379 6268; Fax: ((0)171) 379 5661.
Note: Trade association to promote and protect the interests of the British magazine publishing industry.
Code: *Guidelines*.

Press Complaints Commission
Address: 1 Salisbury Square, London EC4Y 8AE.
Tel: ((0)171) 353 1248; Fax: ((0)171) 353 8355.
Note: Self-regulatory body for the newspaper and periodical industry.
Code: *Code of practice*.

Producers Alliance for Cinema and Television (PACT)
Address: Gordon House, 10 Greencoat Place, London SW1P 1PH.
Tel: ((0)171) 233 6000; Fax: ((0)171) 233 8935.

The Publishers Association
Address: 19 Bedford Square, London WC1B 3HJ.
Tel: ((0)171) 580 6321; Fax: ((0)171) 636 5375.
Note: Trade association for UK book publishers.

Scottish Daily Newspaper Society (and Scottish Newspaper Publishers' Association)
Address: 48 Palmerston Place, Edinburgh, EH12 5DE.
Tel: ((0)131) 220 4353; Fax: ((0)131) 220 4344.

Scottish Publishers' Association
Address: Scottish Book Centre, 137 Dundee Street, Edinburgh EH11 1BG.
Tel: ((0)131) 228 6866; Fax: ((0)131) 228 3720.

Video Standards Council
Address: Research House, Fraser Road, Perivale, Middlesex UB6 7AQ.
Tel: ((0)181) 566 8272; Fax: ((0)181) 991 2653.
Code: *Code of practice rules*.

C.

Institute of Journalists
Address: 2 Dock Offices, Surrey Quays, Lower Road, London SE16 2YS.
Tel: ((0)171) 252 1187; Fax: ((0)171) 232 2302.
Note: Professional body for journalists incorporated by Royal Charter in 1890.
Codes: *Code of professional ethics*; *Professional usage and practice*.

Institute of Public Relations (IPR)
Address: The Old Trading House, 15 Northburgh Street, London EC1V 0PR.
Tel: ((0)171) 253 5151; Fax: ((0)171) 490 0588.
Code: *Code of professional conduct*.

Royal Television Society
Address: Holborn Hall, 100 Gray's Inn Road, London WC1X 8AL.
Tel: ((0)171) 430 1000; Fax: ((0)171) 430 0924.

Society of Authors
Address: 84 Drayton Gardens, London SW10 9SB.
Tel: ((0)171) 373 6642.

Writers' Guild of Great Britain
Address: 430 Edgware Road, London W2 1EH.
Tel: ((0)171) 723 8074; Fax: ((0)171) 706 2413.

D.

Campaign Against Censorship
Address: 25 Middleton Close, Fareham, Hampshire PO14 1QN.
Tel: ((0)1329) 284471.
Aims: To uphold freedom of speech and information, and oppose censorship.

Campaign Against Pornography
Address: 11 Goodwin Street, London N4 3HQ.
Tel: ((0)171) 263 1833; Fax: ((0)171) 272 3044.
Aims: To raise awareness of the harm pornography does to women.

Campaign for Freedom of Information
Address: 88 Old Street, London EC1V 9AR.
Tel: ((0)171) 253 2445; Fax: ((0)171) 608 3325.

Campaign for Press and Broadcasting Freedom
Address: 8 Cynthia Street, London N1 9JF.
Tel: ((0)171) 278 4430; Fax: ((0)171) 837 8868.
Aims: To act as pressure group for a democratic and free media in the UK.
Code: *Media manifesto.*

Freedom Association
Address: 35 Westminster Bridge Road, London SE1 7JB.
Tel: ((0)171) 928 9524.
Aims: To promote defence of freedom and free enterprise.

National Viewers' and Listeners' Association (NVALA)
Address: All Saints House, High Street, Colchester, Essex CO1 1UG.
Tel: ((0)1206) 561155; Fax: ((0)1206) 766175.
Aims: To uphold good standards in TV and radio programming.

The Voice of the Listener and Viewer (VLV)
Address: 101 King's Drive, Gravesend, Kent DA12 5BQ.
Tel: ((0)1474) 352835; Fax ((0)1474) 352835.
Aims: To ensure high standards, diversity and independence in British TV and radio services.

E.

University of Birmingham – Department of Cultural Studies
Address: PO Box 363, Edgbaston, Birmingham B15 2TT.
Tel. ((0)121) 414 3344; Fax: ((0)121) 414 3971.

Bournemouth University – Department of Communications and Media
Address: Dorset House, Talbot Campus, Fern Barrow, Poole, Dorset BH12 5BB.
Tel: ((0)202) 524111; Fax: ((0)202) 513293.

Brunel University – Department of Human Sciences
Address: Uxbridge, Middlesex UB8 3PH.
Tel: ((0)1895) 274000; Fax: ((0)1895) 232806.

University of Central England in Birmingham – School of Media and Communication
Address: Perry Barr, Birmingham B42 2SU.
Tel: ((0)121) 331 5719.

University of Central Lancashire – Department of Journalism
Address: Preston, Lancashire PR1 2HE.
Tel: ((0)772) 893730; Fax: ((0)772) 892907.

City University, London – Graduate Centre for Journalism/Department of Social Sciences and Communication Policy
Address: Northampton Square, London EC1V 0HB.
Tel: ((0)171) 477 8230; Fax: ((0)171) 477 8562.

Darlington College of Technology – School of Journalism and Media Studies
Address: Cleveland Avenue, Darlington, Co. Durham DL3 7BB.
Tel: ((0)325) 467651; Fax: ((0)325) 483843.

University of Dundee – Department of Philosophy
Address: Dundee DD1 4HN.
Tel: ((0)1382) 223181; Fax: ((0)1382) 201604.

University of East London – Mass Communication Research Unit
Address: Romford Road, London E15 4LZ.
Tel: ((0)181) 590 7722; Fax: ((0)181) 519 3740.

University of Essex – Human Rights Centre
Address: Wivenhoe Park, Colchester, Essex CO4 3SQ.
Tel: ((0)1206) 872558; Fax: ((0)1206) 873627.

University of Glasgow – Department of Sociology
Address: Glasgow G12 8QQ.
Tel: ((0)141) 339 8855; Fax: ((0)141) 330 4808.

University of Hertfordshire – Department of Culture and Communication
Address: College Lane, Hatfield, Hertfordshire AL10 9AB.
Tel: ((0)1707) 284000; Fax: ((0)1707) 284115.

Highbury College of Technology – Department of Communication and Media Studies
Address: Dovercourt Road, Cosham, Portsmouth, Hampshire PO6 2DA.
Tel: ((0)705) 383131; Fax: ((0)705) 325551.

University of Hull – Department of Philosophy
Address: Cottingham Road, Hull HU6 7RX.
Tel: ((0)1482) 46311; Fax: ((0)1482) 465936.

Keele University – Centre for Contemporary Ethical Studies
Address: School of Law, Keele University, Staffordshire ST5 5BG.
Tel: ((0)782) 621111; Fax: ((0)7820) 613847.

University of Kent at Canterbury – Department of Communications and Image Studies
Address: Canterbury, Kent CT2 7NZ.
Tel: ((0)1227) 764000; Fax: ((0)1227) 452196.

University of Leeds – Centre for Business and Professional Ethics
Address: Leeds LS2 9JT.
Tel: ((0)113) 243 1751; Fax: ((0)113) 233 6017.

University of Leeds – Institute of Communication Studies
Address: Leeds LS2 9JT.
Tel: ((0)113) 243 1751; Fax: ((0)113) 233 6017.

University of Leicester – Centre for Mass Communication Research
Address: 104 Regent Road, Leicester LE1 7LT.
Tel. ((0)116) 252 5293.
Note: Postgraduate research and teaching unit; contribute to public debate and inform policy on the major media and communication issues of the day.

University of Liverpool – School of Politics and Communication Studies
Address: Liverpool L69 3BX.
Tel: ((0)151) 794 2000; Fax: ((0)151) 708 6502.

University of London, Goldsmiths College – Department of Media and Communications
Address: New Cross, London SE14 6NW.
Tel: ((0)171) 919 7171; Fax: ((0)171) 919 7113.

University of London, Institute of Education – Department of English, Media and Drama
Address: Institute of Education, 20 Bedford Way, London WC1H 0AL.
Tel: ((0)171) 580 1122; Fax: ((0)171) 612 6126.

University of London, King's College – Business Ethics Research Centre
Address: King's College, Strand, London WC2R 2LS.
Tel: ((0)171) 873 2587; Fax: ((0)171) 873 2265.

University of London, King's College – British Institute of Human Rights
Address: King's College, Strand, London WCR2 2LS.
Tel: ((0)171) 836 5454; Fax: ((0)171) 836 1799.

London Business School – Centre for Marketing and Communications
Address: Sussex Place, Regent's Park, London NW1 4SA.
Tel: ((0)171) 262 5050; Fax: ((0)171) 724 7875.

London, Morley College – Department of Philosophy and Mass Media
Address: 61 Westminster Bridge Road, London SE1 7HT.
Tel: ((0)171) 928 8501.

London, Guildhall University – Department of Communications
Address: 31 Jewry Street, London EC3 2EY.
Tel: ((0)171) 320 3086.

London School of Economics and Political Science – Media and Communications
Address: Houghton Street, London WC2A 2AE.
Tel: ((0)171) 955 7710.

University of Luton – School of Media Arts
Address: Park Square, Luton, Bedfordshire LU1 3JU.
Tel: ((0)582) 401401; Fax: ((0)582) 405401.

Manchester Metropolitan University – Department of Communication Media
Address: All Saints, Manchester M15 6BH.
Tel: ((0)161) 247 2000; Fax: ((0)161) 247 6390.

Sheffield Hallam University – School of Cultural Studies
Address: 36 Collegiate Crescent, Sheffield S10 2BP.
Tel. ((0)114) 253 2236.

Sheffield Hallam University – Northern Media School
Address: The Workstation, 15 Paternoster Row, Sheffield S1 2BX.
Tel: ((0)114) 253 4602.

University of Stirling – Department of Film and Media Studies
Address: Stirling FK9 4LA.
Tel: ((0)1786) 473171; Fax: ((0)1786) 463000.

University of Strathclyde – John Logie Baird Centre for Research in Television, Film and Music
Address: Glasgow G1 1XH.
Tel: ((0)141) 553 4150.

University of Strathclyde – Scottish Centre for Journalism Studies
Address: 26 Richmond Street, Glasgow G1 1XH.
Tel: ((0)141) 552 4400-9; Fax: ((0)141) 552 0775.

University of Sussex – Department of Philosophy
Address: Sussex House, Falmer, Brighton, East Sussex BN1 9RH.
Tel: ((0)1273) 606 755; Fax: ((0)1273) 678 335.

University of Wales, College of Cardiff – Centre for Applied Ethics
Address: Cathays Park, Cardiff CF1 3XA.

University of Wales, College of Cardiff – School of English Studies, Communication and Philosophy
Address: PO Box 920, Cardiff CF1 3XP.
Tel: ((0)1222) 874000; Fax: ((0)1222) 874478.

University of Wales, College of Cardiff – Centre for Journalism Studies
Address: Bute Building, King Edward VII Avenue, Cathays Park, Cardiff CF1 3NB.
Tel: ((0)1222) 394069.

University of Westminster – Centre for Communication and Information Studies and School of Communications
Address: Northwick Park Campus, Watford Road, Harrow, Middlesex HA1 3TP.
Tel: ((0)171) 911 5000: Fax: ((0)171) 911 5939.

F.

Association for Cultural and Communication Studies (ACCS)
Address: c/o Department of Literature and Languages, Nottingham Trent University, Clifton Site, Nottingham NG11 8NS.
Tel: ((0)115) 941 8418; Fax: ((0)115) 948 6632.

British Film Institute
Address: 21 Stephen Street, London W1P 2LN.
Tel: ((0)171) 255 1444; Fax: ((0)171) 436 7950.
Aims: To encourage the development of the art of film and television. Library.

Catholic Communications Centre
Address: 39 Eccleston Square, London SW1P 1PD.
Tel: ((0)171) 233 8196; Fax: ((0)171) 630 5166.
Aims: Promotion and training for Christian communication and media work.

Centre for Business and Public Sector Ethics
Address: Lilac Place, Champneys Walk, Cambridge CB3 9AW.
Tel: ((0)1223) 68050; Fax: ((0)1223) 327024.
Aims: To develop teaching and practice of professional knowledge on ethics and corporate responsibility and the upholding of standards of conduct in government, business and the professions; linked with Cambridge and Harvard Universities.

Institute for Public Policy Research (IPPR)
Address: 30–32 Southampton Street, London WC2E 7RA.
Tel: ((0)171) 470 6100; Fax: ((0)171) 470 6111.
Publications: *New media, new policies*; *Reservoirs of dogma.*

Media Studies Association
Address: c/o The School of Communication, Trinity and All Saints College, Brownberrie Lane, Horsforth, Leeds LS18 5HD.
Tel: ((0)532) 584 341.

National Council for the Training of Journalists
Address: Lotton Bush Centre, Southern Way, Harlow, Essex CM18 7BL.
Tel: ((0)274) 430009; Fax: ((0)274) 438008.

Yugoslavia

See **Serbia**; see also **Bosnia-Herzegovina**; **Croatia**; **Macedonia**; **Slovakia**; **Slovenia**.

Africa

B.

Southern African Broadcasting Association
Address: PO Box 4720, Harare, Zimbabwe.
Tel: (+263) (4) 723866; Fax: (+263) (4) 723867.
Aims: Exchange system for African produced programmes.

Union of African Journalists
Address: 12A Haroun Street, Dokki, Giza, Egypt.
Tel: (+20) (2) 3497922; Fax: (+20) (2) 713261.

Union des Radiodiffusions et Télévisions Nationales d'Afrique
(Union of National Radio and Television Organizations of Africa)
Address: 101 rue Carnot, BP 3237, Dakar, Senegal.
Tel: (+221) 211 625; Fax: (+221) 225 113.

West African Journalists' Union
Address: 135 rue Carnot, BP 4130, Dakar, Senegal.
Tel: (+221) 223 625.

C.

Association des Professionelles Africaines de la Communication (APAC)
Address: BP 4234, Dakar, Senegal.

Federation of East African Journalists' Associations
Address: 40–42 William Street, PO Box 14058, Kampala, Uganda.
Tel: (+256) (41) 234 538.
Aims: Organization for journalists in ten East African countries.

Pan-African Writers' Association
Address: PO Box C450, Cantonments, Accra, Ghana.
Tel: (+233) (21) 773062; Fax: (+233) (21) 773042.

F.

African Council for Communication Education – Institute for Communication Development and Research
Address: PO Box 47495, Nairobi, Kenya.
Tel: (+254) (2) 27043.
Publication: *Africa Media Review*.

Algeria (+213)

A.

Ministry of Communications and Culture
Address: Palais de la Culture, Les Annassers, Kouba, Algiers.
Tel: (2) 672420.

Enterprise Nationale de Radiodiffusion
(Radiodiffusion Télévision Algérienne)
Address: Immeuble RTA, 21 Boulevard des Martyrs, Algiers.
Tel: (2) 590700; Fax: (2) 605814.

B.

Union Générale des Travailleurs Algériens (UGTA)
(Secteur Information, Formation et Culture)
Address: Maison du Peuple, Place du 1er Mai, Algiers.
Tel: (2) 685200.

E.

Université d'Alger – Institut de l'Information et de la Communication
Address: 11 Chemin Mokhtar Doudon ITFC, Ben-Aknoun, Algiers.

Angola (+244)

A.

Ministerio da Comunicação Social
Address: Avenida Comandante Valódia, CP 2608 Luanda.
Tel: (2) 342818; Fax: (2) 392649.

Radio Nacional de Angola
Address: Rua Comandante Gika, CP 1329, Luanda.
Tel: (2) 321558; Fax: (2) 324647.

Televisão Popular de Angola (TPA)
Address: Avenida Ho Chi Min, PO Box 2604, Luanda.
Tel: (2) 320240; Fax: (2) 391091.

C.

União dos Escritores Angolanos
(Association of Angolan Writers)
Address: CP 2767-C, Luanda.
Tel: (2) 322155.

Benin (+229)

A.

Ministry of Communications, Culture and Information
Address: BP 120, Cotonou.
Tel: 315 931.

Haute Autorité de l'Audiovisuel et de la Communication
Address: Cotonou.

Office de Radiodiffusion et Télévision du Benin
Address: BP 366, Cotonou.
Tel: 300 359; Fax: 300 448.

Botswana (+267)

A.

Department of Information and Broadcasting
Address: Private Bag 0060, Gaborone.
Tel: 352 861; Fax: 357 138.

Gaborone Broadcasting Corporation
Address: PO Box 921, Gaborone.
Tel: 357 654; Fax: 301 875.

Radio Botswana
Address: Private Bag 0060, Gaborone.
Tel: 352 541; Fax: 357 138.

Burkina Faso (+226)

A.

Ministry of Communications and Culture
Address: 01 BP 2507, Ouagadougou 01.
Tel: 307052; Fax: 307056.

Direction de la Press Écrite
Address: Ouagadougou.

Radiodiffusion-Télévision Nationale du Burkina
Address: 03 BP 7029, Ouagadougou 03.
Tel: 324055; Fax: 310441.

Burundi (+257)

A.

Ministry of Communications
Address: Bujumbura.

La Radio-Télévision Nationale du Burundi
Address: BP 1900, Bujumbura.
Tel: (2) 23742; Fax: (2) 2654.

Cameroon (+237)

A.

Ministry of Communications
Address: BP 1588, Yaoundé.
Tel: 223155; Fax: 233022.

Office de Radiodiffusion-Télévision Camerounaise (CRTV)
Address: Mballa 2, BP 1634, Yaoundé.
Tel: 214088; Fax: 204340.

E.

Université de Yaoundé – École Supérieur des Sciences et Techniques de l'Information et de la Communication
Address: BP 337, Yaoundé.
Tel: 220744; Fax: 221320.

Central African Republic (+236)

A.

Ministry of Communication, Arts and Culture
Address: BP 1290, Bangui.

Radiodiffusion-Télévision Centrafricaine
Address: Avenue des Martyrs, BP 940, Bangui.
Tel: (61) 2588; Fax: (61) 6102.

Chad (+235)

A.

Ministry of Posts and Telecommunications
Address: N'Djamena.

Radiodiffusion Nationale Tchadienne
Address: BP 892, N'Djamena.
Tel: 516071.

Congo (+242)

A.

Ministry of Communications
Address: Brazzaville.

National Communications Council
Address: Brazzaville.

Radiodiffusion-Télévision Congolaise
Address: BP 2241, Brazzaville.
Tel: 815152; Fax: 835152.

Democratic Republic of Congo

See Zaïre.

Côte d'Ivoire (+225)

A.

Ministry of Communications
Address: BP V138, Abidjan.
Tel: 211116; Fax: 222297.

Radiodiffusion-Télévision Ivoirienne (RTI)
Address: Boulevard André Laville, BP 883, Abidjan 01.
Tel: 449039; Fax: 447389.

B.

Association de la Presse Democratique Ivoirienne
Address: Abidjan

E.

Université Nationale de Côte d'Ivoire – Department of Communication Science
Address: 01 BP V34, Abidjan 01.
Tel: 439000.

Arab Republic of Egypt (+20)

A.

Ministry of Information
Address: Radio and Television Building, Sharia Maspiro, Corniche El-Nil, Cairo.
Tel: (2) 974216.

Ministry of Communications
Address: 29 Sharia Ramesis, Cairo.
Tel: (2) 909090.

Egyptian Radio and Television Union (ERTU)
Address: Radio and Television Building, POB 504, Sharia Maspiro, Corniche El-Nil, Cairo.
Tel: (2) 749508; Fax: (2) 746989.

B.

General Trade Union of Press, Printing and Information
Address: 90 Sharia el-Galaa, Cairo.
Tel: (2) 740324.
Code: *Charter of work; Code of ethics in the press.*

Syndicate of Egyptian Journalists
Address: Abdel Khalek Tharwal St, Cairo.
Tel: (2) 3930242.

E.

American University in Cairo – Department of Mass Communication
Address: PO Box 2511, 113 Sharia Kasr El-Aini, Cairo.
Tel: (2) 3542969.

Cairo University – Faculty of Mass Communication
Address: PO Box 12611, Orman, Giza, Cairo.
Tel: (2) 5729584; Fax: (2) 628884.

Eritrea (+291)

A.

Ministry of Information and Culture
Address: PO Box 242, Asmara.
Tel: (1) 115171; Fax: (1) 119847.

Communications and Postal Authority
Address: PO Box 234, Asmara.
Tel: (1) 112900; Fax: (1) 110938.

Voice of the Broad Masses of Eritrea
Address: Ministry of Information, Radio Division, PO Box 872, Asmara.

ERI TV
Address: PO Box 243, Asmara.
Tel: (1) 119100; Fax: (1) 123906.

Ethiopia (+251)

A.

Ministry of Information
Address POB 1364, Addis Ababa.
Tel: (1) 550011; Fax: (1) 553855.
Note: Controls newspapers, radio, TV and Ethiopian News Agency.

Telecommunications Authority of Ethiopia
Address: POB 1047, Addis Ababa.
Tel: (1) 510500.

Radio Ethiopia
Address: POB 1020, Addis Ababa.
Tel: (1) 121011.

Television Ethiopia
Address: POB 5544, Patriot St, Addis Ababa.
Tel: (1) 116701.

B.

Ethiopian Journalists' Association
Address: POB 5911, Addis Ababa.
Tel: (1) 128198.

Gabon (+241)

A.

Ministry for Communication, Culture, Arts and Mass Education
Address: BP 1007, Libreville.
Tel: 763755; Fax: 726054.

Radiodiffusion Télévision Gabonaise
Address: BP 2229, Libreville.
Tel and Fax: 763291.

Gambia (+220)

A.

Ministry of Works, Communication and Information
Address: Half Die, Banjul.
Tel: 228251.

Press Council
Address: Banjul.
Code: *Press code* (covering defamation, right of reply, etc.).

Gambia Television and Radio
Address: Mile 7, Banjul.
Tel: 225060; Fax: 227230.
Note: Non-commercial government service of information, education and entertainment.

Ghana (+253)

A.

Ministry of Information
Address: POB M41 Ministries Post Office, Accra.
Tel: (21) 228011.

Ghana Broadcasting Corporation
Address: Broadcasting House, POB 1633, Accra.
Tel: (21) 221161; Fax: (21) 221153.

B.

Ghana Journalists Association
Address: PO Box 2118, Accra.
Tel: (21) 665135.

Private Newspaper Publishers' Association of Ghana
Address: PO Box 125, Darkuman, Accra.

C.

Ghana Association of Writers
Address: PO Box 4414, Accra.

E.

University of Ghana – School of Communication Studies
Address: PO Box 53, Legon, Accra.
Tel: (21) 667706; Fax: (21) 667701.

Guinea (+224)

A.

Radiodiffusion-Télévision Guinéenne (RTG)
Address: BP 391, Conakry.
Tel: 441411; Fax: 441697.

B.

Association Guinéenne des Éditeurs de la Press Indépendente
Address: Conakry.

Kenya (+254)

A.

Ministry of Information and Broadcasting
Address: Jogoo House, POB 30025, Nairobi.
Tel: (2) 334688; Fax: (2) 333791.

Kenya Broadcasting Corporation (KBC)
Address: Broadcasting House, POB 30456, Nairobi.
Tel: (2) 334567; Fax: (2) 220675
Note: State corporation responsible for radio and television services.

B.

Kenya Publishers' Association
Address: POB 18650, Nairobi.
Tel: (2) 223262; Fax: (2) 339875.

Kenya Union of Journalists
Address: POB 47035, Nairobi.
Tel: (2) 337669.

E.

University of Nairobi – School of Journalism
Address: PO Box 30197, Nairobi.
Tel: (2) 334244; Fax: (2) 336885.

Lesotho (+266)

A.

Ministry of Information and Broadcasting
PO Box 36, Maseru 100.
Tel: 323561; Fax: 310003.

Lesotho National Broadcasting Service
Address: PO Box 552, Maseru 100.
Tel: 323651; Fax: 310003.

Liberia (+231)

A.

Ministry of Information
Address: PO Box 9021, Capitol Hill, Monrovia.
Tel: 222229.

Liberian Broadcasting Corporation
Address: PO Box 10-594, 1000 Monrovia.
Tel: 224984.

B.

Press Union of Liberia
Address: YMCA Building, 12 Broad Street, Monrovia.

Libya (+218)

A.

Libyan Jamahiriya Broadcasting Corporation
Address: PO Box 333, Souk al Jama, Tripoli.
Tel: (21) 3332451; Fax: (21) 3333470.

Madagascar (+261)

A.

Radio-Television Malagasy
Address: BP 1202, Antananarivo.
Tel: (2) 22381.

Malawi (+265)

A.

Department of Information
Address: PO Box 494, Blantyre.
Tel: 620266.

Malawi Broadcasting Corporation (MBC)
Address: PO Box 30133, Chichiri, Blantyre 3.
Tel: 671222; Fax: 671257.

Mali (+223)

A.

Office de Radiodiffusion-Télévision Malienne
Address: BP 171, Bamako.
Tel: (22) 2019; Fax: (22) 4205.

Mauritius (+230)

A.

Mauritius Broadcasting Corporation
Address: PO Box 48, Louis Pasteur Street, Curepipe.
Tel: 675 5001; Fax: 675 7332.

Morocco (+212)

A.

Ministry of Information
Address: Avenue Mohamed V, Place de la Grande Poste, Rabat.
Tel: (7) 766016; Fax: (7) 768755.

Ministry of Posts and Telecommunications
Address: Avenue Moulay Hassan, Rabat.
Tel: (7) 702091; Fax: (7) 705641.

Radiodiffusion-Télévision Marocaine
Address: 1 Zenkat el-Brihi, BP 1042, Rabat.
Tel: (7) 705434; Fax: (7) 722047.

B.

Syndicat National de la Presse Marocaine
Address: rue du Prince Moulay Abdullah, Rabat.
Tel: (7) 69331.

Mozambique (+258)

A.

Televisão de Moçambique (TVM)
Address: 942 Avenida Julius Nyerere, Maputo.
Tel: (1) 491359; Fax: (1) 491059.

B.

Organizacão Nacional dos Jornalistos
Address: Avenida 24 de Julho 231, Maputo.
Tel: (1) 492031.

Namibia (+264)

A.

Ministry of Information and Broadcasting
Legislation: *Broadcasting Act 1991*.

Namibian Communications Commission
Address: Private Bag 13309, Windhoek.
Tel: (61) 222666; Fax: (61) 222790.

Namibian Broadcasting Corporation
Address: PO Box 321, Windhoek 9000.
Tel: (61) 2919111; Fax: (61) 217760.
Code: *Policy code* (1990).

Nigeria (+234)

A.

Ministry of Communications
Address: Headquarters, Lafiaji, Lagos.
Tel: (1) 2633747.

Ministry of Information
Address: 15 Awolo Road SW, Ikoyi, Lagos.
Tel: (1) 680358.

Nigerian Broadcasting Commission
Address: PO Box 55021, Lagos.
Tel: (1) 2647867; Fax: (1) 2647868.

Federal Radio Corporation of Nigeria (FRCN)
Address: Broadcasting House, Ikoyi, PMB 12504, Lagos.
Tel: (1) 2690301; Fax: (1) 2690073.

Nigerian Television Authority (NTA)
Address: Television House, Ahmadu Bello Way, Victoria Island, PMB 21165, Lagos.
Tel: (1) 2615949; Fax: (1) 2610289.

B.

Association of Advertising Practitioners of Nigeria (AAPN)
Address: 18 Amore Street, Ikeja, PMB 1054, Ebute-Metta, Lagos.
Code: *Nigerian code of advertising practice.*

Nigerian Union of Journalists
Address: National Theatre, Iganmu, PMB 12756, Lagos.
Tel: (1) 801290.

Nigerian Publishers' Association
Address: The Ori-Detu, 1st Floor, Shell Close, Onireke, GPO Box 2541, Ibadan.
Tel: (2) 411557.

C.

Nigerian Institute of Public Relations
Address: PO Box 6103, Lagos.

E.

Ahmadu Bello University – Department of Mass Communication
Address: Zaria.
Tel: (69) 50581-5; Fax: (69) 50022.

Bayero University – Department of Mass Communication
Address: PMB 3011, Kano.
Tel: (64) 666021; Fax: (64) 665904.

Enugu State University of Science and Technology – Department of Mass Communication
Address: Independence Layout, PMB 01660, Enugu.
Tel: (42) 451244; Fax: (42) 335765.

University of Lagos – Department of Mass Communication
Address: Lagos.
Tel: (1) 821111; Fax: (1) 822644.

University of Maiduguri – Department of Mass Communication
Address: Bama Road, PMB 1069, Maiduguri, Borno State.
Tel: (76) 231730.

University of Nigeria – Department of Mass Communication
Address: Nsukka Campus, Enugu State.
Tel: (42) 771911; (42) 770644.

Rwanda (+250)

A.

Ministry of Transport and Communications
Address: BP 720, Kigali.
Tel: 72424.

Radiodiffusion de la République Rwandaise
Address: BP 83, Kigali.
Tel: 75665; Fax: 76185.

Senegal (+221)

A.

Ministry of Culture and Communications
Address: 58 Boulevard de la République, Dakar.
Tel: 231065; Fax: 214504.

Société Nationale de Radiodiffusion-Télévision Sénégalaise (RTS)
Address: BP 1765, Triangle Sud, Dakar.
Tel: 217801; Fax: 223490.

B.

Press Club
Address: Rue Carde et Avenue Jean XXIII, BP 117, Dakar.
Tel: 229164.

Syndicat National des Professionels de l'Information
Address: 18 rue Raffenel, Dakar.
Tel: 227509.

Sierra Leone (+232)

A.

Ministry of Information and Broadcasting
Address: Youyi Building, 8th Floor, Brookfields, Freetown.
Tel: (22) 240034; Fax: (22) 240034.

Sierra Leone Broadcasting Service
Address: New England, Freetown.
Tel: (22) 240123; Fax: (22) 240922.

South Africa (+27)

A.

Ministry of Communications
Address: Telekom Towers South, 25th Floor, Room 2523, corner of Bosman and Vermeulen Streets, Pretoria 0001.
Tel: (12) 3261110; Fax: (12) 341 1389.

Directorate of Publications
Address: Pleinpark Building, 13th Floor, Plein Street, Cape Town, Private Bag X9069, Cape Town 8000.
Tel: (21) 45618; Fax: (21) 456511.
Aims: Government agency for censorship of films and video and publications.

Independent Broadcasting Authority (IBA)
Address: 26 Baker Street, Rosebank, Johannesburg.
Tel: (11) 4476180; Fax: (11) 4476187.
Aims: Independent regulatory body for the broadcasting – public, community and private.

South African Broadcasting Corporation
Address: Private Bag X1, Broadcasting Centre, Auckland Park 2006, Johannesburg.
Tel: (11) 7149111; Fax: (11) 7143106.

B.

Advertising Standards Authority of South Africa
Address: PO Box 91550, Auckland Park 2006.
Code: *Code of advertising practice.*

Community Press Association of Southern Africa
Address: 8th Floor, 33 Bath Avenue, Rosebank 2196.
Tel: (11) 4471266; Fax: (11) 4471289.

Newspaper Press Union of Southern Africa
Address: Nedbank Gardens, 8th Floor, 33 Bath Avenue, Rosebank 2196. PO Box 47180.
Tel: (11) 4471264; Fax: (11) 4471289.

Print Media Association of Southern Africa
Address: PO Box 47180, Parklands 2121.
Tel: (11) 4471264; Fax: (11) 4471289.

Public Relations Institute of Southern Africa
Address: PO Box 31749, Braamfontein 2017.
Tel: (11) 7267356.

South Africa Media Council
Address: Nedbank Gardens, 8th Floor, 33 Bath Avenue, Rosebank 2196. PO Box 31559.
Tel: (11) 4032878; Fax: (11) 4032879.
Aims: Formed by Newspaper Press Union and Conference of Editors to promote press freedom.

South African Publishers' Association
Address: PO Box 1001, Kalk Bay 7990.
Tel: (21) 7886470; Fax: (21) 7886469.

E.

University of Natal – Centre for Cultural and Media Studies
Address: Durban Campus, Private Bag X10, Dalbridge 4014.
Tel: (31) 260 2204; Fax: (31) 260 2206.

Potchefstroom University for Christian Higher Education – Institute for Communications Research
Address: Private Bag X6001, Potchefstroom 2520.
Tel: (148) 299 1111; Fax: (148) 299 2799.

Rhodes University – Department of Journalism and Media Studies
Address: PO Box 94, Grahamstown 6140.
Tel: (461) 318111; Fax: (461) 25049.

University of South Africa – Department of Communications
Address: PO Box 392, Pretoria 0001.
Tel: (12) 4293111; Fax: (12) 4293221.

Stellenbosch University – Department of Journalism
Address: Private Bag X1, Matieland 7602.
Tel: (21) 808-9111; Fax: (21) 808-4336/4499.

Sudan (+249)

A.

Ministry of Culture and Information
Address: PO Box 2651, Khartoum.
Tel: (11) 79850.

Sudan National Broadcasting Corporation
Address: PO Box 1094, Omdurman.
Tel: (11) 55022.

Swaziland (+268)

A.

Ministry of Broadcasting, Information and Tourism
Address: PO Box 338, Mbabane
Tel: 4303617; Fax: 42093.

Swaziland Broadcasting Service
Address: PO Box 338, Mbabane.
Tel: 47263; Fax: 42774.

Swaziland Television Authority
Address: PO Box A146, Swazi Plaza, Hospital Hill, Mbabane.
Tel: 4303617; Fax: 42093.

Tanzania (+255)

A.

Tanzanian Broadcasting Commission
Address: PO Box 1516, Dar es Salaam.
Tel: (51) 22186.

Radio Tanzania
Address: PO Box 9191, Dar es Salaam.
Tel: (51) 860760; Fax: (51) 865577.

Togo (+228)

A.

Ministry of Communications and Culture
Address: Lomé.

Radiodiffusion Togolaise
Address: BP 434, Lomé.
Tel: 212493.

Tunisia (+216)

A.

Le Conseil Supérieur de la Communication
Address: Avenue de la Liberté, Tunis.
Tel: (1) 793436; Fax: (1) 794363.
Code: *Press code* (1975).

Établissement de la Radiodiffusion-Télévision Tunisienne
Address: 71 Avenue de la Liberté, Tunis 1002.
Tel: (1) 780088; Fax: (1) 785146.

B.

Association des Journalistes Tunisiens
Address: 15 rue Ali Bach Hamba, Tunis.
Tel: (1) 258374.

C.

Union des Écrivains Tunisiens
Address: 20 Avenue de Paris, 1000 Tunis.

E.

Université des Lettres, des Arts et des Sciences Humaines (Tunis 1) – Institute of Journalism and Information Sciences
Address: 29 rue Asdrubal, 1002 Tunis.
Tel: (1) 788068; Fax: (1) 786776.

Uganda (+256)

A.

Ministry of Information and Broadcasting
Address: PO Box 7142, Kampala.
Tel: (41) 254410; Fax: (41) 256888.

Radio Uganda
Address: Ministry of Information and Broadcasting, PO Box 2038, Kampala.
Tel: (41) 257256; Fax: (41) 257252.

Uganda Television (UTV)
Address: PO Box 4260, Kampala.
Tel: (41) 257256; Fax: (41) 256888.

E.

Uganda Martyrs University – Institute of Ethics and Development Studies
Address: PO Box 5498, Kampala.
Tel: (481) 21894; Fax: (481) 21898.

Zaïre (+243)

This information was compiled before the change of the country's name to Democratic Republic of Congo.

A.

Department of Press and Information
Address: BP 3171, Kinshasa.
Tel: (12) 23171.

La Voix du Zaïre
Address: Station Nationale, BP 3164, Kinshasa-Gombe.
Tel: (12) 23175.
Note: State controlled.

Zaïre Télévision
Address: BP 3171, Kinshasa-Gombe.
Tel: (12) 23175.
Note: Government commercial station.

B.

Union de la Presse du Zaïre
Address: BP 4941, Kinshasa 1.
Tel: (12) 24437.

F.

Institut des Sciences et Techniques de l'Information
Address: BP14.998, Kinshasa.

Zambia (+260)

A.

Ministry of Information and Broadcasting Services
Address: Independence Avenue, PO Box 51025, Lusaka.
Tel: (1) 254658; Fax: 25346.

Zambia National Broadcasting Corporation
Address: Broadcasting House, PO Box 50015, Lusaka.
Tel: (1) 254989; Fax: (1) 254317.

B.

Booksellers and Publishers Association of Zambia
Address: PO Box 31838, Lusaka.
Tel: (1) 222647; Fax: (1) 225195.

Press Association of Zambia
Address: c/o The Times of Zambia, PO Box 30394, Lusaka.
Tel: (1) 229076.

E.

University of Zambia – Department of Mass Communication
Address: PO Box 32379, Lusaka.
Tel: (1) 213221; Fax: (1) 253952.

Zimbabwe (+263)

A.

Ministry of Information, Posts and Telecommunications
Address: Linquenda House, Baker Avenue, PO Box 825, Causeway, Harare.
Tel: (4) 703894; Fax: (4) 707213.

Zimbabwe Broadcasting Corporation
Address: PO Box 444, Highlands, Harare.
Tel: (4) 498630; Fax: (4) 498613.

B.

Zimbabwe Association of Journalists
Address: 88 Union Avenue, PO Box 872, Harare.

C.

Zimbabwe Writers Union
Address: PO Box MP 167, Mount Pleasant, Harare.

Asia

B.

Asia-Pacific Broadcasting Union (ABU)
Address: POB 1164, Jalan Pantai Bharu, 59700 Kuala Lumpur, Malaysia.
Tel: (+60) (3) 282 3592; Fax: (+60) (3) 230 5292.
Aims: Founded in 1964 to assist development of radio and television in the Asia–Pacific area, particularly for educational purposes.

Confederation of ASEAN Journalists (CAJ)
Address: Jalan Kebon Siri, no. 34, Jakarta 10110, Indonesia.
Tel: (+62) (21) 3453131; Fax: (+62) (21) 3453175.

Press Foundation of Asia (PFA)
Address: POB 1843, 1500 Roxas Boulevard, Manila, Philippines.
Tel: (+63) (2) 598633; Fax: (+63) (2) 5224365.
Aims: Founded in 1967 to act as a professional forum for newspaper organizations, to improve editorial and management techniques through research and training programmes, and to encourage the growth of Asian newspapers.

F.

Asia-Pacific Institute for Broadcasting Development
Address: PO Box 1137, Pantai, 59700 Kuala Lumpur, Malaysia.
Tel: (+60) (3) 2821046; Fax: (+60) (3) 2822761.
Aims: To service the professional and training needs of broadcasters in the Asia–Pacific region.

Asian Institute for Development Communication (AIDCOM)
Address: ADDC Building, Persiavan Duta, 50480 Kuala Lumpur, Malaysia
Tel: (+60) (3) 254 2558; Fax: (+60) (3) 254 3785.

Asian Mass Communication Research and Information Centre (AMIC)
Address: 39 Newton Road, Singapore 1130.
Tel: (+65) 251 5106; Fax: (+65) 253 4525.

Afghanistan (+93)

A.

Ministry of Communication
Address: Puli Bag-i-Omom, Kabul.
Tel: 21341.

Radio-Television of Afghanistan
Address: POB 544, Ansari Watt, Kabul.
Tel: 25622.

ASIA 309

B.

Journalists' Association
Address: Kabul, Afghanistan

Union of Journalists of Afghanistan
Address: Wazir Akbar Khan Mena Street 13, Kabul, Afghanistan.

Armenia (+374)

A.

Ministry of Communications
Address: Tumanian Street 5, 375002 Yerevan.
Tel: (2) 561920; Fax: (2) 523922.

State Television and Radio Broadcasting
Address: A. Manukian Street 5, 375025 Yerevan.
Tel: (2) 555033.
Note: Responsible for Armenian Radio and Armenian Television.

Azerbaijan (+994)

A.

Ministry of Communications, Information and the Press
Address: A. Yarayev Street 12, 37001 Baku.
Tel: (12) 926357; Fax: (12) 936536.

Radio and Television Company of Azerbaijan
Address: Mekhti Hussein Street 1, 370011 Baku.
Tel: (12) 924426; Fax: (12) 932470.
Note: Responsible for Radio Baku and Azerbaijan National Television.

E.

Baku State University – Department of Journalism
Address: ul. Z. Khalilova 23, 370145 Baku.
Tel: (12) 390186; Fax: (12) 380582.

Bahrain (+973)

A.

Ministry of Information
Address: PO Box 1075, Manama.
Tel: 781888; Fax: 681544.

Bahrain Radio and Television Corporation
Address: POB 1075, Manama.
Tel: 781888; Fax: 681544.

C.

Bahrain Writers and Literators Association
Address: PO Box 1010, Manama.

Bangladesh (+880)

A.

Ministry of Communications
Address: Bangladesh Secretariat, Bhaban 7, 1st 9-Storey Building, 8th Floor, Dhaka.

Ministry of Information
Address: Bangladesh Secretariat, 2nd 9-Storey Building, 8th Floor, Dhaka
Tel: (2) 235111.

National Broadcasting Authority (NBA)
Address: NBA House, 121 Kazi Nazrul Islam Avenue, Dhaka 1219.
Tel: (2) 410010; Fax: (2) 833927.
Note: Government body responsible for Radio Bangladesh and Bangladesh Television (BTV).

B.

Bangladesh Council of Newspapers and News Agencies
Address: Dhaka.
Tel: (2) 413256.

Bangladesh Federal Union of Journalists
Address: National Press Club Building, 18 Topkhana Road, Dhaka 1000.
Tel: (2) 254777.

Bangladesh Publishers and Booksellers Association
Address: 3rd Floor, 3 Liquat Avenue, Dhaka.

C.

Press Institute of Bangladesh
Address: 3 Circuit House Road, Dhaka.
Tel: (2) 405914.

E.

University of Dhaka – Department of Mass Communication and Journalism
Address: Ramna, Dhaka 1000.
Tel: (2) 505180-9; Fax: (2) 865583.

Cambodia (+855)

A.

Ministry of Information and the Press
Address: 62 Boulevard Preah Monivong, Phnom Penh.
Tel: (23) 426235; Fax: (23) 426059.

National Radio of Cambodia
Address: rue Preah Kossamak, Phnom Penh.
Tel: (23) 723369; Fax: (23) 427319.

Television Kampuchea (TVK)
Address: 19 Street 242 Chatomuk, Phnom Penh.
Tel: (23) 241269; Fax: (23) 426407.

B.

Khmer Journalists' Association
Address: 101 Boulevard Preah Norodom, Phnom Penh.
Tel: (23) 725459.

China (+86)

A.

Ministry of Radio, Film and Television
Address: 2 Fu Xing Men Wai Dajie, POB 4501, Beijing 100844.
Tel: (10) 68512175; Fax: (10) 68512174.

China National Radio
Address: 2 Fu Xing Men Wai Dajie, Beijing 100866.

China Central Television Station (CCTV)
Address: Bureau of Broadcasting Affairs of the State Council, 11 Fuxinglu, Beijing 100859.
Tel: (10) 68506755; Fax: (10) 68513025.

The Press and Publication Administration of the People's Republic of China
Address: 85 Dongsi Nan Dajie, Beijing 100703.
Tel: (10) 65124433; Fax: (10) 65127875.

B.

Association of China Newspapers Association
Address: Beijing

All China Journalists' Association
Address: Xijiaominxiang, Beijing 100031.
Tel: (10) 66023981; Fax: (10) 66014658.

E.

Fudan University – School of Journalism
Address: Handan Road, Shanghai 200 433.
Tel: (21) 5492222; Fax: (21) 5491875.

Nanjing University – Department of Mass Communication
Address: 22 Hankou Road, Nanjing, Jiangsu 210093.
Tel: 6637651; Fax: 3302728.

Xiamen University – Department of Journalism and Communication
Address: 422 Siming Road S, Xiamen, Fujian 361005.
Tel: 225102; Fax: 227402.

F.

Journalism Institute
Address: Chinese Academy of Social Sciences, PO Box 2011, 2 Jintai Road W, Chaoyang District, Beijing 100026.
Tel: (10) 65022868; Fax: (10) 65022868.

Hong Kong (+852)

A.

Department for Broadcasting, Entertainment and Administration
Address: Government Secretariat, Revenue Tower, 5 Gloucester Road, Wang Chai.
Tel: 2827 4672; Fax: 2827 6646.

Television and Licensing Authority
Address: Wangchai Tower III, 5 Gloucester Road, Wang Chai.
Tel: 2594 5731; Fax: 2507 2219.

Radio and Television Hong Kong (RTHK)
Address: Broadcasting House, 30 Broadcast Drive, Kowloon.
Tel: 2339 6300; Fax: 2338 0279.
Note: Government funded.
Codes: *Television code of practice on programme standards*; *Television code of practice on advertising standards.*

B.

Association of Accredited Advertising Agents of Hong Kong
Address: 504–505 Dominion Gate, 43–59A Queen's Road Central, Hong Kong.
Code: *Standards of practice.*

Hong Kong Chinese Press Association
Address: 3/F, 48 Gage Street, Hong Kong.
Tel: 2543 9477.

Hong Kong Journalists Association
Address: Block B, 3rd Floor, Mercantile Building, O'Brian Road, Wan Chai.
Tel: 2291 6692; Fax: 2527 7325.

Hong Kong Publishers' and Distributors' Association
Address: National Building 4/F, 240–246 Nathan Road, Kowloon.
Tel: 2367 4412.

Newspaper Society of Hong Kong
Address: Culturecom Centre 7/F, 47 Hung To Road, Kowloon.
Tel: 2950 7129; Fax: 2763 9691.

Society of Hong Kong Publishers
Address: Worldcom Hong Kong Ltd, Room 502–503 Admiralty Centre, Tower 1, Harcourt Road, Hong Kong.
Tel: 2865 4007; Fax: 2865 2559.

E.

Chinese University of Hong Kong – Department of Journalism and Communication
Address: Shatin, New Territories.
Tel: 2609 6000; Fax: 2603 5544.

Hong Kong Baptist University – Centre for Applied Ethics
Address: 224 Waterloo Road, Kowloon.
Tel: 2339 7400.

F.

Chinese Language Press Institute
Address: Hong Kong.
Tel: 2561 6211.

India (+91)

A.

Ministry of Information and Broadcasting
Address: Shastri Bhavan, New Delhi 110 001.
Tel: (11) 384 340; Fax: (11) 383 513.
Note: Controls broadcasting by All India Radio and Doordarshan India.

All India Radio (AIR)
Address: Akashvani Bhaven, Parliament Street, New Delhi 110 001.
Tel: (11) 371 0006; Fax: (11) 371 4061.

Doordarshan India
(Television India)
Address: Mandi House, Doordarshan Bhavan, Copernicus Marg, New Delhi 110 001.
Tel: (11) 338 9644; Fax: (11) 338 6507.
Note: Public organization.

Press Information Bureau
Address: Shastri Bhavan, Dr Rajendra Prasad Road, New Delhi 110 001.
Tel: (11) 338 3643.

312 DIRECTORY OF SELECTED ORGANIZATIONS

Note: Co-ordinating body of press affairs for government, which represents newspaper managements, journalists, news agencies, and has the power to examine journalists and censor objectionable material.

B.

Advertising Standards Council of India (ASCI)
Address: 2nd Floor, Bakhtawar, Nariman Point, Bombay 400 021.
Code: *Code for self-regulation in advertising.*

All-India Newspaper Editors' Conference
Address: 36–37 Northend Complex, Rama Krishna Ashram Marg, New Delhi 110 001.
Tel: (11) 344 519.

Editors' Guild of India
Address: A2 First Floor, 28 Feroz Shah Road, New Delhi 110 001.

Federation of Indian Publishers
Address: Federation House, 18/1-C Institutional Area, near JNU, New Delhi 110 067.
Tel: (11) 696 4847; Fax: (11) 686 4054.

Indian Languages Newspapers' Association
Address: Janmabhoomi Bhavan, Janmabhoomi Marg, POB 10029, Fort Mumbai 400 001.
Tel: (22) 287 0537.

Indian Newspaper Society
Address: INS Buildings, Rafi Marg, New Delhi 110 001.
Tel: (11) 371 5401; Fax: (11) 372 3800.

Indian Federation of Working Journalists
Address: F-101, M.S. Apartments, Kasturba Gandhi Marg, New Delhi 110 001.
Tel: (11) 338 4956; Fax: (11) 338 4650.

National Council of Advertising Agencies
Address: 45 Panchkuin Road, New Delhi 110 001.

National Union of Journalists (India)
Address: 7 Jantar Mantar Road, 2nd Floor, New Delhi 110 001.
Tel: (11) 332 1610; Fax: (11) 335 2723.

E.

Banaras Hindu University – Department of Journalism and Mass Communications
Address: Varanasi, Uttar Pradesh 221005.
Tel: (542) 311558; Fax: (542) 312059.

Berhampur University – Department of Journalism and Mass Communication
Address: Bhanja Bihar, Berhampur, Orissa 760007.
Tel: (6812) 3404-6.

University of Calcutta – Department of Journalism
Address: 87 College Street, Calcutta, West Bengal 700073.
Tel: (33) 241 0071; Fax: (33) 241 3222.

Karnatak University – Department of Mass Communication and Journalism
Address: Dharwad, Karnataka.
Tel: (836) 42011-8; Fax: (836) 42464.

University of Kashmir – Media Education and Research Centre
Address: University Campus, Hazratbal, Srinagar.
Tel: (194) 52078; Fax: (194) 52357.

University of Kerala – Department of Journalism
Address: University Buildings, Thivuvananthapuram, Kerala.
Tel: (471) 445738; Fax: (471) 447158.

University of Madras – Department of Journalism and Communication
Address: Chepank, Triplicane PO, Madras, Tamil Nadu.
Tel: (44) 568778; Fax: (44) 566693.

Maharishi Dayanand University – Department of Journalism and Mass Communication
Address: Rohtak, Hatyana.
Tel: (1262) 32639; Fax: (1262) 31132.

ASIA

University of Mysore – Department of Journalism and Mass Communications
Address: Crawford Hall, PO Box 406, Mysore.
Tel: (821) 20161; Fax: (821) 21263.

Osmania University – Department of Journalism
Address: Hyderabad, Andhra Pradesh.
Tel: (40) 868951; Fax: (40) 8609020.

Panjab University – Department of Mass Communication
Address: Chandigarh 1600014.
Tel: (172) 541716.

Punjabi University – Department of Journalism and Mass Communication
Address: Patiala, Punjab.
Tel: (175) 822461-6; Fax: (175) 822418.

University of Rajasthan – Centre for Mass Communications
Address: Gandhinagar, Jaipur, Rajasthan 302004.
Tel: (141) 511070; Fax: (141) 511980.

Shiraji University – Department of Journalism and Communication Science
Address: Vidyanagar, Kolhapur, Maharashtra.
Tel: (231) 22571-4; Fax: (231) 24033.

F.

Jamia Millia Islamia – Mass Communication Research Centre
Address: Jamia Nagar, New Delhi 110 025.
Tel: (11) 683 1717; Fax: (11) 682 3190.

Press Institute of India/Research Institute for Newspaper Development
Address: Sapru House Annexe, Barakhamba Road, New Delhi 110 001.
Tel: (11) 331 8066; Fax: (11) 331 1975.

Indonesia (+62)

A.

Ministry of Information
Address: Jalan Merdeka Barat 9, Jakarta 10110.
Tel: (21) 384 1972; Fax: (21) 384 0046.

Ministry of Communications
Address: Jalan Merdeka Barat 8, Jakarta 10110.
Tel: (21) 345 5665; Fax: (21) 345 1657.

Directorate-General of Radio, Television and Film
Address: Jalan Merdeka Barat 9, Jakarta 10110.

Radio Republik Indonesia (RRI)
Address: Jalan Merdeka Barat 4–5, POB 356, Jakarta 10110.
Tel: (21) 384 9091; Fax: (21) 367 132.

Televisi Republik Indonesia (TVRI)
Address: TVRI Senayan, Jalan Gerbang Pemuda, Senayan, Jakarta 10270.
Tel: (21) 573 1122; Fax: (21) 573 3122.

Press Council of Indonesia
Code: Use *Pancasila*, a set of five basic principles – monotheism, humanitarianism, nationalism, democracy and social justice.

B.

Alliance of Independent Journalists
Address: Jakarta.
Note: To promote freedom of the press.

Ikata Penerbit Indonesia
(Association of Indonesian Publishers)
Jalan Kalipasir 32, Jakarta 32.
Tel: (21) 3141907; Fax: (21) 3146050.

Komisi Tata Krama Dan Tata Cara Periklanan Indonesia
(Independent Advertising Standards Commission)
Address: 23 Jalan Taman Tamah Abang III, Jakarta 10160.
Code: *Code of ethics; Code of practice of advertising.*

Persatuan Wartawan Indonesia
(Indonesian Journalists' Association)
Address: Gedung Dewan Pers, 4th Floor, Jalan Kebon Sirih 34, Jakarta 10110.
Tel: (21) 353131; Fax: (21) 353175.
Note: Government controlled.

Serikaat Penerbit Suratkabar (SPS)
(Indonesian Newspapers Publishers' Association)
Address: Gedung Dewan Pers, 6th Floor, Jalan Kebon Sirih 34, Jakarta 10110.
Tel: (21) 359 671; Fax: (21) 386 2373.

Yayasan Pembina Pers Indonesia
(Press Foundation of Indonesia)
Address: Jalan Jatinegara Barat III/6, Jakarta 13310.
Tel: (21) 8194994.

E.

Universitas Ibn Khaldun – Institute of Islamic Mass Communication
Address: PO Box 1224, Jalan Pemuda Kar 97, Jakarta, Timur 13220.
Tel: 48805 99.

Universitas Indonesia – Institute of Mass Communications
Address: PO Box 295, Jalan Salemba Raya 4, Jakarta.
Tel: (21) 330343.

Universitas Islam Sumatera – Faculty of Islamic Communication
Address: Teladan, Medan 20217, Sumatra.
Tel: (61) 716790.

Iran (+98)

A.

Islamic Republic of Iran Broadcasting (IRIB)
Address: Jame Jamm Street, Vali Asr Ave, Tehran.
Tel: (21) 878 8400; Fax: (21) 879 6476.
Note: Semi-autonomous government broadcasting authority operating national and local radio and television stations.

Iraq (+964)

A.

Ministry of Culture and Information
Address: Near an-Nusoor Square, Baghdad.
Tel: (1) 551 4333.

State Organization for Broadcasting and Television
Address: Broadcasting and Television Building, Salihiya, Karkh, Baghdad.
Tel: (1) 537 1161.

Iraq Broadcasting and Television Establishment
Address: Salihiya, Baghdad.
Tel: (1) 884 4412.

B.

The General Federation of Journalists
Address: POB 6017, Baghdad.
Tel: (1) 541 3993.

Iraqi Journalists' Union
Address: POB 14101, Baghdad.
Tel: (1) 537 0762.

Israel (+972)

A.

Ministry of Communications
Address: 23 Jaffa Street, Jerusalem 91999.
Tel: (2) 702 210; Fax: (2) 702 273.

ASIA   315

Israel Broadcasting Authority (IBA) (Radio)
Address: 97 Jaffa Road, POB 6387, Jerusalem.
Tel: (2) 291 888; Fax: (2) 242 944.
Note: National and overseas radio services.

Israel Broadcasting Authority (IBA)
Address: POB 7139, Jerusalem 91071.
Tel: (2) 291 888; Fax: (2) 242 944.
Note: National television service.

B.

Daily Newspaper Publishers' Association of Israel
Address: POB 51202, 74 Petach Tikva Road, Tel Aviv 61200.
Fax: (3) 561 7938.

Israel Journalists' Association
Address: 4 Kaplan Street, Tel Aviv.
Tel: (3) 256 141.

Israel Press Association
Address: Sokolov House, 4 Kaplan Street, Tel Aviv.

C.

Hebrew Writers Association
Address: PO Box 7111, Tel Aviv.
Tel: (3) 695 3256; Fax: (3) 691 9681.

Society of Authors, Composers and Music Publishers in Israel
Address: 118 Rothschild Boulevard, PO Box 14222, Tel Aviv 65271.
Tel: (3) 562 0115; Fax: (3) 562 0119.

E.

Hebrew University of Jerusalem – Smart Family Foundation Communications Institute
Address: Mount Scopus, 91950 Jerusalem.
Tel: (2) 88211; Fax: (2) 322 545.

Japan (+81)

A.

Ministry of Posts and Telecommunications
Address: 3-2 Kasumigaseki 1-chome, Chiyoda-ku, Tokyo 100-90.
Tel: (3) 3504 4411; Fax: (3) 3504 0265.
Note: Government department for television, radio and cable.
Code: Article 3-2 of the Broadcasting Law establishes ethical standards for self-regulation and sets out standards for programming.

Nippon Hoso Kyokai (NHK)
(Japan Broadcasting Corporation)
Address: Broadcasting Centre, NHK Hoso Centre, 2-2-1 Jinnan, Shibuya-ku, Tokyo 150-01.
Tel: (3) 3465 1111; Fax: (3) 3469 8110.
Note: Non-commercial public corporation providing radio and television services; role defined by Broadcast Law (1994).

B.

Japan Advertising Review Organization (JARO)
Address: Kosan No. 3 Building, 16-7 Ginza 2, Chuo-ku, Tokyo 104.
Note: Self-regulation for the advertising industry.

NHK Roren
(Federation of all NHK Labour Unions)
Address: NHK, 2-2-1 Jinnan, Shibuya-ku, Tokyo 150-01.
Tel: (3) 3485 6007; Fax: (3) 3469 9271.

National Association of Commercial Broadcasters in Japan
Address: 3-23 Kioi-cho, Chiyoda-ku, Tokyo 102.
Tel: (3) 5213 7700; Fax: (3) 5213 7701.

Nihon Kokoku Gakkai
(Japan Advertising Society)
Address: 1-6-1 Nishiwasada, Shinjuku-ku, Tokyo 160.
Tel: (3) 3203 4141.

Nihon Shinbun Kyokai
(The Japan Newspaper Publishers' and Editors' Association)
Address: Nippon Press Centre, 2-2-1 Uchisaiwai-cho, Chiyoda-ku, Tokyo 100.
Tel: (3) 3591 3462; Fax: (3) 3591 6149.

Nihon Zasshi Kyokai
(Japan Magazine Publishers Association)
Address: 1–7 Kanda Surugadai, Chiyoda-ku, Tokyo 101.
Tel: (3) 3291 0775; Fax: (3) 3293 6239.
Code: *Canons of journalism.*

Nippon Kisha Club
Address: Nippon Press Centre, 2-2-1 Uchisaiwai-cho, Chiyoda-ku, Tokyo 100.
Tel: (3) 3503 2721.

E.

Keio University – Institute of Communication Research (and Graduate School of Media and Governance)
Address: 2-15-45 Mita, Minato-ku, Tokyo 108.
Tel: (3) 3453 4511.

Komazawa University – Institute of Mass Communication
Address: 1-23-1 Komazawa, Setagaya-ku, Tokyo 154.
Tel: (3) 3418 9010; Fax: (3) 3418 9017.

Nanzan University – Institute of Social Ethics
Address: 18 Yamazato-cho, Showa-ku, Nagoya 466.
Tel: (52) 832-3111.

Tokyo Keizai University – Faculty of Communication Studies
Address: 7 Minamicho 1-chome, Kokubunji, Tokyo 185.
Tel: (423) 28-7711.

University of Tokyo – Institute of Socio-Information and Communication Studies
Address: 7-3-1 Hongo, Bunkyo-ku, Tokyo 113.

F.

Dentsu Research Institute – Nippon Shimbun Gakkai
(Japan Society for Studies in Journalism and Mass Communication)
Address: c/o Institute of Journalism and Communication Studies, University of Tokyo, 7 Hongo Bunkyo-ku, Tokyo 113.
Tel: (3) 8122-111.

NHK Broadcasting Culture Research Institute
Address: 2-1-1, Atago, Minato-ku, Tokyo 105.
Tel: (3) 5400-6800; Fax: (3) 3436-5880.

Nihon Rinrigakukai
(Japanese Society of Ethics)
Address: Department of Ethics, University of Tokyo, Bunkyo-ku, Tokyo 113.

Jordan (+962)

A.

Ministry of Communications
Address: POB 71, Amman.
Tel: (6) 624 301.

Ministry of Information
Address: PO Box 1854, Amman.
Tel: (6) 641 467.

Jordan Radio and Television Corporation (JRTV)
Address: POB 909, Amman.
Tel: (6) 773 111; Fax: (6) 778 578.

Kazakhstan (+7)

A.

Republican Corporation TV and Radio Corporation of Kazakhstan
Address: Republican Square, 13 Almaty 480013.
Tel: (3272) 63 3617; Fax: (3272) 63 6763.

Korea

See **North Korea**; **South Korea**.

Kuwait (+965)

A.

Ministry of Information
Address: POB 193, Al-Sour Street, 13002 Safat, Kuwait City.
Tel: 241 5300; Fax: 245 8948.

Kuwait Broadcasting
Address: POB 397, 13004 Safat, Kuwait City.
Tel: 242 3774; Fax: 241 5946.

C.

Kuwait Association of Journalists
Address: POB 5454, Safat, Kuwait City.
Tel: 484 3351; Fax: 484 2874.

Kyrgyzstan (+996)

A.

Kyrgyzstan State TV and Radio Company
Address: Molodaya Gvardia 59, Bishkek.
Tel: (3312) 254 229; Fax: (3312) 257 726.

Laos (+856)

A.

Radiodiffusion Nationale Lao
Address: PO Box 310, Ventiane.
Tel: 212 457.

B.

Association of Lao Journalists
Address: BP 310, Ventiane.

Lebanon (+961)

A.

Ministry of Information
Address: rue Hamra, Beirut.
Tel: (1) 351 235; Fax: (1) 350 634.
Note: Broadcast licensing by the National Council for the Audiovisual Media.

Radio Lebanon
Address: rue Arts et Métiers, Beirut.
Tel: (1) 346 880.
Note: Government (Ministry of Information)-run radio service.

Télé Liban
Address: PO Box 11, Beirut 5450.
Tel: (1) 424 912.

B.

Lebanese Press Syndicate
Address: PO Box 3084, Immeuble Press Order, Avenue Saeb Salam, Beirut.
Tel: (1) 865 519.

Malaysia (+60)

A.

Ministry of Home Affairs
Address: Jalan Dato'Onn, 50546 Kuala Lumpur.
Tel: (3) 230 9344; Fax: (3) 230 9344.

Ministry of Information
Address: Angkasapuri, Jalan Pantai Bahru, 50614 Kuala Lumpur.
Tel: (3) 282 4590; Fax: (3) 282 1255.

Radio Television Malaysia (RTM)
Address: Department of Broadcasting, Angkasapuri, Bukit Putra, 50614 Kuala Lumpur.
Tel: (3) 282 5333; Fax: (3) 282 4735.
Note: Supervises radio and television broadcasting.

B.

Advertising Standards Authority of Malaysia
Address: Lot 403, 4th Floor, Wisma Mirama, Jalan Wisma Putra, 50460 Kuala Lumpur.
Tel: (3) 719 8195; Fax: (3) 719 7394.
Code: *Malaysian code of advertising practice.*

National Union of Journalists
Address: 30B Jalan Padang Belia, 50470 Kuala Lumpur.
Tel: (3) 274 2867; Fax: (3) 274 4776.

Persatuan Penerbit–Penerbit Akhbar Malaysia
(Malaysian Newspaper Publishers' Association)
Address: 75B Jalan SS21/1A, Damansara Utama, Petaling Jaya, Selangor Darul Ehsan.
Tel: (3) 719 8195; Fax: (3) 719 7394.

E.

University of Science, Malaysia – Department of Communication
Address: 11 800 USM, Penang.
Tel: (4) 657 7888; Fax: (4) 657 1526.

Mongolia (+976)

A.

State Committee for Information, Radio and Television
Address: PO Box 365, Ulan Bator.

B.

Board of Mongolian Journalists
Address: PO Box 11, Ulan Bator.
Tel: (1) 20536.

Nepal (+977)

A.

Ministry of Information and Communication
Address: Singha Durbar, Kathmandu.

Press Council
Address: RSS Building, Prithvi Path, PO Box 3077, Kathmandu.
Tel: (1) 215 521; Fax: (1) 227 698.

Radio Nepal
Address: Radio Broadcasting Service, HM Government of Nepal, Singha Durbar, PO Box 634, Kathmandu.
Tel: (1) 223 910; Fax: (1) 221 952.

Nepal Television Corporation (NTV)
Address: PO Box 3826, Singha Durbar, Kathmandu.
Tel: (1) 228 447; Fax: (1) 228 312.

B.

Nepal Journalists Association (NJA)
Address: Maitighar, PO Box 285, Kathmandu.
Tel: (1) 225 226; Fax: (1) 279 544.

North Korea (+850)

A.

DPRK Radio and Television Broadcasting Committee
Address: Jonsung-dong, Moranbong District, Pyongyang.
Tel: (2) 816035; Fax: (2) 812100.

Korean Central Television
Address: Ministry of Posts and Telecoms, Pyongyang.

B.

Korean Journalists' Union
Address: Pyongyang.

Korean Writers' Union
Address: Pyongyang.

Oman (+968)

A.

Ministry of Information
Address: PO Box 600, Muscat.
Tel: 603 885.

Oman Television and Radio
Address: PO Box 600, Muscat.
Tel: 603 214; Fax: 605 043.

Pakistan (+92)

A.

Ministry of Information and Broadcasting
Address: Block A, Pakistan Secretariat, Islamabad.
Tel: (51) 810021.

Pakistan Broadcasting Corporation
Address: National Broadcasting House, Constitution Avenue, Islamabad.
Tel: (51) 828651/723; Fax: (51) 823466.

National Press Trust
Address: House 16, 7th Avenue, F-6/1 Islamabad.
Tel: (51) 821949; Fax: (51) 820149.
Note: Government controlled.
Code: *Press code of ethics for Pakistan.*

B.

All Pakistan Newspaper Employees Confederation
Address: Karachi Press Club, M. R. Kayani Road, Karachi.
Note: Confederation of all press industry unions.

All Pakistan Newspapers Society
Address: 32 Farid Chambers, 3rd Floor, Abdullah Haroon Road, Karachi 3.
Tel: (21) 521256; Fax: (21) 521310.

Council of Pakistan Newspaper Editors
Address: c/o United Press of Pakistan, 1 Victoria Chambers, Haji Abdullah Haroon Road, Karachi 74400.
Tel: (21) 5682694; Fax: (21) 7735276.

Pakistan Federal Union of Journalists
Address: Dawn Bureau, Lahore.
Tel: (42) 304342.
Aims: To secure freedom of the press and better working conditions.

Pakistan Newspapers and Periodicals Association
Address: 4 Sharea Fatima Jinnah, PO Box 1815, Lahore 54000.

E.

Bahauddin Zakariya University – Department of Mass Communication
Address: Multan, Punjab 60800.
Tel: (61) 520101-4.

University of Balochistan – Department of Mass Communication
Address: Sariab Road, Quetta.
Tel: (81) 440431; Fax: (81)440323.

Gomal University – Department of Journalism and Mass Communication
Address: Deva Ismail Khan, North West Frontier Province.
Tel: (529) 91279; Fax: (529) 4673.

Islamic University, Bahawalpur – Department of Mass Communication
Address: Bahawalpur.
Tel: (621) 80331.

University of Karachi – Department of Mass Communication
Address: University Complex, Karachi 75270.
Tel: (21) 479001; Fax: (21) 473226.

University of the Punjab – Department of Mass Communication
Address: 1 Shahrah-e-al-Beruni, Lahore 2.
Tel: (42) 354428; Fax: (42) 354428.

University of Sindh – Department of Mass Communication
Address: Jamshoro, Sindh.
Tel: (221) 71563; Fax: (221) 613886.

Philippines (+63)

A.

Office of the President
Address: Malacanang Palace Compound, J. P. Laurel Street, San Miguel, Metro Manila.
Tel: (2) 5212301; Fax: (2) 741641.
Note: Implements government policies on information and the media; freedom of the press guaranteed under 1987 Constitution.

Department of Transportation and Communication
Address: Philcomcea Building, Ortigas Avenue, Pasig, Metro Manila.
Tel: (2) 7213781.

DIRECTORY OF SELECTED ORGANIZATIONS

Peoples Television Network (PTN)
Address: Broadcast Complex, Visayas Avenue, Quezon City.
Tel: (2) 9206521-4; Fax: (2) 9204362.
Note: Public service broadcasting.

B.

Advertising Board of the Philippines (Adboard)
Address: L & F Building, 107 Aguirre Street, Legaspi Village, Makati, Metro Manila.
Note: Self-regulatory association of national advertising associations.
Code: *Code of ethics.*

Kapisanan ng mga Brodkaster sa Pilipinas (KBP)
(Association of Broadcasters of the Philippines)
Address: LTA Building, 118 Perea Street, Legaspi Village, Makati, Metro Manila.
Tel: (2) 8151990; Fax: (2) 8151989.
Note: Self-regulation through radio and television codes.

National Press Club of the Philippines
Address: Magallanes Drive, Intramuros, Metro Manila.
Tel: (2) 494242.

E.

Polytechnic University of the Philippines – Department of Mass Communication
Address: Anona Street, Santa Mesa, Manila.
Tel: (2) 616775; Fax: (2) 7161143.

University of the Philippines – College of Mass Communication
Address: Quezon City.
Tel and Fax: 9280110.

Qatar (+974)

A.

Ministry of Information and Culture
Address: TV Department, PO Box 1944, Doha.
Tel: 869 344.

Qatar TV
Address: PO Box 1944, Doha.
Tel: 894 444.

Saudi Arabia (+966)

A.

Ministry of Information
Address: PO Box 57137, Nasseriya Street, Riyadh 11574.
Tel: (1) 406 8888; Fax: (1) 404 4192.
Code: *Press and publication law* (1963).

Saudi Arabian Broadcasting Service
Address: c/o Ministry of Information, PO Box 60059, Riyadh.
Tel: (1) 401 4440; Fax: (1) 403 8177.

Saudi Arabian Television Service
Address: PO Box 7959, Riyadh 11472.
Tel: (1) 401 4440; Fax: (1) 404 4192.

Singapore (+65)

A.

Ministry of Communications
Address: 460 Alexandra Road, PSA Building 36-00, Singapore 0511.
Tel: 279 9707; Fax: 279 9784.

Singapore Broadcasting Authority
Address: 1 Maritime Square, 09-59 World Trade Centre, Singapore 0409.
Tel: 270 8191; Fax: 278 6009.
Note: Licenses and regulates broadcasting services, including overseeing programme quality through guidelines on subject matter and censorship.

Singapore Broadcasting Corporation
Address: Caldecott Hill, Andrew Road, Singapore 1129.
Tel: 256 0401; Fax: 253 8808.
Note: Holding company for Television Corporation of Singapore, Television Twelve, Radio Corporation of Singapore and SIM Communications.

ASIA   321

B.

Advertising Standards Authority of Singapore (ASAS)
Address: Block 164, No. 04-3625, Bukit Merah Central, Singapore 0316.
Code: *Singapore code of advertising practice.*

C.

Institute of Public Relations of Singapore
Address: PO Box 3800, Singapore 9057.
Tel: 734 9903.

E.

National University of Singapore – Mass Communication Programme
Address: 10 Kent Ridge Crescent, Singapore 0511.
Tel: 775 6666; Fax: 778 5281.

Nayang Technological University – School of Communication Studies
Address: Nayang Avenue, Singapore 2263.
Tel: 791 1794; Fax: 791 1604.

South Korea (+82)

A.

Ministry of Culture and Communication
Address: Sejong-no, Jongro-gu, Seoul.
Tel: (2) 720 4929; Fax: (2) 739 4481.

Korean Broadcasting Committee
Address: 14th Floor, Korea Press Center, 25 Taepyongro, Chung-ku, Seoul.
Tel: (2) 735 2640; Fax: (2) 736 6353.
Note: Programme content approval.

Korean Broadcasting System (KBS)
Address: 18 Yoido-dong, Yongdungpo-gu, Seoul 150-790.
Tel: (2) 781 1470; Fax: (2) 781 1497.
Note: Publicly owned corporation providing local and overseas services.

Korean Press Ethics Commission
Address: Korea Press Center, 25 Taepyongro 1-ka, Chung-ku, Seoul.

B.

Journalists Association of Korea
Address: Korea Press Center, 13th Floor, 25 Taepyongro 1-ka, Chung-ku, Seoul.
Tel: (2) 734 3213; Fax: (2) 738 1003.

Korean Federation of Press Unions
Address: Korea Press Center, Room 1802, 25 Taepyongro 1-ka, Chung-ku, Seoul.
Tel: (2) 739 7285; Fax: (2) 735 9400.

Korean Newspaper Editors Association
Address: Korea Press Center, 13th Floor, 25 Taepyongro 1-ka, Chung-ku, Seoul.
Tel: (2) 732 1726; Fax: (2) 739 1985.

Korean Newspapers Association
Address: Korea Press Center, 13th Floor, 25, 1-ka, Taepyong-no, Chung-ku, Seoul.
Tel: (2) 733 2251; Fax: (2) 720 3291.

C.

Korean Broadcasting Institute
Address: 700 Seocho-dong, Seoul.
Tel: (2) 522 0471; Fax: (2) 521 6680.

Sri Lanka (+94)

A.

Ministry of Media, Tourism and Aviation
Address: 45 St Michael's Road, Colombo 3.
Tel: (1) 540221.

Sri Lanka Broadcasting Corporation
Address: Independence Square, PO Box 574, Colombo 7.
Tel: (1) 697491; Fax: (1) 695488.

B.

Press Association of Ceylon
Address: Negris Building, PO Box 131, Colombo 1.
Tel: (1) 31174.

Press Council
Code: *Press Council law* (1973).

E.

University of Kelaniya – Department of Mass Communication
Address: Kelaniya.
Tel: (1) 520164.

Syria (+963)

A.

Ministry of Information
Address: avenue al-Mazzeh, Imm. Dar al-Baath, Damascus.
Tel: (11) 666 4600.

Directorate-General of Broadcasting and Television
Address: place Omayyad, Damascus.
Tel: (11) 720 700.

Syrian TV
Address: Damascus.
Tel: (11) 372 0700; Fax: (11) 223 4930.

B.

Arab Advertising Organization
Address: 28 rue Moutanabbi, PO Box 2842-3034, Damascus.
Tel: (11) 225 219.

Taiwan (+886)

A.

Government Information Office
Address: 2 Tientsin Street, Taipei.
Tel: (2) 351 6625; Fax: (2) 341 6252.
Note: Supervises operation of broadcasting services.

Ministry of Communications
Address: 2 Chiang Sha Street, Section 1, Taipei.
Tel: (2) 349 2900; Fax: (2) 311 8587.
Note: Determines power and frequencies for broadcasting services.

Chinese Public Station Organizing Committee
Address: 5th Floor, 85 Chung Hsiao E Road, Section 1, Taipei.
Tel: (2) 356 6764; Fax: (2) 356 7452.

Chinese Television Company
Address: 120 Chungyang Road, Nan Kang District, Taipei.
Tel: (2) 783 8308; Fax: (2) 783 3069.

National Press Council
Address: 3rd Floor, No. 4, Lane 9, Nan Cheong Street, Section 1, Taipei.

Taipei Association of Advertising Agencies
Address: 2nd Floor, No. 4-1, Lane 217, Alley 3, Chung Shiao E Road, Section 3, Taipei.

B.

Taipei Journalists Association
Address: 209 Sung Chiang Road, Taipei.
Tel: (2) 505 6530; Fax: (2) 502 1069.

E.

National Chengchi University – Graduate School of Journalism
Address: Wenshan 116, Taipei.
Tel: (2) 939 3091; Fax: (2) 939 8043.

National Taiwan University – Graduate Institute of Journalism
Address: 1 Roosevelt Road, Section 4, Taipei.
Tel: (2) 363 0231.

Tajikistan (+7)

A.

Ministry of Culture and Information
Address: 734025 Dushanbe.
Tel: (3772) 27 65 69.

State TV-Radio Broadcasting Corporation of Tajikistan
Address: Kuchai Chapayev 31, 734025 Dushanbe.

ASIA 323

Thailand (+66)

A.

Ministry of Transport and Communications
Address: Thanon Ratchadamoen Nok, Bangkok 10100.
Tel: (2) 281 3422; Fax: (2) 280 1714.

Mass Communication Organization of Thailand
Address: 63/1 Rama Xi Road, Huay Kwang, Bangkok 10310.
Tel: (2) 201 6336; Fax: (2) 245 1435.

Radio Thailand (RTH)
(National Broadcasting Services of Thailand)
Address: Government Public Relations Department, 236 Thanon Vibhavadi Rangsit, Bangkok 10400.
Tel: (2) 277 9125; Fax: (2) 277 0122.

Television Thailand
(National Broadcasting Services of Thailand)
Address: Government Public Relations Department, 236 Thanon Petchburi, Bangkok 10200.
Tel: (2) 314 4001; Fax: (2) 318 2991.

B.

Confederation of Thai Journalists
Address: 538/1 Thanon Samsen, Dusit, Bangkok 10300.
Tel: (2) 241 4795.

Press Association of Thailand
Address: 299 Thanon Ratchasima, Dusit, Bangkok 10300.
Tel: (2) 241 0766.

E.

Chulalongkorn University – Department of Public Relations and Mass Communications
Address: Phyathai Road, Bangkok 10330.
Tel: (2) 215 0871; Fax: (2) 215 4804.

Payap University – Christian Communication Institute
Address: Amphur Muang, Chieng Mai 50000.
Tel: (53) 241 255; Fax: (53) 241 983.

Thammsat University – Faculty of Journalism and Mass Communication
Address: 2 Prachand Road, Bangkok 10200.
Tel: (2) 221 611120; Fax: (2) 224 8099.

Turkmenistan (+993)

A.

Ministry of Communications
Address: ul. Zhitaikawa 36, 744000 Ashgabat.
Tel: (3632) 35 21 53; Fax: (3632) 34 04 20.

National Television and Radio Company of Turkmenistan
Address: pr. Magtyruguly 89, 744000 Ashgabat.

United Arab Emirates (+971)

A.

Ministry of Communications
Address: PO Box 900, Abu Dhabi.
Tel: (2) 651 900.

UAE Radio and Television
Address: Airport Road, PO Box 637, Abu Dhabi.
Tel: (2) 452 000.

Uzbekistan (+7)

A.

Ministry of Communication
Address: ul. A. Tolstogo 1, Tashkent.
Tel: (3712) 33 65 03; Fax: (3712) 39 87 82.

Television and Radio Corporation of Uzbekistan
Address: ul. Khorezmskaya 49, 700047 Tashkent.
Tel: (3712) 41 05 51.

324 DIRECTORY OF SELECTED ORGANIZATIONS

B.

Union of Writers of Uzbekistan
Address: ul. Pushkina 1, 700000 Tashkent.
Tel: (3712) 33 79 21.

Viet Nam (+84)

A.

Ministry of Culture and Information
Address: 51 Ngo Quyen, Hanoi.
Tel: (4) 825 3231.
Note: Responsible for the management of the radio and television services, and supervision of newspapers, news agencies and periodicals.

Viet Nam Television
Address: 59 Giang Vo Street, Hanoi.
Tel: (4) 355 933; Fax: (4) 355 332.

B.

Viet Nam Journalists' Association
Address: 59 Ly Thai To, Hanoi.
Tel: (4) 825 3608; Fax: (4) 825 0797.

Vietnamese Writers' Association
Address: c/o Writers and Artists Union, 51 Tran Hung Dao Street, Hanoi.
Tel: (4) 52694.

Voice of Viet Nam
Address: 58 Quan Su, Hanoi.
Tel: (4) 825 4953; Fax: (4) 826 1122.

Yemen (+967)

A.

Ministry of Information
Address: PO Box 4227, Crater, Aden.

Yemen Radio and Television Corporation
Address: PO Box 2182, Sana'a.
Tel: (1) 230 654; Fax: (1) 230 761.

Americas

A.

Organization of American States (OAS)
Address: 17th Street and Constitution Avenue NW, Washington, DC 20006, USA.
Tel: (+1) (202) 458 3000; Fax: (+1) (202) 458 3967.
Code: *American Convention on Human Rights*.

D.

Inter-American Press Association
Address: 2911 NW 39th Street, Miami, Florida 33142, USA.
Tel: (+1) (305) 634-2465; Fax: (+1) (305) 635-2272
Aims: To guard the freedom of the press and rights of journalists in the Americas.

International Association of Broadcasting (Asociación Internacional de Radiodifusión AIR)
Address: Office 402, 11200 Montevideo, Uruguay.
Tel and Fax: (+598) (2) 488121.
Aims: Founded in 1946 to preserve free broadcasting and defend freedom of expression.

North America

B

North American National Broadcasters Association
Address: 1500 Bronson Avenue, Ottawa, Ontario K1G 3J5, Canada.
Tel: (+1) (613) 738 6553; Fax: (+1) (613) 738 6887.
Aims: Association concerned with providing a framework for the identification, study and research into questions affecting broadcasting.

Canada (+1)

A.

Canadian Radio-Television and Telecommunications Commission/Conseil de la Radiodiffusion et des Télécommunications Canadiennes (CRTC)
Address: Ottawa, Ontario K1A 0N2.
Tel: (819) 997 3430; Fax: (819) 994 0218.
Note: Regulates radio, television, cable and telecommunications.

Canadian Broadcasting Corporation/ Société Radio-Canada (CBC)
Address: 1500 Bronson Avenue, POB 8478, Ottawa, Ontario K1G 3J5.
Tel: (613) 724 1200; Fax: (613) 738 6742.
Note: National publicly funded broadcasting service established by the 1968 Broadcasting Act.

National Film Board
Address: PO Box 6100, Station Centre, Ville Montreal, Quebec H3C 3H5.
Tel: (514) 283 9000; Fax: (514) 283 7564.

B.

Association of Canadian Publishers
Address: 2 Gloucester Street, Suite 301, Toronto, Ontario M4Y IL5.
Tel: (416) 413 4929; Fax: (416) 413 4920.

Canadian Advertising Foundation (CAP)
Address: 350 Bloor Street, Suite 402, Toronto, Ontario M4W 1H5.
Note: Voluntary self-regulatory organization for the advertising industry.
Code: *Canadian code of advertising standards.*

Canadian Association of Broadcasters (CAB)
Address: 350 Sparks Street, Suite 306, Ottawa, Ontario K1R 7S8.
Tel: (613) 233 4035; Fax: (613) 233-6961.

Canadian Broadcast Standards Council (CBSC)
Address: POB 3265, Ottawa, Ontario.
Note: Established by the Canadian Association of Broadcasters to administer industry standards.
Codes: *Code of ethics*; *Voluntary code on violence on television*; *Sex role portrayal code.*

Canadian Daily Newspaper Association (CDNA)
Address: 890 Yonge Street, Suite 1100, Toronto, Ontario M4W 3P4.
Tel: (416) 923 3567; Fax: (416) 923 7206.

Canadian Magazine Publishers Association
Address: 2 Stewart Street, Toronto, Ontario M5V 1H6.
Tel: (416) 362 2546; Fax: (416) 362 2547.

Canadian Publishers' Council
Address: 250 Merton Street, Suite 203, Toronto, Ontario M4S 1B1.
Tel: (416) 322 7011; Fax: (416) 322 6999.

Le Conseil des Normes de la Publicité
Address: 4823 Sherbrooke Street W, Suite 130, Montreal, Quebec H32 1G7.
Note: Self-regulatory body to administer standards and codes of ethics.
Code: *Le code canadien des normes de la publicité.*

Radio Advisory Board of Canada
Address: 880 Lady Ellen Place, Suite 201, Ottawa, Ontario K1Z 5L9.
Tel: (613) 728-8692; Fax: (613) 728-3278.

Radio Television News Directors Association of Canada
Code: *Code of broadcast news ethics.*

C.

Academy of Canadian Cinema and Television
Address: 158 Pearl Street, Toronto, Ontario M5H 1L3.
Tel: (416) 591 2040; Fax: (416) 591 2157.

Canadian Authors Association
Address: 275 Slater Street, Suite 500, Ottawa, Ontario K1P 5H9.
Tel: (613) 233 2846; Fax: (613) 235 8237.

E.

Association of Directors of Journalism Programs in Canadian Universities
Address: The School of Journalism, Middlesex College, University of Western Ontario, London, Ontario N6A 5B7.
Tel: (519) 679 3377.

University of British Columbia – Centre for Applied Ethics
Address: 227-6356 Agric. Road, Vancouver, British Columbia.
Tel: (604) 822 5139; Fax: (604) 822 8627.

Concordia University – Concordia Center for Broadcasting Studies
Address: 1455 de Maisonneuve Boulevard W, Montreal, Quebec H3G 1N8.
Tel: (514) 848 2424; Fax: (514) 848 3494.

Université Laval
Address: Cité Universitaire, Quebec G1K 7P4.
Tel: (418) 656 2131; Fax: (418) 656 2809.

University of Manitoba – Center for Professional and Applied Ethics
Address: 500 Dysart Road, Winnipeg, Manitoba.
Tel: (204) 474 9107; Fax: (204) 261 0021.

McGill University – Graduate Program of Communications
Address: 845 Sherbrooke Street W, Montreal, Quebec H3A 2TS.
Tel: (514) 398 4455; Fax: (514) 398 3594.

University of Ottawa – Institute of Social Communications
Address: 550 Cumberland Street, PO Box 450, Ottawa, Ontario K1N 6N5.
Tel: (613) 562 5800; Fax: (613) 563 5103.

St Paul University – Centre for Techno Ethics
Address: 223 Main Street, Ottawa, Ontario.
Tel: (613) 236 1393; Fax: (613) 782 3001.

Simon Fraser University – Department of Communication
Address: Burnaby, British Columbia V5A 1S6.
Tel: (604) 291 3111; Fax: (604) 291 4969.

University of Windsor – Department of Communications
Address: Windsor, Ontario N9B 7P4.
Tel: (519) 253 4232.

University of Western Ontario – Graduate School of Journalism
Address: London, Ontario N6A 3K7.
Tel: (519) 679 2111; Fax: (519) 661 3388.

York University – Centre for Practical Ethics
Address: 102 McLaughlin College, 4700 Keele Street, North York, Ontario.
Tel: (416) 736 5928; Fax: (416) 736 5436.

F.

Association for the Study of Canadian Radio and Television
Address: 1455 de Maisonneuve Boulevard W, Room N-312, Montreal, Quebec.
Tel: (514) 879 5901.

Broadcast Research Council of Canada
Address: 2 Bloor Street W, Suite 100, Toronto, Ontario.
Tel: (416) 445 9800.

Canadian Center for Ethics and Corporate Policy
Address: George Brown House, 50 Baldwin Street, Toronto, Ontario.
Tel: (416) 348 8691; Fax: (416) 348 8689.

Canadian Institute for Studies in Telecommunications
Address: 35 Place Bergeron, Pierrefonds, Quebec H8Y 1P4.
Tel: (514) 684 2751.

Newspaper Research Center
Address: 42 Charles Street E, Suite 501, Toronto, Ontario.
Tel: (416) 960 5030.

AMERICAS

Westminster Institute of Ethics and Human Values
Address: 361 Windermere Road, London, Ontario N6G 2K3.
Tel: (519) 673 0046; Fax: (519) 673 5016.

United States of America (+1)

A.

Federal Communications Commission
Address: 1919 M Street NW, Washington, DC 20554.
Tel: (202) 632 6460; Fax: (202) 653 5402.
Note: Licensing broadcast and cable services, operating public interest standards.

B.

American Advertising Federation
Address: 1101 Vermont Avenue NW, Suite 500, Washington, DC 20005.
Tel: (202) 898 0089; Fax: (202) 898 0159.
Code: *Advertising principles of American business.*

American Association of Advertising Agencies
Address: 405 Lexington Avenue, 18th Floor, New York, NY 10174.
Tel: (212) 682 2500; Fax: (212) 953 5665.

American Society of Magazine Editors
Address: 22nd Floor, 919 Third Avenue, New York, NY 10022-3801.
Tel: (212) 872 3700; Fax: (212) 888 4217.

American Society of Media Photographers (ASMP)
Address: 14 Washington Road, Suite 502, Princeton Junction, NJ 08550-1033.
Tel: (609) 799 8300; Fax: (609) 799 2233.

National Advertising Review Board (NARB)
Address: 845 Third Avenue, New York, NY 10022.
Note: Adveristing industry self-regulation.

National Association of Broadcasters (NAB)
Address: 1771 N Street NW, Washington, DC 20036-2891.
Tel: (202) 429 5300; Fax: (202) 429 5410.
Note: Trade association of radio and television stations.

National Press Photographers Association
Address: 3200 Croasdaile Drive, Suite 306, Durham, NC 27705.
Tel: (919) 383 7246; Fax: (919) 383 7261.
Note: Founded 1946 for news photographers, editors and other professionals in photojournalism.

Newspaper Association of America
Address: The Newspaper Center, 11600 Sunrise Valley Drive, Reston, VA 22091.
Tel: (703) 648 1000; Fax: (703) 620 1265.

The Newspaper Guild
8611 2nd Avenue, Silver Spring, MD 20910.
Tel: (301) 585 2990; Fax: (301) 585 0668.

Radio and Television News Directors Association
Address: 1000 Connecticut Avenue NW, Suite 615, Washington, DC 20006.
Tel: (202) 659 6510; Fax: (202) 223 4007.
Code: *Code of broadcast news ethics.*

C.

American Society of Newspaper Editors (ASNE)
Address: 11690B Sunrise Valley Drive, Reston, VA 20191-1409.
Tel: (703) 453 1122; Fax: (703) 453 1133.
Aims: Formed in 1922 to aid the professional growth of members, and to encourage them to concern themselves with the ethics, quality and history of editorial and news policy.
Code: *Canons of journalism; Journalism values institute handbook* (1996).

DIRECTORY OF SELECTED ORGANIZATIONS

Public Relations Society of America
Address: 33 Irving Place, 3rd Floor,
15–16th Street, New York, NY 10003.
Tel: (212) 995 2230.
Code: *Code of professional standards for the practice of public relations.*

Society of Professional Journalists (Sigma Delta Chi)
Address: Box 77, 16 S Jackson Street, Greencastle, IN 46135.
Tel: (317) 653 3333; Fax: (317) 653 4631.
Code: *Code of ethics.*

D.

Accuracy in Media (AIM)
Address: 4455 Connecticut Avenue NW, Suite 330, Washington, DC 20008.
Tel: (202) 364 4401; Fax: (202) 364 4098.
Aims: News media watchdog body for promotion of fair and accurate reporting.

Black Awareness in Television (BAIT)
Address: 13217 Livernois, Detroit, MI 48238-3162.
Tel: (313) 931 3427.

Black Citizens for a Fair Media
Address: 156-20 Riverside Drive, No. 131, New York, NY 10032.
Tel: (212) 568 3168.

Center for Investigative Reporting
Address: 530 Howard Street, San Francisco, CA 94105-3007.
Tel: (415) 543 1200; Fax: (415) 543 8313.

Committee for Accuracy in Middle East Reporting in America (CAMERA)
Address: 1828 L Street NW, No. 702, Washington, DC 20036-5104.
Tel: (202) 822 8884.

Committee to Protect Journalists
Address: 330 7th Avenue, 12th Floor, New York, NY 10001.
Tel: (212) 465 1004; Fax: (212) 465 9568.

Essential Information
Address: PO Box 19405, Washington, DC 20036.
Tel: (202) 387 8030; Fax: (202) 234 5176.
Aims: To promote investigative journalism; *Multinational Reporter.*

Fairness and Accuracy in Reporting (FAIR)
Address: 130 W 25th Street, New York, NY 10001.
Tel: (212) 633 6700; Fax: (212) 727 7668.
Aims: National media watchdog for the promotion of the rights of US citizens to free speech and a free press, and encouragement of reportage of the diverse concerns and opinions of the American public by the media; *Extra!*

First Amendment Congress
Address: 2301 S Gaylord Street, Denver, CO 80208.
Tel: (303) 871 4430; Fax: (303) 871 4585.

Free Press Association (FPA)
Address: PO Box 63, Port Hadlock, WA 98339.
Tel: (360) 385 5097; Fax: (360) 385 3704.
Note: Network of journalists, news photographers, editors and publishers committed to liberty and the Bill of Rights, and against all government censorship; *Free Press Network.*

Freedom House
Address: 120 Wall Street, New York, NY 10005.
Tel: (212) 514 8040; Fax: (212) 514 8050.
Aims: Advocacy and monitoring organization on press freedom.

Fund for Investigative Reporting
Address: 1755 Massachusetts Avenue NW, Suite 324, Washington, DC 20036-2102.
Tel: (202) 462 1844.
Aims: To enable writers to investigate abuses of authority and malfunction of

public institutions through the award of grants.

Fund for Objective News Reporting (FONR)
Address: 422 1st Street SE, Washington, DC 20003.
Tel: (202) 546 0856.
Aims: To enable journalists to conduct media research and correct bias in major news media through the award of grants.

Media Access Project (MAP)
Address: 2000 M Street NW, 4th Floor, Washington, DC 20036.
Tel: (202) 232 4300; Fax: (202) 293-2672.
Aims: Public interest law firm working for citizens' rights of access to broadcast and print media, and government information.

Media Alliance (MA)
Address: 814 Mission Street, Suite 205, San Francisco, CA 94103.
Aims: Association of writers, photographers, editors and other media workers who support a free press and independent journalism; *Propaganda Review*.

Media Network
Address: 39 W 14th Street, Suite 403, New York, NY 10011.
Tel: (212) 929 2663; Fax: (212) 929 2732.
Aims: To increase public awareness of the way in which the media influence and define people's lives, suggest alternatives and try to effect change.

Media Watch
Address: PO Box 618, Santa Cruz, CA 95061.
Tel and Fax: (408) 423 6355.
Aims: Activist group to improve image of women in the media, and to combat sexism, racism, violent images of women and pornography in the media.

National Black Media Coalition
Address: 38 New York Avenue NE, Washington, DC 20002.
Tel: (202) 387 8155; Fax: (202) 462 4469.
Aims: Black news advocacy group seeking to ensure access for black and other minorities in the media through employment, ownership and programming.

National Coalition on Television Violence (NCTV)
Address: 33290 W 14 Mile Road, Suite 498, West Bloomfield, MI 48322.
Tel: (810) 489 3197; Fax: (810) 489 8696.
Aims: Educational and research organization committed to decreasing the amount of violence on film and television.

Public Media Center (PMC)
Address: 466 Green Street, San Francisco, CA 94133.
Tel: (415) 434 1403; Fax: (415) 986 6779.
Aims: Public interest advertising agency producing information campaigns on public rights of access to the media.

Reporters Committee for Freedom of the Press
Address: 1101 Wilson Boulevard, Suite 1910, Arlington, VA 22209.
Tel: (703) 807 2100; Fax: (703) 807 2109.
Aims: Upholding the First Amendment and protecting freedom of information rights of working journalists in all media; *News Media and the Law* (quarterly).

Society for the Eradication of Television (SET)
Address: Box 10491, Oakland, CA 94610.
Tel: (510) 763 8712.
Aims: Activist group against television which encourages homes to remove television sets; *S.E.T. Free: the Newsletter Against Television* (quarterly).

Student Press Law Center
Address: 1101 Wilson Boulevard, Suite 1910, Arlington, VA 22209.

DIRECTORY OF SELECTED ORGANIZATIONS

Tel: (703) 807 1904; Fax: (703) 807 2109.
Aims: To protect the First Amendment rights of student journalists.

Telecommunications Research and Action Center
Address: PO Box 12038, Washington, DC 20005.
Tel: (202) 462 2520; Fax: (202) 408 1134.
Aims: To improve the quality of electronic media through concerted public action; *A citizens' primer on fairness in broadcasting.*

Thomas Jefferson Center for the Protection of Free Expression
Address: 400 Peter Jefferson Place, Charlottesville, VA 22901.
Tel: (804) 295 4784; Fax: (804) 296 3621.

Viewers for Quality Television
Address: PO Box 195, Fairfax Station, VA 22039.
Tel: (703) 425 0075; Fax: (703) 425 8143.
Aims: Campaigning membership organization to promote the development of and support for quality programming on television.

Women's Institute for Freedom of the Press
Address: 3306 Ross Place NW, Washington, DC 20008.
Tel and Fax: (202) 966 7783

E.

University of Arizona – Departments of Communication, Journalism and Media Arts
Address: Tucson, AZ 85721.
Tel: (602) 621 2211; Fax: (602) 621 9118.
Note: Awards for Freedom of Press and the People's Right to Know.

Bowling Green State University – Center for Study of Popular Culture
Address: Popular Culture Centre, Bowling Green, OH 43402.
Tel: (419) 372 2981.

Brigham Young University – Communications Research Center
Address: F276 HFAC, Provo, UT 84602.
Tel: (801) 378 4636.

California State University – Department of Journalism
Address: 6000 J Street, Sacramento, California, CA 95819-26945.
Tel: (916) 278 7737; Fax: (916) 278 5722.

University of California, San Diego – Department of Communications
Address: 9500 Gilman Drive, La Jolla, CA 92093.
Tel: (619) 534 8273.

University of California, San Francisco – Hastings College of Law
Address: 200 McAllister Street, San Francisco, CA 94102-4978.
Tel: (415) 565 4600; Fax: (415) 565 4825.

Loyola University of Chicago – National Center for Freedom of Information Studies
Address: 820 N Michigan Avenue, Chicago, IL 60611.
Tel: (312) 915 6549; Fax: (312) 915 7095.

University of Colorado at Boulder – Centre for Mass Media Research
Address: School of Journalism and Mass Communications, University of Colorado at Boulder, Boulder, CO 80309.
Tel: (303) 492 1357.

Columbia University – Freedom Forum Media Studies Center
Address: 2950 Broadway, New York, NY 10027.
Tel: (212) 678 6600.
Note: Formerly Gannett Center for Media Studies; *Media Studies Journal.*

Columbia University – Graduate School of Journalism
Address: Morningside Heights, New York, NY 10027.
Tel: (212) 854 1754.

De Paul University – Faculty of Law
Address: 25 East Jackson Boulevard, Chicago, IL 60604.
Tel: (312) 362 8000.

Emerson College – Department of Mass Communications
Address: 100 Beacon Street, Boston, MA 02116-1523.
Tel: (617) 578 8500.

University of Florida – Brechner Center for Freedom of Information
Address: College of Journalism and Communications, 3208 Weimer Hall, Gainesville, FL 32611.
Tel: (904) 543 1200; Fax: (415) 543 8313.

University of Florida – Center for Applied Philosophy and Ethics in the Professions
Address: 332 Griffin Lloyd Hall, Gainesville, FL 32611.
Tel: (904) 392 2084; Fax: (904) 392 5517.

Florida State University – Communication Research Center
Address: 424 Diffenbaugh Building, R-42, Tallahassee, FL 32306-4021.
Tel: (904) 644 8742; Fax: (904) 644 8642.

Fordham University – McGannon Communication Research Center
Address: Bronx, New York, NY 10458.
Tel: (212) 579 2693; Fax: (212) 579 2708.

University of Georgia – James M. Cox Jr Center for International Mass Communication Training and Research
Address: College of Journalism, 1180 E Broad Street, Athens, GA 30602.
Tel: (706) 542 5023; Fax: (706) 542 5036.

Harvard University – Joan Shorenstein Barone Center on the Press, Politics and Public Policy
Address: 79 John F. Kennedy Street, Cambridge, MA 02138.
Tel: (617) 495 8269.

University of Illinois – Institute of Communications Research
Address: Armory Building, 505 E Armory Avenue, Champaign, IL 61820.
Tel: (217) 333 1549; Fax: (217) 244 7695.

Indiana State University – Center for Communication Research
Address: Reeve 424, Terre Haute, IN 47809.
Tel: (812) 237 3257; Fax: (812) 237 4361.

Indiana University, Bloomington – Bureau of Media Research
Address: Ernie Pyle Hall 212, Bloomington, IN 47405.
Tel: (812) 855 9240; Fax: (812) 855 5678.

Iowa State University – Department of Journalism and Mass Communications
Address: Ames, IA 50011.
Tel: (515) 294 1840.

Johns Hopkins University – Department of Film and Media Studies
Address: 3400 North Charles Street, Baltimore, MD 21218-2008.
Tel: (410) 516 8000.

University of Kansas – William Allen White Foundation
Address: 200 Stauffer-Flint Hall, Lawrence, KS 66045.
Tel: (913) 864 4755.

University of Kentucky – College of Communications and Information/School of Journalism
Address: Lexington, KY 40506.
Tel: (606) 257 9000.

Louisiana State University – Department of Mass Communications
Address: Baton Rouge, LA 70803-0001.
Tel: (504) 388 3202.

University of Louisville – School of Communications
Address: 2301 S 3rd Street, Louisville, KY 40292.
Tel: (852) 588 5555; Fax: (852) 588 5682.

DIRECTORY OF SELECTED ORGANIZATIONS

University of Maryland – Knight Center for Specialized Journalism
Address: College of Journalism, College Park, MD 20742-7111.
Tel: (301) 405 2411.

University of Massachusetts – Department of Journalism
Address: Amherst, MA 01003.
Tel: (413) 545 0111; Fax: (413) 545 2328.

University of Minnesota – Journalism and Mass Communication Center
Address: 100 Church Street SE, Minneapolis, MN 55453.
Tel: (612) 625 5000.

University of Missouri – School of Journalism
Address: Columbia, MO 6521.
Tel: (314) 882 2121.

University of Montana – Department of Philosophy and Ethics in Public Affairs
Address: Mansfield Center, Missoula, MT 59812.
Tel: (406) 243 2988.

New York University – Center for War, Peace and the News Media
Address: Department of Journalism, 10 Washington Place, New York, NY 10003.
Tel: (212) 998 7960; Fax: (212) 995 4040.

New York University – News Study Group
Address: Department of Journalism, 10 Washington Place, New York, NY 10003.
Tel: (212) 998 7978; Fax: (212) 995 4040.

Northern Arizona University – College of Creative and Communications Arts
Address: PO Box 4103, Flagstaff, AZ 86011.
Tel: (602) 523 9011; Fax: (602) 523 4230.

Northwestern University – Medill School of Journalism
Address: 633 Clark Street, Evanston, IL 60208.
Tel: (708) 491 3741; Fax: 491 7973.

Ohio State University – School of Journalism and Communication
Address: 190 North Oval Mall, Columbus, OH 43210.
Tel: (614) 292 2424.

Oklahoma Christian University – Department of Communications
Address: PO Box 11000, Oklahoma City, OK 73136-1100.

University of Oregon – Division of Communication Research
Address: School of Journalism, 310 Allen Hall, Eugene, OR 97403.
Tel: (503) 346 3744.

University of Pennsylvania – Department of Communications
Address: Philadelphia, PA 19104.
Tel: (215) 898 5000.

St Cloud University – Department of Mass Communication
Address: St Cloud, MN 56301-4498.
Tel: (612) 255 2122.
Note: *Journal of Information Ethics.*

St Louis University – Center for the Study of Communication and Culture
Address: 221 North Grand Boulevard, St Louis, MO 63103.
Tel: (314) 658 2222.

Sonoma State University – Center for Critical Thinking and Moral Critique
Address: Rohnent Park, CA 94928.
Tel: (707) 664 2880; Fax: (707) 664 2505.

University of South Florida – The Ethics Center
Address: St Petersburg, FL 33701.
Tel: (813) 893 9579.

Stanford University – Institute of Communication Research
Address: Stanford, CA 94305.
Tel: (415) 723 3696; Fax: (415) 725 2472.

Syracuse University – S. I. Newhouse School of Public Communications
Address: New York, NY 13244.
Tel: (315) 443 3611.

Temple University – Institute for Communication Research
Address: Annenburg Hall 310-C, Philadelphia, PA 19122.
Tel: (215) 787 7433.

Washington State University – Edward R. Murrow School of Communications
Address: Pullman, WA 99164.
Tel: (509) 335 3564.

Washington and Lee University – Department of Journalism
Address: Lexington, VA 24450.
Tel: (540) 463 8786; Fax: (540) 463 8400.

Wheaton College – Department of Communication Arts and Sciences
Address: 501 College Avenue, Wheaton, IL 60187.
Tel: (708) 752 5000.

Yeshiva University – Benjamin N. Cardozo School of Law
Address: 55 Fifth Avenue, New York, NY 10003.

F.

Academy of Television Arts and Sciences
Address: 5220 Lankershim Boulevard, North Hollywood, CA 91601.
Tel: (818) 754 2800.

American Press Institute
Address: 11690 Sunrise Valley Drive, Reston, VA 22091.
Tel: (703) 620 3611; Fax: (703) 620 5814.

Association for Education in Journalism and Mass Communication
Address: c/o University of South Carolina, 1621 College Street, Columbia, SC 29208-0251.
Tel: (803) 777 2005; Fax: (803) 777 4728.

Broadcast Education Center (BEA)
Address: 1771 N Street NW, Washington, DC 20036-2891.
Tel: (202) 429 5355.
Note: *Journal of Broadcasting and Electronic Media*.

Center for Media and Values
Address: 1962 Shenandoah Street, Los Angeles, CA 90034.
Tel: (310) 559 2944; Fax: (310) 559 9396.
Note: Educational organization devoted to development of a media literate citizenry; *Media & Values*.

Center for Media and Public Affairs
Address: 2101 L Street NW, Suite 405, Washington, DC 20037.
Tel: (202) 223 2942; Fax: (202) 872 4014.
Note: Independent organization for research on media coverage of news and media's role in structuring the national and international agenda.

Foundation for American Communications
Address: 3800 Barham Boulevard, Suite 409, Los Angeles, CA 9006.
Tel: (213) 851 7372; Fax: (213) 851 9186.
Note: Training and education for journalists in ethics, law and other issues.

Journalism Education Association
Address: c/o Kansas State University, Kedzie Hall 103, Manhattan, KS 665066-1505.
Tel: (913) 532 5532; Fax: (913) 532 7509.

Media Action Research Center
Address: 475 Riverside Drive, Suite 1901, New York, NY 10115.
Tel: (212) 865 6690.

The Media Institute
Address: 1000 Potomac Street NW, Suite 301, Washington, DC 20007.
Tel: (202) 298 7512; Fax: (202) 337 7092.

DIRECTORY OF SELECTED ORGANIZATIONS

Aims: Independent research foundation to study First Amendment issues and promote excellence in journalism.

Poynter Institute for Media Studies
Address: 801 3rd Street S, St Petersburg, FL 33701.
Tel: (813) 821 9494; Fax: (813) 821 0853.

Radio and Television Research Council (RTRC)
Address: 245 Fifth Avenue, Suite 2103, New York, NY 10016.
Tel: (212) 481 3038; Fax: (212) 481 3071.

Speech Communication Association
Address: 5105 Backlick Road, Building E, Annandale, VA 22003.
Tel: (703) 750 0533; Fax: (703) 914 9471.
Note: *Critical Studies in Mass Communications.*

Washington Journalism Center
Address: 1282 National Press Building, Washington, DC 20045.
Tel: (202) 662 7352; Fax: (202) 662 1232.

Central America and the Caribbean

B.

Caribbean Broadcasting Union
Address: Wilkins Lodge, Two Mile Hill, St Michael, Barbados.
Tel: (+1 246) 429 9146; Fax: (+1 246) 429 2171.
Note: Association of national broadcasting systems of Commonwealth Caribbean and other regional countries.

Caribbean Publishing and Broadcasting Association
Address: Dayrells Road, St Michael, Barbados.
Tel: (+1 246) 436 7715; Fax: (+1 246) (429 2171.

Federación Latinoamericana de Periodistas
(Latin American Federation of Journalists)
Address: Nuevo León 144, 1er Piso, Col. Condesa, 016170 Mexico City, Mexico.
Tel: (+ 52) (5) 2866055; Fax: (+ 52) (5) 2866085.

Latin America and Caribbean Broadcasting Union
Address: PO Box 376, Calle 21, Zapote 2010, Costa Rica.
Tel: (+ 506) 223 4170; Fax: (+ 506) 223 4426.

D.

Central American Committee to Protect Journalists
Address: Byron Barrera, Apartado 736-1007, San José, Costa Rica.
Tel: (+506) 32 82 28; Fax: (+506) 20 24 16.

E.

University of West Indies – Caribbean Institute of Mass Communication
Address: Mona, St Andrew, Jamaica.
Tel: (+1 809) 927 1660; Fax: (+1 809) 927 2765.

Antigua and Barbuda (+1 268)

A.

Antigua and Barbuda Broadcasting Service (ABS)
Address: Directorate of Broadcasting and Public Information, POB 590, Cross Street, St John's.
Tel: 462 0010; Fax: 462 4442.

Bahamas (+1 242)

A.

Broadcasting Corporation of the Bahamas
Address: PO Box N-1347, Centreville, Nassau.
Tel: 322 4623; Fax: 322 3924.

Note: Government-owned organization, controls Radio Bahamas and Bahamas Television.

Barbados (+1 246)

A.

Ministry of Public Works, Communications and Transportation
Address: Herbert House, Fontabelle, St Michael, Bridgetown.
Tel: 426 2669; Fax: 431 0121.

Caribbean Broadcasting Corporation (CBC)
Address: The Pine, PO Box 900, Bridgetown.
Tel: 429 2041; Fax: 429 4795.
Note: Controls CBC Radio and CBC Television.

B.

Barbados Association of Journalists
Address: Bridgetown.

Belize (+501)

A.

Belize Broadcasting Authority
Address: 28 Regent Street, Belize City.
Tel: (2) 78577.

Broadcasting Corporation of Belize
Address: PO Box 89, Albert Cattouse Building, Regent Street, Belize City.
Tel: (2) 77246; Fax: (2) 75040.

Bermuda (+1 441)

A.

Department of Telecommunications
Address: PO Box HM 101, Hamilton.
Tel: 292 4595; Fax: 295 1462.

Bermuda Broadcasting Corporation
Address: 4 Fort Hill Road, Devonshire, PO Box 452, Hamilton.
Tel: 295 2828; Fax: 295 4282.

Costa Rica (+ 506)

A.

Ministry of Information
Address: Apdo 10-127, 1000 San José.
Tel: 221 9524; Fax: 253 6243.

General Directorate of Information and the Press
Address: Casa Presidencial, Apdo 341, 1002 San José.
Tel: 253 4441; Fax: 253 1485.

Control Nacional de Radio
Address: Dirección Nacional de Comunicaciones, Apdo 8.000, 1000 San José.
Tel: 225 7364.

Cámara Nacional de Televisión
Address: PO Avenida 10 y 12, Calle 21, San José.
Tel: 232 7130; Fax: 233 7172.

B.

Cámara Nacional de Medios de Comunicación Colectiva
Address: Apdo 1583, 1002 San José.
Tel: 233 1845; Fax: 253 9483.

Colegio de Periodistas de Costa Rica
Address: Sabana Este, Calle 42, Avenida 4, Apdo 5416, San José.
Tel: 233 5850; Fax: 233 8669.

Sindicato Nacional de Periodistas
Address: Sabana Este, Calle 42, Avenida 4, Apdo 5416, San José.
Tel: 222 7589.

Cuba (+53)

A.

Ministerio de Comunicaciones
Address: Dirección General de
Telecomunicaciones, Plaza de la
Revolución 'José Martí', CP 10600,
Havana.
Tel: (7) 70 6932.

Instituto Cubano de Radio y Televisión
Address: Edificio Radiocentro, Calle 23,
No. 538, entre L y M Vedado, Havana 4.
Tel: (7) 32 7511; Fax: (7) 73 3107.

B.

Unión de Escritores y Artistas de Cuba
(Union of Writers and Artists of Cuba)
Address: Calle 17, No. 351, Vedado,
Havana.
Tel: (7) 32 4571; Fax: (7) 33 3158.

Unión de Periodistas de Cuba
Address: Calle 23, No. 452, esq. L Vedado,
10400 Havana.
Tel: (7) 32 7098; Fax: (7) 33 3079.

E.

Universidad de la Habana – Faculty of Journalism
Address: Calle San Lázaro, esq. L. Vedado,
Havana 4.

Dominican Republic (+1 809)

A.

Dirección General de Telecomunicaciones
Address: Isabel La Católica 73, Santo
Domingo.
Tel: 689 4161; Fax: 682 3493.

Radio Televisión Dominicana
Address: Dr Tejada Florentino 8, Apdo
969, Santo Domingo.
Tel: 689 2120.

El Salvador (+503)

A.

Administración Nacional de Telecomunicaciones
Address: Calle Juan Pablo, Edificio
Administrativo ANTEL, Centro de
Gobierno, San Salvador.
Tel: 771 7171; Fax: 221 5456.

B.

Asociación Salvadoreña de Radiodifusores
Address: Avenida Izalco, Bloco 6, No. 33,
Residencial San Luis, San Salvador.
Tel: 222 0872; Fax: 274 6870.

Asociación de Periodistas de El Salvador
(Press Association of El Salvador)
Address: Edif. Casa del Periodista, Paseo
General Escalón 4130, San Salvador.
Tel: 223 8943.

E.

Universidad Centroamericana 'José Simeón Cañas' – Institute of Human Rights
Address: Apdo (1) 168, San Salvador.
Tel: 273 4400; Fax: 273 1010.

Universidad 'Dr José Matías Delgado' – School of Journalism
Address: Apdo 1849, Carretera a la
Libertad, San Salvador.
Tel: 289 0926; Fax: 289 0927.

Grenada (+1 809)

A.

Ministry of Communications and Works
Address: Young Street, St George's.
Tel: 440 2271; Fax: 440 4122.

Grenada Broadcasting Corporation
Address: Observatory Road, PO Box 535, St
George's.
Tel: 440 3303; Fax: 440 4180.

B.

Press Association of Grenada
Address: St George's.

Guatemala (+502)

A.

Dirección General de Radiodifusión y Televisión Nacional
Address: Edif. Tipografía Nacional, Piso 3, 18 de Septiembre 6-72, Zona 1, 01001 Guatemala City.
Tel: 253 2539.
Note: Government supervisory body for broadcasting.

B.

Asociación de Periodistas de Guatemala
(Press Association of Guatemala)
Address: 14a Calle 3-29, Zona 1, 01001 Guatemala City.
Tel: 232 1813; Fax: 238 2781.

Cámara Guatemalteca de Periodismo
Address: Guatemala City

Círculo Nacional de Prensa
Address: Guatemala City.

E.

Universidad de San Carlos – School of Communications
Address: Ciudad Universitaria, Zona 12, 01012 Guatemala City.
Tel: 760790; Fax: 767221.

Haiti (+509)

A.

Conseil National des Télécommunications (CONATEL)
Address: 16 Avenue Marie Jeanne, Cité de l'Exposition, BP 2002, Port-au-Prince.
Tel: 22 0300; Fax: 23 0579.
Note: Government communications and broadcasting licensing authority.

Radio Nationale de Haïti
Address: Rue de Magasin de l'État, BP 1143, Port-au-Prince.
Tel: 23 8441.

Télévision Nationale de Haïti
Address: Angle Dimas 33 et Route de Delmas, BP 13400, Port-au-Prince.
Tel: 46 0200; Fax: 46 5814.

Honduras (+504)

A.

Ministerio de Communicaciones, Obras Publicas y Transportes
Address: Barrio La Bolsa, Comayagüela, Tegucigalpa.
Tel: 33 7690.

Radio Nacional de Honduras
Address: Apdo 403, Tegucigalpa.
Tel: 38 5478.

B.

Asociación de Prensa Hondureña
(Press Association of Honduras)
Address: 6a Calle (altos), Barrio Guanacaste, Apdo 893, Tegucigalpa.
Tel: 37 8345.

Jamaica (+1 809)

A.

Jamaican Broadcasting Commission
Address: 13 Barbados Avenue, Kingston 5.
Tel: 929 1997.

Jamaica Broadcasting Corporation
Address: Radio and Television Centre, 5 South Odeon Avenue, POB 100, Kingston 10.
Tel: 926 5620; Fax: 929 1029.
Note: Publicly owned statutory corporation providing semi-commercial radio and television services.

DIRECTORY OF SELECTED ORGANIZATIONS

B.

Press Association of Jamaica
Address: 2, 3–4 Ruthven Road, Kingston 10.
Tel: 926 2434.
Code: *Code of conduct of rules of behaviour for the press, radio and TV.*

E.

University of the West Indies – Caribbean Institute for Mass Communications
Address: Mona St Andrew, Jamaica.
Tel: 927 1660; Fax: 927 2765.

Mexico (+52)

A.

Secretaria de Comunicación y Transportes
Address: Xola y Universidad, Cuerpo C – Planta Baya, Col. Navarte,
Mexico City 03028.
Tel: (5) 538 5148; Fax: (5) 519 9748.

Dirección General de Radio, Televisión y Cinematografía
Address: Roma 41, Col. Suarez, Mexico City 06600.
Tel: (5) 420 8106; Fax: (5) 420 8114.

Dirección de Normas de Radiodifusión
Address: Eugenia 197, Col. Vertiz Narvarte, 03020 Mexico, DF.
Tel: (5) 590-4372.
Note: Licensing body.

Instituto Mexicano de Televisión
Address: Periferico Sur 4121, Col. Fuentes del Pedrigal, 14141 Mexico City.
Tel: (5) 568 5684.
Note: State-owned institute controlling television channels and making educational and cultural programmes.

B.

Asociación de Diarios Independientes
(Association of Independent Newspapers)
Address: Nueva York 228, Col. Nápoles, 03810 Mexico City.
Tel: (5) 687 1200.

Cámara Nacional de la Industria Editorial Mexicana
Address: Holanda 13, Col. San Diego Churubusco, 04120 Mexico, DF.
Tel: (5) 688 2011; Fax: (5) 604 3147.

Cámara Nacional de la Industria de Radio y Televisión (CIRT)
Address: Avenida Horacio 1013, Col. Polanco, 11550 Mexico, DF.
Tel: (5) 726 9909; Fax: (5) 545 6767.

Organización Editorial Mexicana
Address: Guillermo Prieto 7, 06470 Mexico, DF.
Tel: (5) 566 1511; Fax: (5) 566 0694.

Prensa Nacional Asociada
(National Press Association)
Address: Avenida Insurgentes Centro 114-411, 06030 Mexico, DF.
Tel: (5) 546 7389.

E.

Universidad Autónoma de Querétaro – School of Journalism
Address: Centro Universitario, Cerro de las Campanas, 76010 Querétaro.
Tel: 16 32 42; Fax: 16 85 15.

Universidad Nacional Autónoma de Mexico – Instituto de Investigaciones Filosoficas
Address: Ciudad Universitaria, Coyoacán, 04510 Mexico City.
Tel: (5) 622 0778; Fax: (5) 550 9017.

F.

Instituo Mexicano de Cinematografía
Address: Avenida Mexico-Coyocán 240, Col. General Anaya, 03340 Mexico City.
Tel: (5) 688 5852.

Nicaragua (+505)

A.

Dirección de Telecommunicaciones
Address: Apdo 2264, Managua.
Note: Government supervisory body for telecommunications and broadcasting.

Radio Nicaragua
Address: Villa Fontana, Contiguo a Telcor, Apdo 4665, Managua.
Tel: (2) 673 630; Fax: (2) 671 448.
Note: Government station.

Sistema Nacional de Televisión (SNTV)
Address: Km3, Carretera Sur, Contiguo a Shell, Las Palmas, Apdo 1505, Managua.
Tel: (2) 660 118/9; Fax: (2) 662 522.

B.

Union de Periodistas de Nicaragua (UPN)
Address: Apdo 4006, Managua.

E.

Universidad Centroamericana – Faculty of Communications
Address: Pista de la Resistencia, Apdo 69, Managua.
Tel: (2) 773 076; Fax: (2) 670 106.

Panama (+507)

A.

Ministry of the Presidency
Address: Valija 50, Apdo 2189, Panama 1.
Tel: 227 5276.
Note: Responsible for the National State Radio Broadcasting Directorate.

Dirección Nacional de Medios de Comunicación Social
Address: Avenida 7A Central y Calle 3A, Apdo 1628, Panama 1.
Tel: 262 3090; Fax: 262 9495.

Asociación Panameña de Radiodifusión
Address: Apdo 7387, Estafeta de Paitilla, Panama City.
Tel: 635 252.

National Censorship Board
Note: Certificates film and media.

Televisora Nacional
Address: PO Box 6-3092, El Dorado, Panama City.
Tel: 236 2222; Fax: 236 2987.

B.

Sindicato de Periodistas de Panama
Address: Avenida Ecuador y Calle 33, Apdo 2096, Panama 1.
Tel: 225 234; Fax: 225 857.

Trinidad and Tobago (+1 809)

A.

Prime Minister's Office – Telecoms Division
Address: 17A Abercromby Street, Port of Spain.
Tel: 623 8060; Fax: 624 3869.

Trinidad and Tobago Television (TTT)
Address: 11A Maraval Road, Port of Spain.
Tel: 622 4141; Fax: 622 0344.

B.

Media Association of Trinidad and Tobago
Address: 35 Independence Square, Port of Spain.
Tel: 623 1711; Fax: 627 1451.

South America

F.

Centro Internacional de Estudios Superiores de Communicación para America Latina
(International Centre of Advanced Communication Studies of Latin America)
Address: Avenida Diego de Almagro Y, Andrade Marin, Quito, Ecuador.
Tel: (+593) (2) 543 011.

Argentina (+54)

A.

Secretariá de Comunicaciones
Address: Sarmiento 151, 1000 Buenos Aires.
Tel: (1) 316 9140; Fax: (1) 316 9432.
Note: Co-ordinates 30 stations and the international service.

Servicio Oficial de Radiodifusión (SOR)
Address: Maipú 555, 1006 Buenos Aires
Tel: (1) 325 1969; Fax: (1) 325 9433.
Note: Controls all state-owned commercial radio stations.

Comité Federal de Radiodifusión
Address: Suipacha 765-6, 1008 Buenos Aires.
Tel: (1) 394 4274; Fax: (1) 394 6866.

B.

Asociación de Entidades Periodisticas Argentinas
(Argentine Press Association)
Address: Chacabuco 314, 3, 1069 Buenos Aires.
Tel: (1) 334 3705; Fax: 334 3707.

Asociación de Teleradiodifusoras Argentinas (ATA)
Address: Córdoba 323, 6 Piso, 1054 Buenos Aires.
Tel: (1) 312 4208.
Note: Association of 23 private television channels.

Cámara Argentina de Publicaciones
Address: Reconquista 1011, 1003 Buenos Aires.
Tel: (1) 311 6855.

C.

Sociedad General de Autores de la Argentina
(Argentine Society of Authors)
Address: J. A. Pacheco de Melo 1820, 1126 Buenos Aires.
Tel: (1) 421 227.

E.

Universidad Argentina 'John F. Kennedy' – Department of Communications
Address: Calle Bartolomé Mitre 1037, 1411 Buenos Aires.
Tel: (1) 476 4338; Fax: (1) 476 2271.

F.

Escuela Argentina de Periodismo
(Argentine School of Journalism)
Address: Uriate 2449, 1425 Buenos Aires.

Bolivia (+591)

A.

Ministry of Social Communication and Information
Address: Avenida Camacho, Edif. La Urbana 1485, La Paz.
Tel: (2) 376350-4; Fax: (2) 371314.

Dirección General de Telecommunicaciones
Address: Edif. Palacio de Comunicaciones, Piso 14, Casilla 4475, La Paz.
Tel: (2) 368789.
Note: Government-controlled broadcasting authority.

Asociación Boliviana de Radiodifusoras (ASBORA)
Address: Avenida Sánchez Lima 2278, Casilla 5324, La Paz.
Tel: (2) 365154; Fax: (2) 363069.

Empresa Nacional de Televisión Boliviana
Address: Avenida Camacho 1486, Edificio La Urbana, Piso 6, POB 900, La Paz.
Tel: (2) 359753; Fax: (2) 375977.

B.

Asociación Nacional de la Periodistas
Address: Avenida 6 de Agosto 2170, Casilla 477, La Paz.

Asociación Nacional de Prensa
Address: Calle Comercio 1048, Casilla 3089, La Paz.
Tel: (2) 369916.

AMERICAS 341

Brazil (+55)

A.

Ministério das Comunicações
Address: Esplanada dos Ministerios, Bloco R, Anexo 3 andar, 70000 Brasilia.
Tel: (61) 223 3229; Fax: (61) 223 3916.

B.

Associaçao Brasileira de Emissoras de Rádio e Televisão (ABERT)
Address: Mezzanino do Hotel Nacional, salas 5 a 8, 70312-970 Brasilia.
Tel: (61) 224 4600; Fax: (61) 321 7583.

Associação Brasileira de Imprensa
(Brazilian Press Association)
Address: Rua Araujo Pôrto Alegre 71, Castelo, 20030 Rio de Janeiro.
Tel: (21) 282129.

Conselho Nacional de Auto-Regulamentação Publicitaria (CONAR)
(National Council for Advertising Self-Regulation)
Address: 1140 Rua Bahia, 01244 São Paulo.
Code: *Codigo brasileiro de auto-regulamentação publicitaria.*

Sindicato Nacional dos Editores de Livros
Address: Avenida Rio Branco 37, 1503/6, 20090-003 Rio de Janeiro.
Tel: (21) 233 6481; Fax: (21) 253 8502.

C.

Confederação Nacional dos Trabalhadores em Comunicações e Publicidade
(Communications and Advertising Workers' Union)
Address: SCS, Edif. Serra Dourada, 7 andar, gr 705/709, Q11, 70315 Brasilia.
Tel: (61) 224 7926; Fax: (61) 224 5696.

Federação Nacional dos Jornalistas (FENAJ)
Address: CRS 502, Bloco A, Entrada 51, 1–2, 70330-510 Brasilia.
Tel: (61) 223 7002; Fax: (61) 321 8640.

E.

Universidade Federal do Rio de Janeiro – Centre of Philosophy and Human Sciences, and School of Communications
Address: Brig. Trompowski s/n, 21941 Rio de Janiero.
Tel: (21) 260 7385; Fax: (21) 260 7750.

Universidade de São Paulo – School of Communication and Arts
Address: Cidade Universitaria, CP 8191, 05508-900 São Paulo.
Tel: (11) 818 42214.

Chile (+56)

A.

Ministerio de Transporte y Telecomunicaciones
Address: Subsecretaria de Telecomunicaciones, Amunátegui 139, Santiago.
Tel: (2) 6726503; Fax: (2) 6995138.

Consejo Nacional de Televisión (CNTV)
Address: Calle Moneda 1020, Piso 4, Santiago.
Tel: (2) 6982306; Fax: (2) 6990031.
Code: *Code of conduct.*

Radio Nacional de Chile
Address: San Antonio 220, Casilla 244-V, Correo 21, Santiago
Tel: (2) 339071.

Televisión Nacional de Chile
Address: Bella Vista 0990, Providencia, Santiago.
Tel: (2) 7077777; Fax: (2) 7077766.

B.

Asociación de Radiodifusores de Chile
Address: Pasaje Matte 956, Of. 801, Casilla 10476, Santiago.
Tel: (2) 6398755; Fax: (2) 6394205.

Asociación Nacional de la Prensa
(National Press Association)
Address: Agustinas 1357, Piso 12, Santiago.
Tel: (2) 6966431; Fax: (2) 6987699.
Code: *Code of ethics.*

Cámara Chilena del Libro
(Chilean Chamber of Publishers)
Address: Avenida B. O'Higgins 1370, Of. 502, Casilla 13526, Santiago.
Tel: (2) 6989519; Fax: (2) 6989226.

Consejo Nacional de Autorregulación Publicitaria
(National Council for Advertising Self-Regulation)
Address: San Sebastian 2812, Of. 608, Las Condes, Santiago.
Code: *Codigo chileno de ethica publicitaria.*

Colombia (+57)

A.

Ministerio de Comunicaciones
Address: Edif. Murillo Toro, Apdo Aéreo 14515, Bogotá.
Tel: (1) 286 6911; Fax: (1) 286 1185.

Instituto Nacional de Radio y Televisión (INRAVISION)
Address: Centro Administrativo Nacional, Avenida El Dorado, Bogotá.
Tel: (1) 222 0700; Fax: (1) 222 0080.
Note: Government-run radio and television network.

B.

Asociación Colombiana de Periodistas
Address: Avenida Jiménez, No. 8-74, Of. 510, Bogotá.
Tel: (1) 243 6056.

Asociación Nacional de Diarios Colombianos
(National Association of Colombian Daily Newspapers)
Address: Calle 61, No. 5-20, Apdo Aéreo 13663, Bogotá.
Tel: (1) 212 8694; Fax: (1) 212 7894.

Asociación Nacional de Medios de Comunicación
Address: Carrera 22, No. 85-72, Bogotá.
Tel: (1) 611 1300; Fax: (1) 621 6292.

Cámara Colombiana del Libro
Address: Carrera 17A, No. 37-27, Apdo Aéreo 8998, Bogotá.
Tel: (1) 288 6188; Fax: (1) 287 3320.

Unión Nacional de Escritores
(National Union of Writers)
Address: Carrera 6, No. 10-42, Of. 402, Apdo 28846, Bogotá.
Tel: (1) 243 9814.

E.

Fundación Universidad de Bogotá 'Jorge Tadeo Lozano' – Faculty of Social Communications
Address: Carrera 4, No. 22-61, Apdo Aéreo 34-185, Bogotá.
Tel: (1) 334 1777.

Universidad del Valle – Department of Communications
Address: Ciudad Universitaria, Meléndez, Apdo Aéreo 25360, Apdo Nacional 439, Cali, Valle de Canea.
Tel: 392310.

Ecuador (+593)

A.

Secretaria Nacional de Comunicaciones
Address: Avenida Amazonas 2415, Quito.
Tel: (2) 446 168; Fax: (2) 446 171.

B.

Asociación Ecuatoriana de Radiodifusión
Address: Casilla 6014, Quito.

Unión Nacional de Periodistas
(National Press Association)
Address: Joaquin Aux e Iñaquito, Quito.

E.

Universidad Laica 'Vicente Rocafuerte' de Guayaquil – School of Journalism
Address: Avenida de las Americas, Apdo 11-33, Guayaquil.
Tel: (4) 392 121.

Guyana (+592)

A.

Ministry of Public Works, Communications and Regional Development
Address: Wight's Lane, Kingston, Georgetown.
Tel: (2) 72365; Fax: (2) 56954.

Guyana Broadcasting Corporation (GBC)
Address: Broadcasting House, 44 High Street, POB 10760, Georgetown.
Tel: (2) 58734; Fax: (2) 58756.

Guyana Television Broadcasting Company
Address: Homestretch Avenue, Durban Park, Georgetown.
Tel: (2) 71566-8; Fax: (2) 62253.

B.

Guyana Press Association
Address: Georgetown.

Paraguay (+595)

A.

Administración Nacional de Telecomunicaciones
Address: Presidencia del Consejo, Alberdi y General Diaz, Casilla 84, Asunción.
Tel: (21) 442 005; Fax: (21) 444 100.

Radio Nacional del Paraguay
Address: Montevideo y Estrella, Asunción.
Tel: (21) 441 542.

Televisora Paraguaya
Address: Rio Paraguay y Guaranies, Lambare.
Tel: (21) 332 823/6; Fax: (21) 331 695.

B.

Cámara Paraguayo del Libro
(Publishers' and Press Association)
Address: Eduardo Victor Haedo, 184 esq., Nuestra Señora de la Asunción, Casilla 1705, Asunción.
Tel: (21) 47053.

Peru (+51)

A.

Ministerio de Transportes y Comunicaciones – Dirección General de Comunicaciones
Address: Avenida 28 de Julio 800, Lima 1.
Tel: (14) 433 0752; Fax: (14) 433 4833.

Asociación de Radio y Television del Perú
Address: Avenida Roma 140, San Isidro, Lima 27.
Tel: (14) 470 3734.

Radio Televisión Peruana (RTP)
Address: Avenida José Gálvez, 1040 Santa Beatriz, Lima.
Tel: (14) 471 9700; Fax: (14) 472 6799.

Radio Nacional del Peru
Address: Avenida Petit Thouars 447, Santa Beatriz, Lima.

B.

Asociación Nacional de Anunciantes
(National Association of Advertisers)
Address: Avenida Commandante Espinar 719, Miraflores, Apdo 3848, Lima 100.
Tel: (14) 446 3070; Fax:(14) 441 7649.

Asociación Nacional de Periodistas del Perú
Address: Jiron Huancavelica 320, Apdo 2079, Lima 1.
Tel: (14) 427 0687; Fax: (14) 427 8493.

Consejo Nacional de Publicidad (CONAPU)
(National Advertising Council)
Address: Alberto Lynch 164, Lima 27.
Note: Self-regulation for the advertising industry.
Code: *Codigo de etica publicitaria.*

Federación de Periodistas del Perú
Address: Avenida Abancay 173, Lima.
Tel: (14) 428 4373.

C.

Asociación Nacional de Escritores y Artistas (ANEA)
Address: Puno 421, Lima 1.

E.

Universidad de Lima – Centro de Investigaciones en Comunicación Social
Address: Apdo 852, Lima 1000.
Tel: (14) 437 6767; Fax: (14) 437 8066.

Uruguay (+598)

A.

Administración Nacional de Telecomunicaciones (ANTEL)
Address: Avenida Daniel Fernández Crespo 1534, Montevideo 11200.
Tel: (2) 404 585; Fax: (2) 486 071.

Dirección Nacional de Comunicaciones
Address: Boulevard Artigas 1520, Casilla 927, Montevideo.
Tel: (2) 954 068; Fax: (2) 963 351.

Servicio Oficial de Difusión Radiotelevisión y Espectaculos (SODRE)
Address: Boulevard Artigas 2592, Montevideo 11600.
Tel: (2) 412703.

B.

Asociación de Diarios del Uruguay
(Association of Daily Newspapers of Uruguay)
Address: Rio Negro 1308, 6, Montevideo 11100.

Asociación de la Prensa Uruguaya
Address: Avenida Uruguay 1140, Montevideo 11100.
Tel and Fax: (2) 913 695.

Asociación Nacional de Broadcasters Uruguayos (ANDEBU)
Address: Calle Carlos Quijano 1246, Montevideo.
Tel: (2) 921 525; Fax: (2) 921 540.

C.

Cámara Uruguayos del Libro
Address: Juan D. Jackson 1118, Montevideo.
Tel: (2) 415 732; Fax: (2) 411 860.

E.

Universidad Católica del Uruguay 'Damaso Antonio Lawañaga' – Faculty of Social Sciences and Communications
Address: Avenida 8 de Octubre 2738, 11600 Montevideo.
Tel: (2) 472 717; Fax: (2) 470 323.

Venezuela (+58)

A.

Ministerio de Transportes y Comunicaciones – Dirección General Sectorial de Telecomunicaciones
Address: División de Radiodifusión, Torre Este, Parque Central, Caracas 1010.
Tel: (2) 509 1111; Fax: (2) 574 8043.

Comision Nacional de Televisión
Address: Edificio MTC, Las Mercedes, Caracas.
Tel: (2) 924 191; Fax: (2) 923 379.

Radio/Televisión Nacional de Venezuela
Address: Apdo 3979, Caracas 1010.
Tel: (2) 746 022

B.

Asociación Venezolana de Periodistas
Address: Edif. AVP, Avenida Andrés Bello, Caracas.
Tel: (2) 782 1301.

Cámara Venezolana de la Televisión
Address: Edif. Torre La Previsora, 7 Piso, cruce Avenida Abraham Lincoln con Las Acacias, Caracas 1050.
Tel: (2) 781 4608; Fax: (2) 781 2702.
Note: Co-ordinates private television networks, programme quality and ensures democratic right of freedom of expression.

Colegio Nacional de Periodistas
Address: Casa del Periodista, Avenida Andrés Bello, Caracas.
Tel: (2) 782 1301.

C.

Cámara Venezolana del Libro
Address: Centro Andrés Bello, Torre Oeste, 11, Of. 112-0, Avenida Andrés Bello, Apdo 51858, Caracas.
Tel: (2) 782 2711.

Asociación Nacional de Escritores Venezolanos
Address: Avenida Lecuna 22, de Velasquez a Miseria, Apdo 429, Caracas 1010.

E.

Universidad Católica 'Andrés Bello' – School of Social Communications
Address: Urb. Montalbán, La Vega, Apdo 29068, Caracas 1021.
Tel: (2) 442 9511; Fax: (2) 442 3897.

Oceania

C.

Association des Journalistes du Pacifique (AJP)
Address: c/o Fiji Times, Box 1167, Suva, Fiji.
Tel: (+679) 314111; Fax: (+679) 301321.

Australia (+61)

A.

Department of Communications and the Arts
Address: Broadcasting Review Section, Bailieu House, 71 Northbourne Avenue, Canberra, ACT 2601.
Te: (6) 6274 6539; Fax: (6) 6274 6564.

Australian Broadcasting Authority (ABA)
Address: Level 15, Darling Park, 201 Sussex Street, Sydney, New South Wales 2000.
Tel: (2) 9334 7700; Fax: (2) 9334 7799.
Note: Created by the Broadcasting Services Act 1992, replacing the Australian Broadcasting Tribunal, the ABA licenses and regulates radio and television services with the aim 'to promote the availability of a range of broadcasting services which is responsive to the diverse needs and interests of all Australians'; activities include licensing, ownership and control, and programme standards.
Codes: *Commercial television industry code of practice*; *Commercial radio code of practice*; *ABC code of practice*; *SBS code of practice*; *Community broadcasting code of practice*.
Library.

Australian Broadcasting Corporation (ABC)
Address: 700 Harris Street, Ultimo, POB 9994, Sydney, New South Wales 2007.
Tel: (2) 9333 1500 (radio), (2) 9437 8000 (television); Fax: (2) 9333 2603 (radio), (2) 9950 3055 (television).
Note: Statutory corporation providing the National Broadcasting and National Television programme services.
Code: *ABC code of practice*; *Charter of corporation*.

Special Broadcasting Service (SBS)
Address: 14 Herbert Street, Artamon, New South Wales 2064.
Tel: (2) 9430 2828; Fax: (2) 9430 3700.
Note: Provides national multicultural radio and television services.

Code: *SBS code of practice.*

B.

Advertising Federation of Australia (AFA)
Address: 140 Arthur Street, North Sydney, New South Wales 2060.
Note: National self-regulation association of advertising agencies.
Code: *Advertising code of ethics.*

Australian Association of National Advertisers (AANA)
Address: Stockland House, Level 11, 1881 Castlereagh Street, Sydney, New South Wales.
Tel: (2) 9283 4620; Fax: (2) 9283 4625.
Aims: To serve the interests of national advertisers.

Australian Journalists' Association (AJA)
Code: *Code of ethics.*

Australian Press Council
Address: Suite 303, 149 Castlereagh Street, Sydney, New South Wales 2000.
Tel: (2) 9261 1930; Fax: (2) 9267 6826.

Australian Publishers Association
Address: Suite 59, Level 3, 89 Jones Street, Ultimo, New South Wales 2007.
Tel: (2) 9281 9788; Fax: (2) 9281 1073.

Federation of Australian Commercial Television Stations
Address: 44 Avenue Road, Mosman, New South Wales 2088.
Tel: (2) 9960 2622; Fax: (2) 9969 3520.

Federation of Australian Radio Broadcasters
Address: POB 299, St Leonards, New South Wales 2065.
Tel: (2) 9906 5944; Fax: (2) 9906 5128.

Media Council of Australia
Address: 98 Arthur Street, North Sydney, New South Wales 2060.
Tel: (2) 9256 5512; Fax: (2) 9954 9806.

Note: Self-regulatory body with member organizations from the press, television, radio and cinema industries required to observe the code.
Code: *Advertising code of ethics.*

C.

Australian Society of Authors
Address: PO Box 1566, Strawberry Hills, New South Wales 2012.
Tel: (2) 9318 0877; Fax: (2) 9318 0530.

Fellowship of Australian Writers
Address: GPO Box 3448, Sydney, New South Wales 2001.

E.

University of Canberra – Faculty of Communication, Media and Tourism
Address: PO Box 1, Belconnen, ACT.
Tel: (6) 201 5111; Fax: (6) 201 5999.

Curtin University of Technology – School of Communication and Cultural Studies
Address: GPO Box U1987, Perth, Western Australia 6001.
Tel: (9) 351 2000; Fax: (9) 351 2255.

Deakin University – Centre for Citizenship and Human Rights
Address: Geelong, Victoria 3217.
Tel: (52) 271 100; Fax: (52) 272 001.

Deakin University – Centre for Research in Cultural Communication
Address: Geelong, Victoria 3217.
Tel: (52) 271100; Fax: (52) 272001.

Edith Cowan University – Department of Media Studies
Address: Pearson Street, Churchlands, Western Australia 6108.
Tel: (9) 383 8333; Fax: (9) 387 7095.

Griffith University – Institute for Cultural Policy Studies
Address: Faculty for Humanities, Griffith University, Queensland 4111.
Tel: (7) 3875 1772; Fax: (7) 3875 5511.

Griffith University – National Institute for Law, Ethics and Public Affairs
Address: Faculty of Law, Griffith University, Queensland 4111.
Tel: (7) 3875 7111.

La Trobe University – Department of Media Studies
Address: Bundoora, Victoria 3083.
Tel: (3) 479 1111; Fax: (3) 478 5814.

Macquarie University – School of English, Linguistics and Media
Address: New South Wales 2109.
Tel: (2) 850 7111; Fax: (2) 850 9476.

Royal Melbourne Institute of Technology – Centre for Media and Telecommunications Law and Policy
Address: GPO Box 2476V, Melbourne, Victoria 3001.
Tel: (3) 662 0611; Fax: (3) 663 2764.

Monash University – Institute for Ethics and Public Policy
Address: Clayton, Victoria 3168.
Tel: (3) 905 4000; Fax: (3) 905 4007.

Murdoch University – Centre for Research in Culture and Communications
Address: Murdoch, Western Australia 6150.
Tel: (9) 360 6000; Fax: (9) 310 2507.

University of Newcastle – Department of Communication and Media Arts
Address: University Drive, Callaghan, Newcastle, New South Wales 2308.
Tel: (49) 215000; Fax: (49) 216922.

Queensland University of Technology – School of Media and Journalism
Address: Gardens Point Campus, GPO Box 2434, Brisbane, Queensland 4007.
Tel: (7) 3864 2111; Fax: (7) 3864 1510.

University of Queensland – Australian Institute of Ethics and Professions
Address: Queensland 4072.
Tel: (7) 365 1111; Fax: (7) 365 1199.

University of Queensland – Centre for International Journalism
Address: Queensland 4072.
Tel: (7) 365 1111; Fax: (7) 365 1199.

University of Queensland – Centre for Media and Cultural Studies
Address: Queensland 4072.
Tel: (7) 365 1111; Fax: (7) 365 1199.

University of South Australia – School of Communication and Information Science
Address: GPO Box 2471, Adelaide, South Australia 5001.
Tel: (8) 302 6611; Fax: (8) 302 2466.

University of Technology, Sydney – Australian Centre for Independent Journalism
Address: PO Box 123, Broadway, New South Wales 2007.
Tel: (2) 330 1990; Fax: (2) 330 1551.

University of Technology, Sydney – School of Humanities (Communication Studies, Journalism and Social Analysis, Media and Text Production Studies)
Address: PO Box 123, Broadway, New South Wales 2007.
Tel: (2) 330 1990; Fax: (2) 330 1551.

University of Western Sydney – Department of Media and Cultural Studies
Address: PO Box 10, Kingswood, New South Wales 2747.
Tel: (47) 360222; Fax: (47) 360714.

University of Woollongong – Graduate School of Journalism
Address: Northfields Avenue, New South Wales 2522.
Tel: (42) 213555; Fax: (42) 213477.

F.

Australian Film, Television and Radio School
Address: PO Box 126, North Ryde, New South Wales 2113.
Tel: (2) 805 6611; Fax: (2) 887 1030.
Library.

Centre for International Research on Communication and Information Technology (CIRCIT)
Address: Melbourne, Victoria.

Fiji (+679)

A.

Ministry of Public Works, Infrastructure and Transport, Information, Broadcasting and Telecommunications
Address: Ganilau House, 7th Floor, Suva.
Tel: 315133; Fax: 301198.

Fiji Broadcasting Commission (FBC)
Address: Broadcasting House, POB 334, Suva.
Tel: 314333; Fax: 301643.

B.

Fiji Islands Media Association
Address: c/o Pacific Islands News Association, PMB, Suva.
Tel: 303623; Fax: 303943.
Note: National press association (operates Fiji Journalism Training Institute).

New Zealand (+64)

A.

Broadcasting Standards Authority (BSA)
Address: NZLC Building, POB 9213, Wellington.
Tel: (4) 382 9508; Fax: (4) 382 9543.

Note: Government-appointed but independent, the BSA ensures maintenance of radio and TV programme standards, and determines formal complaints and approves codes.

Radio New Zealand
Address: Gleneagles Building, The Terrace, PO Box 2092, Wellington.
Tel: (4) 474 1333; Fax: (4) 474 1712.

Television New Zealand
Address: Television Centre, Corner Hobson and Victoria Streets, PO Box 3819, Auckland.
Tel: (9) 377 0630; Fax: (9) 375 0513.

B.

Advertising Standards Authority/ Advertising Complaints Board
Address: PO Box 10-675, Wellington 1.
Code: *Advertising code of ethics*.

New Zealand Press Council
Address: 93 Boulcott Street, PO Box 1066, Wellington.
Tel: (4) 473 5220; Fax: (4) 471 0987.
Code: *New Zealand code of ethics*.

Newspaper Publishers' Association of New Zealand
Address: Newspaper House, PO Box 1066, 93 Boulcott Street, Wellington.
Tel: (4) 472 6223; Fax: (4) 471 0987.

E.

University of Canterbury – Department of Journalism
Address: Private Bag 4800, Christchurch.
Tel: (3) 366 7001; Fax: (3) 364 2999.

Victoria University of Wellington – Department of Communications
Address: PO Box 600, Wellington.
Tel: (4) 472 1000; Fax: (4) 499 4601.

Papua New Guinea (+675)

A.

Department of Information and Communications
Address: National Parliament, Waigani, PO Box 1279, Boroko, NCD.
Tel: 276 681; Fax: 252 298.

National Broadcasting Commission of Papua New Guinea
Address: PO Box 1359, Boroko, NCD.
Tel: 255 233.

B.

Journalists' Association (PNG)
Address: PO Box 85, Port Moresby.
Tel: 212 577: Fax: 212 721.

E.

University of Papua New Guinea – South Pacific Centre for Communications and Information in Development (CENCIID)
Address: PO Box 320, University, Papua New Guinea.
Tel: 267 200; Fax: 267 187.

Index

Numbers without brackets refer to pages in Parts 1 and 3; numbers within brackets refer to item numbers in the Part 2 bibliography. Title entries in italics are for journals and newspapers cited, and films and television programmes. Organizations listed in the Part 3 directory have been selectively indexed, principally international bodies, organizations from the United Kingdom, Ireland, United States, Canada, Australia and New Zealand, and those referred to in the other two parts of the book.

ABC Television (US)   [247], [469]
Abelman, Robert   [590]
Abrams, Floyd   [182]
abstracting services   101, [771]
Academy of Canadian Cinema and Television   325
Academy of Television Arts and Sciences   333
access   11, 13–14, [110], [163]–[170], [173], [177]
accountability   15–16, 18–19, [25], [30], [87], [185]–[193], [551], [563]
accuracy   16, 56–8, 74, 79, [391]–[407]
Accuracy in Media (US)   328
Action for Children's Television   [134]
activist groups *see* pressure groups
Acton Society Press Group   [72]
Adams, Julian   [1]
Adams, Valerie   21, 22, 23, 25, [227]
Adams, William C.   [408], [614]
The Adult Channel   38
adult television channels   38, 50

advertising   6, 27, 29–30, 59, 92–8, [47], [265]–[267], [423], [424], [442], [661]–[696], [697], [766], [782]
and children   96–7, [674]
appeals to fear   92, [605], [675], [694]
codes   95–7, [266], [569], [605], [663], [666], [668], [673], [677], [688], [691]–[692], 258
harmful   94, 96, [663], [669], [675], [693]
offensive   96, [661], [667]
organizations   258, 262, 263, 291–2, 327
periodicals   [697], [727], [728], [739]
regulation   95, [666], [669], [685], [688]
right to advertise   93, [665], [671], [682], [683], [690], [695]
sexual appeals   [673], [679], [694]
use of stereotypes   59, 97, [442], [669]
Advertising   [683], [727]
Advertising Age   [697]
Advertising Association (UK)   97, [696], 291–2
Advertising Federation of Australia   346

INDEX   351

Advertising Quarterly [727]
Advertising Research Foundation (US) [728]
Advertising Standards Authority (NZ) 348
Advertising Standards Authority (UK) 95, 292
Advertising Standards Authority for Ireland 277
advertorials 30, [266], [267]
Afghanistan 308–9
Africa [104], [163], [200], [400], [428], [457], [616], 298–308
African Charter on Human and Peoples' Rights [104]
African Commission on Human and Peoples' Rights [104]
Agee, Warren K. [59], [60]
ageism [422], [431]
Agence France-Presse (AFP) 89, [620], [644]
AIDS 54, [273], [293], [313], [438], [446], [447], [472], [661], [663]
Al-Ahdal, Abdullah [154]
Alali, A. Odasuo [208], [762], [763]
Albania 264
Algeria [238], 298
Allaun, Frank [105]
Allen, Lois [2]
Allen, Walter [337]
Alley, R. S. [591]
Alter, Jonathan [449]
Altheide, David L. [408], [450], [477], [478]
Altschull, J. Herbert 11, 17, [3], [451], [452]
America *see* United States
American Academy of Arts and Sciences [29], [717]
American Advertising Federation 327
American Association for Public Opinion Research [751]
American Association of Advertising Agencies [43], 327
American Convention on Human Rights [106], 324
American Council on Education 256
American Journalism [698]
American Journalism Historians Association [698]
American Press Institute (US) 333
American Society of Magazine Editors 327
American Society of Media Photographers 327
American Society of Newspaper Editors [1], [18], [41]–[43], [50], [177], [525], [704], 327
Amin, Mohamed [428]
Amis, Kingsley [347]
Amnesty International 260
Amsterdam, University of [25], [87], 281
Anawalt, Howard C. [146]
Anderson, Rob [171]
Ang, Ien [74]
Angola 298–9
Ansah, Paul A. V. [163], [615], [616]
Antigua and Barbuda 334
Aquinas, St Thomas 65
Arab Republic of Egypt *see* Egypt
Arab States Broadcasting Union 257

Arab States Regional Broadcasting Centre 261
Argentina 340
Ariel 51
Arizona, University of (US) [183], 330
Armenia 309
Arno, Andrew [228]
Arthur, Chris [592], [661]
Article 19 [699]
Article 19 – The International Centre Against Censorship [107], [108], [209], [229], [699], 260–1
Ashe, Arthur [313]
Asia [126], [224], [228], [567], [614], [624], [647], [649], 308–24
Asian Mass Communication Research and Information Center [784]
ASLIB Proceedings [326]
Aspen Institute for Humanistic Studies [92]
Associated Press 89, [20], [176], [390], [620]
Association for Cultural and Communication Studies (UK) 297
Association for Education in Journalism and Mass Communication (US) [737], [739], 333
Association for the Promotion of the International Circulation of the Press 257
Association for the Study of Canadian Radio and Television 326
Association of Advertisers in Ireland 277
Association of Canadian Publishers 325
Association of Commercial Television 262
Association of Directors of Journalism Programs in Canadian Universities 326
Association of European Journalists 258–9, 263
Atkin, Charles K. [764]
Attorney General's Commission on Pornography (US) [350]
Aubrey, Crispin [409]
Aucoin, James [185]
audience research 49, [325], [367], [368], [369], [718]
audiences 47–50, 82, 83, 84, [21], [76], [185], [586], [614], [764]
Aufderheide, Patricia 60, [453]
Augustine, St 65
Ault, Phillip H. [59], [60]
Australia 18, [13], [84], [114], [126], [174], [301], [305], [319], [524], [622], [647], [700], [743], 345–8
Australian Association of National Advertisers 346
Australian Broadcasting Authority 345
Australian Broadcasting Commission [84]
Australian Broadcasting Corporation 345
Australian Film Television and Radio School [743], 348
Australian Journalism Review [700]
Australian Journalists' Association 346
Australian Media Notes [743]
Australian National University [84], [114]
Australian Press Council 346
Australian Publishers Association 346
Australian Society of Authors 346

352 INDEX

Austria 264–5
Azerbaijan 309

bad language 6, 38, 47–8, [368], [370]
Baehr, Helen [410], [411]
Bagdikian, Ben H. [251]
Bahamas 334–5
Bahrain 309
Bailey, Charles W. [544]
balance 60–1, 74, [458], [460], [468], [469]
Bangladesh 309–10
Barbados 335
Barbrook, Richard [109]
Barendt, Eric [110]
Barnes, Michael [662]
Barnett, Anthony [172]
Barnett, Steven [194]
Barney, Ralph D. 17, 67, 72, 80, [39], [378], [512], [552]
Barnouw, Erik [61], [265]
Barrett, Richard J. [617]
Barry, Vincent [44]
Basnett, David [257]
Bassiouni, M. Cherif [210]
BBC *see* British Broadcasting Corporation
BBC External Broadcasting [639]
BBC World Service 89, [206], [657]
Beard, Charles 61
Beaver, Frank [335]
Beaverbrook, Lord 27
Becker, Charlotte B. [4]
Becker, Lawrence C. [4]
Belarus 265–6
Belgium 46, 266–7
Belize 335
Bell, Martin [491]
Beloff, Nora [51]
Belsey, Andrew 31, 79, 80, [5], [571]
Ben-Yehuda, Nachman [427]
Benet, James [444]
Benetton 96, [661]
Benin 299
Benn, Tony [173]
Bennett, Roger [663]
Benthall, Jonathan [412]
Bentham, Jeremy 9
Berger, Arthur Asa [62]
Berlin, Isaiah 32, 37
Berlusconi, Silvio [252]
Bermuda 335
Berns, Walter [111]
Bernstein, Carl 69, [503]
Bertolucci, Bernardo 47, [357]
Bertrand, Claude-Jean [6], [550], [551], [618]
Biafra [428]
bias 60–3, [239], [248], [449]–[476]
bibliographies [762]–[801]
Bill of Rights (US) 9
Bindman, Geoffrey [136]
Birdwood, Lady 50
Birkett, Lord [337]
Birkinshaw, Patrick [174]

Birmingham, University of (UK) [95], 294
Birt, John [413]
Bishop, F. P. [664], [685]
Bittner, John R. [63]
Black, Charles [164]
Black, Gregory D. [352]
Black, Jay [414], [552]
The Black and White Minstrel Show [437]
Black Awareness in Television (US) 328
Black Citizens for a Fair Media (US) 328
black people [415], [437], [439], [797], 328–9
Blakeney, Michael [665]
Blanchard, Margaret A [112]
blasphemy 6, 38, 39, 47, 48–9, [154], [368], [611]
Bleasdale, Alan 58
Block, Eleanor S. [765]
Blom-Cooper, Louis [553]
Blum, Eleanor 102, [7], [766]
Blumler, Jay G. 85–6, [74], [379], [575]
Blunt, Anthony [207]
Boccardi, L. D. [147]
Boddewyn, Jean J. 97, [666]
Boer War [238], [247]
Boeyink, David E. [554]
Bogart, Leo [148]
Bok, Sissela 15, 17, 35, 53–4, 66, 68–9, [47], [380], [505]
Bolivia 340
Bolling, Landrum R. [230]
Bolton, Roger [211]
books 39, [7]
  censorship of 43–4, [325], [328], [337], [344], [345]
Borden, Sandra L. [492]
Borjesson, Britt [570]
Bosnia-Herzegovina [229], [248], 267
Boston, Ray [786]
Botswana 299
Bourne, Richard [619]
Bournemouth University (UK) 294
Boutros-Ghali, Boutros [113]
Bovee, Warren G. [493]
Bow Group [328]
Bowling Green State University (US) [735], 330
Boyd-Barrett, Oliver 61, 63, 67, 90, [620]–[621]
Boyer, John H. [454]
Bozelli, Richard J. [467]
Bracken, James K. [765]
Braman, Sandra [268]
Branscomb, Anne Wells [269]
Brazil 341
breach of confidence [315], [505], [508]
Breen, Myles [622]
Bremner, Charles [270]
Brennan, Timothy J. [455]
Bridger, Francis [375]
Briggs, Asa 83, [64], [576]
Brigham Young University (US) [733], 330
Brighton, University of (UK) [21]
Brislin, Tom [513]

INDEX   353

British Board of Film Classification (formerly Censors) (BBFC)   43, 46–7, [340], [354], [358], [359], 291
British Broadcasting Corporation   16, 28, 57–8, 87, 90, [64], [214], [408], [409], [578], [580], [588], [589], [738], [778], [783], 291
  external broadcasting   [639], [657]
  government, relations with   23, 24, [209], [211], [214], [239]
  news and current affairs programmes   23, 24, 56, 60–1, [487]
  public service obligations   26, 83–4, [576], [579], [585], [588]
  violence guidelines   [361], [362]
British Columbia, University of (Canada)   326
British Film Institute   [489], [586], 297
British Humanities Index   101
British Institute of Human Rights   296
British Journalism Review   102, [136], [393], [396], [407], [491], [527], [553], [701]
British Sky Broadcasting   28
Brixton (London) riots   65, [483]
Broadcast   [702]
Broadcast Education Association (US)   [729], 333
Broadcast Research Council of Canada   326
broadcasting   16, 20–1, 47–50, 83–6, [47], [49], [61], [62], [64], [70], [75], [77], [82], [84], [86], [93], [103], [160], [192], [212], [214], [280], [347], [361]–[374], [575]–[589], [657]
  accountability   16, [30], [191], [192]
  and freedom of speech   20–1, [49], [115], [160], [164], [166], [211], [214], [217], [218], [221], [223], [226]
  and government   20–1, [93], [103], [211]–[213], [217], [218], [221], [223], [226], [239], [244], [328], [383], [458], [584]
  and society   47–5, 85, [62], [70], [77], [103], [160], [577], [580]
  and truth   57–8, [179], [211], [212], [217], [218], [221], [223], [226], [407]
  audiences   47–50, 83, 84, [185], [280], [459]
  bibliographies   [718], [764], [766]–[768], [773], [777]–[779], [783], [788], [801]
  censorship   20–1, 38, 39, 45, 47–50, [108], [211], [217], [331]–[334], [346]
  codes of practice   45, 47–8, [34], [361], [362], [364], [371], [560], [569]
  fairness   60–1, [413], [453], [458], [463], [565], [602]
  international   [633], [638], [639], [657]
  law   [49]
  moral role   86, [332]–[334], [522], [591], [602], [612]
  organizations   257, 258, 259, 262, 263, 291
  periodicals   [702], [703], [709], [718], [719], [721], [723], [726], [729], [738], [756], [758], [759], [760], [782]
  programming   [66], [321], [365], [459], [477]–[490], [583], [589]
  public service   26, 83–6, [77], [115], [194], [223], [575]–[589], 259
  quality   83–6, [575]–[589]
  regulation   16, 39, [75], [86], [93], [332], [373], [718]
  religious   87–8, [590]–[613], [760], [779]
Broadcasting & Cable   [703]
'Broadcasting Ban' (UK)   20–1, [217], [221]
Broadcasting Complaints Commission (Ireland)   277
Broadcasting Culture Research Institute (NHK) (Japan)   [756]
Broadcasting, Entertainment, Cinematograph and Theatre Union (BECTU)   292
Broadcasting Organization of Non-Aligned Countries   258
Broadcasting Research Institute (UK)   [489]
Broadcasting Standards Authority (NZ)   348
Broadcasting Standards Commission (formerly Council)   39, 45, 47–9, [75], [308], [339], [368], [369], [370], 291
Brogan, Patrick   [555]
Brook, Tom   [271]
Brookside   48–9
Brown, Jennifer E.   [323]
Brown, Les   [577]
Brown, William J.   [514]
Browne, Christopher   [494]
Bruce, Steve   [593]
Brunel University (UK)   294
Bryant, Garry   [272]
BSkyB *see* British Sky Broadcasting
Buchan, Norman   25, [194]
Buddenbaum, Judith M.   [611]
Buerk, Michael   [428]
Bulgaria   267
Bulger, James   [11]
The Bulletin   [704]
Bulletin of the British Psychological Society   [321]
Bunker, Matthew D.   [137], [506]
Burgess, Guy   [207]
Burkina Faso   299
Burnet, David   [5]
Burns, Tom   [578]
Burundi   299
Bush, Alan J.   [667]
Bush, Victoria Davies   [667]
Business and Professional Ethics Journal   [705]
business ethics   [705], [730], 296
Business Ethics Research Centre (UK)   296
Business Periodicals Index   [697]
Butler, David   [212]
Byrd, Gary   [763]
Byrd, Joann   [456]

cable television   38, 50, 84, [28], [164], [167], [344], [377]
Calcutt, David   36, [281], [283], [284], [290], [298], [311], [315]
California, University of   [79], [720], [722], 330
California State University   330
Cambodia   310
Cameron, James   61–2, [247], [457]

354 INDEX

Cameroon   299
Campaign Against Censorship (UK)   294
Campaign Against Pornography (UK)   294
Campaign Against Racism in the Media   [415]
Campaign for Free Speech on Ireland   [213]
Campaign for Freedom of Information   [178], 294
Campaign for Nuclear Disarmament (CND)   [457]
Campaign for Press and Broadcasting Freedom   [65], [73], [105], [217], [721], 294
campaigning groups *see* pressure groups
campaigning journalism   75, [528]
Campbell, Tom   [114]
Canada   18, [52], [174], [583], [647], [706], 325–7
Canadian Advertising Foundation   325
Canadian Association of Broadcasters   325
Canadian Authors Association   325
Canadian Broadcast Standards Council   325
Canadian Broadcasting Corporation   325
Canadian Center for Ethics and Corporate Policy   326
Canadian Daily Newspapers Association   325
Canadian Institute for Studies in Telecommunications   326
Canadian Journal of Communication   [706]
Canadian Magazine Publishers Association   325
Canadian Publishers' Council   325
Canadian Radio-Television and Telecommunications Commission   325
Canberra, University of (Australia)   346
Canterbury, University of (NZ)   348
Cantor, Joel M.   [66]
Cantor, Muriel G.   [66], [444]
Capa, Robert   [405]
Cardozo Arts & Entertainment Law Journal   [707]
Cardwell, Jerry D.   [594]
Caribbean   [623], 334–9
Carol, Avedon   [336]
Carothers, Diane Foxhill   [767]
Carr, Wesley   [595]
Carruthers, Susan L.   25, [249]
Carter, Jimmy   57
Cassata, Mary   [768]
casuistry   [554]
Cates, Jo A.   [769]
Cathcart, Rex   [214]
Catholic Communication Centre (UK)   297
Catholic Media Council   259
Catholicism   87, [352], [609], [611], [760], 259
Caxton, William   [71]
CBS   [481]
censorship   6, 38–51, 53, [75], [116], [125], [303], [323]–[377], [384], [433], [580], [781], 261
  books   43–4, [325], [328], [337], [344], [345]
  broadcasting   20–1, 38, 39, 45, 47–50, [108], [211], [217], [234], [331]–[334], [346], [347], [351], [361]–[374]
  cable television   50, [344], [377]

  film   38, 39, 43, 45–7, [49], [328], [340], [342], [347], [352]–[360]
  government   20–2, 24, [116], [125], [194], [196], [200], [209], [213], [217], [234], [240], [242], [243], [259]
  Internet   50, [344]
  moral   40–1, [75], [323]–[354], [335]–[351]
  periodicals   [724], [746]
  press   21–3, 44–5, [201], [234], [258], [259], [327], [328]
  radio   [217], [370]
  television   [361]–[374]
  theatres   [328]
  videos   43, 47, [375]
Center for Advanced Study in Telecommunications (US)   [772]
Center for Applied Philosophy (US)   [705]
Center for Investigative Reporting (US)   328
Center for Media and Public Affairs (US)   333
Center for Media and Values (US)   333
Center for the Study of Communication and Culture (US)   [713]
Central African Republic   299
Central America   [106], [514], [647], 334–9
Central England, University of   294
Central European Mass Communication Research Documentation Centre   263
Central Intelligence Agency (CIA)   24
Central Lancashire, University of (UK)   294
Centre for Applied Ethics (UK)   [5], 297
Centre for Business and Public Sector Ethics (UK)   297
Centre for Communication and Information Studies (UK)   297
Centre for Contemporary Cultural Studies (UK)   [95]
Centre for Contemporary Ethical Studies (UK)   295
Centre for Interdisciplinary Study of Social Communications (Italy)   [57], 278
Centre for International Research on Communication and Information Technology (Australia)   348
Centre for Journalism Studies (UK)   [406], 297
Centre for Mass Communications Research (UK)   [439], 295
Centre for Television Research (UK)   [575]
Centre for the Study of Democracy (UK)   [573]
Chad   300
Chadwick, Ruth   31, 79, 80, [5], [8], [571]
Chaffee, Steven H.   [349]
Chandos, John   [337]
charity on television   [598]
cheque-book journalism   28, [314]
Chicago, Loyola University of (US)   330
Childers, Doug   [273]
children   45, [186], [295], [348], [351], [444], [522], [591], [674], [764]
  protection of   46, 48, 96–7, [134], [346], [362], [365]
Chile   341–2
Chilton, Paul   [67]

China [224], [228], [647], 310
Chomsky, Noam 27, 31, [429]
Chonko, Lawrence B. [668]
Chrichley, Janine [783]
Christianity 87, [590]-[613], [696], [740], [742], [760], [799], 259, 262, 297
Christians, Clifford G. 12-13, 17, [7], [9], [10], [11], [12], [48], [187], [517], [556], [596], [597], [689], [770]
Churchill, Winston 71, [238]
City University (London) [263], 294
Civil Liberties Union (US) [121]
Clark, James W. [676]
Clean Up TV Campaign (UK) 40, [373]
Clinton, Helen H. [788]
A Clockwork Orange 47, [354]
Clurman, Richard M. [175]
Clutterbuck, Richard [215], [216]
Cmiel, K. [568]
CNN 90, [3]
Cochrane, Wendell [274]
Cockerell, Michael [195]
codes of ethics 16, 73-4, 77-9, 95-7, [15], [18], [20], [31], [43], [47], [58], [88], [187], [228], [274], [295], [326], [490], [550]-[570], [571], [747]
  advertising 95-7, [266], [569], [605], [663], [666], [668], [673], [677], [688], [691], [692]
  broadcasting 45, 47-8, [34], [361], [362], [364], [371], [560], [569]
  journalism 78-9, [5], [42], [204], [295], [533], [534], [536], [539], [554], [563], [648], [747]
  press 73-4, 78-9, [42], [295], [539], [553], [563], [564], [570]
  privacy 36, [274], [281], [290], [295]
  television 45, 47-50, 84, [292], [362], [412], [569]
  violence 36, [290], [361], [362]
Coggan, Donald [347]
Cohen, Phil [415]
Cohen, Roger [252]
Cohen, Stanley 59, 61, 67, [416], [417]
Cohen, Yoel [231]
Cold War 24, [120], [248], [470]
Coleman, A. D. [275]
collectivism 12
Collins, Richard [68], [69], [115], [338]
Colombia 342
Colorado at Boulder, University of 330
Columbia Journalism Review [708]
Columbia University (US) [76], [440], [558], [708], [745], 330
Combroad [206], [709]
comedy programmes [386], [432], [437]
Comm/ent: a Journal of Communication and Entertainment Law [508], [722]
Commercial Radio Companies Association (UK) 292
The Commission on Freedom of the Press (US) 11-12, [3], [153], [155], [161], [529]

Committee for Accuracy in Middle East Reporting in America 328
Committee of Advertising Practice (UK) 292
Committee on Obscenity and Film Censorship (UK) 39-40, 42-4, [342]
Committee on Privacy (1970) (UK) [282], [315]
Committee on Privacy and Related Matters (1990) (UK) 36, [86], [281], [283], [311], [315], [564]
Committee to Protect Journalists (US) 328
Commonwealth Broadcasting Association [709], 259
Commonwealth Journalists Association 259
Commonwealth Press Union 259
Communication [568], [710]
Communication Abstracts 101, [698], [706], [710]-[712], [722], [730], [731], [735], [739], [750]-[752], [771]
Communication Booknotes [772]
Communication Quarterly [711]
Communication Research 102, [637], [712]
Communication Research Trends [425], [713]
communications 89-91, [87], [88], [92], [614]-[660]
  bibliographies [765], [771], [790], [793], [799], [800], [801]
  periodicals [706], [707], [710]-[716], [719], [720], [722], [725], [726], [731], [737], [739]
Communications and the Law 102, [134], [169], [184], [196], [279], [299], [300], [302], [304], [309], [343], [502], [507], [690], [714]
Communications Law [164], [192], [715]
communism 58, [632]
communitarianism 12-13, [10], [378]
competition 26-7, 95, [251]-[267]
Complutense University of Madrid [533], 287
computers [193], [274], [310], [317], [318]
Comstock, George A. [70], [374]
Concordia University (Canada) 326
confidentiality 68-72, 76, [49], [202], [207], [315], [505]-[511], [530]
conflicts of interest 76-7, [266], [544]-[549], [693]
Congo 300
Conseil des Normes de la Publicité (Canada) 325
consensual paradigm 63
Conservative Party (UK) 18, 58, [239]
consumer magazines [266]
consumerism 93-4, [605], [677], [688]
Contempt of Court Act 1991 (UK) 69-70
Cooper, Alison [13]
Cooper, Cynthia A. [363]
Cooper, Kent 14, 17, [176]
Cooper, Thomas W. 102, [14], [15], [381], [773]
Costa Rica 335
Côte d'Ivoire 300
Cotter, Patrick R. [313]

356　INDEX

Council of Europe   [118], [128], [192], [419], [533], [563], 262
councils   16, 77–9, [255], [257], [281], [283], [536], [551], [553], [561], [564], [570]
court cases, reporting of   10, 69, 71, [53], [175], [430], [435], [474], [484], [501], [502]
Court of Human Rights   47, [110], [130], [695]
Courtney, Alice E.   [669]
Courtright, Jeffrey L.   [557]
Cowton, Christopher J.   [670]
Craft, Stephanie   [188]
Cranfield, G. A.   [71]
Crawford, Nelson Antrim   [515]
Creech, Kenneth C.   [16]
Creedon, Pamela J.   [418]
Crimean War   23, [238], [247]
Crispin, Aubrey   [67]
Critical Studies in Mass Communications   [716], 334
Croatia   [229], 268
Cronkite, Walter   14
Cross, Harold L.   14, [177]
Crossman, Richard   71, [203], [662]
Croteau, David   [479]
Crowley, John H.   [671]
Cuba   336
cultural identity   89–91, [616], [622]–[624], [637], [641], [643], [645], [647], [650], [655]
cultural theory   [68], [653], [735], [741]
Culver, Charles   [496]
Cumberbatch, Guy   [339], [420]
Cunningham, Stanley B.   [17]
Cunningham, Stuart   90, [647]
Curran, Charles   [579]
Curran, James   17, 61, 67, 79, 91, [72]–[75], [253], [468]
Current Law Index   [714]
Curtin University of Technology (Australia)   346
Curtis, Liz   [217]
Cyprus   268
Czech Republic   268

D-Notice system   (UK)   [234]
da Silva, Henriques Francisco   [581]
Daedalus   [29], [717]
Dagenais, Bernard   [204]
Dahlgren, Peter   [421]
Daily Express   [95]
Daily Herald   30, [100]
Daily Mail   [71], [247]
Daily Mirror   [95]
Daily Record   [472]
Daniels, Arlene Kaplan   [444]
Dardenne, Robert   [171]
Darlington College of Technology (UK)   295
Dauncey, Hugh   [276]
Davies, Ann   x, [250]
Davies, Christie   [340]
Davis, James A.   [422]
Davis, Lenwood   [779]
Davis, Richard H.   [422]

Daviss, Bennett   [391]
Day, Louis A.   55, 58, [18], [507]
Dayan, Daniel   [382]
De Paul University (US)   [210], [220], 331
Deakin University (Australia)   346
Death of a Princess   24, [440]
Death on the Rock   21, [179], [211], [218], [226]
decency   38, 74, 95, 96, [342], [370], [547]
deception   65–7, [380], [381], [398], [399], [405], [496], [498], [500], [505]
Dee, Juliet Lushbough   [186]
defence reporting   21–4, [227], [233], [234], [237]
democracy and free speech   5–6, 8, 12, 13, 19–21, 27, 85, 93, [127], [141], [145], [148], [199], [200], [204], [216], [221], [262], [263], [307], [434], [503], [533], [571], [573]
Demszky, Gabor   [116]
Denmark   18, 46, 269–70
Dennis, Everette E.   17, 73, 80, [19], [76], [187], [240], [495], [517], [558]
Denton, R. E.   [392]
Department of National Heritage (UK)   [281]
Deutsche Welle   89
Devereux, Eoin   [598]
deviance   [417], [427], [434], [446]
Devlin, Patrick   40, [324]
Dhavan, Rajeev   [340]
dialectics   [156]
Dialog   101
Diffusion   [718]
digital technologies   [395], [401], [403], [404], [406], [541], [572]
Dimbleby, Jonathan   [428]
diplomatic relations   24, [231], [248], [510]
disability, portrayal of   [420], [431], [445]
disasters, reporting of   45, [29], [271], [308], [412], [421], [436], [470]
Dissanayake, Wimal   [228]
docu-dramas *see* drama documentaries
documentary programmes   21, 57, [405]–[407]
Doisneau, Robert   [294]
Dole, Bob   57
Dominican Republic   336
Donahue, Hugh Carter   [458]
Donnellan, Craig   [364]
door-stepping interviews   37
drama documentaries   57–8, [304], [407]
drama programmes   86, [407], [514], [538], [592]
Dray, W.   67
Drucker, Susan J.   [499]
Dublin City University (Ireland)   277
Dundee, University of   295
Dunn, Hopeton S.   [623]
Dupagne, Michel   [376]
Duval, Robin   [365]
Dworkin, Andrea   41–2
Dworkin, Ronald   22, 24, 25, [138]
Dyer, Gillian   [410]
Dyson, Kenneth   [572]

INDEX 357

East London, University of 295
Eastern Europe [112], [116], [120], [259], [632]
Easton, Susan M. [341]
EBU Review [718]
Ecclestone, Jake [73]
economic pressures 6, 26–31, [251]–[267]
Ecuador 342–3
Edelman, Bernard [277]
Edith Cowan University (Australia) 346
effects of television 47–50, 93–5, [325], [339], [346], [347], [351], [362], [365], [367]–[370], [522], [612], [712], [764]
Egypt 300
Eke, Kenoye Kelvin [208]
El Salvador [429], 336
elderly, portrayal of the [422], [431]
elections [65], [383], [451]
electronic church 87–8, [596], [599], [603], [604]
Electronic Communications Privacy Act (US) [307]
electronic mail [307]
electronic publishing [193], [391]
Eldridge, John [77], [459]
Elliott, Deni [431], [496], [516], [517], [559]
Elliott, Nick 44–5, 51
Elliott, Philip [223], [462], [482]
Ellis, John 85, 86
Elsen, Albert E. [303]
Elstein, David [585]
Elvy, Peter [599], [600]
Emerson, Thomas [121]
Emerson College (US) [773], 331
Emery, Edwin [59], [60]
entrapment 65, [50], [492], [498], [500]
Epstein, Edward Jay 64, 67, 70, 72, 74–5, 80, [480]
Eritrea 300–1
Essential Information (US) 328
Essex, University of (UK) 295
Estonia 270
ethical advertising [670]
ethical audit [42]
ethics (general) 3–4, [4], [5], [50], [197]
  applied 3, [8], [44], [512]–[543]
  study of [9], [14], [17], [33], 261
Ethiopia [29], 301
ethnic minorities [415], [431], [439], [660], [797]
Ettema, James S. [497]
Europe 79, 96, 97, [83], [117], [118], [120], [192], [319], [442], [563], [688], [718], [719], [801], 262–97
European Advertising Standards Alliance 262
European Association of Advertising Agencies (EAAA) [688], 263
European Association of Education and Research in Public Relations 263
European Audiovisual Observatory 263
European Broadcasting Union [581], 263
European Christian Radio Conference 261

European Commission 56, [110], [581], [682]
European Committee of Entertainment and Media Unions 263
European Convention on Human Rights 5, 262, 263
European Court of Human Rights 47, [110], [130], [695]
European Institute for the Media [801], 263
European Journal of Communication 102, [25], [57], [276], [292], [387], [437], [438], [528], [533], [563], [571], [719]
European Journalism Centre 263
European Newspaper Publishers Association 263
European Publishers Council 263
European Union 96, [117], [118], [192], 262
euthanasia, reporting of 48
Evans, Harold 14–15, 17, 59, 67, 71, 74, 75, [254]

Fackler, Mark 12–13, [10], [11]
fair trial [52], [53]
fairness 60–3, [449]–[476], [565], [602]
Fairness and Accuracy in Reporting (US) 328
Fairness Doctrine (US) 60, [453], [455], [458], [465], [466], [502]
Falklands conflict 21, 22, 23, [202], [227], [233], [237], [242], [246], [249], [459], [464]
false light intrusion of privacy 33, [304]
Falwell, Jerry [330], [602]
Family Matters [386]
famine, reporting of [29], [412], [428], [436], [441]
fear, advertising appeals to [663], [694]
Federal Communications Bar Journal [720]
Federal Communications Commission (FCC) 60, 87, [78], [131], [191], [366], [373], [453], [455], [467], [602], [703], 327
Federal Communications Law Journal [720]
Federation of Arab Journalists 258
Federation of Australian Commercial Television Stations 346
Federation of Australian Radio Broadcasters 346
Feldman, Charles [366]
Fellowship of Australian Writers 346
Felton, Daniel J. [601]
feminist viewpoints 41–2, 59, [336], [410], [411], [418], [423]
Ferre, John P. 12–13, [10]
Ferry, W. H. 12, 17
Fiddick, Peter [194]
Fiji 348
film [285], [329], [406]
  bibliographies [766], [775], [782], [801]
  censorship 38, 39, 43, 44, 45–7, [49], [328], [340], [342], [347], [352]–[360]
  periodicals [717], [723], [754], [755], [787], [793]
Film Censors Office (Ireland) 277
Filo, John [320]
Financial Times 77, [311]

Fink, Conrad 14, 17, 22, 25, [20]
Finland 270–1
First Amendment (US Constitution) 5, 10, 11, 15, 60, 69, [1], [81], [98], [111], [122], [124], [125], [127], [131], [134], [142], [157], [166], [169], [210], [267], [458], [467], [502], [507], [509], [671], [690], [693], 328
First Amendment Congress (US) 328
Fisher, Desmond [165]
Fisher, Kim N. [775]
Fisher, Mark [278]
Fiske, John 64, 67
Flaherty, Robert [406]
Flaubert, Gustave [344], [345]
Flint, Leon Nelson [518]
Florida, University of (US) [705], [772], 331
Florida State University (US) 331
Foot, Michael [100]
Fordham University (US) 331
Forgan, Liz [139]
Forsyth, Frederick [428]
Forsyth, John [393]
Fortner, Robert S. [596]
Foundation for American Communications (US) 333
France 9, 18, [109], [151], [174], [276], [294], [376], [453], [467], [530], 271–2
privacy [270], [287]
Francis, Richard [149], [545]
Frankel, Maurice 18, 25, [194]
Frazier, Lowell [490]
free market 8, 11, 16, 27
Free Press [721]
Free Press Association (US) 328
Freedman, Lawrence 21
Freedom Association (UK) 294
Freedom Forum Media Studies Center, (US) [76], [745], 330
Freedom House (US) 328
freedom of expression 7, 41–5, [106]–[108], [110], [117], [123], [135], [136], [218], [255], [335]–[351], [424], [632], [682], [699], 261
freedom of information 8, 15, 18, [33], [94], [117], [173], [174], [177], [178], [182], [190], [194], [237], [629], [658], 294
Freedom of Information Act (UK) 8, 15, 18–19, [173], [174], [198], [221]
Freedom of Information Act (US) 15, [302]
freedom of speech 5–16, 52, 60, 78, 90, 93, [5], [104]–[145], [299], [781], 260–1
and advertising 93, [665], [666], [671], [682], [683], [690], 695]
and religion [608]
extent of 10, [146]–[162]
justifications 6–10, [136]–[145]
periodicals [699], [724]
freedom of the press 5, 6, 10–12, 13–14, 14–15, 78, 90, [1], [112], [120], [126], [128], [153], [156], [161], [253], [255], [257], [315], [648], [721], [746], [753]
French, David [624]

French, Philip [354]
Friedan, Betty 59, [423]
Friendly, Fred W. [78]
FT Profile 101
Fund for Free Expression [123]
Fund for Investigative Reporting (US) 328–9
Fund for Objective News Reporting (US) 329
Funiok, Rudiger [21]

Gabon 301
Gabriel, Martin [192]
Galbraith, J. K. 98
Galician, Mary-Lou [460]
Gallagher, Margaret [424], [425]
Gambia 301
Gannett Center Journal [112], [224], [252], [335], [360], [449], [467], [510], [569], [650], [745]
Gannett Foundation (US) [240]
Gannett Media Center, Columbia University [76], [112], [240], [558]
Gans, Herbert J. [481]
Gardner, Carl [415]
Garrett, Thomas M. [672]
Gauntlet, David [325]
Gemini News Service 89, [619]
General Belgrano 19, [202]
Genet, Jean [337]
Gentry, Richard H. [602]
Georgetown University (US) [230]
Georgia, University of (US) [20], 331
Georgia State University (US) [435]
Gerald, J. Edward [150]
Gerbner, George [204], [444], [625], [795]
Germany 56, [151], [287], [528], 273–5
Ghana 301–2
Gibbons, William Futhey [519]
Gilbert, Paul [5]
Gill, Karamjit S. [22]
Gillan, Patricia [340]
Gillmor, Donald M. 17, [187], [776]
Girodias, Maurice [337]
Gitlin, Todd [79], [394]
Gjelsten, Gudmond [597]
Glasgow, University of (UK) [754], 295
Glasgow University Media Group 63, [232], [459], [463]
Glasser, Theodore L. 17, [187], [188], [279], [280], [497], [517], [776]
Godfrey, Donald R. [426]
Goldberg, David [119]
Goldie, Grace Wyndham 84, 86, [383]
Golding, Peter [74], [482], [626]
Goldstein, Tom [498], [546]
Goode, Erich [427]
Goodman, Geoffrey [257]
Goodwin, Gene [520]
Gordon, A. David [23]
Gottschalk, Jack A. [196]
Gould, Stephen J. [673]
government and the media 11, 14, 18–25, 27, 70–1, [75], [94], [97], [103], [129], [142],

INDEX 359

[161], [174], [194]–[250], [260], [383], [390], [529], [543], [576], [584], [750]
censorship 20–2, 24, [116], [125], [194], [196], [200], [209], [213], [217], [234], [240], [242], [243], [259]
Grade, Michael [178], [338]
Graef, Roger 48
Graham-Yooll, Andrew [120]
Granada Guildhall Lectures [182], [584]
Granada Television [182], [584]
Grant, Myrna Reid [179], [218]
Gray, Ann [411]
Greece 275
Greenberg, Karen Joy [24]
Greene, Sir Hugh 49, 51, [334], [487], [580]
Greenfield, Thomas Allen [777]
Greenwood, Catherine [521]
Gregorian University (Italy) [57], [672], 278
Grenada 21–2, 23, 336–7
grief, media intrusion 37, [286], [295], [305], [308], [309], [315], [323]
Grierson, John [406]
Griffith University (Australia) 347
Groombridge, Brian [581]
Gross, Bertram [648]
Gross, Larry [285], [444]
Grossman, Lawrence K. [166]
The Guardian 67, 70, 75, 80, [159], [245], [287], [294], [464]
Guatemala [429], 337
Guild of British Newspaper Editors [152]
Guinea 302
Gulf War 23–4, [204], [240], [243], [244], [245], [249], [250], [459]
Gumpert, Gary [499]
Gunaratne, Shelton A. [286]
Gunter, Barrie [367], [522]
Gurevitch, Michael 67, 85–6, [74], [379], [468]
Gurfein, Judge [58]
Gutierrez, Felix [660]
Guyana 343

Haarsager, Sandra [461]
Habermas, Jürgen 13, [151]
Haefner, Margaret J. [674]
Haiman, Franklyn S. [121], [122]
Haiti [441], 337
Halberstam, David [47]
Hall, Radclyffe 44, [344]
Hallin, Daniel C. [235]
Halloran, James D. [462], [627]
Hamelink, Cees J. [25], [180], [628]
Hampson, Françoise J. [236]
Hannabuss, Stuart [326]
Hannaford, Peter [189]
Hanns Seidel Foundation [629]
Hargrave, Andrea Millwood 48, [368], [369], [370], [419]
harm principle 10, 39–41, 41–5, [181], [335]–[351], [693]
Harmon, Mark D. [167]
Harms, L. S. [168]

Harré, Rom [368]
Harriott, John F. X. [582]
Harris, Christopher R. [395]
Harris, Nigel G. E. ix, 78, 80, [5], [560], 256
Harris, Robert [237]
Harrison, Martin [463]
Harrison, Paul [428]
Hart, Gary 33
Harvard University [440], [748], 331
Haselden, Kyle [26]
Hastings Communication and Entertainment Law Journal [722]
Hawes, William [371]
Hay, Jocelyn [581]
Hays Code (US) [360]
Hazell, Robert [190]
Hearst, William Randolph 10
Heath, Edward [383]
Hebrew University of Jerusalem [427]
Helsinki Watch [123], 261
Hemingway, Ernest [238]
Hennessy, Peter [195]
Henning, Albert F. [523]
Henningham, J. P. [524]
Henry, Georgina [287]
Henry, Harry [662]
Henry III, William A. [27]
Henthorne, Tony L. [679]
Heren, Louis [80]
Herman, Edward S. 27, 31, [429]
Hertfordshire, University of 295
Herzog, William [630]
Hesterman, Vicki [266]
Hetherington, Alastair [464]
Hewitt, Patricia [288]
Hiebert, Ray Eldon [81]
Higgens, Gavin [778]
Highbury College of Technology (UK) 295
Hill, George H. [779]
Hill, Susan M. [780]
Hill of Luton, Lord [152]
Hinshaw, Ed [465]
Historical Abstracts [717]
Historical Journal of Film, Radio and Television [723]
Hitler, Adolf 56, 74
hoaxes in the press 56, 74
Hobbes, Thomas 9
Hocking, William Ernest [153]
Hodges, Louis W. [500]
Hoffman, Frank W. [781]
Hollingsworth, Mark [258]
Hollywood [329], [352], [360], [656]
Holmes, Stephen 8, 17
Home Office [282], [283], [342], [483]
Homolka, Walter [572]
homosexuality [421], [431], [446], [602]
Honduras 337
honesty 61, 73, 75, 79, [5], [380], [503], [533]
Hong Kong [228], 311
Hood, Stuart [82]
Hoover, Stewart [590], [603], [631]

Hopkinson, Tom 22–3
Horsfield, Peter G. [604]
Horvat, Janos [259]
hostage situations 54, [408], [414], [478]
House Committee on Un-American Activities (US) [509]
House of Commons, Defence Committee (UK) [233], [234]
Howard, Michael W. [260]
Howell, Roy D. [668]
Howitt, Dennis [339]
Hoynes, William [479]
Hoyt, James L. [484]
Huffman, John L. [134], [307], [373]
Hull, University of (UK) [174], 295
Hulteng, John L. 72, 80, [28], [525]
Human Rights Centre, University of Essex (UK) [119], [236], 295
Human Rights Watch [123], 261
Humphreys, Peter J. [83]
Hungary [116], 275–6
Hunnings, Neville March [353]
Hunt, Shelby D. [668]
Hutchins, Robert M. 11, 12, [3], [153], [155], [161], [529]
Huxford, Marilyn [793]
Huxley, Aldous 82, [574]
Hyde, H. Montgomery [289]
Hyman, Michael R. [675], [676]

IBA see Independent Broadcasting Authority
Ibsen, Henrik 54
Iceland 276
IDATE see Institut de l'Audiovisuel et de Télécommunications en Europe
Ignatieff, Michael [29]
Illinois, University of [766], 331
image, ownership of 36–7, [277], [275], [285], [294], [295]
impartiality 60–3, 74, [32], [518]
see also bias; objectivity
incest, portrayal of 48
Incorporated Society of British Advertisers (ISBA) 292
Independent Broadcasting Authority (UK) [93], [209], [211], [783]
Independent Radio and Television Commission (Ireland) 277
Independent Television Authority (UK) 84, [93]
Independent Television Commission (ITC) (UK) x, 37, 38, 39, 48–9, 64, 82, 95, [365], [608], 291
Independent Television News (ITN) 45, [463], [464], [470]
Index on Censorship 25, 46, 51, [120], [139], [172], [178], [298], [354], [724], 261
indexing services 101, [782]
India [228], [567], [647], [649], 311–13
Indiana State University (US) 331
Indiana University, Bloomington (US) 331
Indonesia [126], 313–14

information
  freedom of 8, 15, 18, [33], [94], [117], [173], [174], [177], [178], [182], [190], [194], [237], [629], [658]
  personal 32–3, [269], [288]
information society [2], [22], [56], [67], [91], [269], [641], [725], [732], [772], [801]
The Information Society [725]
information technology [642]
Inglis, Kenneth Stanley [84]
Institut de l'Audiovisuel et de Télécommunications en Europe (IDATE) 264
Institut International du Droits de l'Homme 261
Institute for Public Policy Research (UK) [69], [338], 297
Institute of Communication Studies (UK) 295
Institute of Contemporary British History [94]
Institute of Journalists (UK) 277, 293
Institute of Practitioners in Advertising (UK) 292
Institute of Practitioners of Advertising in Ireland 277
Institute of Public Relations (UK) 293
intellectual property rights [2], [180], [269]
Inter-American Press Association 324
InterMedia 102, [129], [158], [165], [168], [261], [297], [301], [306], [310], [317]–[319], [365], [441], [548], [550], [551], [627], [644], [682], [726]
International Advertising Association (IAA) 93, [666], 258
International Association for Mass Communication Research 261
International Association of Broadcasting 324
International Association of Business Communicators Foundation [774]
International Catholic Association for Radio and Television see UNDA
International Catholic Union of the Press 259
International Chamber of Commerce 258
International Christian Media Commission 259
International Committee of Entertainment and Media Unions 258
International Communication Association (US) [731], 259
international data flows [634], [646], [657], [725], [726]
International Federation of Catholic Journalists 259
International Federation of Film Archives (FIAF) [782]
International Federation of Free Journalists 259
International Federation of Journalists 258
International Federation of Newspaper Publishers 258
International Federation of Societies of Authors and Composers 259
International Foundation for Ethical Research 261

INDEX   361

International Freedom of Expression
   Exchange   261
International Humanist and Ethical Union   259
International Index to Television Periodicals   101,
   [702], [719], [723], [726], [729], [731],
   [738], [741], [743], [754], [755], [758], [782]
International Institute of Communications   x,
   [262], [306], [627], [726], 261–2
International Institute of Journalism   262
International Journal of Advertising   102, [663],
   [668], [670], [685], [687], [692], [695], [727]
International Journalism Institute   262
International League for Human Rights   261
International Mass Media Institute   262
International Organization of Journalists   260
international organizations   257–62
International PEN (World Association of
   Writers)   260
International Press Institute   260
International Publishers' Association   260
International Telecommunications Union
   (ITU)   257
Internet   14, 38, 50, 91, [133], [164], [344]
interviews, conduct of   37, 56, 57, [393], [396],
   [492], [496]
intrusion into grief   37, [286], [295], [305],
   [308], [309], [315], [323]
investigative journalism   65–6, [5], [8], [179],
   [205], [211], [252], [311], [496], [497],
   [500], [503], [505], [507], 328
Iowa State University (US)   331
IRA   20–1, [154], [179], [208], [209], [211],
   [218], [221], [226]
Iran   [228], [408], [478], 314
Iraq   23, [240], [243]–[245], [441], 314
Ireland, Republic of   [209], [482], 277
Irish Book Publishers' Association   277
Isaacs, Jeremy   [585]
Ishikawa, Sakae   85. 86, [583]
Islam   [440], [592]
Islamic States Broadcasting Services
   Organization   262
Israel   [24], 314–15
Italy   96, [252], 278–9
ITC *see* Independent Television Commission
ITN *see* Independent Television News
ITV Network Centre   292
Iyengar, Shanto   [30]

Jacka, Elizabeth   90, [647]
Jackson, Jennifer   [5]
Jakubowicz, Karol   [632]
Jamaica   337–8
Jamieson, G. H.   94, 97, [678]
Japan   [583], 315–16
Jassem, Harvey   [280]
Jay, Peter   [413]
Jempson, Mike   [217]
Jenkins, Roy   [584]
Jenkins, Simon   [290], [327]
Jenkinson, Clay   [140]
Jensen, Carl   [384]

Jhally, Sut   98, [677], [681]
Johannesen, Richard L.   [31]
John Logie Baird Centre for Research in
   Television and Radio   [585], [754], 296
Johns Hopkins University (US)   [440], 331
Johnson, Hiram   [238]
Johnson, Nicholas   [191]
Jones, J. Clement   [561], 256
Jones, Mervyn   [291]
Jones, Nicholas   54, 67, [385], [466]
Jong, Erica   [338]
Jordan   316
Journal of Advertising (UK)   [727]
Journal of Advertising (US)   [667], [673], [676],
   [679], [694]
Journal of Advertising Research   [728]
Journal of Broadcasting   [729]
Journal of Broadcasting & Electronic Media   102,
   [267], [280], [307], [330], [366], [373],
   [377], [434], [455], [484], [729], 333
Journal of Business Ethics   [675], [730]
Journal of Communication   102, [146], [186],
   [221], [349], [453], [474], [497], [538],
   [596], [625], [646], [731], [770]
Journal of Development Communication   [615]
Journal of Information Ethics   [732]
Journal of Mass Media Ethics   vi, 102, [6], [14],
   [17], [33], [127], [155], [167], [171], [181],
   [185], [188], [193], [218], [260],
   [272]–[275], [293], [296], [313], [316],
   [320], [323], [378], [386], [395],
   [397]–[401], [403], [404], [414], [426],
   [448], [452], [460], [461], [490], [492],
   [493], [496], [500], [501], [513], [526],
   [530], [531], [537], [541], [549], [552],
   [554], [556], [557], [559], [566], [630],
   [671], [674], [693], [733]
The Journal of Moral Education   [522], [582],
   [589], [612], [734]
Journal of Popular Culture   [735]
journalism   28, 56, 58–9, 61–3, 64–5, 68–9,
   73–80, [5], [8], [33], [40], [42], [52], [86],
   [146], [378], [413], [421], [452], [456],
   [769], [796]
   campaigning   75, [528]
   codes of conduct   73–4, 78–9, [5], [18], [42],
      [204], [274], [295], [533], [534], [536],
      [539], [554], [563], [648], [747], 258
   investigative   65–6, [5], [8], [179], [205],
      [211], [252], [311], [496], [497], [500],
      [503], [505], [507]
   organizations   258, 259, 260, 262, 264, 292–3,
      327–8, 333–4
   periodicals   [698], [700], [701], [704], [708],
      [733], [736], [737], [739], [745], [747],
      [748], [753]
   photojournalism   33, 36–7, [272], [275],
      [294], [295], [309], [312], [395], [747]
Journalism Education Association
   (Australia)   [700]
Journalism Education Association (US)   333
Journalism History   [736]

Journalism Quarterly and Mass Communication [124], [137], [243], [376], [454], [506], [689], [737]
journalists 22–3, 27, 54, 68–72, [456], [468], [508], [542]
 and confidentiality 68–72, [505]–[511], [530]
 and government 70, 75, [197], [199], [543]
 and politics 70, 76
 and the police 70
 as citizens 22, 76, [545], [547]
 conflicts of interest 76–7, 79, [544]–[549]
 ethics 73–80, [27], [255], [380], [546]
 independence of 27, [146], [252], [254], [260], [261]
 methods 54, 56, 58–9, 64–5, 65–7, [498], [545]–[548]
 professionalism 77–8, [550]–[570]
 values of 54, 56, 61, 73–80, [380], [512]–[543], [597]
Joyce, James 44
Junius, Franciscus 5, 6
Jussawalla, Meheroo [798]
Justice for All (US) [430]

Kaldor, Nicholas [662]
Kamp, John [343]
Kansas, University of (US) 331
Kant, Immanuel 65
Kaplar, Richard T. [197]
Kase, K. M. [508]
Katz, Elihu [382], [633]
Katz, John Stuart [285]
Kazakhstan 316
Kazantzakis, Nikos 39
Keane, John [204], [573]
Keele University (UK) 295
Kellner, Douglas [204]
Kelly, Tom [219]
Kendrick, Walter [344]
Kennedy, John F. 33–4, 71, [382]
Kent at Canterbury, University of (UK) [94], 295
Kent State University (US) [320]
Kentucky, University of (US) [529], 331
Kentucky Minstrels [437]
Kenya 302
Khomeini, Ayatollah [154]
Kieran, Matthew [32]
Kilborn, Richard [292]
Killenberg, George Michael [171], [526]
Killory, Diane S. [467]
Kipling, Rudyard [238]
Kirby, Michael [182]
Kirkhorn, Michael J. [527]
Kittross, John M. [23]
Kitzinger, Jenny [77]
Kleiman, Howard M. [377]
Kline, Stephen 98, [681]
Knightley, Phillip 25, [238]
Kocher, Renate [528]
Korea *see* North Korea; South Korea

Korean Press Ethics Commission [37], 321
Korean War 22–3, [238], [247], [457]
Koresh, David [11], [414]
Kruckeberg, D. [562]
Kubrick, Stanley 47, [354]
Kunczik, Michael [634]
Kuwait 317
Kyrgystan 317

La Tour, Michael [679]
La Trobe University (Australia) 347
Labour Party (UK) 36, [257], [576]
Laitila, Tiina 79, 80, [563]
Lake, James Burges [501]
Lambeth, Edmund B. [33], [529]
Lander, Estelle [293]
Lane, Carla 48
Langham, Josephine [783]
language, bad 6, 38, 48, [368], [370]
Lanier, Gene D. [125]
Laos 317
Last Tango in Paris 46–7, [357]
The Last Temptation of Christ 39, 49, [130]
Latvia 279
law and the media 16, 19–21, [16], [43], [45], [49], [110], [130], [159], [174], [182], [303]
 bibliographies [776]
 libel 16, 19, [16], [43], [175]
 obscenity 44, [324], [335], [340], [342], [343]
 periodicals [707], [715], [720], [722], [744]
 privacy 35–6, [282]–[284], [288], [289], [291], [298], [300]
Lawrence, D. H. 44, [344], [345]
leaking information to the media 19, 70–1, [202]
Lebanon [230], 317
Lee, Chin-Chuan [635]
Lee, Philip [636]
Lee, Simon 17, [154]
Leeds, University of (UK) [575], 295
Leggatt, Timothy 85, 86
Lehtonen, Jaakko [680]
Lehtonen, Leena [680]
Leicester, University of (UK) [439], 295
Leigh, David [198]
Leiss, William 98, [681]
Lennon, Peter [294]
Lent, John A. [784], [785]
Leonard, Rosemary [801]
Leslie, Larry Z. [386]
Lesotho 302
Lessing, Doris [396]
Lester, Anthony 8, [682]
Lester, Paul Martin [295], [431]
Levin, Ellen [430]
Levy, H. Phillip [564]
libel 16, 19, [16], [43], [175]
liberalism 11–12
Liberia [441], 302
libertarianism 11, 12, 50, [75]
Liberty Federation 40

Library Quarterly [7]
Libya [239], 302
Lichtenberg, Judith 17, 62, 86, [74], [141], [468]
Liechtenstein 279
Limbaugh, Rush 49–50
Limburg, Val E. 51, [34]
Lind, Rebecca Ann [296]
Linn, Travis [397]
Linne, Olga [438]
Linton, David [786]
Lippmann, Walter 55
The Listener [271], [278], [356], [545], [547], [738]
Lithuania 279–80
Liverpool, University of (UK) 295
Livingstone, Sonia 49, [74]
Lloyd, Peter [328]
Lloyd, Scott [155]
lobby system (UK) 70, [195]
Locke, John 9, 11, 33
Lockerbie air disaster 37, [271]
Loevinger, Lee [565]
Logan, Robert A. [566]
London, University of (UK) 296
London Business School 296
London Film Commission 292
London School of Economics 296
Long, Gerald [199], [297]
Longford, Lord [347]
Lord Chancellor's Department [282], [284]
Los Angeles Times 30
Loughborough University (UK) [221]
Loughney, Katharine [787]
Louisiana State University (US) 331
Louisville, University of (US) 331
Lowenstein, Ralph L. [35], [90]
Lower, Elmer [469]
loyalty 71, [202], [549]
Lubbe, Hermann [572]
Luce, Henry R. [161]
Luton, University of (UK) 295
Luxembourg 280
Luyken, George-Michael [801]
lying 53–4, 65–7, [380], [386]

McAnany, Emile G. [637]
MacBride, Sean 90–1, [146], [204], [621], [638], [648], [658]
MacCabe, Colin 86, [585]
McCarthy, Joseph 58, [509]
McCavitt, William E. [788]
McCormick, Professor D. N. [340]
McCullin, Donald [238]
McDonald, Donald [261]
MacDonald, J. Fred [432]
McDonnell, James [600]
Macedonia 280
McFarlane, Janice J. [433]
McGill University (Canada) 326
McGregor, Professor O. R. [257]
McKenzie, Compton [203]
McKeough, Jill [665]
McKerns, Joseph P. [789]
McKie, David [298]
McLean, Deckle [299], [300], [502]
Maclean, Donald [207]
MacLeish, Rod [485]
McLeod, Douglas M. [434]
McLuhan, Marshall [85], [348]
McMane, Aralynn Abare [530]
Macmillan, Harold [383]
McNair, Brian 61, 62, 67, [86], [470]
MacNeil, Robert [471]
McPhail, Thomas L. [638]
McQuail, Denis [74], [87], [88], [257], [322]
Macquarie University (Australia) 347
Madagascar 302
Madonna [344]
Maines, Patrick D. [197]
Malawi 303
Malaysia 24, 317–18
Mali 303
Mallam, Paul [301]
Malta 280
Manchester Guardian 53
Manchester Metropolitan University (UK) 296
Mander, Jerry 83, [89]
Mander, Michael [683]
Manitoba, University of (Canada) 326
Mansell, Gerard [639]
Manvell, Roger [51]
Mapplethorpe, Robert 44, [344]
Marcuse, Ludwig [345]
Marinovich, Gregory [400]
marketing 29–31, 95, 96, [680]
  periodicals [697], [727], [728]
Marks, Jeffrey A. [531]
Martin, Edwin [398], [399]
Maryland, University of (US) [141], 332
Masmoudi, Mustapha [204]
Mass Comm Review [147], [512], [516], [532], [739]
Mass Media Booknotes [772]
Massachusetts, University of (US) 332
Masterman, Len [239]
Mathews, Cleve [47]
Mathews, Tom Dewe [355]
Mauritius 303
Maxwell, Kimera [302]
Maxwell, Robert 34
media (general) [59]–[103]
  ethics 3–4, [1]–[58], [770]
  ownership 6, 11, 14, 27, 28–9, [65], [83], [251]–[264], [721]
  power of 89–91, [3], [13], [20], [75], [77], [80], [263], [478], [494]
  see also advertising; broadcasting; film; press; radio; television
Media Access Project (US) 329
Media Action Research Center (US) 333
Media Alliance (US) 329
Media & Values 102, [140], [391], [498], [631], [740], 333

364 INDEX

Media Council of Australia 346
Media Culture and Society 102, [68], [253], [598], [632], [741]
Media Development 102, [21], [163], [179], [180], [259], [264], [268], [286], [424], [433], [443], [447], [472], [499], [514], [601], [610], [616], [622], [623], [626], [643], [652], [661], [742]
media ethics 3–4, [1]–[58], [770]
periodicals [733]
media events [382]
media imperialism 89–91, [599], [614]–[660]
Media Information Australia [743]
Media Institute (US) [197], 333–4
Media International Australia 102, [115], [126], [225], [305], [346], [521], [665], [743]
Media Law Reporter [744]
Media Network (US) 329
Media Studies Association (UK) 297
Media Studies Journal 102, [27], [113], [116], [120], [125], [145], [148], [248], [430], [451], [456], [542], [618], [651], [654], [745]
Media Watch (US) 329
Medved, Michael [329]
Meech, Peter [472]
Meeske, Milan D. [267]
Meiden, Anne van der [36], [37]
Meiklejohn, Alexander 8, [142], [299]
Mellencamp, Patricia [473]
mental illness, portrayal of [445]
Mepham, John 80, 85, 86, [586]
Mercer, Derrik [241]
Merrett, Christopher [200]
Merrill, John C. 16, 17, 67, 72, 78, 80, [19], [23], [35], [38], [39], [40], [90], [156], [187], [517], [532]
Merryman, John Henry [303]
Mexico [514], 338
Meyer, Philip 72, 73–4, 77, 80, [41], [42]
Meyers, Christopher [181]
Meyers, Marian [435], [474]
MI5 19, [207]
Miami Herald 33
Michigan State University (US) [688]
Middle East [24], [230], [408], [647]
military and the media 21–4, [196], [227], [233], [240], [244], [249], [250]
Mill, John Stuart 7–8, 10, 33, 39, 41, 52, 65, 93, [47], [121], [143], [341], [342]
Millar, Gavin [356]
Miller, Abraham H. [220]
Miller, Henry 44, [345]
Milne, John [126]
Milner, Don [605]
Milton, John 5, 6, 7, 17, 52, [37], [144]
Minear, Larry [436]
Minnesota, University of (US) [776], 332
Miracle, Gordon E. [688]
Missouri, University of (US) 332
Mitterand, François 36
Moldova 280–1
Mollenhoff, Clark R. [503]

Monash University (Australia) 347
Mongolia 318
The Monocled Mutineer 57–8, [407]
monopoly 11, 14, 28–9, 83–4, 89, [251], [254], [255], [256], [257]
Montana, University of (US) 332
Monthly Film Bulletin [755]
Moore, Roy L. [43]
moral campaigners 40, [330]–[334], [579], [580]
moral censorship 40, [75], [323]–[334], [335]–[351]
moral education [774]
Moral Majority (US) 40, [330]
moral panics [77], [416], [427], [438], [446]
morality [26], [742]
Morality Quarterly 260
morals [324], [329]
Moran, Lord 71
Morgan, Janet [585]
Mormons [611]
Morocco 303
Morris, Colin [368], [606]
Morrison, David [242], [331], [340]
Mowlana, Hamid [640], [641]
Mozambique 303
Muggeridge, Malcolm [347], [607]
Mulgan, Geoff 84–5, 86, [586]
Muller, Ronald [617]
multi-national corporations 28–9, [67], [631]
Mungham, Geoff [241]
Murdoch, Rupert 14, 28, 29, 74, [254], [263], [573]
Murdoch University (Australia) 347
Murdock, Graham [74], [221], [223], [264], [462]
Murphy, Brian M. [642]
Murphy, Paul L. [157]
Murphy, Stephen ix, [347]
Murray, John P. [764]
Murroni, Cristina [69]
Murrow, Edward R. [426]
Myers, Kathy [684]

Nabokov, Vladimir [337]
Namibia 303
naming of victims in court cases 10, 33, [356], [430], [435], [501]
National Academy of Television Arts and Sciences (US) [759]
National Advertising Review Board (US) 327
National Association of Broadcasters (US) [34], [43], [371], [377], [569], [780], 327
National Black Media Coalition (US) 329
National Coalition on Television Violence (US) 329
National Council for Civil Liberties (UK) [288]
National Council for the Training of Journalists (UK) 297
National Film Board of Canada 325
National Geographic [403]

INDEX 365

national identity 89–91, [616], [622]–[624], [637], [641], [643], [645], [647], [650], [651], [655]
National Institute of Mental Health (US) [764]
National News Council (US) [187], [544], [555], [556]
National Newspapers of Ireland 277
National Organization for Women (US) [423]
National Press Photographer [747]
National Press Photographers Association (US) [43], [295], [747], 327
National Religious Broadcasters 260
National Review 17
National Union of Journalists (UK) [255], 277, 292
National Viewers' and Listeners' Association (UK) 40, [332], [340], 294
Navasky, Victor S. [509]
Nayman, Oguz B. [764]
NBC [481]
Negrine, Ralph [420]
Neil, Andrew [201]
Nepal 318
Netherlands 18, 46, 281
Nevett, Terence [685]
New Statesman 86
new technologies 91, [15], [105], [428], [572], [726], [749]
New World Information and Communication Order 90–1, [204], [636], [648], [658], [726], [784]
New York Review of Books [312]
New York Times 71, [183], [273]
New York University (US) 332
New Yorker 35, [617]
New Zealand 18, [174], 348
New Zealand Press Council 348
Newcastle, University of (Australia) 347
Newhagen, John E. [243]
news 44–5, 45, 55–6, 56–7, 58, 60–3, 64–5, 65–7, [20], [28], [74], [86], [205], [389], [390], [413], [417], [421], [428], [434], [435], [456], [459]–[464], [474], [746], [753]
 accuracy 56–7, 74, [395], [397]
 analysis 58, [413]
 as entertainment 64
 bibliographies [763], [789]
 censorship 24, [384]
 fairness 60–3, 74
 gathering 63, 65–7, 74, 78, [76], [417], [487], [491]–[504], [513]
 impartiality 60–1, 74
 interviews 57, [385], [393], [396], [492]
 objectivity 61–3, [481], [482], [491]
 of the Third World 89–90, [619]
 press 55, 58–9, 60, 65, [86], [396], [448], [462], [464], [472]
 radio 60, [393], [426], [614]
 television 23, 45, 57, 58, 60–1, 64–5, [383], [397], [412], [413], [460], [462]–[464], [470], [477]–[490]
news agencies 61, 89, [389], [390], [549], [619], [620], [621], [642], [644], [649]
News Corporation 29
news exchange [621]
News Media and the Law [746]
News Photographer [747]
Newsom, David D. [510]
Newspaper Association of America 327
The Newspaper Guild (US) 327
Newspaper Publishers Association (UK) 292
Newspaper Publishers Association of New Zealand 348
Newspaper Research Center (Canada) 326
Newspaper Society (UK) 293
newspapers 11–12, 13–14, 29–31, 58–9, 73–7, [27], [34], [47], [58], [71]–[73], [75], [80], [86], [94], [100], [170], [177], [238], [263], [311], [464], [518], [519], [619], [786]
 and advertising 30, [678], [679]
 and confidential material 70–2
 and privacy 33–7, [270], [278], [279], [282], [283], [311], [314], [315], [320], [511]
 and the truth 52–3, 54, 75
 censorship 21–3, 44–5, [201], [234], [258], [259]
 commercial pressures 26–7, 29–31, [253], [327]
 independence of 26, 28, [112], [120], [126], [128], [153], [161], [206], [254]
 investigative reporting 15, 65, 67, [47]
 licensing of 7, 14, [144]
 proprietors 10, 11, 27, 29, 34, [45], [80], [252], [254], [792], 263, 292
 right to reply 16, 56
 tabloid [8], [314], [472]
 war reporting 21–4, [234], [238], [240], [247]
 see also journalism; press
Newsweek [273], [481]
Ng'Weno, Hilary [158]
NHK Broadcasting Culture Research Institute [583], [587], [756], 316
Nicaragua [429], [491], 338–9
Nicol, Andrew G. [49]
Nieman Reports [748]
Nigeria [482], 303–4
Noble, Grant [346]
Nordenstreng, Kaarle [567]
Nordic Documentation Center for Mass Communication Research (NORDICOM) [790], 264, 269
Nordic Journalism Centre 264
Nordic Union of Journalists 263
North American National Broadcasters Association 324
North Korea 318
Northern Arizona University [133], 332
Northern Ireland 20–1, 37, [209], [211]–[214], [217], [219], [221], [459], [487]
Northwestern University (US) 332
Norway 18, 282
Notre Dame, University of (US) [736]
nuclear disarmament [409], [457], [459]

366　INDEX

nudity　[295], [329], [336]
Nunez Encabo, Manuel　[533]

Oakley, Giles　13, 17, [73]
objectivity　60–3, [74], [454], [468], [474], [475], [481], [482], [528]
O'Brien, Conor Cruise　[547]
O'Brien, Sue　[400]
obscene publications　40, 43–4, [328], [337], [342], [344], [345], [347]
Obscene Publications Act (UK)　[75], [347]
obscenity　39–41, 43–4, [49], [280], [335], [337], [338], [340], [342]–[345], [347], [366], [368], [373]
　trials　[175], [202], [203], [344], [345]
　see also pornography
O'Dea, Jacqueline　[301]
Odell, S. Jack　[40]
Office of Telecommunications (UK)　291
Official Secrets Acts (UK)　10, 19, [123], [198], [202], [203], [328]
O'Heffernan, Patrick　[244]
Ohio State University (US)　[458], [772], 332
Oklahoma Christian University (US)　332
Olen, Jeffrey　61, 67, [44], [534]
Oman　318
O'Neill, John　27, 31
Open University (UK)　[74]
Oregon, University of (US)　332
Organ, Christine　[643]
Organization of American States (OAS)　[106], 324
organizations, directory of　255–349
Orwell, George　[67]
Oshagen, Hayg H.　[349]
Ottawa, University of (Canada)　326
Overbeck, Wayne　[45]
ownership
　media　6, 11, 14, 27, 28–9, [65], [83], [251]–[264], [721]
　of information　[549]
　of the image　36–7, [275], [277], [285], [294], [295]
　of the press　11, 14, 27, 28–9, [254], [255], [256], [257], [261], [263]

Packard, Vance　93–4, [686]
Paine, Thomas　33
Pakistan　[228], 318–19
Paletz, David L.　[222]
Palmer, Robin　[428]
Pan-Arab Media Association　260
Panama　339
Pannick, David　[682]
Panorama (BBC programme)　[383]
Papua New Guinea　349
Paraguay　343
Pares i Maìcas, Manuel　[387]
Paris-Match　36
Parker, Douglas　[401]
Passarelli, Anne B.　[791]
Pasternack, Steve　[460]

Patterson, Philip　[46]
Pavlik, John V.　[486]
Peacock, Professor Sir Alan　[585]
peer-reviewed journals　[521]
Pennsylvania, University of (US)　332
Pennsylvania State University (US)　[749]
Pergau Dam (Malaysia)　24
Periodical Publishers Association (UK)　293
periodicals　[697]–[761]
personal data　[310], [318]
Peru　343–4
Peters, Bettina　[419]
Peters, J. D.　[568]
Petley, Julian　[354]
Phelan, John M.　[388]
Phelps, Guy　[357]
Philby, Kim　[207]
Philippines　319–20
philosophy　3–4, [32], [40], [46], [110], [114], [132], [171], [534], [588], [749]
Philosophy and Rhetoric　[749]
Phipps, Sue　97
photography　39, 44, 45, 56–7, [47], [272], [277], [285], [294], [295], [309], [312], [320], [323], [344], [400], [405], [531], [733]
　and privacy　33, 36–7, [269], [272], [275], [309], [320]
　and truth　56–7, [395], [398], [399], [403]
photojournalism　33, 36–7, [46], [77], [272], [275], [294], [295], [309], [312], [320], [395], [747]
Pickering, Michael　[437]
Picture Post　22–3
Pierson, W. Theodore　[372]
Pigeat, Henri　[644]
Pilger, John　[245]
Pilgrim, Tim A.　[304]
Pippert, Wesley G.　[504]
Pizzey, Erin　[474]
Plato　53
Playboy TV　38
pleasure　82, [374]
Plotkin, Adam S.　[127]
pluralism　29, [264], [586], [600]
Podesta, Anthony　[602]
Poland　282–3
police　70, [415]
Political Communication and Persuasion　[750]
politicians　33–4, [383], [385], [387], [392], [576]
politics　[450], [451], [750]
Ponting, Clive　19, [130], [202], [203]
pornography　38, 41–4, 50, [52], [154], [335], [336], [338]–[344], [349], [350], [366], [373], [419], [446], [591]
　see also obscenity
Porter, Vincent　[192]
Portugal　283–4
Postman, Neil　82, 83, 86, [91], [348], [572], [574]
Potter, Jeremy　[93]
Powell, Di　[305]

INDEX 367

Powell, Enoch 34
Poynter Institute for Media Studies (US) 334
press 10, 27, 29–31, 52–3, 58–9, 71, 73–4, 74–5, 78, 81, [27], [39], [47], [58], [71], [72], [75], [94], [153], [159], [161], [255]–[257], [311], [553], [766], [786], [801]
 accountability 15–16, [159], [188]
 and the law [159]
 censorship 21–3, 44–5, [201], [234], [258], [259], [327], [328]
 codes of ethics 73–4, 78–9, [42], [295], [539], [553], [563], [564], [570]
 councils 78, [255], [257], [551], [553], [555], [564]
 freedom of 5, 6, 10–12, 13–14, 14–15, 78, 90, [1], [112], [120], [126], [128], [153], [156], [161], [187], [253], [255], [257], [260], [261], [278], [311], [315], [648]
 organizations 257, 259, 260, 263, 292–4, 327–30, 333–4
 ownership 11, 14, 28–9, [254], [255], [256], [257], [261], [263]
 power of [80], [263]
 regulation 16, [75], [94], [251], [263], [281], [282], [298]
 social responsibility 11–12, [148], [150], [155], [156], [161], [529]
 see also journalism; newspapers
Press Association [390]
Press Complaints Commission (UK) 16, 36, 66, 78, [281], [283], [315], [564], [571], 293
Press Council (UK) [257], [553], [564]
press councils 78, [255], [257], [551], [553], [555], [564]
pressure groups in the media 40, [25], [65], [72], [73], [75], [327], 260–1, 294, 328–30
 freedom of speech [699], [721], [724]
 media reform [65], [73]
 moral 40, [332], [357]
 periodicals [699], [721], [724]
Preston, Peter [159]
Prevention of Terrorism Acts (UK) 10
Priestland, Gerald 63, 67, 75, 80, [535]
Princeton University (US) [440]
Pringle, Peter K. [788]
printing 7, [71], [85], [348]
privacy 6, 10, 32–7, 79, [32], [52], [86], [198], [268]–[322], [370], [505], [511], [534]
 codes 36, [274], [281], [290], [295]
Producers Alliance for Cinema and Television (PACT) (UK) 293
professionalism 16, 27, [534], [550]–[570]
Project Censored [384]
propaganda 27, 79, [176], [229], [233], [238], [248], [249], [354], [429]
protest movements, reporting of [394], [434], [457], [459], [462]
Protestantism 87, [611]
Psychological Abstracts 101, [717], [731], [734], [751]
Public Administration [190]
public interest 15, 34–5, 65–6, [74], [286], [453], [479], [576], [577], [691]
Public Media Center (US) 329
public opinion 24, [30], [214], [542], [557], [712], [751], 262
Public Opinion Quarterly 102, [751]
public relations [18], [47], [490], [752], [766], [774], [791], 263
Public Relations Quarterly [752]
Public Relations Society of America [18], 328
public service broadcasting 26, 83–6, [77], [115], [194], [223], [573], [575], [576], [581], [583], [585]–[588], [618], [718], [741], [756], 259
public sphere 13, [151], [171], [568]
Publishers Association (UK) 293
publishing 13, [7], [41], [521], 260, 263
Pulitzer Prize 56, 67, [320], [400]
Pullen, Rick D. [45]
Purnell, James [338]
Putnam, John [246]

Qatar 320
quality 81–6, [5], [571]–[589]
 of journalism 28, 73–6, [527]
 of the press 78, [584]
 of television 8, 82, 83–6, [575]–[589]
Queensland, University of (Australia) 347
Queensland University of Technology [700], 347
The Question of Ulster [576]
Quicke, Andrew [608]
Quicke, Juliet [608]
Quill [753]
quiz programmes [402]
quotas, television programme [354]
quotations, use of 57, [526]

R3/Safety Net 50
Raboy, Marc [204], [583], [587], 256
racism 48, 50, 79, 97, [336], [339], [415], [437], [439], [483], [489], [797]
radio 11, 13, 16, 20, 26, 60, 89–90, [61], [64], [75], [94], [265], [370], [585], [588], [613]
 bibliographies [766], [767], [777], [780], [783], [788]
 censorship [217], [370]
 programmes 49–50, [217], [265], [426]
 periodicals [702], [703], [709], [718], [723], [729], [738], [794]
 regulation 11, 16, 60, [53], [280]
Radio Academy (UK) [783]
Radio Advisory Board of Canada 325
Radio and Television Research Council (US) 334
Radio Authority (UK) 291
Radio New Zealand 348
Radio Telefís Éireann (RTE) 277
Radio-Television News Directors Association (US) [18], [43], [490], 327
Radio Television News Directors Association of Canada 325
Rampton, Richard 21, [226]

368 INDEX

rape 10, 33, 47, [308], [356], [501]
Rarick, David [296]
Read, Donald [389]
Reader's Guide to Periodical Literature 101
Real, Michael [402]
'reality' television 57, 64, [276], [292]
Reaves, Shiela [403], [404]
reconstructions 57, [76], [292]
Red Hot Dutch 38
Redmond, Phil [368]
Reed, John [238]
Rees-Mogg, William [159]
Reeves, Geoffrey 91, [645]
reference books [762]–[801]
refugees [24]
regulation 11, 16, 78, [16], [65], [69], [75], [79], [121], [123], [127], [130], [133], [141], [187], [254], [341], [349], [618], [718], [726], [725], [798]
  advertising 95–7, [666], [688], [691], [695]
  broadcasting 16, 39, [75], [86], [93], [191], [332], [361]–[363], [365], [366], [373], [377], [575], [586]
  films 46–7, [352]–[366]
  press 78, [141], [161], [251], [255]–[257], [281]–[284], [298]
Reid, Traciel V. [169]
Reinsch, Roger [302]
Reith, John C. W. (Lord Reith) 83–4, 86, [588]
relief agencies [29], [412], [436], [441]
religion and the media 49, 87–8, [56], [414], [535], [590]–[613], [696]
  periodicals [740], [742], [769]
religious broadcasting 87–8, [590]–[613], [760], [779], 260, 261
religious cults [11], [414]
reply, right of 16, [175], [187], [192]
reporter–source agreements 69, [506], [508]
Reporters Committee for the Freedom of the Press (US) [746], 329
Reporters Sans Frontières [128], 261
Reuss, Carol [23]
Reuters 89, [199], [389], [620]
Richardson, Alan [73]
Richstad, Jim [168]
Rieken, Glen [687]
right
  of reply 16, [175], [187], [192]
  to advertise 93, [665], [671], [682], [683], [690], [695]
  to communicate [163], [165], [168]
  to fair trial [52], [53]
  to know 14–15, 74, [171]–[184], [194], [202], [225], [242], [505], [671]
  to publish 7, 8
Righter, Rosemary [129]
Rijkens, Rein [688]
riots, reporting of 65, [415], [483], [489]
Rivers, William L. [47], [48]
Roach, Colleen [636]
Robert Schuman Institute of Journalism 264
Roberts, Churchill L. [330]

Robertson, Geoffrey [49], [130]
Robertson, James C. [358]
Robillard, Serge 257
Robinson, Glen O. [92]
Rocheron, Yvette [438]
Rock, Paul 55
Rogers, Everette M. [514]
Rogers, Heather [194]
Romania 284–5
Roosevelt, Franklin D. 5
Roseanne [386]
Ross, Andrew [473]
Ross, Karen [439]
Ross, Sir William David [255]
Roth, John K. [50]
Rotzoll, Kim B. 12, [11], [689]
Royal Commission on the Press (UK) 11, 28, [72], [255]–[257]
Royal Family (UK) 34, 35, 36, [290], [382]
Royal Melbourne Institute of Technology (Australia) 347
Royal Television Society [758], 293
Royle, Trevor [247]
Rubin, Bernard [51]
Rubinstein, Eli A. [374]
Ruby, Jay [285]
Rushdie, Salman [130], [154]
Russell, Bertrand 49
Russell, Nick [52]
Russell, William Howard 23, [238], [247]
Russia [470], [567], 285
Rwanda 37, [441], 304

Sadurski, Wojciech [114]
Said, Edward W. [440]
St Cloud University (US) [732], 332
St Louis University (US) [713], 332
St Paul University (Canada) 326
Samarajiva, Rohan [306]
Samoriski, Jan H. [307], [373]
Sampson, Sally [354]
satellite television 38, 50, 84, 87
Saudi Arabia 24, 320
Scandinavia [790]
Scarman, Lord 65, [182], [415], [483]
Scharf, Albert [581]
Scharff, J. Laurent [131]
Scharlott, Bradford W. [690]
Schauer, Frederick 14, 17, [132]
Schiller, Herbert I. 90, [646]
Schlesinger, Philip 60–1, 64, 67, [223], [477], [487]
Schmid, Alex P. [222]
Schmuhl, Robert [536]
Schoenbrun, David [475]
Schramm, Wilbur [47], [48]
Schudson, Michael 55, 67, [74], [145], [205]
Schultze, Quentin J. [691]
Schwarz, Ted [133]
Schwarzlose, Richard A. [792]
Scorsese, Martin [130], [611]
Scotland 37, 45, [271], [472], 293, 295, 296

Scott, C. P.   53
Scott, Colin   [436], [441]
Scott, George   [390]
Scottish Office   [282], [284]
Scottish Newspaper Publishers Association   293
Scottish Publishers Association   293
Screen   [754]
Screen Education   [754]
Seaton, Jean   [75]
secrecy   19, 21–2, 32, 68–72, [65], [123], [154], [198], [202], [203], [207], [224], [290], [500], [505], [510]
secret services   19, [198], [201], [207]
secret taping   [500]
self-regulation   78–9, [187], [281], [419]
  advertising   95–7, [666], [691]
  broadcasting   [79], [569]
  press   16, [281], [283], [284], [298], [327], [553]
Sendall, Bernard   [93]
Senegal   304
Serbia   20, [229], 285–6
Seven Network (Australia)   37, [305]
sex   38, 41–2, 43, 45, 48–9, [339], [369], [376], [423], [673], [679], [694], [762]
sexism   [47], [437]
sexual minorities   [421], [431], [446]
sexual portrayal   41–2, 48–9, [336], [338], [339], [343], [354], [365], [369]
sexual stereotyping by the media   59, 97, [370], [431], [444], [669]
Seymour-Ure, Colin   55, 67, [94]
Shah, Eddie   29
Shanor, Donald R.   [224]
Sharon, Ariel   [175]
Shaw, George Bernard   16
Shawcross, Lord   [256], [347]
Shearer, Ann   [308]
Shearer, Benjamin F.   [793]
Sheffield Hallam University (UK)   296
Shegog, Eric   [600]
Sherer, Michael D.   [309]
shock jocks   49–50
Sidis, William   35
Siefert, Marsha   [625]
Sierra Leone   305
Sight and Sound   [357], [755]
Signorielli, Nancy   [795]
Simic, Predrag   [248]
Simmons, Charles E.   [310]
Simon Fraser University (Canada)   326
Sinclair, John   90, [647]
Singapore   320–1
Singer, Jane B.   [193]
Singh, Kusum   [648]
Singhal, Arvind   [514]
Sinn Fein   [154]
Sixth Amendment (US Constitution)   [53]
The $64,000 Question   [402]
Slide, Anthony   [794]
Sloan, David W.   [796]
Slovakia   286

Slovenia   286
Smith, A. C. H.   [95]
Smith, Anthony   83, 86, [96], [585], [649], [650], [651]
Smith, Ron F.   [520]
Smith, Victoria   [776]
Snoddy, Raymond   8, 17, 18–19, 25, 69, [311]
Snorgrass, J. William   [797]
Snow, Marcellus S.   [798]
Snow, Robert P.   [450]
snuff films   39
soap operas   48–9, 86, [514], [538], [592]
Sobel, Lester A.   [53]
Social Morality Council (UK)   [734]
social responsibility   11–13, 35, 74, 95, 96, 97, [3], [30], [48], [88], [150], [153], [155], [161], [162]
Society   [62]
Society for the Eradication of Television (US)   329
Society of Authors (UK)   293
Society of Professional Journalists (US)   73, 74, [1], [18], [43], [414], [490], [534], [733], 328
Sociological Abstracts   101, [751]
Soldier of Fortune   [693]
Solzhenitsyn, Alexander   15–16
Somalia   37, [441]
Sonoma State University (US)   [384], 332
Sontag, Susan   [47], [312]
Soukup, Paul A.   [609], [610], [799]
sources of information   68–72, [50], [505]–[511], [530], [554]
South Africa   [200], [400], [457], [652], 305–6
South America   [106], [514], [647], 339–45
South Australia, University of   347
South East Asia   [614], [624]
South Florida, University of (US)   332
South Korea   [37], 321
Soviet Union *see* Russia
Spain   286–7
Special Broadcasting Service (Australia)   345
The Spectator   75
speech, freedom of   5–16, 52, 60, 78, 90, 93, [5], [104]–[145], [299], [781], 260–1
Speech Communication Association (US)   [716], 334
spin-doctors   [385]
  see also government; politicians
Splichal, Sigman L.   [506]
sponsorship   30–1, 84, [265]
spying   19, [198], [201], [203], [207], [322]
Sri Lanka   [228], 321–2
staging events for the camera   56, [397], [405]
Stanford University (US)   332
Stead, W. T.   75
Steele, Bob   [414]
Steele, Robert M.   [537]
stereotyping by the media   59, 97, [370], [371], [431], [435], [444], [669]
Stern, Howard   49
Stewart, Ian   25, [249]
Stewart, Olivia   86, [585]

Stirling, University of (UK) [464], 296
Stout, Daniel A. [611]
Stovall, James Glen [313]
Strathclyde, University of (UK) 296
Street, Harry [130]
strikes, reporting of [459], [466]
Student Press Law Center (US) 329–30
Studies in Broadcasting [587], [756]
Sudan 306
Suez crisis 24, [383]
suicide, reporting of [448]
Summers, John B. [569]
Sumner, Tricia 25, [194]
Sunday Sport 77
Sunday Times 15, 24, 56, 59, 65, 71, 75
Supreme Court (US) 69, 71, 93, [121], [142], [299], [302]
Surgeon General (US) [374]
Sussex, University of (UK) 297
Sutherland, John C. [538]
Swain, Bruce M. [539]
Swaziland 306
Sweden 18, 97, [174], [482], [570], [583], 287–8
Switzerland 289–90
Sydney, University of Technology (Australia) 347
Syracuse University (US) 333
Syria 322

tabloid newspapers 33, 36, [8], [75], [314], [421]
Taiwan 322
Tajikistan 322
Tansey, Richard [675], [676], [692]
Tanzania 306
taste and decency 38–51, 96, [323]–[334], [370], [547]
Tavernier, Bertrand [354]
Taylor, A. J. P. 83, 86
Taylor, S. J. [314]
technical communication [2]
telecommunications [301], [306], [641]
  bibliographies [798], [800], [801]
  organizations 257, 264, 291, 327
  periodicals [703], [706], [707], [714], [715], [720], [722], [725], [726], [739], [757], [761], [798], [801]
Telecommunications Abstracts [697], [703], [757]
Telecommunications Policy [757]
Telecommunications Research and Action Center (US) 330
télé-réalité [276]
telethons [598]
televangelism 87, [330], [593], [594], [596], [599], [600], [602], [606]
television 11, 13, 16, 23, 26, 29–30, 48–50, 56, 57–8, 58, 64–5, 82, 83–6, 89, [29], [61], [62], [64], [66], [70], [78], [79], [82], [89], [93], [94], [102], [166], [167], [192], [239], [265], [370], [383], [402], [407], [413], [522], [575]–[589], [647], [659], [768], [773], [782], [788], [801]
access to 13, [164]
advertising 30–1, 95, 97, [265], [678], [695]
and privacy 37, [265], [276], [285], [292], [296], [304]
and truth 57–8, [386], [402], [407], [413]
censorship 38–9, [209], [211], [226], [243], [244], [326], [364], [366], [371]
codes 45, 47–50, 84, [292], [362], [412], [569]
effects of 47–50, 93–5, [325], [339], [346], [347], [351], [361]–[374], [522], [612], [712], [764]
fairness 60–1
moral role 40, 86, [296], [334], [346], [514], [522], [538]
periodicals [717], [723], [729], [754], [755], [758], [759], [787], [794]
pressure groups 40, [331]–[334]
programmes 29, 57–8, 85–6, [211], [304], [402], [514], [538]
quality 82, 83–6, [575]–[589]
regulation 11, 84, 95, 97, [53], [192], [362], [365], [366]
religious [590]–[613], [779]
stereotyping [420], [422], [439]
violence on 43, 45, [223], [334], [361], [362], [363], [367]
women and [410], [442]
Television: the Journal of the Royal Television Society [334], [758]
Television Mail [702]
Television New Zealand 348
Television Quarterly 102, [131], [166], [244], [246], [371], [372], [402], [465], [469], [471], [479], [480], [485], [486], [495], [565], [577], [759]
Television Weekly [702]
Temple University (US) 333
terrorism 10, 20–1, [5], [204], [208], [210], [211], [215], [216], [219], [220], [222], [223], [225], [464], [535], [763], [795]
Tester, Keith [54]
Thailand 323
thalidomide affair 15, 59, [443]
Thames Television 21, [211], [226], [407]
That Was The Week That Was [383]
Thatcher, Margaret 18, 20–1, [208]
Thayer, Lee [55]
theatres [328]
Third World, reporting of 59, 89–91, [56], [158], [163], [206], [614], [616], [619], [620], [628], [629], [633], [642], [645], [649], [742]
This Week [211], [226]
Thomas Jefferson Center for the Protection of Free Expression (US) 330
Thompson, Margaret E. [349]
Thoveron, Gabriel [442]
Thussu, Daya Kishan [621]
Tickton, Stanley [366]
Time [161], [175], [273], [403], [481]

INDEX   371

Time–Warner   28
The Times   21, 22, 23, 26, 52, [159], [201], [247], [254], [270], [290], [413]
Tindall, Matthew   9
Today   29
Togo   306
Tomalin, Nicholas   65, 67, 73, 75, 80, [540]
Tomaselli, Keyan   [652]
Tomlinson, Don E.   [541], [693]
Tomlinson, John   [653]
Tonight   84, [383]
Towler, Robert   [600]
Traber, Michael   [12], [56], [250], [443]
Tracey, Michael   [331], [340]
trades unions   [65], [465], 258, 263
Trauth, Denise M.   [134], [373]
Treise, Debbie   [694]
trespass   [502]
Trevelyan, John   [359]
trials for obscenity   44, 71, 93, [175], [202], [203], [344], [345]
Trinidad and Tobago   339
Truman, Harry S.   34
truth   4, 6, 7–8, 22, 52–67, 74–5, 79, 80, 95, [7], [8], [378]–[390], [395], [396], [398], [399], [404], [407], [518], [520]
Tuchman, Gaye   [444], [488]
Tulsa, University of (US)   [698]
Tumber, Howard   [242], [489], [548]
Tumbledown   [407]
Tunisia   306–7
Tunstall, Jeremy   90, [97], [263], [654], [655], [656]
Turkey   290
Turkmenistan   323
Turner, Ted   [3]
Tusa, John   23–4, 25, 53, [160], [206], [657]
TV Erotica   38

Uganda   307
UK press gazette   67
Ukraine   290–1
UNDA – International Catholic Association for Radio and Television   [760], 259
UNDA News   [760]
understanding   58–9, [408]–[448]
UNESCO   90–1, 101, [128], [129], [146], [204], [561], [567], [621], [638], [639], [648], [658], [795], [800], 257
Union Internationale des Journalistes et de la Presse de Langue Française   260
United Arab Emirates   323
United Kingdom   10, 11, 14, 15, 18–19, 20–1, 28, 60–1, 70–1, 75–6, 83–4, 87, 88, [13], [49], [65], [75], [77], [86], [94], [95], [97], [99], [103], [105], [130], [139], [151], [179], [182], [194], [195], [198], [211], [213], [214], [216]–[219], [221], [253], [255], [256]–[258], [263], [331]–[334], [342], [353], [357], [358], [409], [415], [416], [438], [459], [462], [464], [470], [483], [528], [560], [576], [578], [579], [580], [583]–[585], [588], [589], [607], [613], [701], [702], [741], [796], 291–7
advertising   30, 92, 95–6, 97, [670]
censorship   20–1, 24, 38–9, 39–40, 46–7, [75], [130], [194], [209], [211], [213], [216]–[219], [221], [226], [340], [353], [355], [357], [358]
films   39, 43, 45, 46–7, [340], [342], [353], [354], [355], [357], [358], [359]
freedom of information   8, 15, 18–19, [173], [174], [190], [198], [203], [214], [226], [237]
government and media   20–1, 23, 24, [211], [221], [226], [227], [237], [239], [383], [385], [543], [584]
laws   10, [49], [110], [130], [174], [182], [303]
media ownership   28–9, [253]
newspapers   10, 11, 16, 27, 28–9, 30, 67, 71, 75, [71], [72], [80], [86], [94], [95], [100], [254], [255]–[257], [263], [281], [311], [314], [472], [553], [564], [786]
organizations   291–7
privacy   33, 35–6, 37, [278], [281]–[284], [287], [288], [290], [291], [298], [322], [327]
radio   16, 20–1, 88, 89, [64], [75], [86], [94], [189], [209], [212], [370], [783]
regulation   16, 46–7, 49, 50–1, [75], [93], [365], [582], [608]
right to know   14–15, [182], [202]
secrecy   18–19, [198], [201], [202], [203], [207]
television   16, 20–1, 24, 30–1, 37, 38–9, 40, 45, 47–9, 50, 57–8, 83–4, 88, [64], [75], [86], [93], [94], [139], [209], [211], [212], [331], [370], [383], [407], [420], [483], [487], [489], [573], [576], [580], [583], [603], [608]
videos   43, 47
United Nations   5, 24, 33, [113], [135], [229], [629], 257
United States   9, 10, 11–12, 14, 15, 21–2, 23–4, 28, 58, 60, 69, 71, 85–6, 87–8, [13], [16], [32], [34], [39], [42], [43], [53], [55], [59], [60], [98], [106], [111], [124], [127], [131], [134], [137], [142], [167], [169], [174], [175], [187], [197], [205], [220], [251], [273], [303], [330], [363], [366], [384], [460], [471], [476], [503], [509], [520], [524], [530], [537], [539], [567], [583], [593], [602], [603], [604], [654]–[656], [660], [698], [703], [736], [745], 327–34
advertising   29–30, [265], [266], [267], [668], [671], [672], [690]
censorship   23, 39–40, 46, [210], [220], [343], [352], [353], [360], [371]
films   39, 45, [329], [352], [353], [360], [654]–[655], [656]
freedom of information   8, 15, 18–19, [174], [302]

government and the media 21–2, [205], [210], [235], [244]
  laws [16], [43], [45], [110], [303]
  media ownership 28–9, [251]
  newspapers 10, 11, 27, 28–9, 30, 56–7, 71, 74–5, [3], [80], [150], [161], [299], [314], [481], [530], [555]
  organizations 327–34
  privacy 33–4, 35, [272], [280], [287], [299], [300], [302], [319], [320]
  radio 11, 49–50, 60, [61]
  regulation 11, [366], [373]
  right to know 14, [184]
  television 11, 87–8, [61], [66], [70], [78], [79], [151], [166], [191], [265], [296], [329], [363], [374], [386], [402], [408], [432], [460], [481], [537], [583], [593]
Universal Declaration of Human Rights 5, 33, [135], [229], 257, 260, 261
Université Laval (Canada) 326
UPI [620]
Uranga, Washington [636]
Uruguay 344
utilitarianism 9, 66, 71, [138]
Uzbekistan 323–4

Vale, Norman 93, 97, [666]
values [637], [740]
  of journalists 27, 73–80, [480], [512]–[570]
Van Gerpen, Maurice [511]
Varis, Tapio [659]
Vaughn, Stephen [360]
Venezuela 344–5
Vergobbi, David J. [549]
victims, treatment by the media 10, 33, 37, 45, [271], [273], [286], [295], [305], [308], [320], [430], [435], [474], [501]
Victoria University of Wellington (NZ) 348
video 43, 47, [49], [375], [473], [490], [623], [643], [652], [787]
Video Standards Council (UK) 293
Viet Nam 324
Vietnam War 22, 61, 71, [62], [205], [235], [238], [429], [432], [462], [491]
Viewers for Quality Television (US) 330
violence 6, 38, 42, 43–5, [32], [62], [186], [308], [325], [336], [339], [342], [356], [361], [362], [363], [367], [374], [419], [435], [474], [591], [795], 329
  codes 45, [361], [362]
Visions of Ecstasy 47, [130]
Vivian, John [98]
Voice of America 89
Voice of the Viewer and Listener (UK) [581], 294
Voltaire, François Marie Arouet de 9, [154]
Voorhoof, Dirk [695]
Voss, Dan [2]
voyeurism [276]

WACC Journal [36], [742]
Wacks, Raymond [315]

Waco (Texas) siege [11], [414]
Wahl, Otto F. [445]
Wain, Christopher 22
Wales, Diana, Princess of 35, 36, [382]
Wales, University of [5], [406], 297
Walker, David [195], [656]
Wall Street Journal 26, 76
Wallace, Edgar [247]
war reporting 10, 21–4, 45, [5], [24], [62], [76], [204], [227]–[250], [426], [428], [436], [441], [443], [459], [464], [491], [540]
Warburton, Nigel [405]
Wardlaw, Grant [225]
Warner Bros 47
Warnock, Mary [162], [612]
Washington and Lee University (US) 333
Washington Journalism Center (US) 334
Washington Post 56, 70, [273], [456], [503]
Washington State University (US) [34], 333
Watergate 69, [205], [477], [503]
Watney, Simon [446]
Weaver, David H. [542]
Wedell, George [633], [801]
Weibull, Lennart [570]
Weiss, Thomas G. [436]
Wenham, Brian [589]
Wesson, John [605]
Western Kentucky University (US) [594]
Western Ontario, University of (Canada) 326
Western Sydney, University of (Australia) 347
Westminster, University of (UK) [573], 297
Westminster Institute of Ethics and Human Values (Canada) 327
Westmoreland, General [175]
Whale, John [99], [543]
Wheaton College (US) 332
Whipple, Thomas W. [669]
whistle-blowers 71
Whitaker, Anthony [201]
Whitaker, Brian [170]
White, Robert A. [57]
Whitehorn, Katharine [58]
Whitehouse, Mary 40, [331]–[334], [340], [580]
Wicker, Tom [183]
Wilhoit, Cleveland [542]
Wilhoit, Frances Goins 102, [766]
Wilkins, Lee [46]
Wilkinson, Kenton T. [637]
Williams, Bernard 39–40, 42–4, [338], [342]
Williams, Betty Anne [476]
Williams, David [696]
Williams, Francis 73, 80, 82, 83, 86, [100]
Williams, Kevin [5], [77], [241], [447]
Williams, Nancy [513]
Williams, Raymond [101], [102]
Wilmot, Chester [247]
Wilson, Harold [383]
Wilson II, Clint C. [660]
Winch, Samuel P. [316]
Windlesham, Lord 21, [80], [103], [226]
Windsor, University of (Canada) 326

Wingrove, Nigel   47
Winn, Marie   [351]
Winsbury, Rex   [317], [318], [319]
Winston, Brian   [406]
Wischmann, Lesley   [320]
Wober, J. Mallory   [321]
Wolfe, Kenneth M.   [613]
women, portrayal of   41–2, 59, 97, [410], [411], [418], [423]–[425], [433], [435], [442], [444], [474], [669], [785]
Women's Institute for Freedom of the Press (US)   330
Wood, Geoffrey   46, 51
Woodward, Bob   69, [503]
Woody, Gloria T.   [797]
Woollongong, University of (Australia)   348
World Association for Christian Communication (WACC)   x, [56], [636], [742], 262
World Association for Public Opinion Research   262
World Association of Women Journalists and Writers   260
World Communication Association   260
World Federation of Advertisers   258
World Intellectual Property Organization   257
World Press Freedom Committee   261
World Press Review   [761]
World War One   57

World War Two   5, 56, 71, [247], [426], [692]
World Wide Ethical Society   260
Wright, Peter   19, [194], [201], [203], [207]
Writers and Scholars Educational Trust   261
Writers' Guild of Great Britain   293
Wulfemeyer, K. Tim   [490]
Wyatt, Will   [362]

Yavas, Ugur   [687]
Yemen   324
Yeshiva University (US)   [707], 333
Yesterday's Men   [576]
York, Sarah, Duchess of   34
York University (Canada)   236
Young, Hugo   [407]
Young, Jock   59, 63, 67, [417]
Young, John B.   [322]
Younger, Kenneth   [282], [291], [315]
Yugoslavia   24, [229], [236], [248], [441]
   see also Bosnia-Herzegovina; Croatia; Macedonia; Serbia; Slovakia; Slovenia

Zaïre   37, 307
Zambia   307
Zerbinos, Eugenia   [184]
Ziesenis, Elizabeth   [448]
Zimbabwe   308

REF P94 .m22 1998